Research on the Laws of Contemporary China

Volume 3: 1992-2009

Editor-in-chief Chen Su

Translated By He Jingjing[1] and Shang Cong[2]

Paths International Ltd

中国社会科学出版社
CHINA SOCIAL SCIENCES PRESS

1 Dr. He Jingjing is an Assistant Researcher at the Institute of International Law, the Chinese Academy of Social Sciences

2. Dr. Shang Cong is a licensed lawyer in both State of California and People's Republic of China

Biography of Editor-In-Chief

CHEN Su, a research fellow in the Institute of Law of Chinese Academy of Social Sciences, and a doctoral supervisor, graduated from Liaoning University in 1985 as a bachelor of law; from the Institute of Law of Chinese Academy of Social Sciences in 1988 as a degree of master of law. At present he has held the office of the Co-Secretary of the Party Committee of the Institute of, and the Research Center of the Chinese Academy of Social Sciences; and executive director of China Law Society and Vice Chairman of the Commercial Jurisprudence Research Society.

He has mainly specialized in civil and commercial law, with works and writings, such as *Special Research on Securities Law, Exploration on Subtle Logic of Spirit of Law, New Development of Society Law*; and with dozens of papers published in professional academic journals such as *Chinese Journal of Law* and *China Legal Sciences*.

Preface

Just like the history of the PRC, the study of jurisprudence over the past 60 years since 1949 has been prosperous through hard times, developing steadily and making brilliant achievements with each passing day. The book describes China's jurisprudence study over the past 60 years in general terms, showing the status and evolution process of the new China's jurisprudence in various development stages, analyzing the background and reason for the formation and evolution of important theories in the course of studying jurisprudence, and manifesting theoretical achievements in development and prosperity of jurisprudence and their practical value. It is expected that the book help readers have a clear impression on the development path of China's jurisprudence, to learn the experience of researchers who have devoted their hard efforts and wisdoms to the development process of China's jurisprudence, and to experience the impulse of the "rule of law" era along with the development of the PRC.

General Introduction

The world today is the midst of unprecedented drastic changes, whereas China has the strategic opportunity of promoting the socialism modernization development with chinese characteristics — a critical period for building well-off society in an all-around way, and for the reform and opening-up. All of above have provided the studies of philosophy and social sciences with great opportunities to attain great prosperity and development. Currently, the development of philosophy and social science enjoy three big advantages: firstly the laudable practice of the Chinese-characteristic socialist development, which provides broad arena, i.e., plenty of opportunities, to the field of philosophy and social science; a steady flow of resources and materials to the research of philosophy and social science; second, the Communist Party of China and the state's strong commitment and support, which guarantees the prosperity and development of philosophy and social science; third, the implementation of the policy of "Encouraging blossoming and contending of all", which creates a favorable environment for new thinking and theory innovation in the field of philosophy and social sciences.

It was clearly put forward in China's "Twelfth Five-year Development Plan Outline" that "promote the building of the philosophy and social sciences innovation system, and implement the philosophy and social sciences innovation project, with prosperity and development of the philosophy and social sciences". And in response to the call the Academy of Social Sciences launched the philosophy and social sciences innovation project, a project designed to make efforts to achieve the innovation based on the direction of Marxism of the philosophy and social sciences system—the innovation mainly involving academic viewpoints and theories, academic disciplines, scientific research organization and management, scientific research methods and means, and personnel systems. The purpose to implement innovation project is to establish the philosophy and social science innovation system, to continue to strengthen research of the philosophy and social science, to produce more high quality results that can stand up to practice test, and to develop high-level talents with proper political ideology, and clear academic direction, all to serve the people, prosperous development of advanced socialist civilization, and the socialism with Chinese characteristics.

One of the important contents to implement innovation project is to follow the natural principles of philosophy and social science research to perfect discipline establishment mechanism, optimize discipline structure, and shape a discipline layout meeting China's needs with Chinese characteristics, reasonable structure and prominent advantages. As a means of displaying great achievements of innovation project, the writing of development reports on varied disciplines of the philosophy and social science, as for accurate grasp of academic frontier development, and for active advance of discipline establishment and innovation, is an important job with long-term fundamental importance.

Since the establishment of the People's Republic of China, the philosophy and social science system with Chinese characteristics has been in the course of its formation and development, in the history of Chinese socialistic revolution, construction and reform and development. Especially since the reform and opening-up, with China's economic and social development, the research on varied disciplines of the philosophy and social science has been expanded and deepened continuously, making remarkable achievements and attracting worldwide attention. In order to promote the further development in idea, method and system of philosophy and social science with Chinese characteristics, style and manner, and to drive excellent achievements and talents of China's philosophy and social science to go to the world, who should more actively participate in international academic dialogues, and raise the voice of China's philosophy and social sciences, so as to strengthen the soft power of Chinese culture, it is urgent to sort out academic ideas in varied disciplines of the philosophy and social science, and to summarize excellent accumulated results of the disciplines, including the proposition of major academic point of views and its impacts, the formation and evolution of important academic schools, the writing and publishing of important academic books and literature, and the emergence of the large numbers of important representative academic figures. Hence, the China Social Sciences Press has organized and compiled a large-scale series of consecutively-published books, thc Report on Disciplinary Development of China's Philosophy and Social Sciences, which is not merely a great event in academic circle, but an important part of the philosophy social science innovation project, too.

The Report on Disciplinary Development of China's Philosophy and Social Sciences is divided into two subseries: *Annual Reviews* and *Frontier Reports*, the former published annually as first-level discipline; the latter published every three years, both consecutively-published in compiled-book form. Contents of the *Annual Reviews* include the latest trends at home and aboard in the current year of the discipline development, important theory viewpoints and methods, hot issues and representative scholars and their masterpieces; contents of the *Frontier Reports* overall status of the discipline development, concerns and matters at home and aboard over the past three years of academic frontier dynamics, the latest theory viewpoints and methods, significant theory innovation and hot issues, and main representative personage and their masterpieces on academic frontier at home and aboard. Each discipline development report should be a high-level and –quality research result, reflecting development and evolution contexts of contemporary important thoughts of disciplines and academies; fruits from hard work in tracking research of the discipline by the author for a long time; and mirror recent development trends of the discipline, to hold accurately academic foreland and to guide disciplinary development. Therefore we believe that the implementation of this publication project will certainly play an important role in promoting construction and development of the various disciplines of the philosophy and social sciences in China, and that the series of books will become important historical literature and teaching materials in academic research of the philosophy and social science, making a significant contribution to China's research of philosophy and social sciences, education and talent preparation.

Table of Contents

Volume I 1949-1978

Volume II 1978-1992

Volume III 1992-2009

Research on the Laws of Contemporary China

Volume III 1992-2009

Introduction

In this Part, we choose the years of 1992 and 2009 as the starting and ending points in this stage. The year of 1992 is a very important year in the history of socialist construction in China that, it put forward clearly in the 14th National Party Congress in October 1992 that, the goal of the economic system reform of our country is to build the socialist market economic system, so as to further emancipate and develop the productivity.[1] The establishment of the socialist market economic system has the influence of changes on not only limited to the economic field, but also all aspects of China's society greatly, the rule of law field particularly evident and huge. The amendment to the constitution in 1993 stipulated "the State practices the socialist market economy", then the legislation and research related to market economy system was launched immediately; In 1997, the 15th National Party Congress put forward "governing the state by law to construct a socialist legal country", that the new concept of rule of law conforms to and looks forward to the new development of Chinese jurisprudence; Since China joined in the world trade organization in 2001, the international vision of Chinese juristic research has been more extended; In 2006, the Party's 6th Plenary Session of the 16th National Party Congress put forward "building a socialist harmonious society", and took "democratic rule of law" as the basic requirements

1 See JIANG Zemin's report on the 14th National Congress of the Communist Party of China, *Accelerate the pace of reform and opening up and modernization construction, seize greater victories of the socialist cause with Chinese characteristics.*

of a harmonious society, that Chinese jurisprudence has expectations of a new era and development opportunities. Visibly, Chinese jurisprudence after 1992 is in a continuous development status with its deeper and deeper concept and richer and richer contents, of which the historic trigger point is the establishment of the socialist market economic system. Choosing the year of 2009 as the ending point in this stage does not mean that the year of 2009 has any special significance in the development history of Chinese Jurisprudence, but it is just because the year of 2009 is the 60th anniversary of the founding of the people's Republic of China, which is worthy of commemorating in a variety of ways, also the temporary deadline year we write the article of "Contemporary Chinese Jurisprudence". The development of Chinese jurisprudence has no end point, as the cause of rule of law in China we are devoted our ideal and effort to.

The words of "progressive, prosperous and flourishing" are the common adjectives to describe the development of Chinese jurisprudence in this period, and so the development of Chinese jurisprudence is. Firstly, the branch discipline division of Chinese jurisprudence is becoming more and more specific, and it has formed Chandelier subject system composed of basic secondary-level subjects, a variety of third-level subjects and lots of interdisciplinary subjects in this period. Decomposition, derivation and combination has become the main ways of subject formation of Chinese jurisprudence, such as, a secondary discipline is decomposed into many secondary disciplines (for example, the commercial jurisprudence is gradually decomposed out of the civil and commercial jurisprudence), many legal secondary-level disciplines are derived out more third-level disciplines, and the labor jurisprudence and the social security jurisprudence are combined into the social jurisprudence, and so on. The differentiation of discipline has also been shown in academic organizations, such as, the civil law and economic law research institute of Chinese jurisprudence society is decomposed into the civil law research institute, the commercial law research institute and the economic law research institute later; the procedural law research society is decomposed into the criminal procedure law research institute and civil litigation law research institute. Chinese jurisprudence with the discipline branch system as the backbone has constructed a huge theoretical system composed of different branch discipline knowledge systems. Secondly, the output of juristic study is very great, such as it published more than 400 academic works (translated), and more than 70,000 academic articles (translated) in 2007.[1] The forms of carrier publishing research results of jurisprudence are various, that there are now more than 200 jurisprudence periodicals, a large number of publications on jurisprudence series, a large number of professional web sites of jurisprudence. Thirdly, the theoretical research of Chinese jurisprudence is multiple polarized, which enriches the annotative jurisprudence in the pursuit of application value, but also expands the theoretical jurisprudence in the pursuit of theoretical construction value. In many disciplines, new philosophical discourse began to be used for expressing thinking and speculation on the jurisprudence issues, that such as constitutional philosophy, philosophy of civil law and philosophy of criminal law all became the best choices for academic tasks. The research situation of multiple-polarization as well as parallel is necessary to construct the abundant and integral theoretical system of jurisprudence. While focusing on discipline basic theory research, juristic researchers also attached importance to suggestions and advice on the legal system, basically realizing the balanced development between the basic theoretical research and the research of application countermeasure on various disciplines. There appeared some academic phenomenons referring to theories, terms and methods of other disciplines to study jurisprudence in this stage, such as critical jurisprudence, economic analytic jurisprudence, law and literature, law and post-modernism, and so on. Fourthly, the topic choice of juristic study is more and more sophisticated, which started to seek to the both more

1 ZHANG Wenxian (editor in chief), HUANG Wenyi (vice editor in chief): *A Report on the Development of Philosophy and Social Sciences in Chinese Universities · Jurisprudence* (1978-2008). Guangxi Normal University Press, 2008 edition, p.9.

abstract and more concrete ends, that the introduction-type and comprehensive jurisprudence knowledge narrative in the intermediate level has been transferred to textbook compiling, and basically quit out of the research field. Fifthly, the course of the jurisprudence education has a rapid development and the number of jurisprudence colleges and departments reaches more than 630 recently.[1]The development of legal education course has trained a large number of legal practical talents and legal research talents, expanding social functions transforming ability of jurisprudence theory and expanding teaching staff continuously is the main force of juristic study. Sixthly, foreign academic exchanges in Chinese law circle including translating works, personnel reciprocal visits, academic conference, etc all have become common means of academic exchange in law circle. The academic exchange with foreign countries in previous period is in a statistical stage[2], while the foreign exchange in Chinese law circle in this period is frequent and diverse, hard to statistics.

In this period, Chinese jurisprudence has the development in theoretical innovation and its initiative in essence, or in which can be called "active independence". Previous Chinese jurisprudence always follows closely the changes of law and policy to choose the focus of theoretical research, thus interpreting law and policy is the main academic task of juristic study. In this stage, Chinese jurisprudence has not been interpretation of theory and principle following the status of reality any longer, but providing the practice of rule of law with a theoretical basis and a guide of theory by social observation, logic analysis

1 See:JI Xiangde, et al: *The Current Situation and Developmental Trend of Chinese Jurisprudence Education*. Chinese Social Science Press, 2008 edition.

2 For example, a statistics shows that, during the ten years after the 3rd Plenary Session of the 11th Central Committee of CPC, the reception of legal delegations from 81 countries and regions are 352, 3389 people in total; various academic conferences with the participation of foreign jurists held in domestic China are 18; there are 164 domestic jurisprudence delegations and 589 people going abroad for academic visit. See: ZHANG Youyu (editor in chief), WANG Shuwen (vice editor in chief): *Forty Years of Chinese Jurisprudence*. Shanghai People's Publishing House, 1989 edition, p.12.

and theoretical elucidation, giving full play to the academic function of "theory goes in advance" and promoting the practice of rule of law in China to progress continuously. Such as, after the establishment of the socialist market economic system, scholars in Law Institute of Chinese Academy of Social Sciences keenly started from the research of regularity, analyzed and researched the relationship between the market economic mechanism and the law mechanism systematically and deep, and proposed the suggestion of building a socialist market economic legal system[1], which not only formed an important hot theoretical issue in law circle then, but also promoted the market economic legal construction in China effectively. A paper of "*On Administering a Country by Law*" published on "*Juristic Research*" in 1996 made an outlining explanation on the significance, conditions, concepts of "Administering a country by law"[2];Law Institute of Chinese Academy of Social Sciences also held a symposium on "Administering a country by law and building a socialist country under the rule of law", in which the scholars made further extensive discussions on the "legal system" and "rule of law", "ruling a country with law" and "ruling a country by law", "formal rule of law" and "substantive rule of law", and so on[3].This theoretical herald of advocating "administer a country according to law" promoted the formation and confirmation of the basic strategy of "Administering a country by law and building a socialist country under the rule of law". In this period, the examples of promoting legal construction by juristic study are abundant, such as the standard of right, human right research, governing by law, governmental information publicity, no penalty without a law, Numerus Clausus, maintaining market free and fair competition, justice of procedure and judicial justice and other issues of

1 Research group of Law Institute of Chinese Academy of Social Sciences: "The Theoretical Thinking and Countermeasure to the Legal System of the Socialist Market Economy", *Juristic Research*, 1993, Issue 6.

2 See: WANG Jiafu, LIU Hainian, LIU Han, LI Buyun, LIANG Huixing, XIAO Xianfu: *On Administering a Country by Law. in juristic Research*, 1996, Issue 2.

3 "Summary of the Academic Symposium of Building a Socialist Country under the Rule of Law of 'Administering a Country by Law'", *Juristic Research*, 1996, Issue 3.

theoretical issues all became directly or indirectly the theoretical pilots of law perfecting in that field.

During this period, the consciousness of participation in the practice of rule of law enhanced unprecedentedly in law circle in China, and juristic researchers participated in legislative practice and legal advocacy activities in a variety of ways. As far as participation in the activities of the legislative practice concerned, the pathways of participation of researchers of jurisprudence probably include: becoming members of drafting a law directly; organizing to write a scholar's suggestion draft as reference by the legislature; participating in legal draft demonstration meeting by the legislative organs; providing legislative suggestions for a specific law or a legal draft; putting forward a theoretical insights, indirectly to affect legislative policy choice. As far as participation in the activities of legal publicity concerned, the participation forms of juristic researcher probably include: getting an entrustment by an organ or an authority to preach the legal system; participating in the legal publicity activities under the organization of academic organizations and their own units. Participation in the legal publicity by juristic researchers is conducive to the popularization of the concept of socialist rule of law, and the realization of the social value of the juristic theory and the social responsibility of the juristic researchers.

During this period, there also appeared a trend to pursue the "independence on culture" of Chinese jurisprudence in law circle in China. There is no denying that Chinese jurisprudence is still depending on the western juristic theory more or less after it frees from the dependence of the Soviet juristic theory. Western juristic theory point of view, spirit and concept, system and technology, professional terminology, research methods have also entered into the knowledge generation system of Chinese jurisprudence in a batch size. Although the origin of Chinese juristic theory is enriched by this, it also brings the risk of annihilating Chinese jurisprudence independence, especially with the spread of economic globalization, law and the trend of internationalization is more obvious, and more popular monopoly of western juristic discourse leads to the alert of cultural independence of Chinese jurisprudence. Since 1990s, it has begun to focus on cultural self subjectivity in China's law circle, and the cultural consciousness and cultural subjectivity consciousness has already begun to strengthen increasingly. In the process of juristic study and theoretical construction, Chinese jurisprudence has walked gradually out of the dominating influence of Soviet theory and western jurisprudence further, focusing on the problems of reality of China and the development road of law, and it has formed Chinese jurisprudence rooted in Chinese society and Chinese hearts, which is the era mission in China's law circle. In a certain sense, the construction and popularization of the concept of socialist rule of law is also one part of the efforts in constructing the cultural subjectivity of Chinese jurisprudence. In the process of pursuit of cultural independence of Chinese jurisprudence, creativity, only creativity is the inevitable road.

Since 1990s, the importance of academic standardization has been generally recognized in the entire Humanities and Social Sciences field including jurisprudence circle, and the standardization level of juristic study has been improved significantly. There are still a lot of phenomenons of disorders in present juristic circle, but it can not be denied that this progress is better than that of 20 or 30 years ago. The promotion of the standardization of juristic study shows in literature citation, academic criticism, academic review, academic ethics, and other aspects.[1]Of course, the standardization of juristic study is still a long way, during which it requires the whole profession circle to make a lot of joint efforts. Such as, there are still a lot of repeated and lack-of-innovation juristic studies and plentiful phenomenons with parallel copies in jurisprudence works, and there still exist the writings for rushing headlong and swarming, and the phenomenon to note for noting makes people doubtful on the value of notes, and dull narrative

1 ZHANG Wenxian (editor in chief), HUANG Wenyi (vice editor in chief): *A Report on the Development of Philosophy and Social Sciences in Chinese Universities •Jurisprudence* (1978-2008). Guangxi Normal University Press, 2008 edition, p.13.

style makes people lose reading pleasure on juristic writings. In particular, the pseudo innovation phenomenon with the lack of demonstration is agonizing, that making innovation of juristic theory requires academic courage before, but now it seems only need to learn to be brave.

Practice has proved and will continue to prove that China's rule of law is still moving forward, the Chinese law is still developing. The hope exists forever, so we must try our best.

Chapter 12

Philosophical Jurisprudence Research in View of Reality

1. Three Theoretical Resources of Chinese Philosophical Jurisprudence

Since nearly one and a half centuries, Chinese academy has been suffering ups and downs all the time. From the mid of the 19th century, Western cultural tide came to raid, thus it triggered the reform movement and the democratic revolution, after that, the socialist ideological trend and its relevant new democratic revolution and socialist revolution rose in China, thus, Chinese traditional culture led to sway in the wind, desolated ultimately in the long-term impact of the two major trends. In the early founding of new China, because Chinese philosophical jurisprudence was impacted violently by the Soviet Union, the Western cultural tide was cut off, but Chinese traditional culture was also further criticized and inhibited. After the reform and opening up, Western culture re-formed a huge cultural trend once again depending on the increasingly open social conditions; meanwhile, Chinese traditional culture also began to coruscate new vitality gradually. Under such a historical background, when Chinese philosophical jurisprudence began to "make up missed lessons" from the "naive" in the early stage of reform and opening up, Western culture, socialist theory and Chinese traditional culture in the process of historical changes had already forged its genealogy of knowledge and academic origin, and restricted and influenced its growth and developing road for a long time.

It can be seen from its names that Chinese philosophical jurisprudence has experienced roughly from "Theory of state and law" to "the basic theory of jurisprudence", then to "philosophical jurisprudence". Such a theoretical evolutionary process not only is affected by our domestic political environment and academic environment, but also more obviously is related to the environmental change of international politics. It can be said in a certain sense that, the theory of state and law is the juristic theory related to state politics in the cold war period, and the jurisprudence basic theory is the juristic theory when China has freed from the Soviet bloc and gradually returned lonely to the world system, and the philosophical jurisprudence is the juristic theory when China walks towards the world era with the gesture of reform and opening to the outside world. In the background of international politics in this period, Soviet theoretical influence was weakened gradually, and the "Western culture" flooded into China again in the environment of reform and opening to the outside world, and became important theoretical factors influencing the development of Chinese philosophical jurisprudence.[1]

---

1 The works focusing on introducing western philosophical jurisprudence in 1980s are: SHEN Zongling: *Western Modern Legal Philosophy*, Law Press, 1983 Edition. ZHANG Wenxian: *Contemporary Western Law•Philosophy*, Changchun Press, 1987 Edition; ZHANG Wenxian: *Contemporary Western Legal Thoughts*, Liaoning People's Press, 1988 Edition. These works have greater influence in the philosophical legal circle. The works (translated) and books with also greater influence in history of theory of ideology in this period are: [Soviet] Mokiqev (editor in chief), the compilation and translation office of Law Institute of Chinese Academy of Social Sciences (translator): *A History of Political Theory*, China Social Sciences Press, 1979 Edition; Law Institute of Shanghai Academy of Social Sciences (compiler and translator): Compilation of Foreign Legal Knowledge, Knowledge Press, 1981 Edition; *Selected Compilation of Reference Materials to The History of Western Legal Ideology*, Peking University Press, 1983 Edition; ZHANG Hongsheng (editor in chief):*The History of Western Legal Ideology*, Peking University Press, 1983 Edition; LV Shilun, GU Chunde: *The History of Western Political and Legal Ideology*, Liaoning People's Press, 1981 Edition (1986 Revised Edition of the 1st Volume and 1987 Revised Edition of the 2nd Volume); [America] Bodenheimer(author), DENG Zhenglai, JI Jingwu (translator): *Philosophical Jurisprudence—Legal Philosophy and Its Methods*, Huaxia Press, 1987 Edition, and so on. In addition, the magazine of *Law Translation* sponsored by Law Institute of Chinese Academy of Social Sciences also translated and introduced a lot of foreign literature of jurisprudence.

After experiencing the hot trend of "thought liberation" after the "Cultural Revolution" and the "cultural fever" in 1980s, Chinese philosophical jurisprudence gained a sustainable and rapid development in the stable political and cultural environment, entering into the most historical developmental period. Compared with the theory of state and law and the juristic basic theory, Chinese philosophical jurisprudence in this stage was not only in the guidance of socialist ideology, also was further influenced by the continuous rapid-development western culture, and got a deep infiltration by re-emerging Chinese traditional culture in the early 1990s. Socialism, especially the theory of socialism with Chinese characteristics, western juristic theory and the traditional legal culture thus became the important theoretical resources for the development of Chinese philosophical jurisprudence. It can be seen from the dozen-year developmental reality that, the three theoretical resources are not incompatible as fire and water and completely opposite as previously thought, but function each other and interact mutually and unify together in the process of China's modernization history in the condition of globalization and China's reform and development actually.

Specifically, the interaction and integration of the three theoretical resources is mainly presented through some historical and cultural events related to the Chinese traditional culture, socialism and Western culture. Firstly, the discussion on "Craze for Chinese traditional culture" emerging in the early 1990s and "humanistic spirit" changed the embarrassing situation that Chinese traditional culture was just criticized in a long term in the radical political and cultural movements since the end of the Qing Dynasty. In the 1960s-1980s, with the development of Confucianism in the overseas and the East Asian "economic miracle", the so-called "Chinese cultural circle", "Confucian tradition" and "new Confucian culture" gradually aroused the concern of the international society, thus Chinese traditional culture also started to be recognized, and there appeared a re-evaluation on Confucius in 1980s, and some non-governmental organizations like Academy of Chinese culture were established. Although it still suffered from setbacks in the "Craze of culture" in the mid-end 1980s, the Chinese traditional culture already became a surging-out subsurface flow in the end of 1980s after nearly 10-year brewing. After "Craze of Chinese traditional culture" in 1990s, the year of 2004 also was known as the "revival year of the traditional culture" for a series of traditional cultural events. During this period, "eliminating vice and exalting virtue", "integrating Chinese and the west" and "seeking for modern transformation of tradition" were the main characteristics of the research on traditional culture. Secondly, China has firstly realized the combination between socialism and market economy, and then realized the combination between socialism and the rule of law since 1992. From the perspective of the traditional theory of Marxism, "socialist market economy" and "socialist country under the rule of law" are described as brand-new creativity in the history of socialism. In this period, both the traditional culture and modern human rights were formally recognized at the national level. In the aspect of traditional culture, Chinese state leaders granted an interview to the representatives of "Memorial for Confucius birth of 2540 anniversary and academic discussion conference" and delivered a speech in October 1989, then "Craze of Chinese traditional culture" sprang up as a consequence; till 2006, Chinese first cultural construction plan of "*Cultural development planning outline in the eleventh Five-Year plan period* " gave a high evaluation on traditional culture: "5000-year long and splendid Chinese culture has made a great contribution to the progress of human civilization, which is the spirit link that Chinese nation breeds in an endless succession and vein of state inherits forever, and the source of strength that Chinese nation faces severe challenges and various complicated environments but stands still, and suffers from disasters but is still indomitable." In the aspect of modern human rights, the human rights, equality, rule of law, freedom were accepted gradually as human civilization achievements, and the human rights was not only called "a great term", but also "The state respects and protects human rights" was definitely written in the Constitution in 2004. Finally, after the1990s, the ideological trend of post-modernism began to emerge, and till the mid 1990s, there also appeared a controversy between the so-called "New Left" and the liberalism. From the perspective of content, the controversy between "New Left" and liberalism presents the integration of socialism and modern academic discourse on the one hand, and it also presents the divergence of the liberalism on the issues of social justice, modernity, publicity, citizens' virtue, and so on. In the mutual influence of the three theoretical resources, "the discourse of modern rights", "the discourse of practical interest" and "the discourse of traditional virtue" exist by turns in Chinese legal practice and the research of philosophical jurisprudence.[1]

The historical and cultural events above reflect rather the unity of practice than theoretical disputes. In fact, they all have strong realistic and historical focuses, attaching importance to the common theoretical and practical problems. This mainly presents that they all involve modern historical practice and "Modernity" theoretical thinking, and eventually all settle in China's development path. Traditionally speaking, why traditional culture in China becomes the problems suffering 100 years of tribulation undoubtedly is directly related to China entering into the world modern process after the "upheaval of more than three thousand years" occurred in the late Qing Dynasty, that it was proposed as a big problem related to a state's cultural vein at the beginning passively. From the perspective of the relationship between tradition and modernity, the knowledge arguments like "body" and "tool", "root" and "end", "doctrine" and "instrument", "saint inside" and "king outside" around the traditional culture clearly shows value elements and spiritual significance of Chinese traditional culture for the historical course of modernization. Even the spiritual values contained in the traditional culture have not only practical significance to modern China, but also have universal significance to the modern world. This is concerned that, "Craze of Chinese traditional culture" as well as the "traditional culture ideological trend" later is recognized as rather a historical movement of carrying forward spiritual value after China entering into the process of world modernization than restoration of ancient culture or cultural conservation. If say that the discussion on human nature

1 See:HU Shuijun: *Political Analysis of Law*, Peking University Press, 2005 Edition, Preface.

and humanism in the beginning of 1980s is related to the political movement in 1970s, so the "Craze of traditional culture" emerging in the early of 1990s as well as the discussion on human nature and humanism shall be related to the commercial tide from the perspective of the short term, and shall be connected to more-than-100-year political turmoil and cultural movement together from the perspective of the long run. After the vicissitudes, the traditional culture finally revived in the 1990s, which presents in a large extent that Chinese society began to inherit rationally Chinese history, to revert to Chinese culture and solidify the body and deepen the root after suffering 100-year political turmoil and cultural movement, which also shows that China began to stand itself on the root, and then re-participate in the world modern history progress as the cultural subject.

The socialist modernization beginning in 1950s was largely influenced by the Soviet Union, with the characteristics of confrontation between socialism and capitalism and trying to go beyond capitalism. After the reform and opening up and with the change in the political pattern of the world, especially China's accession to the world trade organization in 2001, globalization became the international background of China's socialist modernization. Under this background, China absorbed and referred all the excellent achievements of human civilization at all the times and in all over the world including traditional culture and modern human rights in the opening world, and also attached more importance to its own history and practice, and was committed to seek its own path to modernization. In view of the historical experience and lessons, in the process of reform and development, the controversy of "socialism" and "capitalism" eventually depends on Chinese concrete practical effect to judge or inspect, and analyzing the basic category of socialist modernization also follows Chinese historical vein back to tradition and modernization, China and the west. The inheritance to Chinese history can be seen here, and the modern tendency that makes theory in accordance with the trend of times and Chinese practice can be seen, too, therefore, Chinese factors has been emphasized repeatedly, Marxism also has evolved into Chinese socialism with characteristics.

Overall speaking, since the 1990s, the traditional culture, socialism and the western culture have been re-recognized more comprehensively, and the spiritual value of the traditional culture, the theory of the primary stage of socialism, the modernity of the western culture have received high attention, which all have integrated in the Chinese own developmental path in the tide of reform and opening up. As a country in a post developed environment in the process of world modernization, China really needs to learn and refer doubly to the successful achievements of civilization in the modern world, especially Europe and the United States, but this does not mean that "history" will end therefore or herein. Chinese modernization with integration of the factors of traditionalism, socialism, modernism as well as post-modernism has the willing and the hope to explore its own path, similarly, Chinese philosophical jurisprudence with integration of the factors of traditional culture, socialist theory and modernism also can explore out its own road. In one and a half centuries' process of modernization, the theory making Chinese factors prominent and the efforts of practice in the process of political and cultural transformation can always be seen from the combination of "Chinese culture as the body and the western culture as a tool", to "three principles of the people" and "constitution of five powers", till Marxism universal principles with connection to the concrete practice of China. Compared with this situation, the viewpoint of "total westernization" suffers a strong cultural resistance from its beginning, highlighting Chinese factors, based on Chinese reality from the beginning and committed to promote and create universal human factors. Along such historical clues, in the developmental process from the theory of state and law to the basic theory of jurisprudence to the philosophical jurisprudence, Chinese philosophical jurisprudence highlighting cultural consciousness and cultural subjectivity will be bound to appear. In fact, the unremitting efforts that scholars of philosophical jurisprudence have made and the achievements by the efforts so far have proved that the developmental road of Chinese philosophical jurisprudence is feasible, and the goal of building up Chinese own philosophical jurisprudence can be achieved.

2. New Construction and Exploration of Juristic Theory

Since 1992, the research of philosophical jurisprudence showed the characteristics of colorful and continuous presentation, while it was still influenced by the western culture with rapid development, it also began to take efforts to expand and construct subjective culture; there were researches based on Chinese own culture and reality and researches in combination with the background of the world and jurisprudence of other countries, and there also appeared researches such as critical jurisprudence, jurisprudence of economic analysis, law and literature, law and post-modernism, law and globalization, law and political philosophy, law and social theory; the national theory abandoned by juristic basic theory including both the so-called "jurist's philosophical jurisprudence" or "legal man's philosophical jurisprudence" and the so-called "legislators' philosophical jurisprudence"[1] was drawn back to the philosophical jurisprudence by some scholars. While the independence and autonomy of the discipline of jurisprudence got a further consolidation, the comprehensive research about "law and ..." (namely, relationship between law and other social phenomenon) also got development. While philosophical jurisprudence were exploring China's legal philosophy and political path, its research knowledge points were also increasing significantly, and its field and scope were expanding, thus, on the one hand it showed the tendency of practice "all the things in the world are all my own responsibility", on the other hand it also presented knowledge exploration of "to see academy as a purpose", "to administer knowledge for knowledge". In the researches of philosophical jurisprudence, there were some discussions about the value and culture of law, rights and democracy, and there were also researches in combination with department law or the actual practice of law, and there also

1 See: SHU Guoying: *Seeing the Thinking Way by the Rational and Historical Investigation of Law*, in *Ideological Battlefront*, 2005, Issue 4; QIANG Shigong: *The Philosophical Jurisprudence Marching to Lawmakers*, Sanlian Bookstore, 2007 Edition.

appeared the tendency of trying to use social scientific method to study legal issues.[1] Disciplines like comparative jurisprudence, social jurisprudence and other new emerging disciplines were developing continuously, and the crossing researches between law and other disciplines were also increasing.[2] Totally speaking, the aspects of the morality and science nature, the legality and political and the scientific philosophical science and knowledge nature of the philosophical jurisprudence shone mutually and added radiance and beauty to each other, complicated in this stage. Compared with the theory of state and law, juristic basic theory, philosophical jurisprudence is more independent, rich and broad, and also more pragmatic, rational and profound, and the Confucian orthodoxy, political orthodoxy, legal orthodoxy and academic tradition Chinese development depends on gradually became clearer.

However, through the seemingly complicated superficial phenomenon and combined with domestic and international events, the development of philosophical jurisprudence in this period is rule-based in general. In the aspects of economy, "to establish socialist market economic system" was determined in 1993, and China entered into the world trade organization in 2001. In the aspects of politics and law, "administering the country by law, and building a socialist country under the rule of law" and "ruling by law" were respectively proposed in 1997 and 2004; "building a socialist harmonious society" was put forward in 2006 and "democracy and the rule of law" was taken as the basic requirement of a harmonious society; moreover, "implementing socialist market economy in China", "implementing administering the country by law and building a socialist law-administration country" and "respecting and protecting the human rights" were also written in constitution in 1993, 1999 and 2004

1 See: SU Li (editor in chief): *Law and Social Science*, Law Press, 2006, 2007, 2008, 2009 Edition.

2 Such as, SHEN *Zongling:Comparative Research*, Peking University Press, 1998 Edition; ZHU Jingwen: *The Framework and Method of Social Science of Comparative Law—Legalization, Localization and Globalization*, Renmin University of China Press, 2001 Edition.

respectively. In the aspects of culture, “Chinese culture” was recognized highly, then Chinese traditional culture was understood more comprehensively, and gradually got rid of the historical situation suffering long-run critics and strike by political and cultural movements since the modern times. All these aspects reflect that the factors of the “world” and “China” were strengthened in the process of deepening reform and expanding the opening up in the situation of the increasingly close ties between China and the world. In the research of philosophical jurisprudence, these aspects also have been reflected clearly, but on the whole, the two subjects of “law-guided administration” and “the human rights” can be roughly used to summarize the developmental mainstream in this period, closely contact to the political, economic, cultural development since 1992. “Law-guided administration” reflects the deepening of the study of “legal system” in 1980s, and “human rights” reflects the promotion of the research on “civil rights” and “rights based” in 1980s. Market economy, harmonious society and traditional culture jointly contributed to the historical process that such a philosophical jurisprudence develops towards the higher level, especially further resulted in the complete separation of philosophical jurisprudence from “taking class struggle as the key link” in the research paradigm. If summarizing “law-guided administration” to “law” and “human rights” to “logic”, then it can be said, that philosophical jurisprudence in this period was in a historical stage when “juridical logic” was presented increasingly and “law” and “logic” combined more closely. This feature is particularly prominent in the system of textbooks on philosophical jurisprudence. Compared with the old textbooks, textbooks on philosophical jurisprudence in this period especially the 21st century adopted the basic framework of “science” and “juridical logic” in general. In the textbooks, the part of “juristic logic” mainly involves legal mechanisms and legal principle, specifically including concept of law, elements of law, value of law, the origin of law, legal effect, development of law, legal system, legal relationship, legal acts, legal profession, legal liability, legal culture, legislation, law enforcement, judiciary, legal procedures, legal interpretation, legal reasoning, legal technology, human rights, right, obligation, legal system, the rule of law, reflecting the theoretical characteristics of researching law and its development law based on the general principles or basic principles.

Specifically speaking, in terms of the research of law-guided administration, this period is a critical historical stage that law-guided administration achieved a breakthrough in China, and a stage that it unfolded a deep and wide discussion on law-guided administration. From the perspective of the history since the founding of new China, law-guided administration is an old theoretical issue, which there appeared some relevant discussions in the 1950s and the late 1970s to the early 1980s. Taking the *Juristic Study* for example, it had opened up "administration by law and will" column for three times, and published eight articles on the debates between administration by law and will selectively between 1979 and 1981. *Indication on protecting the criminal law and criminal procedure law's implementation firmly* by the central authorities explicitly mentioned "implementing the socialist rule of law" in 1979, but from the eight articles to see, there existed many divergences on the understanding on law-guided administration, and there also existed some vague understandings. For example, some scholars think that the view of law-guided administration is more democratic than the view of will-guided administration in the history; some argue that law-guided administration and will-guided administration can be used parallelly because there is no absolute boundaries; some also believe that both law-guided administration and will-guided administration should be abandoned for it is so prone to unscientific concept with ideological confusion. These divergences and vague understandings have some certain connection with the situation that scholars discussed law-guided administration and will-guided administration mostly around the administrative advocates between ancient Confucian and Legalism. Only from the perspective of "governance" logic, not "politics" system to examine the "law-guided administration" will inevitably lead to the so-called "combination view"of will-guided administration and law-guided administration.

Then till the early 1990s, it can be said that it is a gradually changing period from "legal system" to "law-guided administration".[1] The year of 1996 is the year of establishment of the theory of law-guided administration, and it is also a year when the theory of law-guided administration influences political decision. A paper of "*On Administering a country by law*" published on "*Juristic Research*" in this year made an outlining explanation on the significance, conditions, concepts of "Administering a country by law";[2]Law Institute of Chinese Academy of Social Sciences also held a symposium on "Administering a country by law and building a socialist country under the rule of law", the scholars made further extensive discussions on the "legal system" and "rule of law", "ruling a country with law" and "ruling a country by law", "formal rule of law" and "substantive rule of law", and so on.[3] From the perspective of the situation of the discussion, implementing law-guided administration had been a consensus in the law academic circle then, but the research situation, but some basic theories on law-guided administration are necessary to research deeply. For example, till 1999, some scholars still felt it was necessary to sort out the basic question: "What the law-guided administration is?"[4] In 2007, the relationship between law-guided administration and democracy became a focus problem at the conference of the tenth anniversary of memorial to implementation of law-guided administration held by juristic Research Institute

1 SHEN Zongling: *Analysis on the Words' Meaning of "Legal System", "Administration by Law" and "Administration by Will"*, in *Juristic Research*, 1989, Issue 4; SUN Guohua: *Administration by Law and Administration by Will Should Not Be Confused*, in *Chinese Jurisprudence*, 1993, Issue 3; ZHANG Hao: *Briefly On Administration by Law and Administration by Will*, in *Chinese Jurisprudence*, 1993, Issue 3; LIU Zuoxiang, XIAO Zhoulu: *To Jump Out Of Periodicity Relying On Democracy, But Administration By Law More*, in *Chinese Jurisprudence*, 1995, Issue 2.

2 WANG Jiafu, LIU Hainian, LIU Han, LI Buyun, LIANG Huixing, XIAO Xianfu: *On Administering a Country by Law*. in *Juristic Research*, 1996, Issue 2.

3 *Summary of the Academic Symposium of Building a Socialist Country under the Rule of Law of "Administering a Country by Law"*. in *Juristic Research*, 1996, Issue 3.

4 XIA Yong: *What Is Administration By Law?—Origins, Precepts and Value*, in *Chinese Social Science*, 1999, Issue 4.

of Chinese Academy of Social Sciences.[1]Some scholars think the relationship between them is antagonistic, or that they are two irrelevant paths, thinking that there is no necessary connection between law-guided administration and democracy, and there exists law-guided administration without democracy in the history, so China should go along law-guided administration rather than democracy. And some scholars tend to integration of law-guided administration and democracy, but law-guided administration first and then democracy, or postponing democracy, emphasizing democratic politics must be in the framework of law-guided administration, especially in the restraint of legal system. During this period, the law-guided administration has been the focus of discussion in the field of jurisprudence, and the research scope involves the value, principles, elements of law-guided administration, the social interaction foundation, political and cultural conditions of law-guided administration, law-guided administration and civil society, law-guided administration and democracy, etc, of which topics are wide and various. In these discussions, there are some theoretical reflection on law-guided administration and its practice in China. Such as contradictions between form and substance, determination and change, common and speciality, China and the western, tradition and modernity, state and society, justice and reconciliation, litigation and petition, democracy and law-guided administration, professionalism and democratization, legal facts and objective truth, all became the research subjects of scholars.[2]

In the aspects of the study of human rights, compared with the study of human rights since 1992, the discussions on the category of right and liability as well as

1 "Records on the Commemoration of the 10th Anniversary Implementation of the Basic Strategy of 'Administering a Country by Law'", in *Juristic Research*, 2007, Issue 4.

2 Such as, SU Li: *Chinese Modernization And Administration By Law in the 20th Century*, in *Juristic Research*, 1998, Issue 1; MA Xiaohong: "The Historical Investigation and Thinking of Administration By Law", in *Juristic Research*, 1999, Issue 2; GAO Hongjun: "The Dilemma and Outlet of Modern Administration By Law", in *Juristic Research*, 2003, Issue 2; WANG Hailan: "The Misunderstanding, Deficiency and Flaw of the Form Rationality—In the Perspective of the Criminal Procedure", in *Juristic Research*, 2006, Issue 2.

the discussion on standard of right between the mid and late 1980s and the early 1990s in the field of jurisprudence are more deepened in theory. The researches on human rights and rights in this period develop and expand to international human rights and some specific right such as the right of association, the right of academic freedom, and so on along international and domestic legal system and practice on the one hand,[1] and they focus on philosophical exploration with more theoretical depth and height on the other hand. Philosophical exploration mainly presents the theoretical argument on the fundamental rationale of human rights and rights, the analysis on moral foundation of human rights and the right and its realistic political situation, the philosophical reflection on theory of modern human rights and the right, and the theory of developing modern human rights and the right based on Chinese cultural vein, etc. In proof theory, some scholars try to transfer "subjectivity" to "inter subjectivity", based on "mutual recognition" to establish the foundation of human rights and rights; some scholars try to examine the realistic foundation of human rights and the rights based on "community" except for the natural right, social justice and utilitarianism. In the morality basis, some scholars have established the foundation of human rights on the morality of man, emphasized the "harmless" of human rights, and advocated that human rights should be entitled to the moral standard of "harmless to people". In the political situation, some scholars have mentioned that the discourse of rights actually plays a role of providing proper reasons, the formal boundary and the exercise of the rules for the ruling power snugly. In the philosophical reflection, some scholars have put forward the theoretical criticism, the formal way and the formal law-guided administration on the basis of the institutionalization of human rights and rights. In addition, some scholars have done specific exploration on

1 Such as, LI Lin: "International Human Rights and National Sovereignty", in *Chinese Jurisprudence*, 1993, Issue 1; WAN Exiang: "On International Standard of Human Rights", in *Chinese Jurisprudence*, 1993, Issue 1; XIE Haiding: Academic "Freedom Rights As Legal Rights", in *Chinese Jurisprudence*, 2005, Issue 6; WU Yuzhang: "The Practice of Civil Rights—the Legal Significance of the Phenomenon of Association", in *Juristic Research,* 2005, Issue 5.

the theory of human rights and rights oriented in the West in Chinese language environment. Some scholars emphasize the influence of Chinese and Western cultural differences on the formation and development of human rights and human rights in China. Some scholars believe that Chinese traditional thought has already developed the elements of natural rights, but in the Chinese traditional people-based theory, people-based administration was mentioned more while administration-for-people was mentioned less, and lack of proper abstract concept, and further lack of the specific design of the system. Therefore, it is necessary to transform the traditional people-based theory, to complete the transformation from people's other-based to self-based, and to put administration-for-people into practice of civil rights, and to develop operative civil rights' concept, procedures and mechanism from the legal system. Some scholars also mention to re-integrate justice, ethical and legal rights, and to realize the combination of rights and virtue under modern conditions.[1] Compared with the former analysis of rights from legal system and juristic category, researches on human rights and rights in this period is more deeply involved in the fields of moral philosophy and political philosophy. In the debates on "standard of right" between the late 1980s and the early 1990s, criticizers against "view of standard of right" have criticized that "standard of right" has been the outdated "Enlightenment" theory actually, and believers for "view of standard of right" have also separated their own theory from "natural rights" and "man's natural rights" in the history. And since 1992, especially since

1 See: ZHAO Dingyang: "Paid Human Rights and the Doctrine of Human Being", in *Philosophical Research*, 1996, Issue 9; QIU Ben: "Free Human Rights and the Doctrine of Ordinary Human Being", in *Philosophical Research*, 1997, Issue 2; WANG Haiming: "Paid Human Rights and Free Human Rights", in *Philosophical Research*, 1997, Issue 7; ZHANG Hengshan: "On the Moral Foundation of Human Rights", in *Philosophical Research*, 1997, Issue 6; HUANG Kejian: "At the Gap between Ideological Level and Rights—To See the Humanity Mission of Confucianism in Modern Times", in *Tianjin Social Sciences*, 1998, Issue 4; ZHAO Dingyang: "'Paid Human Rights In Advance': A Non-Western Universal Human Rights Theory", in *Chinese Social Sciences*, 2006, Issue 4; XIA Yong: *Philosophy of Chinese Civil Rights*, in Sanlian Bookstore, 2004 Edition; HU Shuijun: *Political Analysis of Law*, Peking University Press, 2005 Edition.

entering the 21st century, the historical status of human rights and rights in modern history especially the history of modern political philosophy and the history of moral philosophy has got a more full understanding, meanwhile, Chinese scholars have also begun to make a certain reflection and creation based on Chinese language environment.

In addition, there frequently appeared review, summary and outlook on Chinese philosophical jurisprudence in this period, that "Where Chinese jurisprudence will go?" became a problem many scholars considered and argued, especially at the turn of the centuries and the 30th anniversary of reform and opening to the outside world.[1]Generally speaking, Chinese philosophical jurisprudence after the founding of new China has experienced roughly from "theory of state and law" to "the basic theory of jurisprudence", then to "philosophical jurisprudence" as mentioned above. In the "philosophical jurisprudence" stage since 1992, the four basic factors of "Tao" (logic), "Zheng" (politics), "Fa" (law) and "Xue" (academy) used for building and supporting the building of Chinese philosophical jurisprudence have gradually been formed and plump. Moreover, after experiencing more than 30 years of development relying on external theoretical resources, the cultural subjectivity of Chinese philosophical jurisprudence or the political logic and legal principle along their own cultural logic and social reality to develop forward has shown up more and more as historical missions.[2]

1 Such as, "The Philosophical Jurisprudence Walking Towards the 21st Century—A Summary of 1995 Annual National Conference on Philosophical Jurisprudence", in *Chinese Jurisprudence*, 1995, Issue 5; "A Summary of Academic Seminar of Review and Prospect on Chinese Jurisprudence in 20th Century", in *Chinese Jurisprudence*, 1997, Issue 5; "Speech Summary of the Seminar of Chinese Jurisprudence and Legal System in 20th Century", in *Juristic Research*, 1999, Issue 2; "Summary of the Symposium on 'Where Philosophical Jurisprudence will go?'", in *Juristic Research*, 2000, Issue 1; DENG Zhenglai: *Where Chinese Jurisprudence Will Go—The Outline of Constructing the Era of "Chinese Legal Ambition Prospect"*, Commercial Press, 2006 Edition.

2 See:HU Shuijun: "The Presentation of Legal Principle: The Thirty Years of Chinese Philosophical Jurisprudence", in *Chinese Jurisprudence* (Specialty for Commemoration of the 30th Anniversary of the Reform and Opening up); HU Shuijun: "The Thirty Years of 'juristic Research': Philosophical Jurisprudence", in *Juristic Research*, 2008, Issue 6.

In the process of constructing the theoretical system of philosophical jurisprudence in China, compilation of juristic textbooks in the on-going "Marxism theoretical research and construction project" is a great theoretical innovation project."Marxism theoretical research and construction project" was officially launched by the CPC Central Committee directly in 2004, in which it set up 24 main research groups, one of which was on compilation of textbooks on jurisprudence. Since the founding of the research group on compilation of textbooks on jurisprudence, it has established two sub-research groups on "*Philosophical Jurisprudence*" and "*Constitutional Jurisprudence*", in which the system of "chief expert in charge of the project" was adopted. The chief expert of the research group of "*Philosophical Jurisprudence*" was held by ZHANG Wenxian, and the other members included XU Chongde, YANG Jingyu, XIN Chunying, LI Lin, etc. The chief expert of the research group of "*Constitutional Jurisprudence*" was led by XU Chongde, and HAN Dayuan and LI Lin as chief experts, and the other members included TONG Zhiwei, HU Jinguang, MO Jihong, JIAO Hongchang, LIU Maolin, WANG Lei, ZHENG Xianjun, etc. In the compilation process of the two textbooks, it integrated the latest results exploring Chinese Marxism juristic theory actively in juristic circle.[1]

3. The Development of Cultural Subjectivity of Philosophical Jurisprudence

Since the west influence, Chinese philosophical jurisprudence was built up on the basis of basically following or copying foreign jurisprudence and legal theory. At first it was in the influence of European, American and Japanese jurisprudence. After the founding of new China, it was in the influence of the Soviet "theory of state and law". And then since the reform and opening up, it was further influenced by the western culture and science. Compared with foreign theoretical resources, China's philosophical jurisprudence is scarce in the positive use of Chinese traditional cultural resources that the "ancient and modern" historical ties

1 This paragraph is written by MO Jihong in Chinese.

is weakened even cut off obviously by the "Chinese and foreign" communication. This academic situation is inseparable with the global background that the connection between China and the world has been strengthened since the modern times. The integration and communication between different cultures in the world can be regarded as the favorable objective conditions to promote academic development in a country, however, the cultural subjectivity of Chinese academy and Chinese philosophical jurisprudence is highlighted up as a reality problem in the process of historical transformation.

On the one hand, Chinese philosophical jurisprudence shows the lack of its own cultural autonomy since it is largely influenced and even dominated by foreign theories. Research shows that, there appeared about 5500 legal books in domestic China only in the period of the Republic of China, but "the classic works are very few", and "they are mostly the replica of the western legal theory"[1], which reflects the passive situation of Chinese philosophical jurisprudence in the process of modernization. Compared obviously with the critique, devaluation, even destruction traditional culture and system suffered, foreign theory and system have become the main objects to learn, imitate and transplant. We know, learning and reference is not a fault, but it leads the dependence of Chinese academy. Some scholars were worried about this situation in 1903s.Some scholars pointed out:"Jurisprudence is a part of culture, of which quality and quantity is connected with the cultural standard of the country. Chinese modern jurisprudence has already had the history of decades, from the perspective of content and essence, if we say there is no juristic culture in China, that's not a fault. That is because Chinese juristic culture mostly is translation culture or transplanting culture. The natural science can be transplanted, but the jurisprudence can not be copied. Law is a form of national social organizations, which has an inseparable relationship

1 See: HAO Tiechuan: "Legal Students Studying Abroad in Modern China and Modernization of Legal System", in *Juristic Research*, 1997, Issue 6; HE Qinhua: "The Death and Rebirth of Chinese Ancient Jurisprudence—A Thought on Modernization of Chinese Jurisprudence", in *Juristic Research*, 1998, Issue 2.

with its own reality society. Jurisprudence construction coming from translation and copying will wipe out the nation; so-called juristic culture is another name of colonial culture. The construction of Chinese real juristic culture later seems to take the national consciousness and the awakening of the nation as a starting point."[1]This is the historical situation of China's modern jurisprudence that still continues so far. More important, in this situation, a lot of people has gradually formed such a tendency in the understanding: things coming from foreign especially western countries are usually regarded as the new, the progressive, the things worth pursuing; those things in China are usually considered as the old, the backward, the things to be eliminated, while the goal of China's development is to learn from Japan, Europe and the United States and even the Soviet Union to join the world. Just as some scholars have criticized, "Things are divided into the old and the new, and into the West and China, but always taking Chinese things as the old, while taking Western things as the new."[2] Hundred-year humiliation and turmoil has led to such a state of mind by learning from foreign countries and an influence by foreign countries. Till the 21st century, some scholars reflected on Chinese jurisprudence like this:"The development of nearly 30 years of Chinese jurisprudence mainly relies on the modernization paradigm, of which concrete performance is that it provides Chinese law and the development of law with an ideal vision of the western law by transplanting western system or relevant concepts, and it also causes that Chinese juristic scholars can not realize it is not Chinese own legal ideal vision provided by them."[3] It is worth pondering that there still appeared such a judgment in juristic circle after Chinese philosophical jurisprudence experiencing the reform and opening to the outside world especially the decades-development since 1992.

1 CAI Shuheng: *The Self-Conscious Development of Chinese Legal Principle*, Tsinghua University Press, 2005 Edition, p.25.

2 QIAN Mu: *Academic Standard in Modern China*, Sanlian Bookstore, 2001 Edition, Preface.

3 DENG Zhenglai: *The Premise Analysis on the Current Basic Mission of Chinese Legal Philosophy—The World Structure as a Historical Condition,* 2006, Issue 5.

On the other hand, after Chinese jurisprudence has experienced continuous political revolutions and cultural movements in more than 100 years since the late Qing Dynasty, the inheritance of the traditional cultural resources have been almost cut off. As early as the end of the 19th century and the beginning of the 20th century, LIANG Qichao has been aware of the problem, he said, "What we are worried about is not that the western academy is not thrifty, but that Chinese academy will die today"[1], "I'm not concerned that foreign academic thought can not enter into Chinese mind, but I'm concerned that Chinese academic thought does not glow brightly".[2] In the 20th century, "Chinese Academy" was regarded as stale and inferior-to-western-academy knowledge system in quite a long historical period and was criticized and negated by cultural and political movement repeatedly. Since the founding of new China, the theoretical resources of Chinese traditional culture has either been neglected, or been regarded as historical reason of frustration or fault of reality in the sense of lack of democratic legal system tradition in the research of philosophical jurisprudence. It seems that the deep-rooted critical concepts on Chinese traditional culture since the modern times are much more than Looks, winding based on the traditional culture of the formed since modern deep-rooted critique views, far more than the meticulous, clear and sympathy understanding on traditional culture by people, however, the situation of doing judgment along existing theory even vision of western scholars without actual deep study still exists. Some scholars of legal history have a deep feeling about it. Some scholars wrote like this: "when we read works on Chinese traditional legal research since a hundred years ago, especially in recent twenty years, we can not feel the shock of tradition, and we can not find the tradition able to give us confidence. Instead, what we always feel is a bitter and frustration... In

1 LIANG Qichao: Epilogue of "Book List of Western Academy", *The first volume of Collected Works of Yinbingshi* (a name of a studying house of LIANG Qichao).

2 LIANG Qichao: On the General Trend of the Changes of Chinese Academic Thoughts, *The seventh volume of Collected Works of Yinbingshi* (a name of a studying house of LIANG Qichao).

the developmental history of China's five thousand years' civilization, history and tradition is never so dim like that in this hundred-year history, and so doubtful by Chinese people."[1]However, this kind of attitude to treat Chinese traditional culture remaining in studies need to reflect, and that distorted comparative view "to break down the old for the new" in the longitudinal historical comparison and "Chinese academy inferior to the western academy" in the transverse space comparison also need to correct. In fact, "Chinese Academy" can not merely be understood as national historical and cultural form with replacement of the old and the new, but also can be treated as a kind of culture containing common elements crossing all the times and all over the world, like it also contains a certain pervasive factors in western culture. From the perspective of universe, "Academy", as it can really be said, shall not be divided into the Chinese and the western, or the ancient times and the modern times, that is so called "Academy has no difference between new and old and between ancient and modern"[2], however from the perspective of different cognitive paths on the common factors, "Academy" has showed different focuses and the perspective of and from achieving the universal factors of different cognitive path, "learning" in different cultures and showed different focuses and distinctions. Therefore, it can be said that "the culture differs, the academy also varies".[3] For the matter of that, strongly supporting Chinese academy and the cultural subjectivity of Chinese philosophical jurisprudence is the adherence and the pioneering to human's universal culture based on Chinese culture logic and social reality. The view that the pursuit of the cultural subjectivity of Chinese philosophical jurisprudence is to maintain the national performance of its own national culture narrowly is full of the methodological bias and the values of prejudice. Chinese culture went through much suffering in nearly a hundred

1 ZENG Xianyi, MA Xiaohong: *Some Problems in the Study of Chinese Traditional Law*, in *Juristic Research*, 2003, Issue 3.

2 WANG Guowei: *Preface of "Journal of Chinese Literature", Another Collected Works of Guantang* (a respectable name of WANG Guowei), Volume 4.

3 QIAN Mu: *Academic Standard in Modern China,* Sanlian Bookstore, 2001 Edition, Preface.

years of history, but from the point of view of history, "Chinese Academy" has been showing an inclusive and innovative ability all the time. Inheriting and integrating academies "at all times and in all over the world" and making its cultural subjectivity prominent can be said to be a historical task of Chinese philosophical jurisprudence.

Since 1990s, it has begun to present concern on their own cultural subjectivity in Chinese academia and academia of philosophical jurisprudence, and the cultural awareness and the cultural awareness of subjectivity have shown a gradual strengthening trend. For example, some scholars put forward the concept of "cultural consciousness", and pointed out that "cultural consciousness refers only to that people living in a certain culture "know" its culture, understand its origin, formation process, its characteristics and development trend, without any meaning of 'cultural return'. Not 'Involution' or advocating 'all-Westernization' or 'overall-other-changes', knowing-self is to strengthen the autonomic ability of the cultural transformation, and to gain independent status of cultural choice in the new environment and the new era". At the same time, they also pointed out that, "the 'cultural consciousness' refers to people living in different cultures understand other cultures and the relationship with their own culture on the basis of knowing their own culture".[1]This proposal has caused a great resonance in the academic circles. In the circles of philosophical jurisprudence, some scholars have also demonstrated their theoretical attitude of engaging in the philosophical jurisprudence research based on the Chinese cultural theory and social reality. Some scholars pointed out that, "Since more than a century ago, comparative study on the Chinese and the western has mostly been carried out under the strong self deprecating attitude, especially comparative study on Chinese and Western political and legal culture, always seems to illustrate how China is inferior to the west and how to transplant the western system over";[2] "Today, we are trying to

1 FEI Xiaotong: *On Culture and Cultural Consciousness*, Qunyan Press, 2007 Edition, pp.190, 302.

2 XIA Yong: *Asking For Doctrine Day and Night—Political and Legal Notes*, Shanghai Sanlian Bookstore, 2004 Edition, p.8.

walk out a new road, to reacquaint ourselves and the world we live with enough subjective consciousness of Chinese culture. ... While re-knowing and deep research Chinese legal culture, we shall promote Chinese legal culture to the world, and conduct equal and effective dialogue and exchange with other legal cultures including western legal culture."[1] In the perspective of the "subjective China", some scholars also criticized so-called "western modernization paradigm" dominating Chinese jurisprudence, and tried to start a "new era of jurisprudence" of cultural consciousness.[2]

Publicity of cultural subjectivity of Chinese philosophical jurisprudence means making Chinese philosophical jurisprudence walk out of dominated influence of Soviet theory and Western academy gradually in a large extent, focusing on Chinese realistic problems and the path of realistic development of law, following the line of reasoning of Chinese culture to develop the legal principle and the political logic, which can integrate both of Chinese and foreign universal values, also can push forward each other, complement each other and help and move forward in parallel on Chinese and foreign universal cultures. In another word, the key of the cultural subjectivity lies in the conscious awareness on the universal and essential "Tao" and "Li", and the historical development significance of the philosophical jurisprudence also lies in the expansion and development on "Tao" and "Li" along the road of Chinese cultural logic. This means that, cultural consciousness and philosophical jurisprudence with cultural subjectivity is built among the connection of "law" and "Li" (logic) and logical relationship, and what it wants to avoid is to directly copy the "Li" (logic) of the Soviet Union, Europe, the United States or other countries as our own principle or theory, but also to avoid to copy directly so-called "Li" (logic) in the classic works guide practice. At the same time, it also highlights value orientation and pursuit of knowledge to

1 Chinese Legal History Association (compiler): *Chinese Culture and Administration By Law•Preface*, Social Sciences Literature Press, 2007 Edition.

2 DENG Zhenglai: *Where Chinese Jurisprudence Will Go—The Outline of Constructing the Era of "Chinese Legal Ambition Prospect"*, Commercial Press, 2006 Edition.

make political view and legal practice conform to morality and justice and logic. In this regard, cultural consciousness and cultural subjectivity is actually the consciousness and the rise of morality and justice, reason and legal principle.

So-called "philosophical jurisprudence", which can be said, is "science" about "law", and which can also be said, is knowledge and discipline about legal principle, which actually the key of philosophical jurisprudence. As the ancients said, "'law' and 'logic' are two things originally", "the establishment of 'law' must be based on 'logic'. There are truth and fault first, then comes law, not the other way round"[1]; "Where there is legal system, there is 'law and logic' as its original....If you want to develop legislation in a law-disordered country and find 'law and logic' outside legal documents, the effect of jurisprudence will end, so if you want to advocate jurisprudence in today's China, the most important is abstract 'law and logic'"[2]. That "law and logic" is more obvious and conscious to present is the more intensive aspect than the theory of state and law and the basic theory of jurisprudence. The so-called cultural consciousness and philosophical jurisprudence with cultural subjectivity which requires to know the connection of logic and justice and the logical relationship consciously. Compared to the theory of state and law and the basic theory of jurisprudence, drawing law and logic out of such political movement as "based on class struggle" and foreign theory and reconsidering and constructing legal principle and political logic based on Chinese cultural logic and realistic road in the conditions of globalization and the opening world is an important symbol that Chinese philosophical jurisprudence has walked into maturity gradually. These have already been manifested in the textbook system and theories of the rights, the rule of law and so on. In the textbook system, as mentioned before, since entering into the twenty-first Century, textbooks of philosophical jurisprudence have adopted more and more the system

1 YAN Fu (translator): *The Spirit of Montesquieu Law* (Volume 1), Commercial Press, 1981 Edition, pp.1-2. Introductory notes by YAN Fu.

2 LIANG Qichao: *On the Developmental History of Chinese Philosophical Jurisprudence, The fifteenth volume of Collected Works of Yinbingshi.*

structure of "academy" and "legal principle", basically composed of two parts of content: "jurisprudence" and "philosophical jurisprudence", which shows that Chinese philosophical jurisprudence has paid more attention to be based on legal principle and the reality of China, though the scope of philosophical jurisprudence research is actually far beyond the law and logic content listed in textbooks of philosophical jurisprudence. In the theory of rights, compared to the basic theory of jurisprudence to establish the rights and obligations as the basic category of jurisprudence, the philosophical jurisprudence research about rights since 1990s has a significant expansion in the "logic". During this period, scholars have tried to excavate discourse of rights and law-guided administration from the traditional Chinese culture to make the human rights and law-guided administration speak "Chinese", therefore, so-called "rights with morality" concept to try to integrate Chinese and Western culture and to break through rights and morality have appeared, then the academic logic and Chinese style are obviously strengthened.[1]

Based on fundamental and pervasive cultural factors, publicity of cultural subjectivity does not mean that Chinese philosophical jurisprudence will go into a situation of producing cocoon to tie itself, self-closing, observing the sky in a well, even Ignorant Boastfulness. On the contrary, because of the subjective culture in the background of globalization and the open world, it precisely requires to absorb, go through or join other universal cultures in the world with open and tolerant attitude. This means that it needs to turn diaphragm and fracture to more dredging and understanding in the treatment of "ancient" things, and it requires to turn the passive and even conscious acceptance to subjective construction in the treatment of "foreign" things. In other word, "China of the world" not only needs

1 XIA Yong: *Philosophy of Chinese Civil Rights*, in Sanlian Bookstore, 2004 Edition; XIA Yong: *Floating Rule of Law—Chinese Reform Thoughts and Rule of Law in the Late Qing Dynasty and the Early Republic China*, in *Research of Comparative Law*, 2005, Issue 1; XIA Yong: *A Forgotten Civilization—Re-understanding Chinese Ancient Thoughts of Rule of Law, in the seventh volume of Journal of Collected Legal Works* in Tsinghua Journal of Rule of Law (GAO Hongjun as editor in chief), Tsinghua University Press, 2006 Edition.

China to connect with the world so as to absorb the world's culture, but also needs the world to connect with China in order to make China's wisdom and universal value participate actively and join in the process of the history of the world. Emphasizing the cultural consciousness and cultural subjectivity of Chinese philosophical jurisprudence just remains consciously path of Chinese culture and thus highlights and expands the corresponding universal values in the dispute of Chinese, western, new and old cultures, so as to establish Chinese philosophical jurisprudence which truly belongs to China itself and also belongs to the world with its unique characteristics in the woods of world academy.

4. The Theoretical Exploration on Legal Transplant and Trend of Globalization of Law

4.1 The theoretical exploration on legal transplant

Since 1990s, many scholars of the comparative law in China have made an explanation on the theoretical problems of legal transplant in their articles and works. Many Comparative jurists like SHEN Zongling, PAN Handian, WANG Chenguang, LIU Zhaoxing, ZHU Jingwen, HE Weifang, GAO Hongjun, MI Jian, HE Qinhua and many other scholars have published a lot of articles and works, which have set forth the problem of legal transplant from different perspectives by using methods of comparative research.

4.1.1 Different understandings on the implication of legal transplant

There are other terms equivalent to "transplant" used in the articles and works of western jurisprudence, such as borrowing, drawing on, assimilation, imitation, importation, influence, transfer, spread, introducing, and so on. There are four kinds of understandings on the implication of legal transplant by some Chinese scholars on the researches on the issues of legal transplant: The first is acceptance theory or inheritance theory, which thinks that legal transplant is a phenomenon a country accepts or voluntarily accepts foreign law; the second is inputting theory, which says that legal transplant means that part or most part of a national legal system are input from legal system of another country or "legal bloc" of many countries; the third is spreading theory, which explains legal transplant as the dissemination of law; the fourth is migration theory, which argues that legal transplant is a migration of a rule or a legal system from a country to another country.

Some scholars believe that legal transplant means that the law of a country or region can be transplanted into another country or region, like a whole plant being moved to another place to plant; Some scholars believe that legal transplant should be considered in the medical sense, like organ transplantation or part-transplantation; Some scholars think that legal transplant refers to the absorption, reference, integration and assimilation to the international law especially. "transplant" includes to conduct a comprehensive investigation on comprehensive factors like the legal norms, legal enforcement situation, legal operation process of the law to be transplanted, and it also includes transplant experiment after the comprehensive analysis on factors of politics, economy, culture and society of the acceptance country, and it still also includes continuous coordination and integration between the law transplanted after being transplanted and the law of the state.[1]

From the perspective of history to analyze, Some Chinese scholars think that law transplant is a result of a variety of social changes. Some are caused by military invasion, that occupying power transplants the law of their own country to the occupied countries; some are the results of economic and cultural exchanges, the developed countries in economy and culture have influenced the legal system of less-developed countries in exchanges and intercourse, namely, less developed countries have accepted the advanced legal culture.[2]Many scholars believe that law transplant is a kind of process of activities, a process of achieving a scheduled or non-scheduled result in a certain way and procedures. This process of activities includes importation, acceptance, introduction, but also choice, integration and

1 See: *The Law Year Book of China* (1995), The Law Year Book of China Press, 1995 Edition, p.1010.

2 See: ZHU Jingwen: *Introduction to Comparative Law*, Chinese Prosecution Press, 1992 Edition, pp.169, 173.

selection with rationalization, decision-making with control.

4.1.2 Different understandings on the portability of the law

Chinese scholars have three views on the portability of the law: the first thinks law does not have portability, because law is produced in a specific time and space, it can not be transplanted arbitrarily. The theoretical basis of emphasizing on the non-portability of law is actually emphasizing on the specialty of law. The second view is that law can be transplanted, because law is universal, and different laws have some same or similar characteristics. The third point of view argues that law is universal and particular, in a certain sense, law transplant is selective and conditional.

British comparative jurist O. Kahn-Freund who put forward the issue of legal transplant the earliest believes in his "The application and misuse of comparative law" that, the laws of a country are difficult to migrate to another country, of which the obstacle hindering legal transplantation is the political factor. British historian of Scottish legal system, Alan Watson refuted the viewpoint of Freund above in his article of "legal Transplant and Legal Reform", believing that history does not prove the pessimism of legal transplant; legal transplant is often achieved successfully in very different legal systems, even at very high levels of development and in different political circumstances; legal reformers think foreign laws can be transformed into a part of domestic law. Chinese jurist of comparative law SHEN Zongling thinks, differences between Freund and Watson are not whether law can be transplanted, but the different views on the level of transplantation.[1]

In recent years, most scholars in China suggest through academic contention and studies that, in order to adapt to the need of establishment and improvement of the socialist legal system in China, Chinese must refer to, absorb or transplant the experience of foreign legal system construction selectively, and further

1 SHEN Zongling: *Comparative Research*, Peking University Press, 1998 Edition, pp.671-672.

understand the connotation of legal transplant from the deeper level. China as a big developing socialist country has unique social life and economic environment different from western countries and other developing countries. Its characteristics and long historical culture makes it inevitable to refer to successful experiences from the legal systems of other countries, meanwhile it shall absorb the experiences from other countries critically and selectively based on its unique position.

4.1.3 The principle of legal transplant and the condition of live-transplantation in China

In recent years, Chinese scholars of comparative law combined with researches on the specific reference and part-introduction of the departmental laws and pointed out that legal transplant should follow the following principles: The first is the principle of same-construction and compatibility between the foreign law as a donor and the national law as a receptor, to do necessary adjustment to the receptor so as to prevent the emergence of tissue or organ variation after being transplanted; The second is the localization of foreign law that, if we want to make the laws and regulations introduced vital, that the "soil environment" must be truly suitable for the "plant"; The third is the choice of legal transplant, that "What only is suitable for their own, it is the best", we must be based on the reality of the country's national conditions to select the appropriate transplant subjects, the transplanted law is probably the most applicable law; The fourth is that the transplanted law shall have advancement, that is, after necessary improvement, the law can maintain the stability and the advancement of the acceptance country, but also it can be adapted to the needs of its modernization and future development.

Some scholars pointed out in the discussion on the legal transplant localization that a legal system must combine with the local factors like politics, economy, culture and so on in the process of formation and development, if the legal rules and operation mode from other countries can be understood, digested and accepted in the transplanted country, it is the localization of law. The localization of the law requires not only the representation of foreign law, but also recreation on the basis of studying its legal philosophy and rules in legal transplantation.[1]

In some articles and works, some scholars focus on the study of the conditions of live-transplantation of foreign law in China, and point out that the condition of live-transplantation of foreign law in China must be a simultaneous transplantation of the legal system and legal concept. Legal transplant shall try to respect its own unique legal language on the basis of accordance with international commonsense in the institutional level, to make the understanding of its citizens and the implication of western legal system reach a consensus, so as to obtain the rightness in the daily life of citizens. The transplantation in institutional level must also pay attention to the corresponding matching transplant. Legal transplantation is a systematic project, which is composed of three systems: the outsider, inner and internal of legal systems. The corresponding matching transplant outside the law is the premise of the preparation to investigate on the dependent environmental factor of foreign law in order to complete the legal transplant, to specifically examine the politics, economy, traditional culture and national geography, and to get an objective evaluation on the development process and social effect of foreign law. The corresponding matching transplant inside the law means to keep the coordination of the insiders of the transplanted law, which is its own requirement. The corresponding matching transplant between legal systems refers to that the transplanted law as a composition of the legal system must join in the whole legal system and keep consistency with the relevant departmental law. In the legal transplant in the concept level, it refers to that if the transplanted legal concept wants to live in China, naturally it can not be separated from the social basis of the civil society and the economic basis of the market economy. What is the most important is the formation of law-guided administration society in China, namely, that it has a good law and good obedience to the law. The key to the establishment of the law-guided administration society lies in the cultivation

1 See: T*he Law Year Book of China* (2007), The Law Year Book of China Press, 2007 Edition, p.830.

of citizens' legal belief, that the establishment of the law-guided administration in China or the cultivation of legal belief and the localization of foreign legal concept is the process of synchronization. Legal transplant in both system level and concept level need to be rooted in the soil of the law-guided administration society, and the cultivation of legal concept or the formation of legal belief is the focus and the focal point of survival of legal transplant.[1]

4.2 On the theoretical exploration of legal globalization

In recent years, with the development of the process of economic globalization and legal modernization, the theoretical issues of the relevant legal globalization is increasingly becoming a topic of discussion by Chinese and foreign scholars. Some comparative jurist in China had a wide and deep discussion on the theoretical issues of legal globalization combining with the reality of contemporary countries and some foreign scholars' theoretical viewpoints.

4.2.1 On the generation background of the theory of legal globalization and the characteristics of the legal globalization

Some scholars believe that the generation background of the theory of legal globalization mainly has the following several aspects: the first is the formation of the new specialized division in the range of the world with the irreversible economic globalization; the second is the connection of the world financial markets, and the free flow of investment beyond borders; the third is that the world-wide production and other activities by large multinational companies has strengthened their importance in the economic globalization; the fourth is the increasing strengthening of the international trade and regional trade blocs resulted in the increasing influence on the domestic rules by international rules of the international trade; the fifth is that most developing countries are in the reduction of direct participation of countries in economic life, emphasizing on developing the market system, and changing the original legal structure; the sixth is the new liberal concept taking the dominant

1 See: *The Law Year Book of China* (2006), The Law Year Book of China Press, 2006 Edition, pp.806-807.

position in economic relations; the seventh is that the voice of democratization, human rights protection and the rule of law has been increasingly rising.

Some scholars believe that the main features of the legal globalization are manifested as follows: The first is to emphasize the technicality of law. The technical law does not differ because of culture, which can be freely imported and exported, namely legal transplant, including the legislation and the implementation of law. A large number of laws have crossed national borders as a technology, especially the commercial law, intellectual property law, environmental law and so on, then formulation and implementation of legal rules is becoming increasingly dependent on the development of the technology. The second is that the theory of the legal globalization advocates the supranationalism of the development of law. The globalization of law today is now showing the trend of unification of globalization contract law and the commercial law.

4.2.2 Different understandings on the connotation of legal globalization

Chinese scholars hold different theoretical viewpoints on the understanding of legal globalization from different perspectives. (1) Theory of “legal convergence”. It argues that the globalization of law is the convergence of legal philosophy, legal value, legal system, law enforcement standards and principles in the scope of globe; It thinks legal globalization is to form the global norms system based on recognition of national sovereignty, is the assimilation and integration of legal norms.[1] (2)The globalization of law is a reflection and stereotype to global international politics, economy and culture. It thinks that the globalization of law is legal presentation in the ongoing globalization process of world economy, politics and culture, which is not only the results, but also the guarantee of the globalization of economy, politics and culture.[2] (3) The globalization of law is law’s bonding force and influence beyond the borders. It thinks that legal

1 See WONG Guomin: “Globalization and International Unification of Rules of International Commercial Contract”, in *Chinese and Foreign Jurisprudence,* 2001, Issue 3.

2 See ZHU Jingwen: *Globalization of Law: The Basis of Legal Principle and Social Content*, in *Collected Works on Philosophical Jurisprudence*, Volume 1, Law Press, 2000 Edition.

globalization refers to a certain countries and regions refer to each other and transplant in certain legal and cultural traditions and then show influence of law beyond national boundaries.[1]Here, it reflects the legal globalization in the sense of the legal transplant. (4) The globalization of law in a sense of sociology refers to that with the development of economic globalization, some rules of the non-country international organization develop independently in the globe without relying on national laws or international treaties, which such "non-country global law" is different from the national law and international law in the traditional sense.[2] Obviously, the scope of this understand is very narrow. (5) The globalization of law is a westernization or Americanization. It believes that the globalization of law is a process that western countries especially the United States promote their legal value and legal system to the globe. Globalization is dominated by western countries and the history of the process must be searched in the capitalist way and be searched in the secret of the market economy.[3] (6) The essence of legal globalization is "legal globalization in a country (region)". It argues that globalization of law refers to a phenomenon and process that the legal system prevailing in a country or region is accepted universally in the globe with the development of global economy, the development of means of communication and increasingly frequent communication between countries. They mainly include two aspects: the first is the globalization of the contract law and the commercial law; the second is the globalization of public law.[4] (7) The globalization of law is a phenomenon of the solution to the global problems. The global problems are the problems that affect every corner of the globe but not stipulating its scope by the

1 See CHEN Xiaolan, WANG Jinyuan: "On Globalization of Law and the Development of Chinese Legal System", in *Guangming Daily*, on September 14, 2001.

2 See SUN Guohua: *Searching for Legal Principle*, in Chinese Prosecution Press, 2003 Edition, p.864.

3 See YANG Chaoren, HAN Zhiwei: *Globalization, Institutional Development and National Rejuvenation*, in *The Paradox of Globalization* (YU Keping as editor in chief), the Central Compilation and Translation Press, 1998 Edition, p.138.

4 See YAO Tianchong, MAO Muran: *On the Theory of "Globalization of Law"*, in *Academic Journal of Northeastern University* (Social Sciences Edition), 2001, Issue 1.

countries' borders.

Some scholars of comparative law have pointed out in depth that, three kinds of misunderstandings on the globalization of law should be avoided: firstly, don't take the legal globalization as the equalizer to capitalism. Globalization of law causes the connection of politics, economy and culture in the scope of globe as a new way of communication based on the development of information technology enabling peoples from various countries to the mutual exchanges and communication in the global era, with an unprecedented way and through the internationalization of capital and globalization of market. The globalization of law shows that the law and the way of communication of human society have entered a new stage. Secondly, don't take the legal globalization as the equalizer to Westernization or Americanization. In the past and the present stage, many international rules are formulated by western countries or the United States, which reflects the characteristics of their domestic rules in varying degrees. But with the development of economic globalization, they may not always occupy the leading position in the process of globalization of law, and with the development of developing countries and the formation of world multiple-polarization, developing countries will play a more and more important role in the new international politics and the new economic order increasingly, which will continuously change the inequality in politics, economy and law between developed and developing countries in the current international relations, and construct a new world legal order in accordance with the equality and the benign interactive relationship model.[1] Thirdly, don't take the legal globalization as the equalizer to worldlization and internationalization of law. That is to say, the legal globalization can not be considered as a movement from global decentralized legal systems to the integration of global law, or a process of laws in the scope of the globe being integrated into a legal system, and thus be regarded that the law

1 See: *The Law Year Book of China* (2007), The Law Year Book of China Press, 2007 Edition, p.830.

comes from "economic or political forces out of control of any state", and the law is "supranational law", and a legislation process independent of any state.[1] Globalization of law is a mutual coordination between laws of a country and those of other members of international society under the premise of independent sovereignty of a national state, which purpose is to reduce the obstacles of the international political, economic and cultural exchanges.

Some scholars have pointed out in the discussion of relationship between globalization and modernization of Chinese legal system that, the legal development of contemporary China is facing new challenges in process of legal reconstruction in the era of globalization. We must defend the legal sovereignty and oppose the new legal colonialism to prevent the tendency of "marginalization" of the development of Chinese law. The trend of legal globalization has pushed the process of the reconstruction of the global law, but it has not brought humans a "Datong (universal harmony) world" of law, and diversified system of legal civilization still has a profound and extensive global basis and strong vitality.[2]

4.2.3 Different evaluations on the globalization of law

In overview of some articles and works of Chinese scholars of comparative law in recent years, they hold different evaluation views on the legal globalization. Scholars holding a positive view believe that the scope of people's communication in the modern world has been beyond the scope of state and there have been many ultra national organizations, so politics and law in a level of social system must also be globalized. Supranational laws have appeared in a large number, and their applicable scope is larger and larger; there are more and more openness in domestic China, and China continuously absorbs mutually and copies the useful things for ourselves in foreign law by exchanges and transplantation, making laws of various countries more and more common and butt each other. The legal boundary between countries is not clear, and the domestic law is not so pure,

1 Ibid, p.807.

2 See SUN Guohua: *Searching for Legal Principle*, in Chinese Prosecution Press, 2003 Edition, p.864.

which has more and more commonness with the laws of other countries.[1] From the perspective of cultural identity some scholars argues that legal globalization can come true because of people's identity and acceptance to the law culture of globalization, including the following to the common legal concept, reference to the same rule of law and the compliance to the common law norms. In the international political, economic and technological exchanges, the legal culture with the mutual recognition makes this global communication and exchanges into reality, so the common legal culture has become the internal cohesion of this interaction.[2]

Scholars holding negative views on legal globalization believe that the proposition of globalization of law is actually the ignorance of the principle of state sovereignty and the denial of the world trend of political multiple-polarization, which ignored the essential characteristics of law, and tried to describe law as a rule that various countries abide by the process of economic globalization and diluted the differences between the laws of various countries.[3]Advocates of the theory of legal globalization beyond the country have ignored the integrity of the law itself and the trend of multiple-polarization of the world's politics. In spite of the convergence of law in the field of private law between countries, intrinsic properties of various national laws and the principle that various governments deal with international affairs independently has not been changed, and the expansion of the adjustment scope of international law and the growth of commonness in law of various countries has not fundamentally changed the diversified characteristics of legal sovereignty of various countries. In the contemporary countries and regions of the world, there still exist differences in social system, values and concepts, developmental degree, religious belief and

1 See YAN Cunsheng: "Integration and Diversification of Law in 'Globalization'", in *Legal Sciences*, 2003, Issue 5.

2 See WANG Shengwei: "The Cultural Perspective of the Study of Legal Globalization", in *Theory Observation*, 2002, Issue 5.

3 See YAO Tianchong, MAO Muran: "On the Theory of 'Globalization of Law'", in *Academic Journal of Northeastern University* (Social Sciences Edition), 2001, Issue 1.

historical and cultural traditions. And the basic framework of the current law still manifests that people of all countries choose social system and develop their own legal system according to their own national conditions.[1]

By studying the theoretical viewpoints of foreign scholars holding negative attitude to legal globalization (such as Dells Marty from the first university of Paris in France), some Chinese scholars illustrates the influence of globalization of law on the legal system of state, and points out that the globalization of law may also be legal means that some countries carry out the hegemony. The first form is to impose publicly some imperialism of the law to another country, such as "*Holmes—Burton Act*" (March 12, 1996) for the US banning the trade with Cuba, "*Alto—Kennedy Act*" (August 5, 1996) for the US prohibiting the trade with Libya and Iran. The second form is to plug the laws of a country into an international treaty, even export the laws of a country as an ordinary commodity to another country, to impose to this country in an ostensible-agreed way. The third form is to impose to another country in a way of only the market law taking dominant position in a real non-law region, to become the law based on the market beyond the state. On the basis of careful research and analysis on these theories, some Chinese scholars point out that the forms above have destroyed the unity of the legal system of state actually, and have broken the domestic unified legal order in the process of legal globalization.[2] Therefore, we must recognize the difference between the legal globalization and the economic globalization for contemporary China with reform and opening up and rapid development. On the one hand, we need to absorb and refer to the foreign advanced and right legislation, legal system and legal culture suitable to Chinese national conditions continuously for building China into a modern socialist country under law-guided administration, meanwhile adhere to the principle of national sovereignty and the legal principle

1 See LIU Zhaoxing: *Comparative Jurisprudence*, Social Science Literature Press, 2004 Edition, p.126.

2 See: *The Law Year Book of China* (2004), The Law Year Book of China Press, 2004 Edition, p.920.

of sovereignty.

5. A Study of the History of Chinese Legal System in the Process of Modernization

The 14th Party Congress has determined the goal of the central of "to construct the socialist market economy". In the consensus of "market economy is legal economy", the creation of the legal system of the socialist market economy has become a top priority, and accelerating to transplant the legal systems of the developed countries and emphasizing on law in accordance with the international standard and modifying and perfection of China's legal system according to the rules of WTO, have become the mainstream view in the field of jurisprudence. Chinese legislative process has accelerated significantly, that a large number of new laws such as *Corporation Law*, *Contract Law*, *Property Act* and so on have been promulgated and implemented, while a large number of original laws have been amended or abolished. The conflict and integration relationship issue between Chinese and Western legal cultures becomes the focus of people's attention and basic proposition once again just in an era when law and social life changes rapidly. In the legal process of the contemporary China, on earth "How to treat the internal factors and external factors of Chinese law" and "How to deal with the conflict between Chinese and foreign factors", are the questions that all of the jurisprudence scholars witnessing and participating in the modernization process of contemporary Chinese law have to face and answer. Relying on their rich historical heritage and a unique historical perspective, the Chinese legal scholars are trying to answer this question in the field of Chinese legal history.

In this period, there is a relative "trough" in the research process of the history of the legal system. The reason is that the economic law and the civil and commercial law become hot subjects due to meet the urgent needs of the rapid development of market economy, and a large number of legal transplants make the articles and works on introducing western legal model and philosophy full in newspapers and medias, while the subject of Chinese legal history is relatively deserted. But scholars of the legal history still hold fast to their position, and have done the following three aspects of work: to exercise itself and strengthen discipline construction and reflection as well as the work of the excavation, sorting and examination to legal documents; to deepen the study on the division-dynastic legal history and the history of department law, that especially the study of Chinese civil and commercial legal system history, national legal history and modern legal history research has made significant progress; it also has made great progress in the aspects of cultural study of Chinese law and the comparative research between Chinese and western cultures.

How to recognize the history of Chinese legal development scientifically and promote the history of law to the science is a major proposition the contemporary legal history scholars face. "New thinking and new method" of the study of history of law were discussed as the central subject in 1999 and 2000 annual meetings of Chinese Legal History Association. The column of "Chinese legal history's counterattack" was opened in "*Social Science News*" published on February 1, 2002, in which articles of four scholars were published and they proposed new insights on the defects and errors of traditional research mode of legal history and the mission in the turning period, and so on. A few years after that, scholars published a series of papers continuously in the field of Chinese legal history, refuting theory of "the unity of various laws", theory of "no differences between civil and criminal law", theory of "the penalty first", theory of "to break the rule by example" and the view of denying the social function of the ancient law. In the discussion on how to recognize the history of Chinese legal development scientifically, scholars proposed a lot of many new viewpoints: to face the defects of traditional research mode of legal history, and to change research thinking and research methods; to question theories of "the unity of various laws", "the penalty first" and "no differences between civil and criminal law", and to recognize right the ancient Chinese legal system; to question theory of "the stagnation of ancient legal system after Tang Dynasty" and theory of "the declination of legal science", and to state correctly the development of legal system and jurisprudence in the late of ancient times; to correct the theory of "to break the rule by example" and the false theory in case study, and to evaluate the historical role of cases correctly; to state the basic characteristics of Chinese traditional legal system accurately according to the epistemology of seeking truth from facts.

In order to provide abundant basic materials for the study of legal history, many scholars also participated in collation to the legal literature, and achieved significant results. According to incomplete statistics, about a hundred works as collation results on the ancient legal books have been published in the field of academy in China since 1996, in-taking more than 500 species of literature, more than 50 million words in total. The number of the results of the collation of ancient legal literature in the last ten years is more than the sum of the first forty years after the founding of new China. The contents of some legal ancient achievements published in recent years involves the laws and regulations, the local laws, judged cases and materials, legal literature, legal collected works in the promulgation of various successive dynasties. Among them, the relative larger scale of literature and representative results with greater influence are: *Sequel of Chinese Rare Legal Collective of Ancient Books and Records*, *Two-year Legal Decree* and *Zou Yan book* (a submitted report) contained in *Bamboo Slips in Han Dynasty Tombs in Zhangjiashan*, *Revise to the Codex Hidden in Tianyi Chamber* (a copy book in Ming dynasty), *Constitutional Documents Compilation in Yuan Dynasty*, *Literature Summary of China Supervisory System*, *Local Legal Literature of Ancient China* (the first volume), *Compilation and Storage of Ancient Notices*, *Ten Kinds of Legal Literature of Ancient Local Regulations and Local Rules*, *Various Dynasties' Legal Cases and Court-decision Documents*, *Conspectus of Penal Cases*, *Collection of Chinese Legal Science*, *Literature of Chinese Legal Science*, *Collection of SHEN Jiaben's non-carved Works*, *Collection of Jurisprudence in the Modern Times*, *National Legal Ancient Books in Various Chinese Dynasties*, *Compilation of TIAN Zang's Contract Documents*,

Collected Works of Treaties in Qing Dynasty, and so on.[1]

Admittedly, in researches on the history of department law, the research on the history of civil law is less than the history of criminal law all the time. The main reasons are: firstly, some scholars still have doubts whether there exists the civil law in ancient China, and this issue often appears. It causes that the whole research of history of the civil law stays hesitant for they have not reached a consensus on the premise issue. Secondly, that Chinese ancient civil law does not form the legal system with typical Chinese characteristics like "tolerating and concealing between kinfolks" and "convicting crimes by kinship" results in which scholars are difficult to form a focal point in research and conclusion. Thirdly, the situation that the use of Chinese ancient civil law is more active in the common people that in the state affairs, and that a large number of resources and literature of the civil law are scattered in the official judgment documents, civil contracts, the customary laws, and so on brings researchers the difficulty to collect materials. However, the rapid development of Chinese civil jurisprudence in the lately more than 10 years has forced the legal historians to find channels of communication and dialogue, therefore, the research on the history of civil law has had a great progress, and more than 10 monographs of "History of the civil law" as representatives compiled by YE Xiaoxin, ZHANG Jinfan, etc have been published. The appearance of works of history of civil law marks that the research in the field of the history of Chinese civil law has gradually been mature and systematic. Meanwhile, specialized works appear in the field from the property law, contract law to marriage and inheritance system, and a large number of papers makes do supplement, improvement and deepening on the above contents, in which the more outstanding achievements are the researches on the contents of the civil customary law, the contract law, Dunhuang civil documents and so on. But the problem is obvious, copying or using the contents of Chinese ancient

1 See: Legal System History Office of Law Institute of Chinese Academy of Social Sciences(editor): T*he New Development of Science of Chinese Legal History*, China Social Sciences Press, 2008 Edition, pp.2-9.

civil law mechanically in accordance with the contents of the modern civil law system can make it get a standardized reorganization and systematic arrangement, but it exist the danger of acting in a Procrustean way. In fact, it may fail to reach the purpose of communication and dialogue between the ancient and the modern eventually.

The research on Chinese legal culture has gradually formed a climax since the middle of 1990s, that it should be said that this is the inevitable result of the study of Chinese legal history and the development of the history of Chinese legal thought. However, the emergence of this research area and its strong momentum have changed the pattern of disciplines of Chinese legal history, which the legal system composed of history of legal system and history of legal thought as its basic components is gradually being broken, Chinese legal culture research is expected to become a new sub discipline independent of history of legal system and history of legal thought. At the same time, the occasion of the birth of such a new research field in the turning of 21st century has its profound source of social environment. Maybe it is a historical coincidence, China experienced an unprecedented and protracted argument on legal culture in the last turn of centuries, and now we are facing the same proposition once again. The difference is that the debate last time focuses on "the western law as a tool", namely, how to introduce the western legal system to be used in China; the debate this time focuses on whether to "take Chinese legal system dominant" and how to "take Chinese legal system dominant". What scholars pay more attention to is whether China should return to the traditional culture, and how to utilize the natural resources of law. In the perspective of internationalization and modernization, legal historians have conducted a profound review and reflection on Chinese legal culture from the connotation, manifestation forms to the similarities and differences between Chinese and western cultures and modern transformation tact, etc. Currently there are about more than 20 works, more than 1000 papers in this aspect, and formed conclusion can be roughly divided into two groups: some scholars some scholars think Chinese legal culture has many positive factors, so it should be inherited and developed in modern times; the others think Chinese legal culture has too many negative factors, so it should be transformed greatly and abandoned. Whether it is a compliment or depreciation, the purpose of scholars is common: Try to reveal the true nature of Chinese original ecological legal culture and to draw nutrient and resources which can serve the modern times from it.

The researches on the Chinese legal culture are mainly focused on the following questions: (1) The characteristics of Chinese legal culture and its formation reason. Scholars have investigated from the origin, core, stage division, evolution way of Chinese legal culture to its material conditions, ideological roots, the philosophical foundation and so on in a multi-dimension and multi-angle way, and analyzed the characteristics of nature of public law, familization, religiousness and absolutism of Chinese legal culture. (2) The researches on rite and law, the rule by rites and the rule by law, ethics and law. Because of politicization and legalization of the concepts of "rule by law" and "rule by virtue", the relationships between rite and law, the rule by rites and the rule by law, ethics and law that always go through in Chinese legal culture since its emergence have been reexplained and reinterpreted. Scholars provides a train of thought for the developmental direction of Chinese rule of law in the future in the aspects of the origin of rite and law, the relationship between family ritual and state law, the connotation of rights and obligations, and value of moral belief and the belief of rule of law, etc. (3) The researches on the modernization transformation of the traditional culture of law. The topic of "tradition and modernization" has been prosperous all the time since the mid 1980s, though scholars of jurisprudence especially the historians of legal history enter into the prosperity slightly late, the latter's momentum is very high. The discussion in this field is mainly focused on the combination level and the conflict factors of the traditional legal culture and the modern rule-by-law spirit, and how to transform them and so on. Currently there are too many, endless works and papers on the traditional legal culture and the modernization, however the real excellent works with theoretical height are very few. But at least this shows the point: after suffering a series of negative effects brought by legal transplantation, scholars begin to reflect environment of society and ethics that the law runs in China, and thus leads to the wave of regress to the native culture. Among them, the viewpoints of LIANG Zhiping[1] and ZHU Suli[2] are the most representatives, and the most influential.

Since China embarked in modern times after the Opium War in 1840, the relationship between western culture and Chinese traditional culture has been a major source leading to Sino-foreign conflicts and domestic major incidents all the time, and the solution of the problem has been so painstaking for "the creators of history". The solution from "learning from foreign fortes on technology to restrict foreign" of learning "sturdy vessels and powerful cannon" from the western to "seeking to be strong and rich" of the Westernization Movement and from "Hundred Days of Reform" in the pursuit of huge and overall changes to "New Policies of Late Qing" later do not run roughly out of the category of "Chinese culture as the body and western science as tools", although the concept of "western science as tools"(western use, western machine and western science) has been expanded from physical level like weapons, military and economy to institutional level like official system, law, constitutionalism, while the concept of "Chinese culture as the body" (Chinese system, Confucianism and Taoism, Chinese culture) has been shrunk from "the institution of culture and materials" to "virtues", which shows that Chinese "creators of history" attempted to re-explain and re-designate continuously the scope and boundary of "Chinese body" and "western tools" in the levels of materials, institutions and spirit before the May 4th new cultural movement to solve the tension between them. The trend is the continuous expansion of the connotation and denotation of "western tools" while the continuous shrinking of the

1 LIANG Zhiping: *The Cultural Interpretation of Law*, Sanlian Bookstore, 1994 Edition; *The Customary Law of Qing Dynasty: Society and Country*, China University of Political Science and Law Press, 1996 Edition; *Law and Order in Customary Society*, in WANG Mingming, et al: *Order, Justice and Authority in Customary Society*, China University of Political Science and Law Press, 1997 Edition.

2 ZHU Suli: *Rule of Law and its Local Resources*, China University of Political Science and Law Press, 1996 Edition.

connotation and denotation of "Chinese body", and finally retreating to the spirit realm to survive. After the May 4th new cultural movement launched "ideological revolution", Confucianism as the representative of Chinese traditional ethics was criticized, and the trend advocating a radical anti tradition and overall westernization appeared. Ethics and morality is the core content in the spiritual field, and a nation's ethics and morality is the value standard the nation understands and transforms the world. Giving up the scale of the nation itself, it can only take the foreign standard as the standard, losing the national discrimination, and then LU Xun's "copinism" will become just empty talk. So since laws were revised in late Qing Dynasty, what ancient lawmakers from various dynasties advertised do not run mostly out of the principle of "integration of the Chinese and the western" from "compromising good common regulations from various countries, and adopting the latest theory in modern times, and still conforming to the propriety and national conditions of various dynasties in China",[1] but what they actually do or can do is "gaining peace by negotiation and learning from big powers as a goal"[2].Today, the western legal spirit and discourse has become the mainstream of China's legislative system, but it can not be rooted in the land of China, can only float in the sky over China. The system and discourse of traditional law has already gone and nothing left in the form, but it still affects the life of the Chinese people stubbornly and profoundly, and actually dominates the fate of every Chinese people. Chinese and foreign legal cultures have never really been integrated, but existing in the Chinese society in this strange form of binary opposition. This is clearly not what we would like to see, and it is also what scholars of history of the legal system should give explanations and solutions.

1 SHEN Jiaben (*The Law Minister and the Right Assistant in Ministry of Law*): Report on the *Completion List for Draft of Criminal Specific Provisions*, revised on November 26, the 33rd of Guangxu, see the Preface volume of Statutes in Imperial Qing Dynasty.

2 SHEN Jiaben (The Law Minister), et al: *Report on Asking for Compiling the Current Criminal Law So As to Implement New Law Immediately*, revised on January 29, the 34th of Guangxu, see Archive of Ming and Qing Dynasties of the National Palace Museum (compiler):*Preparatory Constitutional Archives in late of Qing Dynasty*, Zhonghua Book Company, 1979 Edition, p.852.

Chapter 13

New Development of Rule of Law and Constitutional Jurisprudence

Since 1993, with gradual acceptance and use of principles of "rule of law" and "human rights protection" in Chinese constitutional jurisprudence circle, which are commonly adopted by the current world, especially in 1999, the statecraft of "Ruling the Country by Law and Building a Socialist Country under Rule of Law" was constitutionalized under the amendment to the current constitution, and in 2004, "the country shall respect and protect human rights" was constitutionalized with the fourth amendment to the current constitution.The "Constitutionalization of Rule of Law" and "Constitutionalization of Human Rights" have both effectively promoted the implementation of Chinese constitution in the system construction, and brought historical opportunity for innovation and great progress of our constitutional jurisprudence. Meanwhile, on the basis of highly recommendation and introduction of the latest overseas theoretical achievements of constitutional jurisprudence, and combined with the specific practice of our socialist legal construction, the Chinese constitutional jurisprudence scholars have made deep and systematic studies on many important theoretical problems thereof. Such efforts and attempts have largely both promoted the perfection of the theoretical system of our constitutional jurisprudence, and upgraded the research level of the theory of constitutional jurisprudence in China.

1. "Awakening of Methodology" of Constitutional Jurisprudence

The research methods of constitutional jurisprudence in China have been influenced by the Soviet Union's constitutional jurisprudence for a long time, which strictly implemented the class analysis method as the fundamental approach, and when analyzing specific problems, such research methods were used to adducingpolitical discourse to interpret articles of constitution, or even taking the opposite track to directly take the articles of constitution as grounds for justifying political decision. Some scholars called the early methodology of constitutional jurisprudence as "unspecific" state thereof.[1]

Distinguished from the above mentioned constitutional jurisprudence methodology concerning traditional purport, other scholars tried to rethink and reconstitute the methodology. For instance, TONG Zhiwei held that "the old class analysis methods and pertinent basic theories of constitutional jurisprudence shall be changed fundamentally, the specific practice of which is to take the social rights as core concepts or fundamental categories, build social rights analysis methods as specific analysis methods of constitutional jurisprudence discipline, furthermore, around the new methodology, to renovate and perfect the existing basic theories, so as to form more systematic and scientific professional basic theories."[2] As a kind of analysis method, "social rights analysis method refers to a kind of theoretical approach, which starts with analyzing social rights, being based on grasping the basic attributes of society, especially the law of analysis and reanalysis, to specify and cognize the constitutional phenomena."[3] Corresponding to TONG Zhiwei's social rights analysis method, ZOU Pingxue held that the

1 LIN Laifan: *From Constitutional Norms to Normative Constitution*, Law Press·China, 2001, p.28.

2 TONG Zhiwei: *Reform of Methodology of Constitutional Jurisprudence, Law,* 1994, Issue 9.

3 Ibid.

economic analysis method should be imported into the study of constitutional jurisprudence, which means from the economic category perspective, to cognize economy and implied economic logic of constitutionalism with the comprehensive thinking of economy and constitutionalism, to explore the interactive relationship and integration mechanism between economy and constitutionalism, so as to seek the internal law of development of constitutionalism. The methodology foundation of the economic analysis method is Marxist economic philosophy, the objective basis of which is established pursuant to the deep and close relationship between economy and law, as well as the relationship between economy and policy; and the theoretical basis of which is economics, constitutional jurisprudence and politics. Furthermore, ZOU Pingxue held that the existing economic philosophy and theoretical basis have provided methodological guiding ideology and necessary conditions for further economic analysis of constitutionalism; in the light of existing knowledge, such subject has not been studied as a systematic subject, so the learning and conclusion thereof are dispersed and fragmentary; the relationship between constitutionalism and economy are objective and internal unified, so the unity of objective object shall be reflected and reproduced through the logical and historical unity between the research method and research object.[1] The economic analysis method shall be imported into the study of constitutional jurisprudence, and the economy and implied economic logic of constitutionalism shall be cognized with comprehensive thinking of economy and constitutionalism.[2]

Actually, the study method of constitutional jurisprudence is not absolutely independent, which is not distinguishable from those of general social sciences. So, the study methods of disciplines, such as philosophy, social science and politics, can be directly and comprehensively used in constitutional jurisprudence. Since the 21st century, as to the methodology, most constitutional scholars

1 ZOU Pingxue, "A Rustic Opinion of Import of Economic Analysis Methods into Constitutionalism Study", *Law and Social Development*, 1996, Issue 1.
2 Ibid.

held that constitutional jurisprudence shall be independent of other adjacent disciplines, especially politics.[1]LIN Laifan, who noticed the methodology of constitutional jurisprudence earlier in the field, has put forward unique insights on the fundamental method and specific method which shall be applied to constitutional jurisprudence in China. He deemed, with respect to the fundamental method, the constitutional jurisprudence is certain to be "scientific", able to reveal "facts". Meanwhile, it contains the constituent elements of "learning". In other words, the constitutional jurisprudence gets entangled in a variety of complex value judgments. So, the strained relation between facts and value, and the specific value orientation of constitution must be faced up. Actually, the specific method of constitutional jurisprudence is the interpretation method thereof. However, in today's China, annotated constitutional jurisprudence is suffering from contempt, and the methodology of constitutional jurisprudence is in an "unspecific" condition.[2] TONG Zhiwei also deemed, the theoretical part of Chinese constitutional jurisprudence, "from discipline specific analysis method to language system, is obviously the mechanical extension of historical materialism, for instance, the class analysis method, or such phraseology as state system, regime, class, revolution, economic base, superstructure, productive force and relation of production. That is, the constitutional jurisprudence in China is still in a backward state, absent of discipline specific analysis method, which is due but not yet available, and basically has been substituted by the methods with respect to world view".[3] ZHENG Xianjun also favored that the methodology of constitutional jurisprudence shall have its independent character. She deemed the methodology is one way to make constitutional jurisprudence into an independent

1 ZHENG Xianjun, "Why the Consciousness of Methodology is Needed in Constitutional Jurisprudence?—Discussion on What the Methodology of Constitutional Jurisprudence is". *Zhejiang Academic Journal,* 2005, Issue 2.

2 LIN Laifan, *From Constitutional Norms to Normative Constitution*, Law Press·China, 2001, pp.7-40.

3 TONG Zhiwei: "Reform of Methodology of Constitutional Jurisprudence", *Law*, 1994, Issue 9.

discipline. Consequently, we should establish a methodology, which shall be independent of the methodologies of politics, or even traditional philosophy and historiography, make it become an irreplaceable professional attempt in dealing with the constitutional issues, and build up its discipline autonomy.[1] But MIAO Lianying was inclined to hold that the traditional constitutional jurisprudence has been far away enough from other methodologies. At present, our constitutional jurisprudence must draw lessons from the methodologies of other disciplines. It is the key to solve actual constitutional issues.[2]

Nevertheless, it has reached a consensus among most scholars that the constitutional jurisprudence shall have a specific methodology. However, scholars have different opinions on how to establish the study method of constitutional jurisprudence nowadays in China. LIN Laifan put forward Theory of Normative Constitution.He held that the constitutional jurisprudence is a knowledge which takes constitutional phenomena as the object of study. Furthermore, the constitutional norm is the axis surrounded by constitutional phenomena. In view of the current situation of constitutional jurisprudence study in China, we must return the constitutional jurisprudence to norms, make it developed surrounding the norms, to be more exact, return it moderately close to normativism, but not entirely fall back to the standpoint of the traditional legal positivism.[3] In the study of constitutional jurisprudence around norms, the importance of constitutional hermeneutics has obtained advocation openly. And it has reached a consensus among many scholars in the circle to take constitutional hermeneutics as the core of constitutional jurisprudence. HAN Dayuan is a scholar who put forward

---

1 ZHENG Xianjun, "Why the Consciousness of Methodology is Needed in Constitutional Jurisprudence?-Discussion on What the Methodology of Constitutional Jurisprudence is". *Zhejiang Academic Journal*, 2005, Issue 2.

2 See LIN Laifan & ZHENG *Lei et al.*, "Fantasy of Dialogue and Arrangement-A Summary of the Round Table Academic Conference about Chinese Constitutional Jurisprudence", *Zhejiang Social Sciences*, 2005, Issue 3.

3 LIN Laifan & ZHENG Lei, "So-Called Centering on Norms", *Zhejiang Academic Journal*, 2005, Issue 4.

such theory earlier. He deemed the development of theory and system of contemporary constitutional jurisprudence largely depends on the development and improvement of constitutional hermeneutics. The contemporary constitutional hermeneutics has reflected the basic direction of development of contemporary constitutional jurisprudence. Furthermore, he has been constantly promoting the study and application of the methodology of constitutional hermeneutics, and has published a series of papers on the methodology of constitutional interpretation.[1] The technicalization of constitutional interpretation methodology easily leads constitutional jurisprudence to be content with the myth of value neutrality, and then become formalistic. ZHANG Xiang, a young scholar, realized the value orientation of interpretation method contained in constitutional hermeneutics must be attached importance to. He pointed out that "it's inevitable to bring the political consideration into constitutional interpretation. Under guides of different political theories, the same constitution article may get entirely different interpretation results." Meanwhile, he held that the constitutional interpretation must be rooted in its domestic constitutional history, regulatory environment and constitutional text, to hold "external demonstration" such as political theory demonstration, and eliminate the damage to constitutional interpretation caused therefrom.[2]

ZHENG Xianjun has summarized the major methods of study on constitutional jurisprudence in China. She deemed such study is mainly conducted at three levels: (i) stopping at the spirit level of constitution; (ii) turning into the study of constitutional principles; and (iii) carrying out normative study. We shall pass through the spirit, ideas and principles, and enter into the norms, we cannot stay too long in the ivory tower of spirit, and mustbase on the norms throughout,

1 See HAN Dayuan & ZHANG Xiang, "Study on the Objectivity and Subjectivity of the Constitutional Interpretation", *Science of Law*, 1999, Issue 6; HAN Dayuan & ZHANG Xiang, "Study on the Boundary of Constitutional Interpretation", *Law Review*, 2001, Issue 1.

2 ZHANG Xiang, "Disenchantment and Self-sufficiency: What Is the Influence of Political Theory on Constitutional Interpretation and to What Degree?" *Political and Legal Forum,* 2007, Issue 4.

without regardless of spirit, to face the reality, and make the society return to justice.[1] But FAN Jinxue put forward different views from this, and he deemed the study on constitutional jurisprudence shall be based on three levels as below: (i) axiological constitutional jurisprudence; (ii) normative analysis constitutional jurisprudence; and (iii) constitutional hermeneutics. Studies of the three levels respectively point to axiological jurisprudence, analytical jurisprudence and hermeneutic jurisprudence. The theoretical base of axiological jurisprudence is natural jurisprudence, the theoretical base of analytical jurisprudence is analytical positivist jurisprudence, and the theoretical base of hermeneutic jurisprudence is philosophy and linguistic hermeneutics. The proposition studied and focused by axiological constitutional jurisprudence is "what the constitutional jurisprudence shall be"? The proposition studied and focused by normative analysis constitutional jurisprudence is "what is constitutional jurisprudence"? And the proposition studied and focused by constitutional hermeneutics is the methodology and skill to construe and interpret the meaning of constitution norms. The proposition varies with the object and methodology of study. Furthermore, in FAN Jinxue's opinion, most of scholars nowadays are in favor of axiological constitutional jurisprudence, and a variety of so-called interpretations on constitutional jurisprudence always stay at the metaphysic level; therefore, he called for the turn of study direction of constitutional jurisprudence to constitutional hermeneutics.[2]

Actually, in the study of constitutional jurisprudence, we shall pay attention to the differences and connections between the study method of constitutional jurisprudence and the general study method of laws, as well as the study method of politics and constitutional interpretation, moreover, establish the constitutional

1 ZHENG Xianjun, "Why the Consciousness of Methodology is Needed in Constitutional Jurisprudence?—Discussion on What the Methodology of Constitutional Jurisprudence is". *Zhejiang Academic Journal*, 2005, Issue 2.

2 FAN Jinxue, "Constitutionalism and Methodology: Moving towards the Interpretation of Constitutional Text Itself-Analysis to the Significance of Constitutional Hermeneutics", *Zhejiang Academic Journal*, 2005, Issue 2.

jurisprudence in China.We shall incorporate the study method with the problem consciousness in China, maintain an objective and neutral point of view on the Chinese constitutional text, deal with the relationship between the universal value in constitutional jurisprudence study and the particularity in China, to correctly handle the problem of "time difference".[1] LI Shuzhong further pointed out, the biggest problem facing Chinese constitutional jurisprudence is "the particularity of Chinese issues". For a long time, our study focused on the absorption of foreign advanced theoretical results, being strange to resolve the Chinese issues from Chinese historical perspective and under Chinese social grounds. The initial fundamental purpose of introduction of constitution in modern-age China was to build China a prosperous and powerful country, even nowadays, with "protecting the freedom and rights of citizens", it's still an important mission to make the country rich and powerful. Against this value orientation, the uppermost priority shall be given to the following issues: how to build a set of constitutional theory system that differs from those of both western capitalist countries and the Soviet Union? How to understand the relationship between the ruling party and constitution? How to regard the People's Congress System? And, how to comprehensively interpret the constitutional text in China?[2] LIU Maolin held that the Scientific Outlook on Development has methodological significance for Chinese constitutional jurisprudence to get out of the trouble. He pointed out, according to Marxist theory of social structure, the constitutional jurisprudence is superstructure of thinking, and the comprehensive, harmonious and sustainable development of society cannot be separated from the development of constitutional jurisprudence. Constitutional jurisprudence shall keep up with the social development and the times, which is upon the request of Scientific Outlook on Development, and is the only road for Chinese constitutional jurisprudence to

1 HU Jinguang & CHEN Xiong, "Thinking about the Study Methods of Chinese Constitutional Jurisprudence", *Zhejiang Academic Journal*, 2005, Issue 4.

2 LIU Hui, "Challenges and Trends of the Development of Contemporary Constitutional Jurisprudence", *Procuratorial Daily*, November 10, 2006.

get out of straits. The Scientific Outlook on Development is not only the scientific outlook on social development, but also the scientific outlook on scientific development. It requires the Chinese constitutional jurisprudence to follow the spirit of "people oriented", being based on principles of people's comprehensive and free development, to integrate the social philosophy theory and hermeneutic theory of constitution, and then to develop itself in comprehensive, harmonious and sustainable ways.[1]

2. Reconstruction of the Theoretical System of Constitutional Jurisprudence

The constitutional system can be basically divided into two parts: the people's rights and obligations, the organization of state organs and their functions and powers. The former includes types and contents of various basic rights, and the latter consist of state legislature, judiciary authority, administrative organs and system of locality.[2] With the formulation of national constitution, the system of constitutional jurisprudence has been developed in accordance with the structure of constitutional code. Such situation lasted for a period of time after the policy of reform and opening up was established. A mainstream version of constitutional jurisprudence coursebook's architecture has once been based on the constitutional code, which was divided into seven chapters apart from the introduction, that is, general provisions, the formulation and development of constitution, character of state,form of state, basic rights and obligations of citizens, electoral system and state institutions.[3] In recent years, the binary model on system arrangement, namely the basic rights and obligations of citizens and the state organs, was generally adopted in the constitution coursebooks, such as Chinese Constitution, written by HU Jinguang and HAN Dayuan, which was divided into three parts:

1 LIU Maolin, *Predicament and Way Out of Chinese Constitutional Jurisprudence*, *Studies in Law and Business*, 2005, Issue 1.

2 See ZHANG Zhiben, *Constitutionalism*, China Fangzheng Press, 2004 (Edition of ancient books collation collated by YIN Xiaohu & LI Li).

3 XU Chongde (ed.), *Constitutional Jurisprudence*, Renmin University Press, 1999.

general provisions, basic rights and obligations of citizens, and the state organs.[1]

With the deepening of reflection and study on the methodology and basic category of constitutional jurisprudence, the scholars devoted themselves to constructing new theoretical system of constitutional jurisprudence. WANG Guanghui pointed out, for a long time, there was no agreement on the definition of the study object of constitutional jurisprudence in China, which obstructed us to find out "what the issues are studied exactly in constitutional jurisprudence", and led to a situation that the theoretical constitutional jurisprudence system could not be constructed, which fundamentally influenced the holding of spiritual essence and core value of constitution. In any event, the connotation of the study object of constitutional jurisprudence shall be based on the regulative object of constitution, which cannot deviate from the relationship between state power and civil rights. Hence, the theoretical system of constitutional jurisprudence shall consist of the theories of principles, state power, civil rights and coordination.[2]TONG Zhiwei also deemed, the teaching and study of constitutional jurisprudence in China since the 1970s have been basically conducted pursuant to the formulation, interpretation, implementation and amendment of 1982 constitution, reflecting the requirements of economic and social development, and certainly largely been confined to the development of the 1982 constitution. The teaching and study of constitutional jurisprudence in China has been developed rapidly, but the overall level of which is still relatively low, the primary cause of which lies in the lags in the reform of political structure in China. For this, the constitutional practice cannot supply necessary and sufficient research resources, which leads to the lack of real driving force for promoting the teaching and study of constitutional jurisprudence.

In recent years, some new development trends in teaching and study of constitutional jurisprudence in China appeared. Such new development trends met

1 HU Jinguang & HAN Dayuan, *Chinese Constitution*, Law Press·China, 2004.

2 WANG Guanghui, "Discussion on the Regulative Object of Constitution and the Theoretical System of Constitutional Jurisprudence", *Jurists Review*, 2007, Issue 6.

the requirements of economic and social development in current China, which would lead the teaching and study of Chinese constitutional jurisprudence in a new direction.[1]ZHU Fuhui deemed our current constitutional jurisprudence system relatively lags behind the times, which cannot meet the requirements of governing the country by law and building a socialist country under the rule of law. It is an important thinking in innovation of constitutional jurisprudence system to take the theory of mutual relationship between civil rights and state power as the main thread of constitutional jurisprudence, divide the contents of which into four parts, such as general provisions, state theory, theory of citizenship and typical case analysis, and take the regulating of state power and protection of civil rights as guidance of each parts.[2] ZHOU Yezhong and ZHOU Youyong also held that the first step for reconstructing the theoretical system of constitutional jurisprudence is to correctly resolve the issues such as ethical foundation, social foundation and logical starting point of constitutional jurisprudence,and they held that the ethical foundation of the constitutional jurisprudence is the superiority and weakness of humanity, the social foundation of which is the dualism between state and society, the logical starting point of which is popular sovereignty, and the basic contradiction of constitutional jurisprudence is civil rights and state power. The theoretical system of constitutional jurisprudence, constructed with the main thread of the relationship between civil rights and state power, shall include such four interrelated components as below: basic theory of constitution, which consists of the theoretical basis and basic phenomena of constitution; the theory of civil rights, which includes the contents such as citizens, human rights and civil rights, the constitutional rights and obligations of citizens; the theory of state power, which includes the state power and state nature, the structural system of

1 TONG Zhiwei, "Teaching of and Study on Constitutional Jurisprudence in China for 30 Years", *Science of Law-Journal of Northwest University of Political Science and Law*, 2007, Issue 6.

2 ZHU Fuhui, "On Innovation of Constitutional Jurisprudence System in China", *Journal of Yunmeng*, 2002, Issue 5.

state power, the organization and procedure for implementing the state power; the theory of constitution operation, which includes constitutionalism, formulation and amendment of constitution, implementation and interpretation, procedure of constitutionalism and constitutional lawsuit.[1]

Some other scholars supported that the theoretical system of constitutional jurisprudence should be constructed on the basis of rights or power. In LV Taifeng's opinion, the constitutional jurisprudence system shall be reconstructed around the rights and power, and which shall be divided into five parts as below: the basic principles of constitution, protection of the citizen's basic rights, supervision for state power, restriction on party power and supervision on implementation of the constitution.[2] However, CHEN Baoyin deemed, the socialist democracy at the primary stage of socialism has been confirmed in a legal form in our constitution, and the nature of which is putting the country under the charge of people. As requested by the people to exercise state power, the constitutional jurisprudence system in China shall be consisted of seven specific legal systems as below: constitutional theory, the citizen's status, state system and regime, state structure, state organs, electoral system and political party system.[3]In the view of ZHAO Shiyi, property right is the historical starting point of constitution and cornerstone of the whole constitutional system. He maintained that the theoretical system of economic constitution shall be built on the basis of property right. This system can be divided into three main parts: (i) general provisions of economic constitution. The relationship between citizens and state can be construed as the conflict between individual property rights and the national financial power. In view of this, the proposition of constitutional jurisprudence, for instance,

1 ZHOU Yezhong & ZHOU Youyong, "Consideration on and Reconstruction of the Theoretical System of Constitutional Jurisprudence", *Chinese Journal of Law*, 2001, Issue 4.

2 LV Taifeng, "Reconstructing Constitutional Jurisprudence System around Rights and Power", *Jurists Review*, 2000, Issue 5.

3 CHEN Baoyin, "Consideration on Constitutional Jurisprudence System in China", *Jurists Review*, 2000, Issue 3.

the market economy is the law that the resources and rights are allocated in the principle of economic neutrality under the constitutionalism economic constitution; (ii) economic rights theory. It is the rights system to take the property right as the starting point of rights, and make dualistic confrontation between economic freedom and economic rights in the logical structure of conflict and coordination between freedom of contract and right to work; and (iii) economic power theory. To build the national economic power system around financial power. The idea is that the state is supported by taxes, and the financial power is fundamental to all state powers. Economic constitutional jurisprudence is an important part of group of constitutional disciplines, which is an inter-discipline of constitutional jurisprudence and economics.[1]

Distinguished from the aforesaid doctrines, some scholars devoted to criticizing and reconstructing the existing doctrines. For example, TONG Zhiwei took the "recht" as the central category to construct the constitutional jurisprudence system and put forward recht constitutional theory. In TONG Zhiwei's opinion, the interests behind rights and power are interlinked. The linkage between rights and power constituted the category of recht, namely, the "social rights", as the central category of recht constitutional theory. For purpose of individual standard and state standard, two opposite poles of the law standard issue, the author put forward that the constitution, even all laws shall not be based on rights or power, and shall be oriented by recht, to pursue the maximization of recht.[2] TONG Zhiwei's recht constitutional theory produced great impact in the constitutional jurisprudence circle, and even in the jurisprudential circle, but not widely endorsed, which has been questioned by some scholars. Some researchers pointed out that lodging the concept of "social rights" and taking it as the study method of constitutional jurisprudence and logical starting point

1 ZHAO Shiyi, "Basic Issues of Economic Constitutional Jurisprudence", *Chinese Journal of Law*, 2001. Issue 4.

2 TONG Zhiwei, *Recht and Constitutionalism*, Shandong People's Publishing House, 2000.

of constitutional jurisprudence system have some major defects as below: it is too abstract and short of categories to compare the relationship between citizen's rights and state power to "social rights", which is unsupported as the logical starting point of constitutional jurisprudence discipline; the "social rights" are neither induced from constitutionalism practice, nor deduced from constitutional jurisprudence theory, but obtained from the simple addition of state power and civil rights by author.[1]

LIU Maolin divided the theoretical system of constitutional jurisprudence into three levels:(i) The social philosophy theory of constitution, including constitutional politics, philosophy of constitution, constitutional sociology, constitutional history and constitutional economic analysis. It is absolutely a jurisprudential theory of constitution, studying on the constitution from the perspective of positive law. (ii) The constitutional interpretation theory. It is to solve the constitutional jurisprudence issues emerging in the development of laws. For instance, what is the constitution as a law? How did the constitution form and constitute? How does the constitution allot and regulate the state power? And how does the constitution confirm and protect civil rights? From the running process of the law, the interpretation theory of constitution is designed to provide theoretical interpretation and technical assistance for the formulation, amendment, interpretation and application of the constitution, to achieve and play the role of constitution as a supreme law. (iii) The relationship between the social philosophy theory and interpretation theory of constitution. In LIU Maolin's opinion, the combination of social philosophy theory and interpretation theory of constitution in complete harmony has forged the academic quality and application value of constitutional jurisprudence as an independent branch of science of law. The social philosophy theory of constitution makes the constitutional jurisprudence a science, and the interpretation theory of which makes it a science of law, distinguished

1 ZHAO Shiyi & ZOU Pingxue, "Query on Reconstruction of Constitutional Jurisprudence System with Social Rights Analysis Method", *Chinese Journal of Law*, 1995, Issue 5.

from the general jurisprudential theory and the legal branches such as criminal jurisprudence and civil jurisprudence.[1]

3. Significant Development of the Theory of Constitutional Supervision

The issue of constitutional supervision is always the focus of attention in constitutional jurisprudence circle. China's constitution has provided for the principle of non-conflict in legislation and supervision system of the government, the court and the procuratorate by the National People's Congress, and other pertinent laws have set forth the filing and review system of laws and legislative interpretation system, even so, the principle of legality in legislation is still difficult to be guaranteed for absence of a special system of review and supervision of constitutionality. For this, some scholars pointed out that "violation of constitution is the most seriously illegal act. To rule the country by law, the first step is to rule the country under constitution. Therefore, constitutional supervision is the core and first important task in the supervision of the People's Congress. However, the function of constitution supervision in China has not been effectively exercised. One of the reasons is that the constitutional supervision system and procedure needs to be further improved."[2]

The earlier study on constitutional jurisprudence was mainly devoted to studying how to build the constitutional supervision system under the National People's Congress System, especially, how to establish constitutional supervision agencies. On the necessity of setting up constitutional supervision agencies, two kinds of different views have been put forward in the constitutional jurisprudence circle. One view taken by scholars was that the constitutional supervision exists in capitalist countries in order to adapt to the needs of pluralistic democracy, which is always put forward by the party out of power, and has become the

1 LIU Maolin, "Predicament and Way Out of Chinese Constitutional Jurisprudence", *Studies in Law and Business,* 2005, Issue 1.

2 CHENG Xiangqing, "On Improving the Supervision System of the National People's Congress", *National People's Congress of China*, 2004, Issue 8.

democratic form by which the opposition party restricts the party in office. The multi-party system does not exist in our country, so there is no need to establish a constitutional supervision system. The other view is that the existence of constitutional supervision is determined by the legal nature of constitution, and without constitutional supervision, the constitution means nothing.[1] With gradual acceptance of the concept of application of constitution, the latter view has prevailed in the constitutional jurisprudence circle. Many scholars suggested setting up a constitutional committee or constitutional supervision committee under or paralleling with the Standing Committee of the National People's Congress. Of course, some scholars held that the constitutional supervision could be implemented without separate constitutional supervision agency.[2] Such view has been criticized by many scholars for ignoring that the core of constitutional supervision is to supervise the constitutionality of the laws.

With respect to how to draw lessons from the constitutional supervision systems of other countries in the world to improve China's socialist constitutional supervision system, some scholars held that China shall establish a supervision system, under which the constitutionality shall be reviewed by general court, that is, drawing lessons from America, to permit the people's court to accept the case of constitutional litigation, and authorize the Supreme People's Court to exercise the power to review the constitutionality in the trial of specific cases. The advantage of this model is that the legislature can be reviewed and supervised independently by an "external agency" through highly specialized and professional division of labor; but it faces difficulties. Specifically, the separation of powers principle does not exist in the People's Congress System; the people's court comes from and is subordinate to the People's Congress, being responsible to and subject to the supervision of the People's Congress. The constitutional relationship between

1 MO Jihong, "Playing the Role of Constitution and Insisting on Ruling the Country by Law", *Legal Daily*, September 20, 1997.

2 Relevant theoretical overviews can See *Study on the Constitutional Issues in China* written by HU Jinguang, Xinhua Press, 1998.

the two agencies can be changed fundamentally if the court turns to supervise the People's Congress for excising legislative power. As a result of this, the court will become a power which can restrict the People's Congress, and further more being on equal terms with the People's Congress. The theoretical logic and real result of this is bound to constitute a challenge to the People's Congress System. It is an insurmountable gap to avoid the head-on confrontation between judicial power and legislative power as well as its adverse effect in exercising the power of incidental review on constitutionality by general courts.[1] There was also a view that China should set up a constitutional court as a special constitutionality review body, independent of the People's Congress, to be responsible for exercising such power. It is necessary to establish constitutional courts system in China, because "the transition cost in immediate and complete reconstruction on a series of current systems such as superior legislative power, the method to exercise judicial interpretation right, the settings of the court institutions and the allocation of burden of litigation can be saved; on the other hand, the distrust on personnel quality and judicial impartiality of local general courts can be prevented from continuing to hamper the constitutionality review, so as to quickly establish a judicial review institution with full policy judgment ability and high divine authority."[2] To implement the constitutional court review system, it also needs to coordinate the relationship with the current People's Congress System, and to reasonably interpret the issues about its status as the highest organ of state power and whether its authority to supervise can be shared. If the breakthrough cannot be made in reinterpretation of this two points, then the rationality and legitimacy of establishing constitutional court will lack; but if we can break through the current system and make a new interpretation and design, then the theory and system of the People's Congress might be faced with disintegration.

1 LI Lin, "Development of China's Legislation in the Context of Globalization", *Study and Exploration*, 1998, Issue 1.

2 JI Weidong, "Review on Constitutionality and Strengthening the Judicial Power", *Social Sciences in China*, 2002, Issue 2.

The constitution provides that, all state organs shall comply to the provisions of constitution, and even the National People's Congress also shall conduct, as a state organ, within the range allowed by the constitution. Because of this, many scholars held that, under current People's Congress System, the constitutional committee can only be set up within the National People's Congress.[1] As to its position, there were two opinions: (i) To set up a constitutional committee being level with the Standing Committee of the National People's Congress, responsible for constitutionality review to the legislative actions of Standing Committee of the National People's Congress and all hierarchies thereunder, but cannot able to review the legislation of the National People's Congress; otherwise, it will be contrary to the system under which the National People's Congress and its standing committee exercise the state power as a unity. The position and authority of the Standing Committee of the National People's Congress will be shaken if a constitutional supervision organ was added and authorized to supervise the constitutionality of legislative work and other actions of the Standing Committee of the National People's Congress. (ii) To set up a constitutional committee with the nature of ad hoc committee in the National People's Congress, the main reason for which is that such organ is in conformity with the basic principles and setup of the People's Congress System; it is conducive to keep the stability of constitution to add a new ad hoc committee, which is not involved in the amendment of constitution and pertinent laws, as the constitution has provided clearly for the establishment of ad hoc committee; it is helpful for making up for the lack of constitutional supervision due to the short session and hard task of the highest organ of state power, and difficulties to balance the constitutional supervision by other ad hoc committee, and beneficial for keeping the specialization and routinization of constitutional supervision to assist the National People's Congress and its standing committee to specially supervise the implementation

1 JI Weidong suggested setting up "constitutional committee" or "constitutionality review committee" to conduct constitution supervision. See *New View on Constitutionalism* by JI Weidong, Peking University Press, 2002, pp.29-50.

of constitution by constitutional supervision committee as a standing body; the constitutional supervision committee can be authorized to review the constitutionality of the laws enacted by the National People's Congress and its Standing Committee, the administrative regulations formulated by the State Council, the department rules and the local regulations.[1]

For purpose of the provisions of constitution itself, the National People's Congress and its Standing Committee are not a pure legislative body. In accordance with the constitution, the National People's Congress has "the authority to supervise the implementation of constitution", and the Standing Committee of the National People's Congress has "the authority to interpret the constitution and to supervise the implementation of constitution". The conclusion deduced from the current constitution that the Standing Committee of the National People's Congress has authority and functions, being independent of the legislative power, to review the constitution will not encounter too many systematic difficulties and resistance. Just because of this, the view that the constitutional supervision conducted by the People's Congress has been implied in the constitution is a powerful theory in the academic circle.[2] The issue of constitutional supervision has been excluded from the *Supervision Law* which has been passed, and the office of regulatory review and filing under the Law Committee of Standing Committee of the National People's Congress is specially responsible for dealing with the unconstitutional and illegal issues in administrative regulations, local regulations and department rules. Undoubtedly, this measure is of positive significance for maintaining the unity of the national legal system and protecting the citizen's constitutional rights. However, since the establishment of this office, it has not made any decision on constitutionality or

1 LI Lin, "Development of China's Legislation in the Context of Globalization", *Study and Exploration*, 1998, Issue 1.

2 CHENG Xiangqing, "Some Controversial Issues about Constitutional Supervision", *Chinese Journal of Law,* 1992, Issue 4; "WANG Shuwen, On Supervision of the Implementation of Constitution",*Chinese Journal of Law*, 1992, Issue 6.

unconstitutionality. At present, there is no lack of applications made by citizens to the National People's Congress for constitutionality review. Some scholars held that, decisions on constitutionality of the state actions not inconsistent with the constitution in such applications can be fully made, so as to eliminate the doubts in the social circle for whether the state actions are constitutional; on the other side, it's helpful for providing legitimate basis for state actions under the constitution, and establishing the authority of the law-based government. And then, in the fullness of time, those clearly and seriously unconstitutional regulations can be directly declared unconstitutional and invalid, and even further to make instructions on amendment to eliminate and rectify the unconstitutional actions, to build and improve the constitutional review system in China.[1]

To promote the application of constitution through studying and interpreting the cases or examples occurred in current society is a general academic strategy adopted by the current constitutional jurisprudence circle. In recent years, the constitutional scholars paid more attention to the implementation of constitution. For example, the research center of constitutional politics and administrative law of Renmin University Law School has published "Ten Major Constitutional Cases Annually in China (2006-2007)", taking the constitutional cases appraisal and election as the opportunity to hold a symposium and to study on the theory for application of constitution. In fact, this trend can be traced back to "The First Case of Constitutional Judicialization "[2], happened at the turn of this century. The reply of Supreme People's Court on this case has aroused the discussions about the application of constitution in the constitutional jurisprudence circle, even in the whole jurisprudential circle. The Supreme People's Court replied that "CHEN Xiaoqi has infringed QI Yuling's basic rights of education granted by constitution by means of infringing the rights to name, causing specific harmful consequences,

1 ZHAI Guoqiang, "Forms of Unconstitutional Judgment", *Chinese Journal of Law*, 2009, Issue 3.

2 See "The First Case of Constitutional Judicialization Incurred by Going to School under Other's Name", *Southern Weekend*, August 16, 2001.

and shall bear the corresponding civil liabilities". As to this reply, the jurists have put forward different views. It was a matter of opinion. One view is that the judicial authority cannot directly apply the provisions of constitution. One reason for that is constitution is rule of conduct rather than rule of judgment. The logical structure of rule of judgment, that is, the provision of constitutive elements and legal effect in the same rules, does not exist in the articles of constitution. After all, the task of constitution is to establish the basic principle and system of the national life, but not to set up referee datum for courts in the trial of civil cases.[1] Especially in the civil trial, because the case involving infringement of basic rights between private parties is regulated by the civil law, to regulate the right infringement case pursuant to the constitution obviously exceeds the regulative range of constitution. In fact, it is the generalization of the concept of unconstitutional act, which is not conducive to maintain the authority of the constitution, but will have opposite effects.[2] But some scholars held that QI's right to education has gone beyond the range of civil law theory, and it is obviously the basic right of citizen under the constitution, if not directly apply the provisions thereof, the judicial remedy will not be realized. Therefore, it is necessary to create a precedent for protecting the citizen's basic rights under the constitution through judicial review by courts in China, to open up the ways of judicial relief for protecting the citizen's constitutional rights, and to create a precedentby taking the constitution directly as the legal basis for trying cases in China's courts. In summary, China shall realize the "constitutional judicialization", and put the constitution into judicial procedure[3].

1 LIANG Huixing, "Sober Reflection on Constitutional Judicialization-No Need to Adjudge the Case about Depriving of Education of a Girl in accordance with Constitution", *Jurisprudence World*, 2002, Issue 4.

2 YIN Xiaohu, "Some Queryies and Considerations about Constitutional Judicialization", *Renmin University of China: Constitutional Jurisprudence and Administrative Jurisprudence*, 2002, Issue 2.

3 WANG Lei, "Constitutional Judicialization-Basic Ideas on the Study of Chinese Constitutional Jurisprudence in 21st Century", *Jurists Review*, 2000, Issue 3.

The constitutional norms shall be directly applied to the trial, and be referenced courageously in legal instruments.[1] The different opinions about this case could be deemed as "a close combat" among the constitutional jurisprudence scholars in analyzing the same case, and such opinions have also embodied the confrontation among different jurisprudential theories. The QI Yuling's case has become a communication media and platform among different jurisprudential theories. And the analysis thereof from the constitutional jurisprudence perspective can also be deemed as a dialogue among the constitutional scholars. In this course of dialogue and confrontation, the constitutional doctrines about the application of the constitution and basic rights have been well developed.[2]

4. Re-exploitation of New Fields of Constitutional Jurisprudence

Since 1990s, more and more scholars have paid attention to and devoted to constructing the subdisciplines of constitutional jurisprudence, and the study on constitutional jurisprudence gradually presented more branches. Among them, philosophy of constitution, i.e. studying on the theoretical system of constitution, constitutional hermeneutics, i.e. studying on the constitutional text, and constitutional politics, i.e. studying on constitutional politics from the state construction perspective have prevailed. The common character of those prevailing studies is the normative study about the constitution, focusing on the issue "what the constitution is". In addition, there are constitutional economics, constitution and literature, constitutional sociology, constitutional anthropology and other branches.[3] Through the hard work of the scholars, the study on constitutional jurisprudence in China has achieved a great number of fruits in many fields, such as the studies on philosophy of constitution, constitutional sociology, comparative

1 LIU Liantai, "Empirical Analysis and Commentary on Direct Application of Constitutional Norms to the Trial in China", *Chinese Journal of Law,* 1996, Issue 6.

2 LIN Laifan, ZHU Yuxia, "Dislocation and Coincidence-Four Thinking Tendencies of the Relationship between the Constitution and Civil Law in Current China", *Zhejiang Social Sciences*, 2007, Issue 1.

3 HOU Meng, "Construction of Subdiscipline System and the Development of Constitutional Jurisprudence in China", *Jianghai Academic Journal*, 2006, Issue 3.

constitutional jurisprudence and constitutional history of China.

4.1 Intellectual Enquiries about "Philosophy of Constitution"

Since entering the new century, in China's constitutional jurisprudence circle, a study on so-called "philosophy of constitution" appeared. In fact, the concept strictly corresponding with the "philosophy of constitution" as a nominatum of certain discipline is relatively rare in the foreign constitutional jurisprudence theories, but there are some similar concepts, for instance, the "constitutional philosophy" or "constitutional law's philosophical foundations". It should be pointed out that its relevant studies are very rich, and the domains related are very extensive, even touching upon the categories of political philosophy and moral philosophy. So far, although there is no conclusion on whether the concept of "philosophy of constitution" can be referred to as a kind of knowledge with independent character, the study in this domain is absolutely essential to the constitutional jurisprudence. Some scholars call the "philosophy of constitution" as "constitutional logics".[1] In MO Jihong's opinion, to bring the China's constitutional jurisprudence to get out of the trouble, we must start from the most fundamental logical issues, in accordance with the respective scientific characteristics of moral philosophy, cultural philosophy and logical philosophy, to construct the philosophy of constitution in order to meet requirements of socialist constitutionalism with Chinese characteristics.[2]

However, whether the philosophy of constitution, as the subdiscipline of constitutional jurisprudence, can stand up is not undoubted. LI Qi held that the constitutional jurisprudence always faces a basic question: what is the constitution? This question can be further transformed into three specific questions as below: Why does human life need constitution? What kind of constitution is needed for human life? How purpose of human life can be realized through

1 MO Jihong, "Examination of the Necessity-A View of Constitutional Logics", *Social Sciences in China*, 2001, Issue 6.

2 MO Jihong, "Goal and Task of Study on China's Constitutional Jurisprudence towards 21st Century", *Jurists Review*, 2000, Issue 3.

the constitution? They are meta problems about constitution, which have been involved in the legitimacy of the constitution per se, and it is reasonable to deem it as the "philosophy of constitution".[1]

Of course, although the philosophy of constitution has philosophical temperament, and needs to subject to the test of philosophy, it itself is not philosophy, but a category of constitutional jurisprudence. In WEN Zhengbang's opinion, the philosophy of constitution is a discipline of theoretical constitutional jurisprudence, from the philosophical perspective, and with the view and method of philosophy, to consider and study the theoretical and practical issues of constitution, which is the highest level of theoretical constitutional jurisprudence, and a very important philosophy of branch law. It summarizes and generalizes the contents and problems from perspectives of the world outlook and methodology, through rethinking and reconsideration on the existing constitutional theoretical results, namely, the philosophical "reflection", and with the philosophical examination, cognition and analysis on the constitutional practice, to reveal the most profound essence and most general regularity of the constitution and constitutionalism phenomena, so as to provide direct philosophical guidance and basis for the development of constitution and construction of constitutionalism. That is, the philosophy of constitution is a theoretical and systematical knowledge about the world outlook and methodology on the issues of constitution and constitutionalism. In general, it is the jurisprudential philosophy theory about the issues of constitution and constitutionalism. For purpose of study on philosophy of constitution, it is helpful for us to take a broad and long view, so as to grasp the overall, macro and strategic issues of constitution development and constitutionalism construction. And it is easy for us to deeply understand the complex essence and foundation of the constitutional and constitutionalism

1 LI Qi, "Philosophy of Constitution: Making a Detailed Inquiry about the Legitimacy of Constitution", *Journal of Xiamen University*, 2005, Issue 3.

issues.[1] In XIE Weiyan's opinion, the philosophy of constitution is a knowledge, being started from the human being's reason, and to explore and construct the "Sollen" constitution on the basis of introspection and criticism to the constitutional science. The introspection and criticism are not to suspect or deny the constitutional science, but not satisfied with the "actuality" in constitutional science (Sein), to inquire "the whys and wherefores", and insisting on diving to the bottom of constitutional science, to find its ultimate basis. The philosophy of constitution is a form more advanced than constitutional science, so that the current constitutional jurisprudence shall move from constitutional science towards philosophy of constitution.[2]LIU Zhigang also held that "the philosophy of constitution is a discipline to study the jurisprudential theory implied in constitution on a philosophical level. As a basic theory of constitutional jurisprudence, philosophy of constitution is deeply meaningful for the development of constitutional jurisprudence. In the field of constitutional jurisprudence in China, philosophy of constitution is a virgin land to be reclaimed."[3]

4.2 The Beginning of the Constitutional Sociology in China

The constitutional sociology is a subdiscipline for studying and identifying the characteristics of constitutional jurisprudence discipline with methodology of sociology.[4] DONG Poyu is a scholar who put forward the concept of constitutional sociology earlier. He pointed out that, the constitutional sociology is an empirical science, taking the constitutional process as social process, and making connections between constitutional phenomena, such as constitutional norms, constitutional system, constitutional awareness, constitutional relationship as well as constitutional movement, and other social phenomena including

1 WEN Zhengbang, "Philosophy of Constitution-New Vision for Deepening the Theory of Constitutionalism", *Procuratorial Daily*, at http://www.jcrb.com/.

2 XIE Weiyan, "Trend of Constitutional Jurisprudence: from Constitutional Science to Philosophy of Constitution", *Journal of Sichuan Normal University*, 2006, Issue 1.

3 LIU Zhigang, "Constitution: A Perspective from Philosophy", *Political Science and Law*, 2003, Issue 3.

4 ZHENG Xianjun, "Sociological View on Constitution", *Science of Law*, 2002, Issue 3.

politics, economy and society, to conduct empirical studies.[1] HAN Dayuan also pointed out, the concept of constitutional sociology emphasizes the connection between constitutional phenomena and other social phenomena, highlighting the social foundation of constitution; within the framework of constitutional sociology, a certain correspondence can be set up between the constitutional jurisprudence as social science and the constitutional jurisprudence as normative science; the constitutional sociology is a dynamic system with historicity; the core of the concept of constitutional sociology is the practice function of constitution, exerting its academic influence via the evaluation system of social life.[2] With respect to the purpose and functions, basic framework and methodology of the constitutional sociology, the constitutional scholars have made a preliminary discussion. They deemed the constitutional sociology as a discipline for studying constitutional jurisprudence with the methods of sociology. The structure of constitution from the perspective of sociology is based upon the connections between public authorities, with the duty to protect freedom, and economic society which is organized in accordance with private laws. The separation between state and society is the premise for establishing the constitutional relationship. The partition between public domain and private domain is the foundation of limited government. The confrontation between public power and private rights embodies the classical basic rights in constitution. The social right is the outcome of interpenetration between state and society.[3]

For purpose of the constitutional jurisprudence in China, the constitutional sociology is obviously still in its infancy. With respect to the independence of constitutional sociology as a discipline, the first problem or question it faces might be what the difference between constitutional sociology and politics or political sociology is. Especially for adopting the methods of sociology, it is

1 DONG Poyu, "Fourteen Years for Constitutional Jurisprudence in China", *Tribune of Political Science and Law,* 1989, Issue 5.

2 HAN Dayuan, "On Basic Framework and Methodology of Constitutional Sociology", *Zhejiang Academic Journal*, 2005, Issue 2.

3 ZHENG Xianjun, "Sociological View on Constitution", *Science of Law,* 2002, Issue 3.

difficult to define the study area of such discipline. For instance, there is no essential distinction between the constitutional system and political system from the perspective of sociology. A host of overlaps exist between the constitutional conception and political conception. Many constitutional phenomena are also the study objects of politics. On such premise, only the study by means of the methods of sociology, and meanwhile, keeping a certain distance with the norms of constitution, can be classified into the study of constitutional sociology. Such method for demarcating may be extended to the division between legal sociology and sociological jurisprudence.

4.3 Continuation of the Study on History of Constitution

The history of constitution is one of the objects of study on constitutional jurisprudence. The study on history of constitution can promote the constitutional scholars to accumulate deep cultural heritage of constitution, and so as to be able to observe the connections between the evolution of constitution and the development of society from the course of the history with a strategically advantageous position, and to deepen the understanding on the current constitution and its system. After the founding of new China, subject to the changes of state nature and the ideology, the study on history of constitution in China has been interrupted with the study thereof during Republican Period. Especially in the expansion of anti-rightist struggle and "the Cultural Revolution" period, the whole jurisprudential education and study have been paralyzed, and of course, the study on history of constitution could not be on the rails.[1]

With the recovery and development of legal education, the study on history of constitution began to receive more attention. A Brief Discussion on History of Constitution in China, written by ZHANG Jinfan and ZENG Xianyi, was an earlier work on history of constitution, which started from the constitutional movement with reformism ideas in modern China, the constitutionality fraud conducted by the government of late Qing Dynasty and the constitution

1 WANG Guanghui, *Destiny and Historical Responsibility of Constitutional Scholars*, at http://www.gongfa.com/, April 5, 2008.

promulgated thereby, taking the constitutional system in Republican period and the development process of constitutional system established after the founding of new China as study objects. On this basis, the author also made a historical classification on the development of constitutional system.[1] *A Brief Discussion on History of Constitutionalism and Constitution in Modern China*, written by JIANG Bikun, was an earlier work on modern constitutional history in China. And it was the first book written by constitutional scholar on China's constitutional history.[2] This was a book on the subject of history of constitutionalism and constitution in modern China, the content of which involves "reform movement conducted by reformists", "constitutional issues of late Qing Dynasty", "provisional constitution of the Republic of China", "constitution under the regime of the Northern warlords", "constitutional documents promulgated by Guangzhou and Wuhan nationalist governments", "constitutional issues of Kuomintang government", "new-democratic constitutionalism movement" and so on. The major historical events and figures in respect of the history of constitutionalism and constitution in the development of China's modern history have been analyzed and evaluated comprehensively. Especially the analysis on contents provided by constitutional documents has always been based on the fundamental standpoint of Marxism as well as the methodology of class analysis. Not only the reveal of sham democracy and true autocracy conducted by Qing government, the Northern warlords and Kuomintang government, but also the illustration of democracy contained by constitutional documents of revolutionary bases under the leadership of the Chinese Communist Party, as well as the comparison between new democracy and old democracy, all those have been proved with a great number of historical documents. With the combination of history and discussion, the profound academic foundation and rigorous academic attitude of JIANG Bikun have been

1 ZHANG Jinfan & ZENG Xianyi, *A Brief Discussion on History of Constitution in China,* Beijing Publishing House Group, 1979.

2 JIANG Bikun, *A Brief Discussion on History of Constitutionalism and Constitution in Modern China*, Law Press·China, 1988.

embodied in this book. XU Chongde, combining with his personal experience in the formulation of constitution, wrote a book with the name of *Constitutional History of the People's Republic of China*[1]. In this book, the author provided a large number of first-hand historical materials about constitution, under which the process of amending the constitution was reproduced vividly, combining with the analysis and comments on the constitutional theory, thus providing rich materials for studying the history and exploring the original intention of constitution. In this academic context, many young constitutional scholars also began to pay attention to the study on history of constitution, and wrote a lot of works.[2]

5. New Development of Theory of Constitutional Rights

After the current constitution got passed, more constitutional scholars began to focus on the clauses of basic rights in constitution, and this change even received the attention of western scholars.[3] Most of these studies are conducted around the enactment of new constitution. Through the "commentary" on the clauses of rights in constitution, to appeal the society to pay attention to and attach importance to the constitutional rights, so as to improve the right awareness of the whole society. Of course, the biggest problem of such study, merely interpreting the clauses of rights in constitution, is that the value proposition has been confused with the fact proposition, and the boundary among Sollen form, legal form and Sein form of the constitutional rights has been obscured.[4] One of the typical view is that regarding the rights provided in the constitution as equal to the rights which have been

1 XU Chongde, *Constitutional History of the People's Republic of China*, Fujian People's Publishing House, 2003.

2 YIN Xiaohu, *History of Constitutionalism in Modern China*, Shanghai People's Publishing House, 1997; WANG Renbo, *Constitutionalism Culture and Modern China*, Law Press·China, 1997.

3 See Ann Kent, *Between Freedom and Subsistence, China and Human rights*, Oxford University Press (1993), p.97.

4 The right exists with three modes. Such theory was first put forward by LI Buyun, and then generally accepted by the jurisprudential circle. See LI Buyun's "On Three Modes of Existence of Human Rights", *Chinese Journal of Law*, 1991, Issue 4.

protected by the constitution.[1]

From the enactment of constitution in 1982 to 1990s, the study on interpreting the clauses of rights in constitution has prevailed in the constitutional rights theories. Strictly speaking, the simple interpretation of the constitutional rights clauses conducted by early constitutional jurisprudence was not academic study, but concepts full of politics and slogans. However, the important role it played in improving the whole society's constitutional rights consciousness, forming the constitutional conceptions of respecting and protecting the rights, and shaping the ideology of state and society, cannot be underestimated and denied. These studies also made the protection of rights be attached importance to in the state's political and legal practices, and then promoted the state to gradually take measures to protect the basic rights of citizens. Some western scholar pointed out that, since the enactment of 1982 constitution, in view of change of conceptions, the freedom actually enjoyed by Chinese citizens for speech, publication, association and migration (although this right has not been clearly defined by constitution) is gradually increasing.[2]

Constitutional rights are the legal form of human rights, hence, the study on constitutional rights is closely bound up with the study on human rights. In our jurisprudential circle, the human rights used to be criticized and rejected as the value of the bourgeois.[3] In the early 1990s, the forbidden zone of study on human rights has been completely broken, such research became the hot issue in jurisprudential circle, and this trend also caused great concern about the constitutional rights theory in constitutional jurisprudence circle. Prior to this, the constitutional theories, before the founding of new China, used to be totally denied

1 See TIAN Jun, "Citizens in China Enjoy Comprehensive and Real Basic Rights", *Jianghai Academic Journal*, 1983, Issue 1.

2 See Ann Kent, *Between Freedom and Subsistence, China and Human Rights*, Oxford University Press (1993), pp.96-97.

3 See XIAO Weiyun & LUO Haocai & WU Xieying, "How to View the Issue of 'Human Rights' from a Perspective of Marxism?" *Red Flag*, 1979, Issue 5; LAN Ying, "Has the 'Human Rights' always been a Slogen of the Bourgeoisie?" *Social Science*, 1979, Issue 3.

without discrimination in our jurisprudential circle, and the "academic study" has always been conducted through simply interpreting the Marxist - Leninist classical works. XU Chongde pointed out, "with respect to the constitutional jurisprudence before the founding of the People's Republic of China, it is not advisable to totally deny it without any analysis."[1] However, the change of political order hasn't completely cut off the historical development of constitutional theories. In the studies of constitutional rights theory after 1990s, with the spring tide of studies on human rights, these works about constitutional rights theory wrote before the founding of new China have been widely cited, which had an impact on the studies on constitutional rights theory in China.[2] This turn made the jurisprudential circle return to the academic context of study on constitutional rights in China, and gradually get rid of the influence of theories of the Soviet Union about the state and the law, meanwhile, courageously draw lessons from the theories and practices of constitutional rights protection in the world. Just as HAN Dayuan pointed out, "in the social development of China, the development paths and logics followed by constitution and constitutional jurisprudence were different, and the politics has no absolute influence on constitutional jurisprudence."[3]

Along with the acceleration of the reform of economic structure, the amendments to constitution have been promulgated respectively by the National People's Congress in April 1988, March 1993, March 1999, to reposition the national economic system constantly. In this process, the jurisprudential circle took the mainstream discourse, "building a socialist market economy", as the entry point, put forward the basic proposition that "the socialist market economy is economy of rights", to demonstrate the close relationship between protection

1 HAN Dayuan & NIU Wenzhan, "Witnessing the Development History of Constitutional Jurisprudence of New China-Professor XU Chongde's Academic Career and Thoughts", *Theoretical Front In Higher Education*, 2004, Issue 1.

2 See the typical masterpiece, such as *Comparative Constitution* written by WANG Shijie & QIAN Duansheng, China University of Politic Science and Law Press, 1997.

3 HAN Dayuan, "Analysis and Reflection on the Basic Categories of China's Constitutional Jurisprudence in 1950s", *Contemporary Law Review*, 2005, Issue 3.

of rights and economic construction.[1] Similar to the inference that "market economy is economy of rights" in jurisprudential circle, the constitutional jurisprudence circle also attached highly importance to this[2]. As the core of establishment and perfection of market economy system is the issue of property right, therefore, the study on constitutional property right has become the hot issue in then constitutional jurisprudence circle.[3] Additionally, all previously amendments to constitution conducted around the reform of economic structure, which further promoted the constitutional jurisprudence circle to pay highly attention to property right. With the continuous deepening of study on the theory of protecting property right under constitution, the scholars began to get rid of the slogans, and turned to study "how to amend the constitution to protect the property right".[4] From late 1990s to early 21st century, the right claims and social conflicts occurred in urban-house removing further stimulated the constitutional jurisprudence circle to attach highly importance to and study on the property right. The study results on constitutional right finally supported the Amendments to Constitution enacted in 2004 from a legal technique perspective. The normative structure of rights protection adopted by Article 22 in this Amendments was just the "mode of protection plus legal (public interests) restriction".[5] The amendment on the protection of property right in Article 22 thereof further stimulated the

1 ZHANG Wenxian, "Brief Discussion on Market Economy and the Spirit of Contemporary Law", *China Legal Science*, 1994, Issue 6.

2 See the studies: SUN Chao & QI Yuan, "On Establishing the Position of Constitution in Market Economy", *Law*, 1992, Issue 12; HAN Dayuan, "Market Economy and the Booming of Constitutional Jurisprudence", *Jurists Review*, 1993, Issue 3.

3 HU Jinguang, "Market Economy and Constitutional Protection of Personal Property Right", *Jurists Review*, 1993, Issue 3.

4 LIN Laifan, "On Constitutional Protection of Personal Property Right", *Law*, 1999, Issue 3; LIN Laifan, "Comparative Study on Constitutional Protection of Property Right", in *Constitutionalism Review* by ZHANG Qingfu (ed.), Law Press·China, 1999, Volume 2; ZHAO Shiyi, "Expropriation of Property and Its Constitutional Constraints", *Studies in Law and Business*, 1999, Issue 4.

5 LIN Laifan, "On Constitutional Protection of Personal Property Right", *Law*, 1999, Issue 3.

constitutional jurisprudence circle to pay attention to the protection of property right again. On the basis of previous studies, the scholars put more emphasis on studying the modes to protect constitutional property right.[1] Since then, the study on constitutional property right protection in constitutional jurisprudence circle reached a new climax. Pursuant to the retrieval and statistics of 143 academic papers, published from 1993 to 2008, with respect to the constitutional property right, there were 93 academic papers with the subject of studying constitutional property right protection in four years from 2004 to 2008, but there were only 50 in 11 years from 1993 to 2004. Overall, the normalization of the study on constitutional property right protection was gradually increasing, which has got rid of the simple "political discourse", and began to put emphasis on the logical structure and applicability of legal provisions.[2]

The reply on "QI Yuling Case" issued by the Supreme People's Court in 2001[3] provided an opportunity for China's constitutional jurisprudence circle to utilize the constitutional right theory to explain the practical cases. In the constitutional jurisprudence circle, this case caused a theoretical discussion on the legal force of constitutional rights in private relationships. Furthermore, the "Incident of SUN Zhigang" and the "Yan'an Pornography Case" also provided analysis samples in reality for studying the constitutional right theory. The discussions on these incidents and cases in academic circle have produced certain effects

1 HAN Dayuan, "Thinking on Constitutional Jurisprudence-Constitutionalization of Personal Property Right", *Law*, 2004, Issue 4; ZHANG Qingfu & Ren Yi, "On Constitutional Protection System of Citizen's Property Right", *Jurists Review*, 2004, Issue 4; HU Jinguang & WANG Kai, "Evolution of the Relationship between Property Right and Right to Life", *Jurists Review*, 2004, Issue 4.

2 WANG Kai, "Historical Change of Constitutionalization of Property Right Protection in New China" (1949-2004), *Nomocracy Forum*, 2006, Issue 1.

3 "*Reply on whether infringement of the citizen's basic rights for education protected by constitution by means of infringement of right of name shall be imposed civil liabilities*" (interpretation of laws [2001] No. 25) issued by the Supreme People's Court, has even received highly attention of foreign constitutional jurisprudence circle. See Thomas E. Kellogg, *Courageous Explorers? Education Litigation and Judicial Innovation in China*, Harvard Human Rights Journal, Volume 20 (2007).

on the practice of constitutionalism. For instance, the abolishment of system of investigation under detention largely depended upon the heated discussions on the protection of constitutional rights in the academic circle[1]. The provision of "State shall respect and protect the human rights" has been incorporated into the Article 24 of Amendments to Constitution in 2004, which made the study on theory of constitutional rights become the focus of study on constitutional jurisprudence.

Throughout the history of protecting constitutional rights all over the world, the modes of constitutional rights protection can be roughly classified into three different types: absolute protection, relative protection and compromising protection.[2] Absolute protection refers to that the constitutional rights shall be protected directly by constitution, even free from restrictions or exclusions set up by legislature, in other words, that is a constitutional protection mode; relative protection, also known as theory for protection of constitutional rights by law, refers to that the protection of constitutional rights needs to be based on specific laws, and the constitutional rights may be restricted by the law; the compromising protection is situated between the above two modes. Pursuant to the doctrine of absolute protection, the constitutional rights are basic rights protected directly by the constitution, which shall not be infringed by any state power, including the legislative power. If a law infringes the constitutional rights, it may be adjudged as violation of constitution by the constitutional review body, and become null and void. Since 2000, more and more Chinese scholars began to hold the theory of absolute protection on constitutional rights, and went further to discriminate the rights respectively protected by constitution and by law[3], so as to study the rights

1 On December 3, 2001, "the Seminar on QI Yuling Case" was convened by Beijing constitutional jurisprudence society. And on June 30, 2003, "the Seminar on SUN Zhigang Case and Review of Unconstitutionality" was held by Shanghai Jiao Tong University.

2 See LIN Laifan, *From Constitutional Norms to Normative Constitution*, Law Press·China, 2001, pp.94-98.

3 MA Ling, "Difference between Constitutional Rights Conflict and Legal Rights Conflict", *Studies in Law and Business*, 2006, Issue 6; MA Ling, "Difference between Constitutional Rights and Legal Rights", *Global Law Review*, 2008, Issue 1.

protection under the framework of the application of constitution. A theoretical presupposition of which is to regard the right norms in constitution as the rules of law which can be directly applied. Therefore, most of the scholars tend to adopt the methodology of constitutional hermeneutics, combining the right norms in constitution with specific application thereof in the constitutional review, to make a refined interpretation and construction. The logical structure theory of the application of constitutional rights, abstracted from the constitutional practices of all over the world, has been generally accepted by scholars.[1] In accordance with the doctrine of absolute protection, "protecting the constitutional rights by laws" and "restricting the constitutional rights under laws" are two sides of the same coin. In most cases, the specific provisions on way to exercise rights in law are always restrictions thereon. For example, under the *Law of the People's Republic of China on Assemblies, Processions and Demonstrations*, the provisions on way to exercise the rights of procession and demonstration obviously are a legal restriction thereon. Like any other rights, the constitutional right is possible to be subject to some legal restrictions instead of entirely unlimitedness. However, as a kind of constitutional norms, the constitutional rights keep all state organs in bounds and also impose restraints on the legislative body. Although the specific way to exercise constitutional right may be provided or restricted in legislation, the restriction itself shall be restricted (restriction on restriction). If the restriction made in legislation on basic rights exceeds the limits permissible by constitution, it will be unconstitutional. In conclusion, the logical structure of protection of constitutional right is as below: protection→restriction→restriction on restriction. Based on this theory, in recent years, some young scholars have made comprehensive comparisons among the specific applications of constitutional rights in the world, and have abstracted the common methods, combined with the right provisions of our constitution and legal system, to make interpretations

1 LIN Laifan & JI Yanmin, "Protection of Human Rights: the Significance of Principles", *Studies in Law and Business*, 2005, Issue 4.

from a comparative law perspective.[1] Of course, in accordance with this doctrine, the constitutional right is not ruled out being protected under law. For instance, the constitutional right also corresponds to the state's duty to protect it. Its achievement depends on the state to enact laws, and constitute specific protection system.[2] If the state fails to enact laws with a negative attitude, which leads to the lack of sufficient protection for achieving the rights, the state may violate its obligation under constitution. As mentioned above, this kind of protection provided by law ultimately depends on the respect, restriction and protection in constitution itself.

At present, in our constitutional jurisprudence circle, the above mentioned constitutional protection theory is being advocated by more and more scholars. However, the condition precedent of direct protection by constitution is to make judgment on the constitutionality of laws by constitutional review body, which is the only way to provide ultimate protection on the constitutional rights. But the biggest institutional bottleneck this theory faces is the lack of review system on constitutionality with timeliness. Subject to this flaw, absolute protection theory in contemporary China could not work for lacking of review system on constitutionality with timeliness, and then slipped into "the skilled-art of slaughtering dragons" which only stopped at the level of doctrine. From the practical needs of protecting constitutional rights, this is also one of the reasons why the hot wave of review of constitutionality occurred in constitutional jurisprudence studies. For this, the studies on constitutional rights conducted by academic circle are also accompanied with the calling for system of constitutionality review. For example, the seminar on "SUN Zhigang Case and Review of Constitutionality" held in Shanghai Jiao Tong University in June 2003 was one of the examples.

1 ZHANG Xiang, *Legal Construction of Fundamental Rights Norms*, China Higher Education Press, 2008.

2 MO Jihong, *Law of Protection of Human Rights and the People's Republic of China*, Law Press·China, the Third Part, 2008.

Just due to lacking in system of constitutionality review to support, some studies on constitutional rights conducted in academic circle still sought to realize the constitutional rights on the general level of law, taking the relationship between constitution and branch law as well as the effectiveness of constitutional rights in the field of branch law as study objects, such as the applicability of constitutional rights in the civil field[1], the effectiveness of constitutional rights in other legal branches[2]. On the premise of lacking in direct institutional protection, it is undeniable that the protection of constitutional rights can also receive good results under the doctrine of indirectly making the basic right take effect and by means of using the methods of interpretation of constitutionality in judicial practices. In view of the lag of real system, it is still positively significant to a certain extent to maintain the relative protection theory in China. Therefore, the scholars, keeping steady on the theories, tend to advocate the compromising protection theory on constitutional rights. That is, admitting that it is an important way to protect the constitutional rights in accordance with the laws, on the other hand, asserting that the direct protection by constitution is the "Sollen" state of protecting the constitutional rights, and going further to devote to studying the principles and arts of application of constitutional rights to support the activation of system of constitutionality review.[3]

Constitutional right is a kind of fundamental right, and to a certain extent, its meaning on protection is open to be upgraded from moral right to institutionalized right based on law, which has a certain attribute of natural right. The constitution

1 XU Zhendong, "Force of Constitutional Basic Rights in Civil Law", *Studies in Law and Business*, 2002, Issue 6; ZHANG Xiang, *Force of Basic Rights in Private Laws: In the Context of Contemporary China, Peking University Law Journal*, 2003, Issue 5.

2 HAN Dayuan, "On Force of Basic Rights in the Period of Social Innovation", *China Legal Science*, 2002, Issue 6; CHEN Yongsheng, "On the Constitutional Protection of Civil Rights in Criminal Procedure", *Criminal Law Review*, 2007, Issue 1; QIN Qianhong, "On Force of Constitutional Principles in the System of Criminal Law-from a Perspective of Human Rights", *Studies in Law and Business*, 2007, Issue 1.

3 See LIN Laifan, *From Constitutional Norms to Normative Constitution*, Law Press·China, 2001, pp.94-98.

got moral relevance through confirming the natural rights in the form of legal norms. It is precisely the moral relevance that enables the reflection and self-improvement of the whole legal system to be realized in itself, through the control under constitutional norms, being situated at the top of the Pyramid, over the inferior legal norms, so as to reduce the tension between the two arguments: "An unjust law is no law at all" and "No law is unjust". For purpose of constitutional norms system, and even the whole legal system with the constitution as the fundamental law, the constitutional right shall be at the heart of the value system. So far, in our constitutional jurisprudence circle, the basic consensus on that the constitutional right is the heart of constitutional norms system has been reached. The study on constitutional jurisprudence in China has gradually turned to the study around the constitutional right.[1] In recent years, under the study on constitutional right theory, the scholars began to instill the conception of protecting constitutional rights into the state organs and a variety of public law systems to study, and then tried to construct the constitutional jurisprudence with the axis of constitutional rights.

Based on this viewpoint, many studies on constitutional system can be reexamined from the perspective of constitutional rights protection. For instance, if the study on system of constitutional review starts from the protection of constitutional rights, the pertinent study won't have to be entangled with the reconstruction of political power structure and the choice of specific institutional model, and will focus on the methods and principles of protecting constitutional rights; other examples include the legislative restriction and theory on the protection of the constitutional rights and legislative systems, such as legislative commission, exercising administrative power under constitution, etc., relief

1 In this regard, ZHANG Qianfan pointed out that the constitutional jurisprudence used to be focused on the macroscopic concepts such as "people","state", "sovereignty"etc. But now, the focus has been diverted to personal constitutional rights. ZHANG Qianfan, *From* "Sovereignty of the People" to "Human Rights"-Transition of Modes of Constitutional Jurisprudence Studies in China, *Tribune of Political Science and Law,* 2005, Issue 2.

principle of constitutional rights and judicial system, theory of institutional protection on constitutional rights and local autonomy, electoral system, university autonomy and news and publication system, etc.

For purpose of the reality of constitutionalism in China, the constitutional jurisprudence study, moving towards and revolving around the constitutional rights, is still facing a problem of value orientation. As mentioned above, the constitutionalism has evolved from modern constitution to contemporary constitution. The first subject of modern constitutionalism was to focus on individual, as a "naked individual" before the state, and to liberate individuals radically[1]. Therefore, non-infringement of the heart of private domain was protected, which has received more attention. After entering into the period of contemporary constitutionalism, the subjects such as concepts of society and the state, and the obligation of state to protect basic rights emerged. At present, most of the major constitutionalism countries in the world have even finished these subjects of contemporary constitution, and tended to move towards "post-contemporary constitution". However, for purpose of the current situation in China, the relatively centralized power structure formed under the system of planned economy still exists in many domains. It is of great importance for the contemporary China to protect the private core domains from infringement by the state, and to complete the modern subjects of the constitutionalism. However, the constitution of socialist country has transcended the value of highest authority of right to freedom in modern constitution, which is of the characteristics of contemporary constitution from meaning of the norms. Furthermore, in view of the urban-rural dual structure and the increasing social polarization between the rich and the poor in China, it is more urgent to protect social rights of vulnerable groups, and the contemporary subjects of constitutionalism also needs to be completed. Therefore, considering the historical development stage of constitutionalism in current China, the double attributes of constitutional right

1 See LIN Laifan, *From Constitutional Norms to Normative Constitution,* Law Press·China, 2001,pp.94-98.

norms as "conditional program" and "purpose-oriented program" shall be taken into account when choosing the value orientation of study on constitutional right in China. More specifically, according to the values of modern constitution, the constitution is a system of norms with restrictions on state power, and the norms of constitutional right are defensive against the state. So, it's necessary to require the state power to comply with certain limits when intervening in civil life. Based on this concept, the constitutional right norms perform a function of conditional program, that is, the corresponding conditions have been set for the act of state by constitutional norms, were these conditions be satisfied, such act would be constitutional, otherwise, they would be unconstitutional. In comparison with this, under the concept that the state has the obligation to protect basic rights, the constitutional right norms are purpose-oriented program[1]. That is, emphasizing that constitutional right is the purpose needs to be realized by the state through a variety of ways, including legislation, public policy, etc.[2] To study constitutional jurisprudence from the perspective of constitutional right, there is a need to regard the constitutional right both as purpose-oriented program and conditional program simultaneously. On this premise, the studies on theories of constitutional right from two different dimensions will be involved, namely, the study on "constitutional rights to restrict state power" and the study on "constitutional rights to be realized depending upon state power".

6. Construction of Theory of "Constitutionalism"

Constitutionalism is an important concept in the development history of constitution. Since early 1990s, the study on issues of "constitutionalism" has been gradually received attention in our constitutional jurisprudence circle, and the concept of "socialist constitutionalism" has also been formed. In recent years,

1 Both concepts of "conditional program" and "purpose-oriented program" were put forward and discriminated by Luhmann. See Niklas Luhmann, *Law as Social System*, Oxford University Press (2004) pp.196-203.

2 This discrimination of constitutional norms originating in German constitutional theory has been generally accepted by scholars. See Nishihara Hiroshi's Constitutional Interpretation of Political Departments and the Courts, *Study of Public Law*, No. 66.

due to differences in understanding of constitutionalism in study on constitutional jurisprudence, a variety of definitions on concept of constitutionalism have been made. Generally speaking, in the constitutional jurisprudence, "constitutionalism" is used as a special term of constitutional jurisprudence or politics. The main connotation of "constitutionalism" refers to the political system established under constitution, which is the result of combination between constitutional norms and political practice for implementing the constitution.

6.1 Discussion on the Connotation of Concept of "Constitutionalism"

MAO Zedong has published the book "*Constitutionalism of New-democracy* in 1940, in which he pointed out: "What is constitutionalism? It is democratic politics", "All previous constitutionalism in the world, whether in Britain, France, America or in Soviet Union, were always admitted after the success of revolution and emergence of reality of democracy, by means of promulgating a fundamental law. That was the constitution."[1] The discussion on the concept of "constitutionalism" by Comrade MAO Zedong shows that, as a concept of institutional science, the term of "constitutionalism" is not the proprietary product of the bourgeoisie, but a neuter concept for describing the basic characteristics of the political system of a country, which can be used both by the bourgeoisie and drawn on by the proletariate to build socialist system after seizure of power.

For a long time after the founding of the new China, despite issuance of four constitutions successively, however, the term of "constitutionalism" no longer referred to the political system of society. The term of "constitutionalism" seldomly appeared in the writings of the leaders or scholars, or the published news or publications.

After the enactment of the current constitution, the constitutional jurisprudence scholars gradually began to discuss the concept of "constitutionalism". ZHANG Youyu, the famous constitutional jurist in our country, has once made an accurate description of the concept of constitutionalism: "The so-called

1 *Selected Works of MAO Zedong*, People's Publishing House, 1991, Volume 3, p.735.

constitutionalism is a form of politics, prescribing the state system, organs of state power, and the relationship of rights and obligations between government and the people, to enable the government and the people to enjoy due rights and bear the obligated duties under constitution. No person may violate or override such provisions to act freely."[1] However, in view of the complexity of the theory of "constitutionalism" per se, different understandings of the concept of "constitutionalism" have been formed in the study of constitutional jurisprudence theory.

6.1.1 Discussion on the Concept of "Constitutionalism" from the Relationship between Constitutionalism and Democracy.

In the *Basic Theory of Constitutional Jurisprudence*, ZHANG Qingfu pointed out that, constitutionalism is democratic politics, politics of constitutionality or constitutional politics. The basic characteristic of it is to fix the reality of democracy obtained through struggle by means of the fundamental law—constitution, and then to consolidate and develop such reality of democracy. Constitutionalism is the democratic political system and its facilities confirmed and regulated by constitution.[2] Similar to the above view, XU Chongde pointed out that the essential nature of constitutionalism is democratic politics, combing with requisites in form, constitutionalism should be the democratic politics to implement the constitution.[3]

LIU Jinghai held that, constitutionalism is the realization of constitution, and the constitution is the most basic normative document with faithful and solemn record of democracy. Constitutionalism is the real state of democratic politics corresponding to the constitution, and spirit of constitutionalism is the democracy consciousness which plays an important role in the course of refining constitutionalism

1 ZHANG Youyu, *Papers on Constitutionalism*, Multitude Publishing House, 1986, Volume 1, p.100.

2 *Basic Theory of Constitutional Jurisprudence (I)*, in ZHANG Qingfu (ed.), Social Sciences Academic Press (CHINA), 1999, Volume 1, p.56.

3 XU Chongde, "Extraordinary Course of Socialist Constitutionalism-the 40th Anniversary of Promulgation of New China's First Constitution", *China Legal Science*, 1994, Issue 5.

to constitution and transforming the constitution to constitutionalism. These three constitute an unity with organic connections and unified movements.[1]

6.1.2 Discussion on the Concept of "Constitutionalism" from the Relationship among Constitutionalism and Democracy, Rule of Law and Human Rights.

In the paper of "Constitutionalism and China", LI Buyun pointed out that the constitutionalism should be consisted of three essential elements, namely, the democracy, rule of law and human rights. For purpose of constitutionalism, democracy is its foundation, rule of law is an important condition, and protection of human rights is the purpose thereof.[2] Similar to LI Buyun's viewpoint, in the paper of "*Brief Discussion on Constitutionalism*, GUO Daohui pointed out that, constitutionalism is the process of political acts, such as establishing the constitution, implementing the constitution, upholding the constitution and developing the constitution, with the purpose of realizing democratic politics and the principle of rule of law and protecting the rights of people and citizens, which is consisted of three elements, namely, democracy, human rights and rule of law. The constitutionalism is a dynamically practical process for establishing the constitution, implementing the constitution, upholding the constitution, observing the constitution and going further to develop the constitution in accordance with the requirements of the times and the practice of constitutionalism.[3]ZOU Pingxue also pointed out, in the *Definition of Constitutionalism*, that the constitutionalism is a mode of politics and a political process which begins from the constitution, with the content of democracy, in principle of rule of law, and with purpose of realizing human rights. It means that not only the constitution exists in form, but the democratic politics, state of rule of law and protection of human rights provided by constitution also

1 LIU Jinghai, "Constitution, Constitutionalism and Spirit of Constitutionalism-Understanding of the Objects in Study of Constitutional Jurisprudence", *Jilin University Journal Social Sciences Edition*, 1989, Issue 1.

2 See *A Comparative Studies on Constitution*, Chinese Democracy and Legal System Press, 1993, Volume 2, p.2.

3 GUO Daohui, "Brief Discussion on Constitutionalism", *Law Science Magazine*, 1993, Issue 5.

exist in the reality.[1]

6.1.3 Discussion on the Connotation of "Constitutionalism" from the Perspective of Restricting the Government Power

DENG Shibao deemed, constitutionalism is a political system, under which the government power would be restricted and controlled, and the civil rights would be protected. The basic requirement of constitutionalism is to determine the boundary of government power, and then to control the government power from three levels: control of norms, control of power, and control of rights (from the perspective of social control). [2] CHEN Duanhong asserted that, the so-called constitutionalism is limited government in short. It points to a set of technologies for establishing and maintaining the effective control on political acts and governmental activities, in order to protect the rights and freedom of people[3].

Unlike the viewpoints that equate the constitutionalism to democracy, YANG Xiaojun and YUAN Jinyi stated emphatically that we must get rid of the thinking model that considers constitutionalism as democracy, but have to cognize constitutionalism from the special functions of it. It is a political system based on the constitution, and the main characteristic of it is that the state power would be restricted by constitution, the unrestraint of state power would be prevented, and even the power of democracy would be restricted by constitution[4]. JIANG Wei held that the core of constitutionalism is to emphasize the restrictions on government power and protection of the civil rights[5].

6.1.4 Defining the "Constitutionalism" from the Perspective of Implementation of Constitution

According to the book of *Constitution*, edited by XU Chongde, the main

1 ZOU Pingxue, "Definition of Constitutionalism", Law Review, 1996, Issue 2.

2 DENG Shibao, "Constitutionalism-the Core of Rule of Law", *Science of Law*, 2000, Issue 4.

3 CHEN Duanhong, "Preliminary Discussion on Constitutionalism", *Journal of Comparative Law*, 1992, Issue 4.

4 YANG Xiaojun, YUAN Jinyi, *Empirical Democracy and Rational Constitutionalism, Research on Rule of Law*, Hangzhou University Press, 1999, p.153.

5 JIANG Wei, "Constitutionalism-the Fundamental Sign of a Country under Rule of Law", *Academic Journal of Zhongnan University of Economics and Law*, 2000, Issue 5.

connotation of constitutionalism refers to the political system established under constitution, which is the result of combination between constitutional norms and political practice for implementing the constitution. Judging from the logical form of emergence, existence and development of constitutionalism, the so-called constitutionalism must be a live constitution or an effective constitution in reality. Based on this, the contemporary constitutionalism shall include four basic contents: legitimacy of constitution, certainty of constitution, functionality of constitution and regulatory mechanism of constitution[1].

According to the book *Basic Theories of Constitutional Jurisprudence*, edited by ZHANG Qingfu, constitutionalism is politics of constitutionality or constitutional politics, the political system established on the basis of constitution, and also democratic political system and its implementation confirmed and regulated by constitution. The basic characteristic of constitutionalism is to fix the reality of democracy, which has been obtained through struggle, by means of the fundamental law constitution, in order to consolidate and develop such reality of democracy.[2]

6.1.5 Exploring the Connotation of "Constitutionalism" as a Dynamic Process

For purpose of the specific system of constitutionalism, one scholar asserted that constitutionalism has embodied the rational allocation and running process of the power. Such scholar pointed out that constitutionalism is mode of politics and political process which begins from the constitution (constitutionality), with the content of democracy, in principle of rule of law, and with purpose of realizing the human rights. It represents a whole system with organic structure of politics and law, and the foremost sign of it is the supremacy of constitution. The system of constitutionalism can be divided into substantial structure and structure of levels. The former includes constitution, democracy, rule of law and human rights; the latter is represented by three levels, i.e. norms of constitutionalism, regime of

1 *Constitution*, in XU Chongde (ed.), China Renmin University Press, 1999, pp.17, 19.
2 *Basic Theory of Constitutional Jurisprudence (I)*, in ZHANG Qingfu (ed.),Social Sciences Academic Press(CHINA), 1999, Volume 1, p.56.

constitutionalism and culture of constitutionalism[1].

Some scholars thought of the constitutionalism as a dynamic process, and pointed out that the theory of justice on constitutionalism is not perfectionism in politics. It doesn't mean the absolute ideal of human being will be realized perfectly under the political style of constitutionalism. It simply means, for the moment, with respect to the instinct of human being, constitutionalism is the most reasonable and legitimate political style, which has more values of humanity than the justice realized by other styles, especially the personality and freedom of more individuals. This theory describes a social and political environment, in which the rights and freedom of individuals would be protected as far as possible[2].

One scholar considered the constitutionalism as a transformation process from conception to reality. They deemed the constitutionalism includes both sides, such as substantive content and formal meaning. The latter refers to the procedural nature of constitutionalism, but the former is represented by three levels of theories: (i) ideal state of constitutionalism, that is values of constitutionalism, including the theory, principle and basic conception thereof; (ii) normative state of constitutionalism, that is, the expression form of constitutionalism ideal in law, specifically expressed as a variety of legal norms of constitutionalism enacted under the theory thereof; (iii) real state of constitutionalism, namely, the degree of realization of the ideal and norms of constitutionalism. These three levels of theories cross, but not overlap, presented by a dynamic transformation process. The scholar also stressed that, with reference to the content thereof, the constitutionalism can be expressed from two aspects, namely, vertical levels and horizontal contents. The former is represented as norms of constitutionalism, reality of constitutionalism and conception of constitutionalism, which cross each other but not overlap. The realization process of constitutionalism is as below: normalization of constitutionalism theories, realization of constitutionalism norms

1 ZOU Pingxue, "Definition of Constitutionalism", *Law Review*, 1996, Issue 2.

2 GAO Quanxi, *Justice of Constitutionalism*, at http://go6.163.com/fanyafeng/xianzhengzhiyixinghgaoqx.htm.

and normalization of constitutionalism reality, idealization of constitutionalism norms and proceduralization of constitutionalism.[1]

The constitutional scholars agreed that, the term of "constitutionalism" is not the fruit of Chinese native culture, whether from the perspective of theoretical concepts, or from the institutional practice. It is introduced and learned from the constitutional culture of western capitalism, so, the utterance related to "constitutionalism" cannot be separated from the context of rule of law and culture of western society. As a product of the evolutionary culture of rule of law in western society, the emphases in connotation and manifestation of constitutionalism were different in different historical periods. However, no matter how much it would change in the connotation and manifestation of constitutionalism, the core value thereof on protecting human rights and restricting government power will not change all along. That is the starting point of study and discussion on issues of constitutionalism.

6.2 Discussion on the Nature of "Constitutionalism"

The constitutional scholars often disagree on whether the "constitutionalism" is in the nature of class, on which there are two opposite viewpoints. One viewpoint is that the nature of constitutionalism is the manifestation of fundamental will and interests of the ruling class, the same as constitution, with purpose of providing service for the ruling class. As a system of democracy and politics, it is only democratic to a certain class, and the "abstract", "supra-class" or "universal" constitutionalism would not exist. In terms of the essential characteristic of constitutionalism, there are two divergent views, respectively corresponding to the capitalist constitutionalism and the socialist constitutionalism.[2] But according to the other viewpoint, the class nature of "constitutionalism" has been clearly objected. Such scholars deemed, the socialist constitutionalism has not been indeed established in China and other socialist countries, and therefore, the studies

1 WU Dexing, "On Substantive Contents and Formal Meaning of Constitutionalism", *Tianjin Social Sciences*, 1997, Issue 1.

2 *Basic Theory of Constitutional Jurisprudence*, in ZHANG Qingfu (Ed.), Social Sciences Academic Press(CHINA), 1999, Volume 1, p.56.

and exposition of socialist constitutionalism are not record and description of the past, but outline of constitutionalism blueprint in the future. So, for socialist countries, which class will be protected by the constitutionalism with class nature? And which class will it be against thereunder? Pursuant to the Maxism doctrine, the privilege of class has always been objected. The nature of socialist country doesn't mean the elimination of class, but rests on the elimination of class oppression and class privilege. So, the socialist constitutionalism shall be the universal constitutionalism for all social classes, not only for one or certain classes. The narrow view on class privilege was the product of society dominated by exploiting classes, which must be abandoned by a socialist society.

After discussion, most of the constitutional scholars agreed that constitutionalism is not the proprietary product of the capitalist political system. After seizure of power and establishment of socialist countries, the proletariate can also build socialist constitutionalism in accordance with the concepts of constitutionalism in terms of restricting the government power and protecting human rights. Certain scholars had different opinions on this, believing that the constitutionalism can only fit in the legal culture of a capitalist society rather than a part of a socialist system.

6.2.1 Connections between Constitutionalism and Constitution

The connections between constitutionalism and constitution have become a subject of heated discussions in constitutional jurisprudence circle, in which lots of different opinions have emerged and many representative viewpoints with distinctive characteristics have also been formed.

Some scholars compared the connections between constitutionalism and constitution to the connections between content and form. For instance, in accordance with the book of *Basic Theories of Constitutional Jurisprudence* edited by ZHANG Qingfu, the connections between constitution and constitutionalism are dialectically united and can be referred to as the connections between form and content. On one hand, constitution must be based on the constitutionalism and with the content thereof, and there will be no constitution without constitutionalism movements; on the other hand, constitution is the manifestation and basis of constitutionalism, meanwhile, it is continuously enriched and developed in the process of implementing the constitutionalism.[1]

Some scholars explored the connections between constitutionalism and constitution from the perspective of implementing the constitution. For example, in the book of *Constitution and Institutional Innovation*, ZHU Fuhui held that constitution is the precedent condition of constitutionalism, and the constitutionalism is the result of implementing constitution. However, there is no necessary correspondence between them. The correspondence is based on the democracy of contents of constitution and effective implementation of constitution. To implement the constitution is the key point of constitutionalism, and it is a reflection of the abnormal state for having constitution without constitutionalism[2].

Some scholars have studied the connections between constitutionalism and constitution by examining the interactions between them. For example, in the *Constitution* edited by XU Chongde, the author held that for a political system established on the basis of constitutional provisions, the establishment, existence, development and change of constitutionalism shall all be ready to serve the purposes of making the constitution on paper become constitution in reality. However, the practice of constitutionalism is not utterly passive when it comes to constitution. With regard to the constitution without legitimacy, certainty, functionality and regulatory mechanism, the practical activities of constitutionalism can in turn make the constitution on paper meet the requirements thereof through a mechanism of counteraction. Therefore, the establishment of constitution doesn't mean that the practice of constitutionalism with practical significance can be produced on the basis of constitutional provisions on paper. In order to provide a correct normative basis for practice of constitutionalism constantly, the constitution must satisfy the requirements of

1 *Basic Theory of Constitutional Jurisprudence (I)*, in ZHANG Qingfu (ed.), Social Sciences Academic Press (CHINA), 1999, Volume 1, p.64.

2 ZHU Fuhui, *Constitution and Institutional Innovation*, Law Press·China, 2000, pp.141-143.

the constitutionalism practice. Of course, without constitution, the foundation of practice of constitutionalism, constitutionalism is out of question. That is, if there is no fundamental law in the name of constitution, or the authority of constitution has been badly neglected by the public, it is absurd to talk about constitutionalism. Therefore, in order to realize constitutionalism, the authority of constitution as a fundamental law must be stressed. The constitution is law, rather than a simple political principle or policy. At the request of the constitutionalism practice, the legal system of a country must be kept uniform and coordinated, of which the constitution shall be at the heart, and become the basic premise for rule of law[1].

Some scholars asserted that the connections between constitutionalism and constitution shall be explored in various ways. For example, according to the book *Constitution* edited by ZHOU Yezhong, the constitutionalism shall start from constitution from the perspective of logic; in terms of content, the content of constitutionalism directly depends on the content of constitution, and the purpose of constitutionality is the purpose of constitutionalism, the establishment, existence, development and change of which shall be subject to the purpose that making the constitution on paper become the constitution in reality; with respect to the value, both the constitution and constitutionalism are products of development of commodity economy, and important manifestation of democracy and politics construction and law-governing country construction, taking the restriction on state power and protection of civil rights as the fundamental spirit and value orientation. So, constitution is the condition precedent of constitutionalism, and constitutionalism is the life of constitution; constitution is the guidance of practice, and the practice of constitutionalism helps perfect the constitution. In both theory and practice, there is a dialectical relationship between the two.[2]

Some scholars have classified the connections between constitutionalism and constitution and pointed out the different modes thereof from the perspective

1 *Constitution*, in XU Chongde (ed.), China Renmin University Press, 1999, p.20.
2 *Constitution*, in ZHOU Yezhong (ed.), China Higher Education Press, 2000, p.180.

of taxonomy. For instance, in the *Brief Discussion on Constitutionalism*, GUO Daohui indicated that there are five modes of connections between constitution and constitutionalism as follows: (i) there is no constitution or constitutionalism; (ii) there are constitution and constitutionalism; (iii) there is constitutionalism but no constitution; (iv) there is constitution but no constitutionalism; and (v) there is constitutionalism but with unconstitutionality. Under normal circumstances, no constitution means no constitutionalism, and constitutionalism is the soul of constitution. Without the spirit and running of constitutionalism, the constitution vainly possesses an empty name; furthermore, and constitutionalism is the driving force of constitution, the running of which promotes to establish the authority of constitution and to protect the powers and rights of the people.[1]

After discussions, most of the constitutional jurisprudence scholars agreed that constitutionalism and constitution are two different concepts with both connections and differences. The original constitutional document is the reflection of values of constitutionalism. It's impossible to formulate constitution without the values, such as democracy, human rights, and rule of law. However, in reality, a constitution may deviate from the requirements of values of constitutionalism, which might not be established, even though there is a constitution. The establishment of constitutionalism is subject to two conditions: (i) to establish a constitutional system in conformity with the values of constitutionalism; and (ii) the constitutional system in conformity with the values of constitutionalism can be effectively operated in real life. Some scholars asserted that constitutionalism is inseparable from constitution, and constitutionalism is the specific state of constitution in reality. According to them, what kind of constitution is established determines what kind of constitutionalism will emerge. The socialist constitutionalism is totally different from the capitalist constitutionalism.

6.2.2 Connections between Party System and Constitutionalism

The party system is closely related to constitutionalism. The biggest

1 GUO Daohui, "Brief Discussion on Constitutionalism", *Law Science Magazine,*1993, Issue 5.

characteristic of contemporary constitutionalism is party politics. However, the historical condition for party system, the purpose and nature, the mission, and the legal status of party in national political life are different for each country, so, the theory and practice of constitutionalism formulated through party system are quite different. In recent years, the constitutional jurisprudence scholars in China have made a relatively thorough discussion on the connections between party system and constitutionalism, and put forward many different academic viewpoints.

In the book *New View on Comparative Constitutional Jurisprudence*, ZHAO Shumin made a more comprehensive exposition on the connections between party system and constitutionalism, and put forward a series of views with academic influence. He held that the connections between party system and constitutionalism can be summarized into the following seven aspects: (i) Constitution is democratic politics, and the party system makes constitutionalism and constitution more vivid, richer and more realistic; (ii) Constitutionalism is not the product of all classes and class warfare, and the party emerges in response to the requirement of the class and the situation of class warfare, and in turn provides service for them; (iii) Although the rise of party cannot be separated from constitutionalism movements and constitution, the party had not been incorporated in constitution for a long time, which reflects the characteristics of party and class warfare of constitutionalism and constitution from one side; (iv) The past activities of party, constitutionalism movements and constitution were in order. To serve the purpose of the bourgeoisie party, its emphases on constitutional usage and the state of separating from constitution in the past have been replaced by constitutionalization of party activities. In socialist countries, the party activities are also characterized by expressions and slogans. Subsequently, the parties of many colonial countries and semi-colonial countries, after achieving their own independence, also incorporated their independent features into the constitution; (v) The development courses of the party, constitutionalism movements and constitution were tortuous; (vi) The party, constitutionalism and constitution are all the most sensitive and sharpest reflections of class warfare after the bourgeoisie and capitalism enter into a certain stage. It is entirely different for the party to center on constitutional common practice or to be based on the constitutional articles, and also different to be incorporated in the constitution as a common party or as a ruling party; and (vii) None of the party, constitutionalism or the constitution is supra-class.[1]

How the party acts in the scope permitted by the constitution and laws is a key issue in discussing the connections between party system and constitutionalism in the constitutional jurisprudence circle. PU Zengyuan asserted that with respect to the problem of solving the institutionalization of activities by the party in the scope permitted by the constitution and laws, except for formulating legislation law and supervision law, it is still necessary to enact the rules to specify how the party should act in the aforesaid scope; to develop the training and assessment methods of legal knowledge for the party's leading cadres at all levels, and a person who is not qualified cannot act as party leader; the party committees at all levels shall put the problem, confining the party activities to the scope permitted by constitution and laws, into the agenda of periodical discussions, and bring the issue to high-level party leardership democratic meetings; the party's discipline inspection organ shall take the inspection of whether the party acts in the scope permitted by constitution and laws as an important duty, and draft specific implementation measures; to regulate the status, roles and activity mode of each party, including the ruling party, in the national political arena through legislation, especially by making it a principle that all parties shall conform to the constitution and laws.[2]

There are two opposite opinions on whether it's necessary to incorporate the party system into the scope of legislation. One view is that legislation for party is an important characteristic of contemporary constitutionalism development, and the legalization of party is the premise and condition to implement constitutional

1 ZHAO Shumin, *New View on Comparative Constitutional Jurisprudence*, China Social Sciences Press, 2000, pp.729-739.

2 PU Zengyuan, *Consideration on Confining the Party Activities to the Scope Permitted by Constitution and Laws*, *Exploration and Free Views*, 1998, Issue 5.

supervision on party. Only when the principles of organization and activities of party are regulated through necessary legislation may it be rendered possible to implement constitutional supervision on party. Whether the party activities in our country can be legalized, or whether the party can be supervised by constitution is a very solemn and realistic subject in our political life. Both the uniformity of the nature of our country and that of the Communist Party of China, and the lessons of international communist movements have proved the necessity and urgency to set up constitutional supervision on parties in China.[1] According to the other view, some scholars disagreed to legislate for the party. They held that it is of positive significance for incorporating the party system into *Constitution* (amended in 1993), so far, we don't need to enact another special *Party Law*.[2] To implement "governing the party by law" will face practical challenges. From the perspective of history and reality, the party has enacted lots of party rules and regulations to regulate the activities thereof. Actually, such party regulations have always been running outside the laws. Incorporating all the rules of party into legal regulations will encounter many problems in the system of formulation and implementation of the laws.[3]

Generally speaking, when it comes to the connections between party system and constitutionalism, the study thereon in constitutional jurisprudence circle is still in its infancy. Many important concepts and categories have not been established, and many significant academic issues have not been effectively discussed. Such problems include the issues in development of the party system towards democracy, rule of law and human rights, inter-party relationship and inner-party democratic relationship, supervisory system for party activities, and

1 CAI Dingjian, *National Supervisory System*, China Legal Publishing House, 1991, pp.137-144.

2 XU Menyou, "Party Legislation of Western Countries and Legalization of Our Multi-party Cooperation System", *Journal of Northwest University* (Philosophy and Social Science Edition), 1993, Issue 4.

3 JIANG Liyou, "Basic Framework and Implementation Steps of Chinese Legal System (Rule of Law) Reform", *Peking University Law Journal*, 1995, Issue 6.

the connections between party leadership and constitutionalism construction.[1]

6.2.3 Connections between Constitutionalism and Rule of Law

The connections between constitutionalism and rule of law involve the issue of whether to establish the principle of "supremacy of constitution". At present, the constitutional scholars agree with the principle of "supremacy of constitution" (supremacy of law) in general, but, as to the specific significance and operative forms of the principle in terms of system construction, there are still some different views.

As to whether the constitution has supreme efficacy or supreme authority, one view is that, the principle of "supremacy of constitution" maintained in constitutionalism actually underlines that constitution shall have the supreme legal effect, that is, the principle of "supremacy of constitution" is expressed from the perspective of law. Under the constitutionalism system, it is necessary for the political system of one country to be controlled by political force in reality. Another view is that, what the principle of "supremacy of constitution" emphasizes is that the constitution shall have supreme authority, because if constitution lacks in supreme authority in governing a country, the principle of rule of law will lose its essential meaning. Apart from the above two views, there is another view. Such scholars deemed, in view of the indeed highest leadership of Communist Party in our political life, to realize the "supremacy of constitution" and to establish the supreme authority of constitution, what matters most is to focus on rationalizing the relationship between the Party and state power, which is an inevitable reality in the course of building socialist country under rule of law. The Party shall play an exemplary role and attempt to enable the supreme legal effect of constitution to be truly realized with its comprehensive political resources, which is the key point of achieving "supremacy of constitution" and building a country under rule of law.[2]

1 *China's Constitutional Jurisprudence Entering into New Century (II)*, in YANG Haikun (ed.), *China Personnel Press*, 2001, Volume 2, pp.571-572.

2 *China's Constitutional Jurisprudence Entering into New Century (I),* in YANG Haikun (ed.), *China Personnel Press*, 2001,Volume 1, pp.68-69.

The relationship between "supremacy of constitution" and "sovereignty of the people" is another important issue involving the mutual relationship between constitutionalism and rule of law. Some scholars held that there is no contradiction between "supremacy of constitution" and supremacy of "sovereignty of the people", both of which are unified. Actually, the best manifestation of "sovereignty of the people" is to build a socialist country under rule of law, and to realize rule of law. The principle of "supremacy of constitution" actually incorporates the idea of the sovereignty of people over the state. Because the socialist laws by nature are manifestation of the will of the whole people, the domination by laws is equal to the domination by people, and the will of people has been directly reflected in constitution and laws, therefore, the socialist laws are superior than state power.[1]

Some scholars assert that governing the country by law is actually governing the country by constitution, which is the foremost basis of rule of law, and it must be conducted in the scope permitted by constitution. To achieve the goal of rule of law, it's crucial to implement the constitution. Governing the country by law is actually governing the country by constitution.[2]

Some constitutional scholars hold that, under the current political system of China, the system of People's Congress is an epitomization of our socialist constitutionalism. The main feature of our current constitutionalism is that the people are masters of the country under governance by the Communist Party. The people elect deputies thereof to organize the organs of state power at all levels, through which the people exercise state power and protect basic rights of the citizens. Therefore, constitutionalism has been reflected in China. But a few scholars deem that the constitutionalism has not been established in China, and it is a long-term objective of construction of socialist rule of law.

1 Ibid. pp.69-70.

2 LIU Xia, "Exploration on the Connections between Implementation of Constitution and Governing the Country by Law", *Modern Law Science*, 2000, Issue 3.

Chapter 14

Modernization of China's Criminal Jurisprudence

1. Criminal Jurisprudence Research Emerging from the Amendment to the Criminal Law

In 1988, the Amendment to the Criminal Law was listed in the legislative plan by the Standing Committee of the National People's Congress. Although the amendment to the Criminal Law had been discussed by some criminal jurisprudence scholars, the comprehensive exploration in the criminal jurisprudence circle wasn't in full swing until the aforesaid move in 1988 by the legislature. The new Criminal Law promulgated in 1997 is an all-round amendment to the Criminal Law formulated in 1979, marking a great stride towards the modernization of China's criminal law system, and many findings and suggestions of the criminal jurisprudence circle were incorporated into the new Criminal Law. Of course, academic studies cannot be all in the same key. There being different opinions on the same issue is absolutely normal, and promotion of healthy academic debates is conducive to the formation of school of thoughts in China's criminal jurisprudence.[1] In addition, although some research findings have

1 Liu Renwen. "Basic Characteristics of the Development of China's Criminal Law over the 30 Years", *Legal Science Monthly,* 2008 (5).

not been adopted by the legislature, their significance cannot be thus neglected. In the long run, such research results will facilitate the modernization of China's Criminal Law. For example, many criminal jurisprudence scholars proposed to address the "re-education through labor" issue when the Criminal Law was amended in 1997, but the legislature deemed that this issue was too complicated and the amendment was an urgent task, so it decided to address this issue in other ways. [1]For another example, the proposal of the criminal jurisprudence circle to significantly reduce death penalties was not incorporated into the new Criminal Law in 1997. In the eyes of the legislature at that time, "it is not time to reduce death penalties because of the grave social security situation and severe economic crime situation", therefore, "the death penalties under the existing laws will be neither increased nor decreased in principle this time".[2] But on 1 January, 2007, the Supreme People's Court finally took back the power to approve death sentences, thus significantly reducing death penalties in judicial practice.[3] So to speak, such progress is related to the continuous attention of the criminal jurisprudence circle to this issue.

1 The reform of the "re-education through labor" system has been included in the legislative plan, and the legislature has been conducting the study and demonstration of the promulgation of the *Law on Rehabilitation for Illegal Activities.*

2 Wang Hanbin. *Explanations of (draft amendment to) the Criminal Law of the People's Republic of China,* March 6, 1997.

3 On March 10, 2008, when Xiao Yang, the then president of the Supreme People's Court, was discussing the Report on the Work of the Supreme People's Court and the Report on the Work of the Supreme People's Procuratorate with the deputies of Guangdong Province, he disclosed that the number of people sentenced to death with reprieve had for the first time exceeded the number of people sentenced to death to be immediately executed. On the same day, when being interviewed to interpret the Report on the Work of the Supreme People's Court, Ni Shouming, the then spokesperson of the Supreme People's Court, said that, in 2007, the death sentences not approved for unclear facts, inadequate evidence, inappropriate sentencing, illegal procedures and other reasons accounted for 15% of all the death sentences, and the unified exercise of the power to approve death sentences by the Supreme People's Court contributed to the improvement of the quality of first instances and second instances.

1.1 Abolition of the Analogy System and the Establishment of the Principle of "Nullum Crimen, Nulla Poena sine Praevia Lege Poenali (No Crime and No Punishment without a Pre-existing Penal Law)"

Whether the analogy system in the Criminal Law of 1979 should be abolished was controversial before the promulgation of the new Criminal Law in 1997. At first, most scholars acknowledged the rationality of the analogy system, but later, more and more scholars proposed to abolish this system. This process reflected the attitude changes in China's criminal jurisprudence circle, i.e., the gradual transition from the stress on the role of the criminal law in social protection to the stress on the role of the criminal law in human right protection. As some scholars remarked, "No matter whether we are aware of it or not, this discussion is reshaping the cultural character of China's contemporary criminal law theories. Its far-reaching influence on China's criminal law theories will be definitely shown over time."[1]

But even when the Criminal Law was about to be amended, some scholars still insisted that the analogy system should be retained mainly for the following reasons: "(1) the analogy system conforms to China's actual conditions, and it is obviously impossible for the Criminal Law to contain express provisions on all crimes; (2) owing to the inadequate legislation experience, it is necessary to retain the analogy system, rather than strictly follow the principle of "no crime and no punishment without a pre-existing penal law"; (3) strictly following the principle of "no crime and no punishment without a pre-existing penal law" is not feasible in both legislation and judicial practice; (4) the analogy system is needed in the market economy; (5) the principle of "no crime and no punishment without a pre-existing penal law" is withering away in the Western countries, and the analogy system is again attracting people's attention; and (6) the analogy system

1 Chen Xingliang. "Contemporary Fate of the Principle of 'No Crime and No Punishment without a Pre-existing Penal Law'", *Chinese Journal of Law*, 1996 (2).

is consistent with China's historical tradition. [1]

The above opinions were not approved by many criminal jurisprudence scholars. Most criminal jurisprudence scholars believed that China should abolish the analogy system. For example, some scholars pointed out that the analogy system was in conflict with the principle of "no crime and no punishment without a pre-existing penal law", essentially not conducive to the rule by law, and not conducive to the effective protection of citizens' rights.[2] Other scholars argued that whether a country should follow the principle of "no crime and no punishment without a pre-existing penal law" was not related to legislation experience, but a question of value orientation and legislative ideas.[3] Based on the in-depth study of the principle of "no crime and no punishment without a pre-existing penal law", some scholars pointed out why retaining the analogy system was wrong: for example, it was inaccurate to conclude that the principle of "no crime and no punishment without a pre-existing penal law" only existed in name in the Western countries; in fact, this principle was in the transition from an absolute one to a relative one, which was a self-improvement and totally different from analogy. Although the strictly restricted analogy was incomparable with tyranny in conviction and sentencing, it was still not conducive to the protection of human rights, and it was unfair for perpetrators to bear the responsibilities which were not foreseen even by lawmakers.[4]

After the full argumentation in the academic circle, the legislature finally abolished the analogy system and expressly established the principle of "no crime and no punishment without a pre-existing penal law" in the Criminal Law. But it

1 Hou Guoyun. "Value Orientation of the Principle of 'No Crime and No Punishment without a Pre-existing Penal Law' and the Criminal Analogy System in the Market Economy", *Chinese Journal of Law,* 1995 (3).

2 Bao Suixian. "The Analogy System should Be Abolished", *Law Review,* 1990 (4).

3 Hu Yunteng. "Abolition of the Analogy System and Scientization of Criminal Law", *Chinese Journal of Law,* 1995 (5).

4 Chen Xingliang. "Contemporary Fate of the Principle of 'No Crime and No Punishment without a Pre-existing Penal Law'", *Chinese Journal of Law*, 1996 (2).

should be noted that the principle of "no crime and no punishment without a pre-existing penal law" is expressed in a still unique way in China's Criminal Law, specifically, it is provided both in an affirmative sentence and in a double negative sentence: in an affirmative sentence, "those carrying out criminal activities expressly provided in laws shall be convicted and punished in accordance with the law"; in a double negative sentence, "those carrying out activities not expressly deemed as criminal in laws shall not be convicted or punished". This is obviously different from there being only a double negative sentence in the criminal laws of other countries and regions: "no activity shall be deemed or punished as a crime unless it is expressly provided in the law". The principle of "no crime and no punishment without a pre-existing penal law" was originally put forward to protect citizens' rights to combat judicial autarchy and arbitrary conviction. Therefore, it must be expressed in a double negative sentence. According to the scholars participating in the amendment to the Criminal Law, the reason for China to set forth the principle of "no crime and no punishment without a pre-existing penal law" both in an affirmative sentence and in a double negative sentence was that according to the traditional opinion, the law was a tool of the ruling class and the criminal punishment was a measure to suppress enemies; if this principle was just expressed in a double negative sentence, it would not be well received among received among the people. In order to ensure that this principle would be accepted by more people and established in the Criminal Law as soon as possible, participants in the amendment to the Criminal Law proposed to express the principle both in an affirmative sentence and in a double negative sentence to reduce resistance.[1]

1.2 Discussion on Changing the "Crime of Counterrevolution" into the "Crime of Jeopardizing State Security"

The "crime of counterrevolution" was provided in Chapter One of the Specific

1 Chen Zexian. *Legislative Defects in and Judicial Misunderstandings of the Principle of "No Crime and No Punishment without a Pre-existing Penal Law"*, *New Reports in Criminal Law* (Vol. III), Publishing House of People's Public Security University of China, 2006.

Provisions of the Criminal Law formulated in 1979, but its rationality became controversial with social development. As early as in 1981, some scholars published articles to point out that the "crime of counterrevolution" was no longer suitable for the situation at present, and they proposed that this crime should be changed into the "crime of jeopardizing state security". [1] Later, other scholars expressed similar opinions. [2] In response to this proposition, some criminal jurisprudence scholars argued that the "crime of counterrevolution" should be retained in the Criminal Law for the following reasons: "The crime of counterrevolution" has always been a feature in China's Criminal Law. It is an effective weapon for fighting against domestic and overseas reactionary forces and hostile elements in light of China's national conditions. The crime of counterrevolution indicates one of the acts targeted at by the Criminal Law and has become a strict legal concept. The crime of counterrevolution reflects the unity of the subjective element and the objective element in the composition of the crime of counterrevolution, and it is needed to truly ensure the realization of "one nation, two systems".[3] But most criminal jurisprudence scholars believed

1 Xu Jian. *Is "Counterrevolution" a Rational Crime Name? Exploration and Free Views*, 1981 (1).

2 Zhao Bingzhi, *A Review of the Studies of the Amendment to the Criminal Law*, Publishing House of People's Public Security University of China, 1990, p.235.

3 He Bingsong. "A Dangerous Choice-My Opinions on the Cancellation of the Crime of Counterrevolution in the Criminal Law", *Tribune of Political Science and Law,* 1990 (2). It is noteworthy that although most people in the criminal jurisprudence circle criticized this article, some scholars said this article was actually valuable for the amendment to the Criminal Law. For example, in the draft amendment to the Criminal Law put forward by the Commission of Legislative Affairs of the Standing Committee of the National People's Congress in 1988, all the provisions in this chapter on overthrowing the dictatorship of the proletariat and socialist system were deleted, but after the publication of this article, the authors' opinions attracted the attention of the CPC Central Committee and lawmakers; therefore, in the "Crime of Jeopardizing State Security (i.e., previously Crimes of Counterrevolution)" Chapter in the Criminal Law after the amendment in 1997, "subverting the state power and overthrowing the socialist system" was kept in some articles, "which proved the importance of giving full play to democracy in academic studies, including criminal legislation". Qu Xinjiu. "A Review of the Thoughts of Professor He Bingsong on Criminal Jurisprudence", *Information and Research of Legal Literature*, 1998 (4).

that changing the "crime of counterrevolution" into the "crime of jeopardizing state security" was more rational for the following reasons: (1) the name of a crime type as a legal concept should be clear, rational and definite in wording, but the "crime of counterrevolution" was obviously defective in this regard, and its ambiguity reflected its imprecision, while the "crime of jeopardizing state security" could more accurately indicate the essential characteristics of this type of crimes. Some people thought that changing the name of the "crime of counterrevolution" would result in the fundamental cancellation of this type of crimes. But actually, no one proposed to abolish the fundamental connotation of the "crime of counterrevolution"; instead, the fundamental contents were still retained in the "crime of jeopardizing state security". (2) The emphasis on the "purpose of counterrevolution" led to the confusion among crimes. For example, it would be more suitable to classify counterrevolutionary explosions, arsons, robberies, hijacks and the like as the crimes of jeopardizing public security, [1]and the "purpose of counterrevolution" was sometimes difficult to ascertain in practice, and many cases were controversial in whether perpetrators acted for the "purpose of counterrevolution"; as a result, judicial officials found it confusing to classify a crime as a counterrevolutionary one or an ordinary one. (3) As the "crime of counterrevolution" was highly political, China was confronted with many avoidable and unnecessary difficulties in seeking international judicial assistance. Taking extradition as an example, China's requests for extradition of criminals convicted of the crime of counterrevolution for hijacking planes/vessels, counterrevolutionary damage or killing were rejected by some countries on the ground of the international , ground of "no extradition of political offenders". Hijacking by Zhuo Changren and other four criminals in 1983 and hijacking by Zhang Zhenhai in 1989 were two cases in point. (4) Changing the "crime of counterrevolution" into the "crime of jeopardizing state security" would be conducive to the implementation of "one nation, two systems", because both

1 This proposal was adopted in the new Criminal Law in 1997.

acts of damaging the socialist system of the Chinese mainland and damaging the capitalist system of Hong Kong and Macao would be viewed as jeopardizing national unity and security, but it would not be rational to judge one as revolutionary and the other counterrevolutionary.[1]

After extensive and in-depth discussions, in the new Criminal Law in 1997, the "crime of counterrevolution" was changed into the "crime of jeopardizing state security", the provision on the subjective purpose of counterrevolution was deleted, this type of crimes were changed and adjusted based on the nature of the crime of jeopardizing state security, and the provisions on the crimes actually being ordinary crimes were transferred to other chapters. So to speak, this amendment was an important step for China's Criminal Law to become more scientific and consistent with the international practices of the modern criminal law, so it was well received both at home and abroad.

2. New Advances in Criminal Law Theories

Since the middle of 1980s, annotations-based criminal jurisprudence had been in the gradual shift to the critical and constructive theoretical criminal jurisprudence, and the achievements were notable. In particular, since 1990s, the great efforts of many far-sighted scholars in the criminal jurisprudence circle had pushed China's criminal law theories to a new height.[2]

2.1 Shift to Theoretical Criminal Jurisprudence

In this respect, the *Philosophy of Criminal Law* [3] played an important role. The approach used in this book to study the philosophy of criminal law considerably impacted the criminal jurisprudence circle: the criminal law could even be

1 Liang Huaren, Zhou Rongsheng. *On the Change of the Name of the Crime of Counterrevolution*, *Tribune of Political Science and Law*, 1990 (4). Cao Zidan, Hou Guoyun. *On the Change of the Name of the Crime of Counterrevolution into the Crime of Jeopardizing State Security*, *China Legal Science*, 1991 (2).

2 Wang Minyuan. *Review of the Studies of Criminal Jurisprudence in 1997*, *Chinese Journal of Law*, 1998 (1).

3 Chen Xingliang. China University of Political Science and Law Press, 1992.

studied in this way![1] The author said in the foreword that he wrote this book to "break through the existing criminal law theories in all aspects from system to contents, and complete the shift from annotations-based criminal jurisprudence to theoretical criminal jurisprudence."[2] This book together with the author's subsequent *Human Nature Basis of the Criminal Law*[3] and *Construction of Values of Criminal Law*[4] formed the trilogy of the author's philosophy of criminal law. This area witnessed the successive publication of some important works, such as the *Spirit and Scope of the Criminal Law*[5].

The study of the philosophy of criminal law marked that China's criminal jurisprudence had gone beyond articles of law and become systematic, academic and scientific. But it should be noted that the theoretical criminal jurisprudence could be studied at different levels and in different dimensions. From the perspective of the development need of China's criminal jurisprudence, what was most lacking were the works linking annotations to criminal law and the philosophy of criminal law, i.e., those works systematically expounding the basic theories of criminal law. The good news was that more and more scholars in the criminal jurisprudence circle had realized this gap and Chen Xingliang published the *Ontological Criminal Jurisprudence*[6], his another book on theoretical criminal jurisprudence. The contributions of this book mainly fell into two aspects: one was the development of the theoretical system of the criminal jurisprudence based on

1 Liu Yanhong. *Justice, Path and Method—Inception, Development and Maturity of the Criminal Law Methodology*, contained in the *Criminal Law Methodology* compiled by Liang Genlin, Peking University Press, 2006.

2 The author later reflected as follows: "improvement" is more accurate than "shift". "At that time, I was deeply concerned that the criminal law theories were limited, confined and restricted to legal provisions. Therefore, the criminal jurisprudence mainly with annotations was somewhat superficial, and changes were urgently needed. So, the transition from the criminal law hermeneutics to the criminal law philosophy was put forward. As 'transition' implied 'replacement' and 'negation', this proposition was biased." Chen Xingliang. *Criminal Jurisprudence towards Philosophy*, Law Press, 1999, p.13.

3 Chen Xingliang. China Fangzheng Press, 1996.

4 Chen Xingliang. China Renmin University Press, 1998.

5 Qu Xinjiu. China University of Political Science and Law Press, 2000.

6 Commereial Press, 2001.

the general doctrines and supplemented by personalized narrations, and the other was the integration of the knowledge of the criminal jurisprudence in different periods and countries.[1]

In the context where metaphysical studies were commonplace, annotations-based criminal jurisprudence was almost a derogatory term. At this time, Zhang Mingkai voiced his different opinion: "Annotations-based criminal jurisprudence is not at a low level. It is also a theory. The application of criminal law depends on annotations. Therefore, without annotations-based criminal jurisprudence, there will be no well-developed criminal jurisprudence. If the criminal jurisprudence of a country is backward, the main reason is that there are no good annotations to the criminal law; if the criminal jurisprudence of a country is well-developed, the main reason is that many efforts have been made in the annotations to the criminal law."[2] Therefore, annotations-based criminal jurisprudence and theoretical criminal jurisprudence run parallel and promote each other. The updated annotations-based criminal jurisprudence was no longer just about discussions of a matter on its merits, because it began to discuss problems from the perspective of methodology, for example, the purposive interpretation in criminal law interpretations, and the judicial syllogism in criminal law dogmatics.[3] In recent years, some scholars noticed that in the current annotations-based criminal jurisprudence, there was

1 Liu Renwen. *Ontological Questioning of the Criminal Jurisprudence, Peking University Law Journal*, 2002 (3).

2 Zhang Mingkai, *Criminal Jurisprudence*, Law Press, 1997, Introduction.

3 "purposive interpretation" means "the interpretation in the light of the purposes, meanings and the to-be-protected legal interests in the application of articles of law", but in the opinion of Wang Shizhou, no (interpretation) method is omnipotent, and the comprehensive method is the best. Wang Shizhou. *Thoughts on the Theories in Criminal Law Methodology,* contained in the *Criminal Law Methodology* compiled by Liang Genlin, Peking University Press, 2006. In the opinion of Chen Xingliang, "judicial syllogism" means identifying applicable laws with the interpretation method—identifying facts with the validation method and the deductive method—deducing the conclusion with the logical deduction method. He believes that this is a basic reasoning tool in criminal law dogmatics to provide the application of criminal law with legal rules. Chen Xingliang, *Methodology of Criminal Law Dogmatics*, contained in the *Criminal Law Methodology* compiled by Liang Genlin, Peking University Press, 2006.

no adequate analysis of the distribution of punishment in the quantification of a criminal punishment, so that "in the sub-pandects (on crimes), the exposition of 'crimes' was negligible and a reader can by itself refer to articles of law to impose a punishment". [1] This is a very concise opinion and also a problem needing to be addressed in the future criminal law textbooks and criminal law annotations.

In recent years, dynamic criminal jurisprudence arose in addition to theoretical criminal jurisprudence and annotations-based criminal jurisprudence. A basic idea was as follows: theoretical criminal jurisprudence is based on concepts and annotations-based criminal jurisprudence is based on texts, and the two are both static. But criminal law exists and develops in operation, and it is essentially dynamic and practical. So, in the light of the nature of criminal law, dynamic criminal jurisprudence emerged in response to the need of criminal law and society.[2] The dynamic criminal jurisprudence provides another method to study criminal law, and its propositions are worthy of attention.

2.2 Explanation of Criminal Integration

Criminal integration was first put forward and defined by Chu Huaizhi in 1989 as "the reasonable internal structure of criminal law (horizontal coordination) and the restrictions before and after the operation of criminal law (vertical coordination)". [3]This "criminal integration" was actually defined from the perspective of criminal policies, and its basic thoughts were extremely close to those in the studies of relationships of criminal law with other factors, because both [4]advocated the internal

1 Feng Yadong: "Constituents of Crimes from the Perspective of the Crime Cognition System", *Chinese Journal of Law*, 2008 (1).

2 Chu Huaizhi, et, al. Mechanism of Criminal Law, Law Press, 2004; Liu Renwen, a "Study of the Operation of Criminal Law", *People's Procuratorial Semimonthly*, 2007 (9).

3 Chu huaizhi. "On the Establishment of the Criminal Integration Thought", *Peking University Law Journal,* 1989 (1).

4 Chu Huaizhi's another important academic thought is to study the relationships of criminal law with other factors in the whole relational network, specifically including: (1) social economy and criminal law; (2) regime structure and criminal law; (3) ideology and criminal law; (4) crime and criminal law; (5) punishment execution and criminal law; and (6) other sectoral laws and criminal law. Chu Huaizhi. "An Outline of the Relationships of Criminal Law with Other Factors", *Law and Social Development*, 1996 (2).

and external coordination in the operation of criminal law from the internal and external relationships. In 1991, Chu Huaizhi further pointed out that criminal law should be studied outside criminal law to improve the breadth of study, criminal law should be studied above criminal law to improve the depth of study, and criminal law should be studied in criminal law as the starting point and the destination of the study. About the study of criminal law outside criminal law, Chu Huaizhi said: criminal law is unable to push itself forward, and it is always restricted and affected by both the crime situation and the penalty execution effect; in other words, the development of criminal law is pushed forward by something outside criminal law. Just because criminal law is determined by crimes, criminal punishment execution is determined by criminal law and crime rate is in turn affected by criminal punishment execution, the criminal law should be studied with both crimes and criminal punishment execution taken into account; otherwise, the study of criminal law cannot be effective. In this very sense, criminal law should be studied from the perspective of criminal integration, and criminal law researchers should have a sound knowledge structure, i.e., certain attainment in criminology and penology.[1] At this point, Chu Huaizhi put forward his preliminary conception of criminal integration from the perspectives of criminal policies and methodology.

Although Chu Huaizhi just simply summarized the explanations of criminal integration and did not expound this concept at length, this proposition exerted unexpected influence on China's criminal jurisprudence circle and won the recognition of many scholars.[2] In 1997, Chen Xingliang established a serial publication named *Criminal Law Review*. So far, over 20 volumes have been published. This publication aims to establish criminal integration as a research

1 Chu huaizhi. "Method to Study Criminal Law", *Peking University Law Journal*, 1991 (1).

2 Chen Xingliang explained that this was related to the particular background where China's criminal law expertise was on the ascendancy in 1990s after a period of recovery and accumulation. Chen Xingliang. "An Old Scholar with Fresh Ideas: Academic Impressions of Professor Chu Huaizhi", *Criminal Law Review* (Vol. 21), Peking University Press, 2007.

model, so it is regarded by reviewers as a practitioner of criminal integration on its own initiative.[1] Chen Xingliang also explained, reinterpreted and expanded Chu Huaizhi's methodology of studying criminal law outside, above and in criminal law. In his opinion, the study of criminal law above criminal law is the philosophical study of criminal law, the study of criminal law outside criminal law is the sociological and economic study of criminal law, and the study of criminal law in criminal law is the normative study of criminal law. In addition, he proposed another dimension: the study of criminal law under criminal law, i.e., the case-based study of the criminal law.[2]

Based on the thoughts on criminal integration, the academia further put forward the "all-dimensional criminal jurisprudence" concept, arguing that criminal law should be studied with pre-crime factors and post-crime handling taken into account, with criminal procedure law and some sectoral laws taken into account, with higher-level laws and consequent punishments taken into account, and with internal interpretation and external interpretation boundaries taken into account. "with pre-crime factors and post-crime handling taken into account" means "with criminology and penology taken into account", "with criminal procedure law and some sectoral laws taken into account" means "with criminal procedure law and sectoral laws such as civil law and administrative law taken into account", "with higher-level laws and subsequent punishments taken into account" means "with higher-level laws (the Constitution and international conventions) and consequent punishments (such as public security administration/punishment and re-education through labor) taken into account, and "with internal interpretation and external interpretation boundaries taken into account" means "internally enhancing the interpretation of criminal law and externally setting necessary boundaries of the

1 Fu Liqing. *Criminal Integration: Refining, Assessment and Outlook - On-scene Narration from the Perspective of Discipline Development*, contained in *Criminal Integration and Criminal Policies* compiled by Chen Xingliang and Liang Genlin, Law Press, 2005.

2 Chen Xingliang. Preface to *Precedents-based Criminal Jurisprudence*, China Renmin University Press, 2009.

interpretation of criminal law".[1] The thoughts on criminal integration and all-dimensional criminal jurisprudence were highly tally with the thoughts in the integrated criminal jurisprudence put forward by German criminologist Franz von Liszt, and their philosophical basis is the viewpoint of universal connection and the system theory. The system theory stresses the principle of integrity, which is similar to the principles of universal connection and interaction in materialistic dialectics. Each pair of categories of criminal integration and all-dimensional criminal jurisprudence are interconnected and interacted to jointly form a system, of which function is stronger than the simple sum of functions of all parts. Criminal law efficiency is the economics basis of the system. Criminal integration and all-dimensional criminal jurisprudence are conducive to the establishment of a healthy criminal law mechanism. The implementation of their ideas will surely save criminal law cost, increase criminal law revenue, strengthen the coordination among legislation, judicature and research, and reduce the resource waste arising from internal friction.

2.3 Free Arguments on Crime Constitution Theory

Crime constitution theory is the theoretical cornerstone in normative criminal jurisprudence. In recent years, hot academic arguments rose from the improvement, preservation or abolishment of traditional crime constitution theory in China. This is, firstly, a result of implementing the "double-hundred policy" of "allowing a hundred flowers bloom and a hundred schools of thought contend" in criminal jurisprudence circle, and secondly, a result of China's implementing the policy of opening up to the outside world and accordingly comparative criminal jurisprudence increasingly thrives. This phenomenon is the source that China's criminal jurisprudence terminates the stage of "silent criminal jurisprudence" to

1 Liu Renwen, "Advocating 'All-dimensional Criminal Jurisprudence'", *Studies in Law and Business*, 2003 (3). Later the author further expanded the thought of "all-dimensional criminal jurisprudence", and changed the statement of "combination of inside and outside" into "internally improve the explanation on criminal law and externally pay attention to the operation of criminal law". (Liu Renwen, *Structure and View of Criminal Law*, the part of "Introduction", Peking University Press, 2009.).

form various schools.

As mentioned above, after 1949 China's crime constitution theory followed Soviet's doctrines for a long term and lacked necessary innovation and free arguments. This issue had not aroused the introspection of criminal jurisprudence circle in China until HE Bingsong published the article *To Establish the Crime Constitution System with Chinese Characteristics* in 1986. Some people remarked that, the article *To Establish the Crime Constitution System with Chinese Characteristics* in the *Chinese Journal of Law*, 1986 (1), involved a series of significant issues of criminal jurisprudence that is blank in the then criminal jurisprudence system, such as the system of crime constitution theory, conviction basis, concept of criminal responsibility and the intrinsic characteristics of crime.[1] In 1993, the *Criminal Law Textbook* compiled by He Bingsong came into being (China Legal Publishing House). The most eye-catching part of the book is that it created a brand-new crime constitution theoretical system, i. e., "The System Theory of Crime Constitution". On this basis, in 1995 He Bingsong published his monograph *The System Theory of Crime Constitution* and further consolidated and improved the aforesaid theory. "The System Theory of Crime Constitution" deems crime a comprehensive, subjective, dynamic, fuzzy, multiple-hierarchy, open and organic integrity. The comprehensiveness of crime constitution refers to deem crime constitution an organic integrity that is composed of various interconnected and interacted constituents specified in China's criminal law and has specific criminal nature and social perniciousness. This opinion overcomes the defect of traditional crime constitution theory to deem crime a closed, planar and static "sum of all objective and subjective constituents". Subjectiveness of crime constitution refers to crime subjects controlling and deciding crime constitution. This opinion overcomes the defect of traditional crime constitution theory to neglect the function of crime subject. Dynamic of crime constitution

1 Chen Xingliang, *Philosophy of Criminal Law*, China University of Political Science and Law Press, 1992, p.678.

refers to deem crime constitution a process. This opinion overcomes the defect of traditional theory to neglect the process of crime constitution. Fuzziness of crime constitution is a reflection of complicatedness and diversification of crime constitution. It utilizes the natural science achievement of fuzzy mathematics to explain the issues of circumstance criminals with "grave circumstances" or "particularly grave circumstances". Multi-hierarchy of crime constitution refers to the position, hierarchy and relationship of crime constitution and crime constitution constituents (sub-systems). Crime constitution is a multi-hierarchy, multi-level and interconnected integrity. This opinion, to some extent, overcomes the defect of traditional crime constitution theory to deem crime constitution a planar conviction specification. Openness of crime constitution refers to the interconnection and interaction between comprehensiveness of crime constitution and external environment. This systematic opinion overcomes the defect of traditional crime constitution theory to study crime constitution in an isolated way. "The presentation of the System Theory of Crime Constitution reveals brand-new, fresh theoretical opinions and research methods".[1]

Today the academic discussion with respect to the improvement of crime constitution theory shows an extraordinary active atmosphere in China's criminal jurisprudence circle, and even comes to the vital turning point. Almost no one insists on invariably sticking to traditional crime constitution theory. The point of controversy is: whether to improve the theory based on tradition or thoroughly abandon the traditional theoretical mode of crime constitution to introduce the holistic German-Japanese crime theory system. Multiple opinions including the foresaid "System Theory of Crime Constitution" insist on reforming traditional crime constitution theory to establish the one with Chinese characteristics. However, the other opinion insists on introducing the holistic crime theory system of continental law system. The latter opinion was filled in the judicial examination syllabus in 2009 by the scholars holding this opinion, arousing the attention and

1 Qu Xinjiu, "Review on Professor He Bingsong's Criminal Jurisprudence Thought", *Information and Research of Legal Literature*, 1998 (4).

shock of the criminal jurisprudence circle in China. [1]Addressing this issue, on June 9, 2009, the College for Criminal Law Science of Beijing Normal University held the special symposium on the theoretical system of crime constitution, and the participants reached a consensus as follows: With potential far-reaching influence and heavy responsibility, the national judicial examination syllabus shall adopt the opinions well received by the academic circle; it is rather unserious for some scholars to take the positional advantages of participating in the formulation of national judicial examination syllabus and compilation of supporting textbooks, to substitute the crime theory system of Three-Level Constituents which is still controversial even in German and Japan for China's well-received Four-Constituent theory system of crime constitution.[2]

Indeed, the German-Japanese crime theory system of Three-Level Constituents advocated by some Chinese scholars is introspected and questioned even in Germany, Japan and some other countries. For example, German Günther Jakobs believed, that German doctrines debated which was better, the theory of cause-and-effect behavior or the theory of purpose behavior, and debated level-based constitution theory, was simply because after the World War II, criminal jurisprudence scholars focused on these technical issues to escape political pressure (As intellectuals in vanquished nation, they would have pressure of self-denial if they discuss the purpose or essentiality of norms). It is meaningless to identify the conformity, illegality and accountability of constituents or identify illegitimacy and guilt. Ultimately they are just about whether an actor should account for his act. [3]Similarly, some Japanese scholars believe, under the influence of absolute idea in German criminal jurisprudence, Japanese crime system theory adopts the ideological, abstract crime theory system such as "constituents",

1 Wang Quanbao, Controversy Aroused from the Forced Nature Alteration of China's Criminal Jurisprudence, *Dongfang Daily*, June 4, 2009.

2 http://www.criminallawbnu.cn/criminal/info/showpage.asp? showhead = &pkid =23440.

3 Xu Yuxiu, *Modern Trend of Thought on Criminal Law,* China Legal Publishing House, 2005, p.53.

"illegality" and "responsibility". As judges have to consider what constituents are, and what the relationship between constituents and illegality & responsibility is, they fall into the strong trend of taking system as sole standard.[1] Certainly, no one is intending to deny the reference significance of the crime theory system of continental law system to China, but in the situation that "problems encountered by German-Japanese level-based crime theory system are likely not less than those encountered by China's crime constitution system", it is hard to say the thought to totally throw away instead of reforming China's crime constitution theory is a precise spirit of introspection and criticism.

Some people argue as China's crime constitution theory inherits the criminal law doctrine formed in Stalin times, there is no doubt such doctrine has political marks and is academically obsolete. [2]In fact, Russian crime theory system was developed by scholars including Tagantsev 100 years ago after they accepted German Feuerbach's crime constitution theory. After the October Revolution, in spite of the influence of legal nihilism, Soviet's criminal scholars still inherited such theoretical system and followed it to date since the collapse of Soviet. Reviewing the overall development of Russian crime theory system, its basic pattern kept unchanged over 100 years in spite of the variation of specific content and structure under different historical conditions. [3]In allusion to the proposition of "De-Sovietization and De-Russianization of Criminal Law Knowledge", Xue Ruilin once pointed out: There are many misunderstanding and misinterpretation of Soviet and Russian crime constitution theory in such opinion, and some assertions are pseudo judgment based on imagination. German and Soviet crime

1 [Japan] The Criminal Law Society of Japan, *Overview on the Theory of Modern Criminal Jurisprudence* (Revised), BOOKS SANSIDO in Tokyo, 1989, p.317, quoted from the *Thinking on Some Issues of Pandect of Criminal Law* (by Li Hong) as a secondary source, China Renmin University Press, 2007, pp.51-52.

2 Chen Xingliang, *The De-Sovietization and De-Russianization of Criminal Law Knowledge, Tribune of Political Science and Law*, 2006 (5).

3 He Bingsong, *The System of Crime Theory*, p.176, document II, the international symposium on the New System of Criminal Law Theory in Globalization Times, held in Beijing in 2007.

constitution systems have their own advantages and disadvantages and some of them are just different in their research means. [1] Moreover, he justifiably instructed: We cannot simply remark former Soviet crime theory system is "a failure in practice, and unconvincing in theory". Otherwise, we will be hard to explain why Soviet original 15 republics inherit existing crime theory system after the collapse of Soviet. [2] Undoubtedly China's crime constitution theory calls for further improvement. However, it is an undesirable action to rush to deny the tradition, especially artificially sever the history of Russian crime theory system deriving from 100 years ago to simply shrink its starting point to 1930s, and then "demonize" the theory with the excuse of "kind of Vyshinsky's criminal theory".[3] It is also not real and true for some people to universalize German-Japanese

1 Xue Ruilin, *Dialogue with the Author of The De-Sovietization and De-Russianization of Criminal Law Knowledge, Tribune of Political Science and Law*, 2008 (6).

2 Xue Ruilin, *Belated Counter Criticism—Dialogue with the Author of Rudiment of Criminal Law Principles*, a thesis submitted to the international symposium "Comparative Study on Russia-Sino and German-Japanese Crime Theory Systems" held in Beijing in 2008. It is worth noting that in the latest writing about Russian crime constitution theory, we still see the basic model involving object of crime, objective aspect of crime, subject of crime and subjective aspect of crime. (He Bingsong, Komissarov, et al, Comparative Study on Russian and Chinese Crime Constitution Theory, Law Press, China, 2008, p.45 and latter), This remind us whether it is unfair to excessively link models of crime theory with ideology, although in fact any model of crime theory is likely impacted by ideology.

3 Dr. Li Haidong stated as this in the preface on behalf of the author of *Rudiment of Criminal Law Principles*, Law Press, China, p.3. However, Xue Ruilin pointed out in the *Belated Counter Criticism—Dialogue with the Author of Rudiment of Criminal Law Principles*: there are no such remarks in Soviet criminal law treatises. He also pointed out: although Soviet criminal theories in 1930s feature strong ideological colors, the system is not closed and ossified but continues to be self-adjusted to keep up with the times. This just proves that more than one decade after Soviet's collapse, the crime constitution theories in nations such as Russia preserve original model. Some people believe this should attribute to knowledge inertia because Russian crime theory system would surely be overturned and be reconstructed if given time. In fact, Russian academic circle is also exploring the improvement of crime constitution theory, but their thought is not simply overturning original theory to reconstruct a new one. For example, Kuznetsova and other scholars utilize contemporary systematic perspective to propose to integrate traditional four-constituent into a united system. He Bingsong, Komissarov, et al, *Comparative Study on China's and Russia's crime constitution theories*, Law Press, China, pp.439-440.

crime theory model as this model was not adopted even in some "traditional" and "emerging" European countries around Germany let alone common law system countries.

With the preconceived prejudice against traditional theory or extremely wonderful expectation toward German-Japanese criminal law theory, some scholars grant too much value and mission beyond their own content to crime constitution theory. For example, some scholars linked the models of crime constitution theory with political systems of states. In fact, even in Germany, although its progressive Three-stage Theory has existed for long term, it is only after the World War II that the theory began to link with constitutionalism required by democratic countries. Some other scholars attributed the frequent miscarriage of China's criminal justice to the state's crime constitution theory, and took for granted that progressive Three-stage Theory can prevent miscarriage of justice. However, with a little deliberation, it can be found that this proposition is less convincing, because the causes of miscarriage of justice are complex and they possibly have closer relationship with judicial system, power intervention, litigation structure, etc.

3. The Rise of Criminal Policy Science

3.1 Reason for the Prosperity of Criminal Policy Science

Since early 20th century, writings about criminal policies have mushroomed in China to "make the study on criminal policies a noted school of thought in China". [1]Some scholar observed: "In addition to textbooks and translations, the findings in theory circle mainly include: *Rudiment of Criminal Policies* (Liu Renwen), *Power Analysis of Criminal Policies* (Qu Xinjiu), *Value Analysis of Criminal Policies* (Hou Honglin), etc.; Liang Genlin's series studies on criminal

1 Lu Jianping, *The Chinese Characteristics in the Study of Criminal Policies, Review of Beijing Normal University on Criminal Policies* (Vol. 2), Beijing Normal University Publishing Group, 2008. The author took statistics of 48 writings on criminal policy study since the reform and opening-up policy in the appendix of the writing, indicating 45 ones published in the 21st century.

policies, including *Criminal Punishment: Methods and Selection, Criminal Policies: Position and Categories, Net of Criminal Justice: Expansion and Shrinkage Limitation*; Chen Xingliang's series studies on criminal policies, including *Study on the Criminal Policy that Combines Punishment with Leniency, Review on China's Criminal Policies*, etc.; Xie Wangyuan and others' series studies on criminal policies, including series of *Report on China's Criminal Policies, Study on China's Criminal Policies*, etc.; Lu Jianping and Zhao Bingzhi's series studies on criminal policies, including series of *Review on Criminal Policies, Special Discussion on Criminal Policies*, etc." [1]

The occurrence of this situation mainly comes from the calling and demand of the society: Normative criminal jurisprudence and annotative criminal jurisprudence cannot satisfy the need of struggling with crimes, and the times calls us to shape scientific criminal policies conforming to crime status and trend, and then guide the formulation and execution of criminal law to enable criminal law to punish crime more efficiently. It is the time for us to reflect the 20-year-long criminal policy of "attacking severely". In addition, the overall background of building socialist harmonious society make the new criminal policy of "combining punishment with leniency" deduced logically. The new topic how to realize "supplementing punishment with leniency" is presented to criminal scholars. Under the new situation of rule of law and human rights are written in the Constitution, how should criminal policies work "in the fence of rule of law" to supplement each other with rule of law. Finally, no matter due to the impact of western criminal policies of "restorative justice" and "letting the light be lighter, the heavy be heavier" or due to local reasons (for example, increased pressure on prisons naturally requires decompression), systems such as criminal reconciliation

1 Wang Mingliang: *New Perspectives in the Study of Criminal Policies*, Law Press, China, 2008, p.280. Liu Yuan, *Philosophical Interpretation of Criminal Policies*, phcppsu.com.cn, 2005; Li Weihong, *Reconstruction and Expansion of the Science of Criminal Policies*, Peking University Press, 2007; Jiang Xuhui, et al: *Reflection and Improvement of Criminal Policies,* China Social Sciences Press, 2008, etc.

and community correction have preceded legislation and showed strong vitality in practice. To give the theoretical interpretation of these new things and respond to them is the bound mission of criminal policies. Therefore, the ascendance of criminal policy in China is unsurprising. [1]

3.2 Basic Issue of Science of Criminal Law

The concept of criminal policy evolved from narrow sense to broad sense. At the preliminary stage the academic circle mainly discussed criminal policies from narrow sense, which was characterized by: 1, understand criminal policies from the aspect of tactics. Although the criminal policies in the context were gradually upgraded from method, activity, means, tactics to strategy, they were still criminal policies in narrow sense; 2, Under the guidance of criminal policy concept in narrow sense, the criminal policy study usually perceived criminal politics as the specific principles concerning crime or criminal penalty, typically such as the policy of "combining punishment with leniency" for offenders, the policy of "education, persuasion and redemption" for juvenile criminals, the policy of "two LESSs and one leniency" (i.e., less killing, less catching, and generally sentencing with leniency—the author noted) for crimes by minority nationality citizens, and the policy of "reforming first and production second" in criminal reforming, showing microcosmic features.[2]

With the deepening of the study, criminal policy concept of broad sense is established, which features the following intrinsic content: the comprehensive art

1 When analyzing why the study of criminal policies is in a grand scale in China today, Lu Jianping instructed: As the public security situation sharply deteriorates after China implements the reform and opening-up policy, traditional thoughts including heavy penalty proposition rapidly grew, which to some extent constrained the system innovation in the field of criminal laws, leading to the increasing insufficiency of system supplies to the field of criminal law. To make up for the insufficiency, criminal policies become the prior selection for the reform of existing criminal legislation and criminal justice. Lu Jianping, *The Chinese Characteristics of Criminal Policy Study*.

2 *The Science of Criminal Policies* compiled by Lu Jianping, China Renmin University Press, 2007, pp.17-18.

or strategy in organizing anti-crime struggles or fighting and controlling crimes, centrally embodying all anti-crime policies, systematically integrating anti-crime mechanisms and comprehensively combining all anti-crime subjects. Criminal policy concept in broad sense mainly contains the following meanings: (1) As an organic integrity composed of elements, targets, measures, etc., criminal policies should not be concluded as the concept or term of singly referred "principles" or "guidelines", but should reflect its "strategic" macroscopic characteristics; (2) criminal policies acted on the entire process that the state fights and controls crime, i.e., the process that the state formulates, implements and evaluates criminal policies; (3) criminal polices not only refer to the policies of criminal law, but contain all governing means of fighting against crime and preventing crime; (4) As criminal policies are the sum of methods in which the entire society organizes to respond to crime phenomena, the science of criminal policies is a compound knowledge carrier involving multiple disciples. [1]

The principles of criminal polices mean the basic guidelines that run through the entire process of criminal policy activity and shall be followed and pursued during the formulation and implementation of criminal policies. Chinese scholars presented various statements to this issue. For example, some scholars believe, there are four principles of criminal policies, i.e., the Constitution and criminal laws shall not be violated; each offender shall be treated pursuant to his individual situation; blowing minorities and wining over, educating and reforming majorities; considering holistic situations to prevent the action of only holding partial aspects. [2]Some scholars argue there are five basic principles of criminal policies, i.e., the rule of law; modesty and restraint; humanity; being scientific; education

1 *Review on the Study of Pandect of Criminal Jurisprudence* compiled by Zhao Bingzhi, Beijing Normal University Publishing Group, 2009, p.46.

2 *Science on China's Criminal Policies* compiled by Ma Kechang, Wuhan University Press, 1992, pp.24-27.

and improvement.[1] Some others elaborate the principles from the perspective of formulation and implementation of criminal policies respectively. Specifically, the principles of being scientific, rule of law and human rights shall be followed in the formulation of criminal policies, and the principles of manners conforming to targets, combining principle adherence and flexibility, and synchronizing monitoring with implementation, shall be followed in the implementation of criminal policies. [2] It can be seen that the rule of law is a recognized principle, i.e., criminal policies must be restrained in the "fence" of rule of law and work within the frame of rule of law.

In terms of the structure of criminal policies, some scholars divide it into microscopic and macroscopic levels. The structure in microscopic level refers to structure of single criminal policy, which is composed of principle thought and action program. For example, "combining punishment with leniency" is the principle thought while a series of severe or lenient sentencing systems are its action program. "Mobilizing social force to improve the quality of reforming criminals" is the principle thought while "three extensions" ("forward extension": extend the activity of reforming criminals to the social environment before they enter prisons; "Outward extension": open the activity of educating and reforming criminals to the society, with regulatory bodies being the major force; "backward extension": regulatory bodies organize various social forces to do well the placement and succeeding help and education activities of ex-prisoners) are its action program. The structure in macroscopic level refers to structure of collective criminal policies, which can be divided into vertical structure and horizontal structure. The former is composed of basic criminal policies and specific criminal policies, and the latter is composed of conviction policies, criminal penalty policies and treatment policies. [3]

1 *Science of Criminal Policies* compiled by Lu Jianping, China Renmin University Press, 2007, p.170.

2 Liu Renwen, *Rudiment of Criminal Policies*, phcppsu.com.cn, 2004, p.171.

3 *Discussion on Criminal Policy* compiled by Yang Chunxi, Peking University Press, 1994, p.15.

Some other scholars describe the structure of criminal policy as the organic combination of constituents such as purpose & value target, criminal policy subject, criminal policy means, criminal policy object, criminal policy process, feedback and operating environment. They believe: criminal policy subjects generates certain purpose during the interaction with environment; under the guidance of certain value target and specific purpose and under the interaction of internal operating environment and external operating environment of criminal policies, criminal policy subjects formulate criminal policy means to apply to criminal policy objects and fulfill the basic process of criminal process; and then apply the feedbacks of all sections of the process and feedbacks of environment to the accommodation and optimization of criminal policy means so as to achieve the purpose and value target of criminal policy subjects. [1]

Deriving from system theory, some scholars divide criminal policies into single criminal policy and collective criminal policies. Specifically, the structure of single criminal policy is: (1) from the perspective of social system, criminal policy system is an organic integrity which is composed of subject system of criminal policy, supporting system of criminal policy as well as feedback system connecting the subject system of criminal policy and criminal policy environment; (2) From the perspective of the operation of criminal policies, criminal policy system is a huge system which is mainly composed of interconnecting, interdependent and interactive sub-systems including information sub-system, policy-decision sub-system, implementation sub-system, evaluation sub-system and control sub-system. The structure of collective criminal policies is: (1) Vertical structure: General criminal policies, basic criminal policies and specific criminal policies; (2) Horizontal structure: Criminal legislation policies, criminal judicial policies and criminal social policies. [2]

1 *Science of Criminal Policies* compiled by He Bingsong , Mass Press, 2002, pp.78-79.

2 Xu Xiuzhong, *System Theory in Criminal Polices*, doctoral dissertation, printed and distributed by China University of Political Science and Law, 2004, p.44.

Some scholars dissect the structure of criminal policy into criminal legislation policies, criminal judicial policies, criminal execution policies and criminal social policies, and point out that the four parts are not isolated and static, but interactive. For example, "Severe Attack" in 1983 was originally a judicial policy, but it led to the amendment of some provisions of the criminal law and made criminal legislation policies tend to adopt heavy punishment, which showed that judicial policies had influenced legislation policies. [1]

In terms of the function of criminal policies, one opinion is: Function of criminal policies mainly refers to the role and effects that criminal policies play or have in the social system of crime control, and to be more specific, it includes guiding and adjustment functions. Guiding function is reflected in: (1) In terms of criminal substantive laws: Delimiting attack scope as well as determining key attack points, attack force and attack methods. (2) In terms of criminal procedural laws: When the target of substantive laws is inconsistent with that of procedural laws: the target of substantive laws is to try to allow criminals to escape unpunished as least as possible, while the target of procedural laws is to efficiently execute substantive laws and generate miscarriage of justice as least as possible; when the target of least escape unpunished is inconsistent with the target of least miscarriage of justice, there will be two policy options of "miscarriage of justice better than connivance" and "connivance better than miscarriage of justice". All systems, specific rules and operating mechanisms ultimately have a close relationship with such policy thought. (3) The guiding function of criminal policies is also reflected in organization laws. Core issue of organization laws is power disposition, which certainly falls within policy scope. Adjustment function of criminal policies is mainly reflected in: (1) Internal adjustment, i.e., the adjustment of criminal legislation and criminal judicature, including legislation adjusting judicature by virtue of criminal policies and judicature adjusting legislation by virtue of criminal policies; (2) External adjustment, i.e., the

1 Liu Renwen, *Rudiment of Criminal Policies*, phcppsu.com.cn, 2004, p.48.

adjustment of the intermediate part (such as criminalization and decriminalization) of criminal laws and social conditions (mainly referring to crime trend).[1]

Another opinion believes that the functions of criminal policies include guiding function, regulation function and intermediation function. Specifically, guiding function refers to criminal policies instructing the activities of crime prevention and crime control and showing general direction, course and ways for crime prevention and control; regulation function refers to criminal policies defining specific action rules for national authorities to prevent and control crime, and further influencing the actions of common citizens and offenders. Intermediation function is reflected in, for one thing, criminal policies being the intermediate section between criminal legislation and judicature, and for the other, criminal policies also being the intermediate section between theory and practice. [2]

Another opinion thinks the functions of criminal policies can be examined from multiple aspects, for example, positive and negative functions, safeguarding (human rights) function and blowing (crime) function; restraint function and expansion function; innovation function and conservation function; punishment function and leniency function; expressly function and ambiguous function; etc. All the functions can be classified into two basic functions: guiding function and symbol function. It should be noted that the idea that "functions of criminal policies refer to the positive effect that criminal policies may take" is inappropriate. In fact, as an objective existence, function may be positive or negative, because "positive" and "negative" are a kind of subjective evaluation. For example, the introduction of a criminal policy breaks the principle of Nullum Crimen, Nulla Poena Sine Lege, and its destructive effect to the rule of law is a negative function.[3]

---

1 Chu Huaizhi, *Concept, Structure and Function of Criminal Policies*, *Chinese Journal of Law*, 1993 (3).

2 *Science of Criminal Policies* compiled by He Bingsong, Multitude Publishing House, 2002, pp.56-57.

3 Liu Renwen, *Rudiment of Criminal Policies*, phcppsu.com.cn, 2004, p.150.

4. International Criminal Jurisprudence in China

4.1 Background of the Prosperity of International Jurisprudence

Since 1990s, international crimes, especially the crimes that severely violate international humanitarian laws in international and non-international armed conflicts have frequently occurred. Meanwhile, the end of the Cold War has decreased and even eliminated the ideological difference of governments in prevention and punishment of international crimes, which makes the establishment of international criminal judicial institutions easier. The United Nations Security Council passed a resolution in 1993 and 1994 respectively, deciding to establish two ad hoc tribunals for ex-Yugoslavia and Rwanda, with an aim to try the perpetrators who severely violated international humanitarian laws in the armed conflict in ex-Yugoslavia and in the ethnic conflict in Rwanda. In 1998, the UN passed the *Rome Statute of the International Criminal Court* (also known as the *Rome Statute*) in the diplomatic conference of states in Rome, Italy; in 2002, the first permanent international criminal court in human history was born based on the Statute. Additionally, the UN established or helped establish various types of international tribunals, such as the Extraordinary Chambers in the Court of Cambodia, which was established pursuant to treaty and specially promulgated domestic laws; the using of international judges and procurators in Kosovo court in accordance with the regulations of the United Nations Interim Administration Mission in Kosovo (UNMIK); the mixed tribunal established by the United Nations Transitional Administration in East Timor (UNTATE) with jurisdiction over grave crimes, Special Court for Sierra Leone set up as a treaty court, as well as constitutional court established in the form of special court in the State Court of Bosnia and Herzegovina. [1]The establishment and operation of these international

1 *Rule of Law and Transitional Justice of Society in Conflict and Post-Conflict*, the report of UN Secretary-General, S/2004/616, August 3, 2004, Note 5, p.2, quoted from the *Comparative Study on the Normalization of International Criminal Judicial Organs*, Weiwu, *Tribune of International Laws and Comparative Laws* compiled by Zhao Haifeng, vol. 1, China Legal Publishing House, 2006.

criminal adjudicatory institutions greatly enriched the theory and practice of international criminal laws.

China has actively participated in the practice of international criminal law. For example, three Chinese judges (Li Haopei, Wang Tieya and incumbent Liu Daqun) once worked/are working for the International Criminal Tribunal for the Former Yugoslavia (ICTFY); China also took an active part in the entire negotiation process of the establishment of the international criminal court. Although China finally failed to become the member state of *Rome Statute*, China has been caring for the development of the international criminal court since its establishment, and has expressed for many times that China holds an open attitude toward acceding to the statute and hopes to accede to the statute at appropriate time. The new dynamics in international criminal law field and the active attitude of Chinese government toward international criminal law practice stimulate China's criminal jurisprudence circle pays more attention to the development of the emerging subject in China. For example, in recent years China's criminal jurisprudence circle has actively studied the *Rome Statute* and relevant international academic conferences were frequently held. International criminal law study presents sound overall development trend. For example, 7 monographs on international criminal laws were published in the single year of 2007, including *International Criminal Law* (Zhu Wenqi, China Renmin University Press), *International Criminal Jurisprudence* (Huang Feng, Ling Yan and Wang Xiumei, China Renmin University Press), *Discussion on the Crime against Humanity in International Criminal Law* (Du Qixin, Intellectual Property Publishing House Co., Ltd.), *Study on the Criminal Responsibilities of War Crime* (Lu Youxue, Law Press, China), *International Legal Control of Corporate Crimes* (Fan Hongqi, phcppsu.com.cn), *Study on Criminal Forfeiture – from the Perspective of International Law and Comparative Law* (He Fan, Law Press, China), and *Study on the Principles of Offenders' Extradition* (Qin Yihe, phcppsu.com.cn).

China has successively signed and ratified a series of international covenant related to international criminal laws, many of which involve criminal legislation and criminal justice. This situation calls for the synchronous development of China's legislation. Therefore, many criminal scholars discuss the improvement of China's criminal laws based on this type of international covenants. For example, some scholars presented proposals on the improvement of death penalty legislation in China's criminal law by reference to relevant provisions in the *International Covenant on Civil and Political Rights* (the covenant has been signed and is to be ratified by China). [1]Another example, since the *UN Convention against Corruption* was passed in 2003 (the convention has been signed and ratified by China), China's criminal jurisprudence circle has also conducted relatively many studies on the gap between the status quo of China's criminal law and the requirement of the convention. [2] Moreover, China's opening up to the outside world facilitates criminals' fleeing to foreign countries. In recent years corrupt officials fleeing to foreign countries has become a prominent issue in China. How to strengthen international criminal justice collaboration and coordinate the relationship between domestic laws and international laws (for example, addressing internationally popular "principle of non extradition of the death penalty", some Chinese scholars proposed to abrogate the death penalty

1 Gao Mingxuan, Li Wenfeng, *Discussion on the Improvement of China's Death Penalty Legislation from the "International Covenant on Civil and Political Rights"*, in the *Study on the New Issues of Criminal Law in the 21st Century* compiled by Gao Mingxuan & Zhao Bingzhi, phcppsu.com.cn, 2001; Zhang Wen, Liu Yanhong: *Influence of "International Covenant on Civil and Political Rights" on China's Death Penalty Legislation*, *Journal of China Youth University for Political Sciences*, 2000 (1) and (2).

2 In April 2007, in the academic symposium of "The Coordination of Criminal Law Mechanism in the Context of Harmonious Society" sponsored by the Research Center of Criminal Law Science of China Renmin University, a special unit of "The Coordination of China's Criminal Law and Relevant International Conventions" was launched. 12 out of 18 theses of the unit explored aligning China's criminal law with the *UN Convention against Corruption* and the improvement of China's criminal law. In October 2007, the 2nd "International Forum on Contemporary Criminal Laws" sponsored by the College for Criminal Law Science of Beijing Normal University took the UN Convention against Corruption, the UN Convention on Human Rights and the UN Anti-Terrorism Convention as three major parallel topics under the theme of "the Implementation of UN Conventions in the Field of Criminal Rule of Law".

for corruption and bribery criminals in China) has become a hot topic in China's criminal jurisprudence circle.[1]

4.2 Delimitation of Basic Principles of International Criminal Laws

Through wide discussion, now most scholars in the academic circle believe the following six principles should become the basic principles of international criminal laws:

First, Principle of state sovereignty. When convicting and punishing international crimes, states shall consider not only the need of combating and preventing crimes but also the legislation status and value orientation of states, and conduct international criminal cooperation on the basis of respecting other states' sovereignty. Otherwise, the implementation of international criminal laws is impossible at all. [2]In international criminal laws, respecting state sovereignty are mainly represented as: sovereignty of all states should be equal before international criminal laws; states have the right to decide legislation procedures on their own in terms of the degree of incorporating international criminal laws into domestic criminal laws; during the course of international criminal judicial assistance and cooperation, individual state's criminal proceedings shall be given sufficient attention. [3]Of course, it should be noted that the boom of international criminal laws brings certain challenges to the idea of absolute state sovereignty. For example, according to the *Rome Statute of the International Criminal Court*, in case the UN Security Council submits a request to the International Criminal Court, procurators of the International Criminal Court are entitled to investigate and prosecute a crime committed within the territory of a non-contracting state or by a non-contracting state citizen and the International Criminal Court owns the

1 *Escapee Pursuit and Recovering Illegal Funds from Abroad and International Criminal Justice Cooperation,* compiled by Huang Feng & Zhao Linna, China University of Political Science and Law Press, 2008.

2 *Review on the Study of International Criminal Laws,* compiled by Wang Xiumei, Beijing Normal University Publishing Group, 2009, p.39.

3 Zhang Jing, *Overview of International Criminal Laws*, People's Court Press, 2004, pp.45-46.

jurisdiction over this kind of events.[1]

Second, The principle of legality. As the basic principle of criminal trial, the principle of legality is necessary to maintain law authority and enforcement fairness and especially in the activities of international judicial organs integrated with the features of various laws, regulations and genealogies of law. People usually consider the principle of legality being equal to the principle of Nullum Crimen, Nulla Poena Sine Lege (No Crime and No Punishment without a Pre-existing Penal Law). However, it should be noted that, while establishing the principle of Nullum Crimen, Nulla Poena Sine Lege, the *International Covenant on Civil and Political Rights* also specifies: "Where the act or omission of any person is deemed crime at the time of occurrence pursuant to internationally recognized general legal principles, this provision shall not obstruct the trial and penalty on him/her due to such act or omission." (Paragraph 2, Article 15) As for the so-called "internationally recognized general legal principles" here, international criminal jurisprudence circle usually interprets it as international customary laws. [2]Charges in customary international laws include war crime, crime against humanity, crime against peace, crime of slavery and crime of torture, etc.[3]

Third, The principle of universal jurisdiction. Some crimes are so serious in terms of their nature and harm that they undermine the common interests and fundamental interests of international community as a whole, therefore each state has the obligation to prevent and punish these crimes to the international community as whole and has the jurisdiction over these crimes

1 Chen Zexian, The Nature of Jurisdiction of International Criminal Court, Chinese Journal of Law, 2003 (6).

2 Manfred Nowak, U.N. Covenant on Civil and Political Rights—CCPR Commentary, 2nd revised edition, p.367, N. P. Engel, Publisher, 2005. Yue Liling, "*The International Covenant on Civil and Political Rights*" and China's Criminal Judicature, Law Press, China, 2007, p.205.

3 Yue Liling, *The International Covenant on Civil and Political Rights* and China's Criminal Judicature, Law Press, China, 2007, p.205.

in spite of the country of crime revenue and the offender's nationality. This is the basic meaning of the principle of universal jurisdiction. The purpose of the principle is to prevent grave offenders from finding hiding place and escaping punishment[1] As one of the basic premises under which international criminal laws were born and exist, the principle of universal jurisdiction provides an action guarantee for states around the world to jointly crack down on perpetrators of international crimes. China's criminal jurisprudence circle had long held a negative attitude toward the principle of universal jurisdiction, taking it as the theoretical basis for hegemonists to arbitrarily trample other states' sovereignty, but later gradually changed the attitude and recognized that conforming to the principle of universal jurisdiction as one of the basic principles of international criminal laws is the bounden international duty of each state. Therefore, when amending the criminal law in 1997, China added the content in Article 9: "This Law shall be applicable to crimes which are stipulated in international treaties concluded or acceded to by the People's Republic of China and over which the People's Republic of China exercise criminal jurisdiction within the scope of obligations, prescribed in these treaties, it agrees to perform."

Forth, The principle of individual criminal responsibility. After the World War I, the Allies and Germany signed the *Treaty of Versailles*, and the international community established an ad hoc international tribunal, preparing to sue the German Emperor Wilhelm II and other German soldiers who were accused of violating laws and customs of war, but the efforts to prosecute these perpetrators came to a premature end because of political reasons. After the World War II, the Nuremberg Trials and the Tokyo Trials established the position of the principle of individual criminal responsibility in international criminal laws. After that, the Yugoslav Tribunal and the Rwanda Tribunal further consolidated and developed the principle of individual criminal responsibility. The *Rome Statute*

1 Zhu Wenqi, *International Criminal Laws*, China Renmin University Press, 2007, p.286.

of the International Criminal Court adopted in 1998 ascertained the "principle of individual criminal responsibility" once again, and designated it as one of the basic principles for the operation of the International Criminal Court, making it an incontrovertible basic principle in the theory and practice of international criminal laws.[1]

Fifth, The principle of human rights protection in criminal proceedings. The principle of human rights protection was reflected in substantive laws and procedural laws in the field of international criminal laws. In terms of substantive laws, it is mainly reflected in designating the acts of infringing human rights in large scale as crimes for punishment; in terms of procedural laws, it is mainly reflected in the rights protection to suspected offenders, defendants and victims. [2]The rights protection measures for suspected offenders and defendants mainly include: the right of presumption of innocence, the right of no re-trial for the same crime, the right of exemption from arbitrary arrest and detention, the right of exemption from torture, cruel, inhuman and degrading treatment or punishment, the right to a fair judgment, including the right to public trial and appear in court, the right to be told the accused crime and the right to speedy trial, equal litigation right as well as the privilege against self-incrimination.[3]

Last, The principle of international criminal cooperation. Provisions of international criminal conventions contain the content of international criminal cooperation with respect to the prosecution pursuit of international crimes, mainly including: (1) to establish the jurisdiction over international crimes pursuant to the principle of universal jurisdiction; (2) to take necessary emergency measures and enforcement measures; (3) the extradition or transfer of offenders; (4) to

1 *Review on the Study of International Criminal Laws*, compiled by Wang Xiumei, Beijing Normal University Publishing Group, 2009, p.53.

2 Zhou Lulu, *Study on the Basic Principles of Contemporary International Criminal Laws*, doctorate dissertation, printed by the Renmin University of China, 2007, p.168.

3 *New Edition of International Criminal Jurisprudence*, compiled by Zhao Bingzhi, China Renmin University Press, 2004, p.39; Zhu Wenqi, International Criminal Laws, China Renmin University Press, 2007, p.345.

carry out bi-directional criminal judicial assistance, such as mutually exchanging information, seeking for and detaining properties, and transferring sentenced persons; (5) jurisdiction transfer of criminal litigations as well as the acknowledge and execution of foreign criminal judgments; (6) to comply with other liable regulations and prohibitive regulations in international treaties.[1]The aforesaid international cooperation modes play a key role during the course of punishing international crimes and transnational crimes. The present problem is that the relatively large gap of criminal systems and criminal litigation systems among states and the difference of ideologies and state systems have impacted the efficient use of these measures.

1 *Review on the Study of International Criminal Laws*, compiled by Wang Xiumei, Beijing Normal University Publishing Group, 2009, p.49.

Chapter 15

Development of Times and Prosperity of the Science of Civil Law

1. The Science of Civil Law with Prosperous Development

Since China established the socialist market economy system, the research on the science of civil law that is naturally and closely related to the market economy system has developed much more rapidly than ever. This stage is mostly featured in two aspects: (i) The science of civil law has become "prosperous" in the jurisprudential circle, the research of which has gone beyond textbooks and continues to be pushed forward in the direction of segmentation and professionalism. (ii) The science of civil law has gradually begun to be in line with the latest trend of international science of civil law and to have a direct dialogue with the international community of civil law. It is reflected not only in the translation of various foreign civil codes and works of civil laws, but also in all kinds of international seminars held in China.

1.1 Great Achievements in the Research of the Science of Civil Law

Since 1992, there have been some landmark events indicating the transformation of the research on the science of civil law: First, *Civil and Commercial Law Review* [Law Press, with several volumes being published by Jinqiao Culture Publication (Hong Kong) Co., Ltd.], with Liang Huixing as its editor-in-chief, was inaugurated in 1994. Its purpose is to "provide a scientific basis of legal principles for the modernization of legislation and scientization of trial practice in civil and commercial law in China, improve China's theories of civil and commercial law, and develop a talent base for the theories of civil and commercial law, by taking into account the actualities of China's reform and opening up and development of modern market economy, extensively learning the successful experiences in civil and commercial legislation of developed countries and regions, exploring the latest case theories, and studying fundamental theories of civil and commercial law and significant law issues." The *Review* has not only facilitated publications of big themed papers of the science of civil law in China, really segmenting the research of the science of civil law, but also led the trend of publishing books instead of magazines of Chinese science of law. These include *Chinese and Japanese Civil and Commercial Law Review* (Ju Tao, editor-in-chief), *Private Law* (Yi Jiming, editor-in-chief), and *Private Law Review* (Chen Xiaojun, editor-in-chief), as well as *Fudan Civil and Commercial Law Review* and *Civil and Commercial Jurists* (Zhang Min'an, editor-in-chief), etc. At present, there are a lot of series of publications of the science of civil law, providing an exchange platform for the big papers of the science of civil law. Second, Liang Huixing, during this time period, edited the *Collection of Research on Chinese Civil and Commercial Law* (Law Press), as its editor-in-chief, which has published more than 60 books pertinent to civil and commercial law so far. Among these books, there are plenty of works having significant influence in the community of the science of civil law, including *Contemporary German Property Law* by Sun Xianzhong and *Modern French Contract Law* by Yin Tian. Many scholars were recognized by the community of civil law after publishing works in this collection. The series of this collection involves a swathe of topics, such as methodological issue, represented by *Research on the Methodology of Codification of Civil Law* (2007) by Shi Jiayou; discussion of fundamental issues of traditional civil law, represented by *Research on the Change of Property Right* (2002) by Xiao Houguo, *Change of Circumstances and Contracting Theory* (2004) by Sun Meilan, and *Research on Trust Liabilities: Taking the Conclusion of Deeds as an Analytic Subject* (2007) by Zhu Guangxin; introduction to overseas legal systems, represented by *Research on the Modern French Tort Liability System* (2003) by Zhang Min'an, *Research on the Principle of Consideration in British and Amercian Laws* (2006) by Liu Chengwei, *Research on French Property Right Backed by Real Property* (2009) by Yu Haiyong, and *Comparative Research on Present and Previous German Law of Obligation* (2006) by Qi Xiaokun; and research on new issues concerning modern civil law, represented by *Research on Law Issues concerning Fund Transfer by Electronic Means* (2001) by Liu Ying and *Research on Law Issues concerning Artificial Reproduction* (2006) by Zhang Yanling. Generally speaking, this set of collections represents the segmentation and delicacy of the research on civil law in China. Third, during this period of time, civil law scholars had widely partaken in legislation. In 1999, *Proposed Draft with Reasons of the Property Law of China* (published by Social Sciences Academic Press in 1999) edited by Liang Huixing was the first proposed draft of civil law scholars on legislation published in China, which includes legislation cases, explanations, and reasons, in addition to the proposed articles. After that, there was *Proposed Draft with Reasons of the Property Law of China* (published by China Legal Publishing House in 2001) edited by Wang Liming. The *Property Law of 2007* was enacted with reference to these two drafts. The drafts on Civil Code prepared by Liang Huixing and Wang Liming were published successively. It indicated that Chinese civil law scholars have gradually increased their involvement in legislation. In addition, there was Draft of Green Civil Code (published by Social Sciences Academic Press in 2004) edited by Xu Guodong.

In summarizing the achievements of civil law in the 30 years of the reform and opening-up, Liang Huixing said that the progress of civil laws mainly represented by: (1) multiple successive targets; (2) change of attitudes to foreign civil laws. The present Chinese science of civil law is no longer blindly following the systems and theories of foreign civil laws, but dares to challenge and trade off the foreign civil laws; (3) daring to design legal countermeasures for the practical issues faced by China; (4) generation of a great many of academic research achievements at a high level; and (5) daring to face the challenges from ideologies.[1] In summarizing the research on Chinese science of civil law, Wang Liming, et al., pointed out that the features of research on Chinese science of civil law are that (1) there is more research on legislation theories than on explanation theories; (2) more research on comparative law than on excavation of domestic resources; (3) more research on countermeasures than on basic theories; (4) more research on legal dogmatics than on the analysis and discussion of cases; and (5) more research on pure civil law than on the discussion of cross-disciplines.[2] These summaries exactly pointed out the achievements and deficiency of China's research on the science of civil law.

1.2 Problems Existing in the Research on the Science of Civil Law

The most important problem in the research of the community of the science of civil law in China is overdependence on the methodology of Begriffsjurisprudenz (conceptual jurisprudence) and has ignored, to some extent, the problems per se. Another prominent issue is repeated selection of topics, lacking awareness of problems and lacking convincing arguments. What China's science of civil law inherited is the tradition of German science of civil law after Pandekten school. In Germany, Pandekten school finally embraced the conceptual jurisprudence and Puchta epitomized the thought of this school. *Methodenlehre der Rechtswissenschaft* (*Methodology of the Science of Law*) by Karl Larenz introduced the theory ancestry of German conceptual jurisprudence at full length, believing that the 19th century is the century of the conceptual jurisprudence. The conceptual jurisprudence was derived from the historical school of law that is an interesting issue in the academic history. The most important feature of the conceptual jurisprudence, which takes *The Digest or Pandects* as its theory system and historical basis of conceptual terms, is systemic thoughts,

1 Liang Huixing, *Historic Review and Outlook of China's Science of Civil Law*, published on Issue 1, *Wangjiang Science of Law*, Law Press, 2007.

2 Wang Liming and Zhou Youjun, *China's Science of Civil Law in the Creation of Civil Code*, Issue 1, *China Legal Science*, 2008.

i.e., uniting diversified things by the association of their meanings to form an entirety. An organism of concept which is a pyramid of concept consisting of both superordinate concept and subordinate concept was formed on the basis of analysis of specific materials. Based on that, Puchta developed the "fomalen Begriffsjurisprudenz". The methodology is closely associated with the rational law school and natural law school, underlying the hierarchy of concepts and rules. Obviously, it was affected by the mainstream methodologies of social science by then, i.e., studying social science as natural science. According to such methodology, there pre-exists a ground theoretic framework in general and other subordinate concepts and rules are induced from some fundamental concepts, theories, and rules within such framework. The merit of such system is that it enables norms of law and legal system to form an organism which is logically consistent and binding. As such, it will be able to restrict the court in a logical and legal system, in order to ensure an objective and fair judgment. In this way, the specification of any civil code is not single, but cohesive and consistent in logic with the end echoing the beginning. By doing so, it is impossible to understand any article of a law in an isolated context. Obviously, the conceptual jurisprudence overestimates the significance of the logical system formed by the hierarchy of generic concepts to the discovery and understanding of law. However, a concept is just a calling and cannot be materialized. If we get entangled in the concept itself, the facts and issues themselves will be shielded by such concept. As a matter of fact, it should be noted that an implanted concept is usually closely related to the historical and social context as the concept system of the civil law system has a continuity, but behind such continuity there exists a fundamental rupture of meaning, as pointed out by some papers. Although, the conceptual jurisprudence has provided a basic methodology for the construction of a scientific system, its defect lies in that it only takes into account the logic of a concept in its form and has ignored the functions and merits it contains. From the historical and present perspectives of the research on the science of civil law in China, the advocation and imitation of the merits of the conceptual jurisprudence has led to a great existence of its theory defects in the research on the science of civil law in China and a continuous existence to a certain extent.

Another common problem is the lack of forceful arguments in both works and papers in the field of the science of civil law. We used to argue from the historical and comparative perspectives, from Roman Law to modern civil law, and from French Civil Code to the General Principle of the Civil Law of China. It is not to say that this argument is not good, but it is often weak, as the explanation of text analysis is always limited. The approach of argument often goes as citing concepts and system in text while ignoring the social, historical, and economic context on which the text is dependent. In civil law, we often use the method of cross-disciplines, but we should be aware of the esteem of the discipline of the science of civil law. We cannot simply implant the knowledge of philosophy, sociology, and economics but should use the knowledge from the perspective of the science of civil law to provide these disciplines with sufficient systems and even ideological resources from another perspective.

Another significant issue is the ubiquity of philosophy in the research on the science of civil law. Undoubtedly, civil law is closely related to philosophy, but it does not necessarily mean that philosophy methods can be used to solve problems of civil law at will. The key lies to how we will use the knowledge of cross-disciplines. If we use the knowledge just for the purpose of introduction of some "big words" and become satisfied with such introduction for seeking a moral and philosophical argument for our points, we must rethink. After all, the civil law is to regulate the real life and will lose its vitality, if it is philosophized. In fact, the civil law as a daily law affects all aspects of our lives and the theoretic contribution might be greater if we see through the social vicissitude from the civil law and explain such vicissitude. It seems common sense that scholars should have observed it, but it remains unobserved till today.

1.3 Problems that Deserve Further Concern in the Science of Civil Law

Although we are discussing the academic history of China's science of civil law, the process of discussing history and experience in observing history is for today. As such, we are better historically grounded to provide some suggestions for the current academic reality and point out the significant issues of the science of civil law that deserves in-depth research in the future.

1.3.1 Research on the Relationship between Civil Code and Special Civil Law. The tradition of early modern civil law is built up on the society which was mainly based on agriculture and its highest value is freedom and efficiency. In modern civil law, however, western countries enacted many special civil laws in addition to the civil code, in order to protect the interests of the underprivileged (such as consumers and laborers). The ideas of these special civil laws are significantly different from those of traditional civil code. At present, China has a swathe of special civil laws. During the formulation of the civil code, a big challenge we faced is how to scientifically and rationally coordinate the relationship of the civil code and special civil laws.

1.3.2 Civil Law and Ecology. The civil laws in early modern times were undoubtedly established on the basis of modern liberalism, which does not concern ecology or, in another word, is powerless to the ecology. The civil law merits liberty and efficiency and the design of its system, such as property right system, liberty of contract, and default liability, is also centered on liberty and efficiency. For the moment, ecology and sustainable development have become globally significant challenges and the environment resource law becomes a formal institutional arrangement in response to these issues. In the international and domestic community of jurisprudence, there has been a calling that the nature (animal, at least) should be taken as a subject of law, which is more or less supported by some foreign legislations. In relation to civil subject, property law, and tort law, there have been scholars attempting to reconstruct the existing system with an ecologist concept. Nevertheless, how the concept of environment law breaks through the dichotomy of subjects and objects involves not only the arrangement of value system of civil law and legislative system, but also the reform of such laws as civil procedure law (such as right to suit in infringement in generations). From the perspective of the whole Chinese academic circle, the theory relating to environment is mainly of breaking through anthropocentrism. At the specific operational level, however, there is little segmented research on institutionalization path, except for general operation of subrogation system in civil law.

1.3.3 Relationship between Public Law and Private Law. Civil law involves a great deal of intersections of private law and public law. For instance, protection on environmental rights under public law and private law, right of claim under public law and private law, the origins of right of personality under public law and private law, state mandate and autonomy of private law in legal acts, and mandate and liberty in the statutory principles of property. It is increasingly important to properly deal with the relationship between the public law and the private law at the transformation of both country and society in China. The division of the public law and the private law directly relates to the dichotomy of political state and civil society. The most ideal state of country and society is mutually developing and promoting, other than growing at the cost of another so as to improve the good governance of a country. The imbalance of both will inevitably cause significant social problems. It is not only the logic of theory, but also the logic of human history. It is important to pay attention to this problem, especially under the circumstance of ubiquitous indifference in politics and public domain among citizens and increasing distance between citizens and the country today. During China's transition period, it should not allow the extremities of emphasizing autonomy of private law while ignoring state functions, nor should it underscore the catalyst effect and proactivity of the state, while ignoring the liberty, imagination, and creativity of citizens and society. Although the division of public law and private law has reached a common understanding in the community of jurisprudence in China, the real clarification of the relationship of public law and private law remains unsolved technically. Civil law scholars have discussed the effects of German constitution on the third party and many scholars noted the tendency of "private law incorporated into public law" and "public law incorporated into private law". Unfortunately, the most discussions were of macro arguments other than in-depth analysis of micro issues. Among all departmental laws, the science of civil law is the best discipline at micro analysis. In the academic context, although the division of public law and private law has reached a common understanding, we need to further discuss the relationship between public law and private law so that practical problems could be resolved more effectively.

2. Development of Research on General Principles of Civil law

During this period, China made great progress in the research on basic theories and general principles of civil law. There were a lot of in-depth and insightful works. (1) Textbooks in relation to general principles of civil law include *General Principles of Civil Law* by Liang Huixing (Law Press, 1996), *General Principles of Civil Law* by Kou Zhixin (China University of Political Science and Law Press, 2000), *General Principles of Civil Law* by Sun Xianzhong, et al (Social Sciences Academic Press, 2004), *General Principles of Civil Law* by Han Song (Law Press, 2006), *General Principles of Civil Law* by Liu Kaixiang (Peking University Press, 2006), *General Principles of Civil Law* by Xu Guodong (Higher Education Press, 2007), *General Principles of Civil Law* by Yang Lixin (Higher Education Press, 2007), *General Principles of Civil Law* (Third Edition) by Fu Jingxin (Sun Yat-Sen University Press, 2007), and *General Principles of Civil Law* by Li Jianhua (Science Press, 2007), etc. (2) Systematic works pertinent to general principles of civil law include *General Principles of Civil Law* by Long Weiqiu (China Legal Publishing House, 2001), *Review on General Principles of Civil Law* by Li Kaiguo (Legal Press, 1996), *General Principles of Civil Law* by Li Yongjun (Legal Press, 2006), *General principles of Civil Law* by Xu Guodong, and Review on *General Principles of Civil Law* by Wang Liming (China Renmin University Press). (3) Monographs in respect of general principles of civil law include *Civil Legal Acts* by Dong Ansheng (China Renmin University Press, 1994), *Discussion on Drafting Thoughts of China's Civil Code* by Xu Guodong (China University of Political Science and Law Press, 2001), *Principles of Private Law and Selection of System* by Yi Jiming (China University of Political Science and Law Press, 2002),

Research on the Formulation of China's Civil Code by Liu Shiguo (Shandong People's Press, 2003), *Research on Civil Codes of Continent Law Countries* by Xie Huaishi (China Legal Publishing House, 2005), *Research on Fundamental Theories of Expectant Right* by Sheng Weixing (China Renmin University Press, 2005), *Research on Action Theories of Absolute Property Right and Property Legal System* by Yu Haiyong (Peking University Press, 2006), *Civil Code and Civil Law Philosophy* by Xu Guodong (China University of Political Science and Law Press, 2007), *Interpretation of Public Order and Good Customs under Civil Law* by Zhao Wanyi (law Press, 2007), *Outline of the General Principle of Civil Law by Xie Huaishi* (Peking University Press, 2007), and *Fundamental Theories of and Research on Legal Acts* by Song Bingyong (Law Press, 2008). (4) Translated works on the general principles of civil law mainly includes the *General Principles of German Civil Law* translated by Shao Jiandong (written by Dieter Medicus, Law Press, 2000), the *General Theories of German Civil Law* translated by Xie Huaishi et al (written by Karl Larenz, Law Press, China, 2004), the *Teaching Materials on Civil Law (I)* translated by Xie Gen (written by Keizou Yamamoto, Peking University Press, 2004), the *Study of Pandect of Science of Civil Law* translated by Jiang Su and Zhang Liyan (written by Omura Atsushi, Peking University Press, 2004), the *Newly Amended General Provisions of Civil Law* translated by Yu Min (written by Sakae Wagatuma, China Legal Publishing House, 2009).

The above brief enumeration of writings on the science of civil law to some extent reveals the prosperity of study on general principles of civil law in this period, and to some extent reveals the academic preference of scholars of civil law for the study of "general principle" issues. During this period, many hot issues and key issues on civil law emerged, which drew the attention of a lot of civil law scholars. They conducted in-depth studies and wide discussions with respect to civil law, which led to the occurrence of achievement on a slew of hot issues and key issues concerning the general principles of civil law.

2.1 Research on Civil Society and Civil Law

With the implementation of the socialist market economy, civil law academic circle no longer needed to demonstrate the legitimacy of civil law, but because the traditional administrative power of control over civil society and market economy inertia still existed, coupled with the heated research attention on civil society in the 90s, there were still a large number of civil law articles discussing the relations between civil society and civil law.[1]The content of these works was largely a combination of the basic theories of civil society and civil law's characteristics, and its main purposes are twofold: the first purpose was the demonstration of an important position of civil law in the legal system, and the second was proof of private autonomy, freedom of contract principle of legitimacy.[2]

It seems today that the greatest significance of these discussions is that it has built the symbiotic relationship between what academia generally recognized as civil society and civil law. So far, almost all civil works have acknowledged civil law as "private". With the characteristics of civil law being demonstrated during that period, civil law has only resumed its political constitution beyond the neutral position. Those studies on civil law have also largely escaped the confines of ideology.

2.2 With Respect to Contemporary Civil law and Modern Civil Law Research

In the 1990s, the distinction between contemporary civil law and modern civil law has been a hot topic within the civil law academic circle, and the civil law papers have also frequently used it as the argument premise. What has triggered this discussion is the paper entitled "from the modern civil law to the contemporary civil law legal thought." According to Professor Liang, with the codification of civil law in the European countries in the 19th century, the modern

1 It is the scholar Xu Guodong in civil law academic circle who was the first to cite the concept of civil society and he holds that the original meaning of civil law is the law for civilians and even suggests changing civil law to the law for civilian. See Xu Guodong, *Civil Society and Civil Law*, published on Issue 4, *Law Study*, 1994.

2 Typical theses such as Su Haopeng, Civil Law Culture: A Preliminary Theoretical Interpretation, published on Issue 3, *Study of Comparative Study*, 1997.

civil law has developed a set of civil law concepts, principles, systems, theories and ideas. Modern civil law related expressions are: specific personality, property ownership restrictions, restrictions on private autonomy or freedom of contract as well as social responsibility.[1]

In fact, in the 1980s, in Xie Huaishi's speech, the distinction between modern civil law and contemporary civil law was already touched upon. As Xie Huaishi proposed, the contemporary civil law society emerged with the following phenomena: the formation of a group law different from "Personal Law"; the establishment of equality in family law and liberalization of change; growing attention on personality right, a matter of a principle of the right to be broken; usufruct increasingly losing its importance with the emergence of more and more types of security interests and contracts; the rapid development of tort law; and the greater extent of securitized debt.[2]Today, when we read the script of Xie Huaishi which was written twenty years ago, probably not only will we be impressed by the lofty vision and incisive discussions by Xie Huaishi, but also be surprised at Xie Huaishi's maneuver to introduce the foreign law with superb summary. In fact, the afterwards development of Chinese civil law is basically in line with Xie Huaishi's summary of foreign law during that period of time.

It should be said, the main difference between the modern and contemporary civil law is not a sequence of time, not even the system (not the existence of such a fundamental change and break). The contemporary civil law is also more reflected in the adjustment and amendment of the basic spirit of civil law, and it is difficult to say that there is a real sense of "contemporary civil law".

By comparing modern and contemporary views, some papers have discussed the problems of contemporary civil law, which is to further deepen the "contemporary" discussions. For China, the word "contemporary" is always a big

1 See Liang Huixing, *Thoughts from Modern Civil Law to Contemporary Civil Law – Review of Civil Law in 1920s*, published in *From Modern Civil Law to Contemporary Civil Law*, China Legal Publishing House, 2000.

2 See Xie Huaishi, pp.13-48, *Essence of Foreign Civil and Commercial Law*, Law Press, 2002.

attractive word. In the change process from "modern" to "modernity", "modernity" is also favored by the civil law academic circle. There are papers devoted to the problem of modern Chinese Civil law. It discusses the problem of modernity in Chinese Civil law. It is necessary to acknowledge the function and value of the civil law. We must adjust the value orientation, pay attention to the national spirit and pay attention to the local people.[1] Overall, these papers actually illustrated a major problem facing Chinese Civil law: As a developing country, China's social environment is different from the Western society, and accordingly, the question is how to adjust the "modernity" of the civil law to reflect China's own characteristics?

2.3 A study on the form and value of the Civil Code

"Compared to criminal law, procedural law and other laws, civil law, civil law is a more vivid reflection of a nation's culture and therefore, only one unified Civil Code could show that the whole nation has reached the peak of the Chinese history." [2] Ever since 1949, the Civil Code has always become a heart knot for civil law scholars. As Liang Huixing pointed out in 2001, China has already developed the five conditions for the Civil Code: the market economy has reached a considerable scale; civil legislation for the civil law code provides the basis and experience; civil trial has witnessed considerable development; and Civil Law Teaching and theoretical research has enjoyed considerable development.[3]

In 1998, the National People's Congress Law Committee commissioned scholars and experts to set up the working group to carry out the drafting of the Civil Code. The government's Civil Code promotion has boosted the discussions around Civil Code, and the debates surrounding the Civil Code have become very heated in the civil law academic circle.

---

1 Li Jianhua, Cai Lidong, Dong Biao, *On Issues of Modernity of Chinese Civil Law: Outlook of Legislation Basis of Civil Code*, published on Issue 1, *Law and Social Development*, 2002.

2 Xie Huaishi, pp.13-48, *Essence of Foreign Civil and Commercial Law*, Law Press, 2002.

3 See Liang Huixing, *Assumption on Formulating Civil Code*, published on Issue 2, *Modern Law Science*, 2001.

Regarding the development of the Civil Code, Liang Huixing proposed the following three ideas: (1) loosely or "federal", that is, the compilation of the Civil Code should not be limited to the form of a single law. (2) the idealistic way, which is in accordance with the idea proposed by Xu Guodong—Latin American Civil practices. (3) the realistic way, which is in accord with the tradition, borrowed from the German model.[1]

As to whether the civil code should emphasize human or objects, there are varying opinions among scholars. Based upon a thorough study of the Roman law and the codification of the civil law in modern European and Latin American countries, Xu Guodong pointed out that the three-system "Law ladder" highlights human law, and our Civil Code should adopt the improved two-facet system, namely, laws on personal and property relations. In order to highlight the centrality of human in private law, we should draw on the Civil Code of the Russian Federation and the Netherlands Civil Code structure to design sub-series, and learn from the Ibero-Latin America Civil Code to set preface, regulate the adjustment object, basic principles, trading, rights protection and so on.[2] This idea of the three-facet system leads to two issues, namely the debate between "material humanism" and "humanist" , and the discussion on the logic and structure of the Civil Code. He believes that the traditional civil law approach which emphasizes on objects, is "focusing on things but not people", and the new approach of civil law highlights the spirit of humanism. Around this view, there have been a heated debate among sholars.[3] The prominent feature of the architecture is to highlight the value of human law, making it a separate provision. According to this approach,

1 See Liang Huixing, *Three Thoughts on Civil Code Compilation*, published on Issue 1, *Peking University Law Journal*, 2001.

2 Xu Guodong: *Basic Structure of Draft Civil Code – Center on Theory of Civil Relations Covered by Civil Law*, published on Issue 1, *Legal Study*, 2000.

3 See Xu Guodong, *Two Drafting Thoughts on Civil Code: New Humanism v.s. Materialism*, published on *War on China's Civil Law Drafting Thoughts – the 4th War on World Civil Code Compilation History compiled by Xu Guodong*, pp.137-183, *China University of Political science and Law Press*, 2001.

the German General Civil Code provision will be incorporated into preface, which is different from what the academic circle has learnt from Germany, Japan and Taiwan District. "General" or "Preface" has become the most important issue of the Civil Code of architecture.[1]

When it comes to whether personality rights should be a separate provision or not, Wang Liming stressed that personality rights cannot be covered by the main system or the tort law, and therefore, the development of personality rights as a separate provision will both enrich and improve the civil code system.[2]Some experts believe that personality rights are naturally linked with qualifications of civil subject, hereditary, and personality rights cannot be separated from civil subject. Having said that, those scholars agree that the specific contents of personality rights and eligibility of the civil subject are two issues that can be respectively addressed.[3] Other scholars oppose the idea of putting personality rights as a separate provision, on the grounds of the presence of the essential relationship of personality rights and personality. According to those scholars, the object of personality rights is present in the subject itself, which does not exist in the relationship between people. Setting up personality rights in a separate provision, confuses the distinction between personality rights and other civil rights, undermining the internal logic of the Civil Code.[4] Some other scholars also argue against the notion of a separate provision for personanlity rights, whose reasoning is that personality rights are based on natural personality and therefore, the resulting "personality relationship" should belong to the legal relationship which is impossible to be adjusted by law. According to this idea,

1 See Chen Xiaojun, *China's Civil Code: Preface Or General Provisions*, published on Issue 6, *Legal Study*, 2004.

2 See Wang Liming, *Status of Personality Rights System in China's Civil Code*, published on Issue 2, *Legal Study*, 2003.

3 See Wang Shengming, *Inevitable Course for Country under Rule of Law – Several Questions on Compilation of Civil Law of People's Republic of China (Draft)*, published on Issue 1, *Tribune of Political Science and Law*, 2003.

4 See Liang Huixing, *Loose and Compilation Style of Civil Code Don't Fit with Chinese National Conditions*, published on Issue 1, *Tribune of Political Science and Law*, 2003.

"general personality rights" with a variety of existing concrete personality are a mutually non-inclusive type of rights which do not belong to each other; and personality rights only have negative protection function, which do not have the characteristics of civil rights.[1] "People's Republic of China Civil Law (Draft)"puts the personality rights as a separate provision.

When it comes to whether tort law should be a seperate provision or not, the Traditional Civil Code puts tort law as part of the debt law, but some scholars believe that in view of the 20th century, the complex social life and high development of science and technology have produced a variety of new contractual relationships, new risks and new torts, resulting in greatly expanded debt law content, so the debt is divided into three categories, and compiled according to the general debt provision of contract claims and tort act. Unjust enrichment and negotiorumgestio system are still defined in the general debt provision.[2] Opponents argue that infringement of the debt has its own characteristics, and it cannot change its belonging to a common debt, which determines the law of tort and the debate not juxtaposed relationship, but affiliation, tort law should not be independent from debt law. Tort law is relatively independent advocate point of view, essentially adopted by our legislature.

Whether to establish a debt law general provision or not, the majority of scholars who claim that tort law should be of a separate series of laws has come to conclusion that the general provision of debt law is not appropriate to be incorporated in the Civil Code.[3] Opponents argue that the Civil Code should include a General Debt Law, in order to guide contract law and tort law, and put unjust enrichment and negotiorumgestio regulations in debt law general

1 See Yin Tian, *On Theory Loopholes of Independent Compilation of Personality Rights*, published on Issue 5, *Law Science Magazine*, 2007.

2 Wang Liming: pp.53-58, *On System of China's Civil Code*, published on *Research on Civil and Commercial Law*, Law Press, 2001. Ma Changhua, *Study on Legal Status of Infringing Acts*, China University of Political science and Law, 2004.

3 Tan Youtu, Ma Changhua, *Retention or Abolition of General Rule of Obligation Law in China's Civil Code*, published on Issue 5, *Law Science Magazine*, 2003.

provisions, "If cancelling debt concept and debt general provision, it will completely destroy the civil law logic and system and even the right to the name will also be an issue ...... "[1] There are scholars in favor of independence on the basis of tort law that should still be the establishment of the General Rules of the debt, liability for breach of the provisions of debt.[2]

The proposal of the "Green Civil Code" concept has been put forward. In terms of the value of Civil Code, one of the greatest innovations of the Chinese scholars is the notion of "Green Civil Code". Xu Guodong pointed out that the object adjustment issue of civil law contains hidden green issues. "Green Civil Code" is the "ecological doctrine of the Civil Code", which rests on a pessimistic belief of the future of humanity and is based on the recognition of the inevitability of resource exhaustion and the possibility of sustainable use of natural resources. This green approach of civil code tries to put restrictions on human's wasteful use of natural resources in order to maintain sustainable human survival.[3]Under the guidance of his green idea, the draft of the Civil Code presided over by Xu Guodong is also known as the "Green Civil Code".

In addition, civil law academic circle has a lot of discussions towards the codification itself. Over the years, civil law scholars have high hopes for the Civil Code. But in recent years, scholars have also discussed the limitations of the codification[4] and, even introduced the foreign thoughts of anti-codification into the country.[5]

2.4 A Study on Civil Rights

Traditional mainland civil law is focused on claim rights to analyze rights.

1 Liang Huixing: p.34, *Struggle for China's Civil Code*, Law Press, 2002.

2 Wei Zhengying: *Integration and Separation of Obligation and Responsibility*, published on Issue 1, *China Legal Science*, 1998.

3 See Xu Guodong, *Analysis of Green in Green Civil Code Draft*, Issue 6, Studies in Law and Business, 2003.

4 Representative works such as the *Codification of Civil Law and Its Limitation*, *Peking University Law Journal*, Issue 4, 2002.

5 See Zhang Lihong, Gao Fuping, *Codification, Decodification And Anti-Codification of Civil Law*, *China University of Political science and Law Press*, 2008.

Claim rights is the focus of research by the civil law academic circle, with endless variety of works,[1] but more focused on the discussion of claim rights. On the specific types of rights, Xie Huaishi has made a precise summary of the civil rights of the traditional system, especially on sorting out the identity rights, which has exerted great impacts on the civil law.[2]

The subject of personality rights has attracted a lot of research attention within the civil law academic circle. Civil law scholars participating in research and discussion have done a comprehensive discussion of the personality rights system.[3] It is worth mentioning that some study of the relationship from the point of view of the Constitution and civil law discussed personality right, enhanced the depth of the issues discussed.[4] Thus, this also led to the legal entity issue of whether or not there is general personality right, with or without compensation for moral damage claims and other issues.

During this period, the common research paradigm of the personality right is to provide proof of some kind of personality rights that has not been recognized in the country. For instance, there have been discussions about publicity right as a new type of personality rights with the legal status of concrete personality rights.[5]

2.5 A study on the civil subject system

During this period, the study on the civil subject within the civil law academic

1 Xu Xiaofeng, *Criticism on Concept of Right to Request*, published on *Legal Methodology*, Tsinghua University Press, 2004; Duan Housheng, *Theory on Right to Request for Civil Law*, People's Court Press, 2006.

2 See Xie Huaishi, *Civil Rights System*, published on Issue 2, *Legal Study*, 1996.

3 Wang Liming, *Study on Personality Rights Law*, China Renmin University Press, 2005. Yang Lixin, *Theory on Personality Rights Law*, China Higher Education Press, 2005. Ma Junju, Lecture Notes on Personality and Personality Rights Theory, Law Press, 2009.

4 See Long Weiqiu, *On Personality of Natural Person and its Contemporary Route – Positivism of Constitutional Order and Civil Law*, published on Issue 2, *Tsinghua Law Review*, 2002. Yin Tian, *On Essence of Personality Rights*, published on Issue 3, *Legal Study*, 2003.

5 Yang Lixin, Lin Xuxia, *On Independent Status of Right of Publicity and its Basic Contents*, published on Issue 2, *Jilin University Journal Social Sciences Edition*, 2006.

circle is mainly reflected in the following aspects: First, based on the foundational theory of natural persons, such as research rights capacity, the relationship between personalities, and "not in the system", etc.[1] Second, the study of legal entity theory. [2] Third, the study focused on public legal entity with less focus on traditional civil law. Some scholars have suggested that China should reshape the administrative body theory, especially the concept of public legal entity should be used in the Civil Code in a more rational manner prescribing public legal entity problems. In addition, national authorities should not have the status of legal and administrative body, the State is the legal and administrative body.[3] Some academics have also introduced the German law on the public legal entity (i.e. public law associations, public creation and public law consortium) system, China should learn from the German law, and acknowledge that to some extent, public legal entities have the capacity to go bankruptcy and that there are bankruptcy filing obligations of the directors.[4] Fourth is the study of institutions. Some scholars have suggested that the legalization of institutions is a historical misunderstanding, and the organization and governance of public institutions should follow the operational mechanism of public authority rather than civil law.[5] In addition, scholars have also made in-depth study towards non-profit organizations, and cooperatives, etc.

2.6 A study on legal acts

Legal act is a core part of the general civil law. Not only is it the most

1 Yin Tian, *On Declaration of Disappearance and Death*, published on Issue 6, *Legal Study*, 2001.

2 Jiang Ping, Long Weiqiu, *Study on Essence of Legal Person and its Basic Structure*, published on Issue 3, *China Legal Science*,1998. Yi Jiming, *Communitarianism Character in Germanic* Property Law, published on Issue 3, *Study of Comparative Law*, 2001.

3 See Ge Yunsong, *Rediscussion on Theory of Legal Entity and Administrative Bodies*, published on Issue 3, China Legal Science, 2007.

4 See Zhou Youjun, *Study on Public Legal Persons System in German Civil Law*, published on Issue 4, *Legal Scholars*, 2007.

5 See Fang Liufang, *Reform of China's Institutional Organizations from Legal Perspective*, published on Issue 3, *Study of Comparative Law*, 2007.

sophisticated and the most brilliant theoretical contribution of the German legal system, but also it is the utmost development of the conceptual jurisprudence. Legal act is not only an important manifestation of the principle of private law autonomy, but also one of the core systems of civil law, which has always been an important part of academic research in China.[1]

In recent years, civil law concerns about legal acts are mainly in such aspects: First, reflect on the concept of "civil legal act" for use in civil law general provision. Such studies are mostly critique of the concept of using civil law general provision system.[2] Second is the legal act of origin and semantics evidence. [3] Mi Jian pointed out that the Chinese translation of "legal acts" is not accurate.[4] Some scholars believe, the emerge of legal act theory, in terms of its substantive content, will be affected by the theory of legal thought; its form perspective, influenced by modern European jurisprudence on human behavior has the legal significance of the theoretical analysis.[5] Third, the distinction between acts of disposition and burdens. We shall address this issue later on in the section of the review of Civil Law property rights. Fourth, in-depth study of the meaning of representation. Meaning of representation is a core element of legal acts. Recent studies have focused on the interpretation of the meaning of representation.[6]

3. The Burst of Progress in the Research of Property Rights of Civil Law

Prior to 1995, property rights of Civil Law have been a weak link in national

1 Representative works such as Dong Ansheng, *Civil Law Behaviors*, China Renmin University Press, 1994.

2 Typically, Sheng Weixing, *Rethinking on Essence of Civil Law Behaviors*, published on Issue 6, *Jilin University Journal Social Sciences Edition*, 1995. Song Bingyong, *Renaming Legal Behavior Concept as Establishment Right Behavior*, published on Issue 2, *Peking University Law Journal*, 1999.

3 Zhu Qinyu, *Comments on Legal Behavior Concept*, published on Issue 3, *Peking University Law Journal*, 2008.

4 See Mi Jian, *On Legal Transaction*, published on Issue 2, *China Legal Science*, 2004.

5 See Xue Jun, *Expression of the Theory of Legal Acts Issues in the History of European Generation and Terminology of Private Law*, Global Law Review, 2007.

6 Zhu Qinyu, *Intention Interpretive Theory*, China University of Political science and Law, 2004.

legal research. Until 1994, China has only published one property law textbook.[1] Since then, the study of property law has gradually entered a prosperous period and until now there are hundreds of books on property law. (1) Works of teaching materials during this period are: Professor Liang and Chen Huabin' *Property Law* (Law Press, 1997, 4th edition 2007), Sun Xianzhong' *China Property Law Introduction* (Law Press, 2003), *Property Law Principle* (Law Press). (2) Property law system of the writings are: Wen Shiyang' *Property Law Theory* (Wuhan University Press, 1997), Liang Huixing' *China Property Law Studies* (Law Press, 1998), Wang Liming' *Property Law Theory* (China University of Political Science Press, 1998), Chen Huabin' *Property Law Principle* (National School of Administration Press, 1998), Gao Fuping' *China Property Law: system design and innovation* (People's University of China Press, 2005), Gao Shengping' *Security Law Theory* (Law Press, 2009 edition) and so on. (3) For property law monographs are: Chen Huabin' *Modern Condominium Ownership System Research* (Law Press, 1995 edition), *Property Law Research* [Jinqiao Culture Publishing (Hong Kong) Limited 2001 edition], *Foreign Property Law* (Law Press, 2004), Sun Xianzhong' Contemporary German Property Law (Law Press, 1997) and *On the Property Law* (Law Press, 2001), Wang Weiguo' *China Land Rights Studies* (China University of Political Science Press 1997 Edition), Yin Tian' *French Property Law* (Law Press, 1998) and *Property Law Theory and Reflections* (People's University of China Press, 2008), Wang Yi' *Property Change Theory* (People's University of China Publishing 2001 Edition), Ma Xinyan' *American Property Law and Case Studies* (Law Press, 2001), Shao Houguo' *Property Change Studies* (Law Press, 2002), Tian Shiyong' *Property Behavior Theory Research* (China Politics University Press, 2002), Mei Xiaying' *Basic Structure of Property Rights Analysis* (People's Court Press, 2002), Cheng Xiao' Theory and Practice of China Mortgage System (Law Press, 2002), Cui

1 Namely the *Property Law Principle* written by Qian Mingxing, Peking University Press, 1994.

Jianyuan' *Quasi Property Research* (Law Press, 2003), *Land Rights Group Study* (Law Press, 2004), *Property: Growth and Forming* (People's University of China Press, 2004), *Fishing Rights Argument* (Peking University Press, 2006), Sun Peng' *Property of Publicity Theory* (Law Press, 2002), Chang Pengao' *Construction and Effects of Property Program* (People's University of China Press 2005 Edition), Fang Shaokun' *Usufruct Basic Research* (Peking University Press, 2006), Liu Baoyu' *Guarantee Law Difficult Issues Studies and Legislation Improvement* (Law Press, 2006 edition), etc. (4) The translation work involves two legal systems, such as Shi Tiantao's translation of *Property Law* (Lawson Laden, Encyclopedia of China Publishing House, 1998), Qu Tao's translation of *Property Change and Confrontation* (Suzuki Rokuwataru, Social Science Documentation Publishing House, 1999), Lu Qingsheng's translation of *Property Law* (Yamada Teruaki, Law Press, 2001 edition), Wu Yue and Li Daxue's translation of *Property Law* (Wolf, Law Press 2004 Edition), Zhang Shuanggen's translation of *German Property Law* (Powell, Law Press, 2004 edition), Zhong Shufeng's translation of *Real Estate* (Bernhardt and Burkhart, Law Press, 2005 edition) and *Understanding Property Law* (John G. Franklin, Peking University Press, 2009 edition), Wang Yan's translation of *Property Law* (Koji Omi, Peking University Press, 2006) and so on.

3.1 Ideological Legitimacy Issue with the Draft of Property Law[1]

On July 10, 2005, the General Office of the NPC Standing Committee published a draft of property law to solicit the views of the community. Some people viewed the draft of property law as unconstitutional, and argued that the draft was a departure from socialism and turned back the clock, and therefore proposed to postpone the legislative process of the property law. This view caused widespread impacts, and become social trend property legislation must seriously face. Until November 2005, a message was spread out that the property law plan enacted in March 2006 would be suspended, and soon the news was confirmed,

1 This section was written by Chen Su.

which is called the "abortion event of Property Law plan." This event formed the biggest controversy since the founding of New China, which gave rise to a lot of fierce reactions in the society. As shown by the comments on the Internet, there were varied opinions regarding this event, ranging from worried, angry, regretful, neutral to thankful. The legal ideology controversy , which has been existed for years in the legal circles, finally erupted during the discussions of the draft of property law.[1]

To sum up, the main arguments against the draft of property law from the experts and scholars outside the civil law academic circle are around the legitimacy of the ideological point of view. Their main reasoning is[2]: Firstly, Article 12 of "socialist public property is inviolable" of the Constitution is one of the most essential features of socialism. But the draft of property law proposed "the state, the collective and individuals enjoy equal protection of property rights", which actually intended to equip private property with the same level of protection as public property of socialism, and according to those experts, this was in confliction with the "Constitution" provisions. Secondly, according to those experts, the draft of property law deviated from the socialist principles by stipulating that on behalf of the State, the State Council or local people's governments could exercise ownership responsibilities, fulfill investors' duties and dispose of state property. They believed that the draft actually led to the legitimize behavior of losing state property, which further weakened the socialist state-owned

1 Sun Xianzhong: *Contemporary Chinese Jurists' Library*, China Renmin University Press, 2006.

2 See Gong Xiantian, *An unconstitutional and away from the basic principles of socialism Property Law (draft)* – for *Constitution* Article 12 and 1986 *Civil Law* repealing written open letter to Article 73, contained in http://www.wyzxsx.com; Gong Xiantian and others on *On Property Law* (draft) revised the proposed draft, contained in http://bbs.jycg.com.cn; Yang Xiaoqing' *My views on the Property Law (draft)*, contained http://www.law.tsinghua.edu.cn; Gong Xiantian and others' *To NPC Standing Committee's open letter - on the sixth after consideration 'Property Law (Draft)' on five major issues of principle still violate the Constitution which must seriously revise opinions*, contained in http://economy.guoxue.com.

economy and the dominant position of public ownership of the economy. Thirdly, Article 8 of the Constitution states that: "In rural areas of the various forms of production, supply and marketing, credit and consumers' cooperative economy is a socialist economy under collective ownership by the working people." The draft of property law scrapped such provision and as a consequence, the property of rural labor masses' collective economic organizations was unprotected by the draft. Fourthly, the draft should specify that the accountability for violations of the state-owned property and collective property is of no time limit, because, otherwise, it will make those criminals who embezzle public property after a certain time turn illegal possession of public property into lawful private property. At the same time, the draft's regulation on bona fide acquisition should not be made applicable to public property.

Our civil law, jurisprudence and constitutional scholars held several meetings to refute the opinions that the draft does not have the ideological legitimacy of socialism. First, the draft of property law not only did not violate the constitution, but was in accordance with the constitution-making, which reflected the constitution, in particular the spirit of the 2004 constitutional amendment. After reviewing the history of the constitutional amendment, and some scholars concluded that the constitution in fact affirmed the equal legal status of "non-public ownership economy", and affirmed that the "non-public economy" is "an important part" of the socialist market economy and an important power to promote the development of social productivity, and therefore, the property law provisions were fully consistent with the constitution. [1] Some other scholars pointed out that the viewpoint that the draft did not have special protection of public property was in fact a misunderstanding of the draft itself. Our Constitution and the Civil Law clearly stipulate the principle of the sanctity of public property,

1 See Liang Huixing "Who misinterpret the Constitution and is unconstitutional?—Correct understanding of Article 11 of the Constitution, expose individual lies from a professor of law jurisprudence" contained in http://www.civillaw.com.cn.

but the Constitution also states that legitimate personal property is to be protected by law. The report of 16th National People's Congress of Communist Party of China also made it clear that "we must unswervingly consolidate and develop the public economy" and "we must unswervingly encourage, support and guide non-public economic development." The spirit of the Constitution and the Congress report clearly said that in order to promote the common development of various economic forms, which means various forms of property development will coexist. Therefore, it is necessary not only to protect public property but also to protect private property. We should not cut the links between the two and should not understand the constitution out of the context.[1] Still some scholars pointed out that we could not draw the conclusion that the draft was unconstitutional simply because the wordings of some specific provisions of the draft are different from those of the Constitution. On closer look, it could be seen that the draft of property law was actually consistent with the Constitution. [2]And some more scholars pointed out that the reason why property law does not restate the relevant provisions of the Constitution, is that property law has a different legal role to play as compared to the Constitution. The Constitution has its own functions, and property law also has its own unique function, and they do not repeat each other and cannot replace each other.[3] Second, the relationship between property law and ownership should be correctly understood, since property law does not solve the problem of priority and inferiority among different ownerships, it is to adjust the property relations formed by the economy operation in the public ownership as the mainstay of ownership environment. Ownership and the ownership rights

1 See Wang Liming "Property Law (Draft) in line with China's national conditions, the era of the process and the people need", http://www.civillaw.com.cn.

2 See "Draft Property Rights Law with Civil Law Authority behind, Directed an Open Letter Questioned Gong Xiantian", http://news.xinhuanet.com; Cui Jianyuan: "*Property Law is to promote the reform and opening up of the law*", contained in http://www.civillaw.com.cn.

3 Sun Xianzhong: *Contemporary Chinese Jurists' Library*, China Renmin University Press, 2006.

are not equal, and unequal ownership does not mean that property rights under ownership should be unequal, because under civil law to obtain property rights in accordance with the respective ownership are the same. In fact, China's jurisprudence especially civil law academic circle reached a consensus that state, collective and individual property rights should have equal protection by property law, no matter what form of ownership rights, as long as they are legally acquired, it should be given equal treatment and protection. Only this can accurately reflect China's basic economic system, safeguard the socialist market economic system, promote growth and economic prosperity of social wealth, reflect the basic spirit of the modern rule of law, and properly handle all kinds of disputes for judges to provide basic legal basis.[1]To think that equal protection of property law protecting the citizen's property will lead to illegal property is actually a misunderstanding of the legal function, because the law only protects legal property, and illegal property can never be protected by law. Third, correct understanding should be made on the relationship between the property law and the loss of state assets. Loss of state assets is a very complex phenomenon, where there are a lot of problems related to the system, not just the law can be resolved, and the draft property law pays high attention to this problem, it first emphasizes the protection of the property of state-owned economy, and specially makes provisions for this issue. Some scholars believe that, taking into account the social needs and legislative policies, the protection of state-owned assets provided by the property law is necessary, but the real solution to the protection of state-owned assets must

1 See Wang Liming: *Study of the Civil Code Major Difficult Issues*, Law Press, 2006, pp.245-250; Sun Xianzhong "*Property Law*", Social Sciences Academic Press, 2005, pp.183-187; Liang Huixing: *Thirds Law or monism - Property Law guiding ideology of struggle*", http://www.civillaw.com.cn; Zhao Wanyi: *Calmly and rationally controversial Property Law*, contained in http://www.civillaw.com.cn; *Draft Property Rights Law with Civil Law authority behind, directed an open letter questioned Gong Xiantian*, http://news.xinhuanet.com; *Law expert interpretation of property law: property is the most important principle of equality*, http://news.xinhuanet.com.

rely on specialized law such as "State-owned Assets Law".[1] Fourth, as for the point of view that the draft property law bona fide system provides convenience to criminal encroaching public property, most scholars believe that this view is the most basic understanding to the civil law concept of bona fide acquisition and lack of function. In property law where it mentions "bona fide", the key lies in the perpetrator's "goodwill" and misappropriation of public property criminals is clearly out of "bad faith", and its encroachment simply cannot apply to bona fide acquisition. If the law does not protect the property under "bona fide" status, everyone will go to fight, and the societal property order will not exist.[2]

After repeatedly focused discussions, according to the published research results from China Law Society of Civil Law Studies, our civil law scholars believe that the draft of property law has been published in spite of the specific content which still have some room for improvement, but property law is one important law for maintaining the basic socialist economic system, guaranteeing the smooth construction of the socialist market economy and promoting the socialist harmonious society. The basic principles of property law and civil law general provisions are the same strain, and it is the inevitable result of the establishment and improvement of the socialist market economy. The civil law academic circle reached broad affirmative consensus for the formulation of property law and the basic spirit and content of the draft property law.[3]

In consideration of the draft of property law, the Standing Committee members

---

1 See Wei Zhenying: *How Property Law should reflect the basic economic system of primary stage of socialism*, http://www.civillaw.com.cn; *Draft Property Rights Law with Civil Law authority behind, directed an open letter questioned Gong Xiantian*, http://news.xinhuanet.com; "*Law expert interpretation of property law: property is the most important principle of equality*", contained in http://news.xinhuanet.com.

2 Sun Xianzhong: *Contemporary Chinese Jurists' Library*, China Renmin University Press, 2006.

3 See Yang Lixin: *Property Law and Chinese socialist harmonious society construction theory seminar closing remarks*, http://www.civillaw.com.cn; Yao Hui and others: "2005 Review and Prospects in Civil and Commercial Legal Study", *China Legal Science*; Civil Legal Study hosted by *Chinese Yearbook of Civil Law 2005*, Law Press, 2006 Edition.

and observers agree that the draft adheres to the correct political orientation based on China's national conditions and the Constitution, reflects China's basic economic system of socialism, follows the principle of equal protection of property rights, intensifies efforts to protect the state-owned assets, reflects the party's basic rural policies at this stage, maintains the fundamental interests of the broadest masses of people and focuses resolving the real life problems urgently to be regulated. Regarding the issue around the equal protection of property rights, the General Office of the NPC Standing Committee at a press conference held on December 29, 2006 stated that the Constitution regulates "the state practices socialist market economy", the draft property law provides equal protection decided by the market economy characteristics. Market economy requires market players enjoy the same rights, the same rules and bear the same responsibility. If market players are unequal, China's market economy would not be able to operate further. The implementation of equal protection helps to improve our competitive equality and survival of the fittest in the market environment. Only with the implementation of equal protection would be able to preserve China's basic economic system.[1] We can say that the legislative approach and practice of the property law from the NPC Standing Committee's already made a clear answer on the legitimate ideology in the draft of property law.

3.2 Research on the Basic Theory of Property Law

Although ownership is already a very familiar legal terminology and concept, Chinese civil law is still in its unique style to acquire ownership basis and carry on philosophy discussion. People acquire property rights seems a matter of course, but it is indeed a very difficult problem if it needs to get to the bottom on "why acquire property rights."During the transition of the basis for human beings to acquire properties from divine basis to secular basis, theory of acquisition by labor is the most important aspect. A thesis expounded the justification of acquisition of ownership in philosophy from the perspective of labor theory of property by

1 "*Draft Property Law has Matured* ", in *People's Daily*, December 31, 2006.

Locke. [1]There are also papers pointed out to explore the root causes of property rights, a process of human experience from outside to inside that in ancient times, the ultimate goal of perfection and the idea of the existence of God determines the ownership of the property, obtainment of evidences and final distribution. Labor theory of ownership rights will establish property in people's own natural basis so that people acquiring property find basis in themselves. Locke's labor thesis paper elucidates the acquired property basis and the meaning of labor based on the course of human history.[2]

The relationship between property law and ecological is the study of modern civil law. Civil law is undoubtedly based on the establishment of the political system of modern liberalism, and liberalism is not concerned about ecological problems, but rather speaking, it is powerless towards ecological problems. Civil law is based on the pursuit of value for freedom and efficiency, the system design such as the property rights system, freedom of contract and fault liability are constructed around this goal. Property law reflects the people and things most concentrated binary oppositions in the law. Modern countries' property law just blindly focused on taking full advantage of the economic benefits of the substance which led to the plundering of resources consumption. Some scholars have pointed out the extreme "anthropocentric" philosophy performs in the areas of quasi-property law system and even property rights, that is absolute ownership and quasi-obligatory weakening of property rights. In the field of tort law such as the need to properly recognize some animals have special rights, as absolute "anthropocentrism" of the amendment, and this is a more realistic option.[3] Some scholars have proposed the following scheme: the future man generations as civil subject to solve the problem of intergenerational equity. The destruction acts of

1 Yi Jiming "On the labor theory of property rights", *Legal Study* in 2000, 3rd issue.

2 See Xiao Houguo "Why should we get property rights? - Locke's philosophical interpretation of labor property", in *Civil and Commercial Law Review*, vol. 25.

3 See Cui Jianyuan "Natural philosophy and the fate of property rights and even quasi-civil law", in *Studies in Law and Business*, 2003, 6th issue.

the ecological environment induce not only administrative punishment, but also on behalf of future generations of people asking them to stop the infringement and bear the cost of ecology restoration and environment management. In addition, animals have become the possibilities of legal subject, and the lack of animals' capacity can be made up through the guardianship system. Civil Code should be divided into ordinary objects and animals, and for the animals, they should be applied to the special law on the protection of animals (including ordinary animals).[1]

Some scholars believe that at the conceptual level of the property, the currency measuring the ecological value can be classified into the subject which not only is feasible but also it should be done. Property rights holders' environmental obligation can be specified in the property rights exercise level. There are three legislative models to achieve environmental protection dimension of the property law: (1) adopt the most abstract general requirement, and add the declaration of norms in the general provisions of the property law; and (2) to explain the legal standards as a starting point, for example, interpreting the provisions of the property law must meet the needs of environmental protection; (3) Property law interpretation shall be to maintain the subject of economic value and ecological value as a standard.[2] Other scholars believe that property law in many countries with types of forest rights, prospecting and mining rights, water rights, fishing rights and hunting rights, etc. have all become the chartered property of a public law nature. While we advocate green property law, but in the structure of the legal system, respecting the private rights is still the necessary logical starting point of

1 Cao Mingde, Xu Yixiang: "Chinese Civil Law codification and ecological protection", in *Modern Law Science* 2003, 4th issue. Zhang Ruiping "From 'intergenerational equity' theoretical reflects civil subject system of value" (*Study of Comparative Law* 2003, 5th issue) article also made a similar point.

2 See Gao Lihong: "Property Law Environmental Protection features: concept and mode", *Law Science Magazine*, 2003, 9th issue.

the value system.[1]

3.3 A study on the Property Rights

Before the introduction of the property law, there is a dispute in China regarding whether it should develop property law or asset law. There are papers devoted to the concept of property rights. According to those papers, if the asset law is developed, the contents of which will go beyond the scope of the traditional property rights of continental countries by including the relevant contents of assets rights, which is bound to disrupt the entire civil law system, causing a huge impact on our legislation model. The biggest advantage of the adoption of the concept of property rights is that a distinct difference could be made between the two basic forms of asset rights, namely, property rights and creditor's rights.[2] In terms of what type of social relations is reflected by property rights, there are two different opinions, namely, relations between people and relations between objects.There are papers arguing that in fact those two are not in opposition, and property rights can be defined as "direct ownership of the property".[3]

There are also thesis papers from a historical perspective of property law, discussing the distinctions among property rights, intellectual property rights and quasi property rights. It is believed that since French law uses the concept of property rights, after a further distinction between property and asset made by the conceptual legal theories, the concept has covered the dimensions of property rights, intellectual property rights and the quasi-property rights. If we view property law and asset law historically and systematically, two conclusions could be drawn: First, three kinds of rights have absolute rights of control over nature, but it differs due to the characteristics of each object. Second, two common features were abstracted from property rights, intellectual property and quasi

1 Xu Diyu: "Reconstruction of the concept of environmental changes and property rights system", *Law Science Magazine*, 2003, 9th issue.

2 Wang Liming: "Re-explore the concept of property rights", *Zhejiang Social Sciences,* 2002, 2nd issue. 2.

3 Yin Tian: Definition and nature of property rights, *Peking University Law Journal*, 2002, 3rd issue.

property rights against property rights. In the future Civil Code, we may learn from the Dutch approach to establish general provisions of asset law in general rules of property rights.[1]

The doctrine of numerus is a basic principle of property law, which reflects the important feature of the property law as imperative law. The formation of the legal principle of the numerus clause can be attributed to the anti-feudal hierarchy, the refinement of property rights, the necessity of safeguarding the basic economic system of a country and the need of facilitating the disclosure of property ownership information to maintain the security of transactions and reduce transaction costs.[2] However, there are some scholars worried about the limitations of this principle, and they argued that the doctrine of numerous may harm the flexibility of the law, inhibits the emergence of new types of property rights and represses the innovative capacity of the civil society. In current China, adopting this legal principle may cause a lot of problems, including the challenges that the law will lose touch with reality, and will damage the existing arrangements for diversification and the innovations in the society.[3]Some also believe that under property rights legal mode, although the party cannot create any property rights other than legally required, there are still freedom of choices in selecting legal type of property rights. Thus, in the property rights legislation, it should be designed to meet a variety of types of social life property rights needed to strengthen the freedom of parties to choose the type of property rights. While promoting subject with benefits and assurances of the economic function, it can also realize certain of its social security and environmental protection features.[4] However, some scholars unequivocally adhere to this principle, that

1 Xu Diyu "Understanding property law historically and systematically", *Law Science Magazine*, 2002 4th issue.

2 Yin Tian "Discussing Property Law principle explanation and its basis", *Henan Institute of Political Science*, 2002, 4th issue.

3 Yang Yuxi "Discussing Property Law legal doctrine", *Study of Comparative Law*, 2002, 1st issue.

4 Xu Diyu "Property rights doctrine and legislation", *Studies in Law and Business*, 2002, 5th issue.

the crux of the current property rights legislation is insufficient with statutory rigidity of the property rights, and only if highlighting the importance of statutory property rights can move forward accordingly. Property rights law can base on the objective requirements of social economic development to regulate new category of property rights, in order to meet the needs of the people to choose the type of property rights.[1]

Since 1995, the change of property rights has become a hot topic within the civil law academic circle, which led to many influential works. The most intensely discussed subject is the real right behaviour theory. The civil law academic circle still has varied opinions on the independence of the property rights act. Proponets for property rights act believe that the property rights act exist in both life and transaction in reality, and no matter whether acknowledged or not by the legislators, its existence cannot be denied. The theory's advocate Sun Xianzhong said: "The creation of non-existent property rights must follow the property rights publicity principle and legal principle, not on the basis of the contract law freedom principle. The creation of the property rights contract should not be summarized as the debt law behavior of contract, nor should we apply debt law contract specifications to guide such property rights behaviour. Creation of property rights must be publicized, and the establishment of property rights must be publicized in order to be valid..... The existence of property acts not only complies realistically but also legally."[2] However, the opponents against this theory argue that the property rights of act is purely fictional by scholars, and it is seriously divorced from social realities of life, contrary to common sense and common sense transaction: "This theory has fabricated the property rights act independent of the debt act, and caused further fragmentation towards the relations between reason and property rights act. This is in line with the German

1 Hong Hailin, Shi Min, "Doctrine of Specific Right in Rem", *Modern Law Science*, No.3, 2003.

2 Sun Xianzhong, *Origin and Meaning of Theory of Property Act*, published in Issue No.3 of *Legal Study*, 1996.

way of thinking towards preference for abstraction, and it is a serious distortion of the realistic law of life process, which is harmful for the applicable law. There is no doubt that it is worthless."[1] "If the transfer of ownership of the subject matter and the price stripped out from the sale of consensual, the sale contract would be gone." [2]With our well established trading market and the needed enhancement of precise adjustment on realistic transaction, our legislation and most scholars especially young scholars showed tendency to accept the theory. *Property Rights Law* avoided the Property Act system, but the occurrence of the entry into force of the debt rights contract and the property rights efficacy using the principle of distinction. Non-cause property rights act is much blamed by civil law academic circle, and objecting the independence of the property rights act is even more serious. Some scholars used German first-hand information, combed in detail the non-cause system of property rights act, and conducted in-depth research on related systems, combined with domestic and international criticism on the non-cause theory point of view in order to have an effective defense for non-cause system.[3]

Defects of real estate registration system have long attracted the attention of scholars. Sun Xianzhong spent years of study of the system and called for the establishment of an improved real estate registration system. As early as 1996, Sun Xianzhong published theory on the basis of registered property and explored civil law of German and French property registration system for both similarities and differences between typical and theoretical foundation, as well as how our future legislation should choose.[4] He also pioneered the country's property

1 Liang Huixing, *Cases and Legislations of Civil Law*, China University of Political Science and Law Press, 1993.

2 Wang Liming, *Theory of Property Law, China* University of Political Science and Law Press, 1998.

3 Tian Shiyong, Study on Theory of Property Act, *Journal of China University of Political Science and Law,* 2002.

4 See Sun Xianzhong, On Registration of Real Estate Ownership, *China Legal Science*, 1996, No.5.

registration of the "five reunification" principle, namely, the legal basis for unified registration, unified registration authority, unified registration effectiveness, unified registration process and on the basis of a unified property registration book of the consolidated ownership certificate.[1] There is also a detailed discussion of scholars on property registration system in various systems (such as dissidence registration, notice of registration, non-registration of legal acts based on acquired ownership of property, etc.). These findings about the property rights registration were adopted by the 2007's *Property Law*.

Property claims as an independent type of rights which are side by side with debt claims are special content in property rights. Civil law academic circle previously focuses on the discussions of property claims nature, statute of limitations, etc.[2]With the launching of Tort Law in legislative work, the current hot discussion within civil law academic circle is the relationship with the property claims rights and tort claims. Most of the scholars advocated that the absolute right of way claims should be separated from and tort liability area.[3]

3.4 A Study on the Theory of Property Law Points

In ownership rights regime, state ownership and collective ownership have always been a problem in the field of property rights law. Most views believe that there should not be a distinction between ownership system and ownership rights, and public ownership should be advocated to redefine public ownership and recognize the legal ownership rights.[4] But another paper from the characteristic angle of state ownership believe that the national ownership legislation should contact through a unified legal mutual and cooperation, in accordance with general

1 Sun Xianzhong, *General Principles on Chinese Real Rights Law*, Law Press, 2003.

2 See Hou Lihong, *On Right of Claim for Real Things*, published in Vol.6 of *Civil and Commercial Law Review*, Law Press, 1997;Yin Tian, *On the Institutional Value of the Right of Real Claim*, Issue No.4 of *Law Science*, 2001.

3 See Wang Liming, Volume I. of *Study on Tort Law*, China Renmin University Press, 2004; Cui Jianyuan, *Claim of Absolute Right or Method of Tort Liability*, published in Issue 11 of *Law Science Magazine*, 2002.

4 See Sun Xianzhong, *Right Structure of Ownership System in China's Property Law*, published in Issue No.5 of *Studies in Law and Business*, 2002.

legislative ideas of publicized private law and privatized public law, cited by the property law generalize formula legislative and state-owned assets management act formula legislative technique, in order to set up national ownership system.[1]In the "Property Law" making process, academic circle had appeared if "Property Law" is with the surname socialism or capitalism, if there is no unconstitutional, if it will encourage and condone the loss of state assets and if it will enable the debate to legalize illegal assets, one of the core arguments is the state ownership issues.[2] "Property Law" finally went on with the practice of civil law general provisions.

Since the 1990s, condominium ownership has become a hot property law research. From such ownership to property management (service) and the owners of autonomy, academic circle have done a lot of research. "Property Law" stipulates this system but did not elaborate in which triggered a lively discussion. In 2009, the Supreme Court adopted the relevant condominium ownership and property services judicial interpretation to absorb the reasonable opinions of these discussions.

Bona fide acquisition during this period is a hot issue for discussion. Scholars focused the discussion on the constituent elements of bona fide acquisition, such as confirmed "goodwill", bona fide acquisition and non-cause property rights act, unauthorized disposition relations, etc. But in the study of the relationship between the traditional civil law bona fide acquisition and real estate registration credibility is still not deep enough, "Property Law" Article 107 made a major innovation and stipulates that real estate can also be applied using bona fide acquisition.

Usufruct law best embodies property rights law to solve the contradiction of modern resources tensions and demand tension system. It embodies the "best use" of property rights law pursuing for value. For usufruct, academic circle put

1 Zhou Linbin, Wang Ye, *On Legislation and Mode Selection of China's State Ownership*, *Tribune of Political Science and Law*, 2002, No.3.

2 Gong Xiantian, '*Property Law Draft*' *Breaching Constitution*, [EB/OL].http://www.Chinaelections.com.

more research on it. But for the land ownership under this background, if usufruct system effect is being used into full play, it is indeed a big problem worthy of deep thinking. The representative view of usufruct is that, based on the development needs of China's market economy system, the fair and orderly use of property, human survival and development needs and China's property law self-property rights and structural rights of other property rights; usufruct system should be constructed including surface rights, agricultural land contract rights, pawning rights, residency rights and easements, etc.[1]But for the kinds of usufruct, the academic controversy is quite large such as whether or not to set the residential area, etc. One of the typical research topic model or argumentation paradigm research is that whether it should put up some kind of usufruct. If there is paper argues that should transform the traditional usufruct to meet new needs, the idea is to first think usufruct has changed a lot in modern time: First, you can have a clear deadline; second, to expand the scope of the subject matter; third, transferability enhancement; and fourth, the function has changed. Chinese civil law can borrow the "shell" of usufruct to construct enterprise usufruct, natural resources and space usufruct.[2] "Property Law" largely absorbed the research result from scholars, and Article 117 provision may stipulate movable property may provide usufruct, which affirmed the view of some scholars.

Security interest is the study of a mature field in China, there are many related writings. Since the 1990s, scholars discussed mainly the security interest not regulated in China, such as system of elimination rights, all mortgage, competing and cooperating property insurance and life insurance, term mortgage, legal mortgage (often combined with "Contract Law" Article 286 discussion), pledge of rights, competing and cooperating guarantee property rights. The cis-position discussion is one of the typical research. There is paper which discusses in detail

1 See Qian Mingxing, *Existence Basis for China's Usufruct System*, *Zhejiang Social Sciences*, 2002, No.2

2 See Qu Maohui, *Origin of Usufruct Right and Reference in China's Civil Law*, *Law Science*, 2002, No.3.

the meaning, principle, form and change of cis-position.[1] Due to space limitations, it will not be elaborated here. *Property Law* embodies the research results of the security interests of academic circle, such as security interest to achieve reforms (Article 170) condition, independence (Article 172) guarantees, competing and cooperating property insurance and life insurance (Article 176), a new kind of pledge of rights (Article 223), etc.

Possession is one of the most complex and core contents in property law, but our overall research is still very weak in this area. In recent years, some scholars have deepened the research on this issue. Some scholars from the perspective of property claims rights discuss the possession of the most sophisticated owner-possessor relationship rules.[2]Savigny's classic book *On the Possession* (Zhu Hu, Liu Zhihui translation, Law Press, 2007 edition) has been translated into Chinese. Liu Zhihui published *Possession System Principle* (People's University of China Press, 2007), Zhou Mei published *Indirect Possession of Restitution* (Law Press, 2007 edition). Possession provisions of the property law are quite simple, and it is expected that there will be a culmination of research in possession system in the future.

4. New Progress on Civil Law Debt Rights Study

4.1 Studies on Contract Law

Contract law is one of the most studied areas in the civil law academic circle. In 1992, especially since the adoption of contract law in 1999, contract law research has entered a new phase. All kinds of textbooks, books and monographs are out there. (1) Textbook works like *Contract Law* (Cui Jianyuan, Law Press, 2004), *General Contract Law* (Zhu Guangxin, People's University of China Press, 2008) and etc. (2) Contract law system works as *The Introduction of Anglo-American Contract Law* (Shen Daming, Foreign Trade University Press, 1993 edition),

1 Chang Pengao, *On Cis-position, Civil and Commercial Law Review,* Vol 25.

2 Wang Hongliang, *On Relationship between Owner and Possessor: Claim for Restitution and Secondary Claim Right*, Volume 1 of *Study on China and German Private Law*, 2006, Peking University Press, 2006.

Modern French Contract Law (Yin Tian, Law Press, 1995 edition), *Contract Law (Part I)* (Cui Jianyuan, People's University of China Press, 2008), Cui Jianyuan coauthored *The New Contract Law General Principles* (Wang Liming, China University of Political Science Press, 1997), *The New Contract Law Sub Principles* (Guo Mingrui, Wang Yi, China University of Political Science Press, 1997), *Principle of Contract Law* (Xie Huaishi, Law Press, 2000), *Principle of Contract Law* (Wang Liming, China People's University of Press, 2003), *Contract Law* (Li Yongjun, Law Press, 2004), *Contract Law Introduction* (Han Shiyuan, Law Press, 2004 edition), etc. (3)Monographs on contract law studies, such as *Breach of Contract Liability Theory* (Wang Liming, China University of Political Science Press, 2003), *Research on Compensation for Breach of Contract* (Han Shiyuan, Law Press, 1999), *Performance Obstacles Law System* (Law Press, 2006), *20th Century Contract Law* (Fu Jingkun, Law Press, 1997), *American Contract Law* (Wang Jun, Foreign Economic and Trade University Press, 2004), *Default Rule of Research* (Ge Yunsong, China University of Political Science Press, 2003), *Cause Theory* (Xu Diyu, China University of Political Science Press, 2005), *New German Payment Obstacles Law Research* (Du Jinglin and Lu Chen, Foreign Economic and Trade University Press, 2006), *Studies on Discharge of Contract in Anglo-American Law* (Li Xianbo, Peking University Press, 2008), *Basic Contract Law: Cases and Materials* (Li Xiang, China University of Political Science Press, 2008 edition), etc. (4) Contract law also has a considerable number of translations, such as Wang Weiguo, Xu Guodong translation of *Corbin on Contracts* (Encyclopedia of China Publishing House, 1997), Zhang Wenzhen such as translation of *English Contract Law and Cases* (Geist, Encyclopedia of China Publishing House, 1998), Wang Shujiang such as translation of *Debt Law Supremacy in Modern Civil Law* (Wagatsuma Sakae, Encyclopedia of China Publishing House, 1999), Zhou Zhonghai translated *European Contract Law* (Hein Klotz Law Press, 2001 edition), Ge Yunsong, Ding Chunyan translation of *American Contract Law* (Vance Worth, China University of Political Science Press, 2004), Zhang Jiayong translation of *The Philosophical Origins of Modern*

Contract Doctrine (James Gordley, Law Press, 2006 edition), Chen Yanming such as translation of *Understanding Contract* (Ferrier, Peking University Press, 2009 edition), Gao Shengping translation *American Uniform Commercial Code and Its Official Comments* (People's University of China Press, 2005), etc.One of the major changes in the 20th century contract law is freedom of contract has been subjected to many restrictions, so that American jurist Gilmer exclaimed contract "death". Civil law academic circle translated related foreign works.[1] In addition, there are a lot of works studying the changes of 20th century contract law, namely the expansion of contractual obligations.[2]Civil law academic circle made a general consensus on the "Duties" of contract law that the results of the research embodied in Article 42 (pre-contractual obligations) contract law, Article 60 (collateral obligations) and Article 92 (post-contractual obligation).

Prior to 1999, the research on the validity of the contract focused on the effectiveness of fraud and duress established contracts. Many scholars believe that the effectiveness of such contracts shall normally be voidable contract, and *Contract Law* Article 52 and Article 54 adopted this conclusion. Just around 1999, the civil law scholars discussed the effectiveness of the contract focused on the non-right disposition. Non-right disposition is considered to be the ghost of law on breeding a lot of trouble and strife. After the *Contract Law* Article 51 of the provisions concerning the introduction of non-right disposition, academic circles attempted to determine "effect pending" behavior of non-right disposition on whether it is a debt contract or property contract and has generated significant controversy. One view insists on the validity of the contract of creditor's rights.[3] Another view insists on property change not taking effect. There is no doubt that

1 Grant·Guillermo, translated by Cao Shibin, *Death of Contracts*, Neitiangui, translated by Hu Baohai, *Regeneration of Contracts*, Volume 3 of *Civil and Commercial Law Review*, Law Press, 1995.

2 Fu Jingkun, *20th Century Law of Contract*, Law Press, 1997.

3 Wang Liming, "On Punishment Without Right", Issue No.3, *China Legal Science*, 2001. Liang Huixing, "Change in Property Right and Punishment Without Right", pp.253-254, *Struggling for China's Civil Code*, Law Press, 2002.

the dispute is related to whether to recognize the independence of property act or not. The scholars not recognizing the independence of property act insist on the first view, and others have insisted on the second view.

After 1999, civil law academic circle made consensus to narrow the scope of the invalid contract. Representative view think that the legal act is invalid systems to safeguard the interests of society as their starting point, prohibit or sanction the abuse of the principle of private autonomy act to repair the damage behavior of private autonomy abuse to society. Reducing state intervention in the field of private law, giving the parties greater freedom of action, and narrowing the scope of an invalid legal act should be a guiding principle.[1] For invalid contracts, civil law academic circle focuses on the discussion of the Contract Law Article 52 (5) provision. Although the article "illegal" limit is "in violation of laws, administrative regulations, mandatory provisions" to correct the past simple idea of "illegal = invalid", but the scope is still too broad. Many papers discussed different aspects of solution. Papers pointed out that invalid imputation guiding principle of illegal public law contracts is: the purpose of public law must be implemented and private law must be subjected to the interests of public law. The effect of violating imperative law on private law relates to the balance between the two values, i.e. try best to achieve the mandatory provisions, as well as fairness, faith and security of transactions between both parties.[2] Many papers also draw on the distinction of traditional civil law "validity criterion" and "ban criterion", creating a variety of names to distinguish criterion types, in order to limit the scope of the criterion. Papers further believed that the illegal law should be limited to public law, and it should distinguish breach of public law invalid and breach of private law "not effective" (the state does not sanction such behavior, but at the time the parties

1 See Zhang Guangxing, "Invalid Legal Act - from General Rules of Civil Law to Civil Code Draft", Issue No.6, *Legal Forum*, 2003.

2 See Jie Gen, "On Effect of Contract Breaching Compulsory Regulations", Issue No.1, *Peking University Law Journal*, 2003.

dispute, use as referee criterion).[1]Contract law judicial interpretation (b) Article 14 absorbed the research achievements of scholars, and invalid process will not be done in violation of the management law.

In contract area, the main issue of concern within civil law academic circle in recent years include: (1) Expected Breach of Contract and Precarious Right to Defense. China's Contract Law Article 94 and Article 108 introduce the system of anticipatory breach of common law from British and American law, Article 68 and Article 69 also provide precarious right to defense system. Both have similar functions and how to distinguish both in its application is a focus of concern from the civil law academic circle. Some scholars have discussed the distinction between the two, reviewed the relationship between precarious right of defense and anticipatory breach of contract that the contract law only provides for refusal to perform as expected anticipatory breach of contract and did not confirm that it is not necessary to confirm not expected to perform as expected breach of contract. The latter is equivalent to the civil law unable to treat the payment, performed by the precarious right of defense, fulfilling right of defenses orderly and at the same time fulfilling the right of defense at the same time, respectively. After the expected default occurs, the creditor may choose to recognize anticipatory breach of contract, or choose not to recognize. However, this right of option should be limited.[2] (2) Relates to other contract (contract for the benefit of third party), that the contracting parties not to set their own right, but for the interests of the third party contracts entered into force on the third person. The key point of the debate focused on Contract Law Article 64 whether it has given a third party independent request right.[3] There are also doctoral thesis papers devoted on the theoretical

1 See Xie Hongfei, On *Applicable Regulations on Effectiveness of Legal Acts*, Issue No.6, *Social Science in China*, 2007.

2 See Lan Chenglie, *Rethinking on Expected Default and Uneasy Right of Pleadings*, Issue No.3, *China Legal Science*, 2002.

3 See Yin Tian, "Talking about Involvement Contract", Issue No.1, *Legal Study*, 2001.

context and legislation of this issue.[1]

Since 1999, civil law academic circle discussions on contract termination focused on the Contract Law Article 96 (the way of contract termination), that is how to recognize the observant directly suing without notifying the defaulting party. Also involved is the relation between termination of contract and damages compensation, especially relation with the termination of the contract and liquidated damages clauses. In terms of breach of contract, civil law academic circle focus of the study is: (1) Predictable Rule. This rule and contract law concept have many conflicts: as full compensation, strict liability principle, there are papers from the principle of full compensation, legislation comparison, the principles of contract breach responsibility, causation, theoretical composition and others addresses this rule.[2] Predictable rules are more favorable to the protection of the interests of creditors.[3] (2) Whether breach of contract can be applied for moral damage compensation. The mainstream view is that, in certain circumstances indemnification must be given to parties for non-pecuniary damage suffered due to breach of contract and proposed categorizing the types of breach of non-material damage.[4] (3) Application of liquidated damages. There are papers arguing that, in principle, delay execution and incomplete execution of the agreed liquidated damages, regarded as appropriate compensation rates.[5]

Civil law academic circle does not have much deep study in contract law subsystem. The monograph in this area mainly include Ge Mingrui and Wang Yi's *On New Contract Law* (China University of Political Science Press, 1997), Liu

1 Zhang Jiayong, *System Structure of Contract for Benefit of Third Persons*, Law Press, 2007.

2 Lan Chenglie, Yan Renhe, "On Foreseeability Rule of Damage Compensation for Breaching", Vol.24, *Civil and Commercial Law Review.*

3 Lan Chenglie, Yan Renhe, "Comparative Study on Foreseeability Principle", Issue No.4, *Learning and Exploration*, 2000.

4 Chen Xiao, "Breach of Contract and Non Property Damage Compensation", Volume 25, *Civil and Commercial Law Review.*

5 Han Shiyuan, "Theory Issue of Delayed Performance", published in Issue No.4, *Tsinghua University Journal* (philosophy and social science edition), 2002.

Jia'an *Legal Structure of Trading* (China University of Political Science Press, 2003), Yi Jun and Ning Hongli *Contract Law Subsystem Research* (People's Court Press, 2003), Fang Xinjun *Modern Society in New Contract Research* (People's University of China Press, 2005) and so on. The academic has studied more on the new types of contract. A typical research paper on the subject, made a comprehensive study of the travel contract to study the rights and obligations of both parties, the third party payment, travel contract change and release, breach of contract and mental damages compensation claims, travel time waste claims, travel contract and format of the contract.[1] The studies are very valuable that contract law is not yet specified in the contract carried out when they appear in large numbers in real life, and can also provide valuable material for the development of the Civil Code.

4.2 Research on Tort Law

Compared with the contract, tort law is a weak link in our country. But after 1995, especially for the push after drafting the *Tort Liability Act*, research on tort law has also made remarkable achievements, resulting in the outstanding research achievements of a large number of tort law. (1) For the materials on tort law, mainly from Wang Liming *Civil Law &Tort Law* (People's University of China Press, 1993 Edition), Wang Liming, Yang Lixin *Tort Law*, Law Press, 1996), Zhang Xinbao *China Tort Law* (Second Edition) (China Social Sciences Press, 1998 Edition), Yang Lixin *Tort Law* (Fudan University Press 2005 Edition). (2) For the tort law system works mainly from Yang Lixin *The Tort Law Theory* (Jilin People's Publishing Press, 1998 Edition), Wang Liming *Tort Behavior Law Research* (People's University of China Press, 2004), Yin Zhiqiang, *The Tort Law Theory* (China University of Political Science and Law Press, 2008 Edition), *Tort Behavior Law Pandect* (Cheng Xiao, People's University of China Press, 2008 Edition). (3) For the tort law related monograph is from *Legal Protection of*

1 See Ning Hongli, "Tourism Contract Study", Volume 22, *Civil and Commercial Law Review*.

Privacy Tort Law (Zhang Xinbao, Chinese Social Science Press, 1995 Edition), *Legal Protection of the Reputation Right* (China University of Political Science and Law Press, 1997 Edition), *The Principle of Tort Liability Law* (People's University of China Press, 2005 Edition), *Research of Japanese Legal System of Compensation for Damages in Motor Vehicle Accidents* (Li Wei, Law Press, 1997 Edition), *Japanese Tort Law* (Yu Min, Law Press, 1998 Edition), *Motor Vehicle Damage Compensation Liability and Contributory Negligence* (Law Press, 2004 Edition), *Research on Legislation of Medical Damage Compensation* (Gong Saihong, Law Press, 2001 Edition), *Principle of Tort Law Liability Study* (Second Edition) (Wang Liming, China University of Political Science and Law Press, 2004 Edition), *Tort Law* (Higher Education Press, 2005 Edition), *Tort Damages* (Law Press, 2008 Edition), *Principle and Practice of Tort Law Strict Liability* (Wang Jun, Law Press, 2006 Edition), *Anglo American Tort Law* (Xu Aiguo, Peking University Press, 2004 Edition), *Research Status of Tort Law* (Ma Changhua, China University of Political Science and Law press, 2004 Edition), *Research of Fault Tort Liability System* (Zhang Minan, China University of Political Science and Law Press, 2002 Edition), *University Tort Liability* (Zhongshan University Press, 2007 Edition), *Walking Down the Altar – Research on Basic Problems of Civil Liability* (Jiang Yunwei, Law Press, 2008 Edition), *Vicarious Liability of Employers* (Cao Yanfang, Law Press, 2008 Edition), *Pure Economic Loss Compensation System Study* (Li Hao, Peking University Press, 2004), *Transaction Safety Obligation Theory* (Peking University Press, 2008 - 2009 Edition), *Communication Security Obligations Study* (Zhou Youjun, People's University of China Press, 2008 Edition), *Causation Theory in Tort Law Research*, (Liu Xinping, Law Press, 2008 Edition) and etc. (4) Translated monographs about the tort law mainly from Zhang Xiaoyi, Zhong Hongming translation of *Pure Economic Loss in Europe* (Bussani and Palmer, Law Press, 2005 Edition), Zhang Xinbao, Jiao Meihua translation of *The Common European Law of Torts* (Von Bar, Law Press 2004 Edition), Qi Xiaokun translation of *Deliktsrecht* (Fukesi, Law Press 2006 Edition) and so on.

In 1920s, civil law circle had the theories of crisis and downfall of tort law as modern tort law, especially no fault liability and all responsibility bearing mechanisms (social guarantee, insurance and compensation) strike the foundation of traditional tort law to a greater extent. A thesis reflects on this issue and holds that traditional tort law has to seek its moral foundation with sense of justice so as to avoid the death, which is the primary mission for 21st century tort law. The liability system of tort law should be integrated into a new fault liability principle system so as to eliminate internal inharmoniousness of tort law. In addition, this thesis combines economic, social and scientific conditions of this century to point out that expansive expression of the 21st tort law is private law relief of human right, environmental tort, specially large hazardous activities, scientific and technological development and international function of tort law.[1]

General provisions of tort law provide the legal norms which are at the core of statute law and become the basis for all right of claim of tort. [2]How to determine general provisions of tort law is a very important theory and practice issue and so civil law circle has many discussions on this topic lately. "General provisions + categorization" has become a development trend of contemporary tort law. The general provisions of tort laws of continental European countries have different modes and civil law experts have big dispute over which mode should be chosen. Some scholars think that the mode of "overall general provisions + overall listing" should be taken. [3] Some scholars think limited general provisions should be taken. In fact, it relates to interest protection of tort law and its extent and the mode of general provisions helps granting the judge with discretionary power and determines the protection of interests in individual cases.

1 Ma Changhua, "Revolution of 21st Tort Law", Issue No.6, *Studies in Law and Business*, 2002.

2 Zhang Xinbao, "General Provisions on Tort Law", Issue No.4, *Law Study*, 2001.

3 Zhang Xinbao, "*Tort Law Legislation Mode: Overall General Provisions + Overall Listing*", Issue No.4, *Jurist*, 2003.

Pure economic loss has been a hot topic in study on tort law recent years and it relates to the scope of rights and interests protected by tort law. A thesis focuses on discussing main types of pure economic losses: tort liability of negligence borne by professional for client, tort liability borne by actor for a third person due to negligence statement, liability of compensation for pure economic losses due to construction or product defect, tort liability of negligence due to relevant economic losses from infringement. [1]The scholars have a consistent view that not all pure economic losses can be protected but nor no pure economic losses are protected. Instead, we should take strict restrictive legislative and judicial strategies. There are different viewpoints on how to make restrictions. Some scholars think that we should restrict by breaching good practices and customs and judicial determination of casual relations should take "principle of proximate cause" and the victim can only claim for direct losses.[2]

The relation between unlawfulness and fault is one of the most complex issues in constituent elements of tort. The academic circle has been disputing over independence of unlawful elements. Most experts stand for the independence of unlawful elements and China's future tort law should specify unlawful elements as meaning and function of unlawfulness are different from those of fault; theoretical basis for justified act can only be unlawfulness; recognizing unlawfulness helps design the rules with unlawfulness not fault as element; categorize unlawful act of infringing other rights and interests than absolute rights and interests and respond to and promote relevant judicial practices.[3] Some scholars pointed out that different from evaluating negligence of subjective attitude of actor, the lawfulness relates to whether the interests protected by law are objectively damaged or

1 Zhang Minan, "Tort Liability for Negligence for Pure Economic Losses for Infringement", Vol.25, *Civil and Commercial Law Review*.

2 Zhu Guangxin, "On Standard Mode for Pure Economic Losses", Vol.25, *Contemporary Law Review*, 2006. Wang Liming also focuses on casual relation restrictions, *Study on Tort Law (I)*, pp.381-384, Law Press, China, 2004.

3 Zhang Jinhai, "On Independence of Constituent Elements of Infringement", Issue No.4, *Tsinghua Law Review*, 2007.

not. In addition, the element has the functions of limiting free space for act, safeguarding legitimate interests and shaping right.[1] Currently, the academic circle has universally accepted the theory of corresponding casual relation and casual relation between composition and scope of liability, and also has in-depth study on the relation between casual relation and fault.

Security obligation theory is a new theory introduced by China's study on tort law recent years. [2]The scholars pointed out that security obligation should be reformed to serve as general provisions for negligence tort and be brought under general provisions for China's fault tort. [3]In 2003, Article 6 of the Supreme Court's Judicial Interpretations on Compensation for Person Damage (FS [2003] No.20) confirms on security obligation and currently, civil law circle has some in-depth researches on this aspect.

Research focuses and important questions on infringement damage compensation are as follows: (1) punitive compensation system. This system is contrary to the principle of full compensation and so it is excluded by civil law system. Some scholars suggested introducing common law system. [4]Some scholars retort from the perspective of social function of tort law and think that punitive function has disappeared in tort law and so China should not introduce punitive compensation system. [5] (2) "Similar life with different price" issue. China takes total objective – abstract standard for death compensation and has less study on death compensation. Social circles have heated discussions on "similar life with different price" set forth in Article 26 and Article 29 of the Judicial

1 Ye Jinqiang, "Positioning of Constitutive Elements of Crime in Tort", Issue No.1, *Law Science*, 2007.

2 Zhang Xinbao, Tang Qinglin, "Operators' Security Obligation in Business Places", Issue No.3, *Law Study*, 2003.

3 Zhou Youjun, "On General Provisions in China's Fault Tort", Issue No.1, *Law Science*, 2007.

4 Wang Liming, "Study on America's Punitive Compensation System", Issue 2, *Tort Law Review*, 2003.

5 Yin Zhiqiang, "Social Functions of Tort Law", Issue No.5, *Political and Legal Forum*, 2007.

Interpretations on Compensation for Person Damage. Some scholars pointed out that legal consequence of damaging right of life is not the compensation for the price of life itself and China's current legislation and judicial practices take an "improved" inheritance system, and this principle is mistaken as "urban and rural dual discrimination" in practice. [1] However, academic circle has no in-depth discussion on this issue. (3) Compensation for mental damage. Mental damage is a hot research topic in China. The scholars have expanded the application scope of compensation for mental damage by making expansive interpretation of the *Product Liability Law* and the *Consumers' Protection Law*. The scholars' theories about compensation for mental damage have been assimilated by the Supreme Court's judicial interpretations on mental damage (FS [2001] No.7). We see relatively fast change in judicial interpretations about the nature of "death compensation" and "disability compensation" and also insufficient discussions in academic circle. Some scholars discussed the damages of "mental shock" in common law system and proposed that China should establish "mental shock" damage compensation system and further improve China's system of compensation for mental damage.[2]

Recent years, China's civil law circle's discussions on special tort are mainly as follows: (1) Employer liability. The academic circle discussed much about liability principle and recently focuses more on special issues of employer's liability, such as labor dispatch.[3] (2) Traffic accident liability for motor vehicles. The scholars opened discussions on Article 76 of the *Road Traffic Safety Law* and China's compulsory traffic accident liability. Still some scholars discussed very important

1 Yao Hui, Qiu Peng, "On Compensation on Damaging Right of Life", Issue No.4, *Journal of Renmin University of China*, 2006.

2 Zhang Xinbao, Gao Yanzhu, "Damage Compensation System of Mental Shock in Common Law System and its References", Issue No.5, *Studies in Law and Business*, 2007.

3 Zhang Ling, Zhu Dong, "On Employer Liability of Labor Dispatch", Issue No.4, *Jurist*, 2007.

issue – liability subject in practice. [1](3) Expert liability, especially expert third person liability, has become the research focus of China's tort law and has been deepened and refined. (4) Medical accident compulsory liability. (5) Internet infringement liability.

5. Research on Law Science of Marriage and Family After Return to Civil Law

For 18 years from 1992 to 2009, it is a period of prosperity in which legal construction and legal study of China's marriage and family has been continuously improved and deepened. Since Marriage and Family Law Research Institute of China Law Society put forward suggestions of amending legislation of the Marriage Law in 1990,[2] it undertook key topic "Research on Legislation of Improving Marriage and Family Law" of China Law Society in 1992 and published topic achievement *Chinese Marriage and Life Toward 21st Century* in 1995.[3] This book was written by all members of the society and makes systematic demonstration of necessity and feasibility of amending Marriage Law, systematic structure of revision and concrete system designing so as to provide theoretical support for legislation organization for revision. In 1994, the NPC Internal and Judicial Affairs Committee held demonstration meeting for amending the Marriage Law and relevant participating department personnel and scholars hold that amending the Marriage Law is not only necessary but also feasible.[4] In October, 1995, 16th meeting of 8th Standing Committee of the National People's Congress passed the decision on amending Marriage Law of the People's Republic of China and listed it under "Ninth Five-year Plan" legislation planning.

---

1 Cheng Xiao, "Study on Liability Subject of Damage Compensation for Motor Vehicles", Issue No.4, *Law Study*, 2006.

2 Wu Changzheng, Wang Deyi, Yang Dawen, *Problems of Contemporary Chinese Marriage and Family*, People's Press, 1990.

3 Wu Changzheng, Yang Dawen, *Chinese Marriage and Life Toward 21st Century*, Jilin People's Publishing House, 1995.

4 Wang Mei, *Marriage Law Should Adapt to New Situation – Interview With Wu Changzheng, Director of Marriage Law Research Institute of China Law Society*, data source: http://www.chinalawedu.com/news/21604.htm2005-2-6.

In November, 1996, leading team and office amending the Marriage Law was set up. Law revision team invited six experts of Marriage and Family Law Research Institute to set up drafting team,[1] finishing the 1st and 2nd draft of Marriage and Family Law from November 1996 to June 1997; soliciting local opinions on the drafts from June to September 1997 and organizing relevant departments and experts and scholars to make demonstration, and finishing 3rd and 4th draft of the Marriage and Family Law from September to December of December 1999.[2] Later, Working Commission for Legal Affairs of Standing Committee of the National People's Congress started amending the draft of the Marriage Law. Through opinions solicitation, discussions and revisions, on April 28, 2001, 21st Standing Committee of the 9th National People's Congress passed the Marriage Law of the People's Republic of China (revision) and implemented it nationally as of April 28, 2001.

Different from previous law amendment, this amendment of the Marriage Law did not only have law experts to participate in but also is a process of national participation in legislation. In January 2001, the Standing Committee of the National People's Congress published the Marriage Law of the People's Republic of China (draft amendment) to solicit opinions nationally. Within one month, Working Commission for Legal Affairs of Standing Committee of the National People's Congress received more than 4000 letters and called regarding suggestions on law amendments from workers, peasants, intellectuals, public servants, judicial workers, students and military. It is unprecedented for the amendment of a law to attract so extensive attentions and ongoing public discussion in China's legislation history. It further indicates that Marriage and Family Law relates to all households and it is a law relating to all women and men and its universal application is just

1 Six experts: Yang Dawen, Wu Changzheng, Wang Deyi, Chen Mingxia, Xia Yinwen, Long Yifei. Convener: Yang Dawen.

2 This proposal is finalized after revisions by experts of drafting group on several annual meetings of marriage law research institute, with 11 chapters and 147 clauses. See Liang Huixing, *Civil and Commercial Law Review Vol.14*, Law Press, 2000. pp.770 -779.

secondary to constitution. [1] Also it reflects that people have changed their opinions and enhanced rights awareness since the reforming and opening up. Years later, Chen Mingxia, one of drafting experts, was still excited at mentioning the law amendment process and she said that to some extent, China's amendment process of Marriage Law is far more significant than the amendment result of the Marriage Law. The amendment process of the Marriage Law will generate profound influence on promoting China's legislation democratic process and also promoting China's democratic and legislative construction and social democratic process.[2]

At the end of 2001, it is said that legislative organization would review the Civil Law Draft of the People's Republic of China for the first time after the amendment of the Marriage Law was implemented for half a year. In the draft Civil Law, prevailing Marriage Law and Adoption Law are respectively two independent parts, which is the demonstration of two-step amendment of the Marriage Law by legislative organization. Entrusted by the Working Commission for Legal Affairs of Standing Committee of the National People's Congress, the experts from Marriage and Family Law Research Institute in Beijing drafted the expert proposal of marriage and family volume of Civil Code in April 2002.[3] In the above context, legislative study is still a priority among priorities at the stage of study and it has two aspects: the study on amendment of Marriage Law and the study on formulating marriage and family volume of Civil Code.

5.1 Study on Amendment of Marriage Law

The academic circle of marriage law carried out study of years on law amendment for years after the Marriage Law is introduced under legislative

1 See Chen Shaoyu, *Report on Procedures and Reasons for Drafting of Marriage Law of the People's Republic of China*, April, 1950.

2 Chen Mingxia, *Review on Amendment to China's Marriage Law*, published on International Visions with Local Practice edited by Xue Ninglan, China Social Science Press, 2008. p.201.

3 Members of drafting group of civil law and marriage and family: Wu Changzheng, Li Zhongfang, Wang Deyi, Chen Mingxia, Xia Yinlan, Li Mingshun. Wu Changzheng is the person in charge.

planning. 1997-2000 annual meetings of Marriage and Family Law Research Institute focused on this topic. By summing up general review of annual meetings and writings of some scholars, we can conclude the hot spots and focus problems which the scholars pay attention to and discuss during law amendment period.

1. Legislation mode and systematic structure of Marriage and Family Law originated from 1997 annual meeting and the scholars have been paying attention to legislation mode. In 1999 annual meeting, scholars have formed initial consistent viewpoints on this and hold that independent code of "Marriage and Family Law of People's Republic of China" should be formulated. Some scholars proposed that the amended Marriage Law should be renamed as Family Law or family code of Civil Law, with the following reasons: (1) In 1986, General Principles of Civil Law solved the belonging of Marriage and Family Law from legislation mode and the legislation mode of amendment on the Marriage Law should based on this. (2) Civil law countries mostly use family law names and take them as one volume of civil code. China's adoption of family law name is consistent with international practice, and is easy to integrate into international practice and also lays a solid foundation for integration of legal systems after unification of across the Straits. (3) For 20 years, evolution trend of China's family law is that marriage partnership is gradually weakened and single families are downsizing. With growing cohabitations outside marriage and divorces, there are more and more illegitimate parent–child relationship and other illegitimate close relative relationships. It requires the Marriage Law to cover more extensive close relative relationships instead of marriage and family relationships. (4) Compared to other social security mechanisms, human relative security mechanism has characteristics of being more natural, direct and human being and so should dominate in personal daily life security mechanisms. Current operation coverage of the Marriage Law or Marriage and Family Law cannot meet these new social needs and only by formulating family law, can these

needs be satisfied.[1]

Also some scholars think that even though it is most scientific to adopt the Family Law names, the difficulty of legislation is huge in terms of feasibility. It requires amending thoroughly the prevailing Marriage Law and the laws with nature of Family Law such as prevailing Adoption Law and then consolidating them into Family Law. It will prolong the process of reform of the Marriage Law. If we adopt the name of Marriage and Family Law, the difficulty of legislation will be much smaller and it is easy to be accepted by Chinese citizens and legislative organizations and also we have relatively sufficient theoretical preparations. Therefore, they agree on and support the names of Family Law in theory but on the other side they think it is feasible and more practical to adopt the names of Marriage and Family Law currently.[2]

Regarding legislation status of Adoption Law, the scholars have two opinions. The first opinion is based on systematic nature and unification of law and stands for introducing the Adoption Law under the Marriage and Family Law. The second opinion is that considering the Adoption Law exists in the form of single law in China, they advocate retaining the Adoption Law but establishing the basic principles of adoption in the Marriage and Family Law.[3]

2. Void marriage system

For the amendment draft to the Marriage Law, the scholars put forward some insightful legislative suggestions for concept definition, institutional composition and legal consequences of void marriage through comparative study. When discussing the concept of void marriage, the scholars think it is necessary to divide

1 Yang Suiquan, *On Reduced Change of Chinese Families and Renaming Marriage Law as Family Law*, published on *Annual Theses of Year 1998 Marriage Law Society*. Yang Suiquan, "On Necessity and Urgency of Renaming Marriage Law as Relative Law", Issue 3, *Social Science Study*, 1998.

2 Chen Mingxia, Xue Lanning, "1998 Annual Meeting of Marriage and Family Law Research Institute of China Law Society", *Law Yearbook of China 1999*, p.926.

3 Yi Nan, "Year 1999 Annual Meeting Review of Marriage and Family Law Research Institute of China Law Society", Issue 6, *China Law*, 1999.

the lines among marriage, legal marriage and illegal marriage in establishing void marriage system, and give up connotations of "validness" of "marriage" concept, expand denotation of "marriage" and make it as a neutral concept, and integrate legal marriage and illegal marriage into marriage concept so as to legal contradiction in legal term[1], as law circle defines marriage concept within legal scope and for a long time and illegal marriage, arranged marriage and mercenary marriage etc. appear often in existing law and Marriage Law.[2] Some scholars think that "void marriage" is a specific concept to negate illegal marriage from effectiveness of legal marriage in marriage legislation and Marriage Law and it is not a kind of marriage.[3] Marriage is an identity and is not wholly applicable to relevant provisions and theories of civil conduct in civil law.

There are viewpoints of single-track system and double-track system regarding composition of void marriage system among the scholars.[4] The scholars standing for unitary structure and setting up void marriage think that as the effectiveness of modern void marriage has developed into multiple forms and is substantially same as revocable marriage, it is not necessary to differentiate them in law but only in claimer and prescription period.[5] The scholars standing for dual structure think that the most main difference between void marriage and revocable marriage lies in legal consequences. Ineffectiveness of void marriage is surely and absolute and is from beginning to end while ineffectiveness of revocable marriage is relative and non-retroactivity. There are multiple reasons causing illegal marriage. If

1 Wen Hui, *Questioning on Marriage Concept, published on Nanjing University Law Review*, 1996 Autumn; Xue Ninglan, *Several Thoughts on Void Marriage, Year 1998 Annual Theses of Marriage and Family Law Research Institute of China Law Society.*

2 Wen Hui, *Questioning on Marriage Concept, published on Nanjing University Law Review*, 1996 Autumn; Xue Ninglan, *Several Thoughts on Void Marriage, Year 1998 Annual Theses of Marriage and Family Law Research Institute of China Law Society.*

3 Yang Dawen, *Family Law*, Law Press. China, 1997, p.100.

4 Xue Ninglan, *Symposium of Difficult Issues in Revision of Marriage Law*, published on *Year 2001 Law Yearbook of China*, 2001, p.1115.

5 Yang Dawen, *Void Marriage*; Wu Changzheng, Yang Dawen, *Chinese Marriage and Life Toward 21st Century*, Jilin People's Publishing House, 1995, p.56; Yang Dawen, *Family Law*, Law Press. China, 1997, p.104.

legal effectiveness of marriage is negated in whatever circumstances, women, minor children and the parties in difficult life are mostly damaged. Therefore, it is the best legal choice to establish dual structure of void marriage and revocable marriage for handling flawed marriage.[1]

Regarding legal consequences of declaring marriage void, the scholars standing for dual structure pointed out that revocable marriage shall be void from the date when the court revokes judgment, with respect to the provision "void or dissolved marriage shall be invalid from its inception" in amendment draft to the Marriage Law. The reasons are: (1) in civil law theory, "voidness" means that civil conduct does not take effect surely and thoroughly in law and "revocation" means that civil subject exercises cancellation right to abolish legal effect of civil conduct. Legal consequences of both two have retrospective effect, namely being void from its inception. Marriage partnership is an identity and is different from contractual relations in formation, content and annihilation. Void marriage shall be void from its inception due to infringement seriousness and public order and good customs shall be void from its inception. Revocable marriage is perhaps void: if the person with cancellation right does not exercise right of cancellation, void marriage will still exist; upon expiration of scheduled period, if the person with cancellation right fails to exercise such right, such right shall be eliminated with elapsed time. Therefore, marriage partnership will continue to exist. (2) marriage partnership itself has the nature of facts leading and all established marriages and families will generate a series of important influences on both parties, children and society. Marriage Law cannot totally ignore existing facts and derived identities and property relations of marriage entity and revocable marriage has legal consequences different from void marriage, that is, the court judgment for marriage revocation shall be void from the effective date and does not have

1 Chen Wei, *Thoughts on Establishing China's Void Marriage System*, Issue 4, Law Science, 1996; Wang Hong, *Study on Hot Spots in Marriage and Family Law*, Chongqin University Press, 2000, pp.67-73; Xue Ninglan, *On How to Establish China's Void Marriage System*, People's Court Daily, February 14, 2001.

retrospective effect.[1]

At this stage, the scholars' discussion on void marriage system is further to 1980s discussion. Though some suggestions fail to be adopted by legislative organizations, they have important academic reference values to the improvement of our future void marriage system of civil code.

3. Spouse right

In 1997, Marriage and Family Law Draft (law expert proposal) added the provision that "citizen's spouse right is protected by the state for the first time following one husband one wife monogamy", arousing extensive attentions and warm discussions in the society.[2]

Controversy focus for Marriage Law scholars is whether to add spouse right and couple fidelity obligation clause in couple relationship chapter. There are pros and cons. [3] The pros make logic analysis of reasonableness of existence of spouse right mainly starting from intrinsic requirements of monogamy. The pros think that the fundamental purpose of adding the provision of spouse right in law is to strengthen self-restraints between husband and wife and their common social responsibilities instead of punishing paramour. The cons think that the core and essence of spouse right is to specify belonging of sex right after women and men get married. It means that after women and men get married, exclusive use right of their certain organ just belongs to their spouses and also means emotions and physical bodies of their spouses are their private properties. It deprives citizen's basic civil right - sex freedom right.

Another dispute over the matter of spouse right is whether to write right of requirement for loyalty for couples (fidelity obligation) as legitimate rights

1 Wang Hong, *Study on Hot Spots in Marriage and Family Law*, p.77; Xue Ninglan: *Void Marriage System Theory - From UK, America law to China law, Global Law Review*, 2001 Summer, p.218.

2 See Li Yinghe, Ma Yinan, *Discussion on Amendment to Marriage Law*, Guangming Daily Press, 1999.

3 Xue Ninglan, *Common Concerning Topic - Overview of Symposium of Difficult Issues in Amendment to Marriage Law*, Issue 1, *Collection of Women's Studies*, 2001.

between husband and wife into laws. Most experts of Marriage Law agree on this viewpoint and think that mutual loyalty and no extramarital sex between husband and wife is internal requirement of marriage, and reflects essence of marriage partnership and is a guarantee for establishing equal and genuine couple relationship. The viewpoint of taking couple loyalty as moral obligation separates the relation between law and moral. The governors can make the moral legalized if necessary out of the need for governing country.[1]

4. Couple property system

The 20 years since the Marriage Law was enacted in 1980 is a transition period of China's reforming and opening up and marching toward modern country. Economic system reform brings out highly advanced social productivity and unprecedented people's living standard. From the implementation of rural family contracting responsibility system to establishment of legal status of non-state-owned economies such as individual economy and private economy, [2]social production function of family has gained historical regression and material assets enjoyed by individuals are unprecedentedly rich in terms of number and variety. These will make family property relations increasingly complex and family property system especially couple property system has increasingly highlighting legal status.

Considering that Year 1980 Marriage Law's provision on couple property system is too simple and brief, [3]the scholars proposed to reconstruct China's couple property system and they think that reconstruction of couple property

1 Lin Jianjun, *Study on the Right of Spouse, 2000 Law Yearbook of China*, Law Yearbook of China Press, 2000, p.1067.

2 See Article 14 of *Year 1999 Amendment to the Constitution to the People's Republic of China.*

3 Article 13 of Year 1980 Marriage Law on legal property rule of couple, "the properties acquired by the husband and the wife during the period in which they are under contract of marriage shall be in their joint possession, unless otherwise agreed by both Parties." "Husband and wife shall enjoy equal rights in the disposition of their jointly possessed properties."

system must meet with our national conditions but also can properly estimate the conditions which will probably appear in the future so that legislation is forward looking. To this end, Marriage Law scholars suggest that (1) legal property system continues to be based on the system of joint property after marriage. The system of joint property after marriage conforms to China's national conditions. It fully recognizes social value of household labor, safeguards legitimate rights and interests of the party with weaker economic capability in a couple (especially woman doing household chores), facilitates equality of couple family status and promotes stability of family relations. We can set up individual specific property system and properly narrow down joint property of couple to improve the defects in joint property system of couple. [1]Some scholars pointed out that for the purpose of expanding individual property scope of couple, legal property system should take joint labor income system in which labor income of male or female or both is jointly owned by the couple and the properties not coming from labor such as succession and gift and interests on individual properties before marriage shall belong to specific individual of the couple.[2] (2) we should strengthen the status of agreed property system in couple property system. By taking authoritative norms and regulations, marriage partners may agree on couple property relation in the form of contract. In case of no agreement or void agreement, legal property system shall prevail. Thus, it specifies that agreed property system and legal property system have equal legal status and agreed property system has application effect over legal property system. When amending law, we should make supplementary provisions on time, effective conditions, establishment procedures, effectiveness, modification and termination of couple properties.

1 Chen Wei, "Legislation Conception on Improving China's Legal Property System of Couple", Issue 1, China Legal Science, 2000; Jiang Yue, "Thoughts on Several Essential Problems Concerning China's Legal Property System of Couple", Issue 6, *Modern Law Science*, 2000.

2 Wang Geya, "Suggestions on Improvement of China's Legal Property System of Couple", Issue 2, *China Legal Science*, 1997.

In order to avoid the possibility of maliciously using agreed property system to evade from repaying the debt using couple joint property, agreed property registration system should be set up. (3) setting up exceptional property system. In 2000, the scholars think China's current couple property system is general property system and we need to establish exceptional property system based on Switzerland couple property system. Exceptional couple property system "is an alternative to original couple property system in special circumstance in order to protect the interests of the couple and the third person, maintain transaction safety and reflect legislation purpose of individual interests and social interests." [1]China's exceptional property system includes declared exceptional property system and rightful exceptional property system. Also some scholars think that "it is perfect in theory to divide couple property system into common property system and exceptional property system, thus meeting special requirements of couple property relations in various complex social environments and facilitating fair maintenance of the interests of marriage partners and the third person." However, it is not realistic to set up this system in terms of China's social conditions (economic environment and legal environment etc.) and citizens' marriage property views at this stage.[2]

5.Standard legislation expression for for divorce judgment

During the period of the amendment on the Marriage Law, the standards for divorce judgment has become once again the focus of discussion for scholars. The scholars' attention on this topic is much different from 1950s and 1980s. The discussions for previous two times focus more on political complexion of the topic and stress its class nature and seek basis for argumentation from

1 Chen Wei, *Legislation Study on Legal Property System of Couple, Switzerland Study on Legal Property System of Couple and its Enlightenment on Improvement of China's Legal Property System of Couple*, Liang Huixing, *Civil and Commercial Law Review*, Vol.15, Law Press China, 2000, p.316.

2 Jiang Yue, *Study on Legal Property System of Couple*; Xia Yinlan, Jiang Yue, Xue Ninglan, *21st New Rules for Marriage and Family Relation - Interpretation and Study of New Marriage Law*, China Procuratorial Press, 2001, p.271.

classics. In 1990s, the scholars focused on this topic again and doubted about the reasonableness of "emotional breakdown" taken as standard for divorce judgment.[1]

Taking breakdownism as basic principle for China's divorce legislation is a progress compared to "warrant theory" dominating in justice in 1950s or 1960s 20 and is consistent with overall development trend of global divorce legislation. However, through practice testing of dozens of years, the defects of this provision in legislation and justice are beyond doubt. Firstly, taking couple emotional breakdown as legal conditions for divorce judgment is contrary to the nature of divorce. As socially recognized form of male and female combination, even though marriage has nature character, it exists in the society in the form of ethical relation and legal relation. In terms of legal relation, both parties are closely related by rights and obligations of the couple. These rights and obligations are not derived from emotions and nor transferred due to existence or concentration of emotion but a result of legal adjustment. The couple's relationship is just the ideological basis for marriage partnership to establish and exist and it cannot generalize all contents of marriage partnership. Therefore, taking couple emotional breakdown as legal conditions for court judgment for divorce exaggerates status and role of marriage nature characteristics, and ignores couple rights and obligations and responsibilities for others and society, which is not consistent with the nature of marriage. Secondly, legal norms should be specific, objective and operable but not abstract, subjective and less measurable. Any law covers certain social relations and the couple's relationship belongs to ideology and it is subjective, vague and capricious so it is hard to become the relations covered

1 In 1987, Chinese scholars questioned the reasonability of taking alienation of mutual affection as the standard for judging divorce for the first time. See Jiang Yue, *Review and Prospect on Study of China's Marriage Law for Thirty Years Since Reform and Opening up*, published on *Research on Family Law* by Chen Wei, 2008, Qunzhong Press, 2009, p.198.

by law. Therefore, it is not scientific to take couple emotional breakdown as legal conditions for divorce judgment in terms of legal norms. Thirdly, in judicial practice, as this legal standard is too abstract, the subjectivity and arbitrariness by which judge handles divorce cases grow, so some judges are not applying law but creating law and even sometimes confuse the cause and the effect: For those couples who are granted a divorce by judgment, it shows couple emotional breakdown; for those couples who are not granted a divorce by judgment, it shows the couple emotions are far from the degree of total breakdown.

The scholars think that "couple's relationship breakdown" in the prevailing Marriage Law should be replaced with "marriage relation break" and we should specify this principle definition and make it operable in application. [1] Specifically speaking, law should cover relative abstract generalization provision, that is "marriage relation break" but also need to list the common and specific circumstances which can prove marriage relation break which can be taken as standard by the court to measure if marriage relation is broken or not. The scholars suggest that we can refer to 14 circumstances enumerated in *Several Specific Opinions of the Supreme People's Court on How the People's Court Determines that Mutual Affection No Longer Exists between Husband and Wife* published by the Supreme People's Court in 1989.[2]

After analyzing relevant national standards for divorce judgment, the scholars pointed out that the combination of breakdownism, objectivism and faultism to differing extent is current global divorce legislation trend. The statutory causes for divorce listed in China's current judicial interpretations not only reflect the fact of marriage relation break but also focus on reasons for break and asking about

1 See Wu Changzheng, Yang Dawen, *Chinese Marriage and Life Toward 21st Century*, Jilin People's Publishing House, 1995, p.10; Li Yinhe, Ma Yinan, *Contestation on Amendment to Marriage Law*, Guangming Daily Press, 1999, pp.113-229.

2 Chen Mingxia, Xue Ninglan, *Standards for Divorce Judging, Law Yearbook of China 1999*, Law Yearbook of China Press, 1999, p.927.

fault of either of the couple, which is actually judicial orientation based on three principles. Therefore, China's divorce standard should change from breakdownism to comprehensive breakdownism including faultism and objectivism ("mixture principle").

Meanwhile, some scholars still stick to taking emotional breakdown as the standard for divorce judgment, [1] with main reasons: (1) Classical Marxist Writers think that divorce is just a confirmation of dead marriage and dead marriage should mean affection disappearance. Emotion negation theory will probably make the same mistake as "warrant theory". (2) Emotional breakdown principle conforms to the people's interests and requirements. We advocate concluding marriage based on love and law should protect love and the marriages without love should be granted a revocation. (3) The viewpoint that law does not cover subject things is wrong. Subject elements for committing crime in criminal law, fault in civil law and no fault principle are subjective mentality of parties and so should be covered by law. (4) Emotional breakdown standard is not ahead of the times. 30% of China's marriages are concluded based on love and law cannot accommodate outdated consciousness and behaviors.

6. Study on parent-child relation

For a long time, the study by China's marriage law scholars on parent-child relation is relatively weaker than the study on marriage system, couple's relation and divorce system. It has direct relation with the practice of China's Marriage Law legislation focusing more on marriage partnership than family relation construction. During the period of amendment of the Marriage Law in 1990s, the legislation study by the scholars on parentage law is gradually developed with

---

1 See Xia Zhen, *Legitimacy of Emotional Breakdown as Legal Reasons for Divorce, Year 1998 Annual Theses of Marriage and Family Law Research Institute of China Law Society;* Xia Zhen, *Unquestionability of Taking Emotional Breakdown as Reasons for Divorce Judging*, published on Li Yinhe and Ma Yinan, *Contestation on Amendment to Marriage Law*, Guangming Daily Press, 1999; Li Zhongfang, *Emotional Theory on Insisting on Reasons for Divorce*, Li Yinhe and Ma Yinan, *Contestation on Amendment to Marriage Law*, Guangming Daily Press, 1999.

growing number of published papers.[1] The scholars focus on the study in basic questions of parentage law, for example, kind of parents and children, concept of parental right, presumption and denial system of legitimate children and claim system of illegitimate children, difference between parental right and custodial right, relationship between stepparents and stepchildren and custodial right of parents for minor children after divorce.

Many papers will put research objective on legislative suggestions on amending the Marriage Law. The scholars pointed out that even though China's Marriage Law stipulates that parents shall discipline and protect minor children, it is too abstract and it does not give the name to parental right. To accommodate the impact of market economy and material interest relation on relation among marriage, family and relatives, it is quite imminent to improve China's parentage

1 Academic writings mainly include Chen Peiqun, *Law Comparisons of Parent-Child Relationship Across Taiwan Straits*, published on Issue 2, *Studies in Law and Business*, 1994; Liu Suping, Chen Mingxia, *Improving China's Parent-Child Law System*; Deng Hongbi, Wang Hong, *Reflections and Reshaping of Parent-Child Legal System*; Wu Changzheng, Yang Dawen, *Chinese Marriage and Life Toward 21st Century*, Jilin People's Publishing House, 1995; Zhang Xuejun, *On Raising Minor Children After Divorce*, Issue 6, *Law and Social Development*, 1996; Meng Leguo, Jiang Hui, Huang Peng, *On Nature of Guardianship and Rights and Interests of Guardian*, Issue 11, *Law Science*, 1996; Chen Mingxia, *Study on Basic Questions of Parentage Law*, Liang Huixing, *Civil and Commercial Law Review*, Vol.6, Law Press China, 1997; Chen Wei, *Study on Parents Guardianship of Minor Children after Divorce*, Issue 3, *China Legal Science*, 1998; Fan Lijun, *On Composition of Parentage Legal Relationship*, Issue 1, *Journal of Central Leadership Institute of Politics and Law*, 1999; Fan Lijun, *Theoretical Study on Establishing Parentage System in China's Marriage Law*, Issue 2, *Journal of Shaanxi Normal University (Philosophy and Social Sciences Edition)*, 1999; Li Wenhui, Gao Xiaoxia, *Discussion on Setting up China's Parentage Legal System*, Issue 3, *Heibei Law Science*, 1999; Fan Fan, *On Nature of Parentage*, Issue 3, *Law Science Magazine*, 1999; Wang Hong, *On Correction and Limitation of Family Relation in Determining Parent-Child Relation*, Issue 4, *Modern Law Science*, 1999; Yang Ling, Yang Suiquan, *On Permission of Love Child under Market Economy Conditions*, Issue 4, *Studies in Law and Business*, 1999; Chen Mingxia, *Improving Legal System for Parent-Child Relation (Guidelines)*, Issue 4, *Studies in Law and Business*, 1999.

law. [1] Therefore, China should establish the system of parental right which is a hot issue for the study on parentage law at this stage. [2]After comparing respective regulations of civil law system and common law system on parentage law, the scholars proposed systematic legislation design on parent-child relation law which is volume of kinship of civil code or single Marriage and Family Law. [3]Also, the scholars made special study on legal issues of artificial reproduction technology and its influence on parentage law.[4]

In 1999, Marriage and Family Law of the People's Republic of China (law expert proposal) submitted by Marriage and Family Law Research Institute of China Law Society to legislative organization specifically stipulates parent-child relation in one chapter, with two aspects covered: kinds of parents and children (presumption and denial of legitimate children, claim of illegitimate children and relationship between step parents and step children (adoptive parents and children relationship in another chapter)) and parental right covering concept and contents of parental right, circumstances in which parents lose parental right, exercising of parental right and visitation right after parents' divorce.[5]

5.2 Study on Marriage and Family Volume (Family) of Civil Code

1. Relation between Marriage and Family Law and Civil Law

China's Marriage and Family Law's regression to civil law in legislation style originates from Year 1986 *General Principles of Civil Law of the People's Republic of China*. Article 2 of the *General Principles of Civil Law* stipulates

1 Liu Suping, Chen Mingxia, *Improving China's Parent-Child Law System*, published on Wu Changzheng, Yang Dawen, *Chinese Marriage and Life Toward 21st Century*, Jilin People's Publishing House, 1995, pp.153-155.

2 Xue Ninglan, *Review and Prospect on Study of China's Marriage Law for Thirty Years Since Reform and Opening up*, published on Chen Wei, *Research on Family Law*, 2008, Qunzhong Press, 2009, pp.143-150.

3 Chen Mingxia, *Study on Basic Questions of Parentage Law*, Liang Huixing, *Civil and Commercial Law Review*, Vol.6, Law Press China, 1997, pp.1-74.

4 Feng Jianmei, *Study on Legal Issues of Reproductive Technology*, Liang Huixing, *Civil and Commercial Law Review*, Vol.8, Law Press China, 1997, pp.63-124.

5 *Marriage Law of the People's Republic of China (legal expert proposal)*, Liang Huixing, *Civil and Commercial Law Review*, Vol.14, Law Press China, 2000, pp.783-787.

that "The Civil Law of the People's Republic of China shall adjust property relationships and personal relationships between civil subjects with equal status, that is, between citizens, between legal persons and between citizens and legal persons." According to this provision, China's Civil Law adjust property relationships and personal relationships between civil subjects, in which, personal relationship between the subjects with equal status except personality relationship is family relationship in family field. In addition, the *General Principles of Civil Law* stipulates marriage freedom right and that marriage and family are protected by law (Articles 103-104).

The academic circle had an earlier discussion on and re-recognition of relationship between Marriage and Family Law and Civil Law, such as Zhang Xianyu, *Tutorial on Marriage and Family Law*, Law Press China, 1995 and Yang Dawen, *Marriage Law Science*, China Renming University Press, 1989. They think that the issuance of the General Principles of Civil Law officially announced that Marriage and Family Law is regressed to Civil Law, and determined that Marriage and Family Law shall belong to civil law in a general sense in terms of legislation system and General Principles of Civil Law has same level of basic legal status as inheritance law, intellectual property right law and contract law.[1] They also pointed out that "whether Marriage and Family Law is an independent legal department or not and whether Marriage and Family Law can become a branch subject of law science are two questions of different natures. In terms of extensive contents of Marriage and Family Law and actual needs for developing Marriage and Family Law, it is preferable to take Marriage and Family Law as a branch subject in law science."[2]

In academic circle's discussions on amendment on the Marriage Law since 1990s, much deeper discussion has been given to the relationship between the Marriage Law and Civil Law due to the need for arrangement for legislation style.

1 Zhang Xianyu, *Tutorial on Marriage and Family Law*, Law Press China, 1995, p.36.
2 Yang Dawen, *Marriage Law Science*, China Renming University Press, 1989, p.52.

There were three viewpoints: firstly, status quo should be maintained and the Marriage Law will still remain independent. In amendment, legal name and basic framework should remain unchanged but just some additions and revisions are made. Secondly, if independent status of the Marriage Law is ensured, its name should be changed to "Marriage and Family Law" and its system and contents are also much changed. Thirdly, it should regress to Civil Law and it is listed as a volume of Civil Law and is renamed as "Family Volume" or "Family Law".

There are two kinds of scholars' understanding of the Marriage and Family Law. The first kind is independent law department theory to which the above first and second viewpoints belong. Though there is difference between two viewpoints, they are based on the precondition that the Marriage Law is an independent law department. The second kind is theory of regression to Civil Law. Many experts thought that considering it takes time to determine legal system of socialist market economy in an overall manner, it is not easy to bring Civil Code under legislation agenda lately. "It is the most ideal to take the second kind as it is in line with China's actual conditions and is practical."[1]

Some scholars interpret China's Marriage and Family Law's regression to Civil Law starting from Marx's civil society theory. [2]Jiang Ping pointed out that the relations among equal entities include three aspects: firstly, production, exchange, distribution and consumption of physical materials; secondly, production and reproduction of human being; thirdly, labor relations. In western countries, these relations are unified and belong to Civil Law. When formulating Civil Code, China should bring marriage partnership and family relation under Civil Law. [3] According to civil society theory, family relation and economic relation are two basic relations

1 Wu Changzheng, Xia Yinlan, *Summary of Viewpoints on Amendments to Marriage Law*, published on Issue 7, *Democracy and Legal System*, 1998.

2 Xue Ninglan, *Trend of China's Marriage Law - Legislation Mode and Structure*, Xia Yinlan, Jiang Yue, Xue Ninglan, *New Rules for 21st Century Marriage and Family Relation - Interpretation and Study of New Marriage Law*, China Procuratorial Press, 2001, pp.196-197.

3 Jiang Ping, *Several Hotspot Issues in Civil Legislations*, published in Issue 1, *Journal of Jiangxi University of Finance and Economics*, 2000.

of civil society: one is production and reproduction of human beings and the other is production and reproduction of physical materials. They are not only basis for civil society but also become basic rules for civil society - relations covered by Civil Law.

Xu Guodong thinks highly of the meaning of Family Law's regression to Civil Code and thinks that it brings change in respective proportion of human law and materials law in Civil Law. In the past, we stressed the importance of Civil Law on the development of commodity economy and we put personal relation ahead of property relation in the relations covered by Civil Law. He thinks that from the viewpoint of civil law of humanism, "If Family Law's regression to civil code (and legislation planning of personality right constituting an independent part) cannot be reflected in the definition of the things covered by Civil Law, then the essence of Family Law cannot be achieved."

2. Style of marriage and family volume

The scholars have different understandings as to whether to call it "Marriage and Family Law" or "Family Law" while formulating China's Civil Code and improving and adjusting legal regulation system of relatives. There is a viewpoint that it can be called "Marriage and Family Law" or "Family Law" in future Civil Code. [1]From the situations of tens of years since China's founding, it is easily digestible, understood and acceptable to call it "Marriage and Family Law". Also some scholars pointed out that "Marriage and Family Law" cannot be equivalent to "Family Law" mainly because Marriage and Family Law mainly adjusts marriage and family relations while Family Law adjusts relatives to some extent including marriage and family relations, including other close relatives. The scopes of social relations covered by the two are different. [2]"Family Law" can

1 Chen Mingxia, *Study on Marriage and Family Legislation (Abstract), Annual Theses of Year 1998 Marriage Law Society.*

2 Xue Ninglan, *Trend of China's Marriage Law - Legislation Mode and Structure*; Xia Yinlan, Jiang Yue, Xue Ninglan, *21st New Rules for Marriage and Family Relation - Interpretation and Study of New Marriage Law*, China Procuratorial Press, 2001, p.198.

accurately reflect status law attributes and characteristics of this legal system.

There are external style and internal style for marriage and family volume of Civil Code. In terms of external style, the scholars have different approaches to the compilation of Civil Code due to different threads of thinking. [1] There are three versions of scholar proposals for China's Civil Code, [2] with different characteristics for style design of marriage and family volume of Civil Code (relative volume). "China's Civil Code Proposal Draft" with the version of Institute of International Law of Chinese Academy of Social Sciences takes German style of five-parts structure (Pandekten System), namely taking legal relations as standard to constitute the parts of Family Law, Property Law, Law of Obligation and Law of Succession as parallel.[3] "China's Civil Code Proposal Draft" with the version of China Renmin University gives primary importance to the protection of personality right and secondary importance to marriage and family volume. [4] "Green Civil Code Proposal Draft" with Xiamen University takes two-parts structure of personal relation law and property relation law. In personal relation law, there are natural person law, legal person law, marriage and family law and law of succession. Personal relation law reflects directly dignity and human rights of people and so it is more important than property law and also

1 Liang Huixing thinks that the scholars have three ideas on the compilation of civil code: firstly, "loose type and union type"; secondly, "idealism"; thirdly, "realism". Liang Huixing, *Three Thoughts on Compilation of Civil Code*; Liu Hainian, Li Lin, *Rule by Law and Legal System Constructing*, China Legal System Publishing House, 2001, pp.165-178.

2 The order of publishing time is *A Propositional Version for Civil Code Draft of China* published by Institute of Law of Chinese Academy of Social Sciences, Law Press China, 2003; *A Propositional Version with Reasons for Civil Code Draft of China* by China Renmin University Press, China Legal System Publishing House, 2004; *Xiamen University version of Green Civil Code Draft*, Social Science Literature Press, 2004.

3 See Liang Huixing, *On Compilation of China Civil Codes, Civil and Commercial Law Review*, Vol.24, Jinqiao Culture Press (HK) Co., Ltd., 2002.

4 Wang Liming, *A Propositional Version with Reasons for Civil Code Draft of China*, China Legal System Publishing House, 2004.

it is put in the first volume to highlight "human law" of Civil Law.[1]

Regarding internal style design of marriage and family volume (relative volume), there is a 4th version in addition to the previous three proposal drafts, i.e., expert proposal for marriage and family (relative) of Civil Code drafted by Marriage and Family Law Research Institute upon thc entrustment by the legislative organization. [2] Yang Dawen thinks that "when we determine systematic structure of marriage and family volume, we should take adjusting actual needs for marriage and family relation as basis and focus on internal relations of various specific systems in marriage and family field in order to make it more scientific and systematic." [3] The scholars have consistent viewpoints that marriage and family (relative) volume set up 9 chapters such as general provisions, relatives, marriage, couples, divorce, parents and children, adoption, guardianship and raising. Regarding legal responsibilities and law application of foreign-related marriage and family relations and interregional marriage and family relations, they don't need to be chaptered in marriage and family (relative) volume but instead of being set forth by contract volume, infringement volume and special international private law in Civil Code. [4] Even though the four versions are different in style designs of marriage and family volume, they have common points in main aspects and provide academic model for references for reconstruction of marriage and family volume of Civil Law by the legislative organization.

3. Basic principles on marriage and family (relatives) volume

As the first volume of civil code, marriage and family volume has threads of

1 Xu Guodong, *Basic Structure of Civil Code Draft - Centering on Relations Covered by Civil Law*, Xu Guodong, *Contestation on Drafting China' Civil Code*, China University of Political science and Law Press, 2001.

2 Drafters of all chapters published explanations on the style and contents of the version on Issue 4 of Journal of China Women's College, 2002.

3 Yang Dawen, *Civil Codification and Overall Improvement of Marriage and Family Legal System, Journal of China Women's College*, Issue 4, 2002.

4 *Guidelines of Civil Code of the People's Republic of China (Draft)*, Liang Huixing, *Civil and Commercial Law Review*, Vol.13, Law Press China, 1999, pp.801-832; Yang Dawen, *Civil Codification and Overall Improvement of Marriage and Family Legal System*, published on *Journal of China Women's College*, Vol.4, 2002.

connections with General Provisions. As a status law, marriage and family system has strong ethic principle which should differentiate from other volumes of civil law. The relationship between marriage and family volume and general provisions of civil law is commonness and personality and the marriage and family volume has its own special principle and system design.

The scholars don't have consistent opinion if basic principles should be set forth for marriage and family volume. The negativists think that the basic principles such as marriage freedom, male and female equality, protection of legitimate rights and interests of women, children and elderly in prevailing Marriage Law have been covered by equality principle of civil subject status and principle of the autonomy of will of general provision as well as relevant principles included in prevailing law on the protection of the rights and interests of women, law on the protection of the rights and interests of the elderly and law on the protection of minors, therefore, no basic principle needs to be set forth in this volume. [1]Positivists think that marriage and family (relatives) volume belongs to specific provision of civil law and it and general provisions of civil law constitute the relation between general law and special law. The basic principles set forth in the general provisions are highly abstract rules and should be specified by the basic principles in specific provisions, and two types of basic principles constitute the relationship between higher level and lower level. Unterprinzipien has more specific connotations and special specification function. For example, even though general provisions include principle of autonomy of will, there is a necessity to determine the principle of contract freedom in the contract volume and the principle of ownership freedom in real right volume and will freedom principle in inheritance volume and marriage freedom principle in relatives volume.[2]

1 Xue Ninglan, *Regression and Improvement of Marriage and Family Law to Civil Code - Year 2002 Annual Meeting Summary of Marriage and Family Law Society*, *New Events and Topics in Issue 11 of Legal Research* by China Law Society.

2 Liang Huixing (topic leader): *A Propositional Version with Reasons for Civil Code Draft of China*, Law Press China, 2006, p.2.

5.3 Current and Future Study on Marriage and Family Law

The study on marriage and family law during this period is characterized with closely providing theoretical support for legislation and is also highlighted with comparative study and empirical study in this stage of the study on marriage and family law. As China's law science study breaks down the barrier of complacent and conservative mindset, it studies and assimilates concepts and instances of legislation of civil law countries and some middle aged and young scholars has been going abroad for further study to make comparative study since 1990s. With expansion of research methods on law science, [1] some scholars stand on native culture and go down to the grassroots to make empirical study and so have published many monographs and translations. [2] Since this century, some scholars have published some pioneering and challenging theses by taking social gender advocated by the united nations as perspective and referring to international

1 Chen Wei pointed out that since new century, Chinese scholars have made many updates on the approach to study marriage and family law from traditional method of studying law science to study methods of law social science and law economic science and also use social surveys and social gender analysis. Chen Wei, *Review and Prospect on Study of China's Marriage Law for Thirty Years Since Reform and Opening up*, Chen Wei, *Research on Family Law*, 2008, Qunzhong Press, 2009, p.109.

2 [Japan] Li Gu Xin Yi, translated by Chen Mingxia and Xu Jihua, *Social Science of Divorce Law*, Peking University Press, 1991; Chen Xiaojun, *Comparative Study of Family Law Across Taiwan Straits*, China University of Political science and Law Press, 1996; Xia Yinlan, *American Modern Marriage and Family System*, China University of Political science and Law Press, 1999; Song Yu, Chen Wei, *Comparative Study of Family Law among Mainland China, Hong Kong, Taiwan and Macao*, Chongqin Press, 2002; Jiang Xinmiao, *Comparative Study of Adoption Law*, Peking University, 2004; Wang Liping, *Parentage Law Study*, Law Press China, 2004; Zhang Xuejun, *Legislation of Raising After Divorce*, Law Press China, 2004; Cao Shiquan, *Study on Guardianship of Minors*, China University of Political science and Law Press, 2004; Li Xia, *Comparative Study of Guardianship System*, Shandong University Press, 2004; Li Xiuhua, *Empirical Study on Legal Status of Women Marriage and Family*, Intellectual Property Rights Press, 2004; Chen Wei, *Comparative Study of Foreign Marriage and Family Laws*, Qunzhong Press, 2007; Xia Yinlan, *Theory of Freedom and Limitation on Divorce*, China University of Political science and Law Press, 2007; Jiang Yue, *Frontline Guidelines on Marriage and Family Law*, Science Press, 2007; Wang Geya, Ethical Theory and Institutional Expansion of China's Family Legislation, Heilongjiang University Press, 2008.

convention on human rights ("international convention on women and children") signed by China to analyze and review China's current marriage and family law and regulations as well as judicial interpretations. [1]These writings cover various fields, with the specificity of research theories and topics being far beyond the reach of the marriage and family law study in previous two stages.

However, there are still some shortages in marriage law science study if we take a developmental viewpoint, such as weak basic theory research, insufficient research on China's national traditional marriage and family culture and lack of comparative study on marriage and family systems in Asian countries. China's future marriage and family law study is full of challenges, as "it is not only from theoretical development of this subject but also from the development of science and technology, and interchanges of different subjects……"[2]

1 Chen Mingxia, *Social Gender Awareness: New Viewpoints on Amendment to Marriage Law* published on *China Women's Newspaper*, June 24, 2000; Xia Yinlan, *Perspective of China's Divorce Property Division Method in the Framework of International Human Rights*, published on Issue 1 of *Global Law Review*, 2005; Chen Wei, Ran Qiyu, *Social Gender in Public Policy - Analysis of Social Gender and Legislation Improvement in Marriage Law*, published on Issue 78, *Journal of Gansu Political Science and Law Institute*, Jan, 2005; Xia Yinglan, *Analysis of Social Gender in Joint Properties of China's Couples - Values of Household Labors*, published on Issue 2, *Law Science Magazine*, 2005; Xue Ninglan, *Legislation Mode and Type Selection of Legal Property System of Couple*, published on Issue 2, *Law Science Magazine*, 2005; Ma Yinan, *On Social Gender Analysis of Divorce Property Division Questions*, *Collection of Women's Studies*, Dec, 2006; Xue Ninglan, *Social Gender Analysis of China's Legal Property System of Couple - Focusing on Property Division of Divorced Couple*, published on *Collection of Women's Studies*, Dec, 2006.

2 Xia Yinlan, 21st Century China's Marriage Law Prospect, published on Issue 4, Studies in Law and Business, 1999.

Chapter 16

Prosperity of Commercial Jurisprudence under the Market Economic System

As the basic law of market transactions, the commercial law takes root in the reality of economic development, and continuous to develop and innovate with the development and innovation of economic marketization. Since the founding of new China, the country has successively experienced three major economic systems, namely, the planned economy, the planned commodity economy and the preliminary socialist market economy. In the highly planned economy period, the real commercial transactions were extremely short, and the commercial legislation was out of the question. Therefore, most commercial laws in China were gestated and developed in the process of constructing market economic system after reform and opening-up. Especially in the 1990s, China's economic system reform entered into a brand new stage. With the establishment of socialist market economic system and development of market economy, the commercial legislation flourished. The successive promulgation of numerous separate laws, such as *Maritime Law (1992), Company Law (1993), Guarantee Law (1995), Negotiable Instruments Law (1995), Insurance Law (1995), Commercial Bank Law (1995), Partnership Enterprise Law (1997), Securities Law (1998), Contract Law (1999), Law on Individual Proprietorship Enterprises (1999), Trust Law (2001), Law on*

Securities Investment Fund (2003), and Law on Specialized Farmer Cooperatives (2006), made the commercial legal institutions with respect to commercial subject, commercial transaction and commercial order rapidly established in China. As a result, the commercial system in our country began to take shape. Accordingly, along with the establishment, development and relative perfection of commercial legislation in China, the commercial jurisprudence, taking the commercial law system as study support, the theory and practice of commercial law and the development law thereof as study object, has rapidly developed, and has become the youngest discipline with fastest prosperity in Chinese jurisprudential circle. However, subject to the changes of social economy and politics in our country, the study on commercial jurisprudence has shown different characteristics in different economic development periods, and has reflected the bumpy process, with ups and downs, of commercial legislation in our country. During the development process, relatively brief, but closely keeping up with the times, of commercial jurisprudence, the thinking about and exploration on basic theories of commercial law, company law, securities law and enterprise bankruptcy law have constituted the mainstream of commercial jurisprudence study.

1. Formation and Development of the Basic Theories of Commercial Law

Due to the lack of tradition and history of commercial law in our country, the study on the basic theories of commercial law seemed weak in history. After the founding of new China, the highly centralized and unified planned economy was imposed. So, there were no grounds for both commercial law and commercial jurisprudence in social lives and academic activities. At the beginning of reform of economic system, the trade-off between civil law and economic law has received more attention in jurisprudential and legal circle. In that period, commercial jurisprudence was only struggling for survival in the crevice of clash between civil jurisprudence and economic jurisprudence. However, the commercial jurisprudence scholars explored the issues persistently, such as the position of commercial law, construction of commercial law system and models of commercial legislation, and commercial credit, attempted to build an independent system of commercial law theories, which can really embody the characteristics of commercial law, so as to promote the development of commercial legislation and practice in our country.

1.1 Argument on the Independence of Commercial Law and Independent Formation of Commercial Jurisprudence

In Chinese legal system, the issue about how to establish the position of commercial law and how to grasp the relationship between commercial law and civil law, and the relationship between commercial law and economic law is one of the most important and fundamental issues of commercial law theory since the 20th century. This issue has epitomized the value of commercial law, and determines the prospect and destiny thereof.[1]

In the field of jurisprudential study in the 1980s, subject to the then special economic system in our country, the "analytic model of dualistic economic relationships" prevailed for a time.[2] Under the predominance of this model, commercial law was "absorbed" by economic law in theory, and "included" by civil law in legislation. There was not an inch of land for commercial law to stand on under the "dualistic structure" of civil jurisprudence and economic jurisprudence when Greek meets Greek.[3]

Since 1992, the legal requirements of socialist market economy and construction of legal system therefor have become a key point of jurisprudential study. Furthermore, under the socialist market economic system, the relationship

1 FAN Jian & WANG Jianwen, *Value, Origin and Noumenon of Commercial Law*, China Renmin University Press, 2007, p.6.

2 The so-called analytic model of dualistic economic relationships referred to dividing the realistic economic relationships into "economic relationship between equal subjects" and "economic relationship between unequal subjects". And, "the civil law mainly regulates the property relationship between equal subjects, that is, the horizontal property relationship. The administration on economy by government, the vertical economic relationships between the state and enterprises or within enterprises, or the relationships between unequal subjects shall be regulated mainly by economic law or administrative law".

3 SHUAI Tianlong, "Trend of Chinese Commercial Jurisprudence in the 20th Century", *Peking University Law Journal*, 1997, Issue 4.

among civil law, commercial law and economic law and their roles and functions are the most important in jurisprudential study. Since the system design and normative structure, starting from "analytic model of dualistic economic relationships", have been gradually broken through by realistic economic reform, with the mainstream of self adjustment in civil jurisprudence and economic jurisprudence, the claim for "transcending the structure of civil law and economic law to explore the legal regulation system of socialist commodity economy"[1], and to renew the knowledge on independent position and special role of commercial law in legal system was increasingly rising. With the joint efforts of both scholars and practitioners, the situation "Greek meets Greek" between civil law and economic law in economic legislation during the coexistence of plan and market, has begun to transit to a new "situation of tripartite confrontation" among civil law, commercial and economic law in the context of socialist market economy.

With the deepening of understanding on the relationship between plan and market, more and more scholars have cast doubt upon the existing prevailing viewpoint about the relationship between economic law and commercial law. After a new examination and reflection, based on the understanding on different roles, positions and purposes of the two systems, the free competition (an invisible hand), and state interference (a visible hand), in socialist market economy, it was gradually realized that commercial law is related to market mechanism, and economic law is the measure of state to intervene economy. Commercial law is a part of private law, which emphasizes the principle of autonomy of the parties, with a relatively strong internationalized characteristic, but the economic law is a part of public law. Economic law cannot supersede commercial law, and vice versa, both of them shall be organically integrated.[2]

1 ZHAO Xinhua, "On Legal Regulation System of Socialist Commodity Economy - Establishment of Commercial Law in China and the Relationship among Commercial Law", *Civil Law and Economic Law, Contemporary Law Review*, 1991, Issue 2.

2 ZHENG Shaohua, "Commercial Law and Economic Law: the Design of Important Legal Institutions in Development of the Market Economy", *Studies in Law and Business*, 1995, Issue 3.

Although the legislative system of civil law in China has once included almost all civil and commercial law systems, in the 1990s, a series of commercial separate laws were promulgated. The principles therein, and the systems established or to be established thereby, have features clearly different from principles and systems of civil law. Some differences in system even lead to the non-application of principles and systems of civil law in the areas of commercial activities. For instance, the "insurance contract" provided by insurance law has been completely standardized, adhesion contract has become a universal phenomenon in contract system under insurance law, and the freedom of contract in civil law has nearly been abandoned. As to the principle of good faith in insurance law, with the unique logical connotation, it is difficult to interpret in accordance with the principles and systems of civil law. In addition, many concepts and institutional designs in trust law are also in conflict with the systems of current existing civil law in our country.[1] The irreconcilable differences objectively exist between the laws, which are referred to as "commercial law", and civil law, make people gradually realize that the commercial law is not simply the by-product of civil law. Even under the major premise of combination of civil and commercial codes, the unique characteristics of commercial law, which are different from civil law, cannot be denied. Especially with the pace of economic reform in China, the necessity and importance for developing commercial law have been pointed out by scholars very early.[2] WANG Baoshu pointed out, in an essay published in 1997, that "commercial law is an independent area of law in legal system", and then he expounded the characteristics of commercial law, "commercial law is an area of law which takes the commercial relationship as regulative object. It is an important part of private law, penetrated with the elements of public law." In this essay, WANG Baoshu has also expounded the relationships between commercial

1 ZOU Hailin, *Several Issues in the Development of Commercial Law in China*, at http://www.iolaw.org.cn/showNews.aspx?id=10228.

2 See GU Gongyun, "Commercial Law is Indispensable for Developing Commodity Economy", *Social Sciences Weekly*, July 6, 1987.

law and civil law, the commercial law and economic law, the commercial law and labor law, and, the commercial law and administrative law.[1] In this essay, WANG Baoshu has systematically and thoroughly discussed the essential characters of commercial law and its manifestation in legal form from the following aspects, such as, the regulative objects, the position and features of commercial law in legal system, commercial subjects, commercial actions and the development trend of commercial law, which has provided systematically and convincingly theoretical basis for scholars and practitioners to clearly distinguish and study the commercial law.

In the mid and late 1990s, with the deepening of understanding on the important role of commercial law in the socialist market economy, its independent position and private nature have been gradually recognized. The jurisprudential circle has reached a consensus on the concept that commercial law regulates the commercial actions or commercial relationships between equal subjects, which is one of the most important laws of market economy.[2] However, there are many substantive works to be done on how to delimit the commercial law, and how to seek the internal bases of independence thereof, so as to make the commercial law really independent from the contents to the form.

At the early stage of the economic system reform, it was a common practice, in the field of jurisprudential study, to integrate both of the civil jurisprudence and commercial jurisprudence. For instance, the Office of Civil Law, Faculty of Law, Renmin University of China published *Selected Papers on Foreign Civil and Commercial Law* in 1986, in which the civil and commercial jurisprudence materials were combined together. However, the relatively independent commercial law has obtained relatively free development in the process of gradually separating from traditional territory of civil law; accordingly, the

1 WANG Baoshu, *Concepts of Commercial Law and Conceptual Commercial Law*, in WANG Baoshu (ed.), *Commercial Law Review*, Vol.1, Law Press·China, 1997, pp.1-14.

2 LI Tieying, *To Emancipate Mind, Change Ideas, and Establish the Legal System of Socialist Market Economy*, *Chinese Journal of Law*, 1997, Issue 1.

commercial jurisprudence, a knowledge connected with commercial law, has also begun to develop with relative independence. After the middle of 1990s, to be exact, after the goal of Chinese economic system reform was determined as building socialist market economic system by the fourteenth Party Congress in 1992 , the study on commercial jurisprudence suddenly flourished in an eruptive state. In this period, a lot of general writings with respect to commercial law which can reflect the position of commercial jurisprudence as an independent discipline have emerged. For example, *Chinese Commercial Law*, in WANG Baoshu (ed.), (People's Court Press, 1996); *Introduction of Chinese Commercial Law*, in DONG Ansheng, WANG Wenqin and WANG Yanping (eds.), (Jilin People's Publishing House, 1994); *Commercial Law*, in QIN Youtu (ed.), (China University of Political Science and Law Press, 1999); XU Xuelu, *Introduction of Commercial Law*, People's Court Press, 1999; *Commercial Jurisprudence*, in ZHAO Wanyi (ed.), (China Legal Publishing House, 1999), etc.

Therefore, in the late 1990s, the scholars no longer simply dealt with and studied the commercial law on the platform of the existing studies on civil law. The studies on commercial law have begun to show relative independence, and gradually moved towards maturity.[1] The commercial jurisprudence system, constructed by commercial law scholars, usually consists of basic theories of commercial law, company law, securities law, insurance law, negotiable instruments law, commercial bank law, trust law and maritime law, etc. In the study on commercial jurisprudence in our country, the *Commercial Law Review*, edited by WANG Baoshu, deserves to be mentioned. In view of the then situation, that "the monographic study is still very short, and the major issues have not been studied", in order to "base on the development and improvement of Chinese commercial law, widely draw lessons from and absorb the experience, precedents and doctrines of foreign commercial legislation, track the development trend of

1 *Trends of and Review on Commercial Law Study*, (November 2001 - July 2002), at http://cn-commercial-law.org.cn/shangfa_4.htm.

foreign commercial law, promote the monographic study on commercial law, accelerate the construction of commercial jurisprudence discipline, and then provide theoretical service for commercial legislation and commercial trial practice",[1] a collection of papers which focuses on commercial jurisprudence was published. Based on this, an influential academic platform has been established for study on commercial law.

In the academic history of study on commercial law in China, a landmark event occurred in 2001, that was, the Research Association of Civil and Economic Law, China Law Society was divided into three, and the Research Association of Commercial Jurisprudence was established separately. This Research Association holds an annual academic conference and several symposiums and publishes a *China Commercial Law Annual* per annum, which has provided a more special platform for commercial law scholars to conduct academic communications.

1.2 Debate on Legislative Style of Civil and Commercial Laws

The legislative style of civil and commercial laws has always been a topic which is dwelled upon by civil and commercial jurisprudence scholars with great relish, but difficult to define. After reform and opening-up in China, the importance of commercial law has shown day by day. The argument about separation of civil code and commercial code or combination of civil code and commercial code has become a prolonged theoretical paradox. In summary, separation or combination thereof refers to the relationship between civil code and commercial code (in nature, it refers to the relationship between civil law and commercial law). Separation of civil code and commercial code means to separately formulate the commercial code beyond the civil code. Combination of civil code and commercial code means to establish only one unified code to regulate civil and commercial relationship. The provisions connected with commercial affairs, which cannot be integrated into civil code, shall be established as separate laws

1 WANG Baoshu (ed.), *Commercial Law Review · Editor's Letter*, Law Press·China, 1996.

and regulations. The scholars who hold the view of "combination of civil code and commercial code" pointed out that, "separation of civil code and commercial code is not a scientific conception, but a product of history", "combination of civil code and commercial code has met the needs of the development of social commodity economy, and has reflected the requirements of large-scale socialized production. It is of progressive significance to a certain degree".[1] Some scholars have also specified the grounds of combination of civil code and commercial code in their writings.[2] The scholars who hold the view of "separation of civil code and commercial code", based on the analysis on foreign practice in respect of commercial law, deemed that "China shall take the legislative style with dualistic structure in private law, that is, taking the legislative style with separation of civil code and commercial code, and separately formulating commercial code beyond the civil code".[3] Some scholars insisted that, "someday, a variety of separate commercial laws will be compiled as a socialist commercial code with Chinese characteristics. It will represent the maturity of legal concepts of modern market economy in our country."[4]

Even now, it is still hard for the scholars and practitioners to give a convincing answer to the issue on whether the civil code and commercial code shall be combined or separated. Some scholars pointed out that, since the arguments on legislative style of civil and commercial laws are value judgments made from the perspective of normative analysis, short of support by empirical analysis conclusion, so, they are not convincing. This is the main reason why the domestic scholars are still in endless dispute on this issue at present.[5] The argument on

1 LIANG Huixing & WANG Liming, *Theoretical Issues about Economic Law*, China University of Political Science and Law Press, 1986, pp.121,122.

2 *Civil Law*, in JIANG Ping (ed.), China University of Political Science and Law Press, 2000, p.56.

3 FAN Jian & WANG Jianwen, *Introduction to Business Law*, China Higher Education Press, 2003, p.210.

4 XU Xuelu, *Introduction of Commercial Law*, People's Court Press, 1999, p.6.

5 REN Erxin & SHI Xuwen, *Theoretical Exploration and Institutional Innovation on Commercial Law*, Law Press·China, 2005, p.177.

whether to combine or to separate the civil and commercial code seems to point at legislative style, but in nature, it is a continuation of the argument on the relationship between civil law and commercial law, and the relationship between civil jurisprudence and commercial jurisprudence, or furthermore, to observe from the perspective of civil law standard, it is the argument on whether the commercial law shall be independent, and whether the commercial jurisprudence shall be independent. In fact, the issue whether commercial law and commercial jurisprudence are independent is not inevitably linked with "combination of civil code and commercial code", or "separation of civil code and commercial code". To explore the relationship between civil law and commercial law with substantive significance from the form of the two legislative styles has seemly lost the focus of logic of argument.

Objectively speaking, since the beginning of this century, with the promulgation of a lot of separate commercial laws and regulations, the phenomenon that the commercial law was completely contained by civil law has disappeared. Therefore, in fact, the civil law and commercial law are hard to be combined. However, in China, due to the reality that there is still no civil code so far and the unpredictability of whether the commercial code will be formulated in the future, the "commercial law" often referenced by Chinese jurisprudential circle, in theory or in practice, only can be considered within the system of "combination of civil code and commercial code". Even the scholar who supported the formulation of merchant law, which was equivalent to the general provisions of commercial law, and referred to as "General Principles of Commercial Law" in the subsequent study and practice,[1] did not deny that commercial law is a special law subordinated to civil law. At the present stage, the institutional norms of the social economic activities in our country are basically subject to the legal system of combination of civil and commercial codes. Today, with the development of

1 WANG Baoshu, *Reform of the Commercial Law and the Changing Economic Law*, Law Press·China, 2003, pp.38-55.

modern commodity economy, a trend of "inter-infiltration" between civil law and commercial law emerges. In the worldwide civil legislation, the phenomenon of "inter-infiltration" between civil law and commercial law has been very prevalent. And the most fundamental reason for this is that the traditional boundary between the two has been broken. With the development of socialization of production and non-specificity of subjects participating in commercial transactions, the range of commercial transactions has extended to such areas as industry, agriculture, real estate, negotiable securities and futures. It is hard to determine whether the laws and regulations applicable to such areas are covered by civil law, or covered by commercial law. In consideration of this, it is really useless and endless to continue to get bogged down the choice between "combination of civil code and commercial code" and "separation of civil code and commercial code". From the relationship between theory and practice, the argument on the relationship between civil law and commercial law has lagged far behind the practice of civil and commercial legislation. The substantive relationship with perfect harmony between civil law and commercial law will not be changed by the opinions of scholars on "separation" or "combination". Furthermore, the commercial legal norms can either be covered by traditional commercial code, or emerged in the form of separate laws beyond commercial code. That is to say, the form of existence of modern commercial law has been of diversity. These cases show that the relationship between modern civil and commercial laws has entered into a new stage.[1]

"Out of three worlds, and beyond five elements". We acknowledge that the issue on how to understand the relationship between civil law and commercial law needs to be solved seriously in the development of commercial law. But we may jump out of the argument on combination or separation of civil code and commercial code, combine the practice of our country in a practical and realistic

1 GUO Feng, "Theoretical Analysis on Separation of Civil Code and Commercial Code and Combination Thereof", *China Legal Science*, 1996, Issue 5.

way, and then work out a feasible plan, to provide authentic theoretical support, based on the situation of our country, for the development of commercial law in China. We even need to rethink the premise of such argument. Under the principle of combination of civil code and commercial code, must the commercial provisions be incorporated in civil code and regardless of the difference between the two? Pursuant to the principles of separation of civil code and commercial code, must commercial code be established separately beyond the civil code? Apart from those, couldn't we have other alternatives and designs? Sometimes, a rigid understanding on concepts will constrain our thoughts, and make us fall into the misconceptions in theory. When we jump out of the argument within the concepts with more practical spirit and more attentions on reality, we may have a new understanding from a new perspective.[1] With this idea in mind, we can acknowledge the premise, that is, substantively speaking, the commercial law is gradually formed from the establishment and development of civil law. No matter how the objective basis of the formation thereof, the traces of civil law have been left in theory and application of commercial law. So, no matter which legislative style is adopted, the commercial law cannot get rid of the connections with civil law, what's different is the focus. Meanwhile, we must be clearly aware that, due to the lack of commercial law tradition but with urgent need to develop commercial law in China, to insist on implementing the concept of combination of civil code and commercial code will certainly hinder the formation of independent commercial law system. The key to maintain a proper relationship between civil law and commercial law and to make a scientific orientation for them is to maximize their respective roles in construction of socialist market economy.

1.3 On Infiltration of Public Law to Commercial Law

Traditionally, as a law on autonomy of merchants, commercial law was a typical private law. Fundamentally speaking, the modern and contemporary commercial

1 PENG Zhenming & JIANG Hua, "Reflection on Codification of Commercial Law", *Journal of Zhejiang Normal University (Natural Sciences)*, 2005, Issue 1.

law, as a law to regulate the relationship of commercial transactions, was also a part of private law. However, with the development of modern economy and enhancement of concept on entire society, the government has gradually changed its attitude towards private legal relationships, and has taken active interventions, as a result, the so-called "infiltration of public law to private law" was formed. The infiltration of public law to commercial law is especially noticeable. The commercial law was established around private legal norms. Meanwhile, in order to guarantee that the norms can be implemented, a lot of clauses with the characteristics of public law have been set up. LI Yichen, a scholar in Taiwan of China, pointed out that, although the contemporary commercial laws in various countries are centered on provisions of private law, in order to guarantee the implementation of judicial provisions, many clauses with the characteristics of public law have emerged in commercial law, which has nearly been inseparable from administrative law and criminal law. The "infiltration of public law to commercial law" has certainly been formed.[1]

As a developmental phenomenon of law, the infiltration of public law to commercial law is honored by scholars as the development trend of modern commercial law, and a great difference between commercial law and civil law.[2] The reason to this is, compared with civil law, that commercial subject needs to assume more duties of care than civil subject, and the dress of commercial actions is of more significance for security of transactions. The better implementation of those needs to be guaranteed by the public power of state. However, the compulsion of the provisions which have the characteristics of public law in commercial law were produced in response to the technical needs of market transactions, which is a technical approach to pursue the efficiency of transaction, but not a product of active interventions in economy by the state. Compulsion is

1 Quoted in ZHANG Guojian, *On Commercial Law*, Taiwan, China: San Min Book Co., Ltd., 1980, p.20.

2 FAN Jian & WANG Jianwen, *Introduction to Business Law*, China Higher Education Press, 2003, p.50.

an intrinsic characteristic of commercial law, which is inherently unified with the autonomy of private law. It is a basic premise of rationalization of commercial law to correctly deal with the compulsion thereof.[1]

In China, with the deep development of market economy activities, like the development trend of commercial laws in other countries, our commercial law has also been infiltrated by public law. The main manifestation thereof is that, in order to secure the healthy economic development and social stability, more and more contents, which could embody economic authority and intervention wills of the government, regulate the economic relationship between individual and the government and society, and protect the social public interest, emerged in commercial legislation. To a certain extent, those contents have all shown the property of public law. It should be noted that, in the process of system construction, the commercial law in our country has absorbed more irregular contents of public law which could embody the active interventions of public authority in commercial activities. Therefore, with respect to the infiltration of public law to commercial law, the Chinese commercial law has gone further, and has shown a characteristic of "pan-infiltration of public law". Judging from the contents of commercial separate laws in China, the Insurance Law has provided regulatory body, China Insurance Regulatory Commission, and its regulatory authority, regulatory contents and manners in details, granting the Commission to carry out comprehensive supervision on insurance industry in legal form; the Securities Law has provided supervision on securities exchange, granting China Securities Regulatory Commission to conduct comprehensive supervision on securities exchange, etc.

The characteristic of "pan-infiltration of public law" in Chinese commercial law emerged with profound economic base and institutional background. Firstly, the economic base determines the superstructure. The economic system established

1 CAO Xingquan, "Seriously Treat the Compulsion of Commercial Law: Annotation in Various Views", *Journal of Gansu Political Science and Law Institute*, 2004, Issue 5.

in our country is the socialist market economy with Chinese characteristics. Under this economic system, there are many specific economic phenomena, such as "Macro-economic Control, and Economic Restructure", which have become the economic base of "pan-infiltration of public law" presented in Chinese commercial law. And the "pan-infiltration of public law" to commercial law will be further reflected in the future legal process. Secondly, the legislative system in our country which was transitioned from planned economy focused on the safety of transactions, and has seriously neglected the expressions of subject wills in commercial activities, which caused the value of the norms on commercial subjects and commercial conducts to be distorted in our country. For instance, the negotiable instruments law not only imposes severely restriction on the category of instruments and the qualification of drawer, but also provides that, a real transaction relationship and the creditor's right and obligation shall exist when the issuance, acquisition and transfer of instruments occur.

Many scholars put forward that the infiltration of public law to commercial law shall be confined to the inactive interventions by public authority on commercial activities in nature, that is, setting up compulsory system which must be followed by commercial subjects, to constrain the autonomy of commercial subjects and aggravate the legal liabilities thereof. From the perspective of building a fair and orderly market economy environment, in the infiltration of public law to commercial law, the active interventions by public authority on commercial activities shall not be advocated. Not only involved in infiltration of public law, such active interventions will change the private nature of commercial law. When public authority actively intervenes in commercial activities, and then changes the nature of commercial law, we might refer to it as "economic law", that is, the law under which the state intervenes in economic activities. In the process of reconstructing market economy laws, for purpose of the construction of structure and content of commercial law, our country didn't make sufficient preparations in conformity with legal principles. The active interventions by public authority on commercial activities, which was a part of "public law", were provided in commercial law, which has caused a negative impact on the reconstruction of commercial law theory in our country. Its rationality should be questioned. Therefore, to study commercial jurisprudence in our country needs to untangle the law of development of commercial law, be aware of the boundary of infiltration of public law to commercial law, pour more strength into expanding the autonomy space for developing commercial law, and prevent the evolution from commercial law into economic law.

1.4 Confusion over Modernization of Commercial Law

There are different views on the understanding of modernization. Generally, people interpret the modernization, from a perspective of relative concept, as "a developmental dynamic process and realistic activity, the difference from tradition on time and space".[1] And the modernization of legal system refers to "a historical process that the entire legal system of a country or region, from spirit (or concept or consciousness) of law to institutions of law, gradually reflects, adapts and promotes the developmental trend of modern civilization".[2] The legal modernization has presented two models, namely, the endogenous model and exogenous model. The basic elements of legal system are legal norms, legal procedure and legal ideology. So, the legal modernization shall also contain the modernization process of such elements. But the two models are different in "nature of driving force, order of reform process, and the degree of actual evolution".[3]

As an important part of a country's legal institutions, the commercial law also includes commercial legal norms, commercial legal procedure and commercial legal ideology. Meanwhile, it also contains the endogenous model and exogenous model.[4] Since the reform and opening-up, China has promulgated a number of

1 ZOU Hailin, *Several Issues in the Development of Commercial Law in China*, at http://www.iolaw.org.cn/showNews.aspx?id=10228.

2 GONG Pixiang, *Law and Modernization*, Nanjing Normal University Press, 1995, p.7.

3 Ibid., p.118.

4 XU Xuelu, *On Modernization of Chinese Commercial Law*, at http://www.privatelaw.com.cn/.

commercial laws and regulations in a short period, which was shown, from the model of modernization of commercial law, as a joint promotion by external force and internal force. As a result, the commercial legal institutions have had the characteristics of modernization in form. Such commercial legal norms have contained the legal procedures and legal ideology of modern commercial law. But the substantive modernization has not appeared in such legal procedures and legal ideology. The reason for that, to a great extent, is the lack of ideology of modern commercial law.

"Reference of legal system is one of the basic laws of modernization thereof."[1] It includes "reference to the spirit (or concept or consciousness) and the specific legal system of modern laws. The former is more fundamental and more substantive, which is the basis of the entire legal system, and also the most difficult and permanent form of reference of legal system", "if the reference of legal system doesn't involve any spirit of law, but only involves specific legal institutions and specific legal system...it will be vulnerable to be repelled, eroded, deconstructed and damaged by the traditional spirits of law".[2] In the context of globalization, the issue on how to draw lessons from, transplant or reconstruct, duly and properly, the commercial legal system and rules in our country, has become an important step of the legal reform. In the process of reference and transplantation of modern commercial law, an issue about goal, focus and choice has been involved. Our goal is to draw lessons from and transplant those concepts and specific institutions of commercial law, which can sufficiently reflect the requirements of development of modern economy. For purpose of the specific institutions and concepts of commercial law, we shall focus on the reference to the concepts of modern commercial law, which is the key to innovate the commercial law in our country. What the choice involves is very rich, not only the specific commercial legal institutions and procedures, but also the concepts of commercial

1 GONG Pixiang, *Law and Modernization*, Nanjing Normal University Press, 1995, p.16.
2 Ibid.

law. We shall choose the institutions, procedures and concepts thereof which can represent the developing trend of times and can follow the international trend.[1]

Furthermore, the revision of commercial law and its modernization should receive more attention. In recent years, since the judgments on regulative object of commercial law and the design of system of commercial law in commercial code have seriously lagged behind the socio-economic development practice, many countries with separation of civil code and commercial code universally make substantial revisions on commercial code, and even expect to realize the thorough modernization through making new laws. In our country, the revision of commercial law and its modernization is an outstanding issue. The "commercial laws" which have been revised in our country include *Company Law*, *Insurance Law*, *Securities Law* and so on. Some of the other laws, which have been classified into "commercial law", have begun to be revised, but more of them have not been scheduled for revision. The revision per se of commercial law in our country implies a tortuous developmental process thereof. Obviously, the purpose for revising commercial law was to improve the legal norms which were absent of propriety. However, even after revision by legislative body, the commercial law still has room for revision. This is maybe an eternal issue that the scholars and practitioners have to face. For this, we must prudently follow the legislative concept and requirements of modern commercial law, and seek a scientific commercial law system which can adapt to the developmental practice of market economy and the legal system in our country, and then base on which to guide the enactment and revision of specific commercial institutions.

1 XU Xuelu, *On Modernization of Chinese Commercial Law*, at http://www.privatelaw.com.cn/.

2. Study on *Company Law* to Meet the Needs of Market Economy Development

As an important law with reference to commercial subjects, the *Company Law* plays a decisive role in the system of commercial laws. From the enactment of *Company Act* by Qing government in 1904, to the promulgation of *Company Law* after comprehensive revision in 2005, the company legal system in our country has experienced one century of vicissitudes.

After the Third Plenary Session of the 11th Central Committee, China entered into the period of reform of economic system. As the micro-foundation of economic system, the company institutions began to restore, and the company legislation has also been gradually propelled. The Company Law of the People's Republic of China was passed by voting in the fifth session of Standing Committee of the National People's Congress on December 29, 1993. The first Company Law of new China emerged. However, due to the late start of company practice and rapid market development in our country, the clauses of Company Law have many defects, such as rigid principle, poor operability, and too many legal loopholes, which have confronted many problems in practical application. Although the law has been amended for two times in the subsequent ten years, it was still unable to meet the needs of the development of the socialist market economy and the adjustment of the relationship between companies. In order to adapt to the global competition faced by enterprises of our country, for purpose of reducing supervision, encouraging investment, improving corporate governance mechanism, and enhancing the flexibility and competitive power of company, the 18th session of Standing Committee of the 10th National People's Congress passed the revised Company Law on October 27, 2005. The new Company Law has made more comprehensive revision on the *Company Law 1993*, further improved the corporate legal institutions, complied with the practical requirements of deepening reform and promoting development, and provided a more powerful systematic support for the development of Chinese socialist market economy.

The promulgation and revision of Company Law and the development of company practice have brought about the prosperity of study on company jurisprudence in China. Objectively speaking, the company jurisprudence has always been the discipline which the commercial law scholars has poured into most passion, and one of the areas of Chinese commercial jurisprudence with earlier development and more study achievements. If the promulgation of Company Law 1993 was a landmark that Chinese company jurisprudence has formed scale, then, it is a the period, from the Company Law began to be revised at the end of December, 1999 to present, that Chinese company jurisprudence has obtained further development.[1] On the surface, the study on company jurisprudence in these two periods was conducted mainly around the revision and improvement of Company Law 1993 and the understanding on and implementation of Company Law *2005*. However, in nature, it was the deep thinking on and integration of the theory and practice of company by scholars, on the basis of drawing lessons from overseas study results, in the major context of worldwide modernization reform of company law in 21st century. The exploration on the issues about legislative concept, governance structure, social responsibility and capital system of company not only has theoretical value, but also has practical significance, which has shown the study framework with integration and interaction between macro concepts and micro institutions in the domain of company law.

From the mutual relationship between the institutions evolution of company law and academic study process of company law, there was an important phenomenon deserved to be paid attention to. That was, before and after the establishment of Company Law in 1993, more scholars participated in annotation and interpretation of Company Law; however, when the Company Law was revised in 2005, the form of participation of scholars was more embodied in designing the normative construction of it, and enabling the contents thereof to show more imagines of

1 *Research on the Development of Chinese Commercial Law*, in ZOU Hailin (ed.), China Social Science Press, 2008, p.39.

scholars. In fall of 2001, when the Commercial Jurisprudence Research Society of China Law Society was established, many attendees suggested that the scholars should propound a revision draft of Company Law. After some years of specialized research conducted by the research group on "revision of Company Law", which was originated by the Commercial Jurisprudence Research Society, the Proposed Revision Draft of Company Law of the People's Republic of China was formed[1], in which some systematic and normative revision suggestions with updated concept were propounded to the then current Company Law 1993. This proposed draft had a great impact on the revision of Company Law, many propositions in which have shown in *Company Law 2005* which was promulgated afterwards. In addition, a number of people involved in drafting this proposed draft have all become members of the expert advisory group of the Legal Affairs Office of the State Council for revising Company Law.[2] It can be fully seen from this phenomenon that the study on commercial law, especially the company law, conducted by commercial law scholars, already had very high proactivity and initiative, which not only can affect the implementation of Company Law, but also can influence the legislative practice thereof.

2.1 Research on the Character of Company Law and Corporate Autonomy

The development of company law in our country has once confronted many problems connected with ideology, position of company, state control and so on. The character of company law directly determines the whole trend of the company law, which is a basic proposition of the theory and practice of company law. In 1993, when the Company Law was formulated, establishment of company was in vogue. Since a large number of high and low-quality companies mixed up, the phenomena of escaping or denying debts through the company and then

1 *Proposed Revision Draft of Company Law of the People's Republic of China*, in WANG Baoshu (ed.), 2004.

2 They are JIANG Ping, WANG Jiafu, WANG Baoshu, ZHAO Xudong, CHEN Su, ZHU Ciyun and YE Lin. See *Research Report on Revisions in New Company Law*, China Legal Publishing House, 2005, p.380.

influencing economic order emerged one after another. Therefore, to prevent abuse of establishment of company, rectify the bogus company and normalize the order of company operation became the institutional goal of company law at that time, the embodiment of which in clauses of company law was the existence of a large number of compulsory norms therein. As a result, the company law in our country basically became a pure law on control of enterprise.

With the continuous improvement of market economy law system and deepening of the practice of enterprise legal system construction, the issue on whether the norms of company law shall be compulsory or arbitrary has caused a broad and profound discussion in the academic circle. Subject to the "contract theory applicable to company", originated from the United States in the 1980s,[1]the company law scholars in our country gradually realized that the modern enterprises are independent legal persons and self-governing enterprises.[2] As a private law, the company law shall emphasize the self-governance of company, give it a right, a choice and room for self-governance. The private law property of company law should be called back, and then promote a fair, efficient and free socialist market economic system to be established. As to company law, in addition to the binding function, more importantly, the stimulative function thereof shall be exerted to stimulate the vitality and business flexibility of the company. Some scholars pointed out that, since the original motive for formulating Company Law 1993 was to solve the problems of state-owned enterprise, therefore, the Company Law 1993 has carried the political task for maintaining the social stability ab

1 The law and economics scholars took company as a kind of economic phenomenon to analyze. They held that enterprise is a series of contractual arrangements, is a kind of collection constituted by many factors, which are jointly bound by a complex contract chain. Pursuant to the "Contractual Relationship Theory", company law is basically a kind of arbitrary law. The government or legislative body shall not impose any compulsory provisions on company through statutory law. Since such compulsory provisions are running counter to the contractual relationship concept which represents the free enterprise and free market.

2 JIANG Ping, "Reform and Improvement of Company Law and Commercial Enterprise", *Chinese Lawyer*, 1999, Issue 6.

initio, subject to which, the pursuit of stability, before becoming a conscious action, must be achieved through compulsion. Such text structure would certainly influence the judgment of academic circle on the character of company law.[1] Some scholar directly expressed the character of company law, in legislative policy, as corporate personality liberalism, corporation establishment liberalism, corporate capital liberalism, corporate governance liberalism and corporate transaction liberalism.[2] The concept for revising company law, infiltrated with such academic thought, is that the corporate legal system of the 21st century shall not simply take the regulation of the corporate actions as core content, but shall provide a set of flexible corporate legal institutions for enterprise, which enables the enterprise to carry out creative activities. To improve the self-developing ability of company through strengthening the self-governing ability thereof has become the new institutional goal of the company law.

The persistent and broad attention of academic circle has finally given rise to the judicial expression of private law character of company law. *Company Law 2005* has fully embodied the concept for constructing enterprise legal system with reducing control and strengthening self-governance. This concept was centrally embodied, in the areas of operational decision-making, investment, financing and investigation of internal responsibility of operators, to expand the room for corporate self-governance and to highlight the important role of articles of association as far as possible.[3] In the previous company operation practice, the articles of association were always deemed as formalized corporate documents, the contents of which were stereotyped. As a result, the internal systematic structures of companies lack individual characteristics. In accordance with the new Company Law, in many areas, the company can arrange its own institutions

1 JIANG Daxing, *On Private Law Character of Company Law*, *Journal of Nanjing University*, 2005, Issue 1.

2 SHI Tiantao, "Liberalism of Company Law and Its Legislative Policy-The Revision of Company Law in China", *Global Law Review*, 2005, Issue 1.

3 SHEN Sibao & SHEN Jian, "Important Position and Role of Articles of Association in New Company Law", *Applicable Law*, 2006, Issue 3.

through its articles of association. For instance, when the registered capital needs to be paid by installment, the timing of capital contributions may be provided by articles of association; whether the legal representative will be served by the chairman of the board, executive director or manager may be set forth by articles of association; in a limited liability company, the allocation of dividends or prior subscription of contribution may be provided not to subject to the proportion of capital contribution by articles of association. The articles of association may also set forth that the shareholders may not exercise their voting rights in accordance with the proportion of capital contribution.[1] It can be said that the broadening of the applicable scope of arbitrary norms, the persistence on the commercial spirit of corporate self-governance by new Company Law are undoubtedly a fruit of theoretic exploration of the academic circle and the practical experience of company.

2.2 Reflection and Choice of Corporate Capital Institutions

Corporate capital institutions are the foundation stone of corporate legislation, which run through the whole process of establishment, operation and termination of a company. The process for choosing a corporate capital institutional mode is not only the confrontation process of different corporate legislative concepts, but also the process for cognizing the function of company law. The developments of corporate capital institutions in different countries are not identical, but the purposes thereof are roughly the same, namely, to promote the development of corporate institutions, to facilitate the company raising funds and to protect the interests of creditors of a company. However, the evolution of different institutions is nothing but to seek the best balance point among different purposes.[2]

In order to balance the interests of creditors of company, and hold them

1 CHEN Su, *Company Law: the Institutional Innovation Advanced with Times*, *Chinese Academy of Social Sciences Review*, December 29, 2005.

2 ZHAO Deshu, *Comparative Study on Capital Institutions of Joint Stock Limited Company after the Revision of Company Laws in Mainland and Taiwan*, in ZHAO Xudong (ed.), *International Perspectives on Company Law Reform*, China University of Political Science and Law Press, 2007, p.263.

harmless from the limited liabilities of shareholders, a set of mechanism on formation, maintenance and withdrawal of corporate capital has been designed in advance in the legislation of traditional company law. This mechanism is summarized as three doctrines of capital certainty, capital maintenance and unchanging capital in theory. But the traditional three doctrines of corporate capital are under more and more fire due to their intrinsic defects. Some scholars have compared the influence of three corporate capital doctrines mode on the interests of shareholders, company and outside creditors, and further introspected the issue on whether the corporate capital institutions in our country should be oriented by the interests of shareholders with the pursuit of flexibility of financing, or should be oriented by the interests of creditors and take the flexibility of financing into account simultaneously.[1] Some scholar held that, in theory, the presupposed functions of corporate capital institutions could be divided into financing function and credit function. The former emphasizes on realization of the financing and employment of corporate capital, while the latter lays stress on protection of the creditor's interests. The traditional theory of company law laid particular stress on the credit function, regardless of the financing function thereof. As a result, the core concept of our corporate legislation was the view on preventing wrongdoings, for protecting the order and safety of transactions, and the legislative rules adopted by which were centered on compulsory rules, with the dominant idea towards protection of the creditor's interests.[2]

Along the functional path, more and more scholars have conducted review and judgment to our corporate capital institutions, and gradually formed a consensus that the eclectic capital system is easy to be accepted by the country in which the company law is under transition.[3] Some scholars pointed out that the guarantee

1 FU Qiong, "Comparison of the Three Corporate Capital Doctrines Mode and The Position of Our Corporate Capital Institutions", *Studies in Law and Business*, 2004, Issue 1.

2 YE Lin, *Study on Company Law*, China Renmin University Press, 2008, p.238.

3 YU Min & TANG Huojian & TAN Lirong, LIAO Zhenzhong, "Summary of 2003 Annual session of Commercial Jurisprudence Research Society of China Law Society", *China Legal Science*, 2003, Issue 6.

function of corporate capital has not played the role for protecting company's creditors in practice, on the contrary, it has limited the room of company to facilitate financing and operate freely. Therefore, the capital institutions of different countries have gradually shifted to be loose and flexible; however, meanwhile, the importance on how to protect the interests of creditors was highlighted. With adaption of the trend of mitigation, the corporate capital institutions in our country shall build effective measures, such as, capital information disclosure, preventing the company's assets from improperly flowing to shareholder, and piercing the corporate veil, to protect the company's creditors.[1] It is not only the corporate capital which can determine the credit of company, the corporate assets play a more important role for this. The basic thread and direction of Chinese corporate capital institutions reform is from capital credit to assets credit, and from statutory capital system to authorized capital system or eclectic capital system.[2] The corporate capital institutions shall be centered on enabling rules, take the promotion of efficient financing of enterprise and enhancement of the national economic competitiveness as ultimate goal, promote the formation of corporate capital with minimum cost, seek flexibility of financing with sufficient autonomy of the corporate management, give the investor tangible return on investment with the attitude of actively responding the real business needs and leave withdrawal channel for investment, and balance the conflict of interests among company participants with the concept of neutral rules, so as to achieve a win-win situation among company participants, develop social resource and create social wealth, and further construct a modern company law in conformity with competitive economy.[3]

From the choice and comparison of various capital institutions ascend

1 ZHU Ciyun, "Concepts on Corporate Capital and Protection of Creditor's Interests", *Tribune of Political Science and Law*, 2005, Issue 3.

2 ZHAO Xudong, "From Capital Credit to Assets Credit", *Chinese Journal of Law*, 2003, Issue 5.

3 XU Xiaosong, "On Defects and Improvement of Chinese Corporate Capital Institutions", *China Legal Science*, 2000, Issue 3.

to reflection on the functional position and legislative concept of corporate institutions, the studies of scholars have provided theoretical support for legislative choice of corporate capital institutions in China. The new Company Law has improved the provisions on company establishment and corporate capital institutions. For instance, it has largely declined the registered capital of company to the minimum amount, expanded the property scope that the shareholders can contribute to the company, and implemented the institution about paying registered capital by installments, etc. Such revisions and supplements have facilitated the establishment of company on system, which are favorable for encouraging investment and startup of a business, and promoting economic development and expanding employment.

2.3 Theoretical Exploration on Improving Corporate Governance Structure

Corporate Governance is a core proposition of company law, which mainly refers to the systematic arrangements on allocation and exercise of powers of the relevant corporate organs. In order to build an effective corporate governance mechanism, the governance structure of a company shall be scientific and reasonable for effectively deploying and balancing the duties and authorities of all relevant stakeholders. Some scholar held that corporate governance is an open system involving the internal and external relationships of a company. For purpose of internal relationship, the corporate governance mainly includes the internal allotment and balance of corporate powers. In this sense, the rules for setting up corporate organs will become an important part of corporate governance. For purpose of external relationship, to conduct corporate governance not only need to define the relationship between enterprise and company, but also need to adjust the relationship between the company and all interest groups.[1]

In China, the evolution of corporate governance structure is closely related to the progress of state-owned enterprises reform. The property right of state-owned

1 YE Lin, *Study on Company Law*, China Renmin University Press, 2008, p.193.

enterprise and external corporate governance had received the attention and concern of scholars for a long time. With accomplishment of the reform of joint-stock enterprise, the research on corporate governance was firstly focused on the positions and authorities of shareholder and general session of shareholders, and then centered on the position of director and supervisor in corporate governance. Afterwards, the independent director became the most concerned issue in studies on governance of listed company.

The accumulation and innovation in theory has directly brought about a great deal of institutional innovations for the new Company Law on improving the corporate governance structure. For instance, the new Company Law has improved the institutions concerning to shareholders meeting and board of directors, and enriched the provisions on convening and discussion procedures thereof; has increased the authority of board of supervisors, improved the institutions with respect to meetings of board of supervisors, and strengthened the function thereof; has supplemented some provisions on establishment of independent directors; and has made more specific provisions on the faithful and diligent obligations of directors and senior executives to the company, and the liabilities for breach thereof, etc. These measures made the authority arrangement of company's organizations more detailed and reasonable, and also made the relationship of rights and obligations among those more specific and fair, which have fundamentally improved the corporate governance level, and have provided institutional guarantee for maximizing the interests of company and all shareholders thereof.[1]

2.4 Advocating Corporate Social Responsibilities

Pursuant to traditional corporate governance theory, the interests of stakeholders other than shareholders were often neglected. As a result, companies frequently broke moral base line to damage the interests of other stakeholders. With rapid

1 LIU Junhai, *Prospect and Retrospect of 30 Years' Corporate Legislation Since Reform and Opening-up*, *Legal Forum*, 2008, Issue 3.

economic development, the issues about resources and environmental protection, safety and decent work, consumer's right have been brought about. Many scholars began to expound the connotation of social responsibility of enterprise. Meanwhile, combined with the current socio-economic development in China, they have analyzed the constraints existed in both of the theory and practice, and the practical significance, concerning to Chinese enterprise social responsibilities.

The studies of scholar showed that the corporate social responsibility can be understood from two aspects, namely, the substantive aspect and the procedural aspect. As a concept with procedural meaning, the corporate social responsibility requires that the social interests and social rights shall be considered and reflected in the corporate decision-making procedures. As a concept with substantive meaning, the corporate social responsibility requires that the result of corporate decision-making shall be able to be responsible for social interests and social rights.[1] The gist of corporate social responsibility is that a company shall not be only taken as a tool for maximizing the profits of shareholders, but shall be deemed as an organizational system or institutional arrangement which can, to the largest extent, give consideration to and realize the interests of all stakeholders, including the shareholders, of the company; the power of a company comes from the delegation of all stakeholders, but not roots in the conferment of shareholders; the management of a company shall be responsible for all stakeholders, but not only the shareholders.[2]

Based on the specific economic and political structure in our country, and following the tide and proposals of scholars, the new Company Law first generally provides that the company shall assume social responsibility. However, the social responsibility of enterprise frequently needs to be implemented through many

1 LIU Junhai, *Several Issues Concerning to Corporate Social Responsibilities*, *Theoretical Research*, 2007, Issue 22.

2 LU Daifu, *Corporate Social Responsibility and Innovation of Corporate Governance Structure*, in GU Yungeng (ed.), *Company Law Review*, Vol.2002, Shanghai Renmin Press.

mechanisms. The actual performance of corporate social responsibility is largely determined by the effectiveness of judicial remedy. At present, the meaning of corporate social responsibility is ambiguous, the burden on judges is too heavy, and the competency for business judgment is absent. As a result, the judges cannot make judgment on the cases concerning to corporate social responsibility with strong flexibility. Currently, China urgently needs to construct a more convincing theoretical framework, and prevents the corporate social responsibility from descending to a "justifiable" basis of "enterprise with social burden" and "apportionment to enterprise by government". Furthermore, it needs to be considered that the Ministry of Commerce and other departments shall organize guild or business associations, pursuant to the actual situation of this industry, to issue Guidelines on Corporate Social Responsibility, in order to facilitate due consideration by judge in deciding specific cases.[1]

Throughout the development of corporate legislation and research state of corporate jurisprudence in our country, the internationalized and uniform characteristics of company law become increasingly apparent, and the transplantation of corporate legal institutions are ubiquitous. Reflected in the research field, the comparative research on related foreign legislation and practice has always been the research trend of company law discipline. The global research perspective of scholars enables our country to draw lessons from international advanced concept and institutions in legislation. However, the particular historical and cultural background and specific social environment in transition period has determined the importance of localization of corporate legal system. Therefore, even the corporate legal system has been highly internationalized, the understanding and grasp of local environment are still the key point for determining the success of corporate legal institutions. Based on local situation, and pursuing international vision, the organic combination between the two will be an imperative road for developing corporate jurisprudence in the future.

1 LUO Peixin, *Dilemma in Judging Corporate Social Responsibility in Our Country and Several Solutions*, *Legal Science*, 2007, Issue 12.

3. Securities Law Research on Stable Development of Capital Market

Securities are the products when commodity economy develops to a certain stage. With the deepening of economic system reform and continuous development of socialist market economy, our capital market grew out of nothing, developed rapidly with the change from quantity to quality. The securities legislation has been accelerated and gradually improved, which has provided a brand new economic base and institutional background for developing securities jurisprudence in our country, and has also provided plentiful materials and broad room for research of the scholars. Based on the correlation and interaction between academic study and securities legislation, taking the promulgation of *Securities Law 1998* and Revision of *Securities Law 2005* as nodes, the study process of securities jurisprudence in our country can be roughly divided into three stages.

3.1 Before the Promulgation of *Securities Law 1998*

The securities market of our country has always been in a state of chaos from its production. The contents of legislation at different levels were irregular, the criteria of law enforcement were different, and the problems in securities market occurred frequently. After 1992, the greater practical development in the two major stock exchanges in Shanghai and Guangzhou has raised an urgent requirement on formulation of unified Securities Exchange Law. In view of the studies on economic law issues in development of then securities market from different perspectives, for instance, the development plight of securities market, the specialization of securities intermediary agency, and so forth, many people have propounded some specific advice.[1] Other scholar has explored the issues about securities supervision, and has propounded some legislative advice with respect to legislative principle, content of legislation, organizational style, main

1 See QIAN Yi, *Underlying Reasons for Troubling the Development of Chinese Market*, *Legal Science*, 1989, Issue 8; LIU Haibo, *Management of Securities Intermediary Agency under Laws*, *Legal Science*, 1991, Issue 8.

institutions and so forth.[1] But for various reasons, the Securities Law has not been promulgated. Since the Securities Law had been absent for a long time and was coming up, the research on securities jurisprudence at this stage was to make preliminary planning around the general legislative thinking and legislative framework of the Securities Law and the basic legal institutions of securities market on the whole.

The basic principles of securities law are of significance in formulation, or even the implementation thereof, which has been generally accepted and highly appraised by scholars. However, as to what specific basic principles are exactly covered by securities law, there were many different opinions. Some scholars held that the basic principles of securities law include: the principles on protecting legitimate interests of investors; principles of openness, fairness and impartiality; and principles of free will, equal value exchange and good faith.[2] Some scholars held that the basic principles of securities law include: principle of openness; principle of fairness; principle of impartiality; principle of high efficiency; principle for protecting securities investors; and principle for implementing moderate macro-control in securities market.[3] Although the perspectives of understanding and judgment on securities law differed from each other, and the generalization of various basic principles conducted by scholars were different, the principles of "fairness, impartiality and openness" has been highly appraised and become research focus. The study then emphasized that the connotation of openness of securities legal institutions should show in three aspects: first, the securities shall be issued to the public; second, after issuance, the securities shall be publicly traded in securities exchange, prohibiting illegal "black market" trade;

1 See MO Zhicheng, *Conception on Formulating Securities Exchange Laws*, *Law Quarterly Review*, 1987, Issue 2; CHEN Ling, *On Securities Management Legislation*, *Law Science Magazine*, 1988, Issue 5.

2 *An Introduction to Securities Law*, in ZHOU Yousu (ed.), Sichuan People's Publishing House, 1999, p.128.

3 NING Xinchen & LIU Junhai, *Formal Securities Market-Legal Analysis on Securities*, Guizhou People's Publishing House, 1995, p.12.

third, all information concerning to issuance and exchange of securities shall be disclosed.[1] Since the development of securities market in our country was still in its infancy, when implementing principle of openness in legislation, the review on information to be disclosed should be specially stressed. That is, the relevant information disclosed by listed company must be reviewed and approved by competent authority, which cannot be disclosed to the market without approval, in order to enhance the seriousness and authority of the information to be disclosed.[2] For purpose of the principle of impartiality in securities law, most scholars held that it refers to the impartiality of formulation and enforcement of pertinent securities legal institutions shall be strove to realize in the formulation and implementation of securities law. In addition, another view was that "principle of impartiality mainly refers to the securities competent authority and self-regulatory organizations of securities dealers, including stock exchange and association of securities dealers, in the supervision and management of securities market, shall be equal and impartial to treat each participant of securities market, and shall not make a difference in treatment due to different status."[3]

Due to the omission of legislation and lack of credit mechanism in our country, the fraudulent conducts in securities market were very rampant. The development of Chinese securities market was accompanied by the research on legal regulation of securities fraudulent conducts, which has become an eternal topic in securities jurisprudence research. At that moment, the domestic scholars have reached consensus on whether to conduct legal regulation on securities fraudulent conducts, such as, insider trading, market manipulation, and so forth. However, there were still some disagreements on the subject scope of insider trading,

1 HUANG Renjie, *Securities Legal Institutions and Practice*, Law Press·China, 1997, pp.19-20.

2 XU Donggen, *Principles of Openness, Impartiality and Fairness in Securities Legal System, Study on Several Legal Issues Concerning to Securities Market*, Shanghai Academy of Social Sciences, 1997, p.210.

3 NING Xinchen & LIU Junhai, *Formal Securities Market-Legal Analysis on Securities*, Guizhou People's Publishing House, 1995, p.13.

definition of insider trading, subjective state of mind of insider trader, subjective elements of market manipulation, etc. Therefore, in this aspect, the study focused on defining the illegal actions in securities market from the perspective of constitutive requirements of criminal jurisprudence, in which the studies on insider trading and market manipulation was more centralized and deeper. Some research showed that there are two kinds of intentional circumstances in insider trading: first, deliberately to conceal insider information, and then conduct securities transactions thereby; second, deliberately to provide others with insider information or steal insider information to conduct insider trading.[1] Another view was that, as long as the actor has been aware of insider information and then conducted pertinent transactions, an insider trading might be constituted. It is not necessary to prove the subjective state of mind of traders in transactions and the result of transactions (whether a profit has been made).[2] In determining whether a transaction constitutes "manipulation", the motivation factor is not of substance, but the purpose factor is a constitutive requirement of manipulation.[3] These studies have all objectively shown the concurrency and interaction between theory and practice of securities law.

Information disclosure system is the core system of securities law. With the development of securities market, the scholars gradually realized that "An open securities market is the basis for forming fair price of securities", "the disclosure of corporate information is an important factor to prevent securities fraud."[4] Securities market failure exists objectively, which is the economic base of information disclosure system. To design the information disclosure system

1 CHEN Xiao, *On Legal Regulation of Securities Insider Trading*, *Civil and Commercial Law Review*, Vol.5, Law Press·China, 1997.

2 YANG Zhihua, *Study on Securities Legal Institutions*, China University of Political Science and Law Press, 1995, p.304.

3 SHEN Houfu, *Legal Analysis on Market Manipulation in Securities Transactions*, *Civil and Commercial Law Review*, Vol.7, Law Press·China, 1997.

4 WANG Baoshu, *Disclosure of Information Concerning to Issuing Company and Protection of Investors*, in WANG Baoshu (ed.), *Commercial Law Review*, Vol.1, Law Press·China, 1997, pp.279, 280.

in our country, the double goals, efficiency and equity, must be simultaneously given consideration to on choice of value, so as to reach a harmonious and intrinsic unity between the two. When the government uses information disclosure system to intervene securities market, it shall lay stress on the following aspects: first, creating a fair competitive environment, and building a formal and sound information disclosure system; second, adjudging disputes, punishing illegal activities and guaranteeing the implementation of information disclosure system; and, third, protecting the interests of investors and promoting development of securities market.[1] The principles relied on by this system can be summarized as three points: first, sufficiency and completeness; second, authenticity and accuracy; third, timeliness. The Chinese securities legislation and securities administration authority shall lay most stress and efforts on the mandatory information disclosure system and the pertinent issues, such as the range, depth, timeliness and comparability of information dissemination, and the issues connected with investigation and punishment of deliberate violation of information disclosure regulations, in order to make the market become more mature, and finally liberate the government from daily economic decision-making and specific market operation with high social cost, huge risk, thankless task and unendurable annoyance.[2] Some scholar has analyzed the basic principles concerning to information disclosure of listed company, and pointed out that the listed company shall, when disclosing its information, implement some major principles, such as principles of authenticity, sufficiency, accuracy and timeliness.[3]

In this period, constrained by the historical background and securities legislative practice, the studies on securities jurisprudence was a mile wide and an inch deep, especially the exploration on specific institutions was relatively

1 ZHANG Zhongjun, *Research on Basic Issues Concerning to Information Disclosure System in Securities Market*, *Journal of Renmin University of China*, 1996, Issue 1.

2 GAO Xiqing, *Theoretical Basis of Mandatory Information Disclosure System in Securities Market*, *Securities Market Herald*, 1996, Issue 10.

3 CHE Su, *Basic Principles for Disclosing Information of Listed Company*, *China Legal Science*, 1998, Issue 1.

superficial and scattered, lacking thorough jurisprudential analysis. However, the attention paid to market practice and exploration with theoretical resources by scholars have provided essential theoretical preparation for promulgation of securities law.

3.2 From Promulgation of *Securities Law 1998* to Revision of *Securities Law 2005*

The promulgation of *Securities Law 1998* is of great significance for the construction of Chinese securities legal system and the development of securities jurisprudential research. Taking the promulgation of Securities Law as a turning point, the securities law and regulations increased rapidly, which caused the securities legal system to become the most enormous and complex collection of regulations in commercial law area. With the rapid expansion of scale of the capital market, the securities jurisprudential research, supported by securities legal institutions, has obtained an unprecedented development opportunity and has shown a pragmatic, innovative, open and progressive research trend.

In the early stage, securities jurisprudential research relatively focused on macro and fundamental theoretical issues. But in this period, the focus has been gradually diverted to exposition of specific micro institutions. Meanwhile, paying attention to drawing lessons from foreign experiences, especially the advanced experiences of mature market in the UK and US, the scholars have began to conduct research, step by step, on the key issues occurred in the implementation of Securities Law. Due to the special national conditions and the operating mechanism of securities market predominated by government in our country, it was urgent to research the position of regulatory concept and function and the reasonable exercise of regulatory authority on securities market pursuant to the national conditions in China. The specific research results mainly included: (i) the research on the basic theories concerning to the supervision of securities market. It involves the use of theory of public choice and theory of incomplete law to search the crux of poor supervision in securities market of our country, and then provide new ideas for management to improve the efficiency of securities supervision and to build fair and efficient investment environment for investors. As to supervisory concept, some scholar put forward that, under the condition with imperfect institutions, if more governmental actions and administrative interventions could be deemed as a general character of the emerging markets in a certain way, then, in this period, with China entering into the post non-tradable share reform period, the marketization trend of capital market has become inevitable. For purpose of supervisory concept, this requires that we must adhere to the direction of marketization, gradually reduce administrative control, divert the ideas on securities supervision from the previous idea, which was presented with the characteristic of planning and designed to control risk, to the idea which is designed to follow the law of market operation and reveal risk,[1] take preventing and punishing improper market actions as the major purpose, and take guaranteeing the liquidity and transparency of market, and the effectiveness of market information as a supervisory focus. Pursuant to this supervisory idea, the regulator of securities market was served by securities supervisory authority. In the context of marketization and internationalization, it could not realize the optimal allocation of resources and the effective supervision on market. Meanwhile, it has constrained the self-regulation of market mechanism, restricted the free actions of market participants, squeezed the market development space, and has influenced the healthy development of market.[2] Second, the research on supervisory system, mode and status quo of Chinese securities market. It was necessary to begin with the analysis on status quo and issues of supervisory system concerning to our securities market, and further to propound some specific reform measures and model design. According to some research, at present, the most defect in supervisory system of Chinese securities market was the displacement of supervisory functions, furthermore, the supervisory authority and supervisory duties were too centralized in governmental supervisory body. The potential risk

1 HUANG Yuncheng, *Theory, Practice and Innovation of Supervision on Securities Market*, China Financial Publishing House, 2001, p.219.

2 GAO Xiqing, *On Securities Supervision Authority*, *China Legal Science*, 2002, Issue 5.

for securities market caused by such displacement was that the securities market relations could not be rationalized, and the market was hard to develop pursuant to market rules.[1] In particular, when the regulator of securities market was served by securities supervisory authority, some rights which originally belong to the market, could not be implemented, and was still retained in the supervisory authority of securities supervisory authority. Such conditions would restrict the free actions of market participants, squeeze the development space of the market, prevent the self-development and self-regulation mechanism of the market from fully functioning, and would influence the healthy development of market.[2] Third, the international comparative study on the specific supervisory institutions concerning to the securities market. The main part of which was to examine the omissions in specific institutional construction connected with Chinese securities market, draw lessons from international experience, absorb beneficial enlightenment from foreign mature supervisory institutions, make good for deficiency and adapt foreign things to satisfy Chinese needs.

The stock exchange, which is the heart of securities market, has received a constant attention from academic circle. For purpose of the nature, reform of organizational structure, and the coordination between administrative supervision and self-discipline management of the stock exchange, the understanding were constantly deepening, and the research results were fruitful. The role played by the stock exchange in securities market is complex: it is not only a centralized trading place but also a market self-regulatory organization which is composed of many securities agencies; it is not only a market operation organization but also a market supervisory body. The stock exchange can be described as a special market subject with both of the market function and supervisory function. The stock exchange is characteristic of the dual attributes and multiple roles, which are being acknowledged and accepted universally. No matter emerging market,

1 *Research Report on the Internationalization of Chinese Securities Market*, Vol.4, *Shanghai Securities News*, September 11, 2003.

2 GAO Xiqing, *On Securities Supervision Authority*, *China Legal Science*, 2002, Issue 5.

or mature market, the basic functions of stock exchange thereof are nothing more than two: (i) to provide relevant place and facilities for concentrated securities trading; (ii) to assume supervisory duties for maintaining transaction order of the securities market.[1] As to the source of supervisory authority of the exchange, according to some scholar, from the perspective of historical development and the theory, the supervisory authority is generally a kind of autonomy that the exchange shall enjoy as an independent subject. The provisions of state laws on this authority means to the acceptance and protection by laws on such autonomy enjoyed by exchange. It is rather a confirmation on self-regulatory "authority" of exchange, than the source of self-regulatory "authority".[2]

As to the organizational form of exchange, the differences between the exchange with corporate system and the exchange with membership system are shown in the following three aspects: the ownership structure, governance structure and management objective.[3] With respect to the reform direction of Chinese stock exchanges, pursuant to the prevailing opinion, we shall draw lessons from the demutualization reform experiences of other exchanges in the world, and conduct stock reform to Chinese stock exchange[4], and then make it align with the trend of corporate system reform on stock exchanges in current world.

As to the issues connected with the relationship between the administrative regulation and self-supervision of exchange in our country, a consensus has been reached among the scholars, that is, the self-supervisory management mechanism and function have not been put in the right place. It shows as follows: (i) In

1 PENG Bing & CAO Lijia, *Study on Supervisory Function of the Securities Exchange, China Legal Science*, 2005, Issue 1.

2 XU Ming & LU Wendao, *From Market Competition to Legal System Foundation: Study on Self-supervision of Securities Exchange, Journal of East China University of Political Science and Law*, 2005, Issue 5.

3 XIE Zengyi, *Recent Development of Organizational Structure and Corporate Governance of Stock Exchange, Global Law Review*, 2006, Issue 2.

4 YU Xugang, *Demutualization of Exchange and Its Influence on Self-supervision*, Peking University Press, 2001, p.201.

law, the self-supervisory management of securities market lacks due status. Pursuant to Chinese Securities Law, the securities market supervision is primarily administrative supervision. However, the self-supervision has not been prescribed systematically. (ii) As to the qualification of subject, the self-supervisory management organization of securities market is not of independence enough. The stock exchange and the Securities Industry Association are characteristic of administration, which are usually regarded as quasi governmental agency. (iii) On the division of duties and responsibilities, the boundary between self-supervisory management and governmental supervision is not clear enough. In the supervision on securities market, the boundary of authorities to supervise securities market between self-regulatory organization and the competent securities administrative agency was not clear enough, the division of duties and supervisory mechanism thereof have not been rationalized, and some phenomena, such as intersection, overlap, vacancy or ultra vires acts appeared.[1]

The civil compensation system is the most important and fundamental way to protect the interests of investors. In the institutional system and theory of civil liability, the securities civil liability has received high attention and comprehensive research of the scholars and practitioners due to its rich contents, complex structure, distinct characteristics and significant role. In our country, the research on this issue was roughly conducted from two levels: (i) technical level, which is to study how to construct civil liability system from the perspective of legislative technique, for instance, how to define the nature of civil liability in securities law, how to determine the constitutive requirements of securities illegal actions, more specifically, how to count the loss caused by securities illegal actions, how to set up specific litigation institutions, and so forth. The scholars combined the specialty of securities market, used the theory of civil jurisprudence, drew lessons from the mature securities legal institutions in the

1 ZHU Congjiu, *To Build and Develop the Self-supervisory Management System of Securities Market*, *Economic Law & Labour Law* (periodical literatures reprinted by Renmin University of China), 2003, Issue 11.

US, and put the securities civil liability into the logical thread of tort law to study.[1] For instance, some scholar has systematically expounded the infringement compensation system concerning to securities fraud through the analysis on the constitutive requirements and detriment of various securities fraudulent conducts.[2] (ii) conceptual level, which is to study and explore why the civil liability institutions shall be provided in securities law from the perspective of legislative concept, how to determine the position of civil liability institutions in supervision mechanism of securities market, what kind of legal effect does the civil liability institutions provided in securities law need to reach, and so forth. These two levels interrelate and interact with each other, and the understanding and choice of the legislative idea will decide the choice and application of legislative technique. Beginning with the exploration on institutional level, the study on securities civil liability has gone deep to the reflection in theory, which has promoted the reform of securities legislation and judicature,[3] more importantly, the fundamental appeal for protecting investors by securities laws was carried out in practice. On January 15, 2003, the Supreme People's Court promulgated the Provisions on Trial of Civil Compensation Cases Arising from False Representation in Securities Market (hereinafter referred to as the "Provisions"). With the promotion of the research results of scholars, a substantial breakthrough has occurred in the trial of civil compensation cases in securities market.

In general, a research trend, from general to specific, and from macro to micro, has shown in the academic research of this period, the outstanding characteristic of which was that the scholars were good at drawing lessons from the successful experience of foreign securities legislation, and keen on monographic research on specific institutions of securities law. This scattered and point-to-point

1 GUO Feng, *Determination and Compensation of Infringement Connected with False Representation*, *China Legal Science*, 2003, Issue 2.

2 For example, CHEN Jie, *Study on Infringement Damage Compensation Arising from Securities Fraud*, Peking University Press, 2002.

3 XI Xiaoming & JIA Wei, *Enrichment and Development of Civil Liability in Securities Law*, *Applicable Law*, 2005, Issue 12.

comparative analysis was certainly good for paying attention to details. However, it was hard to form a systematical integrity, seriously lacking a point-to-plain macro control and exploration and analysis, which is strategically situated, on the future development of certain institution. Such circumstances have highlighted the drawbacks of emergency legislation and occasional academic research caused by the too rapid development of Chinese securities market.

3.3 After the comprehensive revision to *Securities Law 2005*

On October 27, 2005, the eighteenth session of Standing Committee of the tenth National People's Congress revised the Securities Law comprehensively. In this revision, a more suitable institutional space was provided for some items which involve the mechanism of market operation, such as, separate operation or mixed operation, margin trading, securities business license, and so forth. Meanwhile, the authority of securities supervisory agency was increased, the institutions connected with securities administrative responsibility was strengthened, and the system of securities civil institutions was further improved. The mainstream of securities jurisprudence study in this period was to conduct necessary evaluation and rethinking on the revised Securities Law. However, the reflection of this period laid stress on working in concert with legislative and judicial practice. So, it has more theoretical significance and practical value.

Although the revised *Securities Law* has further improved the supervisory system of securities market, analyzing from the perspective of the revised content of the institutions, the current supervisory system of securities market just has been improved in quantity, but without change in quality. In particular, the revised Securities Law has not changed the previous supervisory concept and system. On the contrary, on the premise of retaining the previous supervisory mode, through comprehensively increasing the authority of supervisory agency, the trend that making the securities supervisory agency become competent authority of listed company and industrial competent authority for securities company has been further strengthened. Faced with the phenomena of alienation of relations between the securities supervisory agency and its supervisory objects in the realistic supervisory system concerning to securities market, the moderate supervision on securities has become the focus of attention among scholars. According to some scholar, such conversion from market supervisory agency to industrial competent authority was caused mainly by, with the promotion of market operation and duties for market regulation, the "excessive concern" to supervisory objects and the "deep intervention" of supervisory authority.[1] From the perspective of the relationship between supervisory agency and listed company, the role played by securities supervisory agency in improving the corporate internal governance of listed company is very important, the key of which is to determine the supervisory authority. The position of securities supervision shall be varied with the environments of the economy in different historical periods. In general, for more than a decade, the active guidance of Chinese securities supervisor has played a vital role in enhancing the governance of listed company and in improving the governance mechanism thereof. However, great changes have taken place in the external environment of Chinese securities supervision. In the face of the external environment and challenge which have changed, the position of securities supervision should be adjusted. To resolve the internal conflicts of the supervisory system has become an urgent task faced by securities supervisors. The conflicts in the system caused by transplantation of the institutions from the new to the old were very prominent in the internal governance of listed company. Since the share holding structure of most listed companies has not been changed fundamentally, accordingly, the focus of securities supervision was unlikely to be shifted fundamentally. So, the focus thereof was still the issue concerning to preventing insider control. The internal governance framework of listed company has been constructed preliminarily. Under such conditions, the securities supervisor shall lay stress on supervising the company's senior executives and controlling shareholders.[2]

1 CHEN Su, *Monographic Study on Securities Law*, Higher Education Press, 2006, pp.208-210.

2 JIAO Lvhong & DING Ding & XU Jing, *Determination of the Supervisory Authority of Securities Supervisor on Internal Governance of Listed Company in Our Country*, *Company & Securities Law Review*, 2006, Issue 2.

With the joint promulgation and implementation of amendments of *Company Law 2005* and Securities Law, the basic structure of securities civil compensation institution in our country was developed from pour advocacy to exploration of its specific constitution. The range thereof expanded from fraud representation initially to insider trading and market manipulation. Finally, a relatively perfect theoretical system of securities civil liability was formed.[1] However, many scholars held that, since the institutional system of securities market in our country is predominated by administrative supervision, the civil liability institutions have not obtain the due position, and have not exerted its institutional function that it should play from the beginning. Currently, the most understanding issue faced by securities jurisprudential circle is how to implement such basic institutions. The *Securities Law 2005* has systematically established the mechanism of civil compensation liability arising from misrepresentation, and has systematically arranged and summarized the principles for determining liability, types of liability and subjects of civil liability caused by misrepresentation. In particular, it has specified the principles for determining liability. For instance, as to the civil liability arising from breach of the obligation to disclose information, the *Securities Law 2005* has respectively provided non-fault liability doctrine, presumed-fault liability doctrine and fault liability doctrine pursuant to the positions and roles of the relevant subjects. As to the conducts, such as insider trading, market manipulation and deceiving the clients, the relevant civil liability has been expressly provided therein. But, there is still much room for improving the securities legislative technique. For instance, with respect to the civil liability institutions concerning to insider trading, the provisions connected with the presumption of causal connections between damage action and damage result are still absent, which makes the relevant civil liability institution lack operability in practice.

Analyzing from the status quo of study on securities law in our country,

---

1 *Report on the Development of Philosophy and Social Sciences in Chinese Colleges and Universities*, in ZHANG Wenxian & HUANG Wenyi (eds.), Guangxi Normal University Press, 2008, p.168.

since the scholars often begin with some specific issues in practice, and are often oriented by solving specific problems, so, such monographic studies seem insufficient, whether in breadth, or in depth. In addition, the securities jurisprudential scholars often ponder problems in market practice with scholastic research methods, which makes the voluminous research achievements put on the shelf for being severely separated from practice. It is an important task to assimilate and absorb the new experiences and new forms created in the process of internationalization of China's securities market, then make innovation "with Chinese characteristic", and promote the continuous revision and improvement of securities legislation in our country as soon as possible. Meanwhile, the causes, mechanisms and effect of the change of securities legislative regulation will be also directly reflected in the research of securities jurisprudence. Thus, the interaction between legislation and academy is not only a phenomenon of academic level, but also an important reflection of commercial legal practice.

4. Research on Enterprise Bankruptcy Law Closely Related to Enterprise Restructuring

China is a country that lacks the tradition of bankruptcy law. The economic system reform started in 1980s, prompted people to think about how to deal with the problem of enterprise bankruptcy, and then gave birth to the bankruptcy system to promote the reform and economic development. In early 1983, the Research Center on Economic, Technological and Social Development under the State Council advised the relevant departments, in Proposals on Several Issues Concerning to Striving for Technological Advance and Promoting Economic Development, to promptly draft bankruptcy law. In September of the same year, this center wrote another article, A Tentative Plan on Enterprise Bankruptcy and Reorganization Law, and published it in the abstract of Outlook Weekly (Issue 9) in the following year. This was the first publicly published article on the establishment of bankruptcy institutions.[1] In 1985, pursuant to the guidance of the

1 YE Jiasheng, *Realistic Situation and Future Direction of the Research on Theory of Bankruptcy Law in China*, *Journal of Southwest University of Political Science and Law*, December, 2008.

State Council, the Drafting Group of Enterprise Bankruptcy Law established and has drafted the Outline of Enterprise Bankruptcy Law. Based on comprehensively soliciting advice and discussion, this Group finished the Enterprise Bankruptcy Law of the People's Republic of China (Draft) in 1986.In the same year, after two reviews by the seventeenth and eighteenth session of the Standing Committee of the sixth National People's Congress, the Enterprise Bankruptcy Law of the People's Republic of China (For Trial Implementation) was adopted by voting on December 2. This Law only applied to enterprise owned by the whole people. However, other enterprises were also needed to be regulated by it. Therefore, on April 9, 1991, the fourth session of the seventh National People's Congress adopted the Civil Procedural Law, in the second part of which, the nineteenth part, "Procedure of Bankruptcy and Liquidation of A Business Corporation" was specially set up, which is applicable for the bankruptcy cases of other enterprises with legal personality beyond the enterprise owned by the whole people.

When the *Bankruptcy Law 1986* was formulated, our country not only lacked the historical tradition and necessary theoretical accumulation, but also fell short of technological support by bankruptcy judicial practice. In addition, at that time, the institutional factors of non-market economy have seriously restricted the understanding of people on bankruptcy legislation and application of institutions connected with bankruptcy. Therefore, the *Bankruptcy Law 1986* inevitably had a considerable limitations, from the legislative concept to design of institutions, the defects of which were being more obvious gradually in the process of implementation. In 1994, the Financial and Economic Committee of Standing Committee of the eighth National People's Congress began to draft new Bankruptcy Law in our country. From being organized to draft to the promulgation in 2006, the drafting of this Law lasted for 12 years, which could be described as "ten years for sharpening a sword". With the opportunity in legislation of new Bankruptcy Law, the study on bankruptcy jurisprudence was gradually heating up. In the positive interaction with the legislation of bankruptcy law, by drawing on the mature theories and practical experiences of developed countries, the studies conducted by scholars on basic theories of bankruptcy law and relevant specific institutions have developed rapidly. The practice showed that the bankruptcy legislation has promoted or guided the continuous deepening and development of study on academic theories, meanwhile, the academic research on bankruptcy law has also provided solid theoretical foundation and broad growing space for the complete promulgation of bankruptcy law.

Taking the new Bankruptcy Law as boundary, prior to the promulgation of the new Bankruptcy Law, the studies on bankruptcy jurisprudence was closely centered on bankruptcy legislation to brew and grope. After the promulgation of the new Bankruptcy Law, the studies on bankruptcy jurisprudence mainly focused on the subjects of three aspects as below: (i) understanding and application of the new Bankruptcy Law; (ii) development and improvement of the new Bankruptcy Law; and, (iii) the issues produced in the implementation of the new Bankruptcy Law. It comes down to two threads: (i) the renewal and breakthrough on legislative concept, which have laid a theoretical foundation for the promulgation and improvement of the bankruptcy law; and, (ii) the construction and innovation of specific institutions, which have provided a theoretical support for the implementation and improvement of the bankruptcy law.

4.1 Renewal and Breakthrough on Legislative Concept of Bankruptcy Law

Compared with *Bankruptcy Law 1986*, on the legislative concept, the new Bankruptcy Law, based on scientific legislative technique, sufficient autonomy of the parties and moderate judicial enforcement, established a brand new structure of bankruptcy procedural mode, which takes the corporate regeneration as a main goal. However, this shift of legislative concepts has experienced a long-term theoretical thinking and accumulation of practice.

It is a basic principle of the Civil and Commercial Law that the civil subjects have equal status. But in the process of drafting the enterprise bankruptcy law of our country, whether the bankruptcy procedure should be applied to the debtors other than enterprise legal person has once aroused extensive discussion.[1] One view was that the bankruptcy procedure shall apply to both of the enterprise legal person and natural person. The bankruptcy law without the contents of personal bankruptcy is not an integrated bankruptcy law;[2]China is in the background with a trend of general bankruptcy theory, there is no reason to exclude the natural person from the scope of application of the bankruptcy procedure. We shall expand the scope of application of the bankruptcy law to adopt the general bankruptcy theory.[3] "The purpose of bankruptcy procedure is mainly to ensure the creditor can be discharged in a fair way. The main consideration in the design of procedural institutions is how to guarantee the equal status of the creditors. With respect to a procedure which is designed to ensure the fairness, whether the debtor is legal person or natural person, the result will not be influenced. In substantive law, there is no difference between the legal status of the natural person and legal person. The debts assumed thereby will not be discriminated for the status. Accordingly, in procedural law, both of the natural person and legal person also shall be treated equally. The bankruptcy law applies to legal person, and shall also apply to natural person. The equality of natural person and legal person can be reached on the procedure for liquidating creditors' rights and debts." [4]

Analyzing from the theory of law, as a private law, the bankruptcy law shall embody a spirit of equality among subjects; if the competent authority takes different policies among all subjects to which the bankruptcy law can be applied, especially, discriminates the state-owned enterprise from non-state owned enterprise, and then takes different rules thereon, it will violate the equality of

1 CHANG Min & ZOU Hailin, "Reformulation of the Bankruptcy Law of the People's Republic of China", *Chinese Journal of Law*, 1995, Issue 2.

2 LI Shuguang, "Several Important Issues on the Drafting of the New Bankruptcy Law", *Tribune of Political Science and Law*, 2002, Issue 3.

3 TANG Weijian, "Consideration on Several Issues Concerning to the Revision of Bankruptcy Legal Institutions in China", *Tribune of Political Science and Law*, 2002, Issue 3.

4 ZOU Hailin, "Consideration on the Scope of Application of the New Bankruptcy Law", *Tribune of Political Science and Law*, 2002, Issue 3.

subjects, which is a spirit and basic principle of private law; to adhere to the equality of subjects under the bankruptcy law, not only need to equally treat the causes or conditions of bankruptcy, but also need to reduce the intervention of government in bankruptcy of state-owned enterprise.[1] China is a market economy country that has joined the WTO. Therefore, we must bring all subjects of the market economy into a fair environment. In such context, the bankruptcy law shall be drafted as a private law to reflect and embody that the basic spirits of private law have gradually been recognized. What reflects in the new Bankruptcy Law is that the new Bankruptcy Law has unified the application of bankruptcy procedure to the enterprise legal persons, eliminated the various institutional differences existed therein, and has laid an institutional foundation for the equal application of bankruptcy procedure. The institutional arrangement in Enterprise Bankruptcy Law concerning to the application of bankruptcy procedure to enterprise legal person has comprehensively solved the problems connected with unequal application of the bankruptcy procedure which has been lasted for a long time in our country. Except as otherwise provided in Articles 133 and 134 of Enterprise Bankruptcy Law, there is no difference on procedure for enterprise legal person to apply bankruptcy procedure. No matter what differences the enterprise legal persons have in the nature of ownership, scale, industry or other aspects, they shall be governed by the reorganization procedure, settlement procedure or liquidation procedure prescribed by the Enterprise Bankruptcy Law without distinction.[2]

Of course, the Enterprise Bankruptcy Law has only incorporated the enterprise legal person into the scope of application of bankruptcy procedure. Pursuant to Article 2 of the Enterprise Bankruptcy Law, the bankruptcy procedure only applies to enterprise legal person. The reason is that the issue which the lawmaker finally considers is still about how to control the property of natural

1 LI Yongjun, "Restatement of the Spirits of Private Law in Bankruptcy Law", *Tribune of Political Science and Law*, 2002, Issue 3.

2 ZOU Hailin, *Research on the Development of Chinese Commercial Law*, China Social Science Press, 2008, p.130.

person upon bankruptcy, that is, the individual "property registration system and individual credit system are still in their infancy. It is hard to effectively prevent the individuals from using bankruptcy to dodge creditors. So, at present, the bankruptcy procedure is not suitable for applying to individual bankruptcy".[1]

Under the old Bankruptcy Law, the creditors' meeting was prescribed as a basic form of party autonomy. However, the functional position of creditors' meeting was not accurate, and the way to implement creditor autonomy was too rigid, therefore, in fact, the party autonomy has become an ornament of bankruptcy procedure which was predominated by judge. In addition, pursuant to the old institutional model framework, the position and duties of liquidation team, which is liable for liquidating the debts, was not set up clearly. As a result, in the proceeding of bankruptcy, the judge has basically superseded the liquidation team. According to some scholar, the above phenomena boil down to judge-dominated bankruptcy procedure.[2] In consideration of the effective management on creditors' property and the party autonomy in the proceeding of bankruptcy, based on administrator centrism and creditor autonomy, the new Bankruptcy Law has realized a thorough transformation from the judge-dominated bankruptcy procedure to party autonomy dominated bankruptcy procedure. In which, the creditor autonomy means that all creditors form creditors' meeting or select their delegates to express opinion and make decision on the pertinent major issues occurred in the proceeding of bankruptcy, and to supervise the administrator to duly perform his duties.[3] The creditor autonomy in the bankruptcy procedure is an institution set up for the majority of creditors to participate in the proceeding and exercise their rights equally. The new Bankruptcy Law has clearly defined the scope

1 *Interpretation of the Enterprise Bankruptcy Law of the People's Republic of China*, compiled by the Drafting Group of the *Enterprise Bankruptcy Law of the People's Republic of China*, People's Publishing House, 2006, p.8.

2 ZOU Hailin, *Research on the Development of Chinese Commercial Law*, China Social Science Press, 2008, p.137.

3 See ZOU Hailin & WANG Zhongxing, *On Creditor Autonomy in the Proceeding of Bankruptcy*, *Civil and Commercial Law Review*, Vol. 2, Law Press·China, 1994, p.157.

of creditor autonomy, expanded the ways of creditor autonomy with establishment of the creditors commission system, and has enhanced the effectiveness of creditor autonomy in bankruptcy proceeding.

Enterprise regeneration is a worldwide problem in the reform of bankruptcy law. But in our country, "for a long time, with respect to the bankruptcy of enterprise, there is a concept which seems to be conventional and unshakable, namely, the bankruptcy is liquidation for closure". However, according to some opinion, the bankruptcy concept established by the Enterprise Bankruptcy Law of the People's Republic of China (For Trial Implementation) has received high appraisal. Such opinion held that "in our country, the connotation of the concept of bankruptcy didn't experience a long time of evolution like the West, but has possessed the richest meaning from the beginning, and has been deeply inscribed with modern features".[1] With the emergence and growth of modern reorganization system, "a way for realizing the reconstruction and revival of enterprises which were in trouble on the premise of fair liquidation of debts has been opened, thereby, the concept and structure of bankruptcy law is updated, and the thinking space of civil and commercial law is expanded".[2] The scholars have gradually recognized that, when designing the bankruptcy procedure system, the lawmaker shall hold a value judgment that the reorganization interests of enterprises are in preference to other interests produced in the proceeding of bankruptcy; and based on this, the lawmaker shall make a choice on the legislative policies Some scholar pointed out that all creditors, whether or not be guaranteed, and other persons who have right in the ownership of property or distribution of interests of the debtors shall be governed by the reorganization procedure. In the proceeding of reorganization, even if the obligee of some individual voting group disagrees with the reorganization plan, the court also may, at its own discretion, prolong the reorganization period or approve reorganization plan. Obviously, the protection

1 TANG Weijian, *A New Analysis on the Concept of Bankruptcy*, *Peking University Law Journal*, 1995, Issue 3.

2 WANG Weiguo, *On Reorganization System*, *Chinese Journal of Law*, 1996, Issue 1.

of the debtor, provided by the reorganization procedure, is very generous. The bankruptcy legislation in our country shall adhere to such a position.[1] The new Enterprise Bankruptcy Law has comprehensively implemented the bankruptcy procedure system which takes the enterprise regeneration as a main goal.[2] Based on the concept of enterprise regeneration, the Enterprise Bankruptcy Law has sublated the bankruptcy procedure which was predominated by liquidation of enterprise prescribed in the old bankruptcy law in our country. The reorganization procedure and settlement procedure prescribed in the Enterprise Bankruptcy Law make the bankruptcy procedure system predominated by enterprise regeneration more prominent.

4.2 Theoretical Innovation in the Institutional Construction of Bankruptcy Law

The design of procedural institutions of the new Enterprise Bankruptcy Law, especially the reform or institutional innovation carried out around the design and running effect of procedure of enterprise regeneration are both in depth and powerful. The provisions of Enterprise Bankruptcy Law concerning to bankruptcy procedure are not purely procedural institutions, but to enhance the roles played by bankruptcy procedure, at a higher level, in saving the enterprise which is in financial trouble.

The core of bankruptcy law reform is to build a uniform and professional administrator system and implement the creditors' meeting system with diverse autonomous measures. The administrator centrism refers to that the daily routine in the proceeding of bankruptcy is conducted through administrator. After the bankruptcy procedure begins, the administrator will take over, clear up, take care of and run the debtors' property and conduct necessary disposal thereon in accordance with laws, to better protect the interests of creditors. The introduction

1 ZOU Hailin, *Research on the Development of Chinese Commercial Law*, China Social Science Press, 2008, p.139.

2 ZOU Hailin, *Institutional Innovation on Chinese Enterprise Bankruptcy Law, Chinese Academy of Social Sciences Review*, July 5, 2007.

of bankruptcy administrator system finally became a major innovation of the new Bankruptcy Law. The research made by the scholars after drawing lessons from the West showed that the administrator can not only more effectively protect the interests of the debtor and the creditor, but also greatly reduce the work burden of judge in the proceeding of bankruptcy, and save valuable judicial resources. Pursuant to the pertinent provisions of Enterprise Bankruptcy Law, the administrator has independent status in the proceeding of bankruptcy, and shall independently perform his duties in accordance with the law. Based on this concept, the provisions with respect to the administrator and his status prescribed in Articles 13, 23 and 25 of the Enterprise Bankruptcy Law has basically reflected the administrator centrism in the bankruptcy procedure.

In the process of drafting the Enterprise Bankruptcy Law, it has been suggested that the administrator centrism shall be confined to the procedure of bankruptcy liquidation. According to such view, the roles played by administrator in liquidation procedure and reorganization procedure are different. It will be more reflected in the liquidation procedure, but the role of which played in the reorganization procedure will be limited.[1] However, more scholars held that "the administrator centrism shall run through all links of the untied bankruptcy proceeding. The administrator centrism shall not only play its roles in the proceeding of bankruptcy liquidation, but also shall be effectively applied in the settlement proceeding and reorganization proceeding. The administrator centrism is not contradicted with the status of the debtor for managing its property by itself in the proceeding of reorganization. In accordance with the pertinent provisions of the Enterprise Bankruptcy Law, it's true that the central position of administrator in liquidation procedure and settlement procedure is very remarkable, but in the reorganization procedure, the role of whom is limited. Sometimes, the role of administrator played in the reorganization procedure is not very significant. Such phenomenon is just the alienation of administrator centrism, that is, the function

1 LI Shuguang, "Several Important Issues on the Drafting of the New Bankruptcy Law", *Tribune of Political Science and Law*, 2002, Issue 3.

of administrator has transferred to the debtor in the proceeding of reorganization under certain conditions, which is a denial of the administrator centrism".[1]

As to the creditors' meeting system, in the bankruptcy legislation of our country, the creditors' meeting has independent status in the proceeding of bankruptcy. However, due to the large number of creditors involved in the proceeding of bankruptcy, the absolutization of creditor autonomy may affect the smooth progress of bankruptcy procedure, so, the creditor autonomy shall be subject to the judicial control of courts. "To implement the creditor autonomy principle, the bankruptcy legislation shall be designed and regulated from the perspective of how to realize the legitimate rights and interests of the creditors by means of bankruptcy procedure, rather than from the perspective of how to exercise the judicial power of the People's Court on bankruptcy cases. The judicial power of the People's Court on bankruptcy cases is centrally embodied in the supervisory power and commanding authority thereof, the main purpose of which is to restrict the right of autonomy of the creditors, so as to balance the legitimate rights and interests between the creditors and debtors, and prevent the creditors from abusing the rights in bankruptcy procedure to harm the interests of the debtors." [2] In short, the creditor autonomy is confined to the scope of public relief, the courts can make a ruling finally on the activities of creditor autonomy at its own discretion.[3]

The key to systematic design of bankruptcy procedure in the new Enterprise Bankruptcy Law lies in the creative provision of reorganization procedure and settlement procedure. Indeed, the reform of the new Enterprise Bankruptcy Law is carried out around the design and running effect of the procedure of enterprise

1 ZOU Hailin, *New Enterprise Bankruptcy Law and Administrator Centrism, Journal of East China University of Political Science and Law*, 2006, Issue 6.

2 TANG Weijian, *Consideration on Several Issues Concerning to the Revision of Bankruptcy Legal Institutions in China, Tribune of Political Science and Law*, 2002, Issue 3.

3 ZOU Hailin, *Comparative Study on Bankruptcy Procedure and the Substantive Institutions of Bankruptcy Law*, Law Press·China, 1995, p.129.

regeneration. The design level thereof is often a sign for verifying the modernization of the reform of bankruptcy law. The reorganization system is a judicial procedure, prescribed in Enterprise Bankruptcy Law, by which the enterprises which are in trouble can be saved with active measures. It is an active institution for precluding bankruptcy liquidation. The refinement and optimization of the bankruptcy and reorganization system, as one of the main institutional characteristics and the important institutional achievements of the development of the modern bankruptcy law system, is a complex and delicate institutional arrangement. In the world, based on different historical traditions and economic states in different countries, the reorganization system varies widely throughout the world. The reorganization system prescribed in the new Bankruptcy Law of our country is mainly referred to and transplanted from the Chapter 11 of U.S. Bankruptcy Code. Since the reorganization system in our country is absent of detailed provisions, therefore, the refinement and optimization of the reorganization system is a subject that needs to be solved with great efforts in the future studies. In addition, in order to increase the chance of regeneration of the enterprises which are in trouble, the new Enterprise Bankruptcy Law of China has also provided a "self-settlement" system. The settlement system is a procedure for reaching a package of agreements in order to clean up the creditors' rights and debts upon negotiation and compromise between the debtors and all creditors in the proceeding of bankruptcy in accordance with the enterprise bankruptcy law. Strictly speaking, the self-settlement between the debtors and the creditors are not procedural institution, but the practical value or effect of this institution lies in closing the bankruptcy procedure which has commenced, especially closing the bankruptcy liquidation procedure which might be initiated. The creation of self-settlement system concerning to the debtor not only has the function for preventing the courts from declaring bankruptcy liquidation on the debtor, but also has the function for preventing the property of the debtor being distributed through liquidation procedure.[1]

1 ZOU Hailin, "Institutional Analysis and Application of the Procedure Concerning to the Regeneration of Enterprises in China", *Tribune of Political Science and Law*, 2007, Issue 1.

Chapter 17

Chinese Intellectual Property Jurisprudence in Era of Knowledge Innovation

1. Development Overview of Intellectual Property Jurisprudence

Since 1992, in response to the decision of China to access to the WTO, Chinese intellectual property system is undergoing continuous improvements and integration with international rules. Along with emergence and solution of one after another international trade disputes, resulted by protection of intellectual property right, at home and broad, the "intellectual property right" has changed from a term, only known by researchers and professionals, to a hot topic focused by the whole society. Furthermore, the study on Chinese intellectual property law has also undergone a profound change. As a special subdiscipline of traditional civil and commercial jurisprudence and economic jurisprudence, the intellectual property jurisprudence has gradually separated therefrom, and has formed its own study teams with fruitful achievements. The intellectual property law has entered into a period of discipline's development and maturity.

1.1 Discipline development stage of intellectual property jurisprudence (1992-2000)

In this period, Zheng Chengsi, came from Institute of Law, Chinese Academy of Social Sciences, was still academic leader of Chinese intellectual property jurisprudence, and the Chinese Academy of Social Sciences Intellectual Property Research Center was established formally by whom in September, 1994, which has constantly absorbed some famous scholars in the field of domestic intellectual property jurisprudence. Almost in the meantime, some domestic institutions of higher education and research agencies have also successively set up special educational institutions for study on intellectual property right, for example, the "Intellectual Property Academy" established by Shanghai University and Peking University in 1994. Afterwards, with rapid development of Chinese intellectual property legal system, the disputes relevant to intellectual property right in reality increased sharply. In 1996, the Supreme People's Court established a special tribunal for trying intellectual property right cases, and across the country, some other law schools of major universities have also gradually set up special research and teaching institutions of intellectual property right, and have fostered a number of special talents thereof.

As to the writings, with development of the discipline of intellectual property jurisprudence, special educational and training materials were also produced gradually, such as *Coursebook of Intellectual Property Law*, written by Zheng Chengsi, in 1993. And successive production and modification of a variety of teaching materials have provided fundamental conditions for discipline construction and talent cultivation in the field of our intellectual property law. In addition, the writings which systematically expounded the issues of certain aspect of intellectual property law have been produced in academic circle. For instance, *Computer Law*, written by Tang Guangliang, Dong Binghe and Liu Guangsan, 1993; *Interpretation of Patent Law*, written by Tang Zongshun, 1994; *Agreement on Trade-Related Aspects of Intellectual Property Rights*, translated by Zheng Chengsi, 1994, and *Detailed Discussion on Intellectual Property Law*, written by Zhang Ping, 1994, etc. Around China's accession to the WTO, a major event in social and economic life, especially in 1996, the Sino-U.S. trade war relevant to intellectual property right came to an end, China's study on intellectual property law has begun to go beyond introduction and general exposition on the whole, and entered into a relatively deep level, begun to explore the intellectual property system and its rules. The issues, such as basic conceptions of intellectual property right, the connections between intellectual property right and real right, parallel import and exhaustion of right, intersection between trademark law and anti-unfair competition law, and reverse passing off, etc., have all been discussed relatively sufficiently in academic circle. In this period, apart from *Intellectual Property Studies*, published by China Fangzheng Press, and *Intellectual Property Right Series*, published by China University of Political Science and Law Press, which have collected and discussed such hot issues, there were other typical works, such as, *Trade-Related Aspects of Intellectual Property Rights in WTO*, and *On Intellectual Property*, respectively published in 1996 and 1998, written by Zheng Chengsi; *Study on Difficult and Hot Issues of Industrial Property Rights*, written by Cheng Yongshun, 1997; *Determination of Patent Infringement*, written by Cheng Yongshun and Luo Lihua, 1998; *Protection of Patent Right*, written by Yin Xintian, 1998; *Judges' Opinions on Intellectual Property Right*, written by Chen Xu, 1999; and, "*Special 301*" *and Sino-U.S. Disputes on Intellectual Property Rights*, written by Lin Mingde, 2000, etc. Furthermore, at this stage, the institution on research and teaching intellectual property right of Renmin University of China, represented by Liu Chuntian, began to organize to draw up and publish annual "*Review and Outlook on Study of Intellectual Property Jurisprudence*" from 1998, which provided a reference for understanding the specific state of studies on intellectual property law and development of the discipline in China.

1.2 Maturing and independent stage of the discipline of intellectual property jurisprudence (from 2000 to now)

At the beginning of this period, namely, from 2001 to 2005, in need of accessing to WTO, China's intellectual property legal system has undergone a series of amendments until it reached international protection level; Afterwards, China entered into the transitional period of comprehensive performance of WTO commitments. Accordingly, the study on Chinese intellectual property law at this stage was marked by attaching importance to the following aspects: exposition of WTO rules and its connections with Chinese law, comment on and analysis of new revised intellectual property legal rules, study on related supporting laws and regulations, and discussion on new issues of judicial practice. Such as protection of layout-design of integrated circuits, concept and application of preliminary temporary injunction, and protection of intellectual property right in cyberspace, etc., all have been comprehensively and hotly discussed. Apart from such studies closely related to specific systems, more and more scholars joined in the discussion about basic theories of intellectual property right.

At this stage, the landmark event, which showed Chinese intellectual property jurisprudence was becoming mature, was establishment of Intellectual Property Law Academy of China Law Society, and its effective running annually. In late October, 2001, with approval of China Law Society, the Intellectual Property Law Academy, a discipline academy subordinated thereto, was established formally in Beijing. This was a professional academic organization about intellectual property law, which was composed of key staff, specializing in study on intellectual property law, jurisprudential education, legislation on intellectual property right, judicial and administrative affairs, and other professional staff who engaged in businesses closely related to intellectual property right. The core members thereof almost covered all elites in Chinese intellectual property theory and practice areas. Chinese Academy of Social Sciences Intellectual Property Research Center is in charge of daily affairs of Intellectual Property Law Academy of China Law Society, Zheng Chengsi took the chair in first two terms (2001-2006); and the current president for a third term (2007-2012) is served by Wu Handong, who comes from Zhongnan University of Economics and Law.

From a perspective of academic achievements, the representative works of this period included: *Intellectual Property in the Age of Network*, written by Xue Hong, 2000; *Intellectual Property and Anti-monopoly Law*, written by Wang Xianlin, 2000; *On Intellectual Property* (revised version), written by Zheng Chengsi, 2001; *Studies on Intangible Property Right System*, written by Wu Handong and Hu Kaizhong, 2001; *Legal Protection of Well-known*

Trademark and Famous Trademark, written by Huang Hui, 2001; *Substantial Requirements for Patent*, written by Zheng Chengsi and Zhang Xiaodu, 2002; *On Intellectual Property*, 3rd ed., written by Zheng Chengsi, 2003; *Intellectual Property Law of the U.S.* , written by Li Mingde, 2003; *Basic Theory and Frontier Issues of Intellectual Property Right*, written by Li Yang, etc., 2004; *Intellectual Property-The Exploitation of IPR and the IPR Law Fundamentals*, in Zheng Chengsi (ed.), 2005; *Studies on Basic Issues of Intellectual Property Right*, written by Wu Handong, etc., 2005; *Protection of Patent Right*, written by Yin Xintian, 2005, and some series which have collected the discussions on hot topics of this period, such as *Intellectual Property Right Series*, in Zheng Chengsi (ed.), 2005; *Peking University Intellectual Property Review*, in Zheng Shengli (ed.), 2005; and, the volumes of *Intellectual Property Studies*, in Tang Guangliang (ed.), 2005.

In this later period, that is, from 2006 to present, with deepening of China's economic and political system reform, the intellectual property legal system, providing institutional guarantee for construction of "innovation-oriented country ", is entering into a new stage, that is, from mechanistic and passive rule-making to flexible and active rule application, and taking an active part in making international intellectual property rules. In the course of dealing with international trade disputes, resulted by protection of intellectual property right after "Entry into WTO", Chinese enterprises involved in disputes have accumulated profound experiences and lessons. To protect intellectual property right validly and effectively, is not only a need for China's performance of its promised international obligations, but also an intrinsic need for China to promote its economic and social development, and realize the purpose of constructing innovation-oriented country. Chinese government has realized the decisive position of intellectual property right in future world competition, so, attached highly importance to the protection of intellectual property right, and has promulgated the *Outline of the National Intellectual Property Strategy* in June, 2008, which was designed to actively construct good legal environment, market environment and cultural environment for intellectual property right, and to largely improve our abilities to create, apply, protect and manage the intellectual property right. Accordingly, the theoretical study results at this stage were mainly reflected by the discussions around the intellectual property strategy at all levels, the typical of which was fundamental materials of the Outline of the National Intellectual Property Strategy, the result of 20 monographic studies conducted by a variety of related departments, coordinated by then "*Leading Group Office for Formulating National Intellectual Property Strategy*" in more than two years.

Under direct promotion by formulation of national intellectual property strategy and request of knowledge-based economy, in recent years, our study achievements on intellectual property right are very fruitful, and progress has been made in depth and breadth of field and content of research, which showed a good momentum of rapid development of intellectual property jurisprudence; Especially, the young scholars have published a number of works, which have largely enriched the content of study on intellectual property jurisprudence. In recent years, the representative achievements included: *Study on Legal Protection System of Technological Innovation*, written by Dong Binghe, 2006; *Theory of Interests Balance in Intellectual Property Law*, written by Feng Xiaoqing, 2006; *Intellectual Property Law*, written by Li Mingde, 2007; and, *Copyright Law in Cyberspace*, written by Wang Qian, 2008, etc. In addition, *Intellectual Property Right Series*, in Zheng Chengsi and Li Mingde (eds.), *Chinese Intellectual Property Review*, in Liu Chuntian (ed.), and, *Intellectual Property Rights Annual Journal*, in Wu Handong (ed.) also have consistently produced impact on domestic intellectual property law study.

From the creation of intellectual property jurisprudence in New China, we can see that, from enlightenment to maturity of discipline, our intellectual property jurisprudence has flourished in personnel training and construction of research institutions during 30 years, and has been fruitful in theoretical studies. The older generations of scholars, represented by Zheng Chengsi, have made immortalised contribution to the establishment of our intellectual property jurisprudence[1]. At present, a number of young scholars are working on teaching and studying, who have obtained fruitful results, and have become the backbone of our intellectual property jurisprudence. That shows Chinese intellectual property jurisprudence is moving towards maturity, and has a bright future, without lack of successors. However, the current intellectual property jurisprudence in China shows signs of "hot in the inside, but cold on the outside". That is, a number of academic ideas frequently clash in the inside, but rarely interact with outside disciplines. This can be seen from the summary of academic history around 30 years since the reform and opening-up, conducted by the circle of Chinese jurisprudential study and education in recent years. In the brief summary, there is no monographs about establishment and development of the discipline of Chinese intellectual property jurisprudence[2].That is not adapted to the role played by intellectual property jurisprudence in the current circle of jurisprudential study and education in China.

2. Main Opinions and Discussions Emerged in the Process of Development of Intellectual Property Jurisprudence

It should be mentioned that, at the stage of discipline enlightenment and establishment of Chinese intellectual property jurisprudence, the theoretical discussions mainly focused on introduction of related international systems, but rarely discussed the system per se and its rules profoundly. In this circle, the major achievements in theoretical study were mainly produced in the process of intellectual property jurisprudence's development and becoming mature, especially from the year 2000, before or after, till present. In this period, around

1 See Chen Su&Zheng Chengsi: the First Man of Chinese Intellectual Property Studies, China Trial, 2008, Issue.4.

2 For example, Thirty Years of Studies on Law in China: 1978-2008, China Social Sciences Press, 2008; Thirty Years of Studies on Law in China, in Yang Shu (ed.), Sun Yat-sen University Press, 2009; Report on the Development of Humanities and Social Sciences in China (1978-2008) (Jurisprudence), Guangxi Normal University Press, 2009. The content of intellectual property jurisprudence was not involved nearly in the above mentioned books, and only be summarized briefly in the related exposition of development of civil and commercial law.

a variety of hot issues then related to intellectual property right, a relatively wide range of discussions have been produced both in the community and academic circle. And the establishment and improvement of our intellectual property legal system are always accompanied and influenced by such discussions and the results thereof, such as the definition of intellectual property right, the connections between intellectual property rights and civil law, principles in determining the liabilities of tort, and issues of exhaustion of right and parallel import, temporary injunction, reverse passing off, and conflict of rights, some problems of patent law, the connections between anti-unfair competition law and trademark law, Internet and protection of copyrights, protection of traditional knowledge and intellectual property right, and formulation and application of intellectual property strategy, etc. It should be noted that, the judicial circle has been playing an important role in these discussions, since many hot topics came from concern and discussions on typical cases. There are a number of scholarly researchers among Chinese judges, and this phenomenon is especially prominent among the intellectual property judges. In fact, in the above mentioned Intellectual Property Law Academy of China Law Society, there are a large number of Chinese judicial elites, who are main participators and contributors of previous annual meetings since 2001. This made Chinese intellectual property jurisprudence study keep pragmatic so far, combine theory with practice and devote to solve problems.

2.1 Studies on fundamental theories of intellectual property system

2.1.1 Appellation and connotation of "intellectual property right"

In New China, the term of "intellectual property right" is a borrowed term. Although some scholars held that the translation of this term in Taiwan region of China is more proper[1], due to the translation thereof used in Mainland of China has been comprehensively accepted after many years of use, and has been adopted consistently by related state laws, regulations and policies, most scholars held

1 See Intellectual Property Law, in Guo Shoukang (ed.), The Central Party School Publishing House, 2002, pp.2-3.

that it was not necessary or possible to change the translation of this term. As to the connotation of "intellectual property right", the *World Intellectual Property Organization Convention* and *Agreement on Trade-Related Aspects of Intellectual Property Rights*, which have significant influence in international community, didn't make general definition therefor. So, in our academic circle, there are still many different opinions and arguments on this issue.

Generally speaking, there are three main opinions on definition of "intellectual property right" in our intellectual property jurisprudence circle. (a) Scope or Enumeration Doctrine. The main source of this opinion is that "so far, most countries' jurisprudential monographs and laws, even the international conventions, all start from setting scope to clarify or define intellectual property right"; Pursuant to related international convention, intellectual property right means the rights arising in all intellectually creative activities, such as invention, discovery, works, trademark, trade name and anti-unfair competition, etc.[1] (b) Generalization Doctrine. Earlier, this doctrine has been seen in *Encyclopedia of China (Jurisprudence)*, edited by Zhang Youyu, published by Encyclopedia of China Publishing House in September, 1984, the interpretation of "intellectual property right" in which was: "Intellectual property right refers to the right arising in creative activities based on intelligence (written by Zhao Zhongfu)." Afterwards, the typical opinions included: "intellectual property right refers to the proprietary right that may be enjoyed by people to his intellectually creative achievements in accordance with the laws" [2]; "intellectual property right refers to a general term of the rights enjoyed by creator of intellectual achievements, and owner of marks in production and operating activities under the laws"[3]; "intellectual property right means the right enjoyed by people to his intellectually

1 Zheng Chengsi, Further Research on the Concept of Intellectual Property Right, Intellectual Property, 1997, Issue.1.

2 Zheng Chengsi (ed.), *Coursebook of Intellectual Property Law*, Law Press. China, 1993.

3 Liu Chuntian (ed.), *Coursebook of Intellectual Property Law*, China Renmin University Press, 1995.

creative achievements, or, marks or goodwill in business management activities in accordance with the laws"[1],etc. (c) Intangible Property System Doctrine In recent years, some scholar held that not all rights subordinated intellectual property right are from the field of knowledge, or produced based on intellectual achievements, the term of "knowledge" in translation of "intellectual property right" seems to have been misnamed. Therefore, an intangible property system, wider than the range of intellectual property right shall be established in study of civil jurisprudence, which shall consist of three kinds of rights, such as right to creative achievements, right to business marks and business credit rights[2].

2.1.2 Connections between intellectual property law and civil Law

In China, the intellectual property system was originally a part of *General Rules of the Civil Law*. With development of such disciplines, the intellectual property jurisprudence still kept civil jurisprudence at arm's length. In the process of drafting civil code, the researchers of intellectual property jurisprudence and civil jurisprudence have discussed comprehensively for the connections between the two, and whether intellectual property law shall be compiled into civil code. It should be noted that, this issue has also received attentions from the whole jurisprudential circle at that time.

A number of scholars held that the Intellectual Property Law shall not be compiled into civil code, for its highly technical nature, frequently change, obviously international orientation. And it's difficult to coordinate the rules thereof with general civil rules. For instance, Zheng Chengsi supported "the separation between intellectual property code and civil code as they did in France"[3]. Coincidentally, Liang Huixing, a civil jurisprudence scholar, also held that it's not

1 Wu Handong (ed.), *Intellectual Property Law*, China University of Political Science and Law Press, 2002.

2 Wu Handong, "Some Theoretical Issues of Intangible Property Right", *Chinese Journal of Law*, 1996, Issue.4.

3 Zheng Chengsi, "Chinese Intellectual Property Jurisprudence", in Luo Haocai, Sun Wanzhong (eds)., *Chinese Jurisprudence-Keeping Pace with Times*, China Legal Publishing House, 2001, pp.337-373.

necessary to incorporate the intellectual property law into civil code, so, in the Drafted Civil Code, presided to draft by whom, intellectual property right does not exist as a part[1].

However, the contrary view was that all contents of intellectual property right shall be incorporated into civil code as a separate part, such as, "theoretically, as res incorporales, intellectual property right shall be imported into real rights part and be regulated as res incorporales. Therefore, in our Drafted Civil Code, intellectual property right is stipulated as a part adjacent to real rights part, and has been understood as a special ownership. Such arrangement not only can show the connections between intellectual property right and general real right, but also can reveal the difference between them"[2]. In addition, some scholar held that the position of intellectual property right shall be made clear in civil code. For example, Wang Liming held that, "intellectual property right is still civil right by nature, the inherence of which is property right and personal right. And, intellectual property right has been specially set up as a section in the chapter of civil right in the General Rules of the Civil Law. So, our future civil code shall include the content of intellectual property right".[3] Wu Handong held that, the intellectual property part in civil code shall highlight its difference with other civil systems, but can not lack of generality for applying to various intellectual property rights, and can not influence independent existence of other related civil special legislation. Specifically, the nature, scope, validity, use and protection of intellectual property right shall be provided in this part[4]. Other scholars held that, although not all intellectual property rules can be incorporated into civil code,

1 Liang Huixing, "Outline of Chinese Drafted Civil Code", *Civil and Commercial Law Review*, Law Press·China, Vol.13, 2000.

2 Xu Guodong, "Basic Structure of Drafted Civil Code", *Chinese Journal of Law*, 2000, Issue.1.

3 Wang Liming, "On Formulation of Chinese Civil Code", *Tribune of Political Science and Law*, 1998, Issue.5.

4 Wu Handong, "Legislative Style of Intellectual Property Right and Compilation of Civil Code", *China Legal Science*, 2003, Issue.1.

"we absolutely can provide the intellectual property right in principle in general provisions part, that is, like the *General Rules of the Civil Law*, specifies the types of rights that shall be protected by intellectual property system..."[1]

2.1.3 Principles in determining liability for infringement of intellectual property right

What types of remedies are provided by law against infringement of rights, is very important for protecting rights. In the field of intellectual property jurisprudence, the principles in determining liability for infringement of intellectual property right became focus of debate in late 1990s, which has been discussed in many writings, but whether in theoretical circle, or in practical circle, lots of controversies always exist. One view was that the fault liability principle, not strict liability principle shall be applied in determining tort of intellectual property right[2]; however, other view was that the determination of tort of intellectual property right shall be differentiated, and shall simultaneously apply both fault liability principle and strict liability principle[3]. A majority of scholars held that the tort of intellectual property right shall apply strict liability principle. In view of Zheng Chengsi, not all infringements of intellectual property right are resulted by fault of actors[4]. In addition, in accordance with a compromised view, "subjective fault of actor" is one of the constitutive requirements of intellectual property right tort, but "not condition precedent for bearing all tort liabilities"[5]. In these discussions, theoretical consideration was always conducted combining with cases, and surrounding Sino-U.S. negotiation of intellectual property right

1 Hu Kaizhong, Outline of Connections between Intellectual Property Law and Civil Code, Law and Social Development, 2003, Issue.2.

2 Yao Huanqing, Study on Principles in Determining Liabilities for Infringement of Intellectual Property Right, Zhejiang Social Sciences, Issue.4.

3 Zheng Chengsi, Strict Liabilities for Infringing Intellectual Property Right, China Legal Science, 1998, Issue.1.

4 Zheng Chengsi, Strict Liabilities for Infringing Intellectual Property Right, China Legal Science, 1998, Issue.1; Zheng Chengsi, Misconception about and Development of Chinese Tort Law Theory, China Patents & Trademarks, 2000, Issue.4.

5 Wei Zhi, Copyright Law of China, Peking University press, 1998, p.141.

frequently occurred since reform and opening-up, which had great practical significance. Around the year 2000, in the process of further improvement of intellectual property legal system for China's accession to WTO, as related provisions were detailed, various legal liabilities for infringing intellectual property right were specified, and the difficult problems occurred in previous law application were settled, therefore, the discussion on this issue in our intellectual property jurisprudence circle temporarily came to a conclusion.

2.1.4 Right exhaustion and parallel import

"Right exhaustion" means that once the lawful owner of intellectual property right puts goods, which contain its intellectual property right, into market, he will lose the control for resale of these goods in a certain territory, that is, the right of lawful owner has been exhausted; all persons who have lawfully acquired these intellectual property products can use, resell or dispose these products at their discretion, provided that not to use such products to infringe the exclusive right of intellectual property owner. Right exhaustion is a kind of restriction on rights, which is a general principle in the field of intellectual property law. Its basic starting point is, in a market economy society, which encourages free flow of goods, intellectual property right shall not become a barrier to information dissemination or goods' free flow. At the stage of development of Chinese intellectual property jurisprudence, right exhaustion has been analyzed and discussed in many writings.[1] Since trademark right in international goods trade is a most basic intellectual property right, the discussions focus on exhaustion of trademark right. Some scholars introduced the general international rules of exhaustion of trademark right, and put forward his own opinions; [2]however,

1 For example, Yao Huanqing, On Principles of Right Exhaustion in Intellectual Property Law and the Related Theories of Intellectual Property Law, A Thesis for Master Degree, 1996; Wang Chunyan, Principles to Solve Conflict between Intellectual Property Right and Real Right in Trade, Journal of Renmin University of China, 2003, Issue.1, etc.

2 For example, Zhang Jin, Constraint on Rights in Trademark Law, Studies in Law and Business, 1999, Issue.3; Ma Qiang, Study on Principles of Exhaustion of Trademark Right, Modern Law Science, 2000, Issue.1.

some other scholars held that the right exhaustion doesn't exist in the field of trademark.[1]

Parallel import is an issue closely related to right exhaustion, and the discussions thereto also focus on trademark right. Exhaustion of trademark right refers to the lawful owner, after normally exercising his trademark right, has no authority to intervene others to resell the goods with such trademark. Parallel import (also be referred to as "grey market import") means, in the international trade, the activity of importing the goods in the same class, which are legally licensed to be produced with identical trademark overseas, without permission of domestic trademark owner and trademark exclusive licensee. The scholars relatively agreed upon the principle of exhaustion of trademark right in China, but as to parallel import of the authentic goods produced overseas, there were different opinions. Hence, some scholar has put forward countermeasures corresponding to our situation after analyzing both concepts of right exhaustion and parallel import, and drawing lessons from foreign countries.[2] However, after a period of discussion, the basic conclusion was, unlike the question whether exhaustion of trademark right shall be provided in domestic laws, it is not a legal issue to consider whether parallel import of the authentic goods produced overseas shall be permitted, but choice of policy conducted by a state pursuant to its foreign trade situation. Therefore, it is shall not be specified in laws. Of course, if parallel import is accompanied by the situations such as confusion, or free rider, the legal rules for stopping unfair competition may be applied thereto.

2.1.5 Right conflict on intellectual property right

The legal situation that the same intellectual property right object, under certain conditions, simultaneously belongs to more subjects is very common in this

1 Zhang Yongai, Question for Principles of Exhaustion of Trademark Right , Zheng Fa Lun Cong, 2004, Issue.1.

2 Huang Hui, On Exhaustion of Trademark Right and Parallel Import, China Trademark, 1999, Issue.2; Zhang Jin, Restriction on Rights in Trademark Law, Studies in Law and Business, 1999, Issue.

field, especially in works, trademarks or designs, which are easy to cross. How to deal with conflict of rights or concurrence of rights in the field of intellectual property, has caught interest of the scholars thereof in China. The essence of conflict of intellectual property rights is how to regard the relationship between "prior right" and "later right". Combining with the controversies, arising from the use of copyrighted work as trademarks, in the "San Mao and His Picture" case, an improper registration of trademark case, and in the "Wu Song Fights the Tiger" case, a trademark infringement case, our intellectual property jurisprudence circle has made a heated discussion on conflict of rights. Some scholar started from judicial judgments, and put forward his own opinions on the legal nature, philosophical basis and scope of liability of the two.[1] Some scholar held that the claim lodged by copyright owner to trademark owner shall be reasonably restricted, and make the same intellectual product play its role to the highest extent. In addition, the scholar also put forward substantive and procedural measures thereto.[2] The opposite view was, it is infringement of others' copyrights (right of reproduction and right of issuance) to use their works in industry, even the industrial property right has been acquired, the registered trademark shall be revoked.[3] Some measures were put forward from the judicial perspective.[4] For this discussion, Zheng Chengsi has made some comment. He held that the existence of conflict of intellectual property rights shall not be denied generally; however, a number of cases involving conflict of intellectual property rights, which has been propagandized intensely, indeed, didn't involve the real conflict of rights, it was

1 Liu Chuntian, "Prior Right" and Industrial Property Rights, China Patents & Trademarks,1998, Issue.3.

2 Zhou Huanrun, Reasonably Restricting the Claim Lodged by Copyright Right Owner to Trademark Owner, China Trademark, 1997,Issue.4; Cao Xinming, Maximizing the Value of the Same Intellectual Product, China Trademark, 1998, Issue.5.

3 Wu Yan, Discussion on the Relationship between Copyright and Industrial Property Right, China Patents & Trademarks,1998, Issue.2.

4 Chen Zilong, Conflict of Intellectual Property Rights and Judicial Discretion, in Zheng Chengsi (ed.), Intellectual Property Right Series, China University of Political Science and Law Press, Vol.3, 2000.

actual conflict between lawful owner and infringer.[1]

Furthermore, as to how to solve the conflict of intellectual property rights, the scholars have put forward various related measures[2]. The discussion on conflict of intellectual property rights was extended to the conflict between trademark and trade name[3], and it lasted for a longer time than other topics. In judicial circle, concerning to intellectual property right, this conflict has been discussed enthusiastically for many years with rich fruits.[4] Furthermore, in recent years, a relatively dominant view has been formed, which embodied in *Provisions on Several Issues for Adjudging Civil Dispute Cases concerning to Conflict among Registered Trademark, Corporate Name and the Prior Rights*, adopted and implemented by Supreme People's Court on Feb. 18, 2008, and Measures adopted by other provincial High People's Courts. According to this view, as long as the later trademark or trade name contains other's prior right (trademark right or trade name right), which is enough to make the consumer confused, that will constitute unfair competition.

2.2 Studies in the field of copyright law

2.2.1 Protection of database

Database is a product of highly developed information technology, which is

---

1 Zheng Chengsi, Outlook for Intellectual Property Right Study in 21st Century, Intellectual Property Right Series, China University of Political Science and Law Press, Vol.3, 2000.

2 Cao Xinming, On Principles to Coordinate Conflict between Intellectual Property Rights, Chinese Journal of Law, 1999, Issue.3; Li Yongming&Zhang Zhenjie, Study on Concurrence of Intellectual Property Rights, Chinese Journal of Law, 2001, Issue.2.

3 Hou Shuwen, Analysis of Conflict between Trademark Right and Enterprise Name Right, Intellectual Property, 1999, Issue.1; Tao Xinliang, Conflict of Rights, Balance of Rights and Coordination-Special Seminar concerning to "Zhang Xiaoquan case" Held in Shanghai, China Trademark, 1999, Issue.5; Lin Qianduo, On Conflict between Trademark Right and Trade Name Right and its Solution, China Trademark, 2003, Issue.10; Wu Jian, Several Issues in Conflict between Intellectual Property Rights, China Trademark, 2005, Issue.11.

4 For example, Pan Wei, On Conflict between Trade Name Right and Trademark Right, China Trademark, 2001, Issue.8; Su Chi, Study on Issues concerning to Conflict between Trademark Right and Trade Name Right, Chinese People's Public Security University Press, 2003; Tan Xiaoqing, Study on Theories and Cases of Conflict between Intellectual Property Rights, Suzhou University Press, 2004,etc.

generally defined as a collection of ordered works, data or other materials, and can be accessed in electronic or non-electronic manner. The legal protection of database has received comprehensive attention from international community. Generally speaking, it's unquestionable for the database with creativity or originality to be protected under the laws of all countries, that is, being protected as compiled works or collective works under copyright law; however, when the database, with a great deal of information, being unable to show specific conception of the person who collects such information, is arbitrarily intercepted or reproduced, it's difficult to solve this problem in accordance with copyright law. Therefore, in EU' Directive on the Legal Protection of Databases, protection rules on "sui generis right" has been established, that is, based on "sweat of the brow", providing special protection for the content of databases without creativity, but representing a great deal of labor or financial resources investment. This manner also initiated a heated discussion in China. One view was that, it's not suitable to establish a special protection system for databases, like EU, however, we can consider formulating special provisions in copyright law, to appropriately lower the requirements to creativity of database, but, the content of databases shall not be protected.[1] Another view was that it's detrimental to developing country to protect sui generis right of databases. Pursuant to the existing "copyright law plus anti-unfair competition law" pattern, the maker of database can be protected.[2] According to another view, the database shall be protected in our country mainly by means of protection measures in anti-unfair competition law, and meanwhile, making full use of the relevant provisions of contract law.[3] This issue has been discussed for many years. For now, the unanimous opinions in our intellectual property jurisprudence are in conformity with the copyright laws of many countries and international conventions, that is, the database, which can constitute

1 Dong Binghe, On Special Protection of Databases, Copyright, 1998, Issue.1.
2 Xue Hong, Protection of Databases and Fight against Monopoly, Intellectual Property, 1998, Issue.3.
3 Li Yang, On Legal Protection of Databases, Studies in Law and Business, 2002, Issue.1.

collective work due to its choice or compilation of contents, shall be protected by copyright law. According to judgments of relevant cases, although the protection system concerning to sui generis right of databases has not been brought into legislative schedule in China, our courts still has employed the "copyright law plus anti-unfair competition law" pattern to protect it properly.

2.2.2 Protection of copyright in cyberspace

Since late 1990s, with the rapid development of information technology, the digital transmission technology, which is the key technical support of computer Internet, has brought great convenience to the collection, reproduction and transmission of mass information; accordingly, as any one of the innovations of reproduction and communication technology, information technology has brought impact on the implementation of copyright law. Nowadays, living with digitalization or network has become a basic way of lives. The nature of many behaviors involving reproduction with computer or communication on Internet shall be determined in copyright law; So, it's necessary to discuss in theory. In this regard, just like what Zheng Chengsi has said, the level of our intellectual property jurisprudential scholars is not less than the scholars in other countries, whether judging from the starting point, or from the research achievements. For example, the study on copyright of digital transmission on the Internet has already began in late 1990s. Some scholars have summarized and concluded that, in digital transmission, temporary storage is different from copies stored in hard disk or soft disk, and digital transmission is also different from issuance or rental.[1] For purpose of protecting the moral rights of authors in cyberspace, some scholars held that the level of protection shall be maintained at a moderate level, to make the public participate in the process of improvement or even re-creation of works, so as to enjoy the achievements of human intelligence at a higher level. In addition, such scholars have also put forward specific criterion for restricting the moral rights of

1 Yuan Yong, Study on Copyright of Digital Transmission on the Internet, Peking University Law Journal, 1998, Issue.1.

authors on Internet.[1] Some other scholars have explored the subjects of "electronic creation",[2] and network transmission and right of communication of works.[3]

After entering 21st century, with rapid development of Internet, the problem of copyrights protection in cyberspace has become particularly prominent. Afterwards, in order to realize balance of rights and interests among all parties in the context of network, and achieve legislative goal of copyright law to the largest extent, the adjustments of some basic system in copyright law have received more attention. In addition, researchers found that the usage of technology per se on the Internet is significant for running of legal rules, therefore, some research results concerning to technology protection measure and its standard usage have been produced. Such above achievements were particularly embodied in various monographs or textbooks concerning to intellectual property right or copyright, written individually or updated and modified, such as the volumes of *Intellectual Property Studies*, edited by Zheng Chengsi, and his monograph, *On Intellectual Property*; as well as other monographs on Internet and protection of intellectual property right, introduced and expounded by Xue Hong, etc.[4] Furthermore, in the discussion around this heated topic, a number of academic papers were produced. The earlier discussion mainly focused on finding and analyzing relationship between development of new Internet technology and intellectual property law, especially, the copyright law, and pointed out that the copyright law shall be added relevant provisions in response to new technology, or given

1 Xue Hong, Protection of Moral Rights in Cyberspace, Copyright, 1998, Issue.3.

2 Zhang Ping, Exploration on "Electronic Creation", Intellectual Property, 1999, Issue.3.

3 Dong Binghe, Network Transmission and Right of Communication, Copyright, 1999, Issue.3.

4 Xue Hong, Protection of Copyrights and Relevant Rights on the Internet, China University of Political Science and Law Press, 1999; Xue Hong, Intellectual Property in the Network Age, Law Press·China, 2000; Yan Guizhen, Fair Use of Copyrights on the Internet, Jilin People's Publishing House, 2001; Wang Qian, Copyright Law in Cyberspace, China Renmin University Press, 2008.

further interpretation to the existing and relevant provisions[1]. After amendment of *Copyright Law* in 2001, the relevant articles mainly focused on interpretation of right to network dissemination of information and legislative appraisal and improvement of technology protection measures.[2] In addition, combining with new cases occurred on the Internet, as to some problems that had not been thoroughly explored in previous theories of copyright, we also got some results. For example, with respect to the phenomenon of A Murder Case Caused by a Steamed Bread[3], namely, parody, according to the scholars, "parody works" shall apply the legal rules of "fair use", and shall be protected in accordance with "fair

1 For instance, Wang Huapeng, Protection of Copyrights in Electronic Commerce, Copyright, 1993, Issue.3; Li Yanrong, On Protection of On-line Copyrights under Copyright Law, Intellectual Property, 1999, Issue.5; Zheng Chengsi, Protection of New Technology, Circulation of New Technical Products and Change of Key Points in Civil and Commercial Law, Intellectual Property, 1999, Issue.6; Tian Wenying&Meng Juan, Protection of Copyright in Cyberspace, Contemporary Law Review, 2000, Issue.6; Xu Chao, On Relationship between Internet Communication and Copyright, The Rule of Law Forum(Journal of Shanghai University of Political Science & Law), 2001, Vol.16, Issue.1, etc.

2 For example, Wu Weiguang, Technical Protection of and Restriction on Copyright, in Wang Bing (ed.), New View on Protection of Intellectual Property Rights of High Technology, China Legal Publishing House, 2002; Xu Chunming, Interpretation of "INTERNET Treaties", Electronics Intellectual Property, 2003, Issue.7; Guo He, Analysis on Legal Attribute of Behaviors of Circumventing Technological Measures, in Shen Rengan (ed.), Digital Technology and Copyright: Conception, Rules & Cases, Law Press·China, 2004; Qiao Sheng, Legislative Appraisal and Improvement of Right to Network Dissemination of Information, China Legal Science, 2004, Issue.4; Zhang Geng, A Brief Discussion on Technological Protection Measures of Copyright, Modern Law Science, 2004, Issue.2; Feng Xiaoqin&Hu Shaobo, On Challenging Traditional Copyright System by Internet& Comment upon the New Forms of Fair Use of Copyright in Cyberspace, Science of Law, 2004, Issue.6; Wang Qian, Study on Infringement of Copyright by End-users of P2P Software, Intellectual Property, 2004, Vol.14, Issue.5; Liang Zhiwen, Confusion on and Definition of Right to Network Dissemination of Information, Electronics Intellectual Property, 2008, Issue.4, etc.

3 The details of this case See that a cybercitizen, Hu Ge, clipped and rearranged the frames of a move, The Promise, added some other frames and then re-dubbed, as a result, a short film with burlesque, based on The Promise, but fundamentally different from it in plot, structure and subject, was formed and uploaded to the Cyberspace.

use" doctrine by Chinese Copyright Law.[1]

Generally speaking, in our academic circle, the dominant opinion on protection of copyright in cyberspace is, new technology admittedly has brought unprecedented challenge to implementation of legal rules, but not have substantially changed the legal relationship, arising from use of works, among the lawful owner, user and social public. Therefore, the basic theories and rules of copyright law are still valid in cyberspace; that is, the protection on rights under copyright law shall not be weakened or abolished with development of computer and network technologies. However, in consideration of the facts that the lawful owner is difficult to control reproduction and communication of works in cyberspace, the original legal measures shall be adjusted, to a certain extent, to meet the needs of all parties. At present, *Regulations on Protection of Right to Network Dissemination of Information* has been enacted in accordance with *Copyright Law* in China. "Third-party liability", propounded on the basis of absorbing existing research results and judicial experience, is a good idea. The researchers shall put forward more detailed and scientific rules and application plan accordingly, such as design of notice and takedown system, limitation and counter-limitation for technological measures, application of collective management system, etc.

2.3 Studies in the field of trademark law and anti-unfair competition law

"Anti-counterfeiting" is a core concept contained in both trademark law and anti-unfair competition law. With respect to regulation against "counterfeit" business marks, there are often interactions and overlaps between trademark law and anti-unfair competition law. For this issue, some scholars in our intellectual property field have always been studying. Zheng Chengsi has propounded the relationship very early among anti-unfair competition law and intellectual property law, especially trademark law. Furthermore, combining with the legislative models of foreign trademark law and anti-unfair competition law, he

1 Wang Qian, On Legal Rules for Determining the "Fair Use" Constituted by "Parody Works", Science-technology and Law, 2006, Issue.1; Legal Protection of and Restriction on Parody, China Legal Science, 2006, Issue.3.

made a comparative analysis[1], and pointed out that the anti-unfair competition law has played an "additional" or "fallback" role. In addition, some scholar has made comments on the issue whether "reverse passing off" is unfair competition or trademark infringement[2].

In a period of time, the relationship between domain name and trademark has received much attention. Domain name is a technical function designed to facilitate web users, which provides computer with web site composed by characters, easy to be remembered and identified. In e-commerce environment, in order to facilitate remembrance and identification, the domain name of a merchant is always associated with its business name, trademark, trade name, name of product or service, so, it is closely related to intellectual property right. Since the domain registration and trademark registration belong to different systems, the same mark might be respectively registered as trademark or domain name by different persons. Therefore, one view was put forward that the domain name shall be deemed as a new and independent intellectual property category[3]; but according to another view, there is no actual conflict between domain name and trademark, the domain name shall not affect trademark owner to exercise its trademark right, and shall not dilute the well-known trademark[4]. Judging from the cases of domain name and trademark dispute, before the second amendment of *Trademark Law* in 2001, all domestic courts decided such cases combining with *Anti-unfair Competition Law*. After implementation of *Trademark Law* (Revised in 2001), especially after the Supreme People's Court adopted *Interpretation of Several Issues concerning to the Application of Law in Adjudging Cases of Trademark*

1 Zheng Chengsi, Anti-unfair Competition and Intellectual Property, Legal Science, 1997, Issue.6; A Brief Discussion on Interactions and Overlaps between Anti-unfair Competition Law and Trademark Law, China Patents & Trademarks, 1998, Issue.4; Anti-unfair Competition-Additional Protection of Intellectual Property Right, Intellectual Property, 2003, Issue.5.

2 Zheng Youde, Liu Ping, On Imitations and Unfair Competition, Intellectual Property, 1998, Issue.1.

3 Zhang Naigen, Review of Intellectual Property in the Global Electronic Commerce, Intellectual Property, 1999, Issue.3.

4 Wu Denglou, Settlement of the Conflict between Internet Domain Name and Trademark Name, Intellectual Property, 1999, Issue.3.

Civil Dispute in 2002, the discussion on issues of conflict or dispute over trademark and domain in our intellectual property circle came to a conclusion.

In recent years, especially before and after the adoption of *Interpretation of Several Issues concerning to Application of Laws in Adjudging Civil Cases of Unfair Competition* by the Supreme People's Court in 2007, the focus of Chinese intellectual property circle in this area has changed into exploration of the relationship between trademark and commercial marks, such as trade name, trade dress, and so on[1]; In particular, due to ever increasing relevant cases in practice, the relationship among registered trademark, business name and trade name has received much attention, whether in judicial circle or in academic circle, which has been mentioned in preceding discussion of rights conflict. In addition, either pursuant to trademark law, or under anti-unfair competition law, counterfeiting behaviors are generally targeted at commercial marks with fame. So, the protection of well-known trademark and its problems are always the subjects discussed by our intellectual property jurisprudence circle. The discussion covers modes of protection, procedure of determination and alienation of well-known trademark [2]. The influence of such theoretical discussions on practice was

1 He Xiangju, Protection of Trade Dress-Judging from Trademark Law and Anti-unfair Competition Law, Electronics Intellectual Property, 2005, Issue.1; Qian Guangwen, Sun Jinlin, Discussion on Legal Protection of Trade Dress in China-Centering on Application of Anti-unfair Competition Law, Intellectual Property, 2009, Issue.1.

2 Zheng Chengsi, Several Issues concerning to Protection of Well-known Trademark, Intellectual Property, 1995, Issue.3; Qiu Jian, Legal Issues concerning to Well-known Trademark and the Protection thereon, China Legal Science, 1995, Issue.2; Ren Zili, Discussion on Dilution and Anti-dilution Protection of Well-known Trademark, Intellectual Property, 1996, Issue.5; Zhang Jin, Considerations on Special Protection of Well-known Trademark, Tribune of Political Science and Law,2000, Issue.2; Huang Hui, Legal Protection of Well-known and Famous Trademark, Law Press·China, 2001; Pu Xiang, Consideration on Definition of Well-known Trademark-Comment on Revised Trademark Law, China Trademark, 2002, Issue.1; Gong Hengchao, Alienation in Well-known Trademark Determination Practice and Governance thereof-Discussion based on Theoretical Framework for Determining Well-known Trademark, Study on China Administration for Industry & Commerce, 2008, Issue.5; Yuan Xingtao, Reconstruction of Well-known Trademark Determination System in China, Electronics Intellectual Property, 2008, Issue.12, etc.

embodied in *Interpretation of the Supreme People's Court on Several Issues about the Application of Laws for the Trial of Civil Dispute Cases Involving Protection of Well-known Trademark*, adopted in April, 2009. Obviously, the people's court has taken the mainstream view, with a gradually conservative attitude towards the claims for determination of well-known trademark in civil cases.

In the field of anti-unfair competition law, protection of trade secret is another important issue focused all along by intellectual property jurisprudence scholars in China. The earliest study centered on introducing and commenting foreign (especially, United States) related laws, cases and practices. After the legal protection of trade secret was established in *Anti-unfair Competition Law* in China, the *Criminal Law* (revised in 1997) was also added some relevant terms. So, the research later mainly focused on exploring the basic theories and criminal protection of trade secret.[1] After a period of time, a number of monographic achievements, centering on summarizing previous research results and experiences and lessons in practice, and carrying out comparative study on this issue in and abroad, were produced.[2] The study on trade secret became a branch of intellectual property jurisprudence, the main theories of which involve concept, nature and constitutive requirements of trade secret and its relationship with "non-competition". Some researcher has introduced and analyzed the mainstream opinions, in the era of knowledge economy, on protection of trade secret in the countries, such as United Kingdom, United States and France. She held that "theory of property right " and "theory of secret relation" are basic theories, which are

1 Zhang Yurui, Several Issues about Legal Protection of Trade Secret, Intellectual Property, 1995, Issue.5; Chen Li, Trade Secret and Criminal Protection Thereon, Journal of Anhui Normal University, 1995,Issue.1; Xing Yu, Crime of Infringing Trade Secret and the Perfection of Legislation, Public Administration & Law, 2000, Issue.2.

2 Kong Xiangjun, Protection Theory of Trade Secret Law, China Legal Publishing House, 1999; Zhang Yurui, Trade Secret Jurisprudence, China Legal Publishing House,1999; Zhang Yurui, Legal Protection on Trade Secret, China University of Political Science and Law Press,2003; Zheng Chengsi, On Intellectual Property, Law Press·China, 2003; Li Mingde, American Intellectual Property Law, Law Press·China; Dai Yongsheng, A Comparative Study on Trade Secret Law, East China Normal University Press, 2005.

most helpful for understanding the formation and development of the whole legal system for protecting trade secret[1]. With deepening of the study, currently, our academic circle and judicial circle are laying stress upon judgment of the constitutive requirements of trade secret, and discussion on the difficult issues occurred in the trial of cases.

2.4 Discussion on issues in the field of patent law

In the process of improving our patent legal system, the academic circle had discussed many specific issues, such as enlargement of objects, indirect infringement, the infringement under the doctrine of equivalents, service invention patent, and so on. The results of these studies are of significance to the improvement of patent system in China. The characteristic of intellectual property system, which is closely related to high technology, can be best embodied by patent system. At present, whether software, especially the software related to business methods, can be protected under Patent Law, has become the most noticeable issue in field of patent. The development of information and network technology has brought new business model, which is reflected in the law on protection of business methods, based on computer or network technology. What closely relates to this issue is the patent protection on computer software, which has been controversial for a long time in intellectual property jurisprudence circle. Seeking other protection methods other than copyright, is of significance for competitor to obtain lawful monopoly position by means of functional software with novel, practicable and creative characteristics. This principle has also been gradually clarified in our practice, that is, software, inseparable from hardware devices and integrated with technical solution, can be protected by Patent Law. The argument resulted by the patentability of business methods software, especially computer system in financial and accounting field has lasted to present

1 Shan Hailing, On the Prevailing Theories of Trade Secret Protection in the Knowledge and Economic Era:Theory of Secret Relation and Theory of Property Right, Tribune of Political Science and Law, 2004, Issue.5.

time.[1] In addition, the discussion on patent system arising from development of new technology also involves the patentability of achievements related to biological and genetic technologies.[2]

On the other hand, in recent years after entering WTO, since our enterprises were frequently suppressed in the growth by foreign patentees, and the previous smooth progress has been largely damaged. So, in China, a wave of reflection on patent system, even on the whole intellectual property system, sprang up. Combining with the promulgation of *Anti-trust Law* in China, a number of research results about restrictions on intellectual property right (patent right) or abuse of prohibition system have been produced in our intellectual property law studies. Some scholar has analyzed the reasons for expansion of patent right from a perspective of interests balance.[3] One view was that reform of patent system would obviously be influenced by a country's economic level, political system and legal tradition[4]; and some scholar has specifically discussed the compulsory license system for restricting patent right.[5] Among which, the hottest

1 For example, Zheng Wanqing & Jiang Wenpeng, On the Business Method Patent in E-commerce, Intellectual Property, 2001, Issue.2; Jiang Hongzhen, Patent Protection-the Only Road for Innovation of Electronic Commerce Network, Intellectual Property, 2001, Issue.5; Zhang Ping & Lu Haiying, From Refusing Protection to Providing Facilities-A Chronological Study of Desirability of Computer Software Patent, Peking University Law Journal, 2001, Issue.2; Huang Yi & Yin Long, Business Method Patent, China Financial Publishing House, 2004; Lang Guimei, Determination of Patent Object and Patent Protection of Business Method, Intellectual Property Publishing House, 2008, etc.

2 For example, Zhang Qingkui, View on the Patent protection of Biotechnology in China, Intellectual Property, 2000, Issue.6; Zhang Xiaodu, On the Invention and Discovery Correlated with Gene, Intellectual Property, 2001, Issue.6; Zhao Zhengjiang & Liu Yinliang, A Study of the Legal Implications of Human Genome Project, Peking University Law Journal, 2001, Issue.4, etc.

3 Feng Xiaoqing, Probing into the Expansion of Patent and Its Cause, Journal of Hunan University (Social Sciences), 2006, Issue.5.

4 Liu Hua, Demonstration Study on International Patent System Reformations and Apocalypses, Science of Law, 2006, Issue.1.

5 Guo Shoukang & Zuo Xiaodong, Interests Balance under Patent Compulsory License System, Intellectual Property, 2006, Issue.2; Lin Xiuqin, Patent Compulsory License under the TRIPS Agreement, Law Press China, 2006.

issue was discussion particularly on the relation between abuse of intellectual property right (patent right) and Anti-trust Law. In view of some typical opinions, intellectual property right is a legal monopoly by nature, which generally exists with exemption from application of Anti-trust Law; However, as an exclusive right, intellectual property right is often easy to make the owner thereof form monopoly or dominant position in some certain markets, and more easily limit the competition in such markets, for instance, the lawful owner uses intellectual property system to deliberately exclude or restrict competition, dishonestly poses threat with tort lawsuit or maliciously institutes tort proceedings to restrict others to use technology or information, all such acts shall be regulated by law[1].

Some discussions on other aspects of the patent, such as studies on "junk patent" phenomena, system of design, optimization of various procedures in patent law, system of genetic resources disclosure, substantial elements of patent and criteria for judging infringement, and so on, also have played a certain role in improving the systems of our country. From the perspective of amendment of *Patent Law* at the end of 2008, the results of discussions on a variety of issues in patent field, which have been conducted by Chinese intellectual property jurisprudential scholars, are of practical significance.

2.5 Studies on protection of traditional knowledge

With the acceleration of globalization process, enhancement of concepts of biological and cultural diversity, and deepening of ethnic self-determination consciousness, the subject concerning to traditional knowledge protection has gained access to the field of intellectual property law. According to the findings surveyed by the World Intellectual Property Organization (WIPO) in 1999 in many undeveloped countries and regions, traditional knowledge has been always

1 Chen Liping, Legal Regulation on Patent Abuse, Legal Forum, 2005, Issue.2; Xu Chunming&Shan Xiaoguang, On the Doctrine of Patent Abuse Defense: Based on ITC Philips Disc Case, Intellectual Property, 2006, Issue.3; Wang Xianlin, Study of Abuse of Intellectual Property Rights and Its Legal Regulation, China Legal Publishing House, 2008; Zhang Weijun, Study on Legal System for Regulating Abuse of Intellectual Property Rights, Intellectual Property Publishing House, 2008.

deemed as the resources of modern innovation or creation, that is, the resources of many intellectual achievements. It is closely related to all branches of the current existing intellectual property system. Therefore, since the establishment of WIPO Intergovernmental Committee on Traditional Knowledge, Genetic Resources and Folklore (IGC) in 2000, the connections between traditional knowledge, broadly speaking, including the above three items, and intellectual property system have gradually received more and more attentions in China, and have become a hot topic in intellectual property research circle. From the international perspective, there is a great controversy on this issue among all parties. Basically speaking, the developed countries have always been firmly opposed to protection on traditional knowledge by means of intellectual property right or other special rights similar to intellectual property right. However, the developing countries basically hold that the principles similar to "National Sovereignty, Prior Informed Consent and Benefit Sharing" established in *Convention on Biological Diversity* shall be set up, so as to change the current imbalance, under which the existing intellectual property system only protects current creative results, but ignores the fact that such results are produced on the basis of possession without compensation, or even improper use of traditional knowledge.

From the internal perspective, Chinese researchers tend to hold that the traditional knowledge shall be protected by law, but as to how to design the detailed legal system, there is still much controversy. In early studies, the discussions were conducted from the perspective of protection on national folk culture or intangible cultural heritage. Some policy and legal researchers, who were interested in such an issue, all have written articles to give their opinions.[1]

1 The main research results were published in Intellectual Property Series, in Zheng Chengsi (ed.), China Fangzheng Press, Vol.8, 2002. Other articles, such as, Jia Mingru, Legal Construction and Legislative Conception for Protection of National Folk Culture, China Copyright, 2002, Issue.1; Zhao Rong&Liu Xiaoxia, Legal Protection on Folklore Works, Legal Science, 2003, Issue.10; Jiang Wanlai, On Legal Protection of Our Folklore from a Perspective of Interest Ownership Relation, at http://www.civillaw.com.cn/weizhang/default.asp? id=16643.

The unanimous opinions reached on these studies mainly centered on the aspects, such as, necessity of protection, with essence of preservation, and administrative management measures. For example, some scholar held that, the framework of traditional knowledge protection system shall include the general survey system for establishment and improvement of national folk culture, system for special protection and inheritance of national folk culture, system for use and development of national folk culture, system for protection on cultural ecology, and measures for protection of national folk culture, etc[1]. Although some study achievements involving the relation between ownership and use of traditional knowledge have been produced in academic circle[2], in the whole, the theoretical discussion concerning to the relation between traditional knowledge and intellectual property right is still absent. On the other hand, it was also typical for holding a skeptical or even opposite opinion on protection of traditional knowledge by intellectual property law. For instance, some scholar raised doubts about the view that intellectual property system shall be adjusted for protection of folklore, and pointed out that adjusting copyright law to protect folklore would hamper "free access to public sphere", and then produce an impact on the subsequent creation[3]. In recent years, with the deepening of study, the results produced on this issue have increased day by day. More and more researchers held that the special rights protection system in different forms, similar to intellectual property right, and for different classes of traditional knowledge shall be established in

1 See Wang Heyun, Consideration on Legislative Models of National Folk Culture Protection, in Zheng Chengsi (ed.), Intellectual Property Series, China Fangzheng Press, Vol.8, 2002.

2 For example, Long Wen, On Right Ownership of Folklore, Degree Paper of Juris Master, Heilongjiang University, No.011439; Liu Yinliang, Study on Legal Issues concerning to Protection of Traditional Knowledge, atwww.chinalawedu.com.

3 See Cui Guobin, Abandoning the Notion of Collective Authorship-the End of Problem of Folk Literature Copyright, Law and Social Development, 2005, Part 5.

our country[1]. These research results have produced impact on the policies and laws of our country. For instance, the relevant opinions were incorporated into the *Outline of the National Intellectual Property Strategy*, some suggestions concerning to protection of genetic resources were adopted by the *Patent Law*, revised at the end of 2008, and other laws and rules related to traditional knowledge, such as *Law on the Protection of Intangible Cultural Heritage*, *Regulations on Protecting Copyright of Folklore Works*, are under formulation. However, since the major controversy and difference therein still exist, as to how to combine the protection of traditional knowledge with the material legal terms of intellectual property system, there is no generally accepted consensus among Chinese intellectual property researchers.

2.6 Formulation and implementation of intellectual property strategy

Since entering 21st century, intellectual property right has become strategic resources for major countries to participate in international competition in the era of economic globalization and with explosion of knowledge economy. Intellectual property strategy has become an important development strategy for many countries to enhance core competitiveness. After thirty years of reform and opening up, China has made great progress in various aspects. However, the economic development mode is still inefficient, the cost of resources and environment is too large, the capacity for independent innovation is insufficient, core technology and famous brand are absent, creation of cultural works can not fully meet needs of the people to enrich their spiritual and cultural lives, the fundamental role of intellectual property system in encouraging technological innovation, promoting knowledge dissemination, furthering economic and cultural

1 For example, Yan Yonghe, Protection on Intellectual Property Right of Traditional Knowledge, Law Press·China, 2006; Guan Yuying, Protecting Folklore from the Perspective of Intellectual Property, Law Press·China, 2006; Zhang Xiaoyong, Acquisition and Benefit Sharing of Genetic Resources and Intellectual Property Right Thereto, Intellectual Property Publishing House, 2007; Zhang Geng, Study on Protecting Intellectual Property Right of Folklore, Law Press·China, 2007; Huang Yuye, Legal Protection on Folklore, Intellectual Property Publishing House, 2008.

prosperity, and regulating competitive order has not fully played. Therefore, in early 2005, in order to actively deal with international challenge, adapt to the needs of economic and social development, and implement the national intellectual property strategy, the State Council established the Leading Group on Drafting National Intellectual Property Strategy, and formally initiated the drafting works. Thirty three central ministries, agencies, offices and bureaus, such as Intellectual Property Office, State Administration of Industry and Commerce, Copyright Administration, State Development and Reform Commission, Ministry of Science and Technology, and Ministry of Commerce, have jointly promoted the works for drafting national intellectual property strategy. The national intellectual property strategy covers Outline of National Intellectual Property Strategy (referred to as the "Outline"), and the study and development works on thirty three special subjects. Over the next three years, the leading direction of Chinese intellectual property research circle was basically based on these special subjects, and studied, around the creation, management, protection and use of intellectual property right from five aspects as below: macro issues about intellectual property strategy, major categories of intellectual property rights, legal construction on intellectual property right, the important management process of intellectual property right, and main industries involving intellectual property right. The leading experts and scholars in Chinese intellectual property circle all have respectively devoted to the research works on different special subjects. Under the direct guidance of State Council leaders, after serious study and repeated modification by the departments of Intellectual Property Office, State Administration of Industry and Commerce, Copyright Administration, State Development and Reform Commission, Ministry of Science and Technology, and Ministry of Commerce, the Outline (draft submitted for approval) has finally been formulated, and then tabled to State Council Executive Meeting in early 2008, adopted by State Council Executive Meeting on April 9, and finally promulgated for implementation on June 5. It should be pointed out that the key contents of the above special subjects have been reflected in the published Outline, and many details thereof were summary of the previous relevant views. As to how to implement the national intellectual property strategy hereafter, the relevant experts have made expositions in writings published in succession.

2.7 Improving the law enforcement system of intellectual property in China

After entering WTO and the legal rules on intellectual property right has been fundamentally improved, "law enforcement" began to become the most concerned issue on Chinese intellectual property protection in international community; the effect of law enforcement in intellectual property field has become a key factor, which can affect the international profile of China, and in a certain sense, can determine how does China be accepted by international community. The scientific setup and improvement of law enforcement in intellectual property field are the basic condition for ensuring the effect thereof. Chinese Academy of Social Sciences Intellectual Property Research Center has analyzed and summarized the relevant discussions in this field. Through these studies, the Center held that there are two main aspects of the law enforcement system concerning to intellectual property right need to be improved. The first one involves conferment and management of intellectual property right. According to current setup of administrative agencies in China, the duties of application, conferment and management of intellectual property right are respectively shared by different administrative agencies. And the existing system for conferment and management of intellectual property right has also exposed many problems. For instance, interaction and omission in different areas of protection, inefficiency caused by unsynchronized and inharmonious works, waste of labor and financial resources resulted by excessive establishment of organs, confusion and dissatisfaction of right owners and the public produced by complicated procedures, and so on. The second involves the implementation and application system of law. In China, the law enforcement in intellectual property field shall follow "double track system", which includes administrative enforcement and jurisdiction of courts. In recent years, the position and role of administrative enforcement in the whole law enforcement system concerning to intellectual property right has received more attention from the scholars; and meanwhile, as the heart of law enforcement system concerning to intellectual property right, the reform, with respect to China's judicial protection on intellectual property right, especially the procedures for confirmation of rights, has become the focus concerned by the whole academic circle. Since the professionalization of intellectual property cases is becoming more and more prominent, some persons have put forward their views on different occasions, such as, to establish specialized court concerning to intellectual property right, or resume to use the appellation of intellectual property right tribunal. Furthermore, in coordination with the whole process of judicial reform, the issues, which might be resulted by the fact that intellectual property right cases are respectively governed by civil, administrative and criminal tribunals, have drawn attentions of both scholars and practitioners.[1]

3. Prospect of Development Trend of Intellectual Property Jurisprudence

Growing out of nothing, from depending on other disciplines to independence and maturity, the intellectual property jurisprudence has developed rapidly in China. However, as mentioned earlier, Chinese intellectual property jurisprudence has achieved fruitful results since it appeared. The first generation of intellectual property jurisprudential scholars, represented by Zheng Chengsi, have established the discipline of intellectual property jurisprudence in our country. They have finished some academic tasks, for example, introducing and demonstrating the system and rules, and combining them with national conditions, which made the intellectual property jurisprudence gradually become independent from civil and commercial jurisprudence and economic jurisprudence, and enter a relatively independent development stage.

1 Studies on Reform of System for Protecting Intellectual Property Right in China, in Chinese Academy of Social Sciences Intellectual Property Research Center (ed.), Intellectual Property Publishing House, 2008; Studies on Improving the Law Enforcement System of Intellectual Property Right, in Chinese Academy of Social Sciences Intellectual Property Research Center& China Intellectual Property Training Center (eds.), Intellectual Property Publishing House, 2009.

Around the formulation of national intellectual property strategy, the central issue, Chinese intellectual property jurisprudence study has developed rapidly both in depth and in breadth. Especially in the process of formulating and studying national intellectual property strategy, almost all leading experts and scholars and the promising young scholars in intellectual property circle of China have been mobilized, and a number of research results have been produced, which made Chinese intellectual property jurisprudence move towards maturity. More and more colleges and universities have opened the course of intellectual property law. According to the documents issued by Department of Justice in July, 2006 (Letter No.222[2006], Department of Justice), with approval of the Academic Degree Affairs Office of State Council, the National JM Education Steering Committee contemplates to decide to run pilot training classes concerning to in-service studying for master degree of JM, in direction of intellectual property right, in some colleges and universities, such as Renmin University of China, Peking University, Law Institute of Chinese Academy of Social Sciences, Zhongnan University of Economics and Law, and Huazhong University of Science and Technology, etc. After the first five major institutes, with authority to separately enroll the intellectual property talents, were confirmed, the colleges and universities across the country have applied for and set up JM and JD programs toward intellectual property law. Simultaneously, many local and departmental study organs also made great efforts to carry out strategy study concerning to formulation and implementation of various intellectual property strategies. Chinese intellectual property jurisprudence has entered a stage of vigorous development.

After implementation of national intellectual property strategy, namely, since the second half of 2008, the major research priority in our intellectual property circle was to conduct research and have discussion around the major measures and key tasks specified in the Outline. Judging from the trend of research in this period, the development of intellectual property jurisprudence in our country obviously presents with “polarization”: one pole is that more and more scholars began to focus on macro issues, especially the issues concerning to basic theories of intellectual property system; another view is that more and more scholars began to focus on micro issues, diving into a certain domain, specific system or legal rule with respect to intellectual property right. This trend will last for a considerable period of time. It should be noted that, in the process of establishment and development of intellectual property jurisprudence in China, judicial circle has always been playing a special role. The judgments and analysis made by researchers among Chinese judges on typical intellectual property cases, to a certain extent, are determining the focus and orientation of theoretical study conducted by intellectual property scholars, even leading legislative tendency[1], and this influence will last for a certain period.

In intellectual property jurisprudence, the main studies on macro issues cover: background analysis on emergence and development of intellectual property jurisprudence in China, definition and characteristics of intellectual property right, legislative purpose of intellectual property law, the private nature of intellectual property right, the role played by intellectual property right in the era of knowledge economy, intellectual property right and international trade, intellectual property right and human rights, intellectual property law and civil law, intellectual property law and anti-trust law, enforcement of intellectual property law, and codification of intellectual property law, etc. On the other hand, the contents of study on micro issues in intellectual property jurisprudence are very complicated, and can not be enumerated in detail, which mainly focus on application of patent system in new technologies, Internet and copyright, brand management and protection, and so on. With rapid development of science and technology, and advancement of the integration of international economics and trade, basically speaking, the rich study subjects may be produced at any time in any branch, or any specific system or rule of intellectual property jurisprudence,

1 Of course, for this, some scholar held an negative attitude, see Cui Guobin, Critique on Judge-made Law of Intellectual Property, China Legal Science, 2006, Issue.1.

and then lead the latest research trends. Of course, the study on micro system must be conducted in the macro context. Facing the reality that our country is in an economic and social transformation period, in order to develop the current intellectual property jurisprudence in China, we need the scholars who can focus on reality, and concern about society, but not the ones who simply introduce and transplant the legal rules. In the coming period, the task of Chinese intellectual property jurisprudence circle is to meet the needs of situation, so as to make the intellectual property theory be better service for economic growth. Therefore, it shall be the dominant direction of future development of intellectual property jurisprudence to combine with Chinese national conditions, especially combine with the strategy study on how to implement national intellectual property strategy.

Chapter 18

Reform of Economic Law Advancing with the Times

As a new branch of science in the realm of law, the economic law has rapidly rised conforming to China's reform and opening up, and constantly obtained its theoretical breakthrough and innovation in process of interaction between it and economic legislation, enforcement and judicature. Seen from the internal causes for practice and development of times, China's economic law has put forward lots of theoretical propositions and system constructions over 30 years since its generation, which have agreed with China's economic and social development and affected significantly the economic legislation and government policy concerned, and made an indispensable contribution to promoting the transition and development of China's social economy.[1] Although there are setbacks and hardships in course of the development of the economic law, it is extremely normal and common when some subject on its way to maturity and reasonable prosperity. The tough character of scholars of economic law from generation to

1 See the *Theory Innovation and Contributions of 30-Year Development of China's Economic Law* by YUE Caishen, published in *Journal of Chongqing University*, Issue 5, 2008.

generation has forged the economic law with spiritual quality advancing with the times and striving to develop, making the economic law change continuously, in the guidance of *Scientific Outlook on Development*, obtain trans-century sustainable development, all of which have stimulated the development and prosperity of China's law.

1. From Gradual Maturity to Reasonable Prosperity

In the 1990s, China has begun to boost in an all-round way its construction of the socialist market economy, laying the economic foundation for its legal construction, and asserting a higher claim for its construction of economic legal institutions. From January 18 to February 21, 1992, DENG Xiaoping made inspections of Wuchang, Shenzhen, Zhuhai, Shanghai, etc., delivering important speeches, which kicked off the great construction of China's socialist market economy. In 1992, the 14th National Congress of the Communist Party of China put forward clearly that the objective of China's reform of the economic system was to set up the socialist market economy system, so as to further liberate and develop productive forces. Under the new historical conditions, the economic law confronts with the task of overall reflection and reconstitution in discipline. The adoption of the *Amendment to the Constitution*, 1993, establishes fundamental constitutional principles for the gradual maturity and reasonable prosperity of the economic law.[1]

Decision of the Central Committee of the Communist Party of China on Some Issues Concerns the Improvement of the Socialist Market Economy (1993)—a program of action for the overall planning to establish China's socialist market economy system and to reform its economic system—systematizes and materialize the objective and basic principles of reform of the economic system

1 It is explicitly stipulated in Article 7 of *Amendment to the Constitution of the People's Republic of China* that Article 15 of *the Constitution of the People's Republic of China* is modified as: "The state practices the socialist market economy." "The state strengthens economic legislation, and improves macro-control." "The state shall prohibit any organization or individual from disturbing the social economic order."

established in the 14th National Congress of the Communist Party of China. Since 1993, a series of economic laws have been released, such as the *Product Quality Law of the People's Republic of China*, the *Anti-Unfair Competition Law of the People's Republic of China*, the *Law of the People's Republic of China on the Protection of Consumer Rights and Interests*, the *Company Law of the People's Republic of China*, the *Foreign Trade Law of The People's Republic of China*, the *Law of the People's Republic of China on the People's Bank of China*, the *Law of the People's Republic of China on Commercial Banks*, the *Law of the People's Republic of China on Negotiable Instruments*, the *Insurance Law of the People's Republic of China* and the *Securities Law of the People's Republic of China*, as well as the improvement of macro-control system, all of which marked the maturity and proper location in subject of China's economic law based on primary development before. Leaders in research of economic law subject development, including YANG Zixuan of Peking University, LIU Wenhua of Renmin University of China, LI Changlin of Southwest University of Political Science and Law, and QI Duojun of Wuhan University, have written books and set up theories one after another, promoting the prosperity of China's economic law. With the continuous improvement of China's environment of economy rules of law, theories and doctrines have been much more systematized and perfected, there being a leap from quantity to quality in the research on the basic theory of the economic law and on departmental law, which has born countless rich fruits with respect to academic exchange and discipline construction.

From the point of view of academic exchange, while the seminars by Chinese Society of Economic Law have decreased to some extent after 1992, even basically stopped since, theoretical research events of the economic law nationwide have not suspended for that reason. In April 1993, the first seminar smoothly hosted in Beijing by the Beijing Economic Law Society on socialist market economy and economic law theory, of which the topic was the construction of basic theory of economic law under the condition of socialist market economy, obtained sound desired effects. Later, the seminar has been held once a year, its topics broadly involved in important theories and practices concerning basic theories of the economic law, modern enterprise systems, market regulation laws, construction and teaching reform of the economic law subject, and China Western Development. And starting from the sixth seminar, the name of the seminar has been determined as the "Seminar of National Economic Law Theory", a seminar which not only just filled the gap caused by the decrease and even stop of the activities by China Economic Law Society of organizers of special seminars for national economic law, but only in effect replaced part of functions of national economic law academic organizations, thus making great contributions to boosting China's economic law research in a healthy way.[1] Meanwhile, the China Civil Law Society and China Economic Law Society of the China Law Society insisted on convening one seminar every year, discussing deeply important questions and issues, such as the state-owned enterprise reform, security for an obligation, land system, prevention against financial risk, the Company Law of the PRC, the Securities Act of the PRC as well as the influences on China's

Economic Law after China joined WTO, further deepening the study of economic law from different angles. Furthermore, there are some regional and international seminars across the country with great influence, focused on discussions and exchanges of questions regarding economic law theory frontier, competition law, macro-control law, tax law, financial law and legal education.[2]

Since 1992, the average number of economic law theses published yearly is not less than 1500, among which not less than 2000 in 2000 and 2001. Although many theses have nature of practice, instructor guide and universality, there are many a quality thesis with strong technicality, high

1 See *Studies on China's Economic Law History by* XIAO Jiangping, People's Court Press, 2002, p.113.

2 The annual economic law theory seminar joined by 13 provinces (districts) throughout the country since 1984; the annual seminar of economic law frontier theory since 2000; the international seminar of competition law and competition policy every other year or every three years since 1997.

level and prominent innovation. Compared with prior two periods, there is a great increase in both quantity and quality.[1] Many theses have been published in domestic first-class core journals such as *Chinese Journal of Law, China Legal Science* and *Social Sciences in China*, presenting vigorous vitality and creativity of China's economic law.[2] The most noteworthy is an article, *Theoretical Thoughts, Countermeasures and Suggestions on Establishment of System of Socialist Market Economy Law*, published in *Chinese Journal of Law*, Issue 6, 1993, a programmatic article for paradigm in economic law research, which proposes that it is necessary to discriminate public law from private law, and a state for people with public rights from a state for those with ownership, advocates giving up Laptev's economic law theory and idea as well as idea to take the planning law as the basic law of economic law, and newly

1 See *Studies on China's Economic Law History* by XIAO Jiangping, published by the People's Court Press, 2002, p.115.

2 Such as LI Changlin: *Discussion on Legal Protection of Macroeconomic Regulation and Control Goal of Real Estate Market and Achievement of Such Goal*, published in *China Legal Science*, Issue 6, 1994; QI Duojun: *On the Modern Market-Oriented Economy and Law System*, in *China Legal Science*, Issue 5, 1994; YANG Zixuan: *Discussion on Nature of the Property Rights of Company and Shareholder*, in *China Legal Science*, Issue 2, 1996; LIU Wenhua : *Utilization of Economic Law Theory to Strengthen Economic Legislation*, in *China Legal Science*, Issue 3, 1999; ZHANG Shouwen: *Discussion on Legalization of Tax Revenue*, in *China Legal Science*, Issue 6, 1996; SHI Jichun and DENG Feng: *Contract's Dissimilation and Dissimilatory Contract—On Relocation of Economic Contract*, in *Chinese Journal of Law*, Issue 3, 1997; WANG Xiaoye: *Normalize Market Behavior of Public Utilities Needs Antitrust Law*, in *Chinese Journal of Law*, Issue 5, 1997; WANG Xiaoye: *Regulate by Law Behavior of Administrative Restrictions on Competition*, in *Chinese Journal of Law*, Issue 3, 1998; QIU Ben: *From Contract to Human Rights*, in *Chinese Journal of Law*, Issue 6, 1998; LI Changlin and LU Li: *Several Thoughts on Modernization of Chinese Economic Law*, in *Chinese Journal of Law*, Issue 3, 1999; WANG Xiaoye: *Challenge of Giant Multinational Merger to Antitrust Law*, in *Chinese Journal of Law*, Issue 5, 1999; QI Duojun: *Discussion on Power*, in *Chinese Journal of Law*, Issue 1, 2001; WANG Xiaoye: *Antitrust Law Under the Socialist Market Economy*, in *Social Sciences in China*, Issue 1, 1996; LI Shenglan et al: *Law Cost and Construction of China's Economy System*, in *Social Sciences in China*, Issue 4, 1994; etc.

expounds the concept, properties and system of economic law.[1] As of 1999 and 2000, professional publications, such as *Economic Law Review* (China Fangzheng Press), by editor-in-chief QI Duojun; *Research on Economic Law* (Peking University Press), by editor-in-chief YANG Zixuan; *Economic Law Review* (Law Press China), by editor-in-chief XU Jie; and *Review of Economic Law* (China Legal Publishing House), by editor-in-chief SHI Jichun, have organized and published a great number of valuable papers or translations of economic law, which not just effectively makes up for the deficiency in type and quantity of economic law academic journals, but markedly increases integral social influence of economic law subject.

In 1993, approved by the Academic Degrees Committee of the State Council, XU Jie of China University of Political Science and Law and LIU Wenhua of Renmin University of China became the first advisors of economic-law-subject doctor station in China. After 1994, a lot of economic-law-subject doctoral stations were set up at Peking University and other colleges and universities and scientific research institutions.[2] In 1998, Higher Education Division of the Ministry of Education released *Basic Requirements for Core Curriculum Teaching of Law Major at Institution of Higher Education Nationwide*, in which the economic law has been included 14 core curriculums of laws. In May 1999, "Research Group with Chinese Characteristic Socialism Legal System", which the leaders of Standing Committee of the National People's Congress made instructions to establish, released the information that China's law system would

1 See the *Discussion on Standard and Boundary Point of China's Economic Law History* by WANG Lungang, published in the social scientific edition of the *Journal of Chengdu University of Technology*, Issue 3, 2004.

2 The colleges and universities equipped with doctoral stations of economic law major are mainly as follows: Peking University, Renmin University of China, Wuhan University, Jilin University, China University of Political Science and Law, Southwest University of Political Science and Law, East China University of Political Science and Law, Zhongnan University of Economics and Law, Nanjing University, Xiamen University, Hunan University, Anhui University, Liaoning University, Institute of Law Chinese Academy of Social Sciences, etc.

be divided into seven legal departments, the economic law being one of the seven legal departments. During the period when the economic law becomes mature, a great many of monographs one after another have been published, including outline-type textbooks,[1] "Economic Law Series" textbooks[2] and some books with characteristics of textbook. These textbooks, in terms of structural system, resources or theoretical levels, have been distinctly improved and advanced, compared with those of the first two periods, making the compilation of the

1 For instance, ZHANG Shouwen and YU Lei: *Market Economy and New Economic Law,* published by Peking University Press, 1993; Edited by LIU Wenhua: *Newly-Edited Economic Law*, by Higher Education Press, 1993; Edited by YANG Zixuan and XU Jie: *Science of Economic Law*, by Peking University Press, 1994 and 1997; Edited by XIAO Qiangang and CHENG Baoshan: *Introduction to Economic Law,* by China Business Press, 1995; Edited by SHI Shaoxia: *New Theory of Economic Law*, by Jilin University Press, 1996; LIU Longheng: *Introduction to Economic Law,* by Peking University Press, 1997 and 2001; Edited by QI Duojun: *Science of Economic Law*, by Wuhan University Press, 1998; Edited by ZHU Chongshi: *Economic Law*, by Xiamen University Press, 1998; YANG Zixuan: *Economic Law*, by Peking University Press, and Higher Education Press, 1999; WANG Baoshu: *Principle of Economic Law*, by Social Sciences Academic Press, 1999; PAN Jingcheng and LIU Wenhua: *Economic Law*, by China Renmin University Press, 1999; Edited by LI Changqi: *Science of Economic Law*, by China University of Political Science and Law Press, 1999; Edited by YANG Zixuan and XU Jie: *Introduction to Economic Law,* by Peking University Press, 2000; LIU Wenhua and XIAO Qiangang: *General Theory of Economic Laws*, Higher Education Press, 2000; LIU Ruifu: *Principle of Science of Economic Law*, by Peking University Press, 2000; Edited by GU Gongyun: *Economic Law*, by Higher Education Press and Shanghai Academy of Social Sciences Press, 2000; etc.

2 For instance, "Economic Law Series" edited by the Justice Department of the PRC, and published by Law Press China consists of: SHI Jichun et al: *Pandect of Economic Law*; ZHANG Shiyuan: *Enterprise Law*; LI Changqi et al: *Law on Protection of the Rights and Interests of Consumers*; Edited by ZHONG Mingzhao: *Competition Law*; Edited by LIU Jianwen: *Financial and Tax Law*; edited and written by XIAO Qiangang et al: *Law of Natural Resources*; "Series of textbooks of Law Sciences in the 21st" published by Peking University Press—in which there are economic law series of textbooks: LIU Ruifu's *Principle of Economic Law*; GAN Peizhong's *Enterprise and Company Law Sciences*; *Real Estate Law* of CHENG Xinhe, et al; ZHANG Shouwen's *Principle of Tax Law*; edited by WU Zhipan: *Introduction to Finance Law*; LIU Yan's Accounting Law, etc. "Series of Law Sciences in the 21st" published by China Renmin University Press—in which there are economic law textbooks such as *Economic Law*: edited by PAN Jingcheng and LIU Wenhua.

economic law textbooks reach an unprecedented level.[1] Taking the structural system of outline-type textbooks as examples, the transformation of their system extended between overview and sub-pandect, and between sub-pandect and system, emphasizing the echoing nature and harmony from emphasized object to general system, from overview to sub-pandect; consistency and logicality from form to content, from system to theory. Making a comprehensive survey of the common trend of this period's outline-type textbooks in system arrangement, it may be believed that there have been expansion in pandect of outline-type textbooks based on original state, and shrinkage in scope and contents of their sub-pandect. Expansion of overview is embodied in expansion of study field, going into study level and enriching expounded contents; reduction of sub-pandect in "authentic representation" of contents and precision of its kinds. Be overview or sub-pandect, theoretical property of textbooks becomes stronger and stronger; subject peculiarity of the economic law more and more outstanding; phenomenon of regulations version less and less.[2] It should be mentioned that outline-type textbooks is not separate in a lot of breakthroughs in systematism, which embodies and reflects in textbooks the improvement of integral level of study of economic law science, and indicates from one side that China's economy is becoming mature.

Entering the new century, China has stepped into the new stage of building a well-off society in an all-round way, science of economic law continuing to move smoothly and rapidly in advance with the construction of economic legal institutions. The Sixteenth CPC National Congress in 2002 further perfects China's socialist democracy and socialist legal system, and fully implements the basic strategy for the rule of law, a significant objective to build a moderately prosperous society in all aspects. The Sixteenth CPC National Congress' report put

1 XIAO Jiangping: *Studies on China's Economic Law History*, published by People's Court Press, 2002, pp.128-129.

2 XIAO Jiangping: *Studies on China's Economic Law History*, published by People's Court Press, 2002, p.139.

forward that the primary mission in the first decade of 21st century of economic construction and reform is to perfect socialist market economy system, promote strategic adjustment of the economic structure, basically realize industrialization, vigorously promote informatization, accelerate the development of modernization, keep the national economy sustained, rapid and sound development, and constantly better people's lives. The Third Plenary Session of the 16th Central Committee of the Communist Party of China in 2003 adopted *Decision of the Central Committee of the Communist Party of China on Some Issues Concerning the Improvement of the Socialist Market Economy*, further clarifying the objectives and tasks of improving the socialist market economic system. And the 17th CPC National Congress in 2007 clearly put forward the following: to fully implement the basic strategy of the rule of law, to accelerate the development of the socialist country under the rule of law, and to strengthen the comprehensive deployment for construction of the socialist rule of law. In the years before and after it joined the WTO, China successfully sorted out laws and regulations of largest scale since the founding of the new China, a move which improved the unity and coordination of the system of socialist laws, and propelled the history process of the rule of law in China. China's construction of economic legal institutions, on the one hand, has sorted out nationwide economic laws and regulations concerned; on the other hand, constantly improved economic legislation, on the basis of economic law system which has been set up. Science of economic law, conforming to the times development, has maintained a steady and rapid development momentum.

On October 26, 2002, the China Economic Law Studies Association of China Law Society[1] was established in Changsha, Hunan, the first Chairman of which was WU Zhipan. Eight years since its establishment, annual meetings of the Studies Association have been hosted in succession in the places like Beijing, Guangzhou, Nanchang, Lanzhou, Xiamen, and Shanghai on a consolidation basis with seminars on national economic law theory, which have provided abundant

1 The Association is a nation-wide academic group specially established to engage in the study of economic law.

contents and study results. Each annual meeting has been closely centered around the big picture of economic and social reform and development, grasped the questions and issues concerning important theories and practices in the course of reform and development, and determined the topic of the meeting scientifically to attain the goal of common progress through full expression and free discussion. In order to ensure the quality of the articles of such annual meetings, the Studies Association has also established the selection system and online-submission system for such articles, set up and adhered to the selection system for excellent papers by the youth, and jointly published Economic Jurist with Peking University Press, an action that has made fruitful the theoretical study and organization work of the Studies Association, which both improved the efficiency of the annual meetings and expanded their influences. During this stage, the Young and Middle-aged Doctoral Forum on China's Economic Law since 2004 has become an important platform[1] on which young and middle-aged scholars have reached a common view on scholarism, for it has been successfully held 5 times one after another in Hunan University, China University of Political Science and Law, East China University of Political Science and Law, Southwest University of Political Science and Law, and Shenzhen University. Since 2006, the China's Economic Legal Institutions Forum, held 3 terms one after another in Beijing, Shanghai and Kunming, has carried on the special discussion on themes with respect to "the 11th Five-Year Plan and China's Economy under the Rule of Law", "Harmonious Society and Rule of Law of Regional Economy", "the 30th Anniversary of Reform and Opening-up and China's Economic Law" and "Study of Legal Problem

1 The first forum was initiated and hosted by the Law School of Hunan University, mainly on such contents as "economic law in the correlative development of economy, society and ecology"; the second forum was hosted by China University of Political Science and Law themed on "categories, systems, institutions and methods"; the third forum was hosted by East China University of Political Science and Law themed on "Issues on the Subjective Behaviors and Practices of Economic Law"; the fourth forum was held by Southwest University of Political Science and Law with the theme of "Economic and Legal Behaviors"; and the fifth forum was hosted by Shenzhen University themed on "Rights of Economic Law".

on Economic Cooperation and Development in Mekong Region" respectively, attaining active academic achievements and social effects. Furthermore, of special subjects such as modification of banking laws, anti-monopoly legislation and consolidation of corporate income tax laws, universities and study institutions have convened plenty of academic conferences, making more abundant the academic activities on the economic law, and more profound the theoretical study.

After entering the 21st century, China's study results in the economic law science are extremely abundant with constant renewal in monographs, textbooks, reviews, papers and study reports, which makes the economic law science play an important role in the whole field of law. Basic theory and system study on the economic law develops in the longitudinal and deepening direction, in which the new study fields involved in the WTO have been constantly exploited, and played a more and more outstanding role in economic and social development. The latest frontier theory results in the science of economic law were intensively presented by such articles as Quality Library by Economic Law Doctors jointly launched by Southwest University of Political Science and Law and Law Press China, Economic Law Library by East China University of Political Science and Law and Peking University Press, Contemporary Economic Law Series by China Procuratorate Press. Meanwhile, remarkable achievements have been achieved in the construction of the economic-law professional websites projects. In March 2003, the China Economic Law Studies Association of China Law Society set up a website, named "net of China Economic Law" (CEL), an important network platform for the economic law circle's exchange, communication and study. Moreover, economic law professional websites have emphasized on their features with increasing page view yearly (such as, http://www.ccelaws.com, http://www.lichangqi.com, http://qiduojun.csu.edu.cn/, http://www.cnela.com and http://www.bjela.com).

The rational exuberance of science of economic law is determined by the internationalization and scientization of economic legal systems arising out of China's "accession to the WTO", and realized with study results of high quality to actively affect the national economic legislation. YANG Zixuan once emphasized that, after completely getting rid of the economic law theory under the planned economic system of the Soviet Union, China has established a new economic law theory with Chinese characteristics[1]. Economic law, under the direction of the new economic law theory of China, on the one hand, has paid high attention to the regulation by economic law of the subjective behavior of the market, on the other hand, highlighted the constraint by economic law of the economic management by the government, thus playing an irreplaceable role in terms of avoiding “market failure” and “government failure” and effectively guaranteeing the smooth reform and improvement of the market economy system in China. Academic studies on the economic law have been flourishing as never before, with gratifying situation of a hundred flowers blossoming and a hundred schools of thought contending. Economic law studies and teaching teams have further developed and grown stronger at universities and scientific study institutions, with some doctors and post-doctors of law taking front-line posts timely. Especially the postdoctoral system develops very fast, which becomes an important way of developing rapidly high-level economic law personnel and an important means of strengthening competitiveness among economic law talents. A number of older generations of economic jurists have cultivated a group of students of great eminence, many former doctors become today’s tutors of postgraduates or doctoral candidates, and the training mode of economic law talents has achieved remarkable fruits in the process of continuous innovation, all of which have delivered a large number of economic law talents to China. Over nearly 30 years of restoration, reconstruction, reform and development, an economic law education system has taken shape, of which the subject is education of bachelors, masters and doctors of economic law major combined with law professional education and legal professional education, all of which basically adapting to the needs of the construction of modern socialist country.

2. Discussion and Debate on Basic Theory of Economic Law

From becoming mature to rational exuberance, science of economic law keeps

1 See “China’s Economic Law under the Economic Globalisation” by YANG Zixuan and WU Tao, published in *Journal of Jiangxi University of Finance and Economics,* Issue 1 of 2002.

close to the development of times; based on the comprehensive summary and sublation of the first two periods of academic achievements, experiences and lessons, it actively uses for reference of the study results of foreign economic law theories and other subjects at home and abroad, not just innovating and enriching China's legal theory, and breaking through the paradigm of binary classification of public-private law in the traditional law field, but introducing the value idea of standard of society and collectivism, using the study and analysis methods of multidisciplinary and multiple views, thus increasing the explanatory power and dialectical force of legal theory and effectively promoting the establishment and perfection of socialist market economic system while enhancing the openness and contemporaneity of law study.

For more than one decade, the emphasis of study on the basic theory of the economic law has been reflected in: (1) surveying the appearance and development history of Chinese and foreign economic law, knowing objective and theoretical basis of appearance of economic law, and seeking for experience and principles of economic legal system construction at home and abroad; (2) studying the concept, object of adjustment, adjustment mode, characteristics, system functions and system of the economic law, and discussing the law adjustment mechanism and laws in the economy field; (3) discussing the idea, spirit and value (including view of rights, view of interests, etc.) of the economic law, and introducing and promoting advanced concept of value; (4) analyzing basic principles (e.g., moderate government intervention, social standard and economic democracy) of the economic law, illuminating the relationship between nation and market, and uncovering the substantive characteristics of market economy; (5) discussing the logical starting point, analysis paradigm, study methods and basic category of the economic law, and setting up scientific theory system; (6) studying economic law subject and economic law behavior, etc., and getting to know characteristics and rules of market subject and behavior; (7) analyzing responsibility, right relief and implementation in respect of the economic law, and seeking for scientific legal system and implementation mechanism for economy; (8) studying questions about economic law legislation, to channel efforts to offer advice and suggestions on economic law legislation and decision; and (9) studying issues and questions regarding economic law during transition period, and regarding that in times of economic globalization and knowledge economy, to provide theoretical explanation for China's social and economic transformation.[1]

Painstaking efforts of generations of economic law scholars has been put into the study of economic law basic theory, during which have come into being several relatively independent and mature theories and doctrines of economic law, among which the discussion and debate allows study perspective of the economic law more diverse, and theoretical explanation of it more sufficient. Study of the economic law in this period has not been obstinate in the then existing results, but discriminated economic relations from perspectives of act to form economic relations, of peculiarity of economic relations and of economics, significantly changing study perspective.

First, theory on national coordination. This theory, presented by YANG Zixuan, maintains that it is neither all economic relations nor non-economic relations in society, but economic relations arising in course of a nation coordinating its economic operation, that the economic law adjusts. Formation of a nation's economic coordination is because economic operation needs national coordination, with the coordination of economic operation being to promote the healthy and stable development of economy, also to reflect the role played by, in economic operation, a country's economic management functions, its intervention and "nation's hand". In nation economy coordination, the subject is the nation; object, economic operation; purpose, to have economic operation in line with the requirements of objective laws, including relationship with respect to business organization and management, market management, macro-control and social insurance. This theory emphasizes the connection on object between the

1 See *Report on 30 Years of Development of China's Economic Law* (discussion draft) by the Study Group "Report on 30 Years of Development of China's Economic Law" (written by YUE Caishen and LI Yongcheng), October 31-November 3, 2008, p.9.

economic law and international economic law, the consistency on adjustable object of economic law of coordinated quality and its otherness in nations and regions within specific scope. And this theory believes that the economic law, an independent law department, has its specific objects to adjust. Its basic principles include: principle to coordinate the nation's economic operation as per objective laws; principle to insist on economy priority to efficiency and due consideration to fairness; principle to insist on priority to national overall economic interests and to take into account economic interests of parties concerned; and principle to insist on sustainable development and to take into account current development.[1]

Second, theory of needing nation to intervene. This theory, presented by LI Changqi, maintains that the adjustment object of economic law should be economic relations, with wholeness and society publication, that is to be interfered in by the nation, economic relations that the nation shall interfere in, including relations concerning market subject control, adjustment and control of market order, macroeconomic regulation and control and guarantee of sustainable development, and social distribution. He believes that, under the condition of market economy in China, the nation should do something, and leave something undone intervening in economy. And this theory believes that the economic law is an independent law sector between public law and private law. Its basic principles include: principle to optimize the allocation of resources; appropriate intervention by the nation; standard of society; economic democracy; economic benefit; and

1 For the viewpoint of this theory See the following books and papers by YANG Zixuan: paper *Setting up and Perfecting Legal System Adopting to Socialist Market Economy System and Formulation of 'Economic law Outline'* (2001); paper *"Nation Coordinating" Theory* (2000); paper *Discussion on Socialist Market Economy Legal System* (1998); paper *Discussion on New Economic Law System*; paper *New Exploration of Economic Law Adjustment Object* (1994); paper *Establishment of Socialist Market Economy System Economic Law's Development* (1993); monograph *Theory of "Nation Coordination"* (2009); textbook *Economic Law* (1999, 2006, 2008); textbook *Science of Economic Law* (jointly edited with XU Jie) (1994, 1997, 2001, 2007, 2009).

sustainable development.[1]

Third, theory of the nation regulation. This theory, presented by QI Duojun, maintains that the adjustment object of economic law should be social relations that arise in course of the adjustment of economy by the nation, called for short economic adjustment relations, including obstacle removal in market, anti-monopoly and limited competition as well as anti-illegitimate competition, national investment operation, and macroeconomic regulation and control. And this theory believes that the characteristic of method of the adjustment of economic law is to conduct combination of advocated standards and necessary, mandatory standards; and of sanctions and rewards. Inner ground that the economic law becomes independent departmental law lies in its adjusted object and basic functions and tasks. It emphasizes that the economic law, in terms of values such as order, efficiency, fairness and justice, has particularity different from that of general law. Its center is efficiency and equity; its intrinsic value orientation, standard of society. Core connotation of the basic principle of economic law is: to pay attention to maintaining the social economic overall efficiency and to give consideration to the equity of economic interests of parties concerned in society.[2]

Forth, theory of vertical and horizontal uniform. This theory, presented by LIU Wenhua and SHI Jichun, maintains that the adjustment of economic law should be the relation of economic administration that, in course of social production and

1 For the viewpoint of this theory See the following books and papers by LI Changqi: paper *Discussion on Internal Relation Between Market Economic, Government Intervention and Economic Law* (2000); paper *Several Thoughts on China's Economic Law Modernization* (1999); paper *Discussion on Renewal of Socialist Market Economy and Economic Law Concepts* (1994); textbook *Science of Economic Law* (2007, 2008); textbook *Science of Economic Law* (1999, 2002); textbook *Economic Law Course* (1996); textbook *Economic Law—Basic Legal Form of Government Intervention of Economy* (1995).

2 This theory, also called theory "Three-Three System", maintains that the creation of the economic law is because market has three defeats, the three defeats needing a nation's three adjustments, the three adjustment needing laws' three safeguard. For the viewpoint of this theory See the following books and papers by QI Duojun: paper *Discussion on Three Stages of Market Economy Development and Their Law Protection System* (1999); paper *Discussion on Essence, System and Core of Economic Law* (1997); paper *Discussion on Law Protection System of Modern Market Economy* (1994); textbook *Basic Theory of Economic Law* (1993, 1996, 2004, 2008); and *Science of Economic Law* (1998, 2004).

reproduction, is joined in by organizations as basic participants; and cooperative relations in business within definite range (i.e., economic joint, cooperation and competition), including economic administration, maintenance of fair competition, and transfer and collaboration with organization and management nature). "Vertical" excludes administrative relationship of non-economy, and relationship in business internal management which the will of the nation is not involved in or which should be self-governed by parties concerned; "horizontal", free relationship of transfer and collaboration within public-ownership organizations, and any economic relationship whose substantial interest is not intervened in by a nation. "Unification" means that regulative objects in economic law are unification of property and administrative factors, or that of economy and nation will. The economic law, "attaching most importance to public, and taking into consideration both public and private interests", is divided into economic organic law, economic administration law and economic activity law. Its basic principles include: principle to abide by objective economic laws; principle to consolidate and develop socialist public ownership as well as to protect legal development of economic sectors; unified nation control and organization independence; material benefits; system of economic calculation; economic effectiveness; and economic law responsibility system, among which the basest principle is that of united "duties and powers" and "interests and effects".[1]

1 For the viewpoint of this theory See the following books and papers by LIU Wenhua : paper Basic Theory *Outline of China Economic Law* (2001); paper *Economic Law's Essence: Coordination-ism and Its Economics Foundation* (2000); paper *Application of Economic Law Theory to Strength Economic Legislation* (1999); paper *Economic Law is Product of Ideological Line of Reform and Opening Up* (jointly edited with PAN Jingcheng) (1993). Also See the following books and papers by SHI Jichun: paper *Discussion on Times Span From Civil Society and Civil Law or Business Law to Economic Nation and Economic Law* (2001); paper *Position of Economic Law and Criticism of Traditional Legal Department Division Theory* (2000); paper *China's Science of Economic Law Emerging and Developing in Process of Reform and Opening up and Construction of Economic Legal Institutions* (1999); paper *Economic Law: Unification of Objectivity and Subjectivity in Dividing Legal Department* (1998); paper *Socialist Market Economy and China's Economic Law—Concurrent Discussion on Relationship Between Economic Law and Civil Law or Business Law Under Market Economy* (1995); textbook *Economic Law Pandect* (collaborated with DENG Feng) (1998, 2008); textbook *Economic Law* (2005); monograph *Exploration of True Essence of Economy and Law Interaction* (2002).

Fifth, theory of nation modulation. This theory, presented by ZHANG Shouwen, maintains that the adjustment of economic law should be the macro-control by a nation of economy operation, and the economic relationship arising in course of regulation of market, including macroeconomic regulation and control relationship and regulation of market relationship, respectively. And he believes that purpose of the economic law is to constantly solve contradictions between individual profit-making and social publicity, consideration given to both efficiency and fairness, to promote the stable growth of economy, safeguard social public interests and basic human rights, and promote the benign operation and coordinated development of economy and society. Peculiarity of the economic law depends on its modernity. As modern law, the economic law has material differences from traditional law, in terms of spiritual pursuit, dependence of background and system construction. The basic principles of the economic law include: principle to modulate law in a moderate manner and modulation performance. Operation of the economic law system is not mainly reflected in administrative field but judicial field, and hence many disputes arising in the economic law field have not been resolved in judicial organs. The reasons and values for being of a departmental law standard cannot be judged whether such standard is executed by judicial organs.[1]

Sixth, theory of social publicity economic administration. This theory, presented by WANG Baoshu, maintains that the adjustment of economic law should be the economic administration relationship with social publicity as its fundamental characteristics, including market management relation and macroscopic economy

1 For the viewpoint of this theory See the following books and papers by ZHANG Shouwen: paper *Establishment of Basic Principle of Economic Law* (2003); paper *Basic Assumption of Science of Economic Law* (2001); paper *Modernity of Economic Law* (2000); *Brief Discussion on Modulation of Economic Law* (2000); *Description of Time and Space Dimensions of Economic Law* (1998); paper *Brief Discussion on Purpose of Economic Law* (1994); paper *Legal Economic Analysis of Science of Economic Law* (1992); textbook *Economic Law Pandect* (2009); textbook *Science of Economic Law* (2008); textbook *Introduction to Economic Law* (2005); and monograph *Reconstruction of Economic Law Theory* (2004).

management relation. This theory emphasizes that social publicity, reflected as social universal, communism, commonweal and nation intervention, is core category of the economic law, and determines and is reflected as the creation, value, subject, rights and obligations, and property. The real value of the economic law lies in economic freedom, democracy and order as reflected by social publicity. The economic law is an independent legal branch, a branch important to identify and implement adjustment mechanism of society as a whole. The system of the economic law is imposed of market supervision law, macroeconomic management law, foreign economic law and economic surveillance law. Its basic principle includes: economically fair and just, statutory unlawful act, economic management authority and legal procedures[1]

Theory of adjustment subject of the economic law, core of economic law pandect, has direct relation to existing and developing of the whole subject system of the economic law. The six aforementioned theories have not completely included and covered all the views and opinions in the educational circle, such as original study on adjustment subject of the economic law in "theory of national economic operation"[2], "theory of management and coordination"[3], "administrative subordination"[4], "theory of administrative

1 For the viewpoint of this theory See the following books and papers by WANG Baoshu: paper *Study Method for Position and Function of Civil Law, Business Law and Economic Law* (2008); paper *Outline of Economic Law and Social Publicity* (2000); paper *Development Opportunity of Market Economy and Economic Law* (1993); paper *Discussion on Goal of Legal Interest of Economic Law* (2001); paper *Market Economy and Economic Democracy* (1994); textbook *Economic Law Doctrine* (1999, 2004).

2 See LIU Ruifu's *Principle of Science of Economic Law*, published by Peking University Press, edition 2000 and 2002; LIU Ruifu: *Law of Business Cycle and Counter Cycle*, published in *Act Scientiarum Naturalium Universitatis Pekinensis*, Issue 2, 1996, et al.

3 See CHENG Xinhe's *Economic Law and Government's Economic Management*, published by Guangdong Higher Education Press, 2002, et al.

4 See LI Zhongsheng's *Economic Law: Law of Governmental Economy Management*, published in *Jilin University Journal Social Science*, Issue 1, 1994; *Study on Adjustment of Economic Law*, published in *Study of Law*, Issue 2, 1994, et al.

management"[1]; a lot of opinions on adjustment subject that some studies put forward from point of view of nation participation, adjustment and management, combination of sociability and manageability, integrated social economic benefit, creating a market economy, intervention on the government, and macroeconomic regulation and control relationship, and some studies on adjustment subject that some studies have conducted indirectly from the other side of the pandect who have not studied directly theories of adjustment subject[2]. Generally speaking, these theories and doctrines reveal directly and indirectly the quality of subject of the economic relationships the economic law adjusts, that is, in economic legal relationship, a nation or government always or often a subject; they also uncover the act quality of a nation or government, only words and phrases varying from theory to theory, such as coordination, regulation, intervention, modulation, management, regulation and control, in turn making a difference in method and range of nation or government behavior; and they proclaim the purpose quality as a nation or government acts—to pursue the whole interests of society. Commonality or intercommunity in these qualities provides basest tools and keys for conclusion of consensus in theory of adjustment subject of the economic law.

In 2003, LI Changqi published his paper *Development and Innovation: Method, Path and Sight*, which sorts out and reviews contributions for years made by China's young and middle-aged scholars. This paper makes sense of appreciation from older generation of economic jurists for the study results of young and middle-aged economic law scholars, and meanwhile initiates that the economic law should constantly expand new study field and admission passage. His study conclusions are of value, which are given more attention in the academic circle.

1 See SHI Shaoxia's *New Theory of Economic Law* by Jilin University Press, 1996; Reconsideration of the Concept, Object and System of Economic Lay, published by Social Science Journal of Jilin University, Issue 5, 1998, etc.

2 XIAO Jiangping: *Study on History of China's Economic Law,* published by People's Court Press, 2002, p.168.

He maintains that development of the law is closely related to that of study methods of the law, and that study methods of the law itself are important part of legal theory. The methods China's young and middle-aged scholars study the economic law can be said to add radiance and beauty to each other, in terms of method of philosophy of law, economic analysis of law, sociological jurisprudence, history of law, and history of jurisprudence. And he emphasizes that cognitive angle in multiple dimensions may pave the way for matter analysis. It is through grasping the pair of contradiction and unity of nation and market, and in basis of the relevance of a nation to a market, that studies of the economic law construct theory of platform for the economic law. Young and middle-aged scholars have put theoretical review of the economic law on the basic platform of nation and market, drawing out, in terms of cognitional path of the economic law, 5 main cognition models, that is to say, the economic law: (1) a law to double interference with failure in market and government; (2) a law to dialectically unify civil society and political nation; (3) a law to couple market regulation and macroscopic readjustment and control; (4) a law to coordinate evenly free competition and order control; (5) a law to mingle private law and public law. He points out that, in the course of study of the economic law, there is more or less study tendency of treasuring theoretical deduction, but belittling institutional substantiation; treasuring sector position, but belittling problem solving, which makes it difficult for the economic law to work as intended when it resolves social conflicts and standardizes social order. In recent years, when laying more attention to deepening and expanding basic theory of the economic law, China's young and middle-aged scholars have kept a watchful eye on concrete system study in the economic law field, obtaining a batch of plentiful and substantial results in many fields like competition law, corporate law, consumer protection law, macroeconomic regulation and control law, government procurement law and ecological law, social security, and economic public interest litigation, realizing sound interaction of theory guiding system and system reflecting theory, in process of study and practice of the economic law.[1]

In the period when the economic law comes to mature, continues still study on separability and cooperativity of economic law and civil and business law, but obvious transform happens to study on separability—emphasis changing from adjustment of subject to protection of legal interest, adjustment of function and value orientation, from distinction to connection, and from limited original pandect moderately expanded to sub-pandect.[2] In practical terms, judging from protection of legal interest and adjustment function, civil and business law pays attention to the protection of private interests, while economic law to protection of public interest or whole interest of society. Civil and business law protects interest in reserved lands; while economic law, increasing interest.[3] Judging from protection of value orientation, adjustment purpose and level, civil and business law emphasizes autonomy of will, while economic law values autonomy of will and simultaneously emphasizes limitation of autonomy of will; civil and business law emphasizes equal protection, while economic law particular stress on protection; civil and business law emphasizes promotion of interest of the people in way of micro security of free trading and competition to increase efficiency, while economic law (not all) promotion of interest of the people in way of micro, harmony of interests to decrease destroy by social economic shocks to increase

1 See LI Changqi's *Development and Innovation: Method, Path and Sight of Economic Law—Brief Discussion on Contribution China's Young and Middle-Aged Scholars Make to Economic Law Theory* (part A and B), published in Journal of Shanxi University (Philosophy and Social Science Edition), Issues 3 and 4, 2003.

2 XIAO Jiangping: *Study on History of China's Economic Law,* published by People's Court Press, 2002, p.187.

3 SHI Jichun: *Socialist Market Economy and China's Economic Law—Concurrent Discussion on Relationship Between Economic Law and Civil Law or Business Law Under Market Economy,* published in *China Legal Science*, Issue 3, 1995; CHENG Baoshan: *Rediscussion on Relationship Between Economic Law and Civil and Business law*, published in *Journal of Zhengzhou University* (*Philosophy and Social Science* Edition), Issue 5, 1999; CHEN Naixin: *Economic Law is a Law for Incremental Interest Production and Distribution—Another Comprehension of Economic Law's Essence*, published in *Studies in Law and Business*, Issue 2, 2000.

efficiency; civil and business law emphasizes pays more attention to economic targets, while economic law values not just economic targets, but social goals and ecological goals, too.[1] From the point of view of theoretical assumptions, the market assumed in civil and business law is entirely rooted in classical economics, while that assumed in economic law in modern economics; civil and business law is based on assumptions by government of external market, while economic law on assumptions by government of internal market; civil and business law holds that main market players are equal "economic men" of the same quality, while economic law holds that main market players are not "economic men" concurrently "social men" of personality.[2] As for economic law and civil and business law, certain scholars studied the distinction between adjustment subject, regulatory mechanism and created economic environment condition of both.[3] But meanwhile, the scholars are fully aware of function cooperativity of economic law and civil and business law, and that almost all of the distinguishable study result could be understood and identified by their function cooperativity of them.

There is also varying degrees furtherance in study on separability and cooperativity of economic law and executive law. Some scholars maintain that there is complementarity in many ways in economic law and administrative law, among which the complementarity of economic law to administrative law concentrates reflection on legislation objective, legislative subject and legal means.[4]

There is certainly some study to compare together economic law, civil and business law and executive law. For instance, CHENG Baoshan holds

1 WANG Quanxing and GUAN Bin: Outline of Relationship between Civil Law and Economic Law, published in *Studies in Law and Business*, Issue 5, 2000.

2 LV Zhongmei: *Discussion on Edge of Economic Law*, published in *Studies in Law and Business*, Issue 4, 1994.

3 See *Principle of Economic Law* edited by WANG Baoshu, published by Social Sciences Academic Press, 1999, p.89.

4 SHI Shaoxia (ed.): *New Theory of Economic Law*, published by Jilin University Press, 1996, pp.18-23; LV Zhongmei: *Discussion on Edge of Economic Law*, published in *Studies in Law and Business*, Issue 4, 1994.

that, in terms of protecting of law interest, economic law, civil and business law and executive law protect integrated social economic interest, personal interest and national public interest, respectively.[1] WANG Baoshu maintains that, from the perspective of economic and social regulating mechanism, it is civil law that acclimatizes itself to requirements for self-regulatory mechanism of operating entities; it is executive law that acclimatizes itself to requirements for administrative regulation mechanism; and it is economic law that acclimatizes itself to requirements for adjusting the macro indirect economic relations and market management relations, that is, meeting requirements for social collective mechanism playing its role.[2] QIU Ben et al, with analysis from the role played by law on market economy, believes that market economy's independence is thanks to executive law; its development to civil and business law; and its perfection to economic law.[3]

A series of study results indicates that economic law, civil and business law and executive law are distinguished from and closely associated with each other, and that they complete each other and play respective role synergistically. As QIU Ben says, "economic law is generated after civil law, consulting and supplementing civil law, both laws interdependent. Only primarily grasp regularity of civil law, clearly understands its limitation, and the economic law can be understood, because economic law starts from the place where the civil law has limitation, which overcomes the limitation of the civil law. The economic law is closely related to government intervention and executive power; and because government intervention and executive power is core of regulation by administrative law, which decides that the economic law has innumerable links to executive law. As for their contents, the economic law crosses and mingles each other, therefore, for

1 See CHENG Baoshan's *Discussion on Relationship between Economic Law and Civil Law, Business Law and Executive Law*, published in *Journal of Zhengzhou University* (Philosophy and Social Science Edition), Issue 3, 1999.

2 See WANG Baoshu's *Development Opportunity of Market Economy and Economic Law*, published in *Study of Law*, Issue 2, 1993.

3 See *Discussion on Purpose of Economic Law*, written by QIU Ben and DONG Jinyu, published in *Law and Social Development*, Issue 4, 1996.

the economic law, developing with executive law, cooperating with it and using it for reference are due attitude for the economic law. The civil law, administrative law and economic law are "three-in-hand" to pull market economy forward."[1]

The economic law with rational exuberance is still in process of growth, and in spite of certain divergence of many issues and questions, the following theoretical system and consensus have basically formed: (1) taking the legalization of relationship between nation (or government) and market as basic theory framework study the science of economic law; (2) taking the "market failure" and "government failure" as the theory bases of the economic law; the unity of opposites between economic democracy and economic concentration, economic liberalism and nation interventionism as philosophical basis of the economic law, contending that the emergence and development of the economic law should be analyzed from a multidisciplinary perspective; (3) regarding the economic law as a law laying particular stress on substantial justice, as a law of standard of society, making up and surpassing insufficiency of function of traditional civil law and administrative law system; (4) in terms of profit adjustment, firmly grasping social benefit or social and public interests or whole interests of society to carry out study; (5) considering that the economic law has characteristics such as economy, sociality, publicity, policy, modernity, comprehensiveness, and integrity; (6) taking market regulation law and macro-control law as hard core of economic law system; (7) holding that economic legal relationship should break through and surpass traditional pattern of civil legal relationship;[2] (8) holding

1 QIU Ben: *China's Science of Economic Law Deepening Development in Transform*, published in *Political and Legal Forum*, Issue 6, 2005.

2 It is mainly embodied in that economic law believes that the traditional legal theory emphasizes the correspondence of the rights and obligations in civil legal relationship, because the problem the economic law is to solve is no longer limited to the microcosmic individual behavior and individual social relations, we cannot continue to use the theory model of civil legal relationship to interpret social relations adjusted by economic law. Therefore, the economic law, on the base of the particularity of social relations adjusted by the economic law, proposes the equivalence principle of "economic function and power - economic responsibility", "economic rights - economic obligations", enriching in fact the theory of legal relationship.

that responsibility of the economic law has particularity different from traditional legal responsibility;[1] (9) in terms of the judicial remedy of the economic law right, advocating establishing public interest litigation system; and (10) considering that, the economic law having strong aboriginality, China's economic law differs from western economic law a lot, and hence China's economic law should pay close attention to native resources.[2]

In general, the science of economic law entering rational exuberance phase has completely changed from its past jollification and pomposity to composure and thought, realizing from divergent views to unified theory, from searching-impracticalities to practicability, from drawing lessons from international to developing themselves, emphasizing that the economic law should make social prosperity and the people reside, and based on the market economy, keeping pace with civil and commercial law and administrative law, daring to face their own problems to continue to self-improvement.[3] Historical experience of 30 years of science of economic law indicates that economic law scholars should seek common points while reserving differences, work together to promote economic and social sustainable development, integrate academic resources and power in and with various ways and platforms, continuously innovate concerning study paradigm and study methods, and clench new themes of the times; in advance with the times to realize the economic law's economic and social care and welfare of the people's livelihood ideals and aspirations, so as to promote further reform,

1 namely apart from traditional civil responsibility, administrative responsibility and criminal responsibility, the science of economic law, in the light of characteristics of the modern social and economic structure and characteristic of behavior of actor, puts forward new form of responsibility, such as product recall, structural control (splitting monopolistic concern), reduction of qualification and credit, and behavioral control, thus developing and enriching legal liability theory.

2 See *Report on 30 Years of Development of China's Economic Law* (discussion draft) by the Study Group "Report on 30 Years of Development of China's Economic Law" (written by YUE Caishen and LI Yongcheng), October 31-November 3, 2008, pp.9-10.

3 QIU Ben: *China's Science of Economic Law Deepening Development in Transform*, published in *Political and Legal Forum*, Issue 6, 2005.

development and improvement of socialist market economic system.

3. Study on Market Competition and Its Legal Protection Mechanism

3.1 Study on anti-unfair competition law

Where there is market there is competition, which is an inexhaustible driving force to promote the economic development and social progress, a direct reflection of law of unity of opposites in economic society. In process of market economy development, anti-competitive legislation must envisage positive and negative effects arising from competitive behaviors. Positive effects result from free competition, legitimate competition and fair competition, in which competitive subject, in order to get better position in competition, and with active and effective measures, may promote social progress and economic development, and improve the human survival and development environment; while negative effects from limited competition and unfair competition, in which the few operators, by opportunistic means and violating business ethics, seek competitive advantages and business interests—which not merely damages the legitimate rights and interests of competitors, but seriously disrupts the market order of fair competition. The economic law, especially anti-monopoly law covered by it usually named as "economy constitution", is the foundation stone of establishment and development of market economy. Anti-competition law, with a pivotal position in the economic law system in China, takes anti-unfair competition law and anti-monopoly law as its cores, complemented and cooperated by product quality standard and protection law for consumers' rights and interests.

China's competition legislation and study of China starts relatively late. In October 1980, after the Nation Council promulgated *Interim Provisions on Carrying out and Protecting Socialist Competition*, it provides the opportunity for theoretical study on China's competition legislation and competition law. In the wake of the *Law of the People's Republic of China for Countering Unfair Competition* coming into force, a great number of study results of China's science of economic law are focused on the implementation and application of the *People's Republic of China for Countering Unfair Competition*; and some scholars and the legal workers in practice departments, in way of glossators, have put forward many valuable insights as to specific application in practice of the *Law of the People's Republic of China for Countering Unfair Competition.*[1] Studies by many economic law scholars are extremely thorough and meticulous, such as KONG Xiangjun's paper *Study on Misleading False Expression*, published in *China Legal Science*, with detailed argumentation and analysis of act of misleading false expression. He contends that the "misleading false expression" is a form of "misleading expression", the latter covering large concepts of the "misleading false expression" and "misleading true expression". Judging from legislative intent of the *Law of the People's Republic of China for Countering Unfair Competition,* as for whether false expression or true expression, they should be stipulated of the same class if they may lead to misleading objective consequences.[2]

Theoretical studies during the period on anti-unfair competition law have been mainly focused on as follows: (1) value orientation of anti-unfair competition law. Some scholars have specialized in such questions, maintaining that value orientation of anti-unfair competition law has been mainly presented with three points: first, encouraging every behavioral agent in market to achieve maximum benefits by proper means; second, providing every market operators with fair competition opportunities; and third, making market operators get fair competition

1 For instance, LIU Chuntian's *A Few Problems in Practice of China's Anti-Unfair Competition Law*, published in Patent and Trademark in China, Issue 2, 1995; LU Xiumin's *Inappropriate to Protect Special Name of Well-Known Goods—Commenting Concurrently Article 5.2 of Law of the People's Republic of China for Countering Unfair Competition*, published in *Law Science*, Issue 5, 1996; KONG Xiangjun: *Discussion on Competitive Relation in Unfair Competition Law*, published in *Industrial and Commercial Administration*, Issue 19, 1999; WANG Yanlin: *Basic Principle of Market Transaction—Explanations and Discussions on Article 2.1 of Law of the People's Republic of China for Countering Unfair Competition*, published in *Political and Legal Forum*, Issue 6, 2001.

2 KONG Xiangxi: *Study on Misleading False Expression—Commenting Discussing Perfection of Relevant Provisions of Law of the People's Republic of China for Countering Unfair Competition,* published in *China Legal Science*, Issue 3, 1998.

results.[1] (2) Legal attribute of anti-unfair competition law. Study on this question has two different viewpoints: first believes that anti-unfair competition law is part of economic law, for which the main evidence is that anti-unfair competition law like anti-monopoly law is one of the basest and most important laws that regulates legitimate market competition order; and second believes that anti-unfair competition law is part of intellectual property law, for which the main evidence is the final conclusion (that anti-unfair competition law is part of intellectual property law) by relevant international conventions and international organizations that it is an important supplement to patent law and trademark law, named as "The Third Industrial Property Law" equal to patent law and trademark law. Scholar LI Shunde, engaged in study of intellectual property law, believes that the reason anti-unfair competition law may be called economic law is the natural extension to its objective effect and property; but that, if it is only emphasized that anti-unfair competition law is economic law, and denied that it is intellectual property law in its essential attribute, then it is an act of putting the cart before the horse or of attending to trifles and neglecting the essentials.[2] Another scholar ZHENG Chengsi, engaged in study of intellectual property law, emphasizes in his paper that anti-unfair competition law and trademark law cross and mingle each other somewhat, some of them inevitable or even unavoidable. However when legislation consideration is not thorough, some crossing and overlapping may arise that should be avoided.[3] Scholar WANG Xiaoye, engaged in the study of competition law, believes that, although intellectual property law is closely related to anti-unfair competition law, the two laws are two different

1 CAO Xinming: *Tentative Study on Value Orientation of Anti-Unfair Competition Law*, published in *Studies in Law and Business*, Issue 4, 1996.

2 LI Shunde: *Tentative Study on Legal Attribute of Anti-Unfair Competition Law*, published in *Studies on China's Industrial and Commercial Management*, Issue 11, 1998.

3 ZHENG Chengsi: *Necessary and Unnecessary Definition-Crossing and Overlapping of China's f Anti-Unfair Competition Law and Trademark Act,* published in *International Trade*, Issue 7, 1998.

legal systems, with the main differences in their different purposes of legislations. On the one hand, anti-unfair competition law takes it as its duty to prevent unfair competition and practice and protect fair competition. In addition to curbing the infringement in the field of intellectual property, it prescribes that unfair competition and practice should be forbidden, such as commercial bribe, false advertising, and deceptive prize-giving sales. On the other hand, as a special legal system, intellectual property law must define the limit between intellectual property protected by law and that not protected by law. Just because the two laws have different legislative intents, when one market competition behavior leads to circumstances applying to two laws, it is necessary to determine order of priority of applicable laws.[1] (3) Comparison between anti-unfair competition law at home and abroad and translation of foreign anti-unfair competition laws.[2] As for comparative study on anti-unfair competition law, its scope is mainly involved in Sino-Germany, Sino-Japan, and Mainland China Taiwan, etc. Judging from translation results, such as *Anti-Unfair Competition Model Law*, translated by KONG Xiangjun, with systematic, comprehensive and authoritative contents, reflects trends and directions of then legislation against anti-unfair competition, playing a certain reference role for perfecting the *Law of the People's Republic of*

1 WANG Xiaoye: *Important Supplementary—Relationship Between Anti-Unfair Competition Law and Related Laws*, published in *International Trade*, Issue 7, 2004.

2 ZHENG Youde and TIAN Zhilong: *Status Analysis in the World of Anti-Unfair Competition Law*, published in installments *Intellectual Property*, Issues 4 and 5, 1994; ZHENG Youde: *Historical Evolution of Hungary's Anti-Unfair Competition Law,* published in installments *Intellectual Property*, Issue 6, 1994; LIN Yanping: *Development and Enlightenment of Germany's Anti-Unfair Competition Law,* published in *Science of Law*, Issue 9, 1996; ZHANG Yujuan: *Discussion on Difference Between Anti-Unfair Competition Law of China and Germany and Enlightenment to Legislation of China,* published in *Review of Political Science and Law*, Issue 1, 1997; KONG Xiangjun: *"Anti-Unfair Competition Model Law" and Its Annotations*, published in installments *Industrial and Commercial Administration*, Issues 10, 11 and 12, 1998; WANG Weinong: *Comparative Study on Anti-Unfair Competition Law of China and Japan,* published in *Journal of Zhejiang University* (*Humanistic and Social Science* Edition), Issue 1, 1999.

China for Countering Unfair Competition and administrative enforcement of law.[1] Comparison study is still an important aspect in the study of competition law, such as ZHENG Youde, who specializes in the development and innovation of the anti-unfair competition law in Germany and Poland and its enlightenment to our country anti-unfair competition law.[2]

After 2002, study on anti-unfair competition law has been mainly focused on the two points: first, protection by anti-unfair competition law of intellectual property rights. Before, WANG Xianlin and GUO Kaifeng had carried out study on this question.[3] During this period, WANG Wenying had studied the protection by anti-unfair competition law of commercialization right.[4] YANG Ming puts forward the fact that it is necessary to intensify catch-all protection by anti-unfair competition law of intellectual property, because the scope of unfair competition in the field of intellectual property is very narrow stipulated by the current legislation, lack of regulation and control force of unfair competition and practice emerging in real life; hence it is necessary to strive to overcome the defects of current anti-unfair competition law, in order to strengthen the anti-unfair competition law supplementation and catch-all role in the

1 For concrete content See KONG Xiangjun's *"Anti-Unfair Competition Model Law" and Its Annotations*, published in installments *Industrial and Commercial Administration*, Issues 10, 11 and 12, 1998. Afterward some scholars make a specialty of its reference value for the study to China, and See HONG Wei's *'Anti-Unfair Competition Model Law' and Perfection of 'China's Anti-Unfair Competition Model Law'*, published in *Fujian Science of Law*, Issue 4, 2003.

2 See ZHENG Youde and WAN Zhiqian's *Development and Innovation of Anti-Unfair Competition Law in Germany*, published in *Studies in Law and Business*, Issue 1, 2007.

3 WANG Xianlin: *Tentative Study on Protection by Anti-Unfair Competition Law of Brand,* published in *Intellectual Property*, Issue 5, 1995; GUO Kaifeng: *Perfection of Protection by Anti-Unfair Competition Law of Intellectual Property,* published in *Hebei Law Science*, Issue 2, 1998.

4 See WANG Wenying's *Protection by Anti-Unfair Competition Law of Commercialization Rights*, published in *Public Administration & Law*, Issue 7, 2003.

protection of intellectual property rights.[1] SUN Ying contends that the current protection of intellectual property is not entirely satisfactory, and especially complementary protection by *Anti-Unfair Competition Law* remains to be perfected of intellectual property. Complementing or supplementing protection by *Anti-Unfair Competition of Law* of intellectual property may be reduced to the following points: providing protection for subjects not brought into being protected by intellectual property law; providing protection for subjects which may be protected by separate law but have not been authorized to be protected; providing relief for protection not vested by special law; providing transitional protection for new type of subjects; and resolving right conflicts between various intellectual properties.[2] Second, modification and perfection of anti-unfair competition law. [3]Before the *Anti-monopoly Law of the People's Republic of China* came into force, study on amendment of the *Anti-monopoly Law of the People's Republic of China* had been conducted, scholars, with respect to questions in implementation the Law, had carried out wide and profound study on definition, concrete type and legal liability of unfair competition and practice; furthermore, taking into consideration connection and coordination between it and the *Anti-monopoly Law of*

1 See YANG Ming's *Tentative Study on Catch-All Protection by Anti-Unfair Competition Law of Intellectual Property,* published in *Studies in Law and Business*, Issue 3, 2003.

2 SUN Ying: *Protection by Anti-Unfair Competition Law of Intellectual Property,* published in *Political and Legal Forum*, Issue 6, 2004.

3 WANG Xianlin: *Closure of China's 'Anti-Unfair Competition Law' and Perfection of General Terms*, published in *Study on China Administration for Industry&Commerce*, Issue 8, 2003; LI Shengli: *Related Problems in Modification and Perfection of China's Anti-Unfair Competition Law*, published in *Law Science Magazine*, Issue 2, 2005; LI Yang: *Protection by Anti-Unfair Competition Law of Database and its Evaluation and Analysis*, published in *Application of Law*, Issue 2, 2005; ZHENG Youde and FAN Changjun: *Specific Study on General Terms of Anti-Unfair Competition Law—Discussing Concurrently Perfection of Anti-Unfair Competition Law of the People's Republic of China*, published in *Studies in Law and Business*, Issue 5, 2005.

the People's Republic of China, the study on this field has been enhanced after the issue for enforcement of the *Anti-monopoly Law of the People's Republic of China*. LIU Chuntian's[1] *Complementing and Integrating 'Anti-Unfair Competition Law' by Judicature* makes a specialty of further applying and exerting the complementary and controlling function by judicature, to resolve judicial interpretation the questions existing prior to the modification of anti-unfair competition law—such study suggestion clearly having important practical and long-term significance. On January 12, 2007, the *Interpretation of the Supreme People's Court on Some Issues Concerning the Application of Law in the Trial of Civil Cases Involving Unfair Competition* was issued, which would be put into force on February 1 of the same year, thereby they had resolved in advance in juridical practice field, a lot of practical problems concerning the *Anti-monopoly Law of the People's Republic of China.*

3.2 Study on anti-monopoly law

After the issue for enforcement of the *Anti-Unfair Competition Law of the People's Republic of China*, study on anti-monopoly law has been in full swing, and papers increased greatly, with study perspective broadened constantly.[2] WANG Xiaoye's *Anti-monopoly Law under Condition of Socialism Market Economy*, published in Social Sciences in China, clearly put forward main tasks and contents of anti-monopoly law. Judging from

1 LIU Chuntian: *Complementing and Integrating 'Anti-Unfair Competition Law' by Judicature, Application of Law*, Issue 4, 2005.

2 For instance, CAO Shibing: *Study on Anti-monopoly Law*, by Law Press China, 1996; WANG Xiaoye's *Study on Competition Law*, published by China Legal Publishing House, 1999; WANG Xianlin: *Intellectual Property and Anti-monopoly Law—Problem Study of Anti-monopoly of Intellectual Property Abuse*, by Law Press China, 2001. In the 1980s, there were scholars in China having studied anti-monopoly law, such as LU Daifu (*Strict and Tolerance: Control Policy in Anti-monopoly Law of Business Merger*, published in *Modern Law Science*, Issue 4, 1984); and MIN Celi: *Anti-monopoly Law of Federal Republic of Germany*, published in *Chinese Journal of Law*, Issue 6, 1986), etc.

tasks, the first one is to break the administrative monopoly to establish competitive and unified national market; the second one is to establish effective competition market structure to severely prohibit vertical and horizontal agreements limiting competition, to limit a massive wave of business combination, and to take to pieces large businesses with high degree of monopoly; and the third one is to prohibit abuse of market dominance. Judging from substantive contents, it is mainly composed of the following contents: prohibition of agreed monopoly price; object to a massive wave of business combination; prohibition of limiting competition by public utilities or operators having exclusive status; and prohibition government and its subordinate departments from limiting competition misusing their executive power. As a law, in addition to the substantive law norms, it shall also establish applicable exception system; and define responsible organ, procedure and legal liability. [1]WANG Yi's viewpoint is a little different, which, centering on blameworthiness of monopoly and necessity of protecting competition, raises that contents stipulated in anti-monopoly law cover stipulation of laws of the monopoly nation, of the monopolistic conduct, of the trade or business-restricting conduct and of businesses combination. And he emphasizes that administrative monopoly has more social harmfulness than economic monopoly, which shall be resolved on administrative system.[2] During the period of the science of economic law becoming mature nation, China's scholars have systematically studied questions like functions of anti-monopoly

1 WANG Xiaoye: *Anti-monopoly Law under Condition of Socialism Market Economy*, *Social Sciences in China*, Issue 1, 1996. And some scholars have studied legislation of China's anti-monopoly law, their viewpoints differing only on small points. For instance, QI Duojun: *Study on Legislation of China's Anti-monopoly Law*, *Law Review*, Issue 4, 1997; SHI Jichun: *Complying with Objective Requirement of Competition—Two Basic Problems of Concept and Object of China's Anti-monopoly Law*, *International Trade*, Issue 4, 1998, etc.

2 WANG Yi: *Discussion on General Theory and Basic System of Anti-monopoly Law*, *China Legal Science*, Issue 2, 1997.

law[1], nature[2], value goal[3], legislative mode[4], protection of intellectual property[5], market definition,[6] regulation of utilities' market behavior[7] and law enforcement agency[8]; and studied comparative law with terms of the definition of monopoly; and legislation model, adjustment range, applicable principles, application exception, law enforcement agency and juridical practice of anti-monopoly law.[9]

When science of economic law enters the stage of rational exuberance, study on anti-monopoly law has been rising rapidly as China becomes a "WTO member", discussion on relevant theories becoming more and more meticulous and deep-going. WANG Xiaoye said: "It is a nation's economic system that

1 WANG Xianlin and TANG Dasen: *Considering Function of Anti-monopoly Law in Relativity of Monopoly & Competition, Journal of Central Leadership Institute of Politics and Law*, Issue 6, 1995.

2 Namely uncertainty, irregularity and priority. SHEN Minrong: *Nature of Anti-monopoly Law, China Legal Science*, Issue 4, 1998.

3 Namely economic freedom and economic equality. See TANG Chunlai's *Tentative Study on Position of Value Goal of China's Anti-monopoly Law,* China *Legal Science*, Issue 2, 2001.

4 LI Shengli: *Whether Splitting or Merging: Choice of Instance of Legislation of China's Anti-monopoly Law, Hebei Law Science*, Issue 1, 2000.

5 ZHANG Ruiping: *How Anti-monopoly Law Deal with Intellectual Property, Journal of Tsinghua University* (*Philosophy of the Social Sciences* Edition), Issue 4, 2001.

6 ZHANG Junwen: *Market Definition in Anti-monopoly Law, Modern Law Science*, Issue 3, 2001.

7 WANG Xiaoye: Regulating Market Act of Utilities Needs Anti-monopoly Law, *Study of Law*, Issue 5, 1997.

8 QIU Ben: *Imagination of Law Enforcement Agent of China's Anti-monopoly Law, Law Science Magazine,* Issue 1, 1999.

9 For instance, WU Zhenguo: *Anti-monopoly Law Comparison of the United Nations, Germany and Japan, China Legal Science*, Issue 2, 1994; LIN Yanping: *Applicable Exception system Comparison in Anti-monopoly Law, Law Science*, Issue 11, 1997; WANG Xiaoye: *Telecom Anti-monopoly Law in the European Union and Its Enlightenment to China,* Red Flag Manuscript, Issue 24, 1999; CHENG Jisheng: *Analysis of Development Trend of Anti-monopoly Law on Foreign Corporate Merger Control, Modern Law Science*, Issue 1, 2000; XU Shiying and TAO Xudong: *Several Problems in U.S. Software Anti-monopoly Law Practice, Law Science*, Issue 3, 2000; WANG Changbin: *Business Group at Perspective of Anti-monopoly Law—Study on One Comparative Law, Law and Social Development*, Issue 3, 2000, etc.

decides the nation whether needs anti-monopoly law. If a nation need take market mechanism as essential means to allocate resources, the nation must conduct anti-monopoly, formulate anti-monopoly law and build for businesses a fair and free competitive environment. With China's joining in the WTO, anti-monopoly legislation has been becoming more necessary and pressing."[1] And WANG Xianlin made the same conclusion, pointing out emphatically that fundamental basis that China must formulate anti-monopoly law is rooted in the objective requirement of market economy and the built-in function of anti-monopoly law; however, "China's WTO entry" makes more prominent the necessity and urgency for China to enact anti-monopoly law.[2] For more than two decades years of reform of the economic system, China has had bases and conditions to formulate and implement anti-monopoly law: the first one is that the price monopoly system has been broken under the condition of planned economy; the second is that the pattern of ownership of businesses has become diverse; the third is that nation-owned businesses have be entitled to more and more autonomy in operation, in which they have become independent main market players considerably; and the fourth is that, with China's joining in the WTO, China's economy has incorporated itself into international economy more and more rapidly[3]. In this period, scholars have in no time culminated in consensus on necessity and instancy of the formulation of China's anti-monopoly law. Thereafter, study on anti-monopoly law has begun centering on two points, one about study on concrete systems of anti-monopoly law, the other about argument on draft of anti-monopoly law and opinions on specific

1 WANG Xiaoye: "'China's WTO Entry' and Formulation of China's Anti-monopoly Law", *Chinese Journal of Law*, Issue 2, 2003.

2 WANG Xianlin: "Two Problems about Formulation of China's Anti-monopoly Law on Background of 'China's WTO Entry'", *Law Review*, Issue 5, 2003.

3 WANG Xiaoye and TAO Zhenghua: "Competition Policy of WTO and Its Influence on China—Concurrent Discussion on Meaning of Formulation of Anti-monopoly Law", *Social Sciences in China*, Issue 5, 2003.

amendment and perfection.[1] As for study on concrete systems, their contents are widely involved in relevant market definition[2], abuse of market dominant position[3], concentration of undertakings[4], administrative

1 LIN Xiaojing: *Anti-monopoly Regulation of Cross-border Mergers & Acquisitions—Concurrent Discussion on Anti-monopoly (exposure draft), Journal of East China University of Politics and Law*, Issue 1, 2003; WEI Qiong: *Regulations of Procedure for Law Control of Concentration (or combination) of Corporates—Concurrent View on 2004 'Anti-monopoly Law' Draft for Examination, Law Science*, Issue 11, 2004; WEI Qiong: *Preliminary Study on Claims Procedure in China's Anti-monopoly Law—Concurrent Discussion on 2004 'Anti-monopoly Law' Draft for Examination, Politics & Law*, Issue 1, 2005; SHI Jichun and XIAO Zhu: *Comparative Study and Legislative Suggestion on Relationship Between 'Anti-monopoly Law' and Industry Legislation, and Between Anti-monopoly Organization and Industry Supervising Organization, Review if Political Science and Law*, Issue 4, 2005; WANG Jian: *System of Criminal Sanction of Anti-monopoly Law in Concept of Deterrence—Concurrent Discussion on Relevant Regulation of the Anti-monopoly Law of the PRC (Revised), Studies in Law and Business*, Issue 1, 2006; LI Junfeng: *Study on Anti-monopoly Damages Multiplying Power—Concurrent Discussion on Choice of Relevant System of China's Anti-monopoly Draft, Study of Comparative Law*, Issue 4, 2007; WANG Xianlin: *Study on Legal Regulation of Act of Abuse of Market Dominant Position—Evaluation and Analysis of Relevant Part of the Anti-monopoly Law of the PRC (Draft), Studies in Law and Business*, Issue 4, 2007; and LI Guohai: *Study on Public Interest Idea of Anti-Monopoly Law—Concurrent Discussion on the Anti-monopoly Law of the PRC (Draft), Studies in Law and Business*, Issue 5, 2007.

2 For instance, WANG Xiaoye: *Decisive Precondition—Definition of Relevant Market in Anti-monopoly Law*, published in *International Trade*, Issue 2, 2004; WANG Xianlin: *Definition of Relevant Market in Implementation of Anti-monopoly Law, Legal Science (Journal of Northwest University of Politics and Law)*, Issue 1, 2008; DING Maozhong: *Analysis Approach for Definition of Critical Loss in Relevant Market in U.S. Antitrust Law, Journal of Southwest University of Politics and Law*, Issue 6, 2008.

3 For instance, WANG Lijuan and MEI Lin: *Study on Anti-monopoly Law of Comparatively Dominant Position, Law Science*, Issue 7, 2006; LI Xiaoming: *Study on Identification by Anti-monopoly Law of Illegal Act of Abuse of Market Dominant Position, Hebei Law Science*, Issue 11, 2007.

4 For instance, HU Jian: *Interpretation of Legislation of 'Concentration of Undertakings' in Anti-monopoly Law, Anhui University Law Review*, Volume 1, 2008; WANG Xiaoye: *Evaluation and Analysis on Concentration of Undertakings in the 'Anti-monopoly Law of the PRC', Law Science Magazine*, Issue 1, 2008.

monopoly[1], law enforcement agency and private enforcement mechanism[2], application exception and extraterritorial effect[3], damages[4], and industry regulation relationship[5]. Scholars have expressed their views fully and freely, a move to provide the come-into-force of the *Anti-monopoly Law of the PRC* with full theory preparation. The *Anti-monopoly Law of the PRC,* like the *Real Right Law of the PRC*, is model for public legislation, democracy legislation and scientific legislation. In the process of seeking for opinions for the draft, legislative bodies received many valuable suggestions from economic law circles. One of the most typical seminars are five international seminars on competition law and competition policy organized and convened by the Law Institute of Chinese Academy of Social Sciences, especially the fifth one in 2007—a seminar centering firmly on a meticulous and deep-going study on

1 For instance, HU Guangzhi and WANG Bo: *Economic Analysis of Administrative- and Anti-administrative –Monopoly Law, China Legal Science*, Issue 4, 2004; NIE Xiaohong: *Necessity to Incorporate 'Administrative Monopoly' into the ' Anti-monopoly of the PRC'*, *Hebei Law Science*, Issue 2, 2007.

2 For instance, LI Jian: *Tentative Study on Feasibility for China to Set Up Anti-monopoly Law Enforcement Agencies*, *Modern Law Science*, Issue 1, 2004; SHI Jianzhong: *Private Litigation and Realization of Objective of Anti-monopoly of the PRC, China Development Observation*, Issue 6, 2006; JIAO Haitao: *Discussion on Procedure Dependence of Modern Anti-monopoly Law, Modern Law Science,* Issue 1, 2008.

3 For instance, ZHENG Pengcheng: *Exposure and Analysis of Grouth Trend of Applicable Exception System in U.S. Antitrust Law*, *Modern Law Science*, Issue 1, 2004; HUANG Yong: *Exemption and Exception in China's Anti-monopoly Law*, *Journal of East China University of Political Science and Law*, Issue 2, 2008; WU Hongwei and JIN Shanming: *Discussion on Value Goal of Applicable Exception System of Anti-monopoly*, *Politics & Law*, Issue 3, 2008, etc.

4 For instance, LI Guohai: *Comparative Study on Damages System in Anti-monopoly Law*, *Studies in Law and Business*, Issue 6, 2004.

5 For instance, LIANG Peng: *Discussion on Authority of Insurance Association to Make Rules—Concurrent Discussion on Effect of Anti-monopoly Law on Rule-making by Insurance Association*, *Insurance Studies*, Issue 11, 2008, etc.

the *Anti-monopoly Law of the People's Republic of China (draft)*[1], and setting up an ideal platform for the straightforward dialogues between representatives of experts and scholars and representatives of government officials—some amendment suggestions adopted by legislative bodies later. Symposium made after the seminar *Hot Topics of Anti-monopoly Legislation*[2] aroused a positive response in society.

Before and after the *Anti-monopoly Law of the PRC* coming into force, questions about the legislation and implement of anti-monopoly have rapidly become hot topics of society, for which some important law journals, based on its platform, have organized several monographic studies on anti-monopoly law, carrying out in-depth analysis and demonstration of the formulation and implementation of the law. For instance, *Research on Rule of Law*, Issue 5, 2007, published in an intensive manner 8 anti-monopoly law papers; *Law Science Magazine*, Issue 1, 2008, 6; and *Jurist*, Issue 1, 2008, 8. All in all, the *Anti-monopoly Law*, a landmark in the development history of China's economic law, is a fundamental economic law, whose issue and implementation is of great practical value to protecting fair competition in the market, improviing the economic efficiency, maintaining consumer interests and public interests and promoting the healthy development of socialist market economy.[3]

3.3 Study on law on protection of the rights and interests of consumers

Relative to the consumer protection work in developed countries, China's

1 In June 2006, the Standing Committee of National People's Congress for the first time examined the *Anti-monopoly Law of the PRC (draft)*. In consideration of many puzzling questions in the draft, the conference centered on the draft, divided into eight units, organized respectively keynote address and free question discussion on the following eight topics: (1) position of anti-monopoly law; (2) monopoly agreement; (3) consolidation control; (4) market dominant position; (5) administrative monopoly; (6) law enforcement agency; (7) legal remedy; and (8) economic globalization and regionalization, and competition policies related to it.

2 Edited by WANG Xiaoye: *Hot topics of Legislation of Anti-monopoly Law*, published by Social Sciences Academic Press, 2007.

3 XU Mengzhou: *Discussion on Value and Core Value of China's Anti-monopoly Law*, *Jurist*, Issue 1, 2008.

consumer protection starts later, but grows rapidly. In May 1983, the first county-level consumers' association was established in Xinle City of Hebei Province. And in September 1984, Guangzhou's first urban consumer council was set up, and in December of the same year, the China Consumers' Association, approved by the Nation Council, was founded in Beijing, and meanwhile the *Articles of Association of China Consumers' Association* was formulated, playing a sound sole for protecting the interest of consumers and promoting healthy economic development. In 1987, International Organization of Consumers Union admitted China Consumers' Association as its full member. The coming into force of the *Law on Protection of the Rights and Interests of Consumers of China* has lagged the appearance of consumers' questions and problems; however, it has been established in the end and driven idea of inclined protection, aimed at pursuing substantial justice.[1] LIANG Huixing pointed out that, the essence of China's consumer policy is to recognize the conflict of interest under the market economy condition between businesses and consumers, there being certainly some businesses damage without scruple the interests of consumers. Given that businesses are groups with strong economic power, which it is difficult to compete with for the decentralized consumer with unsubstantial economic power, the nation shall be responsible for protecting the interests of consumers—by legislative and administrative way, providing consumers with special protection and remedying their disadvantaged status—to maintain benefit balance between businesses and consumers so as to establish and maintain a sound order of the market economy, which is focused on remedying negative part in market economy and relieving consumers suffered losses.[2] This conclusion indicates in effect that law on protection of the rights and interests of consumers is an integral part of economic law.

As for special legal protection to consumers, perfect legal system of consumers'

1 LI Yougen: *Moving from Equality to Incline—Retrospect and Prospect of Consumer Protection Law*, *Legal Forum*, Issue 3, 2008.

2 LIANG Huixing: *China's Policy and Legislation Concerning Consumer*, *Legal Science*, Issue 5, 2000.

rights and interest's protection shall be set up at the legislative level. Dominated by basic law of consumer rights and interests protection, on the one hand, economic law, administrative law, criminal law and other legal departments are get involved in the field of consumer protection, that is, in their respective legislation, special protection of consumer rights and interests shall be one of legislative value goal orientations; on the other hand, obligation law shall be improved. Focus and protection of obligation law of consumer rights and interests are to remedy them; while protection and mechanism in other laws for consumer rights and interests are prevention and punishment.[1] Just because of this, a number of civil law scholars have studied this field, but most of them have been with a view to obligation law and civil liability, such as the perspective of consumer contract to study its design of rights and interests, an emphasis studied by civil law scholars; and there have been also some valuable results, such as put forward the right of withdrawal of consumers.[2] In terms of study on punitive compensation system, namely the questions applicable to Article 49 of the *Law on Protection of the Rights and Interests of Consumers of the PRC*, they are an emphasis in study on science of civil law, with very abundant fruits.[3] Among them there are

1 FU Xuqiao: *Special Protection of Consumer by New Development of Obligation Law*, *Journal of Yunnan University*, Issue 3, 1994.

2 DAI Juan: *Does An Operator Have Right to Choose Consumers?*, *Law Science Magazine*, Issue 2, 2004; DONG Wenjun: *Consumers' Right to Know*, *Contemporary Law Review*, Issue 3, 2004; DONG Xinkai and XIA Yu: *Cooling Off Period System and Consumer Protection*, *Hebei Law Science*, Issue 5, 2005; CHI Ying: *Discussion on Right of Withdrawal For Purpose of Protecting Consumers in German Law*, *Politics & Law*, Issue 6, 2008.

3 LIU Rongjun: *Exemplary Damages and Consumer Protection*, *Modern Law Science*, Issue 5, 1996; *Thinking Exemplary Damages Regulations in Law on Protection of the Rights and Interests of Consumers of the PRC*, *Journal of Central Leadership Institute of Politics and Law*, Issue 1, 1998; HOU Xianglei: *Urgent to Amendment of Article 49 of Law on Protection of the Rights and Interests of Consumers of the PRC*, *Law Science Magazine*, Issue 2, 1998; LI Jinyuan: *Understanding of Article 49 of Law on Protection of the Rights and Interests of Consumers of the PRC*, *Hebei Law Science*, Issue 6, 1998; DONG Wenjun: *Discussion on Exemplary Damages in Law on Protection of the Rights and Interests of Consumers of the PRC*, *Contemporary Law Review*, Issue 6, 2006.

discussions on not just identification of fraud, but knowing-fake-buying-fake acts, as well as perfection of punitive compensation system. Study in science of civil on consumers' interest protection law has been deepening, and some scholars even pointed out that the transform, from the rights protection transform by the government to support of customer complaints, shall be orientation of institutional change.[1]

Science of economic law pays more attention to studying on law on protection of the rights and interests of consumers. LI Changqi once said that nation protection, operator self-discipline, and consumer awareness are the three magic weapons to protect interests of consumer. The perfection and in full operation of consumer protection laws, a move to categorically improve consumers' situation, especially relies on all-round improvement involved in the consumer protection consciousness of the staff in nation organs, consciousness of self-discipline of operators and self-protection awareness of consumers.[2] To put it in another way, besides relying on civil law, legal protection of consumers must depend on economic law to put government and consumer organizations to good use and to exert the idea of and adjustment method of economic law. The economic law puts more emphasis on macro-perspective, whole perspective and even subject perspective to study legal questions and issues concerning consumer protection, such as CHEN Yunliang, whose ambiguity analysis of consumers concept, using ambiguity law science, has certain new meaning.[3] XU Mengzhou holds that generalization of economic law subject should reflect provisions of law in force, and that generalization and type of economic law subject must show the special right (power) and obligation of economic law borne by these subjects. Study on economic law subject should be rooted in adjustment object of economic

1 GUO Guanghui: *Economic Analysis of Transition of Consumer Protection legal System in China, Hebei Law Science*, Issue 1, 2008.

2 LI Changqi and XU Mingyue: *Discussion on Consumer Protection Consciousness, Modern Law Science*, Issue 2, 1999.

3 CHEN Yunliang: *Ambiguity Analysis of Consumer Concept—One Application of Fuzzy Law, Law Science*, Issue 10, 2006.

law and the special identity and its characteristic of subject bearing right and obligation, so as to distinguish the subject from that of other departmental laws.[1] Some scholars summarize subject of economic law as operators, consumers and governments.[2] XU Mengzhou maintains that it has more basis of law in force to summarize subject of economic law as consumers, operators, and administrators, which also reflects more the special adjustment object and purpose of legislation of the economic law. Concepts of consumers and operators, who are objects to be protected and regulated by market regulation law, have been used in the *Anti-Unfair Competition Law of the People's Republic of China,* the *Law on Protection of the Rights and Interests of Consumers of the PRC* and the *Price Law of the PRC*, and defined definitely by law. In the view of economic law, consumers should sit at the heart of its subject's system structure; the production and operation purpose of operators is to provide consumers with paid services and products; and administrators should serve consumers and operators. For all operators and administrators, consumers are "God", which is the proper meaning of "People First", and the idea that the legislation of economic law must implement.[3] However, GUAN Bin has analyzed thoroughly from a perspective of rights of consumers, holding that rights of consumers are not just theoretical basis of human rights, but empirical demonstration, too, meeting crucial standards of human rights. Essential attribute of rights of consumers is right to live, right to development and other basic human rights—comprehensive rights including various civil and economic rights like property right and personal right.[4] Studies

1 XU Mengzhou and XIE Zengyi: *Discussion on Position of Consumers and Consumer Protection in Economic Law—New Thought on "People First" Idea and Subject and System of Economic Law, Modern Law Science*, Issue 4, 2005.

2 LI Yougen: *Discussion on Subject of Economic Law*, published in *Contemporary Law Review*, Issue 1, 2004.

3 XU Mengzhou and XIE Zengyi: *Discussion on Position of Consumers and Consumer Protection in Economic Law—New Thought on "People First" Idea and Subject and System of Economic Law, Modern Law Science*, Issue 4, 2005.

4 Edited by WU Hongwei: *Economic Law*, China Renmin University Press, 2003, p.209.

of WANG Yanlin answer directly this question on the other side, who wrote, after issue for enforcement of the *Food Safety Law of the PRC*, articles putting forward that such Law "concealed" consumer protection when purpose of legislation and system are constructed. And he is in the hope that such Law shall pay full attention to this fact in course of implementation thereof, and develop the two-pole game of infrastructure of the *Food Safety Law of the PRC*—supervision/production and operation—into ternary game of superintendent—production operator—consumers, to make the food safety enter a structure of tension traverse from two-pole teeterboard status.[1] And some scholars have studied consumer protection from a point of view of competition law. Take "Prohibiting Customers to Bring Their Own Drinks" for example, whether it infringes the choice of consumers, LI Jian thinks that it is necessary to analyze it from the perspective of competition law, which is not universally regarded as infringement. When the market competitor is able to provide consumers with enough choices of hotel, consumers can "vote with their feet" to choose to go to a restaurant accepting "Bring your own bottle"; if, with insufficient market competition, the hotel has the market dominant position, then it is reasonable that the extra restrictions must be give on the conduct of the hotel to balance the power between the hotel and consumers.[2]

Scholars have carried out study on a lot of questions arising from the law on protection of the rights and interests of consumers, such as questions about how to define living consumption, and whether or not automobile consumption is pertain to living consumption and whether it shall be protected the law on protection of the rights and interests of consumers. Most scholars maintain that automobile consumption shall be protected the law on protection of the rights and interests

1 WANG Yanlin: *Consumer Protection in China's Food Safety Law*, *Oriental Law*, Issue 2, 2009.

2 LI Jian: *Logic of Consumers' Right of Choice, Consumer Psychology and Competition Law*, *Modern Law Science*, Issue 6, 2007.

of consumers, for it is into tens of thousands of households.[1] Furthermore, it is argued whether the law on protection of the rights and interests of consumers should adjust doctor-patient relationship: one view being that such relationship need not adjusting because a hospital is different from an operator; the other being that such relationship need not adjusting because the medical service behaviors of doctors and the hospital are repayable service, with medicines being goods. And some hold eclectic opinions that such law shall apply as a whole; but the non-profit medical organization not having operator identity shall not be applicable to such law.[2]

3.4 Study on product quality law

Study on product quality law, focused on introduction of ecological idea of economic law, keeps up with economic and social development. For the sake of strengthening supervision and administration of product quality to clear responsibility for quality of products, China adopted the *Product Quality Law of the People's Republic of China* in 1993, and its amendment in July 2000. This Law, with many Chinese characteristics as a whole, has not only used for reference the latest theory and practice of American and European countries about product responsibility, acclimatizing itself to international legislation trend on product liability, but in terms of legislation style and legal content taken a full consideration of China's national condition.[3] China's *Product Quality Law* is both a law supervising and managing product quality and a law concerning responsibilities for product quality. The fundamental objective of product quality law is to enhance supervision and administration of product quality, improve

1 WANG Xin et al: *Final Judgment by Chengdu Intermediate People's Court, People's Court Daily*, Fourth Edition, June 13, 2006.

2 LIANG Huixing: *China's Policy and Legislation Concerning Consumer, Legal Science,* Issue 5, 2000; WANG Liming: Concept of Consumers and Adjustment Range of Law on Protection of the Rights and Interests of Consumers, *Politics & Law*, Issue 2, 2002.

3 XU Mengzhou and XIE Zengyi: *A Product Quality Law with Economic Law Idea—Concurrent Discussion on Amendment to China's Product Quality Law, Jurist,* Issue 5, 2001.

product quality, clear responsibilities for product quality, protect legitimate rights and interests of consumers, and safeguard social and economic order. Product liability and responsibilities for product quality are two concepts, both closely related to each other and vastly different. Product liability is a civil liability, namely a civil legal liability arising from product infringement, which is a negative responsibility after a defective product causes actual damage to consumers; while responsibilities for product quality are an integrated responsibility, including civil liability, administrative responsibility and criminal responsibility, which are responsibility both before and after an event. The move from single product liability to comprehensive product quality responsibility, realizing a span from civil law adjusting product quality law to departmental law of economic law, which reflects institutional innovation and progress appropriate for China's national conditions.

CHEN Naixin points out that China's economic law textbooks have usually written and edited in them product quality law as a departmental law, but the textbooks have only expressed product quality law with some brief explanatory notes, without deep explanation of the spirit in product quality law. Therefore, when people have read these economic law textbooks, they have no idea why product quality law has been incorporated in economic law, which is unfavorable for us to understand the essence of product quality law, and consequently it is difficult to grasp its legislative spirit in course of implementation of product quality law, find and acknowledge shortage of product quality law.[1] WANG Lijun et al have put forward that ecologicalization of legal system of product quality is a question worthy of study. We have always treated and handled environmental problems and economic problems respectively, with environment protection legislation being separated from economic legislation, economic sectors seldom assuming environmental protection responsibility, and economic legislation

1 CHEN Naixin: *Discussion on Spirit of Economic Law in Product Quality Law*, *Journal of Changsha University of Science and Technology*, Issue 4, 2004.

seldom taking into account environmental requirement, all of which are a giant obstacle to realization of sustainable development. To remove this obstacle, it must integrate the ecological protection requirements and thought of sustainable development into legal departments. It is essential to set up "Green" quality standards of products, including green technical standards, green environmental labels and green system of sanitation and quarantine to ecologicalize product packaging; to extended producer responsibility, to make them bear responsibility for proper recycling and disposal of products,[1] and to set up respectively perfect green quality standard system concerning agricultural products, electronic information products and transgenic products.[2] The thoughts and viewpoints of them in effect manifest directly economic law ecology.

With the technology progress and economic development, there appear requirements for continuously extending range of application of product quality law, a field where a large amount of scholars have carried out pioneering study. In pace with commercialization, propertilization, digitization and networking of information, the information service industry specialized in collecting, sorting, storing and spreading information has emerged at the right moment, and become a mainstay industry in economic society. Some scholars put forward that, if the product quality law, specialized in resolving liability concerns caused by product quality, excludes information product liability out of adjustment range, it is obviously not conducive to protect information products consumers' rights and interests and sound development of information industry. For this purpose, definition of information product; information product quality standard; nature and doctrine of liability fixation of information products liability; definition of information product liability as well as ground for defense in information product liability, all have been analyzed and argued in a sufficient manner. For instance,

1 See YU Jinxiang's *Circular Economy and Its Legal Regulation, Gansu Social Sciences*, Issue 6, 2003.

2 WANG Lijun and FENG Zhaohui: *Thinking on Ecologicalization of Legal System of Product Quality, Hebei Law Science*, Issue 12, 2006.

as for quality standard of information product, it is emphasized that the standards' requirements shall be of authenticity, accuracy, completeness, and legality; any product not meeting the above requirements shall be deemed as defective, from which the liability for damage arising shall be borne.[1] This study is of significance to product quality law to adapt to the economic life.

After "Sanlu milk powder incident" in 2008, the product inspection-free system in China aroused extensive attention and question from the media and society, which garnered the government's response. Before then, some scholars holds in their study that, as an omission of the government, the establishment of the product inspection-free system destroys the hierarchical nature of force of law and fair and orderly market competition order; therefore, such system shall be abolished on the basis of improving the supervision system of product quality.[2] With respect to this question, YING Feihu, from the view of and by means of law science, economics, sociology and social psychology, has made a specialty of the existence or abolishment and improvement of the inspection-free system, on the basis of its rationality, basic performance of its implementation, and signal function of inspection-free marks. And he maintains that, in course of formulation of inspection-free system, the Administration of Quality Supervision, Inspection and Quarantine causes, due to its static thinking, the setting up of inspection-free conditions to be improper; as for the implementation of the performance, there being a lot of questions in mechanism of action influenced by inspection-free system, the sales growth of exempted products after being qualified may not mainly depend on the quality assurance function of the system, but the improper amplification of semiotic function arising out of inspection-free marks,

1 LI Yang: *Primary Exploration of Information Products Liability*, *China Legal Science*, Issue 6, 2004.

2 See LEI Xinghu, XI Xiaoqin and LV Yafeng: *Reservation and Abolishment of China's Business Products Inspection-Free System*, *Law Science*, Issue 7, 2004.

caused by combined actions of multi-factors, such as governments, businesses, consumers, media and status in quo of quality signals; because it is difficult to perceive functional defects of specific products and to measure their hazards, the implementation of the inspection-free system may exert an inevitable, negative influence on product quality. Taking into overall consideration various factors, he suggests that the inspection-free system be canceled; and that, in case of considering improvement of information providing and law enforcement efficiency, or General Administration of Quality Supervision believing that the inspection-free system must exist, then the system shall be amended necessarily in terms of punishment, supervision and appropriate reservations.[1] Moreover, DU Guoming has specialized in China's agricultural products quality safety, pointing out that there at present are some questions in China's legislation on agricultural products quality and safety, such as undefined scope of agricultural products, unclear prohibited production field and insufficient legal responsibility norms, all of which shall be analyzed deeply so as to build a legal system appropriate for the operation law of produce quality safety in China to raise fundamentally the quality and safety of agricultural products in China.[2]

After entering the 21st century, some scholars, from the point of view of law science and economics, have studied and analyzed the application and perfection of strict liability principle of products, maintaining that the proposal of strict liability has, to some extent, restrained manufacturers and distributors from pursuing economic benefits endlessly, and given humanistic care to vulnerable groups in market economy, so as to promote the realization of the pattern of dynamic balance between the social equity and efficiency, conducive to the sustainable development of market economy in China and even the overall

1 YING Feihu: *Analysis by Synthesis on Inspection-free System: Insistence, Abandonment or Improvement? China Legal Science*, Issue 3, 2008.

2 DU Guoming: *Study on Legislation of Quality Safety of Agricultural Products*, *Hebei Law Science*, Issue 9, 2008.

progress of human society.[1] Also, in the wake of amendment of the *Product Quality Law of the PRC*, some scholars have studied and analyzed relevant clauses, raising suggestion on perfection of relevant regulations. It should be noted that, in terms of study on product quality law, some civil law scholars are absorbed in studying product liability, bringing out a series of research results[2] on comparative law, thus providing important theoretical reference data for amending and perfecting China's *Product Quality Law.*

4. Study on Macro-Control Law in Economic Globalization

As an economics noun, macro control has completely become an acronym of macroeconomic regulation and control, and become one of important legal concepts. Guidance and protection of market mechanism may strengthen the constraint of main market players, coordinate contradiction between individual

1 LIU Dahong and ZHANG Jianhui: *Discussion on Application and Perfection of Strict Liability Principle of Products*, published in *Law Review*, Issue 3, 2004. Similar studies include: QIAN Shengli and XUE Pingzhi: *Analysis on Law and Economics of China's Imputation Principle of Product Liability*, published in *Hebei Law Science*, Issue 2, 2002; ZHOU Xinjun and RONG Ying: *Discussion on China's Imputation Principle of Product Liability*, published in *Political and Legal Forum*, Issue 3, 2002; SUN Bo: *Thinking on Perfection of China's Product Liability Law*, published in *Political and Legal Forum*, Issue 1, 2001.

2 For example, ZHANG Qi's *Comparisons of Responsibility Principle Between Products in China and America, Peking University Law Journal*, Issue 4 of 1998; Li Jing and LI Aiguo's *Brief Discussion on French Product Quality Law,* published in *Peking University Law Journal*, Issue 5 of 1998; ZHANG Guihong's *The Latest Development of American Product Liability Law and Its Revelations on China, Studies in Law and Business*, Issue 6 of 2001; WANG Xiang's *Comparative Studies of Grounds for Defense of Product Liability, Politics and Law*, Issue 4 of 2002; ZHANG Minxian and MA Xusheng's *New Development of Product Liability System in Netherlands,* published in *Comments on Law,* Issue 1 of 2005; LI Hui's *Review and Analysis of Trade Disputes in WTO GM Products and Regulation & Legislation of EU GM Products, Reviews of Global Laws,* Issue 2 of 2007; LIANG Ya's *Analysis of Changes in Responsibility Principal in American Product Liability Law*, published in *Reviews of Global Laws,* Issue 1 of 2008; DONG Chunhua's *On Punitive Damage in American Product Liability Law, Studies in Comparative Laws,* Issue 6 of 2008; WANG Junmin and XU Yongqian's *On Special Exemption Defense of Tort Liability in American Toxic-substances -related Damages and Its Revelations on China's Product Liability Law, Reviews of Global Laws,* Issue 6 of 2008; etc.

interests, overall interests and society interests, and prevent and stop conflict between market mechanism function and macroeconomic regulation and control function. When ensuring normal operation of the market mechanism, and guiding interests of main market players inclining to macro-economic objectives, the economic law lays emphasis on normalizing macro-control measures or government economic behaviors, to optimize macroeconomic regulation and control function. According to historical experience, the more active the micro economics is, the rapider process of marketization is, which requires more strong and effective macroscopic readjustment and control. How to make macroscopic readjustment and control both promote the basic role of market mechanism to give into full play, and control the national economy development in a coordinated and balanced manner, all need to promote coadaptation of market mechanism and macroscopic readjustment and control, to attain their internal coupling.[1] With its position upgrading, macro-control law is becoming the core of the economic law system, in which macroscopic readjustment and control and macro-control law are becoming more socializing,[2] democratizing and internationalizing.[3]

As for study on macro-control law, economic law scholars are focused on fields of the forming reason or objective condition of macro-control law; its definition and characteristics, purpose, essence, basic principles, system, and method of adjustment; macro-control right; and the formulation of the basic law of macro-control. The title of "macro-control law" and its theoretical generalization are originally created for China's economic law, there being no such similar concept whether in continental law system or Anglo-American law system.[4] Macro-

1 XU Mengzhou: *Discussion on Coupling Between Market Mechanism and Macroscopic Readjustment and Control*, published in *Jurists Review*, Issue 2, 1996.

2 XIAO Jiangping: *Study on History of China's Economic Law,* published by People's Court Press, 2002, p.353.

3 QI Duojun: *Characteristics of Legislation of Macroscopic Readjustment and Control and Its New Development*, published in *Politics & Law*, Issue 3, 2002.

4 XIE Zengyi: *New Discussion on Basic Principle of Macro-Control Law*, *Journal of Xiamen University* (*Philosophy and Social Science Edition*), Issue 5, 2003.

control law is a need of socialized mass production, a common requirement of market economy development, and centralized reflection of national economic management functions.[1] The reason market economy needs macroscopic readjustment and control is because it is decided by the nature of the market economy and market failure basically. Those require macroscopic readjustment and control to be strengthened, market economy, which cannot always balance automatically, be self-sufficient, realize social equity, or take the initiative to directly promote the public interest; market regulation, which cannot overcome blindness; and emergence, existence and development of market economy.[2]

In the definition of macro-control law, scholars continue to use the defining methods for economic law, defining concept of economic law through the definition of the nature and connotation of its scope of specific economic relationship. For instance, some is defined as "adjusting economic relations occurring in the course of the adjustment and control by a nation of operation of macro economy"[3]; some as "adjusting variety social relations occurring in the course of the macroscopic readjustment and control by a nation of social economy"[4]; and some as "adjusting economic relations occurring in the course of the macroscopic readjustment and control by a nation of economic operation"[5]. It is obvious that there is a close relationship between macro-control law and macroscopic readjustment and control, definition of the former

1 XU Mengzhou: *Brief Discussion on Macro-Control Law, Jurists Review, Is*sue 4, 1994.

2 QIU Ben: *Introduction on Macro-Control Law,* published in *New Development of Economic Studies* (edited by WANG Xiaoye and QIU Ben), China Social Sciences Press, Issue 4, 1994, pp.232-244.

3 WANG Shouyu and GONG Mengqian: *Legal System on Macroeconomic Control Law*, published by China Economic Publishing House, p.1.

4 QI Duojun: *Study on Macro-Control Law,* published in *Studies in Law and Business*, Issue 2, 1999.

5 XU Mengzhou: *Study on Macro-Control Law,* published in Economic Law Review, Volume 2 (edited by XU Jie), Law Press China, 2001; XU Mengzhou: *Further Discussion on Macroeconomic Control Law, China's Macroeconomic Law Seminar and Communication on Law Institute of Beijing Economic Law Seminar Paper*, 2000.

is directly dependent on that of the latter. QI Duojun maintains that macroscopic readjustment and control is one of economic-function activities that a nation adjusts, by means of variety guidance and advancement, structure and operation of macro economy and society.[1] XU Mengzhou holds that macroscopic readjustment and control means the government readjusts and controls social economy operation so as to realize the balance between social aggregate demand and aggregate supply, and to ensure the sustained, stable and coordinated growth of the national economy.[2] WANG Quanxing and GUAN Bin believe that macroscopic readjustment and control means that control subject, concerning social public interests, and in order to realize the basic balance of macroeconomic aggregate and optimize the economic structure, guides the continuous, healthy and coordinated development of national economy, and adjusts and controls on the whole the national economy.[3] In spite that expressions are not the same, they have many common grounds, such as mention of subject, objective and ways of macroscopic readjustment and control, the differences being whether to clear footholds and essential features. And QIU Ben chooses to abandon the methods to define it, but to conclude regularity of macroscopic readjustment and control, that is to say, macroscopic readjustment and control is to adjust and control market, one that is macroscopic readjustment and control in macro-scopical fields, and that is limited, democratic, mainly controlled by law.[4] It can yet be regarded as a new beneficial exploration and try. In terms of characteristic and essence of macro-control law, relevant studies conclude starting with multiple pathways; some, starting with characteristics of adjustment object and legal relations, believe that macro-control law take as adjustment objects the economic

1 Edited by QI Duojun: *Study on Macro-Control Law*, China Fangzheng Press, 2002, p.10.

2 XU Mengzhou: *Discussion on Coupling Between Market Mechanism and Macroscopic Readjustment and Control*, published in *Jurists Review*, Issue 2, 1996.

3 WANG Quanxing and GUAN Bin: Outline on Macro-Control Law, *Journal of Capital Normal University* (Social Science Edition), Issue 3, 2002.

4 QIU Ben: *Discussion on Macro-Control Law,* China Industry and Commerce Press, 2002, pp.1-7.

relationships occurring between individual businesses or units in operation, but the relationships in the whole national economy, that the subject party of macro-control law relations must be a nation or its authorized economic-function- or comprehensive-economic-departments, and that economic rights and obligations between subjects in macro-control law relations are non-equivalent;[1] some, from point of view of method of adjustment, believes that the method of adjustment of macro-control law is a whole adjustment method in society, which is conscious, constraint and indirect, and which is different from other departmental laws,[2] or believes that it is a method comprehensively applying economy, administration, criminal, substantial law and procedural law, and centers on economic and legal means, mainly adjusting by means of economic law and auxiliary by contributory necessary administrative means;[3] and some, generalizing from point of view of interest standard and regulation subject initiative, believes that macro-control law is a government intervention law, a social standard law, and a law with intermediary and policy-based nature.[4] Macro-control law is also a comprehensive law.[5] And some studies believe that essence of macro-control law depends on that it is involved in sociometrist macro and overall, and a law by which a nation regulates certain key and necessary parts of macro and overall, a more conscientious regulation, reflecting highly subjective initiative of modern countries.[6] All these studies uncover certain attributes of macro-control law from different sides, in spite of which is that "wise see wisdom", jointly draws the

1 WANG Shouyu and GONG Mengqian: *Legal System on Macroeconomic Control Law*, China Economic Publishing House, 1995, pp.3-5.

2 Edited by DONG Jinyu: *Science of Macro-Control Economic Law*, Jilin University Press, 1999, pp.20-25.

3 Edited by YANG Zixuan: *Economic Law*, Peking University Press and Higher Education Press, 1999, pp.268-269.

4 Edited by DONG Jinyu: *Science of Macro-Control Economic Law*, Jilin University Press, 1999, pp.15-20.

5 QIU Ben: Discussion on *Macro-Control Law,* China Industry and Commerce Press, 2002, pp.15-19.

6 QI Duojun: *Discussion on Essence, System and Core of Economic Law*, Paper of the *Fifth Economic Law Theory Seminar Communication* (1997).

outline of macro-control law, helping people know and grasp in an even better fashion the concept and meaning of macro-control law.

The basic principle of macro-control law, leading the whole macro-control law system, concentrates reflection of the essential concept and basic spirit of macro-control law, and is a basest standard of behavior which is must be abode by in macro-control legislation and law enforcement, having general significance for systems in the system of macroeconomic regulation and control law. Hence, studies are greatly important on basic principle of macro-control law. In this regard, there is some difference in scholars' summarizations, for example, some are summarized as legal principle of macro-control functions and powers and procedures, of maintaining national macro-economic interests, and of main division of labor and coordination of macroeconomic regulation and control;[1] some as balance optimization principle, principle of limited intervention and macro benefit principle, and combination of centralization and decentralization principle;[2] some as respect for market principle, principle of social public welfare, sustainable development principle, and principle of economic democracy;[3] some as resource optimization principle, aggregate balance principle, indirect control principle, principle of unified coordination and macro benefit principle;[4]some as indirect control principle, planning guidelines principle, public principle, legal principle, suitability principle, and combination of stability and flexibility.[5] It shows that, respecting this important theoretical problem of basic principle of macro-control law, there arise three theories on three principles, four principles, five principles and even six principles, which have a direct relation to different

1 XIE Zengyi: *New Discussion on Basic Principle of Macro-Control Law*, *Journal of Xiamen University* (*Philosophy and Social Science Edition*), Issue 5, 2003.

2 Edited by PAN Jingcheng and LIU Wenhua : *Economic Law*, China Renmin University Press, 1999, pp.296-298.

3 WANG Quanxing and GUAN Bin: *Outline on Macro-Control Law*, *Journal of Capital Normal University (Social Science Edition)*, Issue 3, 2002.

4 LU Jiongxing: *Macro Economic Law*, Xiamen University Press, 2000, pp.53-55.

5 Edited by YANG Zixuan: *Economic Law*, published by Peking University Press, 1999, pp.267-268.

standards and methods scholars use in course of extracting principles. For macro-control legislation and legal research, importance is self-evident, of refining and abstracting of macroeconomic regulation and control principle, which is in favor of organic unification of systems and provisions to be specified in macro-control law, a sub-department economic law.

As for the system of macro-control law, common view in economic law circle is that the construction of the law covers planning law, financial law, tax law, finance law and industrial policy law, the divergence between which is whether the construction shall cover law of national assets management, law of natural resources, energy law, environmental protection law and social security law. In studies in and before 1991, there were different structural analyses on systems of macro-control law, for example, from the means, it will be divided into macroeconomic decision-making procedure, law of supervision of calculation of operation of macro economy, law of information feedback and adjustment of macro-economy, macroeconomic stability growth promotion law and macroeconomic mistake responsibility law, etc.; from the relevant scope, into national economic planning law, financial law, finance law, investment law, material law, resources law, labor and employment law, wages law, prices law, industry revitalization law, industrial structure adjustment law, foreign exchange law, foreign trade law, science and technology progress law, and environmental protection law; and from legislative angle, into laws concerning macroeconomic comprehensive control function, macroeconomic regulation and control of economic industry department, and macroeconomic regulation and control of their own behavior. After 1992, some researchers have maintained that nation's macroeconomic regulation and control under condition of marketing economy may be divided into three legal levels: direct management by the nation of its economy to decide the legal level of national economy development direction; direct management of or indirect involvement in by the national the economic activities to implement control of main body in economic legal relationship; and direct involvement by the national in the economic activities to achieve, through intervention with specific economic behavior, control of the whole national economy. But those are discussions more economically.[1] Some of later studies maintain, from the point of view of substantive and procedure law, that combination of law and macro-control can show up as adjustment in the sense of entity and procedure, the former applicable to economic normality period, the latter to economic fluctuation period. Thus, legal framework of macroscopic readjustment and control consist of four parts: comprehensive law, centering on planning laws and macro-control law procedures; special laws in connection with overall situation, mainly about finance, financial, investment in fixed assets and foreign trade; law for the revitalization of the economy; and law of social security.[2] Some studies, comprehensively understanding on the whole, maintain that system of macroeconomic regulation and control law include financial budget law, tax law, finance law, industrial structure planning law, investment in fixed assets law, planning law for national economic and social development and foreign economic and trade law.[3] And some, understanding from point of view "national planning-economic policy- regulating measure", maintain that system of macroeconomic regulation and control includes in content laws such as planning law, economic policy law and that about application of regulating methods.[4] Furthermore, recent studies hold that macro-control law is a comprehensive law, which is specifically composed of planning law, financial law, finance law and industrial policy law, with various functions in comprehensive form.[5] Although the results of the study are not identical, they reflect understanding and awareness

1 XIAO Jiangping: *Study on History of China's Economic Law,* published by People's Court Press, 2002, pp.353.

2 MA Shaochun: *Reviewing and Thinking of Legalization Process China's Macro-Control, Paper of* the *Seventh Economic Law Theory Seminar Communication* (1999).

3 XU Mengzhou: *Study on Macro-Control Law,* published in Economic Law Review, Volume 2 (edited by XU Jie), Law Press China, 2001, Volume 2.

4 Edited by QI Duojun: *Study on Macro-Control Law*, China Fangzheng Press, 2002, p.18.

5 QIU Ben: *Introduction on Macro-Control Law,* published in *New Development of Economic Studies* (edited by WANG Xiaoye and QIU Ben), China Social Sciences Press, 2002, pp.253-262.

of the macro-control law system by scholars in different periods. Concerning the core composition of macro-control law, there has been as yet a basic consensus, such as planning law, financial law, finance law, industrial policy law, government investment law, state-owned assets administration law and foreign trade law, environmental protection, social security law and other appropriate law, all of which shall be attributable to emerging social law departments. In spite of blank in some legislation, systematization macro-control law is imperative.

As for adjustment methods of macro-control law, XU Mengzhou maintains that there are three types, guidance, regulation and supervision;[1] QIU Ben maintains that there are society whole regulation method, conscientious adjustment method, constraint method and indirect adjustment method;[2] WANG Quanxing and GUAN Bin divide macro-control law into direct control and indirect control, pre control, control in process, post control, summarized control with not specified object and specific control with specified object. Changes in ownership structure since the reform and opening up bring new challenges against macroscopic readjustment and control. Generally speaking, fundamental transforms take place in control methods, from dual regulation of "administration and economy" to economy-oriented control, with the following transforming tendencies to be paid attention to: transform from (tactical) short-term control-oriented to (strategic) long-term control-oriented; from micro goal-oriented to macro goal-oriented; from total quantity control-oriented to structure control-oriented; from ownership system standard-oriented to industrial standard-oriented; from demand control-oriented to supply control-oriented, with joint transformation together with the former; from control-on-business-oriented to mechanism control-oriented; and from value control-oriented to coordination of physical- and value-control.[3]

1 Edited by PAN Jingcheng and LIU Wenhua: *Economic Law*, China Renmin University Press, 1999, p.298.

2 QIU Ben: *Introduction on Macro-Control Law,* published in *New Development of Economic Studies* (edited by WANG Xiaoye and QIU Ben), China Social Sciences Press, 2002, pp.248-253.

3 See WANG Quanxing and GUAN Bin: *Outline on Macro-Control Law*, *Journal of Capital Normal University (Social Science Edition)*, Issue 3, 2002.

In the course of studies on the macro-control law, some scholars have discussed macro-control power as one of the most important categories of macro-control law theory. For instance, in their analyses on the origin of macro-control power, they have raised three different viewpoints: first, theory of ownership. It maintains that power of nation macro control is rooted in state ownership; second, theory of management right. It believes that macro-control power is rooted in the management function of a nation over social economy, being one of public rights activities; and third, theory of legislation-administrative power. It holds that macro-control power is an independent power parallel in legislation and administration, one that is jointly owned by legislative and administrative organs.[1] ZHANG Shouwen holds that, in terms of form, macro-control power comes from a clear mandate in the view of law. Under the circumstances of understanding the law as enacted law, contents of macro-control power such as its establishment, distribution, and implementation shall be embodied in accordance with law enacted by a state. Furthermore, macro-control power also is crystallized jurisdiction of the state over the economy. As a part of state sovereignty or more concrete jurisdictions, macro-control power basically is one with new-style nature of important powers in whole national overall. Legality of macro-control in terms of economy depends on its economic legality, "regularity" in effect concerning economy. The subject of macro control shall be a state, not government institutions at basic level but highest authority in the state. It must be in prudent way to configure macro-control power, with "Legal principle of control power" to be adhered to, exercise of which should be subject to moderate proportion principle, principle of honesty and credibility and principle of change of circumstances.[2] So far, there have still been many questions to study deeply concerning macro-control power, such as its categories, efficacy, corresponding

1 LU Li: *Discussion on Origin of Power of Macroscopic Readjustment and Control, Economical Legal System*, Issue 4, 1994.

2 See ZHANG Shouwen's *Legal Analysis of Macro-Control Power, Acta Scientiarum Naturalium Universitatis Pekinensis (Philosophy and Social Science Edition),* Issue 3, 2001.

obligation and responsibility as well as coordination of relevant systems, and also to extend to constitutional jurisprudence, structure of legal relationship, theory of macro-control law liability, macro-control procedure and macro-control of right of judicial review.[1]

Before and after establishment of socialist market economy system, study on macro-control legislation has attained universal attention in academic circle.[2]

Macro-control law is not a law to call of the role and function of the government over development of economy, but to push forward economy, develop economy, and intervene in economy, and to ensure objectivity, scientificity and stability of macro control by means of law.[3] In 2000, in the eighth National Economic Law Theory Seminar, study on macro-control law has further warmed. And in Fourth Session of the Ninth National People's Congress, four bills regarding setting up of *Macro-control Law* (namely *Macro-control Basic Law*) were raised, a move led by four deputies including YANG Zixuan, and countersigned by 100-odd other deputies. Afterward, some scholars drafted up the drafts of Macro-control Law respectively. In the middle of July 2001, the Second Session of Economic Law Frontier Theory Seminar in Taiyuan discussed 3 drifts of experts, whose contents were involved in questions and issues such as style arrangement of macro-control law draft, its concept, configuration and exercise of macro-control

1 XIAO Jiangping: *Study on History of China's Economic Law,* People's Court Press, 2002, p.356.

2 LIU Jian and GUO Rui: *Discussion on Question in Strengthening Macro-control of National Economy*, *China Legal Science*, Issue 2, 1990; LI Changqi: *Discussion on Legal Question in Socialist Economic Macro Control*, published in *Modern Law Science*, Issue 3, 1990; JIANG Ping: *Implementation of Spirit of Seventh Plenum to Speed up Economic Legal System Construction—Decision on Macro-control of Economy Shall be Legalized, Scientized and Democratized*, China Legal Science, Issue 2, 1991; XU Shiying: *Legal Safeguard of Macro-control of Economy*, Foreign Laws Translation and Review, Issue 3, 1994; PENG Qixian: *Discussion on Legalization of Macro Control, Modern Law Science*, issue 3.

3 LI Tieying: *Emancipating Mind, Change Ideas; Establishing of Socialist Market Economy Law System*, published in Chinese Journal of Law, Issue 2, 1997.

power, control subject, scope of control, control means, relationship between macro-control law and policy, feasibility study, constitute of macro-control law department and its legal responsibility.[1] Study on necessity for setting up *Macro-control Law* maintains that it is necessary to effectively implement Article 7[2] of *Amendment to the Constitution of the People's Republic of China*, to improve China's macro control system, to enhance harmony of China's macro control, to realize third step development strategy goal, to response to the economic globalization and safeguard national economic security, and to draw lessons from foreign experience in macro control to enhance the level of China's macro control. Feasibility study maintains that, for establishment of *Macro-control Law*, there are both constitutional ground and policy support, and many years of fruitful experience in macro control, larger scale of legislation and rich experience in legislation, with adequate theoretical guidance, academic support and successful foreign experience of the rule of law, for referential use; hence mature legislative factors. As for detailed system design, studies maintain that it is important to take as objective implementation of the aggregate balance and structure optimization of national economy, and promotion of sustainable, rapid and healthy development of national economy; to make clear a regulation of the national macro-control institutions, power configuration and its procedures; to legalize the macro-control procedures; to stipulate basic systems concerning plans for national economic and social development, readjust and control by fiscal and tax, financial control, industrial policy, coordination of regional economy, price adjustment and control,

1 Research groups by principals XU Mengzhou, LU Jiongxing and ZHENG Shaohua have put forward respectively one *Macroeconomic Regulation and Control Law of the People's Republic of China* (draft), See communication materials on the Second Session of Economic Law Frontier Theory Seminar (2001). Afterward, a quality expert's draft based on such three drafts was raised as bills at the Fifth Session of the Ninth NPC in March 2002, with a great influence.

2 This Article explicitly stipulates that Nation shall intensify macroscopic readjustment and control to improve macroscopic readjustment and control.

and foreign trade; and to explicitly stipulate legal liability.[1]

One thing we need to pay attention to is that, along with studies on basic theory of macro-control law, economic law scholars have also carried out intensive studies on special field of macro-control laws like fiscal law, tax law, finance law, industrial policy law, law on administration of state-owned assets, government investment law, and foreign trade law, and obtained a great amount of research result. Taking financial law as an example, WU Zhipan once proposed the "Four color theorem" of financial law, in which he said that, financial law is involved in all kinds of "contractual relationship" and "property right relationship", in terms of capital market to capital market, and insurance market to the foreign exchange market; and that these relationship of rights and obligations will be influenced by external four factors. The four factors are government, market, unit and individual, all of them creating four regulations to financial relations: government's administrative adjustment, market's economic adjustment, unit adjustment and personal fine-tuning. We name the four regulations as "Four color theorem" of financial law.[2]

For the past few years, some scholars put forward that, from the perspective of sociology, economics and a country under the rule of law, and combining with the growing trend of macro regulation reform abroad, the study on China's macro-control law needs to rethink and improve control target, control subject, control principle, control responsibility, control measures and the system construction of macro-control law.[3] ZHENG Shaohua et al consider that the study on macro-control law must start with its theoretical premise, to define applicable boundary

1 See *Bill on Enacting 'Macro-Control Law of the People's Republic of China'* put forward by part of deputies to the National People's Congress in the Fourth Session of the Ninth National People's Congress, published in *Study on Economic Law* (edited by YANG Zixuan), Volume 2, Peking University Press, 2001.

2 WU Zhipan: *'Four-Color Theorem' of Financial Law, Financial Law Forum*, Issue 12, 2000.

3 HOU Zuoqian and PAN Aiye: *Reflection on Several Basic Problems about Macro-Control Law, Law Science Magazine*, Issue 1, 2005.

of theory, and to seek effective study methods. In the macro-control law, its main theoretical premise is the definition of macro-control, formation of market mechanism, modern governmental administration, modern social conflict and solution, and modernization and globalization.[1] It is well known that globalization is global integration-centered in economic globalization, of the economy, ecology, politics and culture.[2] At present, globalization is not any more a trend or theory concept but peculiarity of objective institutions in the world, and condition or situation specified for us. For this reason, each and every national state is one state in the course of globalization, and each and every individual one specified in the globalization, and in the woven network of globalization. In the context of globalization, to change research ideas and update research contents, in the period ahead, has become a question needed to be resolved in the study on China's macro-control law. As for research contents, first, it is necessary to, based on study on existing concrete systems of macro-control system, lay more emphasis on study on basic theory of macro-control law; not to just be satisfied with making explanatory note on existing concrete macro-control system, but to take these systems as case to abstract and extract most general and essential concept, category and rule—an inevitable path to set up basic theory of macro-control law; second, it is necessary to, from a comprehensive, systemic perspective, study the adjusting objects of macro-control law; to be focused on not just controllers but the controlled, not just right of controllers but that of the controlled, not just analysis of static relations of macro control but exact grasp of dynamic movement of macro-control relationship; third, it is necessary to study on rules of macro-control legislation, especially possibility, specific timing and implementation path to formulate macro-control law; fourth, it is necessary to pay attention to studying on framework and specific content

1 ZHENG Shaohua and WU Xiaohui: *Discussion on Premise and Method of Theory of Macro-Control Law, Oriental Law*, Issue 2, 2008.

2 ZHOU Yongkun: *Globalization and Revolution of Mode of Law Thinking, Law Science*, Issue 11, 1999.

of macro-control law; fifth, it is necessary to implement macro-control law, especially the enforcement and the judicial of macro-control law; and sixth, it is necessary to pay attention to studying the internationalization of macro-control law.[1] For science of economic law, there is still a long way to go for studies on the macro-control law.

1 HU Guangzhi: *Study on Macro-Control Law and Its Prospect, Journal of Chongqing University* (*Social Sciences Edition*), Issue 5, 2008.

Chapter 19

The Thriving Environmental Law in the Development of Science

1. The Rapid Transformation of Environmental Law in the Transitional Period of Market Economy

1.1 The establishment of market economy and development of environmental law

In June 1992, the United Nations Conference on Environment and Development was held and legal documents of *Rio Declaration on Environment and Development, Agenda 21, United Nations Framework Convention on Climate Change, United Nations Convention to Combat Desertification* and the *Statement of Forest Principles* were adopted, which confirmed the legal status of sustainable development. After the Conference, China issued action programs of *Environmental Action Plan of China 1991-2000, China's Agenda 21* etc. In that October, the 14th National Congress of CPC clearly put forward that "our goal of economic reform is to establish socialist market economy"; "China adopts socialist market economy" was clearly stated in the *Constitution* revised in March, 1993. In September 1997, "to further extend socialist democracy, improve socialist legal system in order to build a socialist country under the rule of law" was put forward in the report of the 15th National Congress of the CPC, in which the basic strategy of law-based governance was officially presented. The strategy was adopted by the *Constitution* revised in 1999. From then on, market economy, sustainable development together with governance under the rule of law started affecting the mode and way of development of environmental law China.

The National People's Congress set up Environmental Protection Commission[1] in 1993 under the request of sustainable development and market economy, which enforced work of repeal, reform and legislation of environmental laws and led the legal system of environmental laws into rapid development. In response to the demand of sustainable development, China issued programs of *Environmental Action Plan of China 1991—2000, China's Agenda 21*, etc., in which a sustainable environmental law system was put forward and environmental legislation was listed as a new and prior project plan. During this period of time, China promulgated the *Regulations of the People's Republic of China on Nature Reserves* in September 1994, the *Interim Regulations on the Prevention and Control of Water Pollution in the Huaihe River Valley* in August 1995, revised the *Atmospheric Pollution Prevention and Control Law of the People's Republic of China* in August 1995, promulgated *Law on the Prevention and Control of Environment Pollution Caused by Solid Wastes* in October 1995, revised the *Law on the Prevention and Control of Water Pollution* in May 1996, the *Mineral Resources Law of the People's Republic of China* in August 1996, promulgated the *Regulations of the People's Republic of China on Wild Plants Protection* in September 1996, and the *Law of the People's Republic of China on Prevention and Control of Pollution from Environmental Noise* in October 1996. Especially in the *Criminal Law of the People's Republic of China* revised in March 1997, the "crime of violating the protection of environment and resources" was added, making a great breakthrough in environmental crime legislation mode. In order to implement the strategy of sustainable development in the economic construction

1 Later renamed as the NPC Environment Protection and Resources Conservation Committee. Also there's a similar committee in CPPCC.

and social development in China, *Decision of the State Council on Several Issues Concerning Environmental Protection* was adopted by the State Council in August 1996, which set a medium term goal and made a systematic arrangement of the environmental protection in China.

During this period of time, because of the new guiding ideology and developing system, research of environmental law entered into an active stage, when the theory, system and mechanism of sustainable development as well as drawing from foreign mature environmental legislation and their systems became hotspots of researches. Representative books and articles like *Basic Theory of Environmental Law*, *Integration of Environmental Law and Natural Resources Law* promoted the innovation of basic theories of environmental law in China; *Introduction to American Environmental Law*, *Introduction to Japanese Environmental Law*, *European Environmental Law*, as well as the *Russian Ecological Law* filled the gaps in relevant nations in their national environmental law research, while *Guide to International Environmental Law* and *International Environmental Law* filled the gaps of the international environmental law research.

The social and economic development as well as that of the legal system construction after the establishment of market economy provided an opportunity for the development of environmental law in China. And after that, with joint efforts from the academic circle of Chinese environmental law, the Chinese environmental law system was generally established, which not only adapted to the reality of China in line with the international trend, but also met requirements of practice with profound theoretical background. [1]The development of environmental law in China showed obvious characteristics of the times. First, sustainable development as the terminal value of the environmental law has deeply affected the researching mode of environmental law in China, which not only put emphasis on the integrative research of environmental damage and prevention

1 QU Geping: "Preface", ZHAO Guoqing: *Selection of Occidental Environmental Law*. China University of Political Science and Law Press, 2000.

of environmental pollution, but also focused on that of environmental protection and resource conservation; not only emphasized the development, utilization and protection of environmental resources, but also the combined researches on environmental protection laws and its political, economic and social backgrounds. Second, sustainable development as a guide for the research of environmental law led to strengthening the research of legislative system and legal system. Third, with the expanding and deepening international exchanges in the field of environmental law, the popular international ideas like behavior control, scientific use, environmental culture, environmental ethics[1] had a relatively great impact on the construction of environmental legal system and environment law research in China and the idea of environmental democracy and public participation were increasingly affecting the development of environmental law in China. During this period of time, environmental laws in China were fully integrating with the construction of the global environmental law, while China's environmental law ascended the world's forest of environmental law for its great researching power and substantial fruits.

1.2 Major theoretical problems in transformation of environmental law

The guiding ideology and central task of the environmental law in China between the United Nations Conference on Environment and Development (UNCED) and its entering the WTO was to strengthen the macro management, regulate micro behaviors, consolidate the achievements of the reform of the socialist market economy system and guarantee the reform and opening up[2] to promote the sustainable development of economy, society and the environmental protection. The transformation of environmental law in China was caused in fact by the clear guiding ideology and central task, the updated understanding of relationship between man and nature and the implant of concept of sustainable

1 Sean Coyle and Karen Morrow, *The Philosophical Foundations of Environmental Law*, Port-land, Hart Publishing, p.3.

2 LI Lin: "Major Legislation Experience of China in 30 Year's Reform and Opening up", http://www.iolaw.org.cn, September 5, 2008.

development as well as new research methods and sources of theories of environmental law. And the transformation was realized successfully for its continuous achievements of related research on major theoretical issues.

About the public interest of environmental law. The classic view in our legal community is law is a tool, made or approved by the ruling class to protect its entire will and common interests and repress against the ruled class[1]. On the basis of this view, traditional Chinese view in legal community proposed that law had only class nature while served no public interest. Scholars of environmental law analyzed in depth whether it served public interest from the respect of the nature and characteristics of environmental law. The factual premise commonly known and universally accepted by such scholars is that environmental factors of air, water, forests and others are open and therefore ecological degradation is harmful to people and property of any class; while on the contrary, to improve the environment benefits everyone, so the legal measures for environmental protection embody the environmental interest attributed to the public.[2] Besides, to ease the class contradictions, "smart" bourgeois would consider more about the environmental welfare of the proletariat in the legislation. Especially in China, people are the ruling class, accounting for the majority of the population, and to protect their environmental rights in environmental law actually reflects public interest[3]. In the *Rio Declaration on Environment and Development* of 1992, to protect the environment for interests of present and future generations, creating conditions for full participation of all nations was claimed, and it confirmed the public interest of national and international environmental protection. The environmental protection for public interest must be guaranteed by the law, while the meaning and effect of guaranteeing the law for environmental protection are in line with the public interest. With the ongoing practice of environmental

1 *The Collected Works of Lenin*, vol 13. People's Publishing House, 1996, p.304.

2 Marie-Louise Larsson, *The Law of Environmental Damage*, Stockholm, Kluwer Law International, 1999, p.403.

3 CAI Shouqiu, *A Textbook of Environmental Law*. Law Press China, 1995, p.29.

legislation and the deepening research of environmental law, nature of public interest of environmental law has been widely recognized gradually.[1]

About the objects to adjust in environmental law. Article one of *Environmental Protection Law of the People's Republic of China* regulates as "This Law is developed for the purposes of protecting and improving living environment and the ecological environment, preventing and controlling pollution and other public nuisances, safeguarding public health...", on which some scholars of environmental law pointed out that environmental law adjusted not only the interpersonal relations, but also the relationship between human and the environment. While other scholars opposed that the law was a regulator of social relationships made by human, which only reflected the people's will, and adjusted interests among people. Since the environment had no expression of intent, a social relationship between human and the environment could never be formed. Environment belonged to humanity, and therefore the relationship between human and the environment was still social relationship between people in the legal sense. The former scholars continued to contend that the environment included in the adjustment of law was social environment, and its relationship with people was essentially a social relationship; in legal relationship, human was the subject, and the environment was the object, so the relationship between human and the environment was that between the subject and object, which was also a legal relationship. Scholars holding the compromised opinion between those two diametrically opposed views promoted that Marxism law did not assert law could only adjust social relationships, so there's no reason to argue whether that relationship between human and the environment was social or not. For environment law adjusts behaviors of human to human and the environment, and in order to avoid disputes, it's better to study the regulated objects in environmental law from the perspective of behavior.

About the construction of legal system under sustainable development. After

1 CAI Shouqiu, *A Textbook of Environmental Law*. Law Press China, 1995, p.29.

the United Nations Conference on Environment and Development (UNCED) in 1992, concept of sustainable development has been deeply rooted in people's mind, and the construction of environmental legal system promoting sustainable economic and social development has become the focus of society and hotspot of research within the environmental law circle; as the unique guidelines for construction of environmental legal system in an era of sustainable development, the environmental law circle universally holds that sustainable development is the fundamental principle of international and national environmental law. But some mainstream scholars of environmental law believe that the basic principles of environmental law should be relatively clear and workable guidelines, which is applicable and justiciable, while sustainable development lacks them, so it should not be a basic principle. Because sustainable development could be overall, abstract and guiding, it can only be the terminal value of environmental law. Because the intra-generational and intergenerational equity is the standard recognized by the international environmental law for judging the realization of sustainable development, some scholars suggested that intra-generational and intergenerational equity should be regarded as the principle guiding the construction of environmental legal system in China.

About the legal adjustment in marketization of environmental protection. In a society of market economy, only through the combination of law of environmental protection and market mechanisms, making environmental protection professional, industrial and market-oriented, can the initiative of all walks of life be activated in environmental protection[1], which then could partly overcome the tragedy of the commons.[2] Marketization of environmental protection leads to redistribution of rights (and interests) among the government, enterprises providing environmental service and objects being served. And the environmental law circle generally agrees that its content should include

1 ZHAO Guanliang, "*Adhering to Sustainable Development*", *China Environment News*, Issue 1, May 11, 2002.

2 Amy Sinden, *The Tragedy of the Commons and the Myth of a Private Property Solution,* 78U. Colo. L. Rev. 533 (2007).

that: first, means of regulation of the government should be market-oriented, stripping the duties and rights essentially belonging to adjustment scope of the market. For example, to transfer local environmental protection and sanitation keeping departments in levels of governments to market players which are independent accounting, while the relationship between the government and the related companies converted to the regulating and the regulated, the subsidizing and the subsidized. Second, environmental protection and sanitation keeping departments in levels of governments should carry out a full range of marketing services, and their revenue come from government subsidies, fees from served clients and national preferential economic policies, who run completely following the market rules. Third, the burden on enterprises and residents should not be significantly increased, or the costs which should be born by the government as subsidies cannot be passed on to residents and enterprises. Investors, investment direction and diversified mode of environmental protection are the core features of marketization of the environmental protection, for which market-oriented modes of commissioned processing, joint treatment as well as the sulfur dioxide and water pollutant emissions right trading need to be developed, thus flexibly reflecting the requirements of the principle of "polluter pays".

About the exploring of comprehensive and long-term mechanism of regional environmental protection. In order to achieve the emission standards as soon as possible, the state implemented the "Zero" Action to shut down major polluting enterprises in the Huaihe River Valley and Taihu Lake Basin in 1997 and 1998 respectively. The Action did achieve some results in a short time: the annual average concentration of COD dropped by 26.7% in the main rivers entering Taihu Lake in 1998 than the year before.[1] However, there's a powerful pollution rebound shortly after that. Facts proved that special law enforcement with huge investment is generally a failure. The heavy lessons forced China to explore a long-term policy design, which should consider factors of economy, society and environment

1 HUANG Wenyu, YANG Guishan and XU Pengzhu: "Analysis of Environmental Effects of 'Zero' Actions in Taihu Basin". *Journal of Lake Sciences*, 2002, (1).

comprehensively. [1]After the year 1998, when the Yangtze River floods happened in the whole basin, in order to strengthen the ecological construction, China immediately initiated activities of restoring farmland to forestry in upstream of the Yangtze River, the middle and upper reaches of the Yellow River, the Northeast China and Inner Mongolia etc. To protect the enthusiasm of farmers in their restoring farmland to forests in the long run, the State Council put forward the comprehensive measures of "restoring farmland to forest, closing hillsides for afforestation, replacing aid by food and implementing individual contracting" in 1999, and preliminarily regulated that farmers would directly enjoy money for restoring farmland to forest and food subsidies for 8 years.

About the administrative handling of environment related civil disputes. Before 1994, most environmental laws stated the resolving mechanism of the "xingzheng tiaochu" of civil dispute. Some scholars believed that "xingzheng tiaochu" was the abbreviation for "environmental administrative investigation and handling";[2] while some held that it was that of "environmental administrative mediation and handling".[3] The difference in understanding led to different application of the law. In administrative mediation, parties cannot bring an administrative lawsuit, which is of no objection, but environmental law experts have different views on whether parties could loge an administrative lawsuit when refusing to accept the result of administrative handling. In 1992, the Legislative Affairs Commission of the Standing Committee of the National People's Congress replied to the state environmental protection department that, "according to the request of the parties, any party who refuses to accept the liability and compensation for damage caused by environmental pollution may lodge a lawsuit to the people's court. But this is only a civil dispute between the parties and an administrative lawsuit cannot be

1 LI Yan, "Little Achieved in Fight against Pollution by Shutting Down Enterprise Polluters in Taihu Lake Basin for 16 Years", *The Beijing News*, June 11, 2007.

2 JIN Ruilin, *Environmental Law.* Peking University Press, 1994, p.192.

3 CAI Shouqiu, *Environmental Administrative Enforcement of Law and Environmental Administrative Lawsuit.* Wuhan University Press, 1992, p.205.

made with administrative department of environmental protection who made the decisions as the defendant." However, some scholars of environmental studies pointed out that the Legislative Affairs Commission of the Standing Committee of the National People's Congress does not represent the Standing Committee of the National People's Congress, therefore the explanation is not legally binding. In order to solve this problem ultimately, the "*huanjing xingzheng tiaochu*" was changed into "environmental administrative mediation and handling" in the *Law on the Prevention and Control of Environment Pollution Caused by Solid Wastes* enacted in 1995 and other environment related laws enacted later.

2. The Ongoing Thriving Environmental Law under the Guidance of Scientific Development Outlook

2.2 The Prosperous Environmental Legislation and the Ongoing Thriving Environmental Law

China's entry into WTO on December 11, 2001 facilitated Chinese Environmental Law to expand its research field and academic insight in an economically globalized world. In August, 2003, the adopted *Administrative Permission Law* by the Standing Committee of National People's Congress requested the "reduction of items of administrative permission, standardization of the modes of administrative permission and reform of the means of administrative permission". And subsequently, the National Administrative Department of Environment Protection launched a special abolishing campaign of administrative permission by conforming to the request. Early in the 21st century, environmental resources have already become the bottleneck hindering the further development of our national economy and society.[1] In October, 2003, with a comprehensive observation and analysis of the then current situation, as well as a timely prediction of coming changes, the third plenary meeting of the sixteenth National People's Congress of CPC clearly put forward that "we should put people

1 David Hunter, James Salzman & Durrwood Zaelke, *International Environmental Law and Policy*, Third Edition, New York, Foundation Press, 2007, pp.2-3.

first, form such an outlook characterized with comprehensive, coordinated and sustainable development, and strive to achieve an all-round development of our economy, society and people". In October, 2005, the fifth plenary meeting of the sixteenth National People's Congress furthered the goal of establishing a resource-conserving and environment-friendly society. In November, 2005, in the aftermath of the accident of the massive pollution of Songhua River, the State Council immediately issued *The State Council's Decision on Implementing Scientific Outlook on Development and Strengthening Environmental Protection*, which streamlined the goal of establishing an environment-friendly society into the specific task of system construction, and demanded "to carry forward environmental cultures, and advocate ecological civilizations". Since then, as the standards measuring whether or not our economy and society is undergoing a scientific development, and if it's true, then whether or not it's harmonious, scientific development, ecological civilization, resource conservation and friendly environment are the great achievements of learning from the foreign advanced development concepts by our government.[1] Certainly, such important ideas as scientific development, ecological civilization, resource conservation and friendly environment not only act as the theoretical sources of the environmental law study, but also as the nourishing nutrient making the environmental law theory prosperous.

In such a period, Chinese Environmental Law, just like the construction of Chinese economy and environmental system, laid equal emphasis on the quantity and quality of the achievements of the environmental law research. From 2002 to 2008, the number of theses published in periodicals of CSSI concerning the environmental law research was respectively 92, 77, 115, 128, 170, 210 and 153. Among others, both the quantity and quality of the achievements of the environmental law research saw a large-scale increase since the Scientific

1 The Research Room of Lecturers of the Beijing Municipal Committee of the CPC: "Concentrated Reflection of the World View and Methodology That Guide Development", *People's Daily*, June 20, 2007.

Development Outlook was put forward by the Central Government of the CPC. All in all, the paradigm of studying the environmental law that learns lessons from the international experience, takes international practice as reference, and embodies the Chinese characteristics and national conditions began to take shape. A lot of works have given their conclusion and added innovation in terms of the basic theories of China's environmental law, such as *Principle of Ecological Law* (CAO Deming, People's Publishing House, 2002), *Philosophy of Law in Ecology*, (ZHENG Shaohua, China Legal Publishing House, 2002) *Innovation and Improvement of Market Economy and Our National Environmental Law System* (CHANG Jiwen, China Environmental Science Press, version 2006), *Law of Animal Welfare: Contrast between China and EU* (CHANG Jiwen, China Environmental Science Press, version 2006). Many works like *Special Statement on Comparative Environmental Law* (XIAO Jianming, OUYANG Guangming, LING Fanghui, China Environmental Science Press, 2004) have made up the blank of the systematic study of comparative environmental law. According to the statistics made by the Environment and Resource Law Study Center of the Peking University, from 1998 to 2008, there are 18 influential scholars in the fields of China's environmental law including CAI Shouqiu, WANG Xi, LV Zhongmei, WANG Canfa, ZHOU Ke, WANG Jing, CAO Mingde, and CHANG Jiwen.[1]

As for the education of environmental law, in 1994, the Academic Degree Committee of the State Council approved the setting of China's first doctorate program in environmental law by the Peking University. Straight after that, the Environmental Law Research Institute of Wuhan University was also granted the doctorate program in environmental law. In 1996, environment and resource law was credited as the B-class discipline, which uplifted the rank of this disciple into the top ten law majors like the civil law and administrative law. By the end of 2007, there have been 63 qualified institutions entitled to enroll postgraduates of

1 See also the website of Resources, Energy & Environmental Law Institute, Peking University: http://envilaw.pkulaws.com, latest visiting date: September 4, 2009.

environmental law major, as well as over ten to enroll doctors of environmental major.

During this period, the development of China's environment law were characterized with such features as: Firstly, its study not only focused on the demands of domestic livelihood, but also of environment treaty and international trading rules, which embodied its uniform, systematic, deep, people-oriented and international features. One conspicuous phenomenon at this stage is that China's environmental law study didn't focus only on foreign environmental law. Adhering to China's basic conditions, and properly drawing lessons and referring to the foreign environmental legislation and results of academic research have become the mainstream trend of environmental law study. Advanced in guiding thoughts, and clear in target and ideas is the second feature. At this stage, with scientific development, resource conservation, friendly environment, harmony between man and nature and other advanced ideas as its guiding principle, China's environmental law was uplifted to one new height after another upon every other period of time. The third feature is to continuously propose new ideas with respect to the basic principles of environment protection and legal systems. For instance, the idea putting environment first proposed by some scholars was partly adopted by *The State Council's Decision on Implementing Scientific Outlook on Development and Strengthening Environmental Protection*. The fourth feature is to carry forward research work in terms of issues arising from internationalized market economy and rule of environmental law, among which are the establishment of long-term, effective and emergent environment protection mechanism, the diversified investment and money-raising in environment protection, and comprehensive policy in environment economy. The fifth is to continuously advocate environment democracy and promote the realization of a democratic and people-oriented environment legislation.[1] Apart from that, the involved subject of

1 BU Xuelin: "New Breakthroughs in the Construction of Environmental Law", *China Environmental News*, December 28, 2007.

the study also included such issues as the cultivation of environment culture.

However, we still face an austere environmental situation and increasing international pressure. So the task of developing the rule of environmental law and studying the environmental law remains to be daunting and formidable. Under the demands of the Scientific Development Outlook, for some period both at present and in the future, the work of developing our national environmental law should take heeds to the following issues: (1) As for the guiding thought, new and feasible suggestions should be put forward for the sake of a comprehensive and scientific social development in China by conforming to the demands of Scientific Development Outlook, ecological civilization, harmonious nature and socialist rule of law, focusing on the environment protection and actualities of economic and social development and through the innovation and improvement in systems, institutions and mechanisms. (2) With respect to the research subject, in future, we should complete the pivot of key research subject on the protection of urban environment to the protection of both urban and rural environment, to the protection of citizens' environment rights and interests in both rural and urban areas, to the performance of international environment obligations and the specific implementation of domestic environment law, to the government protection and people's participation, and to the administrative regulation and judicial supervision. (3) As for the research contents, we should not only value the leading role of the government, but also motivate the function of public participation and release the potential of the market mechanism; not only study the environment issue of one single project and pay attention to the issues of regional environment pollution and ecological degradation, but also as a whole study both the domestic measures for environment protection and the international cooperation and coordination; not only study the issues of environment pollution and ecological degradation, but also the issues of prevention of environment risk and its safety guarantee; not only study the traditional issues in environmental law such as ecological protection, pollution prevention and management, as well as the conversion of resources, but also the new emerging issues in environmental law such as the structure of green industry, the mode of green production and green consumption, as well as the green transaction and copyright. (4) With regards to the research methods, to develop environmental law, we should not only conduct our study with an all-round and systematic approach, but also be clear-headed in research, as well as find out the key and breakthrough points in overcoming the regional, industrial, departmental and western protectionism, and promoting the system construction of public participation and social supervision; not only embody the internationally homogeneous-tending characteristics of the study in international law, but also refer to China's national conditions and characteristics.

2.2 The study into major theoretical issues of the thriving environmental law

The following issues have become the guiding thought and central task of environmental law since China entered the WTO: consolidating and developing the system and mechanism of trade internationalization and global environmental protection; implementing the requirement of the scientific outlook on development; developing ecological civilization and building an environment-friendly and resource-conserving society. The research of China's environmental law has been developed greatly by embracing such guiding thought and central task.

About integrating WTO rules with China's environmental law. WTO's requirements on China's reform on environmental law focus on trade in goods and in service, which mainly include most-favored-nation treatment and national treatment, unified implementation and transparency, free trade and fair competition, and administrative remedy and judicial review, etc. Because the old environmental law has been printed with the trace of planned economy and economy transformation, the environmental law field reckons that the innovation and reform of the environmental law system in China should meet the following special requirements: building a market-oriented control system of environmental law, opening the environmental protection market step by step in accordance with promises; dealing appropriately with the transparent relations among the Party's documents, the Party and government's internal regulations and environmental laws; combining the legislation and execution of national environmental law; and surmounting local protectionism. Facts have demonstrated that entering WTO can not only prevent the transfer of environmental pollution and ecological damage, but also prevent the over-developing of China's primary resource products and defuse international trade disputes. What's more, entering WTO is good for establishing a sound environmental protection market, developing environmental protection industry and speeding up the reform of the system of environmental administration and judicature.[1]

About establishing environmental emergency laws. The occurrence of SARS and especially the Songhua River heavy pollution made China profoundly realize the importance of strengthening the studying and establishing of environmental emergency laws. In the aspect of comprehensive law, *The Law on Response to Emergencies* in 2007 stressed the importance of preserving environmental safety and stipulated basic systems relating to the identification, elimination and emergency handling of environmental hidden danger. In the aspect of specialized law, currently formulated or modified laws such as *Radioactive Pollution Control Act*, *Law on the Prevention and Control of Environment Pollution Caused by Solid Wastes* and *Law on the Prevention and Control of Water Pollution* made specific stipulations about contingency reserve, emergency disposal and recovery after event. In the aspect of administrative law, the *National General Contingency Plans for Public Emergency* that was published in 2005 explicitly incorporated the destruction of ecological environment into national public emergencies. In the aspect of administration regulations, *The National Contingency Plans for Environmental Emergency* in 2006 refined the following contents: the classification and grading of environmental pollution events, emergency response principles, the commanding and obligations of organizations, prevention and early warning, emergency response, as well as emergency security and after-treatment,

1 CHANG Jiwen: "WTO and the Innovation and Improvement of China's Environmental Law System", *Economic Law and Labor Law*, 2002, (7).

etc. It shows that China's environmental emergency law is systematic, graded, explicit and operable.[1]

About providing legal safeguard to an environment-friendly and resource-conserving society. In the era of rule by law, the building of an environment-friendly and resource-conserving society should begin with the system innovation and improvement in three aspects: production mode, life style and consumption mode. The current environmental legislation does not meet the demand of an environment-friendly and resource-conserving society in terms of system, aim, basis, application scope, concrete content and consistency. Therefore, professionals in the field of environment and law believe that the following major issues should be dealt with from the aspects of innovation and improvement of legal system: the cultivation of environmental culture, the guarantee of environmental information rights, the democratic supervision and orderly participation of the public, the set up of environmental property right system, the establishment of market access and policy-supporting system, making scientific compound decision and market intervention and encouraging technical support and technical transformation, etc.[2]

About cultivating ecological civilization legislation. Unguided use and nonstandard privatization of public land will undoubtedly lead to the degradation of ecological environment and decline of regional civilization. That's why the government should use its public rights to strengthen the construction of environmental culture[3] and to cultivate concept, thinking mode, decision-making model, production mode and life styles that are environment-friendly and resource-conserving.[4] In 2005, for the first time, *The State Council's*

1 CHANG Jiwen: "Earthquake Relief Work and the Establishment of China's Environmental Emergency Laws", *Global Law Review*, 2008, (3).

2 MA Kai: "Developing Circular Economy and Building an Environment-friendly and Resource-conserving Society", *Qiushi Journal*, 2005, (16).

3 GU Lianhong: "From Environmental Crisis to National Crisis", *Chinese Journal of Plant Ecology*, 2007, (3).

4 PAN Yue: "Socialist Ecological Civilization", *Study Times*, September 27, 2006.

Decision on Implementing Scientific Outlook on Development and Strengthening Environmental Protection uplifted the construction of environmental culture to the level of advocating ecological civilization and made it the precondition of strengthening the rule of environmental law. The report of the Seventeenth Congress of the CPC made further contribution to this. Other than restating the thought of ecological civilization, the report also proposed to "build ecological civilization, develop an industrial structure, a growth pattern and a consumption model that are dedicated to saving energy resources and preserving ecological environment", and to "firmly cultivate the awareness of conservation in the whole society". Thus, the ecological civilization would be shifted from pure consumption civilization to a comprehensive civilization that is conducive to environment and resources protection and is supported by the system of production, decision-making and consumption. The report proposed to carry out the requirement of ecological civilization construction all the way into industrial structure and growth pattern. This showed that advanced culture played a guiding role in the rule of environmental law.

About the application of law in regional restricted approval. The one-to-one way of law enforcement to specific projects can't change regional local protectionism, therefore some scholars put forward that China should learn from US Environmental Protection Agency's experience of giving no approval at regional levels to establish regional and industrial law enforcement systems. In January, 2007, national environmental protection administration circulated notices of criticism on 82 projects that seriously violated both the environmental impact assessment and the "three synchronizations" system in fields such as steel, electricity and metallurgy. For the first time, the administration gave the sanction of regional restricted approval to 4 power enterprises including China Guodian Corporation in such 4 cities as Tangshan, Lvliang, Laiwu and Liupanshui according to provisions in the Articles 13th and 21st of *The State Council's Decision on Implementing Scientific Outlook on Development and Strengthening Environmental Protection*. This effectively restrained the blind expansion of high-pollution industries. Compared with project law enforcement, regional law enforcement and industrial law enforcement are closer to the base line of local protectionism and are more difficult to be implemented. Some local governments declared that the provisions of Articles 13th and 21st of *The State Council's Decision on Implementing Scientific Outlook on Development and Strengthening Environmental Protection* are in lack of enforceability for the basis of punishment set by national environmental protection administration is not sufficient. Under this circumstance, the *Law on the Prevention and Control of Water Pollution* modified in 2008 legalized regional restricted approval, stipulating that "in regions where the total emission of key water pollutants exceeds the control quota, related administrative departments of environmental protection should stop examining and approving environmental impact assessment documents to new construction projects that will discharge key water pollutants".

About the innovation of the environmental damage compensation system. The problem of an incomplete environmental damage compensation system has always been troubling the judicial circle. Other than continuously sticking to the principle of no-fault liability, the *Law on the Prevention and Control of Water Pollution* modified in 2008 also made a few innovations. First, in terms of damage suit, the polluter should take the burden of proof to prove that there is no causal relationship between its, his or her behaviors and the damages by referring to the exemptions that are stipulated by law. Second, if the damage is done on purpose by the victim, the polluter does not take the responsibilities. If the damage is caused for the gross negligence of the victim, liability for damage of the polluter can be reduced. Thus, the duty of supervising and the liability for damage of pollution emission firms are strengthened. Third, if the damage is done on purpose or for negligence by a third party, the polluter has the right to claim compensation from the third party after it/he/she assumed the compensation liability. The three innovations mark a breakthrough of the traditional civil law and civil procedural law. They also show the government's well intention to overcome local protectionism, protect the vulnerable and boost social harmony.

About the theory of environmental rights. Environmental rights have been an academic hotspot in the research process of environmental law in China.[1] There are mainly four viewpoints in the study of environmental rights. The first viewpoint holds that the environmental right is a new right of the public law that aims to resolve environmental issues. It's a right that is set up in the environmental law which possesses the nature of social law. Its goal is to protect the environment from being polluted and damaged and therefore public welfare becomes the essential attribute of the right. The second viewpoint holds that the attribute of environmental rights is closely related to human rights, natural rights, moral rights, right of personality and property right. The environmental right is a kind of customary rights in nature. The third viewpoint holds that environmental rights combine the attribute of three rights—ecological right, economical right and spiritual right into one. The fourth viewpoint holds that the environmental right is a kind of human rights in nature. It's a right that mankind as a group possesses towards the environment as a whole. It cannot be separated from mankind and can only be obtained through the active fulfilling of obligations by each subject of duty.[2] At present, there is no obvious embodiment of the environmental right system for no dominant viewpoint stands out in the study into environmental rights and current viewpoints have not been accepted by fields except for the environment protection law field in China's judicial circle. But still, the study of environmental rights possesses great theoretic significance for it can help to set the basic category of environmental protection law and build and perfect the theoretical system of environmental protection law.

1 For example, according to the statistics in 2008, over 200 papers on environmental rights have been published since 1982 and 4 monographs about environmental rights have been published since 2003. See ZHANG Wenxian, HUANG Wenyi: *A Report on the Development of Philosophy and Social Science in Chinese Universities· Legal Science (1978-2008)*, Guilin: Guangxi Normal University Press, 2008, p.223.

2 The induction of the four viewpoints are quoted from ZHANG Wenxian, HUANG Wenyi: *A Report on the Development of Philosophy and Social Science in Chinese Universities· Lagal Science (1978-2008)*, Guangxi Normal University Press, 2008, p.223.

What's more, in the same stage of the period, the circle of environmental protection law in China also put forward such academic hot topics as regional ecological compensation[1], environment public interests litigation[2] and animal welfare protection[3]. Although these topics lead to no final conclusions, they possess great theoretical and practical significance in enriching China's environmental protection law theory and improving the concept of environmental legislation.

By looking at the research course, we can see that since 1990s, the circle of environmental law in China has conducted preliminary studies into the nature and basis of environmental law. At the same time, the issue of environmental rights became the research hotspot, together with the publishment of a great number of related research papers and monographs. Since 2000, there have been influential academic debates in the circle of environmental law in China. Especially when CAI Shouqiu put forward in 2001 that environmental law can adjust the relationship of human and the nature, heated discussions were aroused and a lot of monographs on this viewpoint were published. Since 2003, a new viewpoint that holds obligation constitutes the basis of environmental law gradually formed and became the focus issue of academic debate.[4] What's more, there showed a growing diversity in research methods in the research of environmental law. In the early stage of the research of environmental law, scholars mainly use the research methods of ecology and environmental economics to analyze problems concerning the environment and the environmental system to elaborate basic theories of environmental law. With the spread of ecological ethics and

---

1 For example: DU Qun: "The Legal Relation of Ecological Compensation and Its Current Situation and Problems", *Modern Law Science*, 2005, Issue 3.

2 For example: YE Yongfei: "On Environmental Public Interest Litigation", *China Legal Science*, 2004, Issue 5.

3 For example: CHANG Jiwen: *Animal Welfare Law: A Comparison Between China and EU*, Beijing: China Environmental Science Press, 2006.

4 XU Xiangming, et al: "30 Years of the Study of Environmental Law: Retrospect and Prospect", *Legal Forum*, 2008, Issue 6.

ecological philosophy in China, the study of environmental law absorbs the theoretical research achievements of these disciplines and hence gives more reasonable judgment about environmental problems. At present, the study of environmental law presents the following overall features. First, environmental ethics have become an important part of the epistemology of environmental law. Second, the environmental law theory which is marked by the adjustment of relationship between human and the natural environment have basically become mature now. Third, the theory of sustainable development has steadily become the guiding thought of environmental law. Fourth, environmental justice, environmental fairness, environmental democracy and environmental rights have become the ideological weapons of environmental law.[1] However, compared with other second-class disciplines of the law, the number of teaching staff and research personnel of environmental law is relatively small, which to some degree affects the quantity and quality of the results of environmental law research.[2] Having a comprehensive look at all kinds of textbooks of the environmental law, we can find that they are almost of the same structure, content, style despite of their assorted varieties. It seems that there is already a consensus about how to compile a textbook and this will lead to the suspicion of lack of innovation.[3] But as a new subject, the environmental law is on its way to completeness and maturity. And the thriving study of environmental law theories is showing stronger academic vitality.[4]

1 CAI Shouqiu: "On the Development of Contemporary Environmental Law", *Studies in Law and Business*, 1998, Issue 3.

2 WANG Jin: "The Current Situation and Problems about the Study of Environmental Law in China", *Science of Law*, 2005, Issue 4.

3 LV Zhongmei: *The Theory of Environmental Law*. Shanghai: Fudan University Press, 2007, p.1.

4 This paragraph is written by YU Shaoxiang.

Chapter 20

Administrative Law in the Process of Governance in Accordance with Law

1. Fundamental Construction of General Theory of Administrative Law

Year 1992 is an important milestone for administrative law. The administrative law before and after 1992 marched forward, broadened its research vision and developed its theoretical achievements against different social ideas, institutional environments and knowledge systems. In 1993, China's administrative law circle carried out an unprecedented discussion on the theoretical basis of administrative law, thus greatly promoting and deepening China's administrative law study development. Such discussion gives arise to a common understanding that the administrative law of "strengthening administration" has been almost consistently criticized in the circle. Since then, China's administrative law (at least theoretically) has totally broken away from the concept of strengthening administration of the Soviet Union and broken free from traditional normative analysis, and started marching toward the development stage of promoting humanism spirits, advocating the rule by law and improving theory system.

1.1 Study of administrative law theoretical basis

As early as in 1983, YING Songnian put forward the research problem on administrative law theoretical basis, [1]until LUO Haocai, YUAN Shuhong and LI Wendong published *Theoretical Basis of Modern Administration LawAdministrative Law–Balance of Rights and Obligations of Administrative Organizations and Private Party* in 1993, China's administrative law set up a series of discussions on theoretical basis of administrative law. Such discussions lasting for nearly 10 years are quite heated and open and display a situation of letting a hundred flowers blossom and a hundred schools of thought contend, and also form several representative schools and theories such as "Balance Theory", "Theory of Controlling Power", "Standard Public Interest Theory", "Service Theory", "Public Power Theory", "Standard Responsibility Theory" and "Theory of Government under Rule of Law". The proposal, confrontation, demonstration and correction of different theories and schools and refinement of basic scope of administrative law and construction of theoretical system by scholars have greatly enhanced the overall research level of China's administrative law and marked that China's administrative law has already broken through traditional normative analysis and is marching toward the development stage of rational thinking. It undoubtedly has extremely important significance to promote "deepening of research on China's administrative law and humanistic spirit."

Specifically speaking, main contributions of such discussions are as follows: (1) Establishing basic categories of administrative law. Some core categories of this subject, including administration, administration power, administrative law relationship, subject of administration, administrative counterpart, act of administration, administration procedure, administration illegal behavior, administrative responsibility, administration relief and judicial review have

1 See *Discussion on Matters of Theoretical Basis of Administrative Law* by YING Songnian, ZHU Weijiu and FANG Yan, *Journal of China University of Political Science and Law,* 1983 Issue 2. This topic is also called "Basic Theory of Administrative Law" and See *Reflection, Consolidation and Status for Different Theory Bases of Administrative Law* by ZHOU Youyong, *carried on Year 1999 Issue No.2 of Law Science*, 1999 Issue 2. The debate concerning the above two calling is also a part of such discussions.

basically taken shape. (2) Updating theoretical system of administrative law. An important mission of administrative law theoretical basis is to provide standpoint for constructing theoretical system of administrative law. Almost all schools of theory claim that scientific theoretical system of administrative law can be constructed based on such discussions. (3) Starting philosophy thinking on administrative law. In the process of studying on administrative law, the scholars have no longer been standing on simple explanation of administrative law norms or focusing on discussing countermeasures. Oppositely, they have consciously explored from philosophy perspective what administrative law is, what the essence of administrative law is, what value orientation of administrative law is, what contents and functions administrative law should have, what perspective and method we should use to study administrative law, institutional building and theoretical system of administrative law as well as what concepts should be used as guide.[1]

1 The theses and works arising from such discussions are too numerous to enumerate. WU Buyun: *Theoretical Basis of Administrative Law – Public Power Theory, carried on Year 1994 Issue No.3 of Law Science*, 1994 Issue 3; CHEN Quansheng: *On Theoretical Basis of Modern Administrative Law, carried on Year 1995 Issue No.5 of Law System and Social Development*, 1995 Issue 5; YANG Jiejun: *Comments and Analysies of Several Viewpoints on Theoretical Basis of Administrative Law*, China Law, 1996 Issue 2; WANG Xixin, SHEN Kui: *Re-discussion on Theoretical Basis of Administrative Law*, China Law, 1996 Issue 4; YE Bifeng: *Study on Theoretical Basis of Administrative Law*, 1997 Issue 5 of *Law Review*; GUO Runsheng, SONG Gongde: *Legal Control of Executive Powers – Balance Theory*, 1997 Issue 6 of *China Law*; PI Chunxie, FENG Jun: *Several Thoughts on Omitting Questions on Balance Theory*, 1997 Issue 12 of *China Law*; SUN Xiaoxia: *Analysis of Theoretical Basis of Departmental Law,* 1997 Issue 10 of *Law*; ZHOU Youyong: *Reflection, Consolidation and Status for Different Theory Bases of Administrative Law*, 1999 Issue 2 of *Law Science* etc. The writing in this part also refers to ZHANG Zhiyuan: *Looking Back and Forward: Analysis of Study on Theoretical Basis of China's Administrative Law,* 2004 Issue 3 of Journal of *Guizhou Police* Officer Vocational College; SHEN Kaiju, WANG Hongjian: *Looking Back and Forward on Study on Theoretical Basis of Contemporary China Administrative Law, carried on Looking Back and Forward on China's Administrative Law – 20 Years of China's Administrative Law Bo'ao Forum & China's Law Institute Administrative Law Study Year 2005 Annual Thesis Collection* compiled by China Administrative Law Institute, China University of Political Science and Law Press in 2006.

In recent years, even though we have not seen many discussions on theoretical basis of administrative law, administrative law scholars continue their abstruse theoretical innovation and efforts. Above all else, YUAN Shuhong and LUO Haocai put forward successively, based on grand vision of "public law", the theory of uniformed public law and theory of "soft law" going beyond administrative law but closely relating to study on theoretical basis of administrative law. [1]This topic study has new starting point and intelligence sources with new academic visions growing.[2]

In a latest article on study on theoretical basis of administrative law of "Never Simple Summary", the author sums up that theoretical basis of administrative law has gradually evolved, as an overall view of administrative law, from a rough and simple concept and opinion (statement and guideline) to systematic and theoretical approach, and later, it tries to open a new window on theory, introduce new intelligence resources and enrich the study on this subject. The dispute over the schools of administrative law theoretical basis will perhaps continue. Till now, this competition has given chances to different schools to improve themselves rather than declaring certain winner. Even though all schools complete systematic work to some extent, their assertions still have room to improve.

1 For "uniform public law", See YUAN Shuhong: *Establishing Uniform Public Law*, 2003 Issue 5 of *China Law;* YUAN Shuhong: *Time Significance of Establishing Uniform Public Law – Answers to Possible Questioning on "Uniform Public Law"*, 2005 Issue 5 of *Modern Law Science*; YUAN Shuhong *Fundamental Theory Framework of Uniform Public Law*, 2007 Issue 4 of *Law Forum*; YUAN Shuhong, SONG Gongde: *Original Theory of Uniform Public Law – An Approach to General Theory of Public Law*, published by China Renmin University Press in 2005. For "soft law" theory, See LUO Haocai et al: *Soft Law and Public Governance*, Peking University Press in 2006; LUO Haocai: *Serious Treatment of Soft Law – General Theory and China's Practice of Soft Law in Public Sphere*, 2006 Issue 2 of *China Law*; JIANG Ming'an: *Emergence and Governance of Soft Law*, 2006 Issue 2 of *China Law*; ZHAI Xiaobo: *Demonstration of "Soft Law" and its Concept – Public Governance as Background*, 2007 Issue 2 of *Law Science*.

2 See SHEN Kui: *Looking Back on Theoretical Basis of Administrative Law – Transition of an Overall View*, 2008 Issue 6 of *Journal of China University of Political Science and Law*.

Putting the discrepancies over different schools aside, it is not difficult to find that different schools have reached many common understandings concerning many matters on administrative law. These common understandings have generated more contributions than discrepancies to administrative law, so that China's administrative law has same or similar basic standpoints for administrative right and it has established the research path which faces up to administrative process, setting and realization of administrative objectives and the role of legal regulations on administrative process. Meanwhile, academic practice of contention of different schools of thoughts in this ongoing discussion will be a valuable asset to administrative law science and also implies a possibility of generating excellent school having dialogue with the world.[1]

1.2 Study on administrative law system

The study on theoretical system of China's administrative law involves many fields such as administration, administrative right, administrative law relationship, subject of administration, administrative act, administrative procedure and administrative litigation, as well as theory categories such as central idea, theoretical basis and basic principle. Sophistication of theoretical system of administrative law reflects the sophistication of administrative law science. Since China's administrative law has recovered, theoretical system of administrative law has, similar to the basic principle of administrative law, also experienced a process of getting separated and independent from constitutional law system and administration science system. Since 1990s, the academic circle has consciously searched and discussed theoretical system of administrative law science. Teaching and research office of administrative law of Department of Law of Peking University and Administrative Law Studies of China Law Society held symposiums with administrative law system as topic respectively in 1991 and 1994 so as to promote in-depth development in this field. One scholar summarized the selections and judgments of the following relationships which were

1 Ibid.

experienced or faced with by theoretical system of China's administrative law science: (1) Administrative law and administrative litigation law, namely, whether we should put administrative litigation law outside administrative law and make it become an independent legal department corresponding to administrative law. The academic circle is still analyzing this issue and by taking "whether administrative law includes administrative litigation law" as the standard, "big administration science system" and "small administration science system" have been respectively formed. (2) General theory and dispersed theory of administrative law: this relationship is relatively simple and people's opinions are unanimous. General theory means the rules and principles universally applicable in all fields of administrative law and dispersed theory means the applications of rules and principles of administrative law in all fields of administration management. (3) Single line system and dual line system: "single line system" means the theoretical system which takes administrative right as mainline and focuses on studying subject of administration and legal adjustment of administrative right operation process. In China, most teaching materials and literatures use single line system; "dual line system" means the theoretical system which takes administrative law relationship as mainline and focuses on studying legal adjustment process of relative people of administrative law relationship and their respective acts. "Single line system" and "dual line system" have their respective advantages in which single line system can draw a clear distinction between the primary and the secondary and highlight the center of national administrative right and the dual line system can fully unfold administrative law relationship and covers more comprehensive research topics. It is perhaps the common direction for administrative law circle to connect basic categories in two systems and establish theoretical system of modern administrative law with inherent uniform logics and Chinese characteristics based on the same theoretical basis. The above three groups of relationships are the most important relationships in theoretical system of China's administrative law. In addition, the scholar also discussed several modes of administrative system such as "system (static) administrative law system and principle (dynamic) administrative law system", "microcosmic administrative law system" and "inner line system and outer line system".[1]

2. Overall Update of Theory of Subject of Administrative Law

2.1 Theory of subject of administration

Subject of administration is an extremely important basic category in China's administrative law, and is not only the core concept of administrative organization law but also the basic question in administrative act, administrative procedure, administrative litigation etc. The definition and creation of subject of administration by western countries include "legal personality of exercising public power and independently bearing legal consequences" whether it uses directly the concept of subject of administration or not.

Based on the investigations of some countries and areas, China's administrative law academic circle learned from French practices to introduce the concept of "subject of administration" in late 1980s and took China's actual conditions into consideration to transform and localize this concept. Through comparative analysis of Chinese and overseas concepts of subject of administration, administrative law scholars specified the real meaning of subject of administration as independent legal personality in administrative law, correctly defined subject of administration in China's administrative law and rationalized the relationship among subject of administration, administrative organization and administrative organization personnel in administrative law so as to form the theory of studying subject of administration in an overall, in-depth and multi-dimensional views. In addition to the definition of subject of administration, other basic contents of theory of subject of administration also include scope and classification of subject of administration, rights and responsibilities of subject of administration and qualifications and confirmation of subject of administration.

---

1 See HU Jianmiao's *Model and Judgment of China's Administrative Law Theoretical System,* 1997 Issue 1 of *China Law*; XIONG Wenzhao: *Looking Back on Tough Past and Looking Forward to Important Tasks – 20 Years' development Process Development Process of New China's Administrative Law.*

The scholars have different definitions of subject of administration but their basic cores are consistent: (1) Subject of administration is an organization instead of an individual. This organization includes national administrative organization and the organization authorized by laws and regulations. (2) Subject of administration is the organization which legally has administrative function and exercises functions in its name. Having administrative function or not is an important standard for defining subject of administration. (3) Subject of administration means the organization which can bear legal liabilities resulting from its acts, mainly represented by the ability to participate in administrative litigation both in its own name and as the defendant herein.[1]

On the other hand, the scholars have reflected on the theory of subject of administration. Some scholars pointed out that by positioning subject of administration as subject of administration management, it would cause conflicts between connotation and denotation of this concept and make the study on the theory of subject of administration narrower and shallower. It is concretely embodied as follows: the angle and scope of study on theory of subject of administration is narrower; it does not facilitate uniform and coordination of administrative organization; it causes conflict between connotation and denotation of concept of subject of administration; it unilaterally emphasizes external management role of administrative functional departments but ignores overall control of subject of administration and public servants. Therefore, in order to enrich the studies on theory of subject of administration in China, real meaning of

1 See *New Theory of Administrative Law* compiled by YING Songnian, China Fangzheng Press, 1998, pp.58-62; LI Xin: *Comparative Study on Theories of China and Foreign Subjects of Administration*, 1999 Issue 1 of Administrative Law Study; LI Jixia: *Brief Analysis of China's Subject of Administration Theory and its Practice Significance*; SHI Youqi, SUN Xue: *On Development of China's Subject of Administration Theory – Perspective from State Administration to Public Administration Organization*, carried on *Looking Back and Forward on China's Administrative Law – 20 Years of China's Administrative Law Bo'ao Forum & China's Law Institute Administrative Law Study Year 2005 Annual Thesis Collection* compiled by China Administrative Law Institute, China University of Political Science and Law Press, 2006.

subject of administration as independent legal personality must be specified and subject of administration be correctly oriented. The relationships among subject of administration, administrative organization and administrative organization personnel in administrative law must be rationalized. By studying the theory of subject of administration in an overall, in-depth and multi-dimensional perspective, studies based on common features of public law and private law and the approach of private law as well as those in static organization should be made; and the theory of subject of administration not only from external role of administrative power but also from interior structure of subject of administration should be improved.[1] Some scholars pointed out that the theory of subject of administration has the following troubles: deficiency in determining defendant qualification in administrative litigation; difficulty in confirming the ownership of entity administrative right and administrative responsibility; failure to get adapted to the big trend from state power to social public power.[2] Also, some scholars took state administration and public administration as models to analyze and compare the theory of subject of administration in two different backgrounds and claimed for transfer from theory of state subject of administration to theory of public subject of administration.[3]

Administrative law scholars don't have in-depth studies on the personnel in administration organization, namely, public servants, and generally describe and introduce the system of public servants from perspective of administration organization, according to the previous Provisional Regulations of State Council on Public Servants and *Law of Public Servants of the People's Republic of China*.

1 See LIU Cuixiao: *Year 1999 China's Law Study Review – Administrative Law Study Review,* 2000 Issue 1 of Chinese Journal of Law.

2 GAO Wenying, LI Linlin: *Looking Back on and Reconstructing Theory of Subject of Administration, carried on Looking Back and Forward on China's Administrative Law – 20 Years of China's Administrative Law Bo'ao Forum & China's Law Institute Administrative Law Study Year 2005 Annual Thesis Collection* compiled by China Administrative Law Institute, published by China University of Political Science and Law Press, 2006.

3 SHI Youqi, SUN Xue: On Development of China's Theory of Subject of Administration – Perspective from State Administration to Public Administration.

There are relatively fewer literatures which study the legal status of public servants and state public function relationship between public servants and the state from administrative law perspective.[1]

2.2 Theory of administrative counterpart

When China's administrative law was initially established in late 1970s, the basic idea of administrative law was to strengthen administrative management and administrative law was deemed to be a law regarding administrative management and was recognized as an effective tool of administrative management. The value orientation of administrative law causes administrative law to focus on subject of administration and its administrative power. As a party subject to control, administrative counterpart doesn't have more research values due to its passive role in legal status. Therefore, there are rare literature works which directly narrate administrative counterpart and even rare studies on its system. Some administrative law scholars once pointed out that "traditional administrative law theory is limited to the study on subject of administration without study on administrative counterpart;...it is only limited to study on administrative act but not acts of administrative counterpart." [2] "Traditional administrative law focuses on mostly administrative right or role of subject of administration but ignores the role of administrative counterpart in administrative process."[3]

With modern administrative law gradually developing from traditional mode of checking administrative power by power to the mode of checking administrative power by due process right of administrative counterpart as well as from earlier

1 See *New Theory of Administrative Law* compiled by YING Songnian, China Fangzheng Press, 1998, pp.96-119; *Administrative Law and Administration Litigation Law* (Edition II) compiled by JIANG Ming'an, pp.149-159; Yang Linhong: Essence of Public Servants, Hualing Press, 2005.

2 ZHANG Huanguang, HU Jianmiao: *Principles of Administrative Law*, Labor Personnel Press, 1989, p.371. Quoted from FANG Shirong: On Relative People of Administration, China University of Political Science and Law Press, 2000, p.2 of Preface.

3 *Administrative Law* compiled by LUO Haocai, Peking University Press, 1996, p.99. Quoted from FANG Shirong: *On Relative People of Administration*, China University of Political Science and Law Press, 2000, p.2.

single order administration to order administration and supply administration of modern welfare country, the administrative acts with traditional power decay such as administrative contracts and administrative guidance are widely used and administrative democracy mobilizing active participation of administrative counterpart are greatly favored. With China's political and economic system reform and legislative administration development, the status of relative people is greatly enhanced and this provides empirical foundations and opportunities for administrative law to study administrative counterpart. In the disputes over basic theories of administrative law in 1990s, "balance theory" emphasized the balance of rights and obligations between administrative organization and relative party and provided an important road to correctly understand administrative counterpart and its legal status. Therefore, there arose China's first literature which systematically studies administrative counterpart during this period, namely, *On Administrative Counterpart* by FANG Shirong, which preliminarily sets up theoretical framework of basic categories of administrative counterpart, discusses and studies various related legal issues such as concept, qualification, type, status, right and act of administrative counterpart, and makes scientific theoretical summary of regular phenomenon. [1] Among the theses of administrative law relating to administrative counterpart published during this period, most authors focused on further discussions on legal status and procedural rights of administrative counterpart. In the theory discussions with public participation recent years, administrative law scholars have fruitfully discussed the rights, procedures and relief of relative people in participating in administration process in administrative acts such as administrative legislation and administrative decision-making.[2]

1 See FANG Shirong: *On Relative People of Administration*, pp.4-6.

2 Recent years, for representative theses on administrative counterpart, see FANG Shirong: *Actss and Validity of Relative People of Administration*, 2000 Issue 1 of Studies in Law and Business; ZHANG Xiaoguang: *Participation Right of Relative People of Administration Administrative inCounterpart in Administration Procedures*, 2000 Issue 3 of Study on Administrative Law; WANG Xixin: *Study on Procedural Rights of Relative People of Administration Administrative Counterpart in Administration Process*, 2001 Issue 4 of *China Law*; FANG Shirong: *Cognition of Equal Status of Both Parties for Subjects of Modern Administrative Law – Perspective from Relative People of Administration*, 2002 Issue 6 of Studies in Law and Business etc.

3. Systematic Construction of Theory of Administrative Act

To some extent, basic theory of administrative law (especially traditionally speaking) is mainly theory of administrative act as the task of administrative law is to regulate administrative acts of subject of administration and ensure legality and reasonableness of administrative acts. China's administrative law conducts study on administrative act mostly in two aspects: firstly, general theory of administrative act, mainly including the study on definition, validity and classification of administrative acts; secondly, dispersed theory of administrative acts, namely, the concrete study on categorized administrative acts. As administrative acts are closely related to administration system of a country, the study has strong Chinese characteristics and China's administrative law scholars have original theories for categorization of administrative acts and law formulation and implementation in administrative punishment, administrative reconsideration, administrative licensing, administrative enforcement, etc.[1]

3.1 Study on general theory of administrative act

For effectiveness of administrative acts, the scholars held before 1990s that administrative acts have power of determining, restricting and implementing. [2]In 1990s, YE Bifeng put a lot of efforts in this field by successively publishing *Study on Determining Power of Administrative Acts*, *On Public Power of Administrative Acts and On Implementation Power of Administrative Acts*[3] and published *Study on Effectiveness of Administrative Acts* which is a comprehensive expression of the effectiveness of administrative acts in 2002[4].

1 XIONG Wenzhao: *Looking Back on Tough Past and Looking Forward to Important Tasks – 20 Years development ProcessDevelopment Process of New China Administrative Law.*

2 ZHANG Shangyuan: *China Administrative Law Out of Sluggish*, China University of Political Science and Law, 1991, pp.153-154.

3 The three articles published respectively on Year 1996 Issue 3 of *China Law*, Year 1997 Issue 5 of *Law StudyChinese Journal of Law* and Year 1997 Issue 3 of *Administrative Law Study*.

4 YE Bifeng: *Study on Effectiveness of Administrative Acts*, China Renmin University Press, 2002.

Some scholars had correct and profound insights of this subject, [1]and others preliminarily discussed the effectiveness of acts of administrative counterpart corresponding to administrative acts.[2]

In China's first administrative law teaching material Outline of Administrative Law of higher education institutions, administrative acts are classified into abstract acts (formulating abstract norms) and concrete acts (acts of handling concrete matters, generally referred to as administrative measures). WANG Mingyang classifies administrative acts into two types in French Administrative Law: universal act and concrete act. In terms of naming, we have abstract administrative act and concrete administrative act in which this classification is not generated automatically but by enlightened by relevant overseas theories. As Administrative Litigation Law and its two relevant judicial interpretations involve the definition and differentiation of concrete administrative act and abstract administrative act, the study on this concept has become a highlight in the study on administrative acts. Relevant scholars also carried out discussions and disputers over differentiation standard of abstract administrative acts and concrete administrative acts, categories and suability of abstract administrative acts.[3]

In addition to this pair of category of abstract administrative acts and concrete administrative acts, administrative law scholars focused on discussing multiple pairs of categories such as internal administrative act and external administrative act, administrative act by duty and administrative act by application, restrictive administrative act and discretional administrative act, administrative act and

1 ZHOU Youyong: *Study on Effectiveness of Administrative Acts*, 1998 Issue 3 of *Law Review*; LIU Xin: *Discussion on Effectiveness of Concrete Administration Acts*, 1998 Issue 5 of *China Law*; SHEN Jun: *On Effectiveness of Composing Elements of Concrete Administrative Acts*, 2001 Issue 3 of *Study on Administrative Law*; ZHANG Zhiyu: *Inspection on Theory of Administrative Acts Effectiveness*, 2004 Issue 10 of Hebei Law Science.

2 FANG Shirong: *On Act and Effectiveness of Relative People of Administration*, 2000 Issue 1 of *Studies in Law and Business*.

3 On viewpoints and study depth on the questions, See *Study on Basic Category of Administrative Acts* by HU Jianmiao, Zhejiang University Press, 2005, "Chapter I – Abstract Administrative Acts and Concrete Administrative Acts".

administrative inaction, formal administrative act and informal administrative act, beneficial administrative act and burdened administrative act, intermediate administrative act and final administrative act, administrative legal act and administrative real act, legal administrative act and illegal administrative act and invalid administrative act.[1]

3.2 Study on dispersed theory of administrative act–study on typical administrative act

The scholars carried out rich study on administrative legislation which is a typical abstract administrative act in 1980s. During this period, administrative law scholars continued to focus on this field and there are several monographs making overall studying of administrative legislation, such as LIU Xin: *Study on Administrative Legislation*[2], *Government Ruled By Law, Administrative Decision-making and Administrative Legislation*[3] and ZENG Xianghua: *Properness Study on Administrative Legislation*[4]. *Study on Administrative Legislation* fills the gap in specialized study and widely collects previous norms and expositions relating to administrative legislation study and makes comparative analysis.[5] Government Ruled By Law, Administrative Decision-making and Administrative Legislation discussed the requirements of rule by law on government decision-making and administrative legislation by analyzing government roles and positioning against the backdrop of Chinese social transition and transformation. *Properness Study on Administrative Legislatio*n brings up fundamental value pursuits for administrative legislation from the perspective of studying administrative legislation properness.[6] Recent years, with ongoing legislation practices of local administrative rules and

1 See corresponding chapters of *Study on Basic Categories of Administrative Acts* by HU Jianmiao.

2 LIU Xin: *Study on Administrative Legislation,* Law Press, 2003.

3 LIU Xin: *Law Governance Government and Administration Decision-making, Administration Legislation,* Peking University Press, 2006.

4 ZENG Xianghua: Study on Justifiability of Administrative Legislation, People's Public Security University of China Press, 2007.

5 LIU Xin: *Study on Administrative Legislation*, Preface.

6 ZENG Xianghua: *Study on Justifiability of Administrative Legislation*, Preface.

regulations, the scholars combine the formulation of administrative legislation and public participation into study.

Administrative punishment is an effective measure for state administrative management but also one of administrative acts most probably infringing the rights of administrative counterpart. Therefore, the study on administrative punishment has as always been a focus in administrative law study. There are considerable number of literatures relating to administrative punishment, especially around enactment of Administrative Punishment Law of the People's Republic of China (hereinafter referred to as "Administrative Punishment Law", the scholars have carried out in-depth discussions on the concept and principle (especially the principle of "no offence should be punished for twice", setting up, subject, jurisdiction, kind (especially reeducation through labor), procedure (especially hearing procedure), of administrative punishment, relevant administrative liability for breach and reflections on Administrative Punishment Law.[1] In addition, relevant scholars combined the study on administrative punishment and the study on departmental administrative law and discussed the topics for departmental administrative punishment which is more professional and technological, such as SONG Gongde: Tax Administrative Punishment[2] and SHI Zongzheng: General Theory of Public Security Administrative Punishment[3] etc.

As typical beneficial administrative act, administrative licensing received the attentions of the scholars at the beginning of administrative law study. The initial definition of administrative licensing can be traced back to the Outline of Administrative Law in 1983.[4] As China was still under planned economic system

1 Representative works, Such as, HU Jinguang: *Study on Administrative Punishment*, Law Press, 1998; FENG Jun: *New Theory of Administrative Punishment,* China Procuratorial Press, 2003; YANG Xiaojun: *Study on Administrative Punishment*, Law Press, 2002.

2 SONG Gongde: *Tax Administrative Punishment*, Wuhan University Press, 2002

3 SHI Songzheng: *General Theory of Public Security Administrative Punishment,* People's Public Security University of China Press, 2002.

4 WANG Mincan: *Outline of Administrative Law*, pp.114-115, quoted from ZHANG Xingxiang's *Theory and Practice of China's Administrative Permit*, Edition 2003 of Peking University Press, p.1.

in 1980s, the scholars did not have so many in-depth studies on administrative licensing which is administrative act with typical market economy characteristics. Until socialist market economy system was established in China in 1994, the first literature with overall study on administrative licensing appeared, namely, MA Huaide: Administrative Licensing.[1] Later on, many administrative licensing contents appeared in many teaching books and also the works on administrative licensing emerged in endlessly. After China joined WTO in 2001, the study on administrative licensing has become popular as WTO rules posed considerable challenges to domestic administrative licensing and China made corresponding commitments to entry into WTO and started working on legislation of administrative licensing. The administrative law scholars conducted extensive and in-depth discussions on the concept, nature, classification, creation, implementing organization, implementation procedures, supervision and inspection, charging, legal liabilities etc. of administrative licensing. After Administrative Licensing Law of the People's Republic of China (hereinafter referred to as "Administrative Licensing Law") was officially enacted, some scholars analyzed the profound propositions and significance implied under Administrative Licensing Law such as the path of rule by law and individual freedom starting from but going beyond administrative licensing, in addition to interpretation and explanation of administrative licensing legislation and offering guidance on practices of administrative licensing. For example, some scholars analyzed practical challenges faced by Administrative Licensing Law, put forward policy suggestions on further implementation, and pointed out the law of diminishing marginal utility in China's legislation as well as double dilemma of rule by law caused in the path of politics putting forward rule by law.[2] Some scholars used analysis approach to concept essence and logics of administrative licensing so as to explain individual freedom

1 MA Huaide: *Administrative Permit*, China University of Political Science and Law Press, 1994

2 ZHOU Hanhua: "Administrative Permit Law: Concept Innovation and Practice Challenge", 2005 Issue 2, *Chinese Journal of Law.*

and rights evolution and scope of administrative licensing.[1] Furthermore, still some scholars combined administrative licensing and departmental law to study administrative licensing of all administrative departments, such as YU Lingyun: Police Permit and Administrative Licensing Law[2].

The study by Zhejiang University on administrative enforcement is at the frontline nationally. The Project of the National Social Science Foundation of China regarding "administrative enforcement" chaired by HU Jianmiao published a series of literatures with study on administrative enforcement. Among the literature works, Study on Administrative Enforcement Law by HU Jianmiao[3] systematically discusses and studies the theories and legislations of administrative enforcement; Administrative Enforcement Law System of China by JIN Weifeng[4] systematically studies 15 systems such as China's administrative enforcement inspection, enforced quarantine and anti-epidemic, enforced preservation and enforced shutting down and makes comparative study of their respective administrative enforcement systems of Hong Kong, Macao and Taiwan of China; Administrative enforcement Law System of Overseas Countries by ZHU Xinli[5] mainly chooses to focus on developed western countries with mature administrative enforcement law systems by showcasing the outlines of administrative enforcement law systems of different countries but also highlighting characteristics of administrative enforcement law systems of different countries; Administrative Enforcement Law Study Materials of Foreign Countries and China[6] by ZHANG Jiansheng provides solid, reliable, practical and

1 CHEN Duanhong: *Administrative Permit and Individual Freedom*, 2004 Issue 5 of Chinese Journal of Law; ZHU Xinli, YU Jun: Logic Structure of Administrative Permit Concept – Interpretation of Perspective on Analyzing Law, carried on Administrative Permit and Government Governance by LIU Heng, Peking University Press, 2007

2 YU Lingyun: *Police Permit and Administrative Permit Law*, China University of Political Science and Law Press, 2003.

3 HU Jianmiao: *Study on Administrative Compulsory Law*, Law Press, 2003.

4 JIN Weifeng: *Administrative Compulsory Law System of China*, Law Press, 2003.

5 ZHU Xinli: *Administrative Compulsory Law System of Foreign Countries,* Law Press, 2003

6 ZHANG Jiansheng: *Study Materials of Administrative Compulsory Law of China and Foreign Countries*, Law Press, 2003

convenient literature base for administrative enforcement study. In addition, YU Lingyun made special study of administrative enforcement theory and practice of public security department[1], and WANG Tianxing specially studied administrative emergency enforcement system.[2]

Contemporary administrative law is much different from traditional administrative law. With the economic development, development of democracy, and emergence of welfare countries, administrative law has evolved from authoritarian tool, management means, to control of administrative right and maintenance and safeguarding of civil legitimate rights and interests, and many new systems appear in administrative law field. The scholars have been increasingly focusing on non-power administrative acts which have increasingly noticeable influence on people's life while going ahead with in-depth study on regulating means of traditional administrative law, such as administrative contracts, administrative guidance, administrative planning and administrative supply. However generally speaking, compared to study on traditional administrative acts, we still have no such in-depth study on the administrative acts which follow. In late 1990s, several books filling the gap in relevant study fields came out in China, among others, YU Lingyun: *On Administrative Contracts*, which has in-depth and detailed discussions on basic theories such as concept of administrative contract, conciliation of administrative contract and administrative rule by law, quoting of rules and principles of civil law in administrative contracts, allocation of substantive rights and obligations in administrative contracts and procedural regularization, relief system of administrative contracts, establishes basic framework of administrative contract theory and makes typical exemplification study of concrete administrative contract forms.[3]

1 YU Lingyun: *Theory and Practice of Police Administrative Compulsion*, China University of Political Science and Law, 2003.

2 WANG Tianxing: *Study on Administrative Urgent Forces System*, Intellectual Property Rights Press, 2007.

3 See YU Lingyun: *Administrative Contract Theory*, China Renmin University Press, 2000, 2nd Edition of 2006.

The scholars studied other concrete administrative acts. For the study on administrative award and administrative material help or administrative supply, Chinese scholars mainly study basic theories of administrative supply (concept, nature function, principle and existence form), rights foundation and righting of administrative supply, obligation contents and nature of administrative organization in administrative supply, concrete acts in administrative supply as well as positive analysis of administrative supply in addition to introducing and borrowing relevant overseas systems and schools.[1]

The book making earliest systematic study of administrative guidance in China is On Administrative Guidance by GUO Runsheng and SONG Gongde[2]. In this book, the authors make systematic discussions on basic theory and system structure of administrative guidance and relationship between administrative guidance and rule by law by studying cross disciplines in economy, politics, administration and law (including constitution, jurisprudence, administrative law and economy law) relating to administrative guidance, and makes in-depth and overall investigation of practices of overseas countries and China's administrative guidance system.[3] MO Yuchuan published Outline of Administrative Guidance and his doctorial dissertation Important Theory of Administrative Guidance – Center on Basing Administrative Guidance on Rule by Law. He comprehensively used social science approaches such as material analysis, comparative study, cross study, case study, empirical research and countermeasure research to conduct systematic and focused discussion of administrative guidance.[4] His latest achievement is the book "Administrative Guidance in View of Rule by Law" [5]

1 See LIU Yantao: *Administrative Supply Study*, Shandong People Press, 2006.

2 GUO Runsheng, SONG Gongde: *On Administrative Guidance*, China University of Political Science and Law, 1999.

3 GUO Runsheng, SONG Gongde: *On Administrative Guide · Preface*, p.3.

4 MO Yuchuan: *Administrative Guidance Outline*, Chongqing University Press, 1999; MO Yuchuan: *Theory of Administrative Guide – Administrative Guide by Rules of Law as Center*, People's Court Press, 2002.

5 MO Yuchuan: *Administrative Guidance under Law Governance Perspective*, China Renmin University Press, 2005.

together with his master degree student.

In 1980s, no attention was paid to administrative compensation but in 1990s, several study articles came out.[1] After entering 21st century, with the publishing of JIANG Ming'an "Study on Administrative Compensation System"[2], study on administrative compensation has gradually been emerging in administrative law circle with increasing number of theses and unprecedented width and depth of research. The scholars not only start studying standard, scope and procedures of administrative compensation but also combine administrative compensation with administrative expropriation, private property protection, environment victim, urban relocation, etc. for study.[3] Recent years have witnessed the publishing of several books for administrative compensation.[4] The latest one is XIA Jun's *On Administrative Compensation*[5]. This book uses positive analysis, value analysis, comparative analysis and logical analysis to study systematically concept definition, historical causes, functions, theoretical basis, basic principles, obligations and subject of right, type and mode, accountability principle, standard and procedures, relief, legislation assumption and empirical analysis of administrative compensation.

1 See ZENG Xiangrui: Japan's Theory of Administrative Loss Compensation, 1993 Issue 3 of Administrative Law Study; LIU Siyuan: *Discussion on China's Administrative Compensation System*, Year 1995 Issue 3 of Administration and Law.

2 JIANG Ming'an: *Study on Administrative Compensation System*, 2001 Issue 5 of Law Science Magazine.

3 Representative theses: YANG Jiejun: *Definition of Public Interests Gain and Administrative Compensation Improvement*, 2005 Issue 1 of Hunan Social Science; XIONG Wenzhao: *Trial Discussion on Administrative Compensation* 2005 Issue 2 of Administrative Law Study; SHEN Kaiju: *On Standard for Administrative Compensation*, 2005 Issue 1 of Henan Social Science; MO Yuchuan: *Protection of Private Property Right and Improvement of Administrative Compensation Law System*, 2005 Issue 2 of Journal of Zhejiang Gongshang University.

4 WANG Taigao: *Study on Administrative Compensation System*, Peking University Press, 2004; SHEN Kaiju: *Study on Administrative Compensation Law*, Law Press, 2005; JI Huaicai: *Study on Elements of Administrative Compensation*, Law Press, 2006 etc.

5 XIA Jun: *On Administrative Compensation*, Press of China University of Geosciences, 2007.

4. Booming Development of Study on Administrative Procedure

In China's administrative law circle, the study on administrative procedure law has been the hottest topic for recent decades of years and the books regarding administrative procedure law have sprung up in multitude. Administrative procedure law has become the topic for various high level academic conferences of administrative law. Administrative law scholars use various channels to positively offer advice and major progress has been made in administrative procedure legislation work and procedural illegal acts have been continuously rectified. Promoted by administrative law scholars, new type administrative procedure systems such as administrative hearing and academic openness have been gradually known to Chinese people. The society has greater understanding and demand on administrative procedure. Some scholars claim that the era of administrative procedure law is coming to us.[1]

When looking back on the process of administrative procedure law study, some scholars tried to divide the transmutation path of China's administrative procedure law into three stages later than 1978 and made comprehensive analysis:[2](1) The "initial period" is from 1978 to 1989 when Administrative Litigation Law was implemented. The characteristics at this stage is that China's administrative law scholars did not put enough attention to the study on administrative procedure system and the study by some scholars is only at unsystematic or simple and sporadic introduction stage of administrative procedure system of overseas countries. (2) The "premature period" is from 1989 when Administrative Litigation Law was implemented to 1996 when Administrative Punishment Law

1 XIONG Wenzhao: Looking Back on Tough Past and Looking Forward to Important Tasks – 20 Years Development Process of New China Administrative Law.

2 WANG Chengdong: *Looking Back on and Reflecting on Theory and Practice of China's Administrative Procedure Law*, carried on *Looking Back and Forward on China's Administrative Law – 20 Years of China's Administrative Law Bo'ao Forum & China's Law Institute Administrative Law Study Year 2005 Annual Thesis Collection* compiled by China Administrative Law Institute, published by China University of Political Science and Law Press, *2006.*

is implemented. The implementation of Administrative Litigation Law marks that China's administrative law development enters a brand new stage. With enactment of new law, the theory horizon has given unprecedented attention to administrative procedure system supervising right exercising process of subject of administration and a lot of insightful literatures and theses have sprung up[1]. The overall characteristics at this stage are that although China's administrative law scholars had a higher level study on administrative procedure system, overall study was still at the stage of introducing overseas experience and comparison at a shallow level. Though some scholars have put forward the viewpoint of procedural justice, procedure instrumentalism thinking was still in mainstream, which is the reflection of China's administrative law scholars having narrow understanding of modern legal country at this stage. (3) The "gradual mature stage" is from 1996 when Administrative Punishment Law was issued till now. Administrative Punishment Law is China's first specialized legislation standardizing operation process of administrative act and China's entry into WTO and China's administrative procedure legislation being put on agenda also provide strong impetus to the study on administrative procedure law. At this stage, the scholars had more in-depth and extensive study on administrative procedure and the study on administrative procedure entered relative systematical mature stage, and the concept "procedural justice" had been accepted by more researchers.[2] The research perspective extended from regulating the process of exercising right by subject of administration to the study on procedural right of administrative counterpart in implementation process of administrative act.[3]

At this stage, many scholars made special study on administrative procedure

1 YING Songnian: *On Administrative Procedure Law*, 1990 Issue 1 of China Law; JI Weidong: *Significance of Law Procedures*, 1993 Issue 1 of China Social Science Press.

2 CHEN Duanhong: "Values on Law ProceduresPeking University Law Journal", 1997 Issue 6, *Peking University Law Journal.*

3 WANG Xixin: *Study on Procedural Right of Relative People in Administration Process,* carried on Essence of China's Administrative Law (2002), Machinery Industry Press, 2002.

with countless great achievements, such as the series of research results published by the Project of the National Social Science Foundation of China "Study on Administrative Procedure Law" chaired by YING Songnian, Law Principle of Administrative Procedure[1] and Comparative Study of Administrative Procedure Law[2] by ZHANG Jiansheng, Zhejiang University, Administrative Procedure Codification of China: Study from Perspective of Comparative Study by YANG Haikun, Suzhou University[3], Comparative Study on Administrative Procedure Law by PI Chunxie, China Renmin University[4], Legislation Study on Administrative Procedure: Draft Proposal and Statement of Reasons for Administrative Procedure Law[5] by MA Huaide, China University of Political Science and Law, as well as Concept and System Study of Administrative Procedure and Public Participation and Administrative Process[6] by WANG Xixin which is the latest book for studying administrative procedure and public participation. "Concept and System Study of Administrative Procedure" makes systematic introduction and discussion of administrative procedure theories such as basic viewpoints and elements, procedural values and procedural rights of procedural justice starting from the relationship between government ruled by law and legal procedures, and based on theoretical discussions, and the author makes in-depth analysis of administrative decision-making procedures and administrative legislation procedures of China and sums up experience but also brings up shortcomings as well as put forward

1 ZHANG Jiansheng: "Introduction to Administrative Procedures Law", *China University of Political Science and Law*, 1994.

2 ZHANG Jiansheng: *Comparative Study on Administrative Procedure Law,* Hangzhou University Press, 1997.

3 YANG Haikun: *Codification of China Administrative Procedures: Study from Comparative Law Perspective*, Law Press, 1999.

4 PI Chunxie: *Comparative Study on Administrative Procedure Law*, People's *Public Security University* of *China Press,* 2000.

5 MA Huaide: *Administrative Procedure Law Study: Draft Proposal and Reasons of Administrative Procedural Law*, China Legal Publishing House, 2000.

6 *Concept and Institutional Research of Administrative Procedure Law and Public Participation and Administration Process*, published by China Democratic Legal Press, 2007.

a series of suggestions, through comparing and borrowing the experience of the countries with relatively advanced system of administrative procedure. "Public Participation and Administrative Process" investigates transition in mode of administrative law, analyzes the meaning of public participation in modern administration process as well as puts forward some viewpoints and suggestions to improve China's public participation system in consideration of China's actual conditions, from the perspective of combining law with administration.

5. Administrative Legal Responsibility and Ongoing Administrative Remedy Research

5.1 Study on administrative responsibility

The theory of administrative legal responsibility is an important part of administrative law theory and some scholars described the research process of China's administrative law scholars on this topic:[1] Outline of Administrative Law by Wang Mincan in 1983 does not discuss on administrative legal responsibility; Teaching Book on Administrative Law by YING Songnian in 1988 and Administrative Law and Administrative Litigation Law by JIANG Ming'an in 1989 starts elaborating administrative legal responsibility; Outline of Administrative Legal Responsibility [2] by REN Zhikuan came out in 1990 and it is China's first book regarding administrative legal responsibility; in 1995, China Legal Publishing House published Legal Responsibility Application Book (Administrative Law). Later on, more and more teaching books on administrative law contain the chapters introducing basic theory of administrative legal responsibility. Entering the new century, a batch of

1 See Liang Jinming: *Looking Back and Thinking on Research of Administrative Legal Responsibility, carried Looking Back and Forward on Study on Theoretical Basis of Contemporary China Administrative Law*, carried on *Looking Back and Forward on China's Administrative Law – 20 Years of China's Administrative Law Bo'ao Forum & China's Law Institute Administrative Law Study Year 2005 Annual Thesis Collection* compiled by China Administrative Law Institute, published by China University of Political Science and Law Press in 2006.

2 REN Zhikuan: Introduction to Administrative Legal Responsibility, People's Publishing House, 1990.

famous works on study of administrative legal responsibility came out one after another, such as *Study of Illegal Administration and Legal Responsibility*[1] by YAO Ruiming and YI Fenglan, *Study of Administrative Legal Responsibility: Pluralistic Interpretations* [2] by ZHU Xinli, and Study of Administrative Responsibility[3] by YANG Jiejun.

The scholars' study on administrative legal responsibility includes as follows: (1) concept of administrative legal responsibility. Current mainstream viewpoint is that administrative legal responsibility is negative legal consequences legally investigated or borne by state administrative organizations as subject of administrative law relationship breaches administrative law obligations. The concept of administrative legal responsibility is summed up as 9 viewpoints in Teaching Reference Book on Administrative Law and Administrative Litigation Law by YANG Jianshun and LI Yuan.[4] The core of the concept of administrative legal responsibility is the nature of administrative legal responsibility and administrative law scholars have different insights on this, with representative viewpoints as sanction theory, consequence theory and obligation theory. (2) The basis of administrative legal responsibility is constituent element of administrative legal responsibility. There are currently six viewpoints on it.[5] The common view holds that the constituent elements of administrative legal responsibility mainly include subject element, act element, consequence element and subjective element. (3) Mode of administrative legal responsibility. According to different effects, the mode of administrative legal responsibility can be

1 YAO Ruimin, YI Fenglan: *Illegal Administration and Legal Responsibility Study*, China Fangzheng Press, 2000.

2 ZHU Xinli: *Administrative Legal Responsibility Study: Multi-dimensional Interpretation*, Law Publishing House, 2004.

3 YANG Jiejun: *Study on Administrative Responsibility,* Peking University Press, 2005.

4 YANG Jianshun, LI Yuanqi: *Teaching Book on Administrative Law and Administrative Litigation Law*, China Renmin University Press, 2005, p.385.

5 Ibid, p.399.

divided into punishment mode and remediation mode. According to different subjects, the mode of administrative legal responsibility can be divided into subject of administration, state public servants and administrative counterpart.

5.2 Study on Administrative Remedy

When formulating and implementing Administrative Litigation Law, State Compensation Law of the People's Republic of China (hereinafter referred to as the "State Compensation Law") and Administrative Reconsideration Law of the People's Republic of China (hereinafter referred to as the "Administrative Reconsideration Law"), the scholars have made great progress in the study of administrative remedy system field and administrative remedy accounts for a large proportion in a series of administrative law teaching books, literatures and theses published one after another.[1] We may generally divide administrative remedy study into general theory and dispersed theory.

In the researches for administrative remedy the scholars mainly study administrative reconsideration, administrative litigation and administrative compensation in dispersed theory, and relatively speaking focus less on general theory of administrative remedy. For a long time, administrative law scholars have rarely used the concept of administrative remedy and also rare books have been on this concept while some influential administrative law teaching books and literatures use the concepts such as supervision administration, administration supervisor, administrative legal supervision and supervision over administration for elaboration in special chapters. However, some young and middle aged administrative law scholars have borrowed administrative law theories from UK and France etc. and used the concept of

1 SHI Bolin, SHI Yanan: *Looking Back and Forward on 20 Years Development of China's Administrative remedy LawAdministrative Remedy Law*, carried on *Looking Back and Forward on China's Administrative Law – 20 Years of China's Administrative Law Bo'ao Forum & China's Law Institute Administrative Law Study Year 2005 Annual Thesis Collection* compiled by China Administrative Law Institute, China University of Political Science and Law Press in 2006.

administrative remedy in their books.[1] The administrative law scholars have not formed uniformed viewpoints on the study scope of general theory of administrative remedy. Some scholars mainly study concept, features, mode and classification of administrative remedy (or referred to as supervision over administration and administrative legal supervision etc.) and some included the study on administrative illegality and administrative responsibility.[2]

The word “administrative reconsideration” is the abstract generalization made by administrative law scholars for review and judgment of administrative disputes by state administration organization with the emergence of China’s administrative law[3]. For the positioning of administrative reconsideration, some scholars put it under the “administrative justice” of “administrative act”[4] and some put it under “administrative remedy”.[5] Either one is right and just reflects different perspectives which the scholars take to focus on administrative reconsideration and embodies multiple natures of administrative reconsideration. But generally speaking, more and more scholars tend to take administrative reconsideration as a means of administrative remedy for study. By taking Administrative Reconsideration Law enacted in 1996 as a borderline, we divide into two periods the study on administrative reconsideration later than 1990s. During the first period, the scholars studied various systems of administrative reconsideration and

1 SHI Bolin, SHI Yanan: *Looking Back and Forward on 20 Years Development of China's Administrative remedy LawAdministrative Remedy Law*. The earliest monograph named “Administrative Remedy” is LIU Heng: *Study on Administrative remedy SystemAdministrative Remedy System*, Law Press, 1998. There are more writings named “Administrative Remedy”, such as LIN Lihong: *Theory and Practice of China's Administrative remedyAdministrative Remedy*, Wuhan University Press, 2000; ZENG Xiangrui: *Theory of Administrative remedyAdministrative Remedy*, People’s Publish House, 2002; YUAN Mingsheng, LUO Wenyan: Introduction to Administrative Remedy Law, China University of Political Science and Law, 2004; SONG Yafang: Administrative Remedy Law, Zhengzhou University Press, 2004; BI Kezhi: On Administrative Remedy, Peking University Press, 2005.

2 See YING Songnian: *New Theory of Administrative Law*, pp.371-391.

3 Ibid, p.313.

4 XU Chongde, PI Chunxie: *Research Summary of New China Administrative Law.*

5 JIANG Ming’an: *Administrative Law and Administrative Litigation Law* (Edition II).

relationship, similarities and differences between administrative reconsideration and administrative litigation. After Administrative Reconsideration Law was officially enacted in 1996, the scholars had more in-depth study of administrative reconsideration but also paid more attention to practical questions in the implementation of administrative reconsideration.[1] Furthermore, some scholars concretely paid attention and made study of administrative reconsideration system of specific departments or fields.[2]

China's study on administrative compensation starts later than China's study on other parts of administrative law and administrative litigation law. Before 1990s, there were few books on administrative compensation and there were the chapters with systematic descriptions of administrative compensation in the books for administrative law and administrative litigation law but with rare in-depth and detailed study on concrete matters of administrative compensation. Some scholars analyzed the reasons in early 1990s.[3] Since the *State Compensation Law* was enacted in 1994 and was implemented in 1995, the study by scholars on administrative compensation have made significant progress in width and depth and the scholars have focused their attentions on the scope, standard, principle of administrative compensation and the revisions of the State Compensation Law. In sum, the academic theses and books carrying weight are still few.[4]

1 ZHOU Hanhua: *Administrative Reconsideration Jurisdiction: Theory, Practice and Reform*, Peking University, 2005; XU Jing: Analysis of Administrative Reconsideration Cases and Practices, Wuhan University Press, 2007.

2 LI Shishan, YANG Hua: *Tax Administrative Reconsideration*, Wuhan University Press, 2002; Liu Jingdong and YAO Zhen: *Theory and Practice of Administrative Reconsideration and Judicial Review System of Anti-dumping Cases*, People's Public Security University of China Press, *2004*.

3 See ZHANG Shangyuan's *China Administrative Law Out of Sluggish*, China University of Political Science and Law, 1991, p.579.

4 Representative theses: MA Huaide: *Constituent Features of Administrative Compensation Liability* (1st&2nd), 1994 Issue 3 & 4, Political Law Forum; ZHANG Zhiyuan: "Conception of China's Administrative Compensation System Improvement", 2005 Issue 2, *Journal of Guizhou Police* Officer Vocational College.

6. Multidimensional Unfolding of Study of other Aspects of Administrative Law

6.1 Departmental administrative law

The study of previous topics constitute general theory of China's administrative law and dispersed theory relates to departmental administrative law (also called special administrative law) which means the application of administrative law rules and principles in all concrete administrative management fields and is an important component of China's administrative law system. In-depth studies of departmental administrative law will not only help enriching and going deeper into the study of administrative law general theory but also improving administrative law science system. Therefore, carrying out in-depth and classified study of departmental administrative law is of great significance to China's administrative law science construction.

China's study on departmental administrative law starts from the book *Outline of Administrative Law* by Wang Mincan in 1983. This book is composed of introduction, general theory and dispersed theory. The dispersed theory outlines the departmental administrative laws such as military, public security, national economic operation and education, science, culture and health and pioneers the study on departmental administrative law. Later on, although most administrative law books hold that departmental administrative law is a component of administrative law, they have no detailed discussions on it and administrative law scholars tend to stop in front of departmental administrative law with strong professional and technical requirements. Since then, China's study on departmental administrative law has entered dispersed research stage and practical workers in all administration fields have published some unsystematic and sporadic research results of departmental administrative law consciously and unconsciously in their respective administration publications. It is worth mentioning that under the organization of departmental administrative law editorial board of higher education institutions with Yu Shutong as consultant and LUO Haocai as director,

15 "departmental administrative law series teaching materials" including Custom Administrative Law, Industrial and Commercial Administrative Law, Administrative Law of Civil Affairs, Audit Administrative Law and Environment Administrative Law were compiled and published in 1990s, promoting the study of departmental administrative law. Those series of books focus on the introduction of concrete system of departmental administrative law, being far from reaching the level of "study of departmental administrative law". It can be seen that the study of departmental administrative law lags behind social realistic life and also curbs further development of departmental law. Some unsatisfying places in China's departmental legislation and law enforcement have something to do with it.

Recent years, with legislation strengthening of administrative activities, administrative law scholars have increasing in-depth study on all questions in dispersed theory of administrative law and some books on departmental administrative law have come out. For instance, the study of departmental administrative law fields such as public security administrative law, industrial and commercial administrative law, land administrative law, tax administrative law and environment administrative law have achieved results to some extent. They make systematic discussions on legal issues in national administrative activities from different perspectives and played an active role in promoting gradual improvement of China's administrative law system. In the aspect of education administrative law, we have fruitful results in the researches of administrative legal status of higher education institutions, relationship between judicial review and university autonomy and empirical study of students suing judicial review of higher education institutions.[1]

6.2 Government supervision (regulation)

Government regulation study has close relation with the study on

1 CHENG Yanlei: "Looking Back and Forward on Administrative Law Study in Higher Education Field", 2006 Issue 1, *Administrative Law Study*.

departmental administrative law. China's attention and study on government regulation is marked with late start. Around early 1990s, economy scholars started studying economics of regulation. Later on, with further deepening of economic system reform, government organization reform is increasingly pressing and the fields of law and politics start focusing on regulation. ZHU Xinli from Zhejiang University, LIU Heng from Zhongshan University, ZHU Mang from East China University of Political Science and Law, YU An from Tsinghua University, YANG Jianshun from China Renmin University and ZHOU Hanhua from Institute of International Law of Chinese Academy of Social Sciences etc. are Chinese scholars who are earlier to focus on government regulation from the perspective of administrative law.

With the hard studying and promotion of the above scholars, the study on government regulation and application of empirical method and sociology of law in administrative law study has become a highlight recent years. Also we need to point out that the introduction of government regulation theory and method by modern administrative law and the attention to administrative process won't cause termination of administrative law but increase vitality for administrative law study. For instance, in government regulation theory, regulation is basically deemed as a process of mutual alliance and bargaining among the government, enterprises and customers, which promotes us to reflect on traditional theories of administrative counterpart and relationship between administration and law. Many emerging independent regulation organizations promote us to review and correct traditional subject of administration and administrative organization law theory. Many brand new government regulation patterns appearing in modern society will promote us to reflect on and reconstruct formal and informal administrative activities theories of administrative acts. Government regulation theory should not be parallel to traditional administrative law and the study will help us renovate concept framework and theory system of traditional administrative law and gradually establish modern administrative law system having interpretive power on administrative process of the real world.[1]

6.3 Administrative law and comparative administrative law of foreign countries

China's contemporary administrative law study has always been focusing on learning from extraterritorial administrative law and it is glorious tradition to read western books, assimilate and transplant western administrative law system and use this to criticize and construct China's administration ruled by law.[2] From 1980s till now, Chinese scholars have translated countless books and introduced translations of administrative laws of foreign countries or discussed on the articles of administrative laws of foreign countries,[3] and it is also a trend to quote foreign literatures in administrative law theses. In sum, there are still some weak links when the scholars translate books of administrative laws of foreign countries. In terms of types, the books of administrative laws of foreign

1 ZHU Xinli, SONG Hualin: "Construction of Modern Administrative Law and Emergence of Government Regulations Research", 2005 Issue 5, *Law Science.*

2 YU Lishen: *Looking Back and Forward on Five Years of Administrative Law Study of Five Years at Turn of Centuries*, 2001 Issue 1 of Law System and Social Development.

3 Influential works published after 1992 include WANG Mingyang's *American Administrative Law*, China Legal Publishing House, 1995; HU Jianmiao: *Comparative Study on Administrative Laws of Ten Countries*, China University of Political Science and Law, 1993; [UK] Weid: *Administrative Law*, translated by XU Bin, Encyclopedia of *China* Publishing House, 1997; [French] Maurice Hauriou: Precis De Droit Administratif et de Droit Public, translated by GONG Mi et al., Liaohai Press, Chunfeng Art and Literature Press, 1998; [Japan] Yan Yehong: *Administrative Law*, translated by YANG Jianshun, Law Press, 1998; [German] Maurer: *General Theory of German Administrative Law,* translated by GAO Jiawei, Law Press, 2001. LUO Haocai: Summary of the Series of Translating *Famous* Works of Public Law, Commercial Press (China); CHEN Duanhong, ZHAI Xiaobo: *Ancient and Modern Constitution*, Law Press; LUO Haocai, ZHANG Zhijian: Liaohai Press, Chunfeng Art and Literature Press "French Public Law and Public Administration Famous Works"; CHEN Duanhong: *Legal Procedures and Administrative Process*, Higher Education Press; JIANG Ming'an, LI Honglei: Law Science · Public Law Collection, China Renmin University Press; "Foreign Laws Collection", Encyclopedia of *China* Publishing House, as well as translation books with topic as administrative law.

countries translated are mostly teaching type books but fewer topical type books. In terms of countries, these translated books are basically limited to UK, USA, France, German and Japan with obvious blind areas. For example, we still lack understanding of the administrative law of Russia in its transitional period; in terms of time effectiveness, we still have obvious "time difference" with overseas latest developments. For example, we don't have alternative ideal works after *French Administrative Law* by WANG Mingyang so that the book is still often quoted after it is published for 20 years. We can say that in comparative administrative law study, there is undoubtedly an "era of WANG Mingyang" in China's contemporary law, and it shoes we still haven't walked out of the "era of WANG Mingyang" as his book is still frequently quoted.[1]

A scholar studied the influences of extraterritorial administrative law on China's administrative law development since 1978 from the perspective of an "aerial photographer". The author compares the Development Process of China's administrative law as building a property and generally divides the influence into three periods. From 1978 to 1989, we are at the period of "laying foundation and setting up framework" when administrative law is at the stage of initial creation and academic framework is initially established and macro system of extraterritorial administrative law is introduced. From 1989 to 1998, we are at the period of "paving, walling and building" when we transferred the introduction of administrative law from its macro system to construction of concrete systems. Administrative law theory has gradually become mature and when we introduce extraterritorial administrative law, we focus on its legislation and especially serve the characteristics of judicial review. From 1999 till now we are at the stage of "refining decoration and seeking for innovations" when administrative law study goes booming and academic system framework is further established. The study of extraterritorial administrative law creates the situation where the books

1 See YING Songnian: "New Look of Administrative Law: 2005-006 Administrative Law Research Review", 2007 Issue 1, *China Law*.

of all schools are booming together and a great number of translated literatures and articles are introduced in China, which promotes the development of administrative law to go toward the direction of focusing more on administrative process and dispersed theory of administrative law.[1]

1 ZHU Xinli, LUO Meiying: *No Obstacle Ahead – Development of Comparative Administrative Law and China Contemporary Administrative Law*, carried on on *Looking Back and Forward on China's Administrative Law – 20 Years of China's Administrative Law Bo'ao Forum & China's Law Institute Administrative Law Study Year 2005 Annual Thesis Collection* compiled by China Administrative Law Institute, published by China University of Political Science and Law Press in 2006.

Chapter 21

Social Law Emerging from the Harmonious Society Construction

Social law is a new-rising discipline. With the development of productive forces, science and technology, the modern society manages to possess more material wealth, but is forced to confront with an increasing number of social problems and negative influences, such as extreme disparity between the rich and the poor, difficulty of subsistence suffered by disadvantaged groups, destroy of natural and human environment, etc. Therefore, the traditionally dual structure of legal theories cannot satisfy the needs of law practice any more. In other words, the state must pay attention to those problems concerning labor, social relief, welfare, education, economy, etc., which were irrelevant to it in the past. In addition, the state should apply administrative and legal means to adjust and interpose various social problems. As a result, the realistic social reasons and system formation logic for social law come into being. As a new legal area to cover the shortage of private laws and inherent defects of market economy, social law adheres to the fundamental conception that the relative equality and fairness shall be pursued based on the inequality of social reality with a view to promoting and realizing the overall social benefits.

1. Emergence of Chinese Social Law

As a legal phenomenon, there were certain studies on social law in China prior to 1949. For instance, those relatively profound books written by HUANG Youchang, LI Jingxi, WU Chuanyi, etc. are handed down from ancient times. For various reasons, the studies on social law and some sub-disciplines experienced a long-term interruption since 1949. The study on social law and discipline construction was recovered successively until China adopted the policy of reform and opening up. Based on the existing literatures, the concept of "social law" was initially proposed in a research report titled as *Theoretical Thinking and Approach Suggestions on the Construction of Socialist Market Economy Law System* published by the Institute of Law under Chinese Academy of Social Sciences in 1993. According to this report, the legal system of socialist market economy was mainly composed of civil and commercial law, economic law and social law, considering that "social law is another significant law of market economy, a general term of legal norms to adjust various social relations arising from the protection of labor rights and deliverance to job hunters, whose legal nature is between public law and private law".[1] Later on, social law began to enter the research fields as a juristic discipline. However, it failed to attract sufficient attention from the Chinese jurisprudential circle.

After entering the 21st century, the Central Committee of the Communist Party of China proposed the concept of "people oriented" and advocated to construct a "harmonious society". Therefore, the relevant theories of "social law" became the hot spot of academic circle. In May 2015, the Institute of Law under Chinese Academy of Social Sciences established the first research institute of social law. In May 2016, the institute prepared and held the first session of "Forum on Chinese Social Law", and advocated to study the basic theory of social law. Up to now, the Forum has been convened for three sessions. In September 2005,

1 Research Group of Institute of Law under Chinese Academy of Social Sciences: *Theoretical Thinking and Approach Suggestions on the Construction of Socialist Market Economy Law System*, Issue 6, *Chinese Journal of Law* (1993).

Social Law Institute of China Law Society was established with JIA Junling as the first president. In October of the same year, the annual conference of Social Law Institute of China Law Society titled as "Study on Labor Standards Law" was held in Suzhou University, where over one hundred scholars throughout the country were present. By August 2009, the Institute managed to hold four sessions of its annual conferences. Currently, the National People's Congress has positioned social law as one of the "seven legal departments" in parallel with civil and commercial law, administrative law, economic law, criminal law, etc.

Proceeding from the research status of social law, the development of Chinese social law is featured with the following characteristics. Firstly, the research on the pandect of social law is in arrears of that on some sub-disciplines such as labor law, social security law, environment protection law, etc., the research of each of which was started earlier than that on the pandect of social law with relatively mature development. Secondly, the talents engaged in the research on social law are gravely insufficient, and quite a few theoretical problems haven't been raveled out. In the past four sessions of the annual conferences already convened, the participants were almost all scholars dedicated to studying labor law and social security law, among whom few were engaged in the research on the pandect of social law. In addition, there are many disputes over the definition of social law in academic circles, a jurisdiction or a legal department. Thirdly, compared with other juristic disciplines, the overall level of the study on social law is relatively backward. Rare theoretical articles concerning social law can be found in the high-end periodicals such as *Social Sciences in China*, *Chinese Journal of Law,* etc.

With regard to the research on the basic theory of social law, the social jurisprudential circle has made beneficial exploration and contributions over the past decades and produced some influential articles. For instance, the *Original Dissertation of Social Law* by DONG Baohua offers a systematic analysis and interpretation for such matters of social law as its generation and development, objects, principles, legal relations, enforcement procedures and legal liabilities. In this book, the four domains, i.e. social benefits, social fields, social standard and social law, are explored from the perspective of new technology, and a relatively unique theoretical standpoint on social law is included, which creates sound research approaches for Chinese social law. The *General Theory of Social Law* by TANG Lihong clarifies the position and roles of social law in a systematic manner, holding that social law is the product arising from the settlement of social problems and has played a significant role in solving social problems and maintaining social stability in modern history. Apart from proclaiming the basis, process and form of social law discipline systematically, the *Social Law* recently edited by TANG Lihong also expounds the research objects of this new emerging discipline roundly, namely theories about the connotation, theoretical basis, scope, formation, origin, value, basic principle, system, etc. of social law, and summarizes the social legal systems are composed of the legal system supporting disadvantaged groups, the legal system promoting social welfare and the legal system maintaining social stability. The *Social Law* by SHI Tanjing makes a detailed introduction to social law as well as the basic concepts, basic framework and basic theories of all laws within the scope of social law, reviews and rethinks the process of social legal construction, analyzes hot social issues, difficult points and focal points with people's attention objectively, conducts a depth study on various problems reflected and explores the corresponding solutions. *On Social Law,* another work of SHI Tanjing, states the pandect of social law as well as the labor law, trade union law, social security law, contract law, economic law and contents in other aspects profoundly, offers a theoretical analysis and exposition in every way, and has a higher academic value.

In addition, the academic circle of social law has realized certain achievements in the theoretical research of its sub-disciplines. Those achievements are reflected at multiple theoretical levels, such as the contracting theory of labor relation, theory of weak laborers, category theory of labor right, legislative theory of labor contract, construction theory of social security system, reform theory of labor dispute settlement system, regulation theory of atypical labor relation, etc. The study on the basic theory of social law, by contrast, is very weak. Only 3489 articles can be detected from CNKI, CMFD, CCND, CDFD and CPFD (hereinafter referred to as "Five Databases") if taking "social law" as the index, and such number is far below that of other disciplines. The quantity of the books concerning social law in the National Library of China and CNKI are only 91 in total. In short, the study on the basic theory of social law is a virgin land awaiting for development and just breaks ground.

It is expected that the 21th century will witness the significant development of Chinese social law. Firstly, the Chinese economy experiences a sustainable, stable and coordinated development with GDP per head exceeding $3,000. Currently, China has become the fourth largest economic entity worldwide and is capable of solving quite a few social problems unsolved in the past. From the international aspect, the development of social law is also related to the economic development level. Secondly, the Party Central Committee demands to attach importance to people's livelihood politically, and to maintain equality both in the primary distribution and in the second distribution. In the report of the 17th Party Congress, it was explicitly indicated that the social construction aimed at improving people's livelihood should be accelerated with a view to promoting social equality and fairness, realizing such phenomenon where every kid is in school, every work is made paid, the sick are treated, the elderly are taken cared of and everyone has a roof over the head, and promoting the construction of a harmonious society. From the perspective of legislation, social legislation has been accelerated. For instance, *Social Insurance Law*, *Public Assistance Act*, *Law of Charity Promotion*, etc. have entered into the legislative programming successively, which undoubtedly promotes the research on social law substantially. Thirdly, China has preliminarily established the perfect organizational network for study on social law, which effectively promotes the study and development of disciplines concerning social law. Apart from the Social Law Institute established by China Law Society, some provincial law societies have established social law institutes in succession, offering a powerful organizational guarantee for the study on social law. To strengthen the discipline construction of social law, series of comments on *Labor Law* compiled by Renmin University of China have been revised to *Comment on Social Law*, and China University of Political Science and Law has also initiated to compile *Series of Social Law*, both of which have exerted certain social influence. Currently, the theoretical articles concerning social law and relevant seminars continue to rise year over year with a sound development momentum. As LIN Jia says, "the research on Chinese social law ushers its vibrant spring".[1]

2. Theoretical Basis of Social Law Developed in Discrimination

From the foregoing, social law has become a hot topic in recent years, so that some scholars confuse the concept of social law, law of sociology and legal sociology .[2] According to the works already published, the hot issues researched by the pandect of social law include concept orientation, property characteristics, system principles, etc. However, the academic circle fails to reach an agreement or a consensus on each issue, which is similar to the status of other disciplines in their early phases of development.

As to the concept orientation of social law, some scholars hold that social law is a jurisprudential conception or a legal theory, namely a folk law corresponding to individual law and national law. For instance, WANG Weinong considers that social law can be deemed as a kind of "legal theory, namely a concept corresponding to 'individual law'", or the word "social law" can be used as "inspecting and recognizing the source of law from the perspective of social law". Compared with the legal norms formulated by national and local legislative bodies – national law, the so-called social law is a code of conduct formulated by social groups and only applicable to the same. In other words, the so-called national law includes all positive laws formulated by the state, while the social

1 *Series of Social Law* edited by LIN Jia, Vol. 2, China Renmin University Press, p.1 (2007)

2 See YAN Cunsheng: *Essential Issues of the Research on Social Law*, from Issue 5 *Catena at Law* (2006). WANG Yong: *Theory and Practice of Social Law and Modern China Law – A Tentative Self-Criticism and Conception*, Issue 1, *Peking University Law Journal* (1996).

law, in addition to those unwritten customs and rules, also covers the internal "legal norms" formulated by social groups as their rules, agreements and some code of conduct instead of being subject to the legislative procedure of national law.[1] Some scholars propose that social law is an independent third jurisdiction between public law and private law. For instance, SUN Xiaoxia holds that as the traditional existence of two structural elements cannot adapt to the modern society, the legal system has witnessed a major revolution that the third structural element of legal system, i.e. social law, emerges in the modern market economy society.[2] According to DONG Baohua et al, if we take public law oriented at the state as the first jurisdiction and private law oriented at individuals as the second jurisdiction, the social law oriented at society arising from the combination of private law and public law shall be deemed as the third jurisdiction.[3] Some scholars consider that social law is a legal department in parallel with the constitution, criminal law, civil law and administrative law and the like. As a "law of the same category", social law, together with the constitution, administrative law, criminal law, procedure law, civil and commercial law, and economic law, constitutes with the socialist legal system with Chinese characteristics. For instance, CHEN Su holds that as a legal department in parallel with civil and commercial law, economic law and administrative law, social law has both realistic system basis and significant theoretic importance.[4] ZHENG Shangyuan holds that the result of opposing or integrating the "public" and the "private" is not "society", and it is impossible to generate social law by combining public law with private law. The combination result shall be a "third jurisdiction" beyond public law and private law, which

1 WANG Weinong: *Essential Issues of Social Law: Conception and Characteristics*, from Issue 11, *Research on Financial and Economic Issues* (2002).

2 SUN Xiaoxia: *Merciful Intervention and Neutral Law – Law Required by Chinese Market Economy Society*, Issue 11, *Law Science* (1993).

3 DONG Baohua: *Social Law – Exploration to the Third Jurisdiction*, from Issue 1 *Journal of The East China University of Politics and Law* (1999).

4 Edited by CHEN Su: *New Development of Social Law*, China Social Sciences Press, (2009).

cannot be deemed as social law.[1] Generally speaking, there is no unified understanding on the conception of social law in academic circles at present.[2] Scholars have presented diverse opinions on those issues on what is social law, and what are the system of social law as well as the position of social law in the overall legal system.

With regard to the property characteristics of social law, some scholars propose that social law is oriented at the society as private law advocates individual orientation and public law advocates state orientation. For instance, according to LI Long, the interests involved in legislation can be classified into four categories, i.e. state public interests, social community interests, family community interests and individual interests. Correspondingly, laws and their systems can be divided into national law, social law, family law and autonomous legislation. Therefore, environmental & natural resources law, science & education law and economic law are included into social law.[3] Besides, some scholars consider that social law equals to labor law and social security law, a law applied by the state to adjust labor relation, social security and social welfare relation. For instance, according to QIN Youtu and FAN Qirong, the narrow social law refers to the social security legislation established since Bismarck, including social insurance and social welfare legislation. However, in the case of understanding social law narrowly, many norms of social law can be included into the form-meaning laws and regulations as labor law, housing law, consumer protection law and environmental law in actual fact. Therefore, the recognition on the system of social law shall be made from the perspective of real legal norms and departmental laws rather than in a broad or narrow sense.[4] In addition, some scholars hold that social

1 ZHENG Shangyuan: *Existence and Theoretical Exploration of Social Law*, from Issue 3, *Law Science* (2003).

2 DONG Wenjun: *Harmonious Society Construction and Social Law Guarantee*, Issue 6, *Contemporary Law Review* (2007).

3 LI Long: *On the Scientific Construction of Socialist Legal System with Chinese Characteristics*, from Issue 5 *Law and Social Development* (2003).

4 QIN Youtu: *Social Security Law*, 1997, Law Press.

law, taking the concrete and different people in social life as the subject of legal relation and acknowledging the differences among individuals in capability, gift and resources occupation, includes the necessary restrictions on public law on private law with a view to promoting the equality and fairness in the substantive sense based on the current inequity. The guarantee of the right to existence constitutes the essence of social law. In other words, everyone has the right to survive upon birth. As the connotation of survival right has witnessed continuous recognition and breakthrough, social law manages to be developed.[1] According to the *Law Base of the People's Republic of China* prepared by the Supreme People's Court, social law, as the basic legal norm of social security system, includes the systems to guarantee the rights and interests of laborers, the unemployed, and other social members losing the capability to work or needing social subsidy, and is mainly characterized with sticking to the social equity, maintaining the social public interests, protecting the legal rights and interests of disadvantaged groups, and promoting the whole advancement and development of the society. Obviously, the words concerning social law used by Chinese scholars are less definite as compared with the fixed and mature terms of civil and commercial law, administrative law and criminal law.[2] As a result, some scholars even advocate that what we should do is to understand, identify and master the word "social law" from certain perspectives and at designated levels rather than get into the concept of social law seriously or achieve a generally accepted definition.[3]

With regard to the system principle of social law, some scholars equal social law as social security law, one of the legal departments, such as ZHANG Shouwen, LIU Cuixiao, LIN Jia and QIN Youtu. ZHANG Shouwen once pointed out, "The social legislation in each country is oriented at its social security

1 YU Shaoxiang: *Concern Social Law, Promote Social Harmony*, from *Proceedings of Chinese Academy of Social Sciences* on Aug. 31, 2006.

2 WANG Weinong: *Essential Issues of Social Law: Conception and Characteristics*, Issue 11, *Research on Financial and Economic Issues* (2002).

3 ZHU Xiao: *Consideration on Using the Word "Social Law" by Mainland Scholars*, Issue 4, *Modern Law Science* (2004).

policies and social security systems. It is the common point that causes social law to be comprehended as social security law".[1] In addition, LIN Jia takes German as an instance and indicates that social law, including social insurance, social compensation, social facilitation, social relief and other regulations to adjust citizen relationship, has not been included into social security law despite its purpose of protecting disadvantaged social groups.[2] Besides, some scholars consider that social law is the sum of social security law and labor law. For instance, CHEN Haisong holds that social law can be interpreted in a broad, medium and narrow sense. The medium social law is between the abroad one and the narrow one. "Based on the common sense reached by the jurisprudential circle, social law shall be positioned between labor law and social security law".[3] According to ZHU Xiao, the essence of social law is the "sum of labor law and social security law", whose understanding of social security relationship includes social welfare relation and other fields.[4] In addition, some scholars state that social law is the generic term of remaining laws in the third jurisdiction, except for economic law. For instance, XIE Pengcheng divides the legal system structure into basic structure, departmental law structure, sub-departmental law structure and legal system, and then the basic structure of socialist market economy law system with Chinese characteristics is divided into three "categories", namely private law, public law and social economic law.[5] Apart from the above, some scholars hold that social law as legal concept shall include the socialization of law in private law and public law in addition to the third jurisdiction.[6] As to the basic principles

1 ZHANG Shouwen: *On Social Law*, Issue 6, *Peking University Law Journal* (1996).

2 LIN Jia: *On Social Law Essence of Social Security Law*, Issue 1, *Jurists Review*, (2002).

3 CHEN Haisong: *Opinions on the Relation between Economic Law and Social Law*, from Issue 4 *Journal of South-Central University for Nationalities* (2003).

4 ZHU Xiao: *Whether There is the Medium Social Law in the Legal System*, Issue 2, *Science of Law* (2005).

5 XIE Pengcheng: *Analysis on the Basic Structure of Market Economy Law System*, Issue 4, *Chinese Journal of Law* (1994).

6 WANG Quanxing: *Study on Social Law Shall Take Warning from that on Economic Law*, Issue 1, *Zhejiang Academic Journal* (2004).

of social law, some scholars advocate equal protection, while some prefer inclined protection.[1] At present, there is no dispute that labor law, social security law and special group protection law belong to social law in academic circles. However, whether economic law, environmental and resources protection law, and consumer protection law shall be included into social law still bear different opinions. According to some scholars, the broad social law shall include labor law, social security law, economic law, environmental law, population and family planning law, law of science and technology, education act, health law and public utility law; the medium social law is positioned on labor law and social security law; the narrow social law means social security law.[2] It is thus clear that the academic circle has had different opinions on the basic system of social law for long. By the end of 2006, Chinese Academy of Social Sciences once took the "Innovation and Perfection of Social Law System" as a key subject for research. However, the opinions held by research group members are different.

Generally speaking, the theoretical research on Chinese social law is extremely weak at present and at the initial stage of exploration and discussion. Neither the quantity nor the quality of scientific payoffs can live up to the requirements of the new situation. As to the basic theoretical problems concerning social law, many issues are worthy of exploration such as extension and connotation of social law, legal characteristics, value idea, legal principles and functional goals. It is unavailable to avoid those major problems urgent to be solved.

3. Study on Science of Labor Law with Humanistic Concern

The study objects of science of labor law include *Labor Law*, *Labor Contract Law*, *Employment Promotion Act*, *Law on Medication and Arbitration of Labor Disputes*, *Production Safety Law*, *Law on Prevention and Control of Occupational Diseases*, *Trade Union Law* as well as other laws and regulations. Taking the

1 YU Shaoxiang: *Social Law – Law to Maintain the People's Livelihood*, Issue 1, *China-Today Forum* (2009).

2 ZHU Xiao: *Whether There is the Medium Social Law in the Legal System*, Issue 2, *Science of Law* (2005).

formulation of *Labor Law* in 1994 as a limit, the development of contemporary science of labor law in China experienced two significant phases: previously, the planned economy had a profound influence on labor policies and regulations. The theories of science of labor law are corresponding to the planned economic system, whose opinions, systems and methods still bear the influence of Soviet science of labor law; later on, the labor rules and labor law in China experienced a fundamental transition, and the theories of science of labor law corresponding to the market economic system were gradually established. In the last decade, the study on science of labor law has achieved great development. On the one hand, the society attaches more significance to the study on science of labor law. On the other hand, the professional staff engaged in the study on science of labor law has been substantially improved. However, science of labor law is still a vulnerable subject on the whole, and the research resources available to it are much less than those of other disciplines. According to the current discipline classification standard, labor law is still a third-level discipline rather than an independent legal department.[1]

Discipline research and development of labor law. In the early years of the new China, science of labor law once attracted the attention of the public. In the summer of 1950, the department of sociology in some universities had set the labor group, and labor law had been listed as a main subject in the teaching program. In 1951, the department of law of Renmin University of China opened the lesson of science of labor law for undergraduates and cultivated a dozen of graduate students in succession. Around 1954, the major departments of law and some departments of economics opened the lesson of science of labor law. In addition, some colleges also established the teaching-research offices for science of labor law. In 1958, Institute of Law, Department of Philosophy and Social Science, Chinese Academy of Sciences established the research group of science of labor law. At that moment, the research group of labor law was equipped

1 Edited by CHEN Xinyong: *Labor and Social Security Law*, Zhejiang University Press.

with certain scale. In the end of the 1950s, influenced by the left mistakes, some departments of law began to adjust their courses, and many law specialized courses were cancelled. Except for individual colleges, the course of labor law was suspended, and the study on science of labor law was trapped in the utter stagnation status.[1] Upon 3rd Plenary Session of the 11th Central Committee of the Communist Party of China, the study on science of labor law was gradually recovered. In April 1982, Institute of Labor Science, Ministry of Labor and Personnel established the research laboratory of labor law. Shortly after, some colleges and universities initiated the construction of labor law department or teaching-research office. In July 1983, the first national academic discussion of labor law was held, on which the institute of Chinese science of labor law was established. In 1984, the law volume of Encyclopedia of China listed labor law as a sub-discipline. In the meantime, some colleges prepared the teaching materials and lecture notes of labor law as well as the reference data for labor law teaching. The problems explored and argued in the study on labor law witnessed an increase. By the 1880s, quite a few departments of law and departments of economics nationwide had opened the lesson of labor law.

With regard to the discipline construction of labor law, in 1998, JIA Junling from Peking University School of Law began to enroll doctoral students major in labor law and social security law. It was the first doctor station of labor law and social security law in China, which greatly pushed the intensive study on labor law and social security law. By the end of the 20th century, in addition to the research institutions expert in labor law, the institution of political science and law in all institutions of higher learning was equipped with teachers major in labor law, and courses concerning labor law were set successively. At that moment, relevant academic activities and communication turned into an unprecedented flourish stage, which vigorously promoted the growth of labor law.

1 Edited by ZHANG Youyu: *Four Decades of China Law*, Shanghai People's Publishing House, p.436.

In the 21st century, the successive promulgation of those significant laws as *Employment Promotion Act* and *Labor Contract Law* greatly promoted the research on science of labor law and its development. Around the promulgation of *Employment Promotion Act*, there once were enthusiastic discussions. Particularly, the research on *Labor Contract Law* received much concern. From the basic theoretical problem to various detailed problems concerning labor contract, a great deal of works were published. Taking the definition of collective contract as an example, several kinds of representative opinions were formed from the 1990s to the beginning of the 21th century. The first opinion is that a collective contract is a collective agreement, namely a kind of agreements formulated by enterprise administration and trade union to adjust the labor relation of this enterprise. Sometimes, the industrial collective contract can be formulated by the labor union organization or enterprise organization in a region.[1] The second opinion holds that a collective contract refers to the written agreement formulated by employers or employer groups with corporate capacity and trade union with corporation capacity or representatives of employees with a view to regulating the labor relation. As to employers, the party involved in a collective contract may be individuals or groups. As to employees, the party involved in a collective contract must be groups.[2] The third opinion holds that a collective contract refers to the written agreement enacted and entered into by and between trade unions, enterprises and public institutions, business enterprise sectors, employers and employer groups on labor remuneration, working time, rest and vacation, safety and sanitation, insurance and welfare upon negotiation. The parties involved in a collective contract are composed of the trade union organized by employees of their own accord, the legal representative of enterprises or employers and

1 SHI Tanjing: *Labor Law*, Economic Science Press.

2 QIANG Lei, LI Ezhen: *Current Labor Contract in China – Collective Negotiation and Collective Contract*, China Prices Press.

employer groups.[1] The fourth opinion holds that a collective contract refers to the written agreement enacted and entered into by and between trade unions, employee representatives, enterprise operators and representative organizations of the both parties on labor remuneration, working time, rest and vacation, safety and sanitation, employee's welfare, insurance and other matters upon equal negotiation.[2] The discussion of those different opinions has greatly promoted and enriched the study on collective contract.

As formulating the *Labor Contract Law*, the academic circle once carried out hot debates on some focus issues. For instance, the party advocating labor-capital balance represented by DONG Baohua and the party advocating worker priority represented by CHANG Kai once conducted sustainable discussions on the assessment of *Labor Contract Law*, appraisal of labor standards, whether the current labor relation impairs employees or employers and other essential issues. As to the issue whether unfixed-term labor contracts shall lead to an "iron bowl", WANG Quanxing held that it was available to terminate unfixed-term labor contracts as the *Labor Contract Law* made no exceptions for them, which bore substantial differences with the "iron bowl" of the "big rice bowl" system. As to the issue whether the *Labor Contract Law* restrained the demand of employees as a result of rising labor cost, GU Xiaomin considered that enterprises would become more and more cautious on employment, which may lead to the shrinking of employees. ZHANG Shicheng pointed out the implementation of *Labor Contract Law* would raise the labor cost of illegal enterprises substantially, which had less influence on that of legal enterprises. As to the issue whether the *Labor Contract Law* would influence the investment environment, ZHANG Wuchang held that some foreign enterprises had decided to move to India, Vietnam and other countries due to the influence of the *Labor Contract Law.* However,

1 LIU Jicheng: *Collective Negotiation and Collective Contract System*, China Workers Publishing House.

2 Compiled by All China Federation of Trade Unions: *Training Course for Trade Union Officials*, China Workers Publishing House.

according to XIANG Wenbo, the emigration of those foreign enterprises taking advantage of various preferential policies formulated by China at the early era of reform and opening-up to import foreign capital, enjoying super-national treatment, sharing Chinese population dividend, impairing the environment in China and consuming China's limited resources was an essential result as the state improved the quality of economic operation, transformed the mode of economic growth and adjusted the industrial structure. It's nothing to be surprised about.[1] At this stage, the academic circle of social labor studied such hot issues as characteristics of labor contract, how to distinguish labor contract, civil contract and employment contract, position of labor contracts in labor relation and unilateral termination of labor contracts by employees etc.[2] Currently, the main deficiency of the study on the science of labor law is the in-depth and advanced theoretical exploration is relatively weaker. The present study is mainly aimed at solving various practical problems or accommodating to urgent legislation demands. Therefore, it is necessary to conduct further study on those basic theories, which will bring directional and fundamental guiding significance on the development of labor legislation.

Prior to the 1980s, the traditional science of labor law represented by the teaching materials prepared by the Ministry of Justice prevailed in China, a kind of labor law theories corresponding to the mechanism of high concentration and uniform management. Almost all significant scopes of the traditional science of labor law indiscriminately imitated the Soviet science of labor law in the 1950s. Upon the 1990s, the economic system in China was reborn. However, some old concepts in the science of labor law not suitable for market economy development had not been eliminated radically. For instance, some local governments raised labor standards and intensified administrative management under the veil of protecting employees. Therefore, the modern science of labor law shall only be established by sublating the traditional science of labor law. The *Labor Law*

1 See CUI Jiuheng: *Five Focus Issues of Labor Contract Law*, http://www.enpctn.com.cn.

2 QIAN Fei: *Research Overview of Labor Contract*, Issue 7, *China Labor* (2004).

published in 1990 by SHI Tanjing began to realize the transition of science of labor law from planned economy to market economy. It was the first work concerning labor law after China promoted the market economic system, which initiated the new ideology to study the science of labor law. Upon the publication of *Science of Labor Law* by GUAN Huai in 1996 and 1997, domestic scholars in labor law published a series of labor law teaching materials and works in 1998 and 1999, among which *On the Labor Law* by DONG Baohua was relatively conspicuous. This book is a new work concerning labor law, which states the generation and development of labor law, proposes some valuable opinions and offers reference value to the later study on labor law. In the past twenty years, the academic circle of labor law published a batch of weighty teaching materials, monographs, essays and reference books. For instance, the interpretation of labor law in *Law Dictionary* and that in the "Law" volume of *Encyclopedia of China* conducted beneficial exploration for the study on labor law. In addition, the publication of *Labor Law Dictionary* and *Labor Law Encyclopedia of the People's Republic of China* made great contributions to the study on labor law.[1] Taking "labor law" as the subject, there are 2892 essays in the "Five Databases", the number of which is apparently bigger than that of many other disciplines of social law. However, there are quite a few significant problems to be settled in the study on labor law, such as how to perfect the settlement mechanism of labor disputes to dispose labor disputes in a legal, effective and fair manner, further promoting collective contract system, establishing an independent negotiation mechanism of labor relation practically, and perfecting the tripartite coordination mechanism of labor relation.[2]

4. Study on the Science of Social Security Law Caring for Disadvantaged Groups

From 1949 to the beginning of the 1980s, the social security of China always

1 GUAN Huai: *Development of Chinese Labor Law since the Third Session of the Eleventh Congress*, Issue 1, *Jurists Review* (1999).

2 WANG Dongjin: *Study on Labor Security Law in the New Era*, Issue 2, *China Labor* (2005).

belonged to the labor insurance and welfare scope of urban employees. The labor insurance and welfare problem of employees was adjusted via policies rather than laws. Therefore, there was no social security law in the planned economy period academically. Upon the 1980s, social security law was once deemed as one component of labor law. At that moment, the content of social security was included into the science of labor law in quite a few works and textbooks.[1] Until September 1985, the central government proposed the concept of "social security" in the *Seventh Five-Year Plan of China for National Economy and Social Development* formally and incorporated social insurance, social assistance, social welfare and social special care into the social security system, and then the format and pattern of the study on the science of Chinese social security was gradually developed.

The social security legislation in China is always taking the style of "decentralized legislation". In consequence, there are no comprehensive laws concerning social security. The current laws concerning social security are characterized with incomplete system, low level and shortage of uniformity, stability and authority. In terms of research, there are many disputes over the legislation mode of social security and two mainstream opinions have been gradually developed. The first opinion advocates the mode of "one law controlling other law" and considers that the legislation of social security under market economy conditions shall turn to the comprehensive legislation mode as "one law controlling other law" from the decentralized legislation mode as "coexistence of multiple laws". In other words, the fundamental law of social security shall coordinate, unify and guide various separate rules and local legislation at macro level.[2] The other opinion advocates the mode of "coexistence and parallel of multiple laws" proceeding from the demands of social security system operation

1 YU Weiming: *Social Security Law*, China Fangzheng Press, p.45 (2002).

2 SEN Yongyu: *Legislative Construction of Chinese Social Security System*, Issue 5, *Sociological Studies* (1994).

instead of taking the mother-child legal structure as the best choice.[1] Although the International Labor Office recommends to "combine and integrate decentralized social security laws as much as possible", it shall be determined in accordance with the concrete national conditions of each state. Currently, the academic circle has reached an agreement that social security law is an independent legal department. However, they still hold different opinions on the connotation and extended understanding of "social security", and the concepts of social security law are various. For instance, some scholars equal social security law to social insurance law, considering that social security law refers to the laws offering certain material assistance to employees as they are trapped in particular difficulties, regulating the collection and application scope of social security funds, and applicable for those situations as oldness, diseases, occupational injuries and unemployment.[2] In addition, some scholars hold that social security law means those laws applied to adjust relevant social security and social welfare.[3] Some scholars consider that social security law is the general term of laws and regulations applied to adjust social security relationship.[4] Some scholars think that social security law refers to all laws and regulations applied to adjust the social relations taking the state and society as the subject with a view to guaranteeing the basic living of employees with difficulties, other social members and special social groups, and gradually improving the living quality.[5] It is observed that there are many basic theoretical problems awaiting for complete settlement in the study of social security law such as the definition, nature, object of study and scope of social security law. We have to admit that the discipline is still under the relatively

1 International Labor Office: *Development of Social Security in the 21th Century*, Labor and Personnel Publishing House, p.7 (1998).

2 Research Group, Institute of Law, Chinese Academy of Social Sciences: *Theoretical Consideration and Countermeasure Suggestion on the Establishment of Socialist Market Economy Law System*, Issue 6, *Chinese Journal of Law* (1993).

3 Edited by SHEN Zongling: *Jurisprudence*, Higher Education Press, p.337(1994).

4 QIN Youtu et al: *Social Security Law*, Law Press, p.69 (1997).

5 SHI Tanjing: *Several Theoretical Problems Concerning Chinese Social Security Law*, Issue 4, *Chinese Journal of Law* (1998).

weak condition.[1]

The contents covered by social insurance law are abundant, including but not limited to endowment insurance, unemployment insurance, medical insurance and work-related injury insurance. At the planned economy period, the urban medical insurance system in China was composed of labor protection medical care and free medical service, while villages adopted the system combining "cooperative medical care" and low-price charged medical service. It should be mentioned that relevant studies are vulnerable spots of law study. According to statistics, there were only 7 literatures concerning social insurance from 1949 to 1955, among which, 6 literatures were interpreted from Soviet social insurance. From 1956 to 1979, there were no translation introductions and researches on social insurance. By the 1980s, the works relating to social insurance were still rare. From 1949 to 1978, there were only two essays concerning social insurance, which were filled with strong ideology colors. Since the 1990s, the number of relevant essays witnessed an increase. However, social insurance was still in the marginalized position and stage rather than the hotspot or emphasis of academic circles[2]. Correspondingly, the law study was rarer. According to No. 33 Decision issued by the State Council in 1991, China began to explore how to establish the multi-level endowment insurance legal system including basic endowment insurance, occupational pension and individual pension saving. In 1998, the State Council issued a series of laws such as *Regulations on Establishing a Basic Medical Care System for Urban Employees*, and then the relevant study on social insurance law was initiated. But so far, the study conducted by the academic circle is not deeper. With regard to the endowment insurance, the theoretical study is always the weak link, which hinders the reform and legislation of China's pension system.[3] With

1 CHEN Xinyong: *Several Problems Relating to the Discipline of Social Security Law*, Issue 2, *Study & Exploration* (1999).

2 See ZHANG Yongli: *Source and Development of Research on Social Security in the Chinese Mainland (1931-2007) – Document Analysis Based on NLC and CNKI*, Intellectual Property Publishing House, pp.94-97(2008).

3 YANG Yansui: *Social Insurance Law*, China Renmin University Press, p.104(2000).

regard to the medical insurance, the legal system of China's medical insurance has experienced four major reforms since the 1980s, but "it is a failure in general".[1] There are many problems in such aspects as medical care level, system design and management operational mechanism. With regard to unemployment insurance, work-related injury insurance and maternity insurance, both the legislative theory research and institutional constitution are at the exploration stage. There are many problems in necessity of exploration. Generally speaking, the study on social insurance law in the domestic is equipped with the following characteristics as starting relatively late, weak foundation, deficient in theoretical depth, level and forward looking, which cannot satisfy the crying need of maintaining economic life order. After entering the 21st century, the Chinese government, experts and scholars have conducted some international study and comparison concerning social insurance legislation for the purpose of enhancing the theoretical study on social insurance legislation as well as the breakthrough of critical problems. For instance, the construction of the legal system for social insurance in villages is under discussion. In accordance with the legislative rules formulated by the Standing Committee of National People's Congress, the draft of *Social Insurance Law* is under discussion and consultation. On the whole, there is still a long way to go for the establishment of a legal system of social insurance conforming to the situations in China. It is necessary to strengthen the legislation of social insurance as well as the exploration of relevant theories, and establish a social insurance theory system in conformity with the realistic needs.

Social welfare includes housing, public facilities, compulsory education, state subsidies, welfare institutions, disability nursing and other aspects. Prior to the reform and opening-up, social welfare referred solely to various welfare matters in the charge of civil administration departments, traditional occupational welfare arranged by employers and price subsidies for urban citizens. The former takes

1 Development Research Center of the State Council: *Comment and Suggestion on China's Health System Reform*, from *China Development Review*, Supplement, 2005.

social relief as the main content, while the latter, oriented at urban employees and on the basis of occupation, cares the life of employees in all aspects with all expenses needed provided by national finance. Upon the reform and opening-up, the welfare projects sponsored by the state and the society are characterize with rapid development, continuously expanded social welfare scope and unremittingly increased welfare projects. For instance, the community services for the aged, living security for disabled persons, female welfare and child care have been included into scope of social welfare. From the perspective of study, the study on social welfare in the domestic was sporadic in the 1950s, and witnessed an over 20-year break-period from the 1960s to the 1980s. Later on, the relevant study managed to have a slow recovery and development. As to the development course, social welfare system, policy model and theoretical study were recovered and reconstructed from 1978 to 1985. During this period, the study on sociologism welfare experienced the gradual transition from "sociologism theory" to "social lifelization". From 1986 to 1999, social welfare theory and policy study experienced their social security period. During this period, specialized institutions concerning social welfare were continuously increased; works and journalistic articles titled as social security overwhelmed with a large number; national and international seminars on social security theories and policies increased day by day. However, articles and books titled as social welfare were rare; the influential research finds relating to social welfare theory were still few; the academic circles failed to pay due attention. The third period is from 2001 up to now. In December 2000, Division of Social Welfare and Social Affairs under the Ministry of Civil Affairs joined hands with United Nations International Children's Emergency Fund (UNICEF) and other units to hold the "First Session of National Seminar on Social Welfare Theory and Policy", which marked that the study on welfare theories and policies the social welfare period. The study during this period is equipped with the following characteristics as taking experts in social welfare rather than sociologists as the subject, active participation by welfare decision-makers and welfare workers, application of welfare theories and methods to study welfare theories and policy problems from the perspective of living status and meeting demands.[1] On the whole, the domestic study on social welfare started late with slower development and lower research level. By contrary, it is observed that the study on relevant problems of social welfare conducted by the jurisprudential circle is more deficient and in necessity of vigorous enhancement.

Although social relief always exists in the history, the history of Chinese social relief is characterized with "absence of legal definition" in general. From general principles to concrete content operation, there are neither legal regulations nor constant procedures, only featured with subjectivity and arbitrariness.[2] In the traditional concept of Chinese people, poverty is an individual matter, and the view on individualism poverty is always recognized by the society. The concept that "if one does more work, one should get more, and less pay for less work. He does not work, and neither shall he eat" enjoys popular support, which has been indicated in and intensified by the laws and regulations formulated since the foundation of the new China. According to the current research, there were no works concerning social relief in China prior to 1996. From 1992 to 2004, the study on social relief in the academic circle was always backwards and at the hover state without any obvious advancement. Subsequently, the number of relevant articles was rapidly increased, while the academic research and theoretical essays were still rare. Some researchers hold that the domestic study on social relief until now is still featured with late beginning, slow development and long-term dead state. In accordance with their current position in the academic circle, only several scholars engage in the study on this aspect, who stay in the "status of being neglected" rather than the "marginal place".[3] In addition, the study on social special care and compensation is always deficient. From 1949 to the outbreak of the Great Cultural Revolution,

1 LIU Jitong: *Life Quality and Need Satisfaction: Research Overview of Chinese Social Welfare in Five Decades*, Issue 1, *Social Sciences in Yunnan* (2003).

2 ZHONG Mingzhao: *Study on Social Security Legal System*, Law Press, p.352 (2000).

3 See ZHANG Yongli: *Source and Development of Research on Social Security in the Chinese Mainland (1931—2007) – Document Analysis Based on NLC and CNKI*, Intellectual Property Publishing House, p.281 (2008).

the uniform special care and settlement system was formed nationwide to cure the long-term war wound and arrange for the large-scale demobilized soldiers. In the past 30-plus years from the ending of the Great Cultural Revolution up to now, the special care and settlement work has achieved significant development, while the theoretical circle pays less attention and makes few studies. Social compensation includes not only the compensation for disabled soldiers, but also the reproductive compensation for females and damage compensation for Samaritans. As the Chinese legislation in this aspect is insufficient, both theoretical study and material work are extremely backward, and few researchers of law are involved.

This status is reflected by articles and works researched as well. The articles titled as "social relief" in the Five Databases are as follows: 12 articles in CNKI, 1 article in CMFD, 25 articles (the majority of which are news reports) in CCND, none in CDFD and 1 article in CPFD. There are only five books titled as "social relief" in National Library of China and CNKI. Correspondingly, the articles titled as "law on social special care" and "law on social compensation" in the Five Databases are as follows: 3 articles in CNKI, none in CMFD, CCND, CDFD and CPFD. There are no books with such titles in National Library of China and CNKI. It is observed that the research findings of this problem are extremely rare. In recent years, as the study on social law is getting more dynamic, the study on social relief law–a significant component of social law has been gradually concerned by the academic circle.[1] Based on the articles already published, the hotspots of social relief study include the definition and standards of social relief, models and implementation effect and etc. In the meantime, the concepts of social relief have transformed from the theory of mercy to the rights theory, from the simple material assistance to the combination and material assistance and ability enhancement, from the stigma relief to the humanization relief.[2] Special social

1 YANG Sibin: *Status Analysis and Countermeasure Study on the Legal System Construction for Social Relief*, Issue 4, *Probe* (2008).

2 ZHAO Shulan et al: *Dynamic Overview of Study on Social Relief*, Issue 9, *Social Work* (2007).

care and compensation is over-emphasized in policy research, while articles concerning law study are still few.

As a whole, the study on the science of social security law shall be enhanced in many aspects. From a general survey of the contemporary study on social security law, there are no effective theoretical guidance and policy practice systems already formed, which cannot get rid of the fetter of "transition", seems very weak in the exploration of social security theories and is in short of long-term development.[1] According to the current discipline classification standards, science of labor law and that of social security law are included into the science of civil and commercial law, and some scholars prefer to comprehend social security law as a component part of economic law, which is caused by the backward study on the basic theory of social law. In the legal education, social security law is still in the marginal status and considered as dispensable and "even excluded from the legal education".[2] For instance, social security law was absent in the 14 main courses of law major determined by the Ministry of Education in 1998. Currently, few law schools have the course of social security law. Although some schools open this course, it is deemed as an optional course. As the study on the science of social security law is initiated late, it is still a three-level discipline among legal disciplines. Instead of forming mature theoretical frameworks, the number of high-standard research articles and works is extremely limited and the study on corresponding basic theories is still weak.[3] According to the works already published, *Ideology, System, Practice and Critical Thought of Social Security Science* by ZHENG Gongcheng and *Ideology, Practice and Innovation of social security law* by LIN Jia have exerted certain social influence. It is worth mentioning that *A Big Thing: Study on the Social Security System for Chinese*

1 WAN Guoming: *Market Span of Social Security*, Social Science Academic Press, p.1 (2005).

2 ZHANG Wenshan: *Study on Several Problems Concerning Social Security Law*, Issue 1, *Journal of Guangxi University* (2002).

3 Edited by CHEN Xinyong: *Labor and Social Security Law*, Zhejiang University Press, p.3 (3007).

Farmers by LIU Cuixiao states the development and current situation of the social security system for Chinese farmers systematically, explains the reasons for the failure to achieve social security by Chinese farmers, dissects the wrong regions of establishing social security system for farmers, and demonstrates the necessity and urgency of establishing social security system for farmers during the process of industrialization, which ranks to be a masterpiece to study the social security problems of farmers. In short, the legal system of social security in China is in the course of exploration and establishment, both opportunities and challenges for the future academic research and discipline development.

5. Continuously Developed Study on other Aspects of Social Law

5.1 Study on the Protection Law for Special Groups

As to the protection law for special groups, the object of study refers to the special social groups, including but not limited to the aged, females, disabled persons and juveniles. Compared with other problems of social law, the matters concerning the special group protection started earlier and are equipped with the following two characteristics. Firstly, the study on relevant career development is more, while the law study is fewer. Secondly, the theoretical study is more, while the application study is fewer. Taking "the aged", "female", "juveniles" and "disabled persons" as titles to conduct retrieval in the aforesaid Five Databases, the articles of each study exceed 5,000. However, the study on relevant laws is obviously decreased, which is reflected by the books in National Library of China and CNKI as well.

As to the *Law on the Protection of the Rights and Interests of the Aged*, *Law on the Protection of Women's Rights and Interests* and *Law on the Protection of Disabled Persons*, the research subject is always professional associations or groups (as Committee on Aging, All-China Women's Federation, China Disabled Persons Federation and their subordinate bodies) as well as some special agencies (as China Association of Gerontology and China Research Center on Aging). In accordance with the articles and works already published, the study on relevant jurisprudence mainly focuses on how to understanding, studying, advertising and implementing relevant laws as well as principal achievements already created. By contrary, the articles from the academic perspective are few. As one branch of jurisprudence, it has not been established into the discipline system. In fact, there once were some theoretical opinions concerning the aged, females and disabled persons in China from 1949 to 1978, but no systematic theories were formed. The theory of comparative system was developed upon the reform and opening up. At present, the academic circle has established some specialized institutions. For instance, Center for Gender and Law Studies, Institute of Law, Chinese Academy of Social Sciences mainly study the legal problems of female protection. In 2007, Disability Research Center of Shandong University, Disability Research Center of Peking University and Disability Research Center of Renmin University of China were established successively. Regrettably, the subject of relevant researches is still sociologists rather than jurists. To be exact, the study on related business has achieved great success, while that on jurisprudence is pale by comparison. In particular, the study on the undertaking of the aged and disabled persons has created a series of compelling achievements. By the end of 2005, there were 24 kinds of elderly newspaper with circulation as 2.8 million and 23 kinds of elderly periodicals with circulation as 3.058 million. At present, more than 50 institutions are engaged in the prevention and control of aged diseases.[1] With regard to the study on the undertaking of disabled persons, China Disabled Persons Federation (the "CDPF") has organized to publish a lot of works. In 2002, the CDPF established special laboratories and took new measures, which enabled the theoretical research to witness new situations and become prosperous. As a result, some research results managed to attract more social attention and play a significant guiding role.[2] *Study on Legal Protection of Women's Rights and Interests* published by LI Mingshun in August 2003 makes a relatively systematic

1 Information Council of the State Council: *China Aging Development Report* in December 2006.

2 GUO Peiping: *New Step of Theoretical Research on Chinese Handicapped Utilities*, http://www.cnki.net/index.htm.

statement on the construction of women's legal system as well as the security of women's rights and interests involved in *Law on the Protection of Women's Rights and Interests*, *Marriage Law*, *Criminal Law* and *Anti-Family Violence Law*, which can be honored as one masterpiece in the research field.

On the contrary, the study on the law concerning minors by the jurisprudential circle is more active by compared with the above three matters. The research achievements are better both in quantity and influence. In addition, the research institutions are more diversified. Apart from the China Society for Research on Juvenile Delinquency established earlier, China Law Society also set the special Society for Legal Education of Juveniles in 2004. Besides, some institutions of higher learning established the department of juvenile criminology or similar research centers as well. *Juvenile Jurisprudence* published by KANG Shuhua in 1986 was deemed as the beginning of the era that juvenile jurisprudence appeared in China as an independent discipline. In 1995, KANG Shuhua and XIANG Zexuan joined hands to compile the *New Theory of Juvenile Jurisprudence*, which was deemed as one of the relatively novel and authentic law books. As to the study on the *Law of the People's Republic of China on the Protection of Minors*, it is necessary to mention China Society for Research on Juvenile Delinquency, which was established in June 1982 with Chinese Academy of Social Sciences as the superior administrative unit (currently changed into the Central Committee of the Communist Young League). It has established the magazine titled as *Research on Juvenile Delinquency*, organized and compiled the teaching material – *Juvenile Criminology* and published a batch of professional books relating to the research on juvenile delinquency, which lays a solid foundation to form the theory system relating to juvenile delinquency problems. Currently, China Society for Research on Juvenile Delinquency is equipped with 12 professional boards, and has established the society for research on juvenile delinquency in 22 provinces, autonomous regions and municipalities directly under the central governemnt. Entrusted by the National People's Congress, State Council and other relevant units, China Society for Research on Juvenile Delinquency has carried out several times of large-scale investigation, undertaken multiple national key research topics, published 245 proceedings and over 24 million characters of academic achievements and materials accumulatively, established long-term cooperative relations with some research institutions in the overseas, Hong Kong and Macao, participated in the juvenile legislation as *Law of the People's Republic of China on the Protection of Minors* and *Law of the People's Republic of China on the Prevention of Juvenile Delinquency*, and organized legal assistance to juveniles.[1] In short, the work conducted by China Society for Research on Juvenile Delinquency has made great contributions to the study of the jurisprudence relating to Chinese juveniles. However, there are two obvious defects in the study of the jurisprudence relating to Chinese juveniles all the time. Firstly, *Youth Protection Law* and *Law on the Protection of Minors* are confused. Secondly, the crime problems have been stressed, while the right protection is always neglected.[2] In 2000, TONG Lihua wrote the *Juvenile Jurisprudence*, where the concept "juvenile jurisprudence" was initially proposed and which claimed that the study on juvenile jurisprudence should be conducted from the perspective of right protection rather than anticrime on the basis of distinguishing minors and youngsters. It may be the new development direction of the study on juvenile jurisprudence in China.

Upon the founding of new China in 1949, the once popular corporate philanthropy disappeared in China, which was mainly caused by the absolute monopoly of resources by the state. Accompanied with the reform and opening up, charitable cause began to recover in the 1990s after undergoing a long-term "winter" and "there are certain signs of obtaining great development" forward into the 21st century.[3] 1994 witnessed the formal establishment of China Charity

1 YANG Yue: *Report on the Fifth National Convention of China Society for Research on Juvenile Delinquency* on Oct. 21, 2004.

2 TONG Lihua: *Reflection on the Law Study Concerning Juveniles*, Issue 6, *Tribune of Political Science and Law* (2001).

3 ZHENG Gongcheng: *Development of Chinese Charities and Direction of Efforts*, Issue 3, *Academic Bimestris* (2007).

Federation. In 1996, ZHENG Gongcheng published *On the Essential Laws of Charitable Cause* on *China Social News* and proposed the social position that charitable cause was a private social redemptive enterprise based on social donation. To strengthen relevant researches, cultivate and popularize charity awareness, China Charity Federation founded the magazine titled as *Philanthropy* in 1998, edited and published *The Almanac of China Charity* in 1999, cooperated with TV stations, broadcasting stations, newspapers, websites and other media to set the special column of charity, and took advantage of various channels and resources to service charitable cause.[1] Proceeding from the study until 2006, the understanding of charitable cause by the academic circle and the theoretical circle had been gradually converged, and that charitable cause was still at the initial development stage was concluded. In recent years, the study on charitable cause has set off a new upsurge. In addition to an increasing number of personnel paying attention to charitable cause in theory circles, the personnel in political circles and in the media also engage in the development of charitable cause. Both the number of articles published and the scope of charitable cause involved are unprecedented. However, the charitable cause in China is still at the initial development stage from a general view, and relevant researches are waiting for further deepening and perfection. At present, China has no special *Law of Charity Promotion*. There are only three corresponding regulations, namely *Welfare Donations Law of the People's Republic of China*, *Regulations Governing the Registration of Social Organization* and *Regulation of the Administration of Foundations*. It is reported that the Ministry of Civil Affairs is engaged in the draft of *Law of Charity Promotion* as scheduled jointly with relevant departments of the State Council and specialists and scholars of all walks of life.

In practice, many economists and sociologists had attached great significance to anti-discrimination study at the beginning of the 1990s. In 1994, GUO Zhengmo

1 ZHOU Qiuguang et al: *Review of Development Trace of Chinese Charities and Its Prospect*, Issue 5, *Cultural Journal* (2007).

issued the *Initial Exploration of Labor Discrimination* on the Issue 2 *Economic Science* and began to think highly of the discrimination in the employment field. However, the relevant study in the jurisprudence filed was started at the early 21st century. In addition, direct study is less than indirect study, and systematic study is less than monographic study. According to journal articles, the general characteristic of anti-discrimination study is more phenomena reported while few methods offered, and more legislation regulations required while less academic study completed. It cannot be denied that the social discrimination problem in China is extremely serious. Taking employment discrimination as an instance, it not only impairs the equal employment right of job seekers, but also destroys the level playing field seriously. Therefore, it is essential to study and formulate anti-discrimination laws with a view to protecting the equal employment right of employees and maintaining the fundamental social equality. In recent years, the relevant researches on anti-discrimination are mainly focused on the definition of discrimination, current situations and classification of domestic discrimination, reasons for relevant discrimination, deficiencies existing in legislation and methods to eliminate employment discrimination.[1] Academically, the science of anti-discrimination law has not been established. Currently, China has approved some international conventions concerning anti-employment discrimination, while the anti-discrimination legislation is always extremely weak.

5.2 Study on Family Planning Law and Public Health Act

Upon the founding of new China, guided by the ultra-left ideology as "many hands make light work", the population theory proposed by MA Yinchu was always criticized. Until the 1970s, China began to practice the family planning policy. Particularly, China attempted to have an integrated approach to the population issue with its own national characteristics under the circumstance that the social economic development level was relatively lower after the reform and

1 ZHU Dongli: *Research Overview of Employment Promotion and Anti-Discrimination*, Issue 2, *China Labor* (2004).

opening up. In the late period of the 1980s, as the effect of the family planning policy was declined, the academic circle began to pay attention to the legislation and standardization of family planning, while the relevant articles are few. In 1994, GU Baochang and MU Guangzong published *Recognition of Chinese Population Problem* on the Issue 5 of *Population Research*, and began to discuss the effect elimination problem of family planning policy. Generally speaking, the study on population legislation in China was started earlier and can be divided into three stages. The first stage was from the mid-term of the 1980s, during which a preliminary strategic research on population legislation was conducted. The second stage means the beginning of the 1990s, during which some scholars in the demography circle, jurisprudence circle and legislation circle proposed the theoretical supposition of constructing population jurisprudence in China respectively. The third stage refers to the integrated study period around the implementation of the population and family planning law. It is observed that the above three study stages are identical with the basic progress to implement the legal system of family planning in China. From the first national population science symposium (1978) up to now, the population study is mainly conducted along the principal line from "small population" to "large population" and from "discussion of population based on population" to "discussion of population based on development". During this process, the study on population theory has exerted sound guiding function on the practice, whose subject status and function has been continuously improved. The population and family planning law belongs to a new law, which is explored by quite a few countries worldwide in an active manner.[1] Some scholars hold that the formulation and discussion of the *Population and Family Planning Law of the People's Republic of China* seems to be limited in a "certain scope". "At least, the academic circle has no deepening and extensive discussion of this problem". As to the special law involving many complicated

1 CHEN Mingli: *On the Milestone Meaning of Population and Family Planning Law of the People's Republic of China*, Issue 1, *Journal of Sichuan Administration College* (2002).

problems, "it is deficient to depend on the wisdom of legal experts only", while "a law in short of extensive discussion and theoretical support is bounded to bear some hidden danger".[1] In addition, there are new targets, new standards, new mechanisms and new requirements in the new time, which constitute the new subjects the study on the science of population and family planning law will confront with.

Upon the founding of new China, the health legal construction in China suffered certain zigzags, yet experienced a gradually developed and improved process. Specially, the health legislation managed to achieve breakthrough progress after the reform and opening up. With regard to the academic research, there were scholar views and legal problems arising from the health work in the early 1980s. The *Fundamentals of Management* edited by ZHU Xiying in 1985 listed "health legislation" as a special chapter and included the relevant health laws at the end of the book. That the health jurisprudence shall be established as an independent discipline was earlier proposed in the *Medical Science and Health Legislation* published by CAI Weisheng in 1987. 1992 witnessed the foundation of *China Health Law*, a nationally professional journal of health jurisprudence, and 1993 witnessed the formal establishment of China Health Law Society[2], which marked that the study on health jurisprudence began to normalize. However, the study on Chinese health jurisprudence is still at the initial stage generally. In particular, "the study and exploration of theories of health jurisprudence is far from enough".[3] Proceeding from the current situations, the study on health law is deficient either in the research team or in the research power. The concrete representations are as follows: firstly, the theoretical study is blind and the discipline boundary

1 MU Guangzong: *Background, Connotation and Prospective Analysis of Population and Family Planning Law of the People's Republic of China*, Issue 3, *Chinese Journal of Population Science* (2002).

2 CAI Weisheng: *Review on the One Decade Development of Chinese Health Law Study*, Issue 6, *Medicine & Philosophy* (1995).

3 JIANG Baisheng: *Historical Development and Social Function of Health Law*, Issue 4, *Journal of Nanjing Medical University* (2001).

is obscure; secondly, the research modes are diversified with science and art confused; thirdly, the research perspective is narrow with medical science and laws fragmented.[1] As new science and technology has been applied for medical domains unremittingly, the contemporary medical science proposes a series of new subjects against the study on health jurisprudence. Therefore, the science of health law has not been established. Currently, some medical colleges and law schools have offered the courses concerning health law. In addition, some colleges and universities also established the major in health law. However, this emerging discipline fails to reach consensus on adjustment object, research direction and even discipline name. Specific to discipline construction, teaching mode, textbook system and curriculum designing, there is no uniform specification. As to the research achievements, "there are few deepening and creative achievements and many of them are repeated".[2] There are only 22 essays in the Five Databases if taking "health law" and "disease prevention and control act" as topic for retrieval. In addition, there is only one book on this topic in National Library of China and CNKI. It is observed that the relevant research is extremely inadequate.

1 SHI Dongfeng: *Discussion on Problems Existing in Chinese Health Law Study*, Issue 3, *Chinese Journal of Public Health* (2008).

2 WANG Senbo: *A Tentative Analysis of Health Law, Medical Law and Life Law*, Issue 3, *China Health Law (2009).*

Chapter 22

Procedure Law Jurisprudence Developing along the Path of Procedural Justice

1. Procedure Law Jurisprudence Developing in Foresight and Reflection

From 1992 to date, studies on China's procedure law (for the purposes hereof, referring to the science of criminal procedure law and civil procedure law) have been thriving, and fruitful results have been achieved in the studies of criminal procedure law and civil procedure law. According to incomplete statistics, more than 10,000 academic papers and over 2,000 academic articles have been published to date on newspapers and magazines across the country.[1] These publications cover an extensive range including all aspects of theoretical jurisprudence of procedure law, empirical studies on the litigation system and judicial practice, as well as studies on comparative procedure law, overseas procedure laws and international conventions. These publications also take a variety of forms, including papers, translations, survey reports, summaries, briefs, books, translation works, and collected works. Meanwhile, many textbooks have

1 Search results through the "Collected Resources" database of the National Library of China.

been published, including those compiled by the Ministry of Education, the Ministry of Justice, core curriculum textbooks, as well as procedure law textbooks for universities, colleges, and schools of political science and law.

In the research area of criminal and civil procedure law, the Procedure Law Research Society (PLRS) of China Law Society has played a significant role in promoting the research on China's procedure laws and academic exchange. Founded in 1984, the PLRS is a national academic society dedicated to procedure law research in the jurisprudence and law circles. In 1986, it started to hold an annual national procedure law conference, and since the 1990s, it has organized several seminars on international criminal procedure laws, playing a significant role in promoting the research on China's procedure laws. The PLRS not only organizes experts and scholars for academic discussions and research findings exchange through the annual conference but also works out summaries of the papers submitted to and topics discussed at the conferences and publishes them on *China Legal Science*, *New Developments of Legal Research*, and *Law Yearbook of China*. Since 1994, the PLRS has also successfully held six editions of the Award for Young and Mid-Aged Researchers with Outstanding Research Findings on procedure laws, which motivates waves of promising procedure law researchers. With its unique functions in terms of exchange, orientation, and organization, the PLRS has greatly promoted scientific research on procedure laws and its development in China. In March 1997, two professional committees were established for the research on criminal procedure law and civil procedure law, respectively, under the PLRS, to better promote academic research activities in various professional areas. Since then, the two professional committees have held several symposiums or seminars each year, apart from the annual conference, creating a good academic atmosphere and accumulating rich research data. In 2006, a new leadership of PLRS was elected, and the society was divided into two independent societies: the Criminal Procedure Law Research Society and the Civil Procedure Law Research Society. This further professionalised procedure law research.

Presently, there are a considerable number of procedure law researchers. They are mainly experts from universities, research institutes, judicial authorities, and law firms. Teachers and researchers from universities and research institutes, among others, are the backbone of procedure law research, while experts from the judicial authorities represent an indispensable research force. To date, 615 regular higher education institutions have established law schools or major, with criminal procedure law and civil procedure law being the main courses. Procedure law teachers at these schools and researchers at institutions such as the Chinese Academy of Social Science are the primary workforce on procedure law research. Presently, 52 of such schools and research institutions have launched postgraduate programs for procedure law, and 15 have launched doctorate programs. As such, the mechanism for cultivating high-end talents including masters, doctors and post-doctors is being increasingly refined. These masters, doctors and post-doctors are dedicated to theoretical and practical studies under the guidance of their mentors. Particularly, they often focus their doctoral dissertations on specific areas where relevant research is weak, achieving fruitful results in theoretical innovation and filling one gap after another.[1] A significant number of young scholars holding advanced degrees in procedure law are becoming the backbone of procedure law research.

In general, the achievements in criminal procedure law and civil procedure law research in China take on three characteristics: (1) academic research oriented to legislation and policymaking. The development of China's procedure law jurisprudence and relevant achievements are closely related to the development of China's legislation of criminal procedure law and civil procedure law and the legal construction thereof. To a large degree, the research findings of China's

1 CHEN Guangzhong, etc.: *Creation and Development of Criminal Procedure Law Jurisprudence in 50 Years Since the Foundation of the People's Republic of China*, contained in *50 Years of Development: Criminal Procedure Jurisprudence*, CHEN Guangzhong (the chief editor), 1999, Police Education Publishing House.

procedure jurisprudence circles mainly derive from extensive and in-depth academic research and exploration into the legislation and enforcement of criminal procedure law and civil procedure law and demonstrate that each time the overall development and deepening of procedure law research takes the opportunity of the enactment of criminal and civil procedure codes. It has always been an important task for procedure law research in China to enforce criminal and civil procedure laws in an all-around manner.[1] Besides the research on legislation, the procedure jurisprudence circles in China are, in general, carrying out their research work in line with the CPC's policies. For example, the 14th National Congress of the CPC set the target of establishing a socialist market economy; the 15th National Congress further put forward the requirement of governing the state by law to adapt to the internal requirements of the market economy; the 16th National Congress clearly defined the objective and task of promoting the reform on the judicial system; the 17th National Congress established the goal of building a harmonious society. The policy objectives of these four periods also orient the procedure law studies in China. (2) Countermeasure research centered on judicial reform. China's judicial reform was conceived from the early 1990s and officially commenced in the mid-1990s. The reform has carried an important mission to consolidate and promote our nation's market economy, political democracy, and governance of the country by law. Starting from the reform on civil trial methods, our nation's judicial reform has taken the following development path: during the transition from planned economy to market economy, the number of economic and civil disputes is on the rise, exerting staffing and financial pressure on the courts and evoking the reform of burden of proof on the part of the courts; issues such as the judge's power as involved in the reform of burden of proof leads further to the reform of the trial methods; since the reform on trial methods would naturally involve the roles and powers of attorneys and procurators, it is followed closely by

1 "Minutes of the Founding Meeting for the Criminal Law Association and Procedure Law Association of the China Law Society", the *New Events and Topics of Legal Research*, Issue 22, 1984, China Law Society, 1984.

the reform on litigation system. As such, the reform on the entire judicial system has gradually become an overwhelming trend.[1] During the process, the theoretical research on civil procedure law and criminal procedure law not only faces challenges from the reform practice, but also needs to respond to the requirements of judicial practice reform, as theories serve as guidance for practice. Therefore, judicial reform has not only been a hot subject for procedure law research but has also been the main thread of it. Taking an overview of the achievements in the procedure law research in China since 1992, we will see that the research centred on juridical reform almost cover all aspects of the jurisprudence of civil and criminal procedure laws. (3) Research based on China's particular national conditions and by referring to overseas theories and experience. As China is further opened to the world, our procedure law research circles have increasingly deepened the exchange and communication with other countries as well as regions including Hong Kong, Macau, and Taiwan. To promote the modernisation of China's procedure law, we must grasp the development and jurisprudence of the procedure law systems in other countries. Meanwhile, the Chinese government signed or sanctioned a number of international documents including the *International Covenant on Civil and Political Rights* and the *International Covenant on Economic, Social and Cultural Rights*. These international documents have established a series of international standards regarding criminal judicial criteria, and the internationalisation of civil procedure represents a brand new trend of justice worldwide. Regarding the relationship between relying on China's national conditions and referring to overseas theories, many scholars advocate the adoption of gradual or aggressive approaches to prompting China's procedural judicial system towards the international criteria, while a few scholars still emphasize making full use of "local resources" to improve judicial system. In general, the former has the upper hand, but the debate between the two has

1 *Reforming the Judiciary, the Retrospect and Prospects of Judicial Reform in China*, compiled by the Judicial Reform Research Group, Social Sciences Academic Press, 2005, pp.3,5.

never ceased. Over the recent years, the research by the Chinese academic circles on procedure laws has been caught up in the tense relationship between the internationalised "western-centralism" trend of thought that appears in the form of universality and the localised sense.

In only 60 years, the research achievements made by China's procedure law scholars have been undoubtedly enormous. They have not only preliminarily established a basic theoretical system for the jurisprudence of modern criminal and civil procedure law but have also played an important role in promoting legislation and judicial reform for criminal and civil justice. Looking back at the 60 years of development for China's research on judicial and civil procedure laws and into the future, we will see that besides deepening the findings achieved from previous research, China's academic circles on procedure laws should reflect on more profound issues in the future.

First, they'd better reflect on the paradigm of legislation- and policy-oriented countermeasure research. Due to specific historical background, China's procedure law scholars have devoted most of their time to academic research dominated by legislation and policies in the past 60 years, thus forming a fixated countermeasure research formality and a specific way of thinking. For this, critics in the academic circles on procedure laws have sharply pointed out that scholars tend to position themselves as "legislation experts" that take as the final purpose of their research identifying legislation problems, putting forward countermeasures for improvement, and promoting judicial reform, while few would reflect on what theoretical contributions have really been made by the jurists.[1] In fact, it is blameless that scholars may play their role in the legislation and policy-making process. From the aspect of effective interaction between academics, theories and practices, this is rather a very positive move. Regarding this matter, what really needs attention and reflection is that the long-term fixated

1 CHEN Ruihua, "Reflection on the Formality of criminal procedure Law Research", *Political and Law Science Forum*, May 2005.

countermeasure research formality has made scholars totally forget about the position of legislation-policy orientation deeply rooted in their mind, leading to the ignorance of other numerous participants and their positions besides the legislators and policy-makers during system construction. As we can see, among the abundant researches regarding legislation modification and countermeasure recommendations, most are theoretical and general, while those raising specific questions and putting forward detailed solutions are actually few. This can easily lead to a doubt: to what extent would the research method that raises questions first and then proposes a detailed solution provide effective theoretical support for solving the problems existing in the litigation system in our country?

Second, the existence and passing down of academic tradition should be clarified. Among the abundant findings from the procedure law research today, a common issue deserves our attention, which is the absence of academic tradition. In research, people tend to be satisfied with randomly putting all kinds of concepts together or drawing a simple comparison among various terms, instead of conducting analysis and making demonstration in the context of a specific theoretical tradition. Therefore, as the opinions we referred to are based on different philosophical ideas, our discussion about freedom has contained an internal tension or conflict from the very beginning. This situation shows that although we have seriously cited the opinions of many different theorists to support our own view about a certain issue, we don't really know what academic context or philosophical tradition we are in when doing so. In other words, we are speaking outside the academic tradition.[1] Such research conducted in the absence of an academic tradition is to break down the academic theories of the predecessors into separate components and then put them together into the researcher's own works, papers, or other forms of research findings to meet the specific purpose of the researcher himself. This breaking down only destroys

1 DENG Zhenglai: "Research on Academic Independence and China's Jurisprudence", *Social Science Front*, Issue 4, 2007.

all the cited theories without possibly achieving any valuable research findings because one cannot expect to get the answers from the components themselves. Only by conducting research in the context of an academic tradition or theories can the components of the theories lead to meaning and value of thoughts in the specific research.

Third, establishing means of self-criticism and rebuilding for academic research. Through 60 years of research and accumulation, the procedure law research circles in China have achieved findings that cover many fields in question, and these findings are ladled with repeated research at the same time. As we can see, once a topic captures attention, it will be followed by numerous papers and repeated researches, which more or less reflects the opportunism and utilitarianism of the academic research. The plague of repeated researches, with many papers staying at the textbook level or even lower, is hardly real academic research.[1] To change this situation, we not only need to reflect on the current research formality and mindset but also have to establish means of self-criticism and rebuilding for academic research. Otherwise, we can have no way to carry out scientific and systematic research on procedure laws. To that end, as a fundamental premise, we must conduct serious academic analysis and criticism on the thoughts and academic opinions of our predecessors and the contemporary ones. This includes researches by Chinese scholars as well as those by foreign scholars. On the other hand, the introduction of many research methods and perspectives plays an important role in enriching the procedure law research. But likewise, these new research methods and perspectives must accept serious academic criticism, so as to avoid simple draft when other cross-discipline methods are used or regarded as a sensational academic "decoration" to show academic innovation. Presently, there is also a clear opportunism tendency for China's procedure jurisprudence

1 XIONG Qiuhong: "The Status of criminal procedure Law Research in 2003", published in *The Rule of Law Blue Book—Report on the Rule of Law Development in China (2004)*, Social Sciences Academic Press, 2004.

circles in the interaction between theoretical research and practice. To view from the surface, it seems that the theoretical views are totally aligned with the reform practice and that the two prove each other. But in fact, the theories are not systematic, while the practice is mechanical and partial. The superficial match between the theories and practice has hidden the detachment between the two at a deeper level. In this aspect, what is to be done to vitalise our academic research while maintaining its power of criticism beyond reality is thus an issue that our procedure law scholars have to deal with seriously in the future.

2. Research on the Basic Theoretical Issues of the Jurisprudence of Criminal Procedure Laws

During this period, China's criminal procedure jurisprudence circles held relatively thorough discussions on the theories and conducted judicial practices with respect to the criminal procedure laws at all times and in all countries. Research books and publications are available for each aspect of this field. Experts and scholars have made groundbreaking achievements in some issues, reached consensus thereon, and deepened their understanding through academic exchanges. In the following, the main research content and findings will be discussed in four aspects. Undoubtedly, the research findings achieved by the criminal procedure jurisprudence circles in China during this period are far from the following aspects. The content below is only a fraction of the research findings which are representative in the criminal procedure law research and which have played a constructive role in prompting the improvement of China's criminal procedure law research and the criminal law system.

2.1 Basic theories regarding the jurisprudence of criminal procedure laws

In China's criminal procedure jurisprudence circles, scholars originally viewed the purpose of criminal procedure from a single perspective, holding that the criminal procedure is mainly aimed at cracking down on, proving and punishing crimes, and that the purpose is to accurately and promptly find out the truth, combat crimes and ensure the innocent is free from criminal liabilities. As research on this aspect deepens, some scholars have raised a dual point of view for the purpose of the criminal procedure, holding that the ultimate goal of the criminal procedure is to punish crimes accurately on the one hand and to safeguard basic human rights on the other hand. Presently, the dual purpose of punishing crimes and safeguarding human rights represents the mainstream point of view regarding the purpose of criminal procedure.[1]

The "dual purpose" theory has greatly promoted the criminal procedure law research. Particularly, pinpointing the safeguarding of human rights as one of the two major purposes of criminal procedure is not only of significant academic importance but has also exerts positive and extensive impacts on China's social democracy and its rule of law process. The existing criminal procedure law in China has incorporated this academic view to a large extent. However, in recent years, some scholars have raised questions about this. They hold that this theoretical formality deviates from the value objective system of modern laws; it goes against the basic principle of the criminal procedure; there are many defects by taking the punishment of crimes as the purpose of criminal procedure; it is contradictory to the presumption of innocence, reinforces the nation-oriented tendency of the criminal procedure, and directly inhibits the important criminal procedure subject of "defence"; furthermore, it is easy to give rise to legal and procedural nihilism in the judicial practice, thereby leading to continuous injustice and seriously threatening the constitutional order and citizen rights. Therefore, they demand

1 Reference: CHEN Guangzhong and XU Jingcun (chief editors): *The Jurisprudence of Criminal Procedure Laws*, published by China University of Political Science and Law Press, 2002; *The Principles of Litigation*, compiled by FAN Chongyi and published by Law Press, 2003; SONG Yinghui: *The Purpose of Criminal Procedure*, published by Chinese People's Public Security University Press, 1995; LI Xinjian: *The Structural Theory of Criminal Procedure*, China University of Political Science and Law Press, 1992; SONG Shijie: *Theoretical Research on Criminal Procedure*, Hunan People's Publishing House, 2000.

that this formality be abolished. Re-establishing new jurisprudence on criminal procedure laws, with legitimate procedure and the safeguarding of human rights being the formality of the procedural purpose, is the most urgent academic task at present.[1]

Before 1980s, China had implemented the system of planned economy. At that time, few in the jurisprudence circles mentioned the value of procedure. It is not until 1990s when the theoretical discussions on procedural justice and the independent position and value of procedure laws rolled out had the criminal procedure value research become a basic theoretical issue that captured the attention of the procedure jurisprudence circles. Regarding the value issue in the criminal procedure, scholars initially absorbed the theories on political philosophy to explore the relationship between the nation and the defendant as an individual, as well as issues relating to the mode of coordinating the national and individual interests. Afterwards, their focus shifted to the justice and benefits in the criminal procedure, raising many theories of the ideal procedure value and its composition mechanism, including dualism, pluralism, etc.[23] The research conducted by procedure law scholars on the criminal procedure value is aimed at analysing such value, rationally regulating the distribution relationship between individual rights and national power, as well as fully studying and analysing the position and role of the criminal procedure law and the criminal procedure throughout the legal system construction.

---

1 For details of relevant expositions, see HAO Yinzhong: "Criticism and Re-establishment of the Dual-Purpose Theory of the Criminal Procedure", *Studies in Law and Business*, Issue 5,, 2005; LI Changcheng: *New View of the Purpose of Criminal Procedure*, published in *Criminal Science*, Issue 1, 2006; MA Mingliang: "Several Thoughts on 'Criminal Governance' as the Purpose of Criminal Procedure", *Science of Law*, Issue 4, 2006, etc.

2 CHEN Ruihua: "20th Centry Chinese Jurisprudence of Criminal Procedure Law", *Chinese and Overseas Jurisprudence*, Issue 6, 1997.

3 E.g. CHEN Ruihua: *Criminal Justice Principles*, Peiking University Press, 1997; SUO Zhengjie: *Legal Philosophy Principle of the Criminal Procedure*, Chinese People's Public Security University Press, 2002; CHEN Jianjun and LI Lihong: *Criminal Procedure Axiology*, China South University Press, 2006, etc.

The structure and mode of criminal procedure essentially take the form of the statuses of and legal relationship of the plaintiff, the defendant, and the judge. In this regard, most scholars in China believe that there have been the forms of impeach procedure and inquisitional procedure in human history. Following the Bourgeois Revolution, the mixed type of procedure system was established, wherein the criminal procedure in countries such as Britain and the United States took the adversary system, while the criminal procedure in countries of the Continental Legal System took the inquisitorial system. As for the type of our nation's criminal procedure structure and mode, the theoretical circles of the procedure law jurisprudence generally hold the view that the structure of our nation's criminal procedure structure has its own characteristics that significantly differ from the adversary mode of the Anglo-American Law System and are not the same as the inquisitorial mode of Continental Legal System whatsoever. For example, it emphasises the division of responsibilities, collaboration and mutual conditioning among people's courts, people's procuratorates, and public security organs. As a public prosecution organ, the people's procuratorate is not a party involved, while the investigation authority has the right to impose mandatory punishments, etc. The criminal procedure mode built on the criminal procedure Law in 1979 has a typical inquisitorial characteristic, while the current criminal procedure law has led to the reform on the mode of our nation's criminal procedure by introducing and absorbing the adversary criminal procedure mode, showing an "adversary" tendency. Regarding the research on the procedure structure, the procedure law jurisprudence circles in China have also raised "regular triangle structure", "inverted triangle structure" or "linear structure" views. Regarding the structure and mode of the criminal procedure, since early 1990s when scholars conducted specialised research on the "structure of criminal procedure" as a basic category of the criminal procedure, "structural analysis" or "mode analysis" have become a basic research method for our nation's criminal procedure law jurisprudence. This research angle has exerted certain impact on the theoretical exploration of the criminal procedure law jurisprudence.[1]

Regarding the subject and function of the criminal procedure, research mainly focuses on the relationship between the scope, functions, and rights of the subject of the criminal procedure and the criminal procedure itself. In the criminal procedure, the division and coordination of various procedural functions are an important issue in the basic theoretical research of the criminal procedure jurisprudence. But for a prolonged period in the past, the ignorance of the division of the procedural functions gave rise to the advocating of "joint case handling" in the judicial practice, which was promoted as a positive experience. Therefore, the research by criminal procedure law scholars for the purpose of clarifying the border of procedural functions is of great importance to streamlining the legal relations of the criminal procedure. In our nation's procedure theories, the conception of civil procedure subject has been widely recognised, but in terms of the criminal procedure theory, the research on the criminal procedure subject in our nation's criminal procedure law jurisprudence has gone through a process from rejection through major divergence to common ground. The criminal procedure subject can be essentially regarded as an individual image and an epitome of the social structure and a nation's political power structure.[2]As the research on issues such as the conceptual category and the relevant procedural functions of the criminal procedure subject itself as well as the criminal procedure

1 Representative works: LI Xinjian: *Structural Theory of Criminal Procedure*, China University of Political Science and Law Press, 1992; ZUO Weimin: *Value and Structure — Dual Analysis of Criminal Procedure*, Sichuan University Press, 1994; WANG Haiyan: *Evolution of the Criminal Procedure Mode*, Chinese People's Public Security University Press, 2004; CHEN Ruihua: *The Chinese Mode of Criminal Procedure*, Law Press, 2008; WAN Yi: "Constitutional or Centralized Type: Orientation Analysis of the Criminal Procedure Mode", *Politics and Law*, Issue 1, 2006; GUO Zhiyuan: "Opposition and Cooperation: Mode Positioning for the Reform of China's Criminal Procedure", *Justice of China*, Issue 12, 2006, etc.

2 See FAN Chongyi: *Move Towards Rational criminal procedure Law Jurisprudence,* Chinese People's Public Security University Press, 2006.

subject, object, behaviour and legal relations, the criminal procedure jurisprudence circles in China have strengthened discussions on the meaning of the criminal procedure subject, the attributes of the criminal procedure functions themselves, as well as on the relationship and the guaranteeing mechanism between the procedure subject and the procedural functions, thus carrying the research on this issue to a deeper level.[1]

2.2 Criminal Procedure System, Principles and Proceedings

Research in this regard covers all aspects of the entire criminal procedure system and proceedings, including the basic principle system of the criminal procedure, jurisdiction system, evidence system, procuratorial system, lawyer system, criminal coercive measures system, criminal trial system and procedure, special criminal procedure, criminal procedure history, overseas criminal procedure system, comparison criminal procedure studies, etc. The research by criminal procedure scholars in these fields includes both general basic theoretical research and specific empirical research, and both in-depth discussions on the specific issues in China and comparison research and leverage research on foreign criminal procedure systems and proceedings.

Regarding the research on the privilege of silence, Chinese scholars originally focused on the translation and analysis of the foreign regulations on the privilege of silence and its operation status. Since 2000, the focus of research has shifted to whether China should establish the privilege of silence. The criminal procedure jurisprudence circles had had heated debates on this issue. Among others, scholars who advocated that our country should establish the privilege of silence system in the criminal procedure law tried to demonstrate its necessity from the following aspects: the international human rights protection standards; the important principle for the criminal justice of modern countries under the rule of law that nobody shall be forced into self-incrimination; the value of procedural justice in the privilege of

1 Representative works include: LIU Tao: *Procedure Subject Discussions*, Chinese People's Public Security University Press, 2005.

silence; the micro outlook on China's rule of law and social development. Those who hold a positive view not only demonstrated the necessity of introducing the privilege of silence but also argued its feasibility from constitutional, criminal procedure law and other perspectives. They also point out that it is insufficient to only bestow the privilege of silence on the criminal suspects and defendants; there must be systematic and procedural guarantee in place. Those who hold a negative view believe that the privilege of silence system is not suitable for our country, as the negative impacts of this system will lead to inefficiency of the judicial system, and many countries are trying to restrict the privilege of silence; furthermore, the privilege of silence may not inhibit forced confession; meanwhile, the existing criminal procedure system has already contained some content of the privilege of silence.[1] The debate on the privilege of silence has never ceased to date.

Judicial reform has been a hot topic in the procedural jurisprudence circles. The discussions on the judicial reform started from early 1990s, and in the first 5 years, they were mainly focused on the criminal procedure, particularly on the reform of the court's criminal trial methods. The Report of the CPC's 15th National Congress clearly indicated the goal of "ruling the country by law and building a socialist country under

1 For relevant discussions, See SUN Changyong: *Studies on the Privilege of Silence System*, Law Press, 2001; YI Yanyou: *The Freedom of Silence*, China University of Political Science and Law Press, 2001; CHEN Guangzhong (chief editor): *Research on Issues Concerning the Privilege of Silence*, published by Chinese People's Public Security University Press, 2002; LIU Genju: *Research on Several Issues Regarding the Establishment of the Privilege of Silence in China*, published in *China Legal Science*, Issue 3, 2000; WANG Jiangling: "Brief Analysis of the Privilege of Silence System in Criminal Procedure", *Journal of National Prosecutors College*, Issue 3, 2000; SHI Xianqun: "Thoughts on the Legal Principles of the Privilege of Silence", *Chinese Journal of Law*, Issue 1, 2002; ZHOU Hongbo: "The Question of Privilege of Silence: New Theory Surpassing Two Theoretical Lines", *Science of Law*, Issue 5, 2003; XIE Xiaojian: "On the Privilege of Silence and the Obligation of Truthful Confession", *Journal of National Prosecutors College*, Issue 1, 2000; YUE Weidong: "My Opinions on the Establishment of the Privilege of Silence in China", *Law and Society*, Issue 4, 2000; XIONG Qiuhong: "Differentiation Between the Privilege of Opposing Self-Incrimination and the Obligation of Truthful Confession", *Foreign Law Review*, Issue 3, 1997; ZHOU Guojun: "Exploration on Several Issues Regarding the Prohibition of Forced Confession", *Political and Legal Forum*, Issue 1, 1999, etc.

the rule of law" and pointed out the requirements of "promoting judicial reform and ensure the judicial authorities may exercise the power of trial and prosecution independently and fairly according to law." Following this, the criminal procedure jurisprudence circles diverted their attention to research on the more macroscopic judicial reform. To ensure judicial justice and efficiency, the criminal procedure jurisprudence circles have carried out all-around theoretical explorations and practical research and put forward various kinds of countermeasures and solutions through research. The research content and findings cover the basic theories on the judicial power, system guarantee for judicial independence, the concepts of judicial reform, value orientation, macro objectives and specific steps, trial system reform of the court and judge system, reform of the prosecution system, the relationship between the police, procuratorate and court, the monitoring system of the people's congress for the judicial authorities, the mechanism for rectifying and preventing wrong cases, etc.[1]

1 The research findings in this aspect are rich, such as CHEN Ruihua: *The Nature of Judicial Power*, published in *Chinese Journal of Law*, Issue 5, 2000; XU Jingcun: *A Few Issues about Chinese Judicial Reformation*, published in *Journal of Southwest University for Nationalities (Philosophy and Social Sciences Edition)*, Issue 1, 2000; GU Peidong: *Macroscopic Thoughts on the Judicial Reform of China*, published in *Chinese Journal of Law*, Issue 3, 2000; JI Weidong: *Constitutional Review and Reinforcement of Judicial Power*, published in *Chinese Social Sciences*, Issue 2, 2002; ZHANG Peitian: *Theory and Practice of the Democratic Choice of Judicial Trial — Comparison Between the Jury System and Assessor System*, published in *Journal of National Prosecutors College*, Issue 1 and Issue 2, 2000; DENG Siqing: *Conception on the Improvement of the Discretion Restriction Mechanism for Prosecutors in China*, published in *Studies in Law and Business*, Issue 5, 2003; XIE Youping: *Judicial Trial Principles in the Perspective of Criminal Procedure*, published in *Peking University Law Journal*, Issue 1, 2003; SUN Qian: *Prosecution Reform in China*, published in *Chinese Journal of Law*, Issue 6, 2003; CHEN Guangzhong (chief editor): *Judicial Justice and Reform*, published by *China Democracy and Law Press*, 1999; ZHANG Wen etc.: *Studies on the Criminal Justice System and Reform in China*, People's Court Press, 2000; ZUO Weimin: *Changes and Reform — Modern Studies on Court System* (Law Press, 2000) and *Between Power Discourse and Power Technology: New Thoughts on China's Justice* (Law Press, 2000); GUO Chengwei and SONG Yinghui (chief editors): *Studies on Modern Judicial System*, China University of Political Science and Law Press, 2002; TAN Shigui (chief editor): *Principles and Reform of Criminal Procedure*, Law Press, 2002; ZHANG Jianwei: *Principles of Criminal Justice System*, Chinese People's Public Security University Press, 2002; LIU Genju: *Multi-Dimensional Perspectives on the Reform of Criminal Procedure*, Chinese People's Public Security University Press, 2006, etc.

Since judicial reform is a complicated social system project and our country is still at the preliminary stage of the rule of law that lacks certain basic conditions for modern rule of law, scholars point out that the judicial reform in China should follow the methodology of "relative rationalism" and only take progressive steps from technical reform towards system reform.[1] This "theory of balance," which emphasises equal importance of justice and efficiency, as well as local resources and overseas experience in the reform of the criminal judicial system, is the mainstream view of the criminal procedure jurisprudence circles.

Procedural sanction has been a highlight of the criminal procedure research in recent years. The research focuses mainly on the legal consequences of procedural violations and demonstrates that the basic principle of the procedural sanction mechanism is to deprive procedural violators of their illegal gains, so as to force them to observe the legal proceedings required by law. The research analyses the main deficiencies in China's current procedural sanction system and puts forward a systematic theoretical assumption regarding the improvement of the procedural sanction system and the restructure of such systems as the related procedural judgment, procedural defence, procedural appeal, and constitutional remedy, forming a procedural sanction theory centred on right relief.[2]

As a procedural system under which the victim and the offender reach an agreement and reconciliation so as to allow the government authorities to no longer impose criminal liabilities or reduce penalties, Criminal reconciliation has been a hot topic in China's criminal procedure law research in recent years. In the very beginning of the criminal trial reform, while the adversary procedure mechanism was constructed, the reconciliation issue in the criminal procedure gradually gained attention for the original purpose of increasing procedural

1 LONG Zongzhi: "On the Relative Rationalism in Judicial Reform", *Chinese Social Sciences*, Issue 2, 1999.

2 For relevant discussions, See WANG Minyuan: "Legal Consequences of Violating the Procedural Acts of the criminal procedure Law", *China Legal Science*, Issue 3, 1994; CHEN Ruihua: *Procedural Sanction Theory*, China Legal Publishing House, 2005;

efficiency. Ever since then, in the context of building a harmonious society, criminal reconciliation has been regarded to provide a brand new line of thoughts for our country's judicial reform and the integration process of the entire criminal law sector.[1] For this, some theorists believe that the criminal reconciliation system has put forward a private cooperation mode that is different from the traditional adversary justice, which places the defendant-victim relationship at the centre of the criminal procedure and breaks the limits of crime and infringement in terms of criminal procedure and civil procedure, resulting in significant impact on the traditional criminal procedure theories. In the long run, criminal reconciliation will become a special procedure independent of the formal criminal procedure. However, theorists have also pointed out that as a new movement for criminal justice reform, restorative justice, is sweeping the world with its brand new concepts and good experimental results and has received extensive attention from the theory circles and practice circles. However, restorative justice has many flaws in terms of its orientation, concepts, function and system design. Full consideration shall be given to these issues when whether the restorative justice system is to be introduced into China is decided.[2]

Evidence system has been an important area of research by China's criminal procedure jurisprudence circles. In this area, criminal procedure law scholars have launched research that mainly aims to promote criminal evidence legislation. Organised by the procedure law Research Centre of China University of Political

1 CHEN Guangzhong and GE Lin: *Preliminary Exploration into Criminal Reconciliation, China Legal Science*, Issue 5, 2006.

2 For relevant discussions, See WANG Zhiyuan etc.: *Mode and Procedure of Criminal Reconciliation*; CHEN Qingguo etc.: *Theoretical Basis of Criminal Reconciliation*; ZHANG Zhihui and SONG Yinghui: *Research Review on Criminal Reconciliation, Journal of National Prosecutors College*, Issue 4, 2007; CHEN Ruihua: *Private Cooperation Mode of Criminal Procedure — Emergence of Criminal Reconciliation in China, China Legal Science*, Issue 5, 2006; TANG Fang: *The Distress and Surpassing of Restorative Justice, Science of Law*, Issue 4, 2006; ZHEN Zhen: *Theoretical Analysis of the Feasibility of Criminal Reconciliation, People's Procuratorial Semi-monthly*, Issue 14, 2006, etc.

Science and Law, numerous domestic criminal evidence experts conducted special research on the criminal evidence legislation and completed an academic criminal evidence code — Expert's Draft for the Criminal Evidence Law of the People's Republic of China (Articles, Notes, and Demonstrations);[1]meanwhile, the criminal procedure jurisprudence circles have also conducted in-depth research on the fundamental theoretical issues of the evidence jurisprudence such as case facts and evidence, evidence types, object of proof, standard of proof, rules of evidence, etc.[2] In this aspect, some scholars shifted the base point of discussions on case facts and evidence issues from ontology to epistemology and drew the conclusion by using history and modern philosophy as analysis tools that "whether the perception of case facts and evidence facts is right or wrong can only be judged by science and common knowledge while it cannot be solved by abstract rules." It is of great theoretical value for our procedural jurisprudence circles to review the functions of evidence rules and build an evidence rule system that is meaningful to the judicial practice.[3]

1 CHEN Guangzhong, etc.: *Expert's Draft for the Criminal Evidence Law of the People's Republic of China (Articles, Notes and Demonstrations)*, China Legal Publishing House, 2004.

2 Representative works include ZHOU Guojun and LIU Genju: *Theory and Practice of Criminal Evidence Types and Classification*, China University of Political Science and Law Press, 1992; FAN Chongyi, etc.: *Principles and Application of the Criminal Evidence Law*, Chinese People's Public Security University Press, 2001; WANG Jinxi: *On the Criminal Testimony of Witnesses*, Chinese People's Public Security University Press, 2002; WEI Xiaona and WU Hongyao: *The Principles of Procedural Evidence*, Law Press, 2002; SHEN Deyong and SONG Suijun: *Criminal Evidence System and Theory*, Law Press, 2002; YANG Yuguan: *Research on the Exclusion Rules for Illegal Evidence*, Chinese People's Public Security University Press, 2002; SUN Changyong (chief editor) *Criminal Procedure Evidence and Proceedings*, China Procuratorate Press, 2003; BIAN Jianlin (chief editor): *Criminal Evidence Theory*, Chinese People's Public Security University Press, 2004; WANG Jiancheng: *Ideal and Reality — New Exploration of Criminal Evidence Theory*, Peking University Press, 2006; ZHANG Zhihui (chief editor): *Studies on the Exclusion Rules for Illegal Criminal Evidence*, Peking University Press, 2006, etc.

3 WANG Minyuan: *One Fallacy, Two Sentences of Nonsense, Three Theories — Philosophical and Historical Analysis of Case Facts and Evidence, Public Law*, Volume 4, Law Press, 2003.

2.3 Revision and Improvement of the criminal procedure Law

Countermeasure research aimed at issues existing in the criminal procedure legislation and judicial practice has always been the focus of China's criminal procedure jurisprudence circles. As the criminal procedure Law in 1979 was promulgated shortly after the end of the "Cultural Revolution", it has inevitable historic limitations. In the mid-and-late-1980s, the criminal procedure jurisprudence circles called increasingly strongly for revising the criminal procedure Law to solve the numerous problems arising from the implementation thereof. Since early 1990s, the Procedure Law Association has organised many academic meetings regarding the revision and improvement of the Criminal Procedure Law, centralising the discussions among scholars on this issue. In 1992, the book titled *Revision and Improvement of the Criminal Procedure Law* was published, which was edited by the procedure law Association of the China Law Society. This book presents all-around discussions on the systems, principles, and procedures that need to be revised in the criminal procedure Law, giving rise to public opinion in support of the revision thereof.

In October 1993, CHEN Guangzhong, entrusted by the Legislative Affairs Committee of the National People's Congress, organised criminal procedure law scholars of the China University of Politics and Law to conduct research and work out draft amendments to the Criminal Procedure Law. More than 20 criminal procedure law professors, associate professors, lecturers and doctoral students summarised and studied the comments and suggestions provided by the criminal procedure jurisprudence circles on the reform of the criminal procedure system, and according to the particular conditions of China and the common tendency of the criminal procedure system reform in different countries, they drafted a *Proposal for Amending the Criminal Procedure Law*, which was then submitted to legislative departments and relevant judicial departments. This proposal produced major impact on the amendment of the

Criminal Procedure Law at the time. In March 1996, the Criminal Procedure Code of the People's Republic of China was enacted, which referred to and absorbed many contents of the Proposal.[1]

Afterward, the criminal litigation law circle has kept an eye on questions and issues occurring in the implementation of amended the criminal procedure law, and summarized and reviewed continuously in terms of its theories, offering advice and suggestions on its re-amendment and at the same time empirically studying in many ways, for instance, pilots of the "project of reform of investigative interrogation procedures," "project of disclosure of evidence," and "reform experiment of minors released on bail pending trial and deliberated no prosecution" presided by the China University of Politics and Law Procedural Law Research Institute and Criminal Law Research Center, extensive social survey and empirical analysis on reform of procedure of second instance carried out by the Research Center of Procedure System and Jurisdiction of Renmin University of China, "project of amendment China's criminal procedure law and of human rights protection platform" organized by Institute of Law of Chinese Academy of Social Sciences, the Human Rights Center, Guangzhou University, Beijing Haidian District People's Procuratorate, and Beijing Kingdom Law Firm, and discussions, focusing on the amendment to criminal procedure law, organized by Criminal Business Committee of All China Lawyers Association, from the point of view of defence, all of them reflecting the gradual identification and active exploration, by the criminal litigation law circle, of the importance of empirical research methods. The introduction of empirical research methods will certainly exert important and far-reaching influence on the development of criminal procedural law study in China and the improvement of lawsuit

1 See *Amending Advice Draft and Argument of the Criminal Procedure Law of the People's Republic of China*, July 1995, jointly edited by CHEN Guangzhong and YAN Duan, and written by all the criminal procedure law scholars taking part in drafting of Advice, published by China Fangzheng Press.

system.[1]

In addition to the aforementioned fruits, in the criminal litigation law circle, a large number of studies on legislation, amendment, and improvement of criminal procedure law have been conducted. Because they are so huge in number with wider scope concerned, they will not be listed here one after another. As a matter of fact, in the basis of the said characteristics of legislation-and-policy-led academic research, it is frequent to touch upon the modification and improvement of the relevant legislation in China's criminal litigation law scholars' research results when they discuss questions in all ways.

2.4 As for comparative science of criminal procedural law

China's criminal litigation law scholars have carried on full and thorough discussion on a series of international conventions and other documents, adopted by United Nations Assembly and its subordinated organizations, related to standards of criminal judicature, especially important standards of criminal

1 For amendment of criminal procedure law and the fruits of these empirical research projects, See CHEN Guangzhong's *Research on the Issues in Implementation of the Criminal Procedure Law*, published by China Legal Publishing House, 2000; FAN Chongyi's *Study on Problems and Countermeasures in Implementation of Criminal Procedure Law*, published by Chinese People's Public Security University Press, 2001; CHEN Weidong's *Model Code of Criminal Procedure*, published by China Renmin University Press, 2005; XU Jingcun's *Scholars' Draft and Legislation Cause of Chinese Criminal Procedural Law* (2nd Bill of Amendment), published by Law Press China, 2005; CHEN Guangzhong's *Experts' Suggestion Draft and Argumentation on Re-amendment of Criminal Procedure Law of the People's Republic of China*, published by China Legal Publishing House, 2006; FAN Chongyi's *Empirical Study on Reform of Criminal Pre-trial Process—Presence of Layers in Procedure of Investigation and Interrogation (Test)*, published by Chinese People's Public Security University Press, 2006; GUO Zhiyuan and et al's *Pilot and Reform: Empirical Study Method of Improvement of Judicial System*, published by Peking University Press, 2006; Research Team of Amendment of Chinese Criminal Procedural Law and Human Rights Protection Project: *Legislative Suggestion and Argumentation on Several Rights in Criminal Procedural Law*, published by Democratic Legislative System Press of China, 2007; Edited by TIAN Wenchang and CHEN Ruihua: *Layers' Suggestion Draft and Argumentation on Re-amendment of Criminal Procedure Law of the People's Republic of China*, published by Law Press China, 2007.

judicature focusing on *International Covenant on Civil and Political Rights*, such as the presumption of innocence, prohibition of torture, no arresting or detaining of any person willfully, fair and independent trial, the right to defence, no privilege against self-incrimination, special procedures applied to minors cases, compensation for wrong judgments, and double jeopardy, research results from all of which provides an important reference for the further development and betterment of China's criminal procedure system.[1]

China's criminal procedure law scholars have also achieved fruitful results with respect to the study on foreign criminal lawsuit systems and comparative science of criminal procedure laws. They have also conducted preliminary comparative studies on criminal lawsuit systems of Britain, the United States, France, Germany, Japan, and the Soviet Union, in addition to the translation and publication of criminal procedure codes of other nations such as the Soviet Union and Russia, Japan, France, Germany, Italy, the United States, etc. For China's criminal procedure law scholars, such studies have played a large role in expanding their scope of knowledge, broadening their horizons, and improving theory systems of criminal procedural laws; especially in recent years, studies on foreign criminal lawsuit systems and comparative science of criminal procedure laws have no longer rested on the level of system introduction but rather studied in depth the context, background, and practice process of operation concerning the

1 Representative works, such as XIONG Qiuhong's *Interpretation of Just Jurisdiction, published in Chinese Journal of Law*, Issue 1, 2001; XIONG Qiuhong's *Theory of Criminal Defence,* published by Law Press China, 1998; Edited by CHEN Guangzhong: *A Study on the Issue of Ratifying and Implementing of International Covenant on Civil and Political Rights*, published by China Legal Publishing House, 2002; Edited by XIE Youping: *Study on Criminal Proceedings International Norms*, Law Press China, 2002; Edited by CHENG Weiqiu: *Training Manual on International Covenant on Civil and Political Rights—International Standards and China's Rules for Fair Trial*, published by China University of Political Science and Law, 2002; Edited by CHEN Guangzhong: *'Covenant on Civil and Political Rights' and China's Criminal Proceedings*, published by Commercial Press, 2005; YUE Liling: *'International Covenant on Civil and Political Rights' and China's Criminal Justice*, Law Press China, 2007; etc.

evolution of their legal systems.[1]

3. Study on Basic Theoretical Issues about the Science of Civil Procedure Law

Because of the influence of idea, that is, China's socially long-term "attaching great importance to criminal law but looking down upon civil law" and "attaching great importance to substantial law but looking down upon procedural law," the study on the science of civil procedure law in China has been in the edge position for a long time, the condition of which mainly incarnates in two aspects: first, in the field of the science of procedure laws, the study on science of civil procedure law has been "attached" to that on criminal proceedings for a long time; second, in the field of civil law, the study on civil substantive law has been paid more attention to due to being a famous theory, while that on the science of civil procedure law is an implicit theory with less concerns, which, for a long time, has caused civil procedural law to be significantly behind civil and commercial law, economic law and criminal procedural law and other disciplines, in terms of research team and discipline construction.

On the other hand, perhaps due to this marginalized status, Chinese civil procedure law scholars have been able to soberly realize the difference and deficiency in study on law science and to learn and absorb with an open mind

---

1 Representative works, such as OUYANG Tao et al's *Introduction to British and American Criminal Law*, published by China Social Sciences Publishing House, 1982; Edited by CHEN Guangzhong: *Comparative Researches on Foreign Criminal Procedure*, Law Press China, 1988; Edited by WANG Yizhen: *Foreign Science of Criminal Procedural Law*, published by Peking University Press, 1994; BIAN Jianlin and LIU Mei: *Foreign of Criminal Procedural Law*, published by China Social Sciences Publishing House, 2002; Edited by CHEN Guangzhong: *Recent Developments of Criminal Procedure Law Outside Mainland China in 21st Century*, published by China University of Political Science and Law, 2004; Sun Changyong: *Exploring Due Process of Law: Comparative Criminal Procedure*, published by China Legal Publishing House, 2005; Zhou Wei: *Mainland China and Taiwan, Hong Kong and Macao: Comparative Study onCriminal Procedure*, published by Chinese People's Public Security University Press, 2002; SONG Shijie: *Comparative Study on Foreign Criminal Procedural Law*, published by China Legal Publishing House, 2006.

beneficial essence theory and practical experience.[1]Meanwhile, because they are left out on the edge, Chinese civil procedure law scholars have seldom been controlled by political legal discourse of non-theories or anti-theories, which has been a mainstream ideology in some periods, from which they could free their mind and explore courageously.[2]Therefore, although the study on China's civil procedural law begins late with a lack of strength, it brings a lot of valuable research results to other subjects such as science of civil law and criminal procedural law.[3]

1 For instance, in order to promote development of study on science of civil procedure law and train personnel, February to June, 1983, "qualified teachers' class for advanced studies in the third phase of the national legal profession by Justice Ministry (civil procedural law)" was held in Southwest University of Political Science & Law, which engaged domestic first-class experts and scholars to teach and train the teachers; July to August, 2000, "international seminar of comparative civil procedure law" in Renmin University of China Law School, which engaged senior specialists and scholars from Germany and the United States to give instruction to and make mutual discussion with a group of middle-aged and young researchers as backbones in China in civil procedure law. A substantial part of personnel attend training then have been foregoers of civil procedure law subject in the unit where they work with. Moreover, it is rare in Chinese legal science circle to organize young and middle-aged scholars to learn and discuss in so large-scale, scientific way at home and abroad.

2 For all main stream research paradigms in science of procedure laws circle are counter-measure study focused on Legislation and policy, some scholars, in course of study, haven't very early adopted angle of view of "requirement" or "opinion" but attached importance to "description" and "perspective", for which representative works See WANG Yaxin's *Discussion on Reform of Adjudication Method in Civil Economic Case*, published in *Social Sciences in China*, Issue 1, 1994; XU Xin's *Discussion on Self-protection*, published by China University of Political Science and Law Press, 2005; and RAN Jingfu's *Researches on the Changes of Civil Litigation Rate in China*, published by China Renmin University Press, 2005.

3 For instance, civil procedural law scholars have early demonstrated the rationality basis on which unincorporated society is as a party in civil action, their acknowledgement of the party of unincorporated society's capacity not just independent of provisions of the civil legislation, but far early than civil law scholars. And thanks to effort of civil procedural law scholars, it is a big breakthrough to generally acknowledge the position of parties in "other organizations" without corporate capacity in civil procedural law and China's juridical practice—*General Principles of the Civil Law of PRC* doesn't See juridical status of "other organizations", except for stipulations with respect to partnership organizations, individual businesses and individual peasant households (i.e. 2 Hu and 1 Huo). Furthermore, civil procedural law scholars' studies on theories, such as burden of proof, just claim and res judicata, extend great reference value to development of science of criminal procedure law; for more information See CHEN Ruihua's *Reflection of Research Paradigm of Science of Criminal Procedure Law*, published in *Political and Legal Forum*, Issue 3, 2005.

3.1 Basic theory on the science of civil law

Since the 1990s, civil procedure law scholars have preliminarily set up basic theoretical system of China's civil procedural law. This theory system consists of, in civil procedure, value theory, purpose theory, procedure guarantee theory, legal relation theory, just claim theory, object of action theory and res judicata theory. The reconstruction of basic theory of civil procedure lays a theoretical foundation for further development of China's science of civil procedure law.

Discussion on the value of civil procedure has begun in the late 1980s and early 1990s. In terms of subject classification, study on the value of civil procedure falls into the overlapped field of study on law philosophy, jurisprudence, and civil procedure theory, which has not been deemed as part of basic theory of civil procedure system in the study on the science of civil procedure law in civil-law countries and regions with a reputation for rigorous logical structure. However, China's scholars maintains that value theory of civil procedures is the most profound and abstract lawsuit theory at the core of the basic theory, that in civil procedure, purpose theory, just claim theory, object of action theory and res judicata theory and other basic theoretical plates, all have their own value implications, and that for the whole architecture of civil procedure and judicial practical operation the value of civil procedure has fundamental significance, so the value theory of litigation shall serve as part of basic theory system of China's civil procedural law science, based on which one is to rethink and construct China's civil litigation theory system and remodel the existing system of civil procedure. As for the discussion on civil litigation procedure value, scholars generally believe that value criterion of civil proceedings should not be single but polybasic and what makes them different is different knowledge of the standard of classification for civil litigation procedure value as well as of what basic value criterions should be included in it. It has yet to carry out locating lawsuit viewpoint of value to emphasize combination of procedure and entity.[1]

China's civil procedure law scholars have inherited or accepted theories on the purpose of civil litigation in civil law countries, on the basis of which they have raised their own main theories in respect of civil lawsuit purposes such as dispute resolution theory, procedure guarantee theory, interests guarantee theory, resolving disputes theory (to maintain social order), protection of civil rights, dual teleology, and multivariate theory. In this respect, the focal point of disputes over civil lawsuit purpose between civil procedure law circles in Germany, Japan, and China are: whether the purpose of civil procedure is unitary or polynary, how to define this purpose in case that it were unitary, and which purpose should be covered if it is polynary. In China's science of civil procedure law circle as yet, the pluralism maintaining to cover substantive purpose and procedural purpose has been the dominant theory.[2]

Just claim theory, always regarded important by civil procedural law of civil law circle, has been a basic theoretical problem in national civil procedural law of civil law system all the time, and practical problems pertaining thereto have

1 For relevant discussion See edited by JIANG Wei: *Monograph on Civil Procedural Law*, published by China Renmin University Press, 2005; GU Peidong: *Social Conflict and Litigation System*, Sichuan People s Publishing House, 1991; Edited by CHAI Fabang: *System Reform and Improvementof Litigation System*, published by Chinese People's Public Security University Press, 1991; CHEN Guiming: *Litigation Justice and Procedure Guarantee*, China University of Political Science and Law Press, 1996; JI Weidong: *The Rule of Law, Order and Its Making*, China University of Political Science and Law Press, 1999; LIU Rongjun: *Theoretical Perspective of Procedure Guarantee*, Law Press China, 1999; and XIAO Jianguo: *Discussion on Civil Litigation Procedure Value*, China Renmin University Press, 2000, et al.

2 For details of these theories and viewpoints See LI Zujun's *The Theory of Litigation Purpose*, Law Press China, 2000; JIANG Wei's *Mission of Market Economy and Science of Civil Procedure Law*, *Modern Law Science*, Issue 3, 1996; LIU Rongjun: *Discussion on Purpose of Civil Action*, *Political and Legal Forum*, Issue 5, 1997; CHEN Gang and WENG Xiaobin: *Discussion on Purpose of Civil Action*, published in *China Legal Science*, Spring 1997; HE Wenyan and LIAO Yong'an: *Brief Discussion on Purpose of Civil Action*, Procedural Law Review of Law Press China, Volume 2, 1998; and ZHANG Wusheng and WU Zeyong: *Discussion on Purpose of Civil Action*, *China Legal Science*, Issue 6, 1998.

been also paid much attention to in British and American case law. Just claim theory is put forward and arises from the separation of the civil procedure law and civil substantive law on the legal system and the dividing line between the civil procedural law and civil substantive law. In this process, it has always been one of the disputes that focus on how to handle and look upon correctly the relationship between civil procedural law and civil substantive law and to define the purpose of civil litigation. Just claim has always been a question of dispute with numerous schools and theories, and essential issues regarding its connotation and function have become long-standing topics in the civil-litigation-theory circle of many countries. In existing China's civil-litigation-theory circle, dual theory of just claim is a mainstream theory, which maintains that just claim is in nature a basic right with both procedural connotation and substantive connotation, procedural connotation meaning the right to apply to a court for exercising judicial power, and substantive connotation meaning the request for protecting civil rights and interests or solving a civil dispute.[1]

Res judicata is at the core of the theoretical system of relevant judgment, albeit all of the res judicata, executive force and formal power fall into substantive

1 For relevant works See JIANG Wei, SHAO Ming and CHEN Gang: *Study on Civil Litigious Right*, published by Law Press China, 2002; JIANG Wei and SHAN Guojun: *Study on Questions about Litigious Right*, published in Procedural Law Review of Law Press China, Volume 1, 1998. For more other representative academic point of view See editor-in-chief CHAI Fabang's *System Reform and Improvement of Litigation System*, published by Chinese People's Public Security University Press, 1991; GU Peidong: *Discussion on Litigious Right*, published in GU's *Exploration of Law and Science of Economic Law* by Chinese People's Public Security University Press, 1994; ZHANG Jiahui: *Reply to Litigation Right—Theory Basic Point of Relationship between Procedural Law and Substantive law, Law Review*, Issue2, 2000; GUO Weihua: *Abuse of Litigation Right to Exercise Right and Responsibility, Chinese Journal of Law*, Issue 6, 1998; ZUO Weimin and ZHU Tonghui: *Citizens' Litigious Right: Study on Constitution and Judicial Safeguard, Law Science*, Issue 4, 2001; MAO Wei: *Discussion on Litigation and Litigious Right, Journal of Chinese Institute of Management Cadres of Political Science and Law*, Issue 1, 1998; FAN Mingxin: *Humble Opinion of Litigation and Action Right, The Jurist*, Issue 4, 1998; and Li Xiangqin: *Protection of Action Right, China Legal Science*, Issue 2, 1991, et al.

effect of judgment. The concept of res judicata and system design related to it has become a key to understanding the finality of judgments. If we further study from that point, it can be seen that all of the particular characteristics of judicial decision, relative to other authoritative decisions like executive decision, are closely related to the idea of res judicata through major theoretical propositions like law order, constructed with judicial proceedings and with solution to dispute by realized judgment. Just because of this, with respect to traditional procedural law theories on Western European law, theories on res judicata have always played an important role, and doctrines on res judicata have always been deemed as one of the basic theories of procedural laws. But for the study field of China's science of civil procedural law, due to its conflicting with mainstream lawsuit ideas such as "objective reality" and "to rectify whatever is wrong," the science of civil procedural law has been given the cold shoulder for a long time, after which with the study on civil litigation theories such question has got the attention of civil procedure law circles in the mid-1990s. Afterwards, on the basis of introduction of relevant theories of Germany, Japan, and Taiwan, scholars have conducted discussions on concept, function, nature, grounds, subjective scope, objective scope, time limit (standard time), and the relationship between res judicata and object of action, so as to set up China's res judicata theories.[1]

1 For relevant research contents and results by Chinese scholars See: YE Ziqiang: *Discussion on Essence of Res Judicata* and *Discussion on Res Judicata of Judgement*, *Chinese Journal of Law*, Issue 5, 1995 and Issue 2, 1997 respectively; JIANG Wei and XIAO Jianguo: *Discussion on Objective Scope of Res Judicata,* published in *Chinese Journal of Law*, Issue 4, 1996; MA Xianyan: *Discussion on Retrospective Scope of Res Judicata, Civil and Commercial Law Review*, Issue 11, 1997; LI Long: *Discussion on Res Judicata* of Civil Judgement, published in *Law Science*, Issue 4, 1999; Edited by JIANG Wei: *Monograph on Civil Procedural Law*, published by China University of Political Science and Law, 1998; LIU Rongjun: *Theoretical Perspective of Procedure Guarantee*, Law Press China, 1999; Edited by YANG Rongxin: *Theory on Civil Procedure*, Law Press China, 2003, et al.

3.2 System, principles, and procedure concerning civil litigation

Study on the foresaid covers all aspects of the whole civil litigation system and procedures, including basic principle system of civil lawsuit, jurisdiction system, party system, evidence system, mediation system, civil litigation cost system, civil trial system and procedure, non-lawsuit procedure, civil execution system, and civil litigation history, as well as foreign civil litigation system and comparative civil litigation.

International academic discussion abroad began in the wake of World War II on the relationship between civil procedure law and constitution, with the 7th Conference of the International Association of Procedural Law taking it as its central subject under discussion; while it is since 2000 that China's scholars have systemically studied the constitutionalization of civil litigation constitution and the relationship between civil procedural law and constitution. Study on that respect has now been carried out from the point of view of protection of judicative claim, civil judicial protection of constitutional rights, and the guarantee by constitution of judicial organization. Especially from the point of view of protection of judicative claim, study includes judicative claim in constitution and the right of claim in the civil lawsuit, the relationship between litigation rights and jurisdiction, and civil judicial protection of constitutional rights.[1]

As China makes transition from a traditional society to a modern one, law is also faced with historical changes from a traditional model to a modern one, a course named "modernization." China's civil procedure law scholars believe that judicial modernization has an obvious tendency of sequencing. As an intermediary agent connecting law and social life and a link connecting general and specific

1 Representative results such as: LIU Min: *Study on Judicative Claim—Constitution Idea of Civil Action*, published by China Renmin University Press, 2003; and CHEN Gang and WANG Sanmao: *Constitution and Civil Action*, published in *Comparative Civil Procedural Law*, China Renmin University Press, 2001.

principles, justice's legitimacy has only come from judicial proceedings. To this end, civil procedure law scholars have carried out systematic research on civil judicial modernization, including litigation concept, principle, main body system of litigation, procedure of litigation. They have not only introduced the concept but also explored concrete system, which not only clarifies its theoretical basis but also combines program with the construction of system. Research achievements, therefrom, has a positive effect on China's science of procedure law theory and judicial practice.[1]

Since the late 1980s, starting from intra-system of courts, reform from top to bottom of adjudication method in civil and economy has put in motion the study on judicial reform in civil procedure law circle. Scholars have carried out studies with broad contents and scopes, including not only the study on reforms of the judicial system, such as macro policies of judicial reform, judicial system reform, court system and jury system reform, and the reform of judicial identification system but also that on civil justice system itself in all kinds of specific reform policies and measures. Study on reform of civil litigation and judicature has developed along with reform of civil trial mode, whose results mainly give expression to (1) intensifying the burden of proof of parties concerned to establish and improve evidence system and to remodel the relationship between parties concerned and the court, (2) setting up pre-trial preparing procedures to intensify the function of court trials centered in public trial (3) promoting procedural justice to vest parties concerned with more procedural rights to reconstruct civil litigation mode and (4) improving the application of civil summary procedures to provided parties concerned

1 Representative results such as ZHANG Wusheng et al: *Construction of Judicial Modernization and Civil Litigation System*, Law Press China, 2000; and SONG Bing: *Procedures, Justice and Modernization*, China University of Political Science and Law Press, 1998.

with convenience.[1]

All the time, evidence system has been one of the important fields studied by China's civil procedure law circle, in which civil procedure law scholars have carried out study led by the promotion of civil evidence legislation, a study that finally headed by Jiang Wei at Renmin University of China Law School, who has been based in Science Research Center of China's Civil and Commercial Law and who has called together specialists and experts in legal profession of jurisprudential circle, court, procuratorate and law firm, all of them spending three straight years completing *Draft of China's Law of Evidence (Suggestion Draft) and its legislative reason Letter*. The study has summarized the latest research results of civil evidence legislation in China in recent years and analysed the current evidence law system and the experience and lessons from the use of the system in the judicial practice; on the basis of the study of basic theory of evidence; it has been used for reference evidence legal systems from home and abroad and regions including Taiwan, Hong Kong Special Administrative Region, and Macao Special

1 Representative works, such as JIANG Wei and YANG Rongxin (editors-in-chief): *Reform of Civil Litigation Mechanism*, People's Court Press, 1998; JIANG Ping and CHEN Guiming: *Reform and Development of Mode of Civil Trial*, China Legal Publishing House, 1998; Edited by QI Shujie: *Study on Civil Judicial Reform*, Xiamen University Press, 2000; WANG Yaxin: *Civil Litigation in Society Reform*, China Legal Publishing House, 2001; Edited by TIAN Ping'an: *Study on Hot Topics of Reform of Civil Procedure*, China Procuratorial Press, 2001; YE Ziqiang: *Change in Civil Litigation System*, published by Law Press China, 2001; HE Wenyan and LIAO Yong'an: *Exploration into Theory and Reform of Civil Litigation,* China's Procuratorial Press, 2002; JING Hanchao: *Questions and Themes on Justice Reform in China*, China's Procuratorial Press, 2002; HUANG Songyou: *On Modem Civil Trial Power*, Law Press China, 2003; Supreme People's Court Civil Procedure Law Research Group: *Report on Reform of Civil Litigation Procedure,* published by Law Press China, 2003; ZHANG Weiping: *Transformed Logic: Analysis of Transition of Civil Litigation System,* Law Press China, 2004; FAN Yu: *Tide and Trend of Judicial Reform in the World and China's Reform on Civil Proceedings*, The Jurist, Issue 2, 1998; GU Peidong: *Macroscopical Thinking in China's Judicial Reform*, Chinese Journal of Law, Issue 3, 2000; LI Hanchang: *Grasping Essence of Judge's Quality and Education on Background of Judicial System Reform*, *China Legal Science*, Issue 1, 2000; and FU Yulin: *Division between Complex and Simple and Procedure Guarantee, Chinese Journal of Law*, Issue 1, 2003, et al.

Administrative Region to compare law perspective; it has been combined with evidence of Chinese legal culture tradition and reality to determine the concept and basic principle of new evidence idea; it has put forward the mode and contents of the evidence legislation in China.[1] In the meantime, civil jurisprudential circle has carried out in-depth study on basic theoretical problems about civil evidence like the burden of proof, proof standard, and rules of evidence.[2]

3.3 Amendment to and improvement of China's civil procedure law

From beginning to end, it has been the main study subject in China's civil procedure law circle to learn countermeasures concerned to questions in practice of civil litigation legislation and judiciary. Whether it is the *Civil Procedural Law of the Peoples Republic of China (trial)* issued for enforcement in 1982 or the code of civil procedure officially issued for enforcement in 1991: the *Civil Procedural Law of the Peoples Republic of China*, civil procedure law scholars have been their active participants and contributors. Since the issuance of the *Civil Procedural Law of the Peoples Republic of China (trial)* in 1982, Mainland China's civil procedure system has entered the stage of codification of "there

1 JIANG Wei: *Draft of China's Evidence Law (Suggestion Draft) and Legislation ReasonPaper*, published by China Renmin University Press, 2004.

2 For Representative works See LI Hao: *Burden of Proof on Civil Proceedings*, published by China University of Political Science and Law Press, 1993; BI Yuqian: *Civil Evidence Law and its Procedure Function*, Law Press China, 1997; CHEN Gang: *Study on Law of Burden of Proof*, China Renmin University Press, 2000; YE Ziqiang: *Study on Civil Evidence*, Law Press China, 2002; CHEN Jierong: *Evidence Law: Study on Burden of Proof principle and Rule,* China Renmin University Press, 2004; ZHAO Gang and LIU Xuezai: *Practical Interpretation and Theoretical Criticism—Experience from Preliminary Study of Some Provisions of the Supreme People's Court on Evidence in Civil Procedures*; WANG Liming: *Several Questions about Judicial Interpretation of Civil Evidence Rules, Legal Science*, Issue 1, 2004; LI Hao: *Several Questions about Civil Evidence: Concurrent Comment of the Judicial Interpretation about Civil Evidence of the Supreme People's Court's Rules on Civil Evidence, Chinese Journal of Law*, Issue 3, 2002; TANG Weijian: *Theory of Evidence Exchange System*, published in *Procedural Law Review*, Volume 8, China's Procuratorial Press, 2003; XIONG Zhihai: *Discussion on Nature of Evidence, Modern Law Science*, Issue 4, 2002; and XIAO Jianguo: *Discussion on Value Implication of Distribution of Burden of Civil Evidence, Law Science*, Issue 3, 2002, et al.

must be laws for people to follow." However, the political meaning of the *Civil Procedural Law of the Peoples Republic of China (trial)* is greater than that in law. Since 1988, civil trial mode reform has been officially started within the court system. Partial results of civil trial mode reform have been reflected in the code of civil procedure officially issued for enforcement in 1991—the *Civil Procedural Law of the Peoples Republic of China.*

As far as the former *Civil Procedural Law of the Peoples Republic of China (trial)* is concerned, in spite of major amendment and supplement in many ways to the *Civil Procedural Law of the Peoples Republic of China* in force, which is produced before the establishment of China's market economy, the hysteresis quality of the Law has become prominent, with huge changes in the international environment, social structure, and market economy that have followed its issuance. In practice, the civil trial mode reform has been involved in basic principle and system of law, a reform that has broken through the provisions of current laws in many ways. The existence of the questions has required amendment to the current *Civil Procedural Law of the Peoples Republic of China.*

In the study on amendment to civil procedural law, the most influential is *Suggestion Draft of Amendment to Civil Procedural Law (Draft 3)* launched by Research Team of Amendment to and Improvement of China's Code of Civil Procedure, headed by Jiang Wei.[1] It has taken three years to complete the Amendment, joined by many scholars and senior judges. In the course of the creation of the Suggestion Draft, there have been intense exchanges and interactions between judges and scholars, as well as practice circle and theory circle. In addition to *Suggestion Draft of Amendment to Civil Procedural Law (Draft 3)*, there have remained in China's civil procedure law circle a quantity of studies on legislation, modification, and improvement of civil procedural law, the studies that are more often than not

1 Research Group to Modify and Improve Chinese Code of Civil Procedure: *Suggestion Draft (3nd) and legislation Ground on Amendment of Civil Procedure Law of the People's Republic of China,* the People's Court Press, 2005.

combined with those on judicial reform and civil trial mode reform, all of them enriching the discussion on the modification and perfection of legislation of civil procedural law from different perspectives and to varying extents.[1]

3.4 On comparative science of civil procedural law

In the wake of World War II, the internationalization of essential procedure guarantee of parties concerned and of civil procedure has become a trend. After the 1970s, internationalization is quite universal of basic rights and procedural safeguards of parties concerned in civil procedure. From civil law countries to common law countries, constitutional or international documents have stipulated the provisions with respect with the rights and guarantees concerning adjudication procedures. The research field by civil procedural law scholars has extended to the study on such questions as great efforts to seek for cross-border civil procedural principles predominant in civil procedural, the ability to communicate with each other in the world, the effective right of prosecution and the right to response to suits, the effective right to obtain judicial justice, and substantive equality of two parties concerned, including legal aid, litigation delay, litigation costs, and small request, all once neglected. In the field, China's civil procedural law scholars have been studying step by step, while docking and communicating with international

1 For instance, LIAO Yong'an and FENG Shu: *Several Questions about Amendment to China's Civil Procedural Law:Concurrent Comment of Experts' Suggestion Draft(3nd) on Re-amendment of Civil Procedural Law*; TANG Weijian, LIU Jian and XU Shanghao: *Basic Trend of Amendment to Civil Procedural Law, Jianghai Academic Journal*, Issue 2, 2005; SHAO Ming: *What Kind of Code of Civil Procedure We Need? Procedural Law Research*, Volume 8, 2005; CAI Yanmin: *Consider the situation: Thinking on Amendment to Civil Procedural Law in Force, Jurists Review*, Issue 4, 2002; FU Yulin: *Basic Ideas to Amend China's Civil Procedural Law, Soochow Law Review*, Autumn 2004; ZHANG Weiping: *System Transition: Elemental Work of Amendment to Civil Procedural Law, Jurists Review*, Issue 3, 2004; CHEN Guiming: *Addition, Deletion and Amendment to Civil Procedural Law, Jurists Review*, Issue 3, 2004; ZHAO Gang and ZHU Jianmin: *Violent Change or Gradual Advance?—Brief Discussion on Keynote to Civil Procedural Law, Jurists Review*, Issue 3, 2004; JIANG Wei and SUN Bangqing: *Brief View of Amendment to Civil Procedural Law, Jurists Review*, Issue 3, 2004; ZHAO Gang and LIU Xuezai: *Several Basic Question About Amendment to Civil Procedural Law, Jurists Review*, Issue 4, 2004, etc.

cutting-edge studies to some extent.[1]

China's civil procedural law scholars have obtained plenteous fruits in the study on foreign civil litigation system and comparative science of civil procedural law, who have translated and published plenty of works on modern lawsuit system and theories of civil litigation from the United States, Germany, Italy, France, and Japan; the reform on the judicial system and particular discussions on the connotation of "adversary system" and on the pattern of litigation of China have greatly progressed the introduction of modern western civil procedure system; the study on comparative civil law and the reform of the judicial system in China has indeed stated almost at the same time the compiled and published series of collected translated works on the study of comparative science of civil law, of which the results have widened the views of China's civil procedural law scholars and which has played an important role in establishing and improving the theory system of China's science of civil procedure law.[2]

1 Representative works such as XU Hui's *Study on Conflict of Jurisdiction in Foreign-related Civil and Commercial litigation*, China University of Political Science and Law Press, 2001; LI Wang: *International Civil Procedure Law*, Tsinghua University Press, 2003; XU Xin: *International Harmonization of Civil Procedural Law: Between Effort and Romance*, *Tsinghua Law Journal*, Volume 2, 2003; FAN Yu: *Study on Small Claims Procedure*, *Social Sciences in China*, Issue 3, 2001.

2 Representative works such as SHEN Daming's *Initial Exploration in Comparative Civil Procedure Law*, CITIC Publishing House, 1991; ZHANG Weiping: *Conflict and Balance in Realization of Procedural Justice: Introduction to Study on Foreign Civil Procedure*, Chengdu Press, 1993; BAI Lvxuan: *Civil Procedural Law of the United States*, the Economic Daily Press, 1996; SONG Bing: *Textbook: Judicial System and Procedure of the United States and Germany*, China University of Political Science and Law Press, 1999; CAI Yanmin and HONG Hao: *Legal Analysis of Due Procedure—Study on System of Civil Procedure of Contemporary America*, China University of Political Science and Law Press, 2000; CHEN Gang: *Brief of Socialist Civil Procedure law—Evolution, Subject of Litigation and Evidence System*, Law Press China, 2001; XU Xin: *Civil Procedure and Civil Justice Reforms in UK*, China University of Political Science and Law Press, 2002; WANG Yaxin: *Confrontation and Determination: Basic Structure of Japan's Civil Litigation Law of Japan*, Tsinghua University Press, 2002; TAN Bing (editor-in-chief): *Study on Foreign System of Civil Procedure*, Law Press China, 2003, etc.

4. Science of Administrative Proceeding Law with the Expansion of Theoretical View

Since the promulgation of the Administrative Procedure Law of the People's Republic of China, academic achievements have emerged endlessly. Based on the summaries by scholars,[1]since 1989, China's science of administrative procedure law may be divided into two phases, with boundary point of time of promulgation of the *Judicial Interpretation of the Supreme People's Court on Some Issues Regarding the Enforcement of the Administrative Procedure Law of the People's Republic of China* in March 2000 (hereinafter referred to as *Interpretation on Some Issues*).

4.1 Phase of study of glossators and science of positive law (1989 to promulgation of Interpretation)

With the promulgation of *the Administrative Procedure Law,* subjects in regard of the science of administrative procedure law have become temporary hot topics discussed in the jurisprudential circle. On the one hand, administrative procedure system and its spirit have been widely known to the public in society; on the other hand, extensive discussions have been carried out in the jurisprudential circle on the questions arising out of the process of implementing *the Administrative Procedure Law* and on those existing in legislative regulations. Topical subjects concerned focus on: in administrative cases, the scope to be accepted by the court, the concept of concrete act of administration and its justiciability, burden of proof, plaintiff qualification, court hearing mode, application of administrative judgment, third party, and administrative litigation with incidental civil action. Questions and issues in the course of practice, especially those about ordinary people's "not wanting to accuse or daring not accuse" and "law enforcement difficulty", have become

1 YANG Haikunand and CAO Daquan: *Study on China's Administrative Procedural Law Developing Gradually, Zhejiang Academic Journal*, Issue 6, 2006.

topics discussed the most in that period.[1] Study on China's jurisprudence of administrative procedure has especially featured an empirical research method, widely applied in the jurisprudential circle, which is of annotation type and superficial. Rarely discussing deep theoretical problems arising out of legislation practice, scholars have been especially keen on analysing deficiencies in the practice. For instance, discussion in the jurisprudential circle on the scope of accepting cases has specifically centered on the connotation of legislative clauses of the *Administrative Procedure Law,* as well as status quo of unclear scope of acceptance of administrative procedural law in practice, caused by insufficient legislative regulations,[2] instead of aiming at the study on theoretical basis of scope of accepting cases. Study on form of judgment in the jurisprudential circle mainly aims at the discussion of basic questions like how to apply the form of judgment in practice,[3] without any deeper theoretical research results. The results of practice in the jurisprudential circle in the period are intensively reflected in the *Judicial Interpretation of*

1 In 1999 (on the 10th anniversary Day of the Issuance of the *Administrative Procedure Law* of the People's Republic of China), an annual meeting of China Administrative Law Society was held in Zhuhai, the main topic of which was "Establishment, development and improvement of China's administrative litigation system". At the meeting, scholars widely discussed questions concerning "not wanting to accuse, or daring not accuse" and "law enforcement difficulty", summarizing in an all-round way achievement and deficiency on and in the ten years' of implementation of China's administrative litigation act. For more See *Law Yearbook of China* (2002), pp.1048-1049.

2 See LIU Shangchun's *Exploration in Theory and Practice Scope of Accepting Cases in Administrative Litigation*, published in *Political and Legal Forum*, Issue 3, 1995; LU Wushi: *Thinking on Several Defects in Provisions of Scope of Accepting Cases in Administrative Litigation, Journal of Guangxi University (Philosophy and Social Science Edition)*, Issue 1, 1994,etc.

3 See ZHUANG Jiaxiang: *Discussion on Application of Changing Decision in Administrative Litigation, Administrative Law Review*, Issue 4, 1995; YAN Huiren: *Relevant Administrative Provisions that Should be Quoted in Administrative Judgement and Ruling, Administrative Law Review*, Issue 2, 1995; PAN Changfeng: *Discussion on Boundedness of China's Form of Administrative Judgment and Its Improvement, People's Judicature*, Issue 10, 1997; LI Daoqing: *Administrative Procedure Should Set Up Partial Judgment, Administrative Law Review*, Issue 3, 1997, etc.

the Supreme People's Court on Some Issues Regarding the Enforcement of the Administrative Procedure Law of the People's Republic of China, in March 2000 (hereinafter referred to as *Interpretation on Some Issues*). It may be said that *Interpretation on Some Issues* has summarized such results, which is also the best testimony of research methods of the science of positive law and glossators combined then.[1]

Plenty of textbooks of administrative procedure law[2] have been published during that period. However, there has been a common characteristic in the textbooks. That is, all have been laid out in accordance with the style of the *Administrative Procedure Law.*[3] Treatises and textbooks[4] of that period on foreign administrative procedure systems translated or compiled in the jurisprudential circle have paid more attention to giving an outline of foreign administrative procedure systems, with insufficient introduction of results on theoretical basis

1 It is generally acknowledged that provisions concerning scope are mainly focused on Article 2, 11 and 12 of accepting cases in administrative litigation. This legislation mode has been reduced by the circle to "principle + enumeration + exclusion mode", of which the malpractice is vague boundaries of scope of accepting cases, thus leading to circumstances whether the scope falls into that of accepting cases in administrative litigation. Hence, Section 1 of *Interpretation of Several Questions* exclusively provide for scope of accepting cases, the provisions that meet the need of practice, and can also be summary of academic research results.

2 LUO Haocai (editor-in-chief): *China's Judicial Review System,* Peking University Press, 1993; YING Songnian (editor-in-chief): *Science of Administrative Proceeding Law*, China University of Political Science and Law Press, 1994; XUE Gangling (editor-in-chief): *Science of Administrative Proceeding Law*, Sino-Culture Press, 1998; PI Chunxie (editor-in-chief): *Administrative Procedure Law Tutorial*, China Renmin University Press, 1993, etc.

3 For evaluation of administrative procedure law textbooks, See YUAN Shuhong and SONG Gongde: *Original Theory of Science of Unite Public Law—Another Mode of Pandect of Science of Unite Public Law* (A), published by China Renmin University Press, 2005, pp.308-312.

4 WANG Mingyang's *Administrative Law of the United States*, China Legal Publishing House, 1995; *Foreign Administrative Litigation System*, People's Court Press, 1991; *Administrative Law*, written by William Wade, translated by XU Bing et al, Encyclopaedia of China Publishing House, 1997; YANG Jianshun's treatise *General Theory on Administrative Law of Japan*, China Legal Publishing House, 1998, et al.

research on administrative procedure laws, which could explain a lot about the immaturity of study on China's jurisprudence of administrative procedure as a whole. In the period, a small number of treatises of the jurisprudential circle were published[1], together with some academic papers meeting high standards for theories[2], but unfortunately, such results did not played a key role in the study on administrative procedure at the time.

4.2 Phase during which basic theory has been preliminarily constructed of administrative procedure (since promulgation of *Interpretation*)

The promulgation and implementation of the *Interpretation on Some Issues* has promoted further study on jurisprudence of administrative procedure. In the period, on the one hand, with related issues left over by the *Administrative Procedure Law* and new ones in practice initiated by the *Interpretation on Some Issues*, the study of annotation-type law has culminated on administrative procedure system;[3]on the other hand, since the *Interpretation on Some Issues* has further improved the *Administrative Procedure La,* and put into practice many study results then, the jurisprudential circle has begun distracting attention onto reinforcing study on the background of creation, reason, and advantages and disadvantages of the concrete system of administrative litigation and turning its attention to basic theories on administrative procedure.

1 LIU Shanchun: *Theory on Value of Administrative Procedure* (Law Press China, 1998); XUE Gangling: *Study on Administrative Right of Suit* (Sino-Culture Press, 1999); HU Xiaohua: S*tudy on Basic Theory of Administrative Procedure* (Hunan People's Publishing House, 1999), et al.

2 ZHANG Jiansheng: *Analysis About Theories on Scope of Accepting Cases in Administrative Procedure*, published in China Legal Science, Issue 2, 1998; CHEN Duanhong: *Standoff: Way out of China's Constitutional Government in the Eye of Administrative Procedure, Peking University Law Journey*, Issue 4, 1995.

3 There are the following three representative books, JIANG Bixin: *Development of China's Administrative Procedure System—Judicial Interpretation of Administrative Procedure Law*, Gold Wall Press, 2001; GAN Wen: *Comment on Judicial Interpretation of Administrative Procedure Law—Reason, Opinion and Problem* (China Legal Publishing House, 2000); GAN Wen: *Comment on Judicial Interpretation of Administrative Procedure Law—Reason, Opinion and Problem*, China Legal Publishing House, 2003.

For study on administrative procedure law during this period, the most outstanding features are that the study methods in the jurisprudential circle have become diversified from the study of glossators and the science of positive law and that the main emphasis of study has turned into the analytical investigation going deep into advantages and disadvantages, existence or abolishment, and the improvement of existing concrete system of administrative litigation from concerns about regulations of the *Administrative Procedure Law* and its implementation. In the period, study methods linking theory with practice have been exerted in a broad way, with discussions on questions in their practice by and large, such as the scope of accepting cases, plaintiff qualification, judicial system[1], and withdrawal[2]; the jurisprudential circle has begun realizing the relevance between administrative procedure system and other systems, forming a basic trend of trans-field study on administrative litigation system like investigation into the influence of WTO system on administrative litigation system,[3] and the study on administrative litigation system from the point of

1 For instance, YING Songnian and XUE Gangling: *Investigation Report on Administrative Trial System Reform* (A and B) made based on their questionnaire in Beijing, Shanghai, Zhejiang, Hunan and Guangdong about "Reform of the administrative judicial organ, of administrative law judge system, of operation condition of the administrative litigation, of administrative litigation system and recognition and evaluation of administrative lawsuit system". See *Procedural Law Research*, published by China Procuratorial Press, Volume 4, 2002, pp.291-320; *Procedural Law Research*, published by China Procuratorial Press, Volume 4, 2003, pp.367-409.

2 For instance, HE Haibo: *Study on Dismissal in Administrative Procedure*, published in *Peking University Law Journal*, Issue 2, 2001; *Scope of Accepting Cases in Administrative Procedure: A Chapter of Practice History of Judicial Power (1990-2001)*, published in *Peking University Law Review*, Album 2 of Volume 4, Peking University Press, 2002, pp.569-587.

3 XIAO Wei: *Study on WTO and China's Judicial Review*, published in *Journal of Wuhan University of Technology (Social Sciences Version)*, Issue 1, 2005; MA Huaide and GE Bowei: *WTO and Development of China's Administrative Procedure System—Concurrent Discussion on Amendment to Administrative Procedure Law in Force*, published in *Political and Legal Forum*, Issue 2, 2002; KONG Xiangjun: *Establishment Judicial Review System Suitable for WTO Requirements*, published in *China Legal Science*, Issue 6, 2001; YANG Jiejun: *China's accession to the WTO and Reform of Administrative Procedure System*, published in *Legal Science*, Issue 4, 2002, et al.

view of constitutional government;[1]comparative study methods are wielded widely in the jurisprudential circle; some scholars consciously employ economic analytical method,[2] value analysis method[3]and so on to inspect administrative litigation system. In other ways, the study on administrative litigation system has made progress in depth and breadth. More than anything else in the period, the jurisprudential circle has begun to attach great importance to basic theory on questions about jurisprudence of administrative procedure,[4] such as administrative right of suit[5] and its value,[6]interest of action in administrative

1 For instance, HU Xiaohua: *Constitutional Analysis on Scope of Accepting Cases in Administrative Procedure,* and *Theory and Practice of Procedural Law 2003 Civil and Science of Administrative Procedure Law Volume (B)*, China University of Political Science and Law Press, 2003, pp.485-489; as well as *Discrimination of Relationship Between Administrative Procedure and Constitution, "Game Between Right and Power"—Free Discussion on Amendment to Administrative Procedure law*, China Legal Publishing House, 2005, pp.11-20; DAI Jianzhi: *Administrative Procedure Means Contacting with Constitution up Close* (published in *People's Judicature*, Issue 9, 2002), p.22; LI Weigang: *Constitutionalism Meaning of Administrative Procedure, Contemporary Law Review*, Issue 2, 2003, et al.

2 For instance, LIU Xia and ZHANG Dan: *Economic Analysis on Transition of China Administrative Relief System*, published in *Journal of Fujian School of Administration and Fujian Institute of Economics and Management*, Issue 4, 2003. Also See WANG Yong's *Economic Analysis on Main Procedure in Administrative Litigation, Modern Law Science*, Issue 1, 2004.

3 For instance, ZHANG Jiansheng: *Discussion on Application of Interest Measurement Methods Used in Judgment for Confirmation in Administrative Procedure, Law Science*, Issue 6, 2004.

4 Here are two concepts need to be discriminated: one being "basic issue"; the other being "basic theory". In the Chapter, this refers to basic issues in science of administrative procedure law, such as value and purpose; that basic issues in the system, such as scope of accepting cases.

5 For instance, ZHAO Zhengqun: *Generation of Administrative Right of Suit in Mainland China and Challenge Facing It*, published in *Procedural Law Review*, Volume 6, and by Law Press China, pp.753-775, et al.

6 For value of administrative procedure, some scholars have summarized fully that of administrative procedure of western countries in ancient times and today, putting forward, on the basis of analyse results of generative mechanism of administrative procedure value, an administrative procedure value system in order of human rights, order, efficiency and justice. For instance, LIU Shanchun has written *Discussion on Administrative Procedure Value* based on his doctoral dissertation, Law Press China, 1998.

procedure,[1]categorization of administrative procedure,[2] intension of judicial review[3], and review standards[4]. In terms of the purpose of administrative procedure, the jurisprudential circle has produced "three main categories and no fewer than dozens of kinds" of viewpoints.[5]These have been published in succession a batch of quality treatises,[6]doctor and master theses, as well as periodical research papers. It should be mentioned that the study in the jurisprudential circle in the period on basic theory of jurisprudence of

1 For instance, LIU Zhigang's *Discussion on Interest of Action in Administrative Procedure*, published in *Procedural Law Review*, Volume 9, and by Law Press China, 2004, pp.512-547, et al.

2 For instance, XUE Gangling: *Research on the Administrative Procedure Category*, published in *Procedural Law Review*, Volume 1, and by China Procuratorial Press, 2002, pp.346-378, et al.

3 See YANG Weidong's *Study on Judicial Review Intensity on Administrative Act—Longitudinal Study on Administrative Jurisdiction*, published by China Renmin University Press, 2003; XIE Zhiyong: *Discussion on Examination Standard for Administrative Procedure—Concurrent Discussion on Precondition Review in Administrative Procedure*, published by Chinese People's Public Security University Press, 2004.

4 For instance, XIE Zhiyong: *Discussion on Examination Standard for Administrative Procedure—Concurrent Discussion on Precondition Review in Administrative Procedure*, published by Chinese People's Public Security University Press, 2004.

5 See LIU Dongliang: Discussion on Purpose of Administrative Procedure: *"Safeguard Rights and Interests of the People" and "Amendment to and Improvement of China's Administrative Procedure Law"*, doctoral dissertation at China University of Political Science and Law, 2004.

6 For instance, LV Liqiu's Burden of Proof in Administrative Procedure (China University of Political Science and Law Press, 2001); XIE Zhiyong: *Discussion on Examination Standard for Administrative Procedure: Concurrent Discussion on Precondition Review in Administrative Procedure*, Chinese People's Public Security University Press, 2003; YANG Weidong: *Study on Judicial Review Intensity on Administrative Act—Longitudinal Study on Administrative Jurisdiction*, China Renmin University Press, 2003; WANG Xuehui (editor-in-chief): *Comparative Study on Administrative Procedure System,* China's Procuratorial Press, 2004; WANG Baoming et al: *Judicial Review of Abstract Administrative Act,* People's Court Press, 2004; MA Huaide (editor-in-chief): Principle of *Administrative Procedure,* Law Press. China, 2003; YANG Haikun and HUANG Xuexian: *Basic Principle of Administrative Procedure and Its System Improvement*, Personnel of China Publishing House, 2005.

administrative procedure has made greater progress than the pervious period; however, the study on basic theory has yet to become the core in the period.

It can be seen on the basis of the foresaid analyses that the study on China's jurisprudence of administrative procedure has experienced a gradual process from the establishment condition of brief study on administrative litigation system to the reasoning reflection of living basis of China's administrative litigation system and to the study on basic theory of jurisprudence of administrative procedure. So far, the phased objectives have been achieved of study on jurisprudence of administrative procedure, which shows not only diversified research methods and widened research perspectives but also the study in the jurisprudence circle on basic theory on administrative procedure, with the trend of going further. But we should realize soberly that there have been so many questions and difficulties in study on jurisprudence of administrative procedure: (1) a theory system, which has not been formed but surpasses legislation system, is relatively mature and stable, without criticizing and reflecting ability due to theoretical study. (2) Study on comparative law has not been conducted effectively all the time, with the study on jurisprudence of administrative procedure lacking basic international vision. (3) There are few effective academic exchanges and dialogues. On the one hand, it is due to ubiquitous replicated studies; on the other hand, it is difficult to make breakthroughs in major theoretical issues.[1] It is safe to say that study on China's jurisprudence of administrative procedure still has a long way to go.

5. Study Focusing on Judicial Reform

Beginning in the late 1980s, today's China judicial reform, guided by reform of mode of adjudication in civil trial of people's court, taking the opportunity of the report at the 15th NCCPC in 1997, has been one of the hot topics on theory.

1 LIN Lihong and ZHAO Qinglin: *Review and Examination: New Development for About 7 Years of China's Science of Administrative Proceeding Law*, published in *Review and Prospect of China's Administrative Law: Collected Papers of 2005 Annual Conference on "Twenty Years of China's Administrative Law" Boao Forum and China Administrative Law Society*, compiled by China Administrative Law Society, China University of Political Science and Law Press, 2006.

As a grand topic, study on judicial reform is involved in extensive contents with rich research results.[1] As a whole, research on China's judicial reform has been enlarged constantly. Some questions were once deemed as forbidden zones of theories studied to a large extent, such as judicial independence, judicial review, separation of powers, and checks and balances. Research teams have been strengthened ceaselessly, with scholars of constitution, procedure law, legal principle, judicial system, and civil law joining the teams. Meanwhile, main research field has been developed from the macroscopic theory narration to the concrete judicial management, but there are still very few micro and empirical researches on judicial reform and management.

5.1 Study on basic theory of judicial power

Study is mainly involved in the concept of judicature, the nature of judicial power, the influence of globalization on China's justice, and international standard of justice. Among them, representative points of view include: as for the comprehension of judicial meaning and the judicial composition, to break original comprehension of "Grand Judicature" is not limited to official narratives by courts and procuratorates, the "Two Big Judicial Offices", but to locating judicial power on judgment and execution.[2] In terms of the study on independence of judicature, we have discussed the following: why independence of judicature is necessary, revolutionary teachers' discussions on independence of judicature, the relationship between independence of judicature and media supervision, the relationship between media supervision and leadership of the Party, relatively independent ability of procuratorial power, independence of judicature and adjustment of court structure, independence of judicature and a judge's independent judicial personality, independence of judicature and reform of judge management system,

1 The following is quoted from WEI Qunlin's *Study Review on China's Judicial Reform*, published in *Journal of Chongqing Vocational and Technical College*, Issue 5, 2007, which did an induction and conclusion in detail of study on China's judicial reform.

2 For details See SUN Wansheng's *A Jurisprudential Interpretation of Judicial Power*, Law Press China, 2002; HU Xiabing: *Judicial Power: Analysis of its Nature and Structure*, the People's Court Press, 2003.

and starting from proposition of judicial independence to elaborating other questions about judicial reform.[1]

With the purpose of using ideas, experience, or lessons from foreign judicial reform for reference in the course of reforming China's judicature, many scholars have carried on comparative study on judicial reform, the scope of which covers both countries whose rule of law is perfect such as the United States, Britain, France, Japan, Germany, and South Korea and those whose judicial system is under reconstitution such as Russia and even African countries with backward judicial systems.[2]

5.2 Concept and planning of judicial reform

Study in this respect is involved in discussions on two principal themes of "Justness and Efficiency" raised by the Supreme People's Court, on fundamental value orientation of the judicial reform in China, on judicial reform steps, as well as on the establishment of Judicial Reform Committee to lead the Chinese judicial reform in a unified way. Among them, representative points of view maintain: in contemporary advanced judicial spirit and ideas, the most important is to attach great importance to the security of human rights, adhere to judicial justice, strengthen judicial authority, and strive for judicial efficiency;[3] in search of modern judicial ideas, it is appropriate guidance to abandon traditional

1 TAN Shigui: *Study on Judicial Independent*, published by Law Press China, 2004.

2 For instance, PAN Jianfeng: *From Point of View of Japan's Third Judicial Reform, See Question About China's Judicial Reform, Law Science*, Issue 8, 2000; HAN Dayuan: *Foundation and Meaning of Constitutional Government in East Asian Countries' Judicial Reform: Centered in Experience of South Korea's Judicial Reform, Zhejiang Social Sciences*, Issue 3, 2004; QI Shujie: *Enlightenment to China of Civil Judicial Reform in England and Germany, Journal of Xiamen University (Philosophy and Social Science Edition)*, Issue 1, 2004; QI Shujie: *Germany's Civil Judicial Reform and its Reference Significance, China Legal Science*, Issue 3, 2002; YANG Yafei: *Discussion and Evaluation on Russia's Judicial Reform*, published in *Law and Social Development*, Issue 2, 1999; YAN Yunqiu: *Localization and Foreignization of Africa's Judicial System, West Asia and Africa*, Issue 4, 2000, etc.

3 GUO Daohui: *Judicial Reform and Reformation of Judicial Idea (B), Jianghai Academic Journal*, Issue 5, 2001.

view of "Objective Reality" so as to restore the idea of "Procedural Justice," it is important to adhere to "Justice is preferential to giving consideration to efficiency," with justice being the priority selection of judicial reform value target; judicial reform is unlikely to be a kind of social phenomenon existing in isolation, but in essence it falls into the category of political management and presents to amplify the political system reform in China, so that the relationship is great with the overall progress of the political system and must be developed synchronously with political system reform in China so as to achieve an ideal effect. Under the current political conditions, judicial reform cannot be only progressive, which must undergo a longer historical process.[1] As for the systematism and integrity of judicial reform considered, learning from foreign experience, numerous scholars maintain that it is necessary to set up a unified judicial reform committee or a similar institution, which will be submitted as a bill to the National People's Congress for examination and approval.[2]

5.3 Judicial review and scope of jurisdiction

To this, mainstream views maintain that it is necessary to expand the field of judicial review and that of the jurisdiction of a court, to build a complete legal system with justiciability, to provide constitution and political legislation with justiciability respectively, and whereby to set up judicial examination power over political behaviour.[3]In terms of concrete systems, it is necessary to set up a constitutional committee only responsible for the Standing Committee of the National People's Congress, with the constitutional court being established step

1 XU Jingcun: *Questions About China's Judicial Reform*, *Journal of Southwest Nationalities College (Philosophy and Social Science Edition)*, Issue 1, 2000; LONG Zongzhi: *Discussion on Relative Rationalism in Judicial Reform*, *Social Sciences in China*, Issue 2, 1999.

2 GU Peidong: *Macroscopic Thoughts on the Judicial Reform of China*, *Chinese Journal of Law*, Issue 3, 2000; DAI Qi: *Bill to Establish "National Commission on Judicial Reform" (Summary)*, *China Lawyer*, Issue 5, 2002.

3 XIE Hui: *Independent Judicature and Actionable Law*, *Science of Law*, Issue 1, 1999.

by step on the basis of setting up another constitution.[1] In terms of jurisdiction of court, there is no scope of accepting cases in general criminal proceedings. However, in administrative litigation, some acts can't be reviewed and examined, such as abstract administrative act, "final" administrative act, and internal administrative act, which is a move far from the concept of the rule of law and requirements of WTO and also far from the practices of advanced countries in the rule of law in the world. Administrative litigation law believes that beyond being excluded by express provisions in constitution and law, an administrative counterpart has the right of just claim not subject to any restrictions.[2]In terms of civil procedure, there is not too much an issue on the scope of accepting cases. However, serious phenomena of "Judicial omission" in actual judicial practices are well worth learning and studying, so are the the phenomena like limitation of just claim with "Judicial interpretations" and other judicial documents or the like, for reasons such as local protectionism, no accepting of the cases filed, no deciding of the cases accepted, or no executing of the cases decided.

5.4 "Administration mode of justice"

Study on such question is mainly involved in theses including questions about administration of judicial management system and improvement of court administration, localization of court financial supply system and "regional protectionism," judicial committee and the People's jury system, judge professionalism and setting up of clerk's array in a smaller unit of clerk, and reform and improvement of China's judicial identification system. Among them, representative points of view cover criticism on the bureaucratization of judicial management in China's court and on the administration of management system of court,[3] which propose that with the development of division of labour in society

1 JI Weidong: *Constitutionality Examination and Strengthening Judicial Power*, *Social Sciences in China*, Issue 2, 2002.

2 WEI Qunlin: *Study on Scope of Accepting Cases of Administrative Litigation in China under WTO Environment*, *Academic Dissertation of Suzhou University School of Law*, 2003.

3 HE Weifang: *Two Questions about China's Judicial Management System*, published in *Social Sciences in China*, Issue 6, 1997; *Relationship Between Upper and Lower Courts in Judicial Reform*, *Science of Law*, Issue 9, 1998.

it should be noted that the court's administrative function should be separated from its judicial function,[1] with the reform in the court of property right and personnel system, restriction on court should be relieved from the administrative body,[2] separate judge establishment and judicial budget should be set up and legal protection should be achieved,[3] separate duty array of clerk should be set up to highlight the difference in the division of professional role between judge and clerk, and in the meantime clerk's nature in profession, technology and service should be emphasized.[4]The judicial committee should be remolded and even canceled out completely, or the role of the system in judgment should be indeed intensified to make it peeled from the existing administrative system of court, at least to weaken the administrative features of "the system of leading cadre's responsibility" existing in court now to a great extent.[5]To meet the requirements of nature in law, science, and openness, it is necessary to straighten up judicial expertise system, improve procedures of management, and evaluate the qualification of judicial expert witness, especially the improvement of matters concerning appearance in court by a judicial expert witness.[6]

There are studies on judicial management mode, judicial quality evaluation mechanism, and judicial corruption prevention mechanism. Numerous procedural

---

1 ZHU Suli: *Discussion on Trial Functions and Administrative Management of Court*, *Peking University Law Journal*, Issue 5, 1999.

2 JIANG Huiling: *Discussion on Management Function of Court*, *Journal of Law Application*, Issue 8, 2004.

3 XU Xianming: 20 Questions about *Judicial Reform,* published in *Science of Law*, Issue 9, 1999; TAN Shigui and SHU Hai: *Discussion on Judge's Independent Judicial Personality*, *Journal of Hainan University*, Issue 4, 2003.

4 LIU Wujun: *Management System of Court Clerk and its Change*, *Review of Rule of Law*, Issue 1, 2004.

5 HE Weifang: *Idea and System of Judicature*, published by China University of Political Science and Law Press, 1998; SU Li: *Deliver Knowledge of Law to the Rural Areas: Study on China's Judicial System at Local Level*, published by China University of Political Science and Law Press, 2000; ZHU Suli: *Discussion on Trial Functions and Administrative Management of Court*, *Peking University Law Journal*, Issue 5, 1999; LIANG Huixing: *13 Suggestions on Judicial Reform*, *Science of Law*, Issue 5, 2003.

6 HONG Jian: *Reform and Improvement of China's Judicial Authentication*, *People's Procuratorial Semi-monthly*, Issue 2, 2003.

law scholars have conducted systematic studies on the evaluation principle of judicial justice and status quo, case, cause and prevention mechanism regarding China's judicial corruption, some of them suggesting the establishment of the science of incorrupt government.[1] Some scholars have suggested the support of new culture and system,[2] while others have conducted in-depth studies on the omission such phenomena in China's judicature.[3]

5.5 Study on the construction of a diversified dispute resolution mechanism

An alternative dispute resolution method has become one of the vital components of the mechanism of resolving civil disputes; it and civil procedure have supplemented each other. Facing the contradiction between shortage of judicial resources and surge in case number, procedural law scholars have carried on study on dispute resolution methods of alternative litigation at the same time, such as compromise and arbitration, and that on reform of the system of civil justice. In this respect, in view of the problems in the development of the rule of law in China and in the matter of problems in the development of China under the rule of law, scholars have systematically expounded the value, significance, and reasonable system construction of diversified dispute resolution mechanism consisting of judicial, administrative, and civil dispute resolution mechanism, and have carried on empirical research and analysis of the role of the current basic-level justice, litigation mediation, petition letter, and administrative remedy mechanism, people's mediation and "big mediation" and the habit and other folk social norms. They advocate the guarantee of sustainable development of the rule of law and

1 TAN Shigui: *Discussion on Prevention and Control of Judicial Corruption*, published by Law Press China, 2003.

2 SHEN Muzhu: *Discussion on Judicial Institutional tort and its Prevention*, *Journal of Gansu Institute of Political Science and Law*, Issue 4, 2001.

3 LIAO Yong'an: *Thinking on "Omission" of Court in Divil Procedure*, *Studies in Law and Business*, Issue 4, 1999. W\EI Qunlin and TAN Shigui: *Preliminary Discussion on Omission in Judicature and Judicial Management Countermeasures*, *Journal of Gansu Institute of Political Science and Law*, Issue 6, 2005.

society with diversified dispute resolution mechanism and the promotion of social harmony, autonomy through negotiation, and healthy development of public society.

As for the basic form, system construction and legislative framework of diversified dispute resolution mechanism, mainstream point of view maintains that the mechanism means an application and dynamic adjustment system to meet a variety of needs of social subject, composed of diversified dispute resolution ways (including those for litigation and non-litigation) in a society, which coordinate with each other and coexist with their specific functions. Diversified dispute resolution mechanism includes both non-lawsuit mechanism and judicature and litigation mechanism in its concept. In terms of theory, it emphasizes the study on the relationships between litigation and non-litigation, the control over legal mechanism and other social control, state judicial power and social autonomy, public remedy and society, as well as self-protection. In terms of system and practice, it focuses on structuring dispute resolution mechanism for the coordination and interaction between legal and non-legal procedures.[1]

Study on folk dispute resolution mechanism and self-protection mainly involves questions such as public-private dualistic division to ternary structure, conditions and issues of operation of folk dispute resolution mechanism, definition, characteristic and classification of self-protection, and legitimacy of self-protection and its limit. Among them, a representative point of view maintains that with the development of the contemporary judicial socialization and dispute resolution practice China's policies to limit or forbid self-protection have changed. Some important principles need to be followed continually such as those forbidding violent and illegal self-protection and limiting self-protection within jurisdiction scope of public power. Nonetheless, some measures and intensities have remitted. For example, in recent years, administrative reconciliation and mediation have no longer been taboos; legitimacy of criminal reconciliation and

1 FAN Yu: *Theory and Practice of Dispute Resolution*, published by Tsinghua University Press, 2007, p.221.

plea-bargaining has been approved, although it doesn't mean the revolution of China's limitation on self-protection. For this, in a broader field, self-protections have been recognized by society increasingly and incorporated into social relief system. In the meantime, China and the jurisprudential circle's attitudes and policies have become more and more tolerant over various kinds of reasonable self-protections.[1]

As for the construction of a diversified resolution mechanism in contemporary China, the main research contents include the path to construct a diversified resolution mechanism, the reconstitution of lawsuit mediation system, and the development of ADR and judicial reform. Mainstream point of view maintains that the rationality of the diversified disputes resolution mechanism lies in its adaptability and effectiveness, and specific standards vary from the actual situations of different countries and regions. Given that the current judicial ability and self-control ability are weak in China, it is important to avoid simply copying the judicial mode and access of western nations. Our country should make the best use of traditional resources for mediation and at the same time try to establish all kinds of new types of dispute resolution mechanisms. The docking mechanism of lawsuit mediation under the current big mediation pattern is both the result of the reflection of justice policy and the relation to its interests. Mediation has its significant advantages for the improvement of judicial dilemma that courts are involved in, while such interests may be in accordance with those of parties concerned and society. Therefore, mediation should become an important component of the policy of "judicatory for people", so as to make full use of social resources to resolve disputes and widen the channel of the mediation of dispute and ways of dispute resolution.[2]

1 See XU Xin's *Discussion on Self-protection*, published by China University of Political Science and Law Press, 2005.

2 For relevant discussions See FAN Yu: *Theory and Practice of Dispute Resolution*, Tsinghua University Press, 2007; *Study on Dispute Resolution Mechanism in Non-litigation*, published by China Renmin University Press, 2000; HE Bing: *Dispute Resolution in Modern Society*, Law Press China, 2003.

Postscript

On the occasion of the 60th Anniversary of the founding of the People's Republic of China (P.R.C.), Subject Group of Institute of Law of Chinese Academy of Social Sciences has widely collected and sorted academic information in a systematic manner, on the basis of which it has updated the academic history of 60 years of law of the People's Republic of China as a memorial of the 60th Anniversary of the founding of the People's Republic of China. In this book, we have carried out a summary description China's legal research of the past 60 years, thus demonstrating the present situation of law science and its evolutionary process during different stages of the development in new China, analysing the background and reason for the important theoretical formation and evolution in the study of law, and manifesting the theoretical achievements of development and prosperity of law and its practical value. It is hoped that with the Book readers can clearly understand China's trajectory of law and experience the hardship and wisdom that the researchers have delivered in the process of the development and prosperity of law science, so that they can feel era development resonating with the fate of P.R.C.

The division of labour in writing the Book is as follows: CHEN Su: editor-in-chief, introduction to Part A, B and C; HU Shuijun: 1 and 4 of Chapter 1, 1, 2 and 3 of Chapter 4, 1, 2 and 3 of Chapter 12; LIU Zhaoxing: 2 of Chapter 1, 4 of Chapter 4, 4 of Chapter 12; GAO Hancheng: 3 of Chapter 3, 5 of Chapter 5, 5 of

Chapter 12; MO Jihong and ZHAI Guoqiang: Chapter 2, 5 and 13; Liu Renwen: 1 of Chapter 3, Chapter 6 and 14; SUN Xianzhong and XIE Hongfei: 2 of Chapter 3, 1 and 2 of Chapter 7, 1, 2, 3 and 4 of Chapter 15; XUE Ninglan: 3 of Chapter 3, 3 of Chapter 7, 5 of Chapter 15; XI Yuemin: 4 of Chapter 3, Chapter 8 and 18; XU Hui: 5 of Chapter 3, 1, 2 and 3 of Chapter 10, 1, 2, 3 and 5 of Chapter 20; GUAN Yuying: 4 of Chapter 7, Chapter 17; CHANG Jiwen: Chapter 9 and 19; JIANG Jing: Chapter 10, 14 and 20, 4 of Chapter 24; CHEN Jie: Chapter 16; YU Shaoxiang: Chapter 21.

The knowledge system of law science is so huge and the evolutionary path of legal theory is so complex with so many minor matters concerning major academic event that this scientific research process need to be accepted or rejected for many times and repeatedly deliberated on, with limited pieces of writing, which cover central trajectory and comprehensive characteristics of China's law development. Each member of the Subject Group only pays more attention to the professional field he/she is familiar with, so as to achieve the goal of fully disclosing the legal history of new China by expressing the historical evolution and development of each major legal field as accurately as possible. The Book does not plan to have the authority to classify subjects. Therefore, chapter arrangement just provides members of the Subject Group with a given scope within which they write, who will express the history of legal research that he/she grasps as a writer as far as possible, on the basis of his/her own knowledge structure and theoretical vision. In the process of writing the Book, XI Yueming, Associate Research Fellow, has undertaken the work of Secretary of the Subject Group, made great efforts to organize discussions, collect articles, adjust styles, and proofread the manuscripts. As for uniformly compiling the manuscripts, the Editor-in-Chief has made great efforts to unify the style of the writings in all chapters, abridged narrations herein that have no significant connection to academic history, adjusted the weight of content in the fields herein, balanced analytical evaluations concerning academic background and influence, and filled major omissions in all chapters. Yet, due to our limited academic views and research capabilities, it is impossible to make a complete list, and it is also unavoidable to imbalance theories inappropriately. Thus, we would like to ask for understandings from the academic colleagues who read the Book.

We would like to commemorate and thank the people who have been putting efforts into and making contributions to the rule of law progress and prosperity of law of the People's Republic of China!

Research Group of *Modern Studies on Jurisprudence of China*

This book is the result of a co-publication agreement between China Social Sciences Press (China) and Paths International Ltd (UK)

This book is published with the financial support of Chinese Fund for the Humanities and Social Sciences (本书获中国国家社科基金中华学术外译项目资助)

Research on the Laws of Contemporary China Volume 3: 1992-2009
Editor-in-chief Chen Su
Translated By He Jingjing and Shang Cong
ISBN: 978-1-84464-502-2
Ebook ISBN: 978-1-84464-503-9

Paths International Ltd
PO Box 4083
Reading
United Kingdom
RG8 8ZN
www.pathsinternational.com

Published in the United Kingdom

CPSIA information can be obtained
at www.ICGtesting.com
Printed in the USA
LVHW101927060619
620427LV00004B/9/P

9 781844 645022